COMMUNITY-BASED
CORRECTIONS

Second Edition

COMMUNITY-BASED
CORRECTIONS

Second Edition

BELINDA RODGERS MCCARTHY
University of Central Florida

BERNARD J. MCCARTHY, JR.
University of Central Florida

Brooks/Cole Publishing Company
Pacific Grove, California

Brooks/Cole Publishing Company
A Division of Wadsworth, Inc.

Printed in the United States of America

10   9   8   7   6   5   4   3   2

Library of Congress Cataloging-in-Publication Data
McCarthy, Belinda Rodgers.
    Community-based corrections / Belinda Rodgers McCarthy, Bernard J.
McCarthy, Jr. — 2nd ed.
        p.   cm.
    Includes bibliographical references and index.
    ISBN 0-534-15510-3
    1. Community-based corrections—United States. 2. Criminal
justice, Administration of—United States. I. McCarthy, Bernard
J., [date] . II. Title.
HV9304.M17 1991   90-47532
364.6′8—dc20   CIP

SPONSORING EDITOR: Cynthia C. Stormer
MARKETING REPRESENTATIVE: Charlie Delmar
EDITORIAL ASSOCIATE: Cathleen S. Collins
PRODUCTION COORDINATOR: Fiorella Ljunggren
PRODUCTION: Sara Hunsaker, Ex Libris
MANUSCRIPT EDITOR: Elliot Simon
PERMISSIONS EDITOR: Mary Kay Hancharick
INTERIOR AND COVER DESIGN: Terri Wright
ART COORDINATOR: Sara Hunsaker
INTERIOR ILLUSTRATIONS: Lori Heckelman
TYPESETTING: Bookends Typesetting
COVER PRINTING: Phoenix Color Corporation
PRINTING AND BINDING: The Maple-Vail Book Manufacturing Group

For Megan, Matthew, and Roxie,
who brought us perspective and patience

Preface

In this revised edition, we examine a wide array of correctional programs commonly referred to as community-based corrections and describe the applications of these programs to specific offender groups as well as to the larger population of adult male offenders. This examination views community-based corrections as a component of the larger system of corrections, which is in turn a major component of the criminal justice system. Throughout this text, community-based correctional strategies are compared to traditional and/or institutional strategies. The interconnectedness of law-enforcement activities, judicial practices, and corrections is continuously emphasized.

Our reasons for writing this book are simply stated. As faculty members in criminal justice departments, we teach a variety of corrections, criminal justice, and research courses. We wrote this book because we were unable to find any single text that addressed all of the major programs, problems, and offender groups that we considered necessary for a comprehensive discussion of community-based corrections. We encourage the reader to approach this text as a sourcebook on community-based corrections—a guide to "how the programs developed, why they grew in popularity and variety, where they are now, and how they can be used most effectively."

We consider community-based corrections to be a dynamic, exciting, and complex approach to offender change and justice-system reform. To illustrate this view, we have included interviews with program staff members and clients and case studies of program operations in each chapter. Frequently we have found that the program participants themselves can best communicate the benefits, trials, and tribulations of program operations. In addition, community-based correctional programs offer promising strategies to reduce the problem of overcrowding in institutional corrections while, at the same time, ensuring the safety of the community.

Throughout the text, we have focused on the interplay among program cost, community protection, and offender change—a focus that encourages readers to continuously question program objectives and results. By adopting an attitude of curiosity mingled with healthy skepticism, the reader can achieve not only an understanding of the current status of community corrections but also an ability to anticipate future correctional dilemmas and to evaluate alternative proposals for problem resolution.

The organization of this text parallels the flow of persons through the criminal justice system. We examine each program in accordance with the sequence of decisions governing criminal justice processing.

Chapters 2 through 8 describe seven community-based correctional programs used for adult offenders, defining them and examining their unique histories. Contemporary forms of the programs are described, and both exemplary and typical programs are represented for purposes of illustration. Guidelines for program development and administration are offered for programs that require extensive citizen involvement and/or are particularly likely to encounter citizen resistance. Problems and issues are discussed in a manner designed to provide a guide for local program assessment.

Research and evaluation studies of community-based programs are an important part of each chapter. Although many programs have not yet been subjected to intense and comprehensive study, what *is* known is presented, and suggestions for future research are offered where appropriate. Prospects for the future are examined at the end of each chapter. These prospects are not our predictions but simply our attempt to assess a program's potential for further development and expansion.

Chapters 9 through 11 look at special problems and needs of female, juvenile, and drug- and alcohol-abusing offenders and the community-based correctional programs designed to meet these needs. Chapter 12, which examines the role of volunteers, paraprofessionals, and ex-offenders in community-based corrections, is especially important because it addresses the process by which the community can become involved in the various aspects of correctional planning and programming. In chapter 13, we look at the future of community corrections by focusing on efforts to plan, organize, and unify correctional efforts.

We are indebted to the following reviewers for their diligence in reading the manuscript of this second edition and for their useful suggestions. They are Robert Fosen of The American University, Donald Gilbert of Hudson Valley Community College, Hilary Harper of the University of South Florida, Robert Heiner of Spring Hill College, William E. Osterhoff of Auburn University at Montgomery, and Stan Stojkovic of the University of Wisconsin–Milwaukee. We would also like to thank Cindy Stormer for her patience during the revision process and Cat Collins for her persistence in making sure that the manuscript would be completed on time.

Belinda Rodgers McCarthy
Bernard J. McCarthy, Jr.

Contents

COMMUNITY-BASED
CORRECTIONS

Second Edition

1: A Reintegrative Approach to Corrections

Objectives of Community-Based Corrections
  Reintegration
  Community Protection
  Intermediate Punishments
  Cost-Effective Sanctions
Development of Community-Based Corrections
  Transition from Soldier to Civilian
  Labeling Theory
  Dissatisfaction with the Criminal Justice System
  The Great Society
  Criminal Justice: A System and an Academic Discipline
  Contemporary Community-Based Corrections
Systems Analysis
Critical Issues
  Alternatives
  Eligibility Requirements
Summary

COMMUNITY-BASED CORRECTIONS is the general term used to refer to various types of noninstitutional correctional programs for criminal offenders. These programs, including diversion, pretrial release, probation, restitution and community service, temporary release, halfway houses, and parole, form a continuum of options for dealing with offenders in the community. Although each program offers different services and serves different groups of offenders, their similarities outweigh their differences.

Objectives of Community-Based Corrections

All of these programs attempt to sanction and control the offender without the use of confinement. These strategies permit the offender to maintain existing ties to the community and to establish new ones. This latter objective is known as *reintegration*.

❏ Reintegration

The most eloquent summary of the meaning and purpose of reintegration as a correctional policy is found in the 1967 President's Commission on Law Enforcement and Administration of Justice:

> The task of corrections therefore includes building or rebuilding solid ties between offender and community, integrating or reintegrating the offender into community life—restoring family ties, obtaining employment and education, securing in the larger sense a place for the offender in the routine functioning of society. This requires not only efforts directed toward changing the individual offender, which has been almost the exclusive focus of rehabilitation, but also mobilization and change of the community and its institutions.[1]

Reintegration is based on the premise that crime and delinquency are as much symptoms of community disorganization as they are evidence of the psychological and behavioral problems of individual offenders. The community's failures are seen as "depriving offenders of contact with the institutions that are basically responsible for assuring development of law-abiding contact: sound family life, good schools, employment, recreational opportunities, and desirable companions."[2] The psychological problems that offenders often manifest are viewed, at least in part, as the products of the environment in which the offender lives. Although this approach to explaining criminal behavior is most frequently used when considering the street crime of ghetto residents, it is also applicable to middle-class and suburban delinquency. Poor schools, family problems, and a lack of meaningful activity can be found in any community, in any social stratum.

Reintegration has its theoretical roots in the social sciences. Social factors have long been considered influential in producing criminal behavior, both directly and indirectly. Factors such as the impact of delinquent associates and the criminal subculture and the lack of opportunity for legitimate success play a significant role in most contemporary theories of crime. These factors are all evidence of the community's failure to promote the development of law-abiding behavior.

The National Institute of Mental Health has likened reintegrative programs for inmates to decompression:

Such programs are not dissimilar in motif from those used with tunnel workers who do day-long construction work in caissons far underground. These workers—so-called "sand-hogs"—must go through an exacting process of readjustment in decompression chambers if they are to adjust satisfactorily to normal air conditions at ground level. Otherwise, they may suffer aeroembolism ("the bends"), an excruciating torment resulting from the release of nitrogen bubbles into the blood. So, too, in corrections the assumption prevails that unless an inmate can be satisfactorily decompressed he is apt rather quickly to manifest the criminal equivalent of "the bends," a kind of environmental malaise that is likely to result in renewed criminal activity.

Programs of "graduated release" are designed to reduce the severity of impact of an abrupt transition between two divergent and possibly antagonistic climates.[3]

To achieve the objectives of reintegration, community-based correctional programs must meet the following requirements:

1. A location within and interaction with a meaningful community. (A meaningful community may be defined as an environment that offers opportunities that fit the offender's needs. Generally, the offender's home community or an environment similar to the one in which the offender will eventually live will be appropriate.)

2. A nonsecure environment—for example, the offender's home, a surrogate home, or a communal residence in which the offender lives as a responsible person with minimal supervision.

3. Community-based education, training, counseling, and support services. (These are provided by noncorrectional public and private agencies as well as by correctional staff and are organized into a comprehensive service-delivery network.)

4. Opportunities to assume the normal social roles of citizen, family member, student, and/or employee.

5. Opportunities for personal growth. (Such opportunities are made possible by the provision of experiences that test a person's ability to function independently. Such testing should occur in an environment that responds to failure with tolerance, encouragement, and guidance, and rewards success by increasing responsibility.)

Staff in reintegrative community-based correctional programs have responsibilities different from those in nonreintegrative programs. Although they may continue to provide supervision, support, and therapy to their clients, they are expected to refer as many persons as possible to noncorrectional community programs that specialize in employment, education, mental health, and recreation services. Acting as *resource brokers,* they are expected to link offenders to the appropriate services and monitor their progress after assistance has been initiated. Often it will be necessary to act as *advocates,* working to ensure that the offenders' rights are protected and that a high quality of service delivery is maintained.

❏ Community Protection

Although reintegration may be the most distinctive feature of community-based correctional programs, these programs have other objectives as well. Such programs attempt to *control* offenders while they remain in the community, as a means of protecting the public from further harm. Control may be accomplished in a variety of ways, such as through the use of prescriptive and proscriptive restrictions on offender behavior. Conditions may include curfews as well as requirements that the offender attend school, get a job, and avoid alcohol and drugs and any contact with persons engaged in illegitimate activities. Sometimes offenders are required to live in a supervised environment, such as a halfway house or a diversion center that provides daily structure.

Enforcing these conditions can be difficult, often requiring frequent telephone calls and personal visits to the offender at work and at home, and contacts with family members, employers, and other associates. The purpose is to use rules and rule enforcement to both deter the offender from inappropriate conduct and identify, before crime occurs, those persons who cannot be maintained in the community.

Although it is impossible to achieve the level of incapacitation that prisons provide, community-based programs attempt to provide offender monitoring sufficient for the degree of risk posed by each program participant. Identifying and classifying offender risk and developing levels of structure and supervision sufficient for each level of risk are the greatest challenges confronting community-based corrections today.

❏ Intermediate Punishments

Many community-based correctional programs serve as *intermediate punishments,* that is, alternatives to traditional probation or incarceration. In the continuum of sanctions, which range from probation to incarceration, selected community-based programs such as intensive supervision, house arrest, electronic monitoring, and boot camps provide mid-range dispositions that better reflect the severity of the offense than prison or probation alone. While many offenders require reintegrative efforts to facilitate a law-abiding way of life, and many persons cannot be safely released to the community without supervision, many offenders deserve a punishment that is less harsh than prison but more severe than a fine or minimum supervision probation. (See table 1-1.)

Consider, for example, the second- or third-time property offender who is placed on probation for prior offenses. How should he or she be handled? At some point it becomes necessary to do more than was done the last time, both as a means of discouraging further criminal conduct and in recognition of the failure of prior dispositions. It is important to demonstrate a desire to accomplish something with each sanction, something other than "more of the same."

Intermediate punishments are also frequently employed as alternatives to revocation for probationers and parolees who run into difficulty in the community. Although it is legally possible to put any probation or parole violator in prison, it is often not desirable to do so. An individual who is obeying the law and holding down a job but who continues to have problems with the use of drugs probably should not be sent to prison, since so many aspects of his or her life are working out. There is a clear need to respond to probation and parole violations, even those that involve new crimes, with efforts that recognize what positive steps the offender may have achieved.

TABLE 1-1 A Model Continuum of Sanctions

Restrictions	Level I	Level II	Level III	Level IV	Level V	Level VI	Level VII	Level VIII	Level IX
Mobility in the community	100% (unrestricted)	100% (unrestricted)	90% (restricted 0-10 hours/week)	80% (restricted 10-30 hours/week)	60% (restricted 30-40 hours/week)	30% (restricted 50-100 hours/week)	20% (restricted 100-140 hours/week)	10% (90% of time incarcerated)	Incarcerated
Amount of supervision	None	Monthly written report	1-2 face-to-face/month; 1-2 weekly phone contacts	3-6 face-to-face/month; weekly phone contacts	2-6 face-to-face/week; daily phone contact; weekly written reports	Daily phone contact; daily face-to-face; weekly written reports	Daily onsite supervision 8-16 hours/day	Daily onsite supervision 24 hours/day	Daily onsite supervision 24 hours/day
Privileges withheld or special conditions	100% (same as prior conviction)	100% (same as prior conviction)	1-2 privileges withheld	1-4 privileges withheld	1-7 privileges withheld	1-10 privileges withheld	1-12 privileges withheld	5-15 privileges withheld	15-19 privileges withheld
Financial obligations	Fine; court costs may be applied (0- to 2-day fine)	Fine, court costs, restitution; probation (supervisory fee may be applied; 1- to 3-day fine)	Same (increase probation fee by $5-10/month; 2- to 4-day fine)	Same (increase probation fee by $5-10/month; 3- to 5-day fine)	Same (pay partial cost of food/lodging/ supervision fee; 4- to 7-day fine)	Same as Level V (8- to 10-day fine)	Same as Level V (11- to 12-day fine)	Fine, court costs, restitution payable upon release to Level VII or lower (12- to 15-day fine)	Same as Level VIII
Examples (*Note:* many other scenarios could be constructed meeting the requirements at each level)	$50 fine, court costs; 6 months' unsupervised probation	$50 fine, court costs, restitution; 6 months' supervised probation; $10 monthly fee; written report	Fine, court costs, restitution; 1 year's probation; weekend community service; no drinking	Weekend community service or mandatory treatment 5 hours/day; $30/month probation fee; no drinking; no out-of-state trips	Mandatory rehabilitation skills program 8 hours/day; restitution; $40/month probation fee; no drinking; curfew	Work release; pay portion of food/lodging; restitution; no kitchen privileges outside mealtimes; no drinking; no sex; weekends home	Residential treatment program; pay portion of program costs; limited privileges	Minimum-security prison	Medium-security prison

SOURCE: Pierre S. duPont IV, "Expanding Sentencing Options: A Governor's Perspective," *Research in Brief*, National Institute of Justice, January 1985, Washington, D.C.

❑ Cost-Effective Sanctions

Finally, community based correctional programs are frequently viewed as *cost-effective sanctions*. The current level of prison overcrowding is such that any feasible alternative to new prison construction must be considered for its financial benefits. There seems to be a growing recognition that increased prison construction only leads to higher levels of incarceration, with no discernible impact on crime. This means that many programs originally valued for their reintegrative potential for less serious offenders are now being reassessed in terms of the economic benefits that can be achieved when prison-bound offenders are accepted into the programs.

It should be obvious that there are potential conflicts among the goals of community-based correctional programs. Intermediate punishments will cost more than current practice, if current practice is to utilize traditional probation or ignore probation or parole violations. Reintegration requires real efforts to assist offenders, a carefully calculated strategy that involves much more than control of offenders. Electronic monitoring may accomplish this goal, but alone it will do little to assist the offender in developing a crime-free lifestyle.

These conflicts are ever-present in community-based corrections, often making it difficult to determine which program components are accomplishing what objectives and how the programs fit into and alter the current scheme of correctional dispositions. Much of this conflict can be better understood by examining the chronological sequence in which each objective was identified, promoted, and "tacked on" to existing program purposes. As we will see, each new objective was promoted to address a newly identified problem. Assembled in pell-mell fashion, community-based correctional programs seem to offer something for everyone.

Development of Community-Based Corrections

The community has not always been viewed as holding the answers to offender problems. In fact, for many years, the community was viewed only as harboring the causes of crime; the evil influences of drink and bad companions were seen as the principal sources of criminal behavior. Not surprisingly, correctional institutions seemed to offer a respite from temptation; removed from a corrupting environment and placed in solitary confinement, an offender could repent and change his ways. Many early community-based correctional efforts were criticized because they were contrary to the "reform through isolation" approach. It was believed that bringing ex-offenders together in halfway houses or group therapy would be asking for trouble because behavior would inevitably sink to that of the lowest common (criminal) denominator. It took many years to overcome this view of crime, criminals, and the community.

Each type of community-based correctional program has its own unique history. Some programs, such as halfway houses and restitution, have been in existence for centuries. Others, such as alcohol detoxification programs and citizen dispute settlement centers, are relatively new developments, although the desirability of such efforts has long been recognized. In the late 1950s and 1960s, however, the general *concept* of community-based corrections began to gain recognition and support. Gradually, the diverse programs now known under the umbrella term *community-based corrections* began to be viewed as distinct and essential components of the correctional policy of reintegration. Several social currents were responsible for the contemporary emergence of community-based corrections.

❑ Transition from Soldier to Civilian

Community-based corrections can be traced back to the years following World War II, when returning veterans encountered adjustment problems as they attempted to reenter civilian life. It was soon realized that many persons required assistance in making the transition from soldier to civilian.[4] This assistance ranged from informal outpatient counseling, to education and job preparation, to intensive therapy offered in residential settings. One concern was overriding—to prepare veterans for civilian life as quickly and effectively as possible. It was soon realized that it was necessary to expose men to civilian life while assistance was being provided. Trying to help persons in isolation was found to be less than useless; it only encouraged institutionalization and dependence. Reintegration, the replacement of the individual in the community and the reestablishment of community ties, required a community-based effort. Reintegration came to be viewed as a process not unlike that of replanting an uprooted tree—something that could not be achieved in a greenhouse or by dumping the tree in even the most fertile soil. One had to work with both tree and soil to nourish the roots and stimulate growth.

A parallel development was occurring in the field of mental health. Careful observation of persons confined for years in mental hospitals revealed a general pattern of learned dependency—an inability to function outside the institution. Although treatment in confinement might "cure" some aspects of mental illness, mental health required an ability to interact with one's environment positively and effectively. The symbiosis required to achieve mental health could not be learned in an authoritarian environment where independence and personal responsibility were lacking. At best, the mental hospital could provide only a way station through which some individuals might have to pass on the way to mental health. It was gradually recognized that the environment most conducive to mental health was the environment in which healthy individuals lived—the free community.

❑ Labeling Theory

At the same time, a relatively new sociological theory was receiving considerable attention from criminologists. *Labeling theory,* which focuses not on the criminal's behavior, but on society's reaction to crime, eventually influenced how we perceive deviance and crime-control strategies. According to labeling theory, societal reactions to crime that stigmatize the offender and emphasize his differences from other men, rather than his similarities, serve to excommunicate him (in the secular sense of the word) and encourage subsequent criminal behavior. Removed from society, having no stake in obeying its laws and mores, offenders have no reason to refrain from crime. Such individuals can only seek out persons like themselves, who have nothing left to lose. Together, they establish new reference groups that reward deviant, rather than conforming, behavior.

The labeling theorists viewed formal processing through the criminal justice system and incarceration in prisons and jails as the most serious forms of excommunication. Cut loose from law-abiding society and forced into schools of crime, the offenders understandably left the system more antisocial in attitude and behavior than when they entered.

Labeling theory showed us how the criminal justice system could encourage crime by stigmatizing offenders and removing them from the larger community, thus encouraging the development of criminal reference groups. At the same time, labeling theory provided a series of answers to the correctional dilemma of how to respond to crime in a deviance-reducing manner. Correctional programs that avoided stigmatizing offenders and enabled them to maintain ties to the larger community could be expected to encourage responsible, law-abiding behavior.

❑ Dissatisfaction with the Criminal Justice System

Labeling theory focused attention on the impact of the criminal justice system, and most observers did not like what they saw. Research produced evidence that the criminal justice system unfairly discriminates against poor and disadvantaged members of society. Pretrial confinement, too often the fate only of poor defendants, was found to increase the likelihood of conviction and a prison term in situations where a person able to buy freedom prior to trial often received only probation. Observers saw a slowly working system that allowed offenders to languish in jail and to bargain for justice, a system that penalized persons who exercised their right to trial.

Studies of incarceration revealed that little resembling rehabilitation was occurring in United States prisons; they were generally warehouses that were barely able to control their captives and keep their residents busy. Although the myth of the "hotel prison" gained some popular acceptance, few such facilities could be found. "Luxuries" such as nourishing food, adequate health care, and the education and training necessary to achieve functional literacy and self-sufficiency were unavailable to all but a few prisoners.

❑ The Great Society

All these developments reached culmination during the 1960s, when the words *country* and *community* took on a new meaning. The Great Society was envisioned as a nation whose greatest resource was its people, a nation that was enriched by every effort to enhance the status and position of disadvantaged persons and to integrate them into the community. The goal was to make economic opportunity and self-sufficiency available to all persons without regard to color, creed, or sex. Numerous federally funded programs were established throughout the United States, especially in urban areas, where the problems of disenfranchisement and disaffection were the greatest. Many of these community-based programs permitted or encouraged offender and ex-offender participation.

❏ Criminal Justice: A System and an Academic Discipline

The 1960s witnessed changes in how many societal institutions were viewed. Our perception of the agencies devoted to crime control, justice, and correction changed during this period. Before the late 1960s, law enforcement agencies, the courts, jails, and prisons were basically viewed as independent organizations with separate administrative problems and objectives. Sparked by the President's Task Force Reports on Law Enforcement and Administration of Justice, this perception began to change.

In the quest for reform, we realized that the achievement of an effective and efficient system of justice required more than independent, isolated efforts to change police officers, judges and district attorneys, guards and wardens. Reform required a comprehensive examination of the interrelationships among the agencies. An "offender's eye view" of the system slowly developed; it focused on the process of justice and how the agencies affected each other, as well as the problem of crime. This increasingly sophisticated view of the justice process led to our current conceptualization of the criminal justice system.

The conceptualization of criminal justice as a system required the development and expansion of academic criminal justice studies. An intensive study of the problem of crime and the policies and practices of the agencies of justice was essential if legislation, administrative policy, and programming were to be designed and implemented effectively. Efforts to professionalize criminal justice agency employees, from law enforcement officers to prison guards, took on new meaning as college-level criminal justice studies expanded. Growing research capabilities and an increasingly complex view of their responsibilities prompted many criminal justice employees to search for more effective and efficient strategies to reduce crime and rehabilitate offenders. Community-based correctional programs provided many of the answers for which they were looking.

❏ Contemporary Community-Based Corrections

The preceding description of the development of community-based corrections may seem overwhelmingly optimistic. It was. Community-based programming seemed to offer the solution to so many problems that it was too often represented as solving them all. Just as the Great Society came to be viewed as a dream that was never fully realized, so we have discovered that community-based corrections is a strategy with many strengths, but also some real limitations.

During the 1970s, community-based correctional programs sprang up across the country. Many were funded by the federal government through such agencies as the Law Enforcement Assistance Administration (LEAA), the Office of Juvenile Justice and Delinquency Prevention (OJJDP), the Department of Labor (DOL), and the Department of Health, Education and Welfare (HEW).

Some of these new programs were carefully planned to fit the needs, resources, and objectives of the communities in which they were established. Others, encouraged by the availability of federal funds, were only vaguely conceptualized and poorly implemented. Some early efforts that had been identified as model projects were subsequently tried in new areas without adequate attention to important differences between the originating community and the new sites. Community-based programs

Chaos in the Courts

by William Glaberson

NEW YORK, Jan. 15 — A din-filled courtroom 941 at State Supreme Court in Brooklyn the other day as Justice Nicholas Coffinas looked down from the bench. Before him was a spindly young man who had been caught with an unregistered pistol. Minutes before, an admitted burglar had his turn before the judge. Then had come a purse snatcher, a man accused of selling drugs and a man charged with splitting another man's lip in a street brawl.

The judge accepted guilty pleas, sent cases off to other judges and imposed jail sentences. Lawyers milled about. Court clerks shuffled papers. All the while, four wide rows of seats were filled with people murmuring among themselves as they waited for their cases to be called. The defense lawyer and the prosecutor in the gun case were each saying something that was lost in the commotion.

Justice Coffinas looked up. "Everybody else, please! Keep quiet!" he shouted in the worn, windowless room.

"Nearly Out of Control"

New York City's criminal courts have always been bustling places. But in the last few years places like the Criminal Term of State Supreme Court in Brooklyn have become frayed institutions, overwhelmed by drug cases and troubled people, where rough justice is often dispensed in rapid fashion. Just last month, the state's Chief Judge, Sol Wachtler, called the situation in New York State courts a "crisis nearly out of control."

A few days in the Brooklyn criminal court over the last few weeks demonstrated the monotonous cacophony of courtrooms throughout the city.

For a few minutes after Justice Coffinas shouted for quiet in his courtroom, the din subsided. Then it was back, as it usually is, like the constant whir on a factory floor signaling that the production line is still rolling.

Justice Coffinas worked his way through a calendar that listed more than 70 cases, as it does almost every weekday. Gabriel Plumer, the chief clerk of the court, which handles the most serious of the criminal charges against adults in Brooklyn, said he figured recently that Justice Coffinas has an average of four minutes to attend to each case.

Like other city courts swamped with drug-related arrests, the Brooklyn court is struggling with a mountainous caseload. In the first 11 months of 1989, the Brooklyn District Attorney presented the 41 judges on the court with 13,460 felony cases. In 1986, 40 judges handled 7,863 felonies.

Court administrators nationwide have complained about similar increases. In its most recent annual report, the National Center for State Courts found the trend to be a strong one nationwide. From 1981 to 1987, the most recent year for which statistics were available, felony filings in California increased by 41 percent, in Connecticut by 43 percent, in New Jersey by 32 percent and in the District of Columbia by 138 percent.

Pressure to Plea Bargain

Judges and prosecutors fight backlogs by exerting pressure to plea bargain. With the enormous caseloads, judges say, they have little opportunity to study the cases before them.

"You really can't give them the real attention that these cases deserve," Justice Coffinas said in an interview. "You do justice the best way you can." As a consequence, the very heart of the criminal-justice system—the trial—is all but vanishing from the courts where the most charges are brought.

Most of the people in this burdened system are poor. In 1989, only 6.2 percent of all cases before the State Supreme Court in Brooklyn ended with trial verdicts, a decline from 10.6 percent three years ago. In 78 percent of the cases, defendants were represented by

were often "tacked on" to the criminal justice system with too little consideration of the role of eligibility criteria and the impact of the new program on existing programs and components of the criminal justice system. Because of these factors, many communities found themselves paying more for corrections than before because they were supervising and servicing offenders who previously would have received little or no assistance.

Legal Aid Society lawyers or private lawyers paid with government funds because they were judged unable to pay for their own defense.

In an annex of the same courthouse on a recent day, Acting Justice Albert Tomei was presiding at a routine hearing. Harold Ortiz, 18 years old, stepped up to the scuffed witness stand. He was there to answer questions about whether he had violated his probation by failing to attend a drug-treatment program.

Mr. Ortiz turned to Justice Tomei. "This is for you," he said, according to court officials. Then, with a razor blade he had hidden, he slashed his own neck so deeply that stitches were required to close the wound.

Two days later, Justice Tomei sat talking in his chambers, where vast slices of paint hung off a yellowing ceiling. Mr. Ortiz's act of hopelessness, he said, was one of many things that make him question whether the courts can meet the demands that society makes of them.

Overwhelmed as it is, Justice Tomei said, the Supreme Court in Brooklyn does not much resemble the lofty legal institutions envisioned by the Constitution. "This," Justice Tomei said, gesturing outside his door where two prisoners waited in a cell the size of a closet, "is not what the Founding Fathers meant when they wrote the due-process clause."

In another courtroom that week, Acting Justice Joseph Slavin was hearing narcotics cases. "Typical," he said wearily, as one drug-sale case followed another.

The Legal Aid lawyer for a 35-year-old man arrested on drug charges proposed a one-year prison term for violating his probation by being arrested again. Too brief, Justice Slavin said. "No way in God's creation," he told the lawyer.

"Judge, it's not a strong case," the Legal Aid lawyer said. A brief negotiation followed. Justice Slavin settled on one to three years. "I'm being nice," he said.

Then, a 19-year-old man that Justice Slavin had given probation on a drug charge last January was back, this time for theft. Justice Slavin told the young man that the prisons upstate are not nice places.

"I'm trying to save his life," said the judge, referring to the defendant as if he were out of earshot, which he

was not. "If you frighten him enough, you might have a chance of having him stop it."

Then another lawyer was at Justice Slavin's bench. "This is an individual who is very unique," she said, with a wave toward her client. Miguel Echevarria, a 23-year-old business-school student, with slender glasses high on his nose, stood at the defense table. He had been caught with four vials of crack on the roof of his apartment building.

Probation, Justice Slavin said. "Remember," he said, "the next time you fool around with this stuff, you're going to wind up in state prison."

"There won't be a next time," Mr. Echevarria said. As he left the drab courthouse in his green parka, there was a look of relief on his face.

A few minutes later came a 17-year-old, arrested for the second time on a charge of selling drugs.

His Legal Aid lawyer told the boy about the offer that Justice Slavin had approved. No deal; the client wanted a trial.

Justice Slavin rebuked the lawyer for filing a lengthy legal motion. Then, fury in his voice, the judge loudly read the note about the plea offer that he scrawled in big letters in the file: "Refused. Do Not Re-offer."

Later, the Legal Aid lawyer, Jonathan Sokolow, said the offer had been for 8½ to 25 years in jail. Defense lawyers, he said, are frequently treated as irritants.

"The pressure is: 'You are part of the system, and you should grease the wheels of the system,' " Mr. Sokolow said. "The counterpressure is to remember why you went to law school and to deliver vigorous representation to your clients."

During his time in the narcotics part of the court, Justice Slavin kept next to him on the bench four 8-by-11 writing tablets. The list of drug deals he heard about in his courtroom filled every line of each one of them.

SOURCE: "Din of Assembly-Line Justice in New York," *New York Times*, January 16, 1990. Copyright © 1990 by The New York Times Company. Reprinted by permission.

In the mid-1970s, research results of studies evaluating the effectiveness of community-based corrections began to appear. In general, the findings of these studies, many of which were federally funded, were less positive than expected. Although it was demonstrated that community-based correctional programs could operate at a lower cost than such traditional practices as incarceration, many programs were found to be relatively costly when compared to the alternative of doing nothing. Because there was little documented proof that community-based programs significantly reduced criminal recidivism, some observers began asking, "Why community-based corrections?"

This question echoed across the nation. Crime continued to increase; the economic recession deepened; and concern for criminal offenders' futures declined. As a result, many communities allowed federally funded programs to die rather than to assume their funding. There was growing support for increased prison construction and growing belief on the part of the states that the federal government should provide economic assistance for it.

By the time the Reagan administration came into office, the impetus for growth in community-based corrections had significantly declined. The Carter administration had virtually eliminated LEAA and its massive funding program. The Reagan policy supported budget cuts in all branches of federal government, including the Bureau of Prisons, the National Institute of Corrections, the Office of Justice Assistance, Research, and Statistics (a significantly scaled-down version of LEAA), the U.S. Parole Commmission, and OJJDP. President Reagan proposed a new federalism in which states would assume greater responsibility for funding and administering all social programs. In addition, Reagan's Task Force on Violent Crime supported the building of new prisons, but the administration indicated that the money for construction must come from the states.

Throughout the 1980s it became increasingly clear that there would never be enough money for new prisons. While the courts were increasingly requiring state correctional systems to meet minimum standards in regard to the space allotted each inmate, increased conservatism fostered a growing willingness to rely on prisons as a correctional sanction. Laws that mandated minimum sentences for specific offenders, such as habitual criminals, and determinate-sentencing statutes that limited judicial discretion also had the effect of increasing prison populations. When the war on drugs escalated at the end of the decade, it was more than apparent that while it was possible to increase arrests, convictions, and sentences to prison, the end product was not a reduction in crime but a system in chaos.

An examination of Washington, D.C.'s effort to contain drug crime provides a vivid illustration of the problem. A 1988 study by the Rand Corporation indicated that drug arrests increased from 11,478 to 19,502 between 1981 and 1986; arrests for drug sales rose from 408 to 5274 during that same period (table 1-2). Prosecutions and convictions similarly increased, so that by 1986 more than half of all prosecutions and convictions were drug offenses. Increased arrests, prosecutions, and convictions were followed by increases in prison commitments and sentences. The average length of stay increased 83 percent during the five-year period; the minimum sentence length increased more than 450 percent.

What was the effect of this crackdown? Unfortunately, indications are that drug enforcement had little impact on either the level of drug use or the crime rate.[5]

As results such as these filtered in, there was growing interest in reducing the demand side of the drug-use equation through greater development of prevention and treatment programs. These same steps can be expected to reduce incarcerations rates.

At present, there is no end in sight to the problem of prison overcrowding. If our jail and prison population continues to grow as it has in recent years, we will

TABLE 1-2 Drug-Selected Enforcement Statistics for Washington, D.C., Criminal Justice System, 1981 and 1986

Activity	1981	1986
Sale and manufacture arrests	408	5,274
Felony drug prosecutions	734	5,101
(% of all felony prosecutions)	(13.1)	(52.6)
Felony drug convictions	273	3,309
(% of all felony convictions)	(9.6)	(52.6)
Drug commitments to correctional facilities	1,025	4,333
(% of all commitments)	(12.5)	(36.5)
Average minimum sentence (months)	5.5	25.6
Total minimum prison years for drug commitments	469.8	9,243.7

SOURCE: Peter Reuter, John Haaga, Patrick Murphy, and Amy Praskac, *Drug Use and Drug Programs in the Washington Metropolitan Area* (Santa Monica, Calif.: Rand Corporation, 1988). Reprinted by permission.

soon have over 1 million persons in confinement. In the first six months of 1988 alone, the federal and state prison population grew by 4 percent, creating a demand for about 900 new prison beds every week (figure 1-1). Such costs simply cannot be met.

The 1990s have brought forth discussion of a "kinder, gentler nation." It may be anticipated that such talk will include a renewed willingness to apply less punitive and less costly correctional sanctions against those offenders who can be safely maintained in the community. There is no interest in returning to the days when community-based corrections was touted as the solution to every correctional problem. There is a need to improve and enhance the community-based strategies that we now employ, to identify less costly alternatives to current practice, and to protect the public from the crimes of convicted offenders released to the community. In many ways we may now have achieved a more mature approach to corrections. Reintegration is not easily achieved, neither is community protection. Saving money requires firm commitment to pursue the least costly alternative, and the use of intermediate sanctions requires a clear understanding of alternative parameters. The goal of all these efforts is to achieve a continuum of cost-effective sanctions that benefit the offender while protecting the community.

Systems Analysis

An understanding of community-based correctional programs requires an understanding of the factors that influence the programs and the manner in which the programs exert influence. This two-way examination of input and output is referred to as *systems analysis*. When only the program's internal characteristics (such as personnel requirements and administration) are examined, a closed system approach is being employed. An open system analysis considers both the internal and external factors.

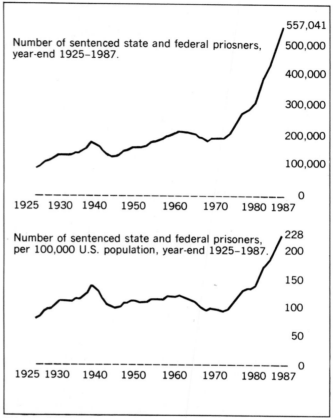

Number of sentenced state and federal priosners, year-end 1925–1987.

Number of sentenced state and federal prisoners, per 100,000 U.S. population, year-end 1925–1987.

Note: Prior to 1977, prisoner reports were based on the custody populations. Beginning in 1977, focus is on the jurisdictional population.

FIGURE 1-1 The Use of Incarceration: 1925–1987

SOURCE: Bureau of Justice Statistics, *BJS Data Report, 1988* (Washington, D.C.: U.S. Department of Justice, 1989).

A key concept in systems analysis is interdependence. Each component or subsystem influences other components and affects the functioning of the entire system. Change in one component can be expected to require change in others.

Figure 1-2 is a model of the criminal justice system. It is an open system because it depicts outside influences and influences to the outside. The police, courts, institutional corrections, and community-based programs are interdependent. All the organizations are influenced by the nature of crime and criminals; each organization influences the functioning of the others.

To illustrate the interdependence of criminal justice agencies, suppose there were a significant increase in the number of arrests made by police. This action could produce any of the following results:

1a. Jail overcrowding
1b. Increase in use of pretrial release programs

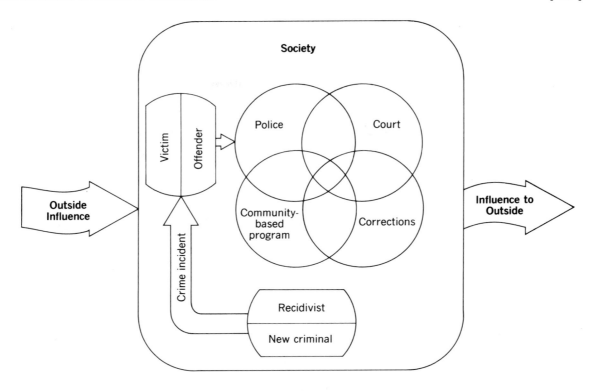

FIGURE 1-2 Elements of the Criminal Justice System
Source: "Criminal Justice Planning: A Practical Approach," by M. E. O'Neill, R. F. Bykowski, and R. S. Blair. Copyright © 1976 by Justice System Development, Inc. Reprinted by permission.

    1c. Relaxation of bail requirements
    2a. Increase in number of prosecutions
    2b. Increase in court backlog and delay
    2c. Increase in use of plea bargaining to reduce the number of trials
    3a. Increase in number of persons sentenced to prison
    3b. Prison overcrowding
    3c. Relaxation of parole requirements and increase in number of early releases from prison granted
    3d. Backup of state prisoners in local jails (when state prisons are under court order restricting overcrowding)
    3e. Increase in use of probation
    3f. Less supervision of probationers as size of caseloads swells

       A different picture of the influences affecting community-based corrections would be obtained if they were viewed as a subsystem of local government or of a community's social welfare network. For example, community-based correctional programs for juveniles may be viewed as just one component of a community's child welfare system. The efforts of juvenile probation officers and residential and nonresidential correctional programs would then be seen as part of a larger network of programs and services for troubled families and physically, emotionally, and socially disadvantaged youth. Any significant change in practice by one component of the child welfare system would necessarily alter the activities of the remaining components. If status offenses were decriminalized, then the problems of truants, runaways, and incorrigible youths would fall much more heavily on the remaining social programs because juvenile court staff and correctional programs would no longer be working with these children.

All assessments of community-based corrections within the context of systems analysis, regardless of the type of system under study, provide a greater understanding of how and why community-based correctional programs function as they do. No system conceptualization is right or wrong; its usefulness can be judged only by assessing the information and insight it provides.

We consider community-based corrections as a subsystem of local government or social welfare at various points in the following chapters; our primary and most consistent analysis, however, focuses on community-based correctional programs within the criminal justice system. The interdependence of criminal justice agencies and the function of community-based programs within the criminal justice system are the predominent themes of this book.

Critical Issues

Many issues need to be addressed if the function and impact of community-based correctional programs are to be understood. Two issues, which affect every aspect of programming, from legislative intent to budget matters, seem especially critical: the *alternatives* and *eligibility* questions.

❑ Alternatives

Community-based correctional programs are often viewed as an alternative to formal criminal justice processing, pretrial detention, or a commitment to jail or prison. This view is, in part, correct. Many persons are diverted from the criminal justice system because arrest and/or prosecution are considered unnecessary and unwarranted. Pretrial release is an alternative to pretrial confinement for persons who are unlikely to abscond prior to trial. Probation and parole are alternatives to imprisonment or continued incarceration for persons who can benefit from community supervision and assistance and who pose no threat to the community.

However, viewing community-based corrections as an alternative is misleading because it misrepresents the current operation of our criminal justice system. Without the involvement of a single organized diversion program, many offenders (especially juveniles) are diverted from the justice system because police, prosecutors, or juvenile intake staff do not believe that arrest, prosecution, or filing a petition is necessary or desirable. Many persons are currently released prior to trial because they have the money to make bail; pretrial release programs do not so much keep criminals out of jail as equalize the opportunities for freedom between poor and not so poor offenders. Finally, if we consider an alternative to be something other than the norm, then incarceration and release after completion of the maximum sentence are really alternatives to probation and parole. Today there are more than four persons on probation or parole for every one inmate in a state or federal prison.[6] Although the use of probation, prison, and parole varies from crime to crime and from jurisdiction to jurisdiction, most of the offenders processed through our criminal justice system commit crimes for which probation is the standard disposition; the remaining offenders enter institutions from which parole is the typical method of release.

When we evaluate a new community-based correctional program, it is important to consider what would have happened to the offender in the absence of the new alternative. If there were no diversion program, no supervised pretrial release program, if no special counseling program or halfway house were available for probationers or parolees, what type of treatment would the offender have received?

In some communities, offenders have been placed in new community-based correctional programs when little or no correctional intervention was really needed. This practice often occurs when a program appears to offer so much benefit that "it couldn't hurt" to provide the offender with counseling or supervision, even though it is really not essential. Such practices may be well intended, but they invariably change the objectives of the programs affected. If the clients of community-based corrections are offenders who don't really need help, instead of persons who would otherwise be formally processed or institutionalized, then community-based corrections can become a costly luxury rather than a low-cost reform. In the end, social control rather than reintegration will become the program's function.

❑ Eligibility Requirements

The issue of how community-based programs are used—as an alternative to what?—is directly related to the issue of program eligibility requirements. Whom we choose to divert, to release prior to trial, or to supervise in the community directly affects both the offenders and the role of community-based corrections in the correctional system. Programs that accept only low-risk offenders who need little assistance can easily demonstrate high success rates, but they are not very useful correctional efforts. Such programs offer a helping hand to those who do not really need it; the criminal justice system is left substantially unchanged.

Summary

Community-based correctional programs have many rationales, but their most distinct correctional goal is to reintegrate offenders into the community. The correctional policy of reintegration assumes that crime is a manifestation of both offender and community failure and that both community change and individual rehabilitation are required if subsequent crime is to be avoided. Additional objectives include community protection, and serving as intermediate punishments and cost-effective correctional sanctions.

To achieve reintegration, community-based correctional programs must provide opportunities for personal growth through education, vocational training and counseling, as well as opportunities for assuming normal social roles. This requires a location in the community and a nonsecure environment. Community tolerance for non-conforming but law-abiding behavior is also important if offenders are to find the acceptance necessary for reintegration. Staff in community corrections must work to educate the public and to expand community opportunities. They also serve as offender advocates and community resource brokers, who link offenders to the community programs they need.

Community-based corrections developed as a result of dissatisfaction with institutional confinement, and in recognition of the problems encountered by inmates re-entering society after prolonged incarceration. Criminological theories that emphasized the stigmatizing effects of criminal justice processing encouraged the search for less debilitating alternatives. The adoption of a systems approach to the analysis of the criminal justice process and the professionalization of criminal justice employees also stimulated a willingness to explore new directions.

The 1970s witnessed phenomenal growth in community-based corrections. Often this growth was poorly planned and/or implemented. When research began to demonstrate that community-based correctional strategies were valuable but not invariably effective, program growth slowed. The political conservatism and economic recession of the 1980s also contributed to the decline in program growth. Yet even as new program development slowed, the need to find less costly alternatives to incarceration prompted a reexamination of community-based corrections. Prison construction, once promoted as a correctional policy, began to sap the resources of a nation. Not only was the task never-ending, but it was proving an ineffective means of dealing with the crime problem. The war on drugs revealed a need to do more than simply lock up troubled substance abusers, who came to account for greater and greater proportions of the population in confinement.

The 1990s are witnessing renewed interest in the potential of community-based corrections. Today the challenge is to develop, implement, and evaluate appropriate alternatives for the diversity of criminal offenders.

KEY WORDS AND CONCEPTS			
	advocates	intermediate	resource brokers
	community-based	punishments	systems analysis
	corrections	labeling theory	
	cost-effective	reintegration	
	sanctions		

NOTES

1. President's Commission on Law Enforcement and Administration of Justice, *Task Force Report: Corrections* (Washington, D.C.: U.S. Government Printing Office, 1967), p. 7.
2. Ibid.
3. National Institute of Mental Health, *Graduated Release* (Washington, D.C.: U.S. Government Printing Office, 1971), p. 1.
4. H. G. Moeller, "Community-Based Correctional Services," in *Handbook of Criminology*, edited by Daniel Glaser (Chicago: Rand McNally, 1974).
5. Peter Reuter, John Haaga, Patrick Murphy, and Amy Praskac, *Drug Use and Drug Programs in the Washington Metropolitan Area* (Santa Monica, Calif.: Rand Corporation, 1988).

6. U.S. Department of Justice, *Correctional Populations in the United States, 1986* (Washington, D.C.: U.S. Government Printing Office, 1989).

FOR FURTHER READING

McAnany, Patrick D., Doug Thomson, and David Fogel, *Probation and Justice: Reconsideration of a Mission* (Cambridge, Mass.: Oelgeschlager, Gunn and Hain, 1984).

McCarthy, Belinda R., ed., *Intermediate Punishments: Intensive Supervision, Home Confinement and Electronic Surveillance* (Monsey, N.Y.: Criminal Justice Press, 1987).

O'Leary, Vincent, and Todd R. Clear, *Directions for Community Corrections in the 1990s* (Washington, D.C.: National Institute of Corrections, 1984).

Petersilia, Joan, and Susan Turner, with Joyce Peterson, *Prison vs. Probation in California* (Santa Monica, Calif.: Rand Corporation, 1986).

2: Diversion Programs

Diversion in the Criminal Justice System
  Traditional Diversion
  Avoidance of Unnecessary Arrest and Prosecution
  Contemporary Diversion
Forms of Diversion
The Philosophy of Diversion
Objectives
  Offenders
  Criminal Justice System
The Diversion Controversy
Types of Diversion Programs
  Alcohol Detoxification Centers
  Diversion of Public Inebriates and the Development of Alcohol Programs
  Family Crisis Intervention Units
  Programs for the Vocationally Disadvantaged
  Programs for Youthful and/or Multiproblem Offenders
  Programs for Drug-Abusing Offenders
  Community Dispute-Resolution Programs
  Neighborhood Justice Centers
  Night Prosecutor Program
Problems and Issues in Diversion
  Problems in Deferred Prosecution and Pretrial Intervention Programs
  The Rehabilitative Ideal
  Diversion and the Victims of Crime
Alternatives to Diversion
New Directions in Diversion Programs
  Need for Alternatives
Summary

DIVERSION PROGRAMS PROVIDE alternatives to the criminal justice process. They offer alleged criminal offenders an opportunity to avoid arrest and/or prosecution and to obtain assistance in the form of medical services, counseling, education, and vocational training.

Although diversion programs do not serve convicted offenders, they may be considered correctional programs because they do serve persons who are accused of crimes by providing them with various forms of assistance in the community. In this sense, diversion programs present the community's first chance for intervention, a chance to provide the deserving defendant with whatever aid he needs and to individualize his treatment so as to resolve the problems that led to his alleged criminal behavior.

Diversion programs are controversial. Many observers of the criminal justice system believe that the primary function of diversion programs is to coerce into treatment those individuals who would not normally be prosecuted. These critics view diversion programs as "widening the net" of social control through the unwarranted expansion and formalization of discretion. In this chapter, we examine both views of diversion and the empirical evidence to support each.

Diversion in the Criminal Justice System

❏ Traditional Diversion

The concept of diversion is as old as our system of criminal justice. Although it is a well-established principle that our society should be governed by the rule of law rather than by the rule of men, it is acknowledged that the administration of our laws needs to be flexible enough to meet our citizens' diverse and sometimes complex problems and needs. With this in mind, our criminal statutes generally are broadly formulated to cover a wide range of behaviors that may be considered offensive to social norms. Criminal justice system officials are authorized to use considerable discretion or subjective judgment in their efforts to enforce the law. The criminal statutes may be interpreted in terms of the problems and needs of the individual offender, the impact of his offense, or the expectations of the community in which the crime occurs. Officials may evaluate the advantages and disadvantages of various courses of action.

Neither police officers nor prosecutors are required to invoke the criminal justice process every time a crime is committed. Police officers may arrest an alleged criminal or they may choose to dismiss him with a reprimand, refer him to a social service agency, or ignore his offense entirely if it is not a serious one. Prosecutors may file criminal charges against an alleged offender or pursue an alternate course of legal action (such as initiating civil commitment proceedings against a defendant who is believed to be mentally ill) or seek some informal remedy to the problem (such as permitting a defendant to make restitution in order to avoid prosecution for shoplifting). Whenever a criminal justice system official chooses not to invoke the criminal justice process, he is diverting that individual from the criminal justice system. Contemporary diversion programs resulted from attempts to expand and formalize traditional diversion.

The Labeling Perspective

"Social groups create deviance by making the rules whose infraction constitutes deviance, and by applying these rules to particular people and labeling them as outsiders. From this point of view, deviance is not a quality of the act the person commits, but rather a consequence of the application by others of rules and sanctions to an offender. The deviant is one to whom that label has successfully been applied; deviant behavior is behavior people so label."

SOURCE: Howard Becker, *The Outsiders* (New York: Free Press, 1963), p. 9.

❏ Avoidance of Unnecessary Arrest and Prosecution

Today many believe that the criminal justice system does very little well and does most things rather poorly. Its rehabilitative efforts have repeatedly been judged as unsuccessful, and, even if this evaluation is inaccurate, the perception of failure is widespread. In addition to failing to put most offenders back on the right path, the system is commonly viewed as steering many of its clients in the wrong direction.

Acceptance of the labeling theory, which focuses on the consequences of the formal and informal labeling of behavior and individuals as deviant, has resulted in a closer examination of the impact of criminal justice system processing. Convicted offenders frequently lose their jobs, and their families and friendships are disrupted. If incarcerated, they are forced into debilitating living conditions with the worst of role models—other criminals. Finally, these offenders are forced to live with the symbolic and real effects of a criminal conviction—the stigma of being an ex-convict and the loss of civil rights that conviction often brings.

These consequences of criminal justice processing can be expected to provide more, not less, criminal behavior. The acknowledgment of the criminal justice system's failure to assist offenders and its often harmful impact on them has prompted the development and expansion of various alternatives to the criminal justice system for all but the most serious offenders. This desire for options other than arrest and prosecution led to the development and expansion of formal diversion programs.

❏ Contemporary Diversion

The perceived need for formal diversion programs has been met with action from many government agencies. The Department of Labor began funding pretrial intervention programs for vocationally disadvantaged offenders in 1967 and funded additional projects in the early 1970s. The Law Enforcement Assistance Administration funded experimental alcohol detoxification centers at about the same time. In 1971, the White House Special Action Office for Drug Abuse Prevention developed a diversion model for drug abusers—*Treatment Alternatives to Street Crime (TASC)*. Several states quickly followed this effort with the development of special legislation for the diversion of drug abusers from the criminal justice system.

Other diversion programs that developed during this period focused on interpersonal disputes rather than on the nature of a defendant's problems. Family crisis intervention units were developed in several urban police departments. A dispute settlement mechanism for more general categories of interpersonal disputes was established in Columbus, Ohio, in 1971.

These new diversion programs received considerable support from professionals in the field of criminal justice and from commissions established to study the problems and needs of the criminal justice system. In 1967, the President's Commission on Law Enforcement and the Administration of Justice reported that "it is more fruitful to discuss not who can be tried as a matter of law, but how the officers of the administration of criminal justice should deal with people who present special needs and problems."[1] This commission recommended the early identification and diversion of offenders in need of treatment, but who did not require criminal dispositions.

Further support for diversion was provided by the President's Task Force on Prisoner Rehabilitation, the American Bar Association, and the American Correctional Association. Criteria and procedures for diversion were outlined in the 1973 report of the National Advisory Commission on Criminal Justice Standards and Goals. National and state organizations were established to promote the expansion of pretrial intervention programs. The number and types of diversion programs grew throughout the 1970s. During that time, the Law Enforcement Assistance Administration alone funded over 1,200 diversion programs for adults and juveniles at a cost of over $112 million.[2] In the 1980s much of the federal aid for diversion programs was withdrawn. However, state and local governments, in many jurisdictions, assumed the costs of many of these programs.

Forms of Diversion

The concept of diversion is as old as our system of criminal justice, but the forms of diversion programs today are very new. Consequently, there is considerable confusion about the precise meaning of the term *diversion*. Some persons use this term interchangeably with prevention, traditional diversion (the routine use of official discretion), or efforts to minimize the penetration of an individual into the criminal justice system.

Our definition was developed by the National Advisory Commission on Criminal Justice Standards and Goals, which defines diversion as "formally acknowledged and organized efforts to utilize alternatives to initial or continued processing into the justice system. To qualify as diversion, such efforts must be undertaken prior to adjudication and after a legally proscribed action has occurred."[3]

Viewed in this sense, diversion programs are distinct from prevention efforts. Diversion must follow a criminal act, but prevention attempts to prohibit a crime from occurring. Contemporary diversion also is distinguishable from traditional diversion or the routine use of official discretion, which is informal and unorganized in focus. Finally, diversion may be differentiated from minimization of penetration efforts. Such efforts attempt to promote the utilization of the least restrictive alternative available at each stage of the criminal justice process. Programs aimed at promoting the use of probation may be accurately placed in this category. Diversion programs, however, are limited to efforts to halt or avoid the processing of an offender through the criminal justice system.

Diversion programs may be characterized as conditional or unconditional. Those that remove the offender from the criminal justice process and place no condition on his postdiversion behavior are *unconditional diversion* programs. Those that restrict the offender's postdiversion behavior, monitor his progress in the community, and provide for reinstatement of prosecution if the conditions of diversion are not met are *conditional diversion* programs. Often these latter programs require offenders to participate in treatment programs. Because such programs maintain the option of returning the offender to the criminal justice system for prosecution, they are sometimes referred to as *deferred prosecution* programs.

The Philosophy of Diversion

Athough the philosophy of diversion is often unstated, it is implicit in virtually all diversion efforts. It emphasizes informal, administrative decision making in efforts to determine: (1) if nonjudicial processing is warranted, (2) if a particular defendant needs treatment, (3) what type of treatment is required, (4) if the treatment chosen has been successful, and (5) if charges against the defendant should be reinstated or dropped. It is assumed that such decision making is "better" than the decision making that occurs within the criminal justice system because it is more individualized and needs-oriented and less restricted by due process requirements. It is also assumed that the questions asked in diversion programs are "better" questions than those asked within the criminal justice system. Rather than asking what acts were committed and what punishment is deserved, the questions of diversion concern the person's problem and how his needs and those of the community can best be met.

Objectives

The principal objectives of diversion programs fall into two general categories: offender change objectives and criminal justice system objectives. Although these objectives are interrelated and interdependent, they focus on different aspects of the problems of crime and the appropriate responses to criminal behavior.

❏ Offenders

The criminal justice process and its unavoidable punishments seem inappropriate for many offenders. What is needed instead is a conscientious and professional evaluation of the problems that led to the individual's criminal behavior and sustained efforts to resolve them. The criminal justice system is poorly equipped to provide either diagnostic or helping services. Not only are its resources limited, but lengthy delays often precede whatever treatment is available. The optimum point for intervention often has passed and cynicism has set in by the time a convicted offender receives any assistance.

Diversion programs attempt to overcome all these problems. Their objectives are as follows:

1. Initiate evaluation and intervention efforts immediately upon identification of an eligible defendant
2. Provide specialized program services beyond the range of those available in the criminal justice system
3. Minimize the social, emotional, and economic disruption experienced by a defendant who faces criminal prosecution
4. Avoid the stigma and loss of civil liberties experienced by individuals convicted of criminal acts
5. Provide a noncoercive environment for the provision of services

Through achievement of these objectives, diversion programs can more effectively meet the general goal of offender rehabilitation and reintegration.

❑ Criminal Justice System

If persons who require and merit treatment or some other form of assistance can be removed from the criminal justice system, both the speed and quality of justice should improve. If the number of defendants processed through the criminal justice system is reduced, system resources can be focused on the remaining individuals and their more serious crimes. Police officers, prosecutors, public defenders, probation officers, and judges can direct their efforts toward identifying, convicting, and sentencing those defendants whose acts necessitate a punitive response. Correctional agencies can focus their limited educational and therapeutic services on those individuals who are so dangerous or so deserving of punishment that they cannot be handled outside the criminal justice system. In this way, diversion programs can promote a more effective criminal justice system by permitting it to serve as a measure of last resort rather than a port of entry for all offenders.

The Diversion Controversy

In the following sections, we examine a variety of unconditional and conditional diversion programs and research on the effectiveness of diversion efforts. Before examining various program models, the reader should be aware of the tremendous controversy currently surrounding diversion programs. In the last few years, a number of research studies have concluded that diversion has fallen far short of its objectives. Using experimental research designs, with subjects randomly assigned to diversion programs and control groups, these studies have found that diversion often has an insignificant effect on recidivism and may increase the cost of handling and supervising offenders.[4] These negative results seem to be a consequence of the process by which offenders are selected for diversion. Too often, only nonserious offenders, who in lieu of diversion would have had their cases dismissed or would have received only minimal sanctions, are selected for diversion program participation.[5] In addition, there is serious concern that when divertees are required to admit guilt as a prerequisite to diversion, they may suffer an irretrievable loss of due process guarantees under current diversion program operations.

All research findings are not so discouraging; we discuss positive as well as negative results in greater detail at various points throughout this chapter. At this point, the reader is simply advised to examine closely the various program models presented and to consider their potential both for success and for abuse.

Types of Diversion Programs

Diversion programs can be classified by the stage of the criminal justice system at which diversion occurs and the types of clients or the problems served by the particular diversion program. Figure 2-1 presents the diversion alternatives available at each stage of the criminal justice process.

Diversion programs that provide alternatives to the arrest of persons suspected of crimes are often referred to as *police-based* or *arrest-stage diversion* programs. These programs may be administered by law enforcement agencies or by public or private organizations working closely with police. Juvenile diversion programs, for example, are often administered by law enforcement agencies.[6] When police do not directly administrate these diversion programs, they often work closely with the independent public or private agency to establish eligibility criteria and diversion procedures. Police then refer suitable candidates to the program as an alternative to arrest. Because police-based diversion programs generally rely on police officers to make the diversion decision, arrest-stage programs do not reduce the police work load. They do, however, reduce the costs of jail detention, prosecution, and correction.

Diversion programs that focus on individuals who have been arrested but not convicted of their criminal charges may be referred to as *pretrial* or *court diversion*. These programs may focus on any stage of the criminal justice process following arrest but preceding adjudication. Typically, the prosecutor makes the decision to divert prior to filing criminal charges or the court makes it prior to initiating the trial. Over two hundred pretrial diversion programs are in operation today.[7] Over half these programs are administered by the prosecutor's office, the court, the probation department, or the public defender's office; the remaining programs are operated by private or public noncriminal justice agencies.[8]

Most pretrial diversion programs are conditional; defendants are required to comply with certain stipulations, such as refraining from criminal activity and participating in a rehabilitative program. Over two-thirds of all programs require defendants to make restitution or perform community service.[9] If the intervention program is not successful, criminal charges may be filed or reinstated against the defendant.

Pretrial diversion may serve as a substitute for arrest-stage diversion if no alternative to arrest is available within the jurisdiction. In such cases, arrest costs are not avoided, but some jail detention, prosecution, and correction costs can be reduced. In communities that have both police and pretrial diversion programs, the pretrial programs are generally reserved for more serious offenders whose offenses merit arrest and careful consideration before a decision to divert is made.

Diversion programs do not have to focus on any single group of offenders or specialize in the nature of services they offer. Many pretrial diversion programs primarily provide diagnostic, referral, and monitoring services. They identify offender

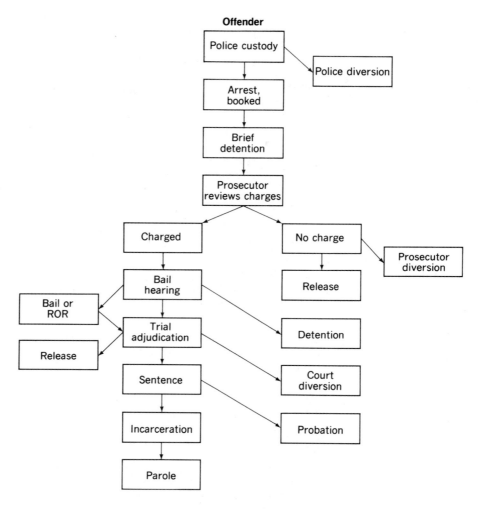

FIGURE 2-1 Diversion Process for Adults

SOURCE: National Council on Crime and Delinquency, *Drug Abuse and the Criminal Justice System* (Davis, Calif.: 1974), p. 143.

needs, refer defendants to appropriate community resources, and report back to the prosecutor's office on the defendants' progress in treatment. Such programs may deal with any type of offender, although most tend to focus on youthful defendants, persons accused of nonserious crimes, and/or first offenders.

❏ Alcohol Detoxification Centers

In many communities, arrests of adults for public intoxication far outnumber any other single category of arrest. Not surprisingly, drunks tend to occupy a large proportion of the jail cells in such communities. Jails shield the inebriate from public view, but they offer the offender little else. Alcohol detoxification programs

What Is the Cost of Drunkenness, and Who Is the Public Inebriate?

It is estimated that:

- There are 300,000–500,000 public inebriates in the United States.
- Public inebriates account for one out of three misdemeanor arrests.
- The processing of these cases costs approximately $500 million a year.

The Public Inebriate is typically a 45-year-old white male, unemployed, with nine years of education, divorced or never married, homeless, receiving no public assistance, and having a prior arrest for drunkenness and/or prior admission to a treatment program or detoxification center.

SOURCE: National Institute of Alcohol Abuse and Alcoholism, *Complex Issues Surround Services to Public Inebriates* (Washington, D.C.: National Institute of Alcohol Abuse and Alcoholism, Information and Feature Service, #95, April 1982).

provide this same service, but in a more secure and therapeutic environment. They also can provide medical treatment, psychological counseling, and referrals to long-term care when necessary.

There are two basic models of detoxification centers. The first is the *medical model*; it provides extensive medical diagnostic and treatment services and maintains a staff of medical professionals. The second model is commonly known as the *social setting detoxification program* because it provides only limited medical services. Paraprofessional staff are trained to identify persons in need of more extensive medical care; such persons are then taken to local hospitals. Otherwise, only routine first-aid and the dispensing of physician-prescribed drugs are provided.

Many of the early experimental alcohol detoxification centers adhered to the medical model, which proved to be quite expensive. When it was recognized that many inebriates did not require extensive medical care, many programs adopted the social setting model, which is less costly because it utilizes existing community medical resources.

❏ Diversion of Public Inebriates and the Development of Alcohol Programs

In 1971 the National Conference of Commissioners on Uniform State Laws published the Uniform Alcoholism and Intoxication Treatment Act. The intent of this model act was to encourage states to decriminalize public drunkenness and shift the responsibility for the care and treatment of public inebriates from the criminal justice system to the public health system. The Secretary of the U.S. Department of Health, Education and Welfare (the forerunner of the present Department of Health and Human Services) expressed the concern behind this movement when he wrote:

> For too long, public intoxication has been the responsibility of the criminal justice system. Experience has demonstrated that existing laws and existing ways of handling alcoholic persons only helped to perpetuate human misery and suffering and to create burdens for their families, local communities, police departments, courts and other agencies. The failure to provide for the medical and social needs of alcoholic persons on the other hand has contributed to high rates of recidivism and the evolution of a revolving door system of ineffectiveness.[10]

Working with Chronic Alcoholics

Jim Kelly's official title at the Seventh Street Center is social research assistant, but his activities are not limited to research. He is one of three persons on the center's management team, which is responsible for the program administration; he is also responsible for all employee training, staff development, and employee services.

He became interested in alcoholism while in college. "At Yale, you could buy a student activities card that would get you into parties where you could drink free for two or three hours a night." Some of his friends developed drinking problems during this time. As a psychology major, Jim began to focus his studies on alcoholism and its impact, and he found that alcoholism has been linked to virtually every contemporary social problem. "Suicide, violent crime, marital and family problems, illness, automobile accidents—alcoholism touches so many lives. They say that for each alcoholic, four other persons are affected—family, friends or co-workers. Nationally, there's about 10 million alcoholics, add about 40 million other persons and you've got the most significant social problem today."

He says that working with alcoholics is frustrating. There are few successes and death comes early to the chronic inebriate. "But we do have a few successes—some who come back to visit—some friends who help us when they can."

By diverting common drunks from the criminal justice system, it was believed, the resources of the criminal justice system could be shifted to more serious offenses, and by diverting these offenders to the health care system they would be provided with the appropriate treatment services.

Since 1971, thirty-four jurisdictions have decriminalized public drunkenness, and evaluation studies have reported that the passage of the act has been followed by a downward trend in arrests for public drunkenness in jurisdictions that changed the law.[11]

The Seventh Street Detoxification Center in Charlotte, North Carolina, is representative of social setting detoxification centers.[12] Only about 8 percent of the persons local police bring to the center require medical services not available there, and most of these are transferred to a nearby hospital for treatment.

The Seventh Street Center is larger than most detoxification programs. It has fifty-two beds and usually operates at about 50 percent capacity; over 5,500 persons are admitted to the program annually. Most of these individuals are brought to the center by local police; others are brought by friends, family, or members of Alcoholics Anonymous.

The center provides chronic alcoholics with three meals a day, snacks, and a bed. During their stay, which averages about 4.5 days, residents have a social history taken by a center employee, are evaluated by counselors, and participate in the development of a treatment plan. That plan identifies the community program to which participants will be referred upon their release from the center.

Most residents sleep for the first few days of their stay at the Seventh Street Center. For those who are interested, motivational counseling is available and is designed to stimulate the individual's determination to seek further help. Individual and group counseling, family counseling, films, and lectures are also available. The center has a recreational area that consists of a pool table, television, playing cards,

The Minneapolis Detoxification Center Civilian Intake Services: Observed Contacts with Potential Inebriates

1. A call over the police radio notified them that some man was sleeping on the sidewalk in front of a business. No police were on the scene when the van arrived. They woke him by calling his name and shaking him. They asked if he wanted to go to detox and told him that he could not sleep on the sidewalk. There was a hotel in the building he was sleeping in front of and they asked if he was living there. He answered yes and then said no. They asked where he lived; he responded that it was close by. At first he appeared unconscious and very drunk. He did not want to go to detox and he looked like he was getting clearer on where he wanted to go. The staff was undecided about the seriousness of his condition and decided, in an unspoken manner, to let him go on his way. Once in the van they talked over the situation—still unsure of what the proper action should have been. They then followed the person to make sure he could get around without getting into or causing trouble. As he walked, he staggered around but kept going in the general direction that he had indicated his home was. He went down an alley and across a vacant parking lot. The decision of the staff was that he would make it. However, after two blocks he came to a corner and was unable to negotiate the curb. He stumbled and nearly fell. The decision to pick up was made at this point. While crossing the intersection he appeared to panhandle a motorist. This confirmed the prior decision to pick up. They indicated to him that he shouldn't bother people. On the form to admit him, they wrote he was moderately intoxicated and disturbing people.

2. As they were driving down an alley behind an in-famous bar (Dolly's) frequented by Native Americans, the van stopped since there was a man down with about three people around him. The man had been beaten severely and possibly stabbed around the eye. The staff called for an ambulance, which arrived within a few minutes. The van staff mentioned that this bar generally had incidents similar to this.

3. The staff pulled up to a man called Tony. He was at a busy intersection, unsteady on his feet. They asked if he wanted to go to detox; he declined the invitation. About an hour later the van went by the same inter-section and Tony had made it to the opposite corner.

4. A police call came in for the "Bear's Den" bar. This bar is on Franklyn Ave., in the heart of the Native American section. The bar's clientele is mostly Native American. The van pulled up and the staff saw two men in front and immediately recognized Francis "S." The "S" family, about four of them, are regular clients at detox; Francis is the worst of them according to the staff. Since Francis was unconscious they just picked him up and put him in the van. The bar's manager, a white man, came out and appeared thankful that the van had come. He explained that the pint bottle that the second man had was Francis's. The second man was conscious and fairly well dressed. He was very belligerent and very big. The staff asked if he wanted to go to detox. He asked them if they wanted to take him—it seemed he was im-plying that he would put up a fight. Then his wife came out of the bar. She wanted him to keep his mouth closed and every time he would mouth off to the staff she would yell at him ("Do you want them to take you?"), and slap him in the face. The staff decided to leave him with her. While he was drunk it appeared that his wife could care for him. The owner looked like he wanted both of them picked up.

Source: "The Impact of Decriminalization on the Intake Process for Public Inebriates: Third Project Report" (Washington, D.C.: NCJR'S Microfiche Collection, 1976), pp. 86–88.

and books. The center avoids serving as a "flophouse" by regulating the number of times an individual may enter the program.

The Seventh Street Center has attempted to develop orientation sessions for local police to familiarize them with the services it provides. North Carolina recently decriminalized public intoxication; many people expected the number of persons brought to the center to increase drastically, but this did not occur. Police can still arrest drunks for blocking public thoroughfares and bring them to the local jail for detention. It appears that police officers who chose to transport public drunks to the center prior to decriminalization of the offense are continuing to do so and officers who previously ignored such persons or arrested and transported them to the local jail have not yet begun to divert public drunks to the Seventh Street Center.

Generally speaking, whenever police officers serve as the principal source of referral to alcohol detoxification programs, several problems may arise. First, the handling of public drunks may be a low-priority service within the police department. Unless there is pressure "clean the streets," police may ignore drunks and only rarely transport them to the detoxification center. Second, unless police officers are convinced of the benefits of detoxification services, they may well elect to arrest and detain public drunks as statutes permit. Finally, whenever police officers are utilized as a major source of referral to detoxification programs, the objective of minimizing the burden on criminal justice system resources may be sacrificed. Except for the reduction in jail detention costs, no other significant savings may be possible; when such persons were previously ignored, transporting drunks to the detoxification center might even result in an additional loss of public personnel resources. It may well be advantageous to follow the practice of detoxification centers in Boston and Minneapolis, where centers provide their own "pick-up and delivery services" to public inebriates.

❑ Family Crisis Intervention Units

Intrafamily disputes are not only one of the most common problems facing law enforcement officers today, they are also one of the most dangerous. Research has shown that a large proportion of police officers injured or killed in the line of duty are attacked during efforts to respond to violent family quarrels. To make matters worse, although calls for police assistance in such disputes are highly repetitive, with many families repeatedly experiencing the same conflicts and making the same complaints, these complaints often do not lead to successful prosecutions. Charges frequently are dropped after tempers have cooled and the complainant withdraws his or her accusation. Such actions often have led police departments to respond only reluctantly, if at all, to calls for assistance in family disputes. Consequently, endangered persons are sometimes denied needed assistance. Thus, family crisis intervention units (FCIU) have been viewed as a valuable component of police services.

Most such programs operating today have been modeled after Morton Bard's pioneering effort within the New York City Police Department. The New York FCIU was established as an experimental program in the late 1960s.[13] A specially selected team of eighteen officers was provided with 160 hours of intensive training in crisis intervention techniques and comprehensive information about community counseling resources. The training included lectures and field trips, human relations workshops, and "learning by doing" through family crisis lab demonstrations. In these labs, professional actors depicted family crisis situations and the police officers intervened. Their interventions were later discussed and criticized. This initial training was followed by additional inservice training. The officers worked in pairs, providing 24-hour coverage in a racially mixed, economically disadvantaged neighborhood. Over a two-year period, they handled 1,388 disputes within 962 families.

Efforts to evaluate this program were limited by the lack of a control group of officers without FCIU training who worked in a similar precinct.[14] It did appear,

Steps in Effective Family Crisis Intervention

1. Prevent violence by separating the disputants.
2. Allow only one person to talk at a time.
3. Take the disputants into separate rooms.
4. Switch officers so that the stories can be checked out.
5. In listening to the stories, try to find out in each case what each individual contributed to the conflict.
6. If one of the disputants holds himself to blame, find out in what ways the other shares the blame.
7. Ask questions so as to get the details as clear as possible.
8. Find out if there has been a previous history of this kind of behavior.
9. See if the history dates from before the marriage, and if the behavior applies to past relationships or to similar relationships in the present.
10. Give each person the opportunity to speak in detail.
11. Bring the couple together to tell their stories to each other. Again, make sure only one person speaks at a time.
12. Point out similarities and discrepancies in the stories.
13. Point out the part that each is playing.
14. Get a reaction from both about what the officers say they see is going on.
15. Ask what the couple plan to do in response to what has transpired and to the officer's reactions. If they seem to understand and say they want to try to work it out, accept it.
16. If you disagree with their response, suggest that they seek other help. If necessary, make the referral.
17. Tell them that if there is another dispute and they see that they are coming close to violence or to repeating the same pattern, they should go again for counseling or contact the FCIU.
18. While noting that there will be further difficulties, assure them that if they sit down and talk, at least they can come out in the open and try to resolve it.
19. If not in the beginning, then before you leave, make sure that they know your name.

SOURCE: Morton Bard, *Training Police as Specialists in Family Crisis Intervention* (Washington, D.C.: U.S. Government Printing Office, 1971), p. 19.

however, that the officers in the experimental program were more willing to respond to intrafamily disputes than officers in a different precinct selected for comparison. Officers in the experimental precinct experienced no family dispute-related deaths or injuries during the research period. The FCIU officers made referrals to local counseling services in about 75 percent of their interventions, but only about one-fifth of those families actually applied for assistance.

FCIUs exist today in a number of urban police departments. Many departments also have broadened the scope of training to provide all police officers with general skill development in the areas of interpersonal relations and crisis intervention. Many family quarrels have been successfully diverted from the criminal justice system. Although such diversion may increase demands upon the police, the ability to resolve family disputes skillfully in a nonviolent fashion, as well as to avoid what often becomes a pointless arrest, may well prove beneficial both to the disputants and to the police officers.

The practice of mediation is not without its critics. In the mid-1980s, the Police Foundation conducted a research study focusing on the handling of domestic disputes

The Minneapolis Experiment

A major experiment was recently conducted by the Police Foundation in Minneapolis to learn whether mediation, separation, or arrest works best at reducing subsequent violence against the victim. The premise was that police practice should be guided by knowledge about the actual effects of using one policy instead of another.

Why Was the Experiment Done by Lottery?

The experiment was done by police officers who agreed to give up their discretion in domestic assault cases and to take whatever action was dictated by a random system of employing arrest in some cases, mediation in others, and so on. This method attempts to ensure that those arrested, those advised, and those ordered out of the house were roughly comparable in average age, education, income, rate of offending, percent black or white, and whether they were intoxicated. Otherwise, the police would have arrested only the most "serious" offenders, who might then have had the highest rate of repeat violence—not because they were arrested, but because they were unusually violent people.

What Did Police Do?

Police practices varied somewhat from officer to officer. The arrests were probably the most consistent police action, with the offender spending at least one night in jail. Separation varied somewhat, because if the offender refused to leave the house, the officer was instructed to arrest him. Advice or mediation varied the most widely, because some officers put much time into it while others put very little. None of them received special training for the experiment, since the purpose was to test the "typical" police approach to advice or mediation.

What Were the Results?

After the police completed their work on a case, Police Foundation researchers contacted the victims and attempted to interview them every two weeks for the next six months. The main focus of the interviews was to discover if the offenders had repeated their assault. Repeat violence was also measured by tracking, for six months, all of the official records of repeat contacts between police and offenders (or victims).

What Were the Findings?

Under both methods of measurement, the arrested offenders were about half as likely to commit repeat violence as the nonarrested offenders. The official records showed that about 18 percent of *all* offenders repeated their violence, while only 10 percent of the *arrested* offenders repeated it. Findings from the interviews with victims were similar.

How Believable Are the Findings?

The results of the experiment seem to indicate that a policy of arresting many or most domestic assailants will spare many victims from future violence. However, all social science research has limitations and leaves questions unanswered; this project is no exception. The main questions about the Minneapolis findings are whether the victims of arrested offenders were threatened and thereby discouraged from calling the police if they were attacked again (which would affect the official measurement) and whether the victims failed to tell the interviewers about the repeat violence. Another possibility is that the arrest policy discouraged victims from calling the police again because what they wanted from the police was emergency help and not to have their companions arrested and possibly prosecuted. Yet another possibility is that the arrested men were likelier to move out and possibly later to treat other women violently. Whether the findings of the Minnesota research will stand up will be known only after similar experiments elsewhere attempt to replicate its findings.

SOURCE: Lawrence Sherman, "Domestic Violence," *Crime File Study Guide* (Washington, D.C.: National Institute of Justice, U.S. Department of Justice, undated).

by the police. The results of this study called into question the mediation approach followed by many police departments in handling domestic disturbances. The Minneapolis study basically found that when an arrest was made, the offender was less likely to commit a subsequent assault or disturbance. The U.S. Department of Justice is currently sponsoring replication studies to determine whether the Police Foundation's findings are reliable and valid.

❏ Programs for the Vocationally Disadvantaged

The initial efforts to divert unemployed and underemployed persons from the criminal justice system were funded by the Department of Labor in 1967. The original projects, the Manhattan Court Employment Project (MCEP) and Project Crossroads in Washington, D.C., were considered very successful and have served as models for diversion programs in over thirty cities, including nine additional programs funded by the Department of Labor. An examination of MCEP provides an interesting illustration of the evolution of a program for the vocationally disadvantaged.

Manhattan Court Employment Project. The original MCEP eligibility standards were designed to ensure the success of diversion—alcoholics, drug addicts, people who make large sums of money illegally, persons with numerous prior arrests, and individuals charged with serious felonies were excluded. In 1970, six eligibility criteria had been established:

1. Males and females between the ages of 16 and 45
2. Unemployed, or, if employed, not earning more than $125 per week
3. Residents of New York City, except Queens and Staten Island, with verifiable addresses
4. Not charged with a violation (a petty criminal offense), a homicide, rape, kidnapping, or arson
5. Not alcoholics or identifiable drug addicts (although those charged with possession of marijuana or hashish may be considered)
6. Individuals who have not spent more than one continuous year in a penal institution[15]

By 1976, only persons charged with felonies were considered for the program.[16]

Participants were selected for the diversion program by project staff, who reviewed the prior records of all persons brought to the Manhattan Criminal Court. Potentially suitable defendants were interviewed to determine eligibility and interest in the program. If the defendant and his attorney agreed to participate, a recommendation was made for adjournment.

The prosecutor and the presiding judge both approved all recommendations for diversion. When a recommendation was approved, the defendant's case was adjourned for four months. At the end of that time, the defendant returned to court with an MCEP progress report that recommended (1) dismissal of the charges, (2) further adjournment to permit additional counseling, or (3) termination of the defendant's participation in the project and the resumption of prosecution.[17] To qualify for a recommendation for dismissal, a defendant must not have been rearrested or used narcotics during the period of adjournment; he also must have behaved responsibly, become involved in any counseling sessions attended, and made a satisfactory vocational adjustment during the 90-day period.

MCEP offered clients individual and group counseling, career development services, education, training, and job placement. Counseling was provided by ex-addicts or ex-convicts, who had been trained to serve as counselors and role models for the defendants. Career development services were provided by persons with academic training or job experience in vocational planning; they worked with defendants to formulate vocational objectives and monitored the client's progress in academic, training, or employment referrals. A social service unit was also established to assist clients in managing financial, housing, and medical problems.

During the first three years of the project, 2 percent of all defendants appearing before the court were diverted at a cost of $731 per case. Almost half the participants were considered successes—they were satisfactorily terminated from the project and charges against them were dropped. Defendants who successfully completed the project had a recidivism rate 50 percent below that of unsuccessful participants. Almost 80 percent of the successes were employed at termination; less than half had been employed at project entry.

Because of questions raised about the research methodology of the study, these findings were subjected to a second review, which concluded that half the defendants who had had their charges dropped after participation in MCEP might have had their charges dropped even without program involvement.[18]

In 1977, a new evaluation of MCEP was begun. It utilized an experimental research design that called for random assignment of defendants eligible for MCEP into an experimental group of MCEP participants and a control group of routinely processed offenders. A 12-month follow-up revealed that both experimental and control subjects increased the amount of time they spent at work, in school, and in other constructive activities and that about one-third of each group had been rearrested.[19] MCEP participants were no more successful in these areas than control subjects.

The failure of diversion services to make a difference was attributed to two factors. First, it was determined that prosecutors were only recommending defendants for diversion in cases in which the evidence was so weak that a conviction was unlikely. Diverted clients were not being "saved" from the harms of prosecution, conviction, and incarceration, but instead were being "spared" unconditional release. Second, the diverted offenders were so extremely disadvantaged in terms of education and work experience that four months of attention and services could not turn them around. As a result of these findings MCEP was terminated in 1979.

Monroe County Pretrial Diversion Program. All evaluations of diversion programs are not so dismal. For example, consider the following description of a New York State diversion program that appeared in *Corrections Magazine*. What does the Monroe County program have going for it that the MCEP project lacked?

> "Everyone's looking for instant gratification, even attorneys and judges. They all want to clear up their paperwork. They all have agendas. If diversion fits into their agenda, they'll use it."
> If Bruce McDaniel sounds cynical, it is because his four years as a pretrial diversion counselor have taught him some realities about the criminal justice system, about

how it can be used and misused by the whole gamut of participants. McDaniel and the other staff members of the Monroe County (N.Y.) Pre-Trial Diversion Program are dedicated to deflecting offenders out of a criminal justice system that would eventually lead many to jail or prison. As in all diversion programs, the Monroe County staff must often work with severely troubled defendants, suspicious and uncooperative judges and prosecutors, and defense attorneys who are sometimes less than devoted to the welfare of their clients. "We fight constantly to hold to our standards," McDaniel said.

But the Monroe County Program is more fortunate than most. It has the support of the district attorney, the public safety commissioner, and at least some judges. Clients of the program have access to a multitude of community services. The program's staff is highly qualified. And at a time when even the operators of pretrial diversion programs around the country have doubts about their effectiveness, Monroe County's, judging by one research report, appears to be a success. . . .

The Monroe County program is one of the few in the country that has been subjected to a rigorous evaluation. The study, done in 1978 by the Center for Governmental Research, a private consulting firm in Rochester, compared 137 people who were not exposed to the program. It was shown that while 21 percent of the program participants were convicted on their original charges, 64 percent of the nonparticipants were convicted. And of the 80 percent of the clients who successfully completed the program, only seven percent were convicted on the original charges.

The program was also found to have had an impact on subsequent arrests and convictions. Within one year, 24 percent of the program participants and 37 percent of the comparison group were rearrested. Of this number, 12 percent of the program participants and 22 percent of the nonparticipants were convicted. Of those who had successfully finished the program, 19 percent were rearrested and eight percent convicted. Of those studied who actually served jail sentences on their original charges, 274 days were served by program participants and 2,412 days by non-participants.

The results of the cost effectiveness analysis showed that the program had a benefit-to-cost ratio of 1.3 to 1, based on one year of diversion and one year of recidivism benefits. Most of the program benefits were attributed to savings from reduced probation and jail sentences, reduced presentence jail custody, and reductions in the number of presentence investigations. Other cost savings resulted from reductions in the number of trials and grand jury presentments. . . .

When an applicant comes to the diversion program's office for the first time, a counselor takes information about his family, job interests, work history, treatment history, criminal record, and so on. Most clients, according to McDaniel, "are cooperative, obedient and compliant. Their attorneys are likely to tell them that if they go over (to the pretrial diversion office) and cooperate, their charges will be dropped in court. The attorneys mostly are responsive to getting help for people but sometimes they say, 'Just go sit there for a while and bullshit and you'll get out of it.'"

But the counselors want the client to know that he is responsible for his behavior. "I tell them they have a right to go to trial," McDaniel said. "Some attorneys tell them they will go to jail for something they won't. Attorneys need to be up-front with them."

If, after two or three interviews, it seems clear to McDaniel that intervention is not going to make a change in the defendant, "I have to put him back into the system," he said.

The counselors try to instill in the client the motivation to change. "I try to build up a picture in his mind of what brought him here," said Andrea Valerio, another counselor. "Can he see any problems?" The counselor helps the clients recognize the connection between his problems and the offense with which he was charged.

"We're advocates for change," Valerio said. "It means being tough with them. I've been counseling for seven years now. I can't be a pure therapist here. I have some power over the clients because I make recommendations to the court."

McDaniel said: "I tell them, 'If you don't do this (fulfill the terms of the contract), something is going to happen to you. Even though you're an adult, there's a force greater than you out here, and that's the court.' "

Before the client signs his diversion contract, his counselor asks him to visit the community agencies where he will receive services. "If, after a few weeks, they don't keep appointments or do what they're supposed to do, we say goodbye," said McDaniel. But even before he sends a client to an agency, McDaniel often gives him some assignments to test his motivation. What the counselor expects the client to accomplish, McDaniel said, "depends on his level of capabilities. I might go so far as taking someone to an agency if he can't figure out how to follow directions. They all start at different levels. Everything has to be put in the perspective of what can be done for this person in the space of a diversion program"[20]*

New Developments.   Nationally, the trend has been toward decreased specialization in diversion programs for the vocationally disadvantaged. The changes made in Operation de Novo, a Minnesota project originally funded by the Department of Labor, are indicative of this trend. After the expiration of the original grant, plans were developed for a dispute mediation program, and a chemical dependency program (for chronic alcoholics and drug-dependent individuals) and a restitution program were established.[21] Operation de Novo also began accepting defendants with stable employment histories. This latter development was prompted by "equal protection" concerns of the court; it appeared discriminatory to exclude defendants from diversion because they had good employment records.[22] These defendants receive virtually no program services and are monitored only for rearrest.

❑ Programs for Youthful and/or Multiproblem Offenders

To illustrate the diversity of programs for the multiproblem and/or youthful offender, we describe two very different pretrial diversion projects, the Citizens Probation Authority (CPA) in Michigan and Operation Midway in New York State.

Citizens Probation Authority.   The CPA program is one of the oldest diversion programs in the United States. It began offering pretrial probation to youthful, nonviolent offenders in Flint, Michigan, in 1965.[23] Originally, CPA relied on volunteers to fill all project positions, but a professional staff was hired in 1968.

The program focuses on situational offenders; defendants with a documented "continuing pattern of antisocial behavior" are not eligible for diversion.[24] Program participation requires a defendant to accept moral responsibility for his crime, pay a service fee if he is financially able to do so, accept probation supervision for up to one year, and sign a treatment contract indicating the rehabilitative program in which he will participate or other self-improvement steps. Some defendants are also required to make restitution. Successful completion of the program enables the defendant to avoid prosecution and permits the expungement or destruction of his police record.

*SOURCE: "Advocates for Change," by J. Potter. Copyright 1981 by *Corrections Magazine* and Criminal Justice Publications, Inc., 116 W. 32 Street, New York, N.Y. 10001.

The CPA program serves relatively "advantaged" clients. Almost two-thirds receive no referral to community services and most receive only about one hour of counseling per month.[25] Only 17 percent of the clients are economically deprived. Because of the nature of their clients and services, CPA is able to divert offenders at relatively little expense. A caseload for a counselor might go as high as eighty-nine defendants; the cost for diverting a case from the criminal justice system is extremely low.[26]

Operation Midway.   Operation Midway in Nassau County, New York, focuses on defendants charged with serious felonies.[27] Only persons charged with homicide or sale of narcotics are excluded from participation. Not surprisingly, the screening of appropriate candidates for diversion is fairly rigorous—extensive interviews and discussions with the arresting officer are reviewed prior to selection. The following is an example of a typically rejected defendant:

> Defendant A was charged with possession and sale of marijuana. He had two recent convictions on drug charges, serving a two-year sentence in one case. Another drug case was pending against him. Interviews established that the defendant experimented with "virtually every known narcotic drug." No strong motivation for treatment was noted. Midway recommended that "the interests of society and of this individual would best be served by confinement in a residential setting where his deep-seated drug addiction would receive the intensive care and therapy indicated.[28]

The screening process tends to produce clients much like these:

> Defendant B was 17 years old. He was charged with burglary and petty larceny. He had two prior adjudications as a juvenile delinquent (both involving burglary), one conviction for possession of stolen property and two arrests (both dismissed) for burglary.
>
> His family environment was poor. The mother was dominant and possessive. The father had alcohol problems. His attitude was to blame others for his problems.
>
> Defendant entered the program while in jail. Testing indicated average intelligence and attitude problems. His early performance in program was marginal—there were failures to keep appointments and a general disinterest. His family problems continued.
>
> Gradually, counseling built a new attitude. Defendant obtained employment at a gas station. He developed independence from parents. With continued assistance he obtained employment at a hospital. Defendant was married and participates in Fortune Society.
>
> Defendant C was 24 years old. He was single and a college graduate. He lived in the county for eight months. Charge was possession of a dangerous drug. He had a prior record of drug offenses.
>
> Testing established that C was in upper one-third in intelligence. He had some involvement in hippie culture. He suffered from a speech impediment (stutter). His future plans were ambiguous.
>
> Midway arranged speech and hearing evaluations for the defendant. These revealed no emotional cause. The defendant was placed in an oral communications course. His speech difficulty lessened.
>
> During preliminary portions of the program, the defendant held several jobs. Testing and interviews revealed an aptitude and interest in a legal career. Defendant applied to law school. His career plans have crystalized. He now refrains from the use of drugs.[29]

Probation officers with reduced caseloads provide counseling, using a variety of psychological and aptitude tests. Program philosophy stresses that crime is a product of maladjustment, which may be remedied in a number of ways—for example:

> Client was frightened of his first contact with college. Counselor drove him to school and assisted him in settling into dormitory and during orientation.
> Client discouraged by administration of Welfare Department. Counselor accompanied him to intake and secured services.
> Client's employment terminated because of arrest (on which Midway entry was based). Midway officer met with employer to have client re-instated.[30]

Successful completion of Operation Midway does not always lead to dismissal of the charges. If the crime charged is extremely serious, the judge and prosecutor sometimes insist on a conviction, although frequently on a reduced charge. After a conviction, successful participants usually receive unconditional discharges.

> Defendant D has been charged with possession and sale of LSD. He was in the program for twelve months. The Midway recommendation was dismissal. It described the defendant as a 19-year-old alien youth. He had become involved in the drug culture. During the program, he developed independence from this influence and obtained employment. He was more acclimated to our society.
> In the case of D, the district attorney did not follow the Midway recommendation. A guilty plea to disorderly conduct was entered and the defendant received an unconditional discharge (amounting to conviction with no sentence).[31]*

The practice of continuing to prosecute successful divertees represents departure from the original conception of diversion. Although such practices result in confusion over diversion program philosophy and objectives, they are not uncommon. A 1979 study of 131 diversion programs revealed that many do not provide for the automatic dropping of charges upon successful program completion.[32] Other contemporary diversion program practices have also produced confusion and debate regarding the commitment of today's programs in comparison to the original objectives.

❏ Programs for Drug-Abusing Offenders

The two major approaches to the diversion of drug-abusing offenders are statutory diversion and the Treatment Alternatives to Street Crime (TASC) diversion model. Both approaches generally provide for the deferred prosecution of drug users. The principal distinction between the models is that the statutory approach utilizes legislative authorization to establish a channel of diversion for drug users; the TASC model provides for the establishment of liaison services between the criminal justice system and drug treatment programs to encourage diversion.

Statutory Diversion. California's P.C. (Penal Code) 1000 legislation is probably the best known and most widely researched statutory diversion program. Under this framework, the local prosecutor is responsible for the selection of appropriate candidates for diversion. Defendants excluded from eligibility include:

*SOURCE: *Diversion: The Search for Alternative Forms of Prosecution,* by R. Nimmer. Copyright © 1974 by American Bar Foundation. This and all other quotations from the same source are reprinted by permission.

1. Persons with prior drug offense convictions
2. Persons whose current offense involves violence
3. Probation or parole violators
4. Former drug offense divertees
5. Persons who traffic in drugs
6. Persons convicted of a felony within the last five years[33]

Eligible candidates apply for diversion to the county probation department, where they are screened for suitability. The results of these investigations are reported to the court, which makes the final selection of program participants. Selected defendants generally have proceedings against them suspended for six months to two years, during which time they normally participate in drug education or treatment programs. In the absence of a new conviction, satisfactory completion of the education or treatment program results in a dismissal of the charges.

The California legislation prompted the development of a massive statewide diversion program administered at the county level. In 1974, 23 percent of all arrested drug offenders were diverted; almost half of all marijuana cases were diverted.[34]

The programs to which defendants were referred varied considerably. In at least one county, 80 percent of the divertees were drug-dependent persons with multiple problems; in others, three-fourths of the clients were situational offenders with little or no severe difficulties.[35] In 1976, when the penalties for marijuana use were reduced to a maximum fine of $100, marijuana arrests and connected diversions declined considerably. The California programs then began to serve individuals with more serious drug dependencies.

Massachusetts and Connecticut both have diversion statutes that focus exclusively on drug-dependent individuals. Medical confirmation of dependency is required. In Massachusetts, diversion is mandatory for all first offenders not involved in drug sales. In both states, diversion is utilized frequently. It appears that prosecutors favor the use of a conviction as a stimulus to treatment, and there is a general belief that many drug-dependent individuals would prefer a conviction and sentence to what may be a lengthy period of treatment.[36] The requirement that defendants admit to drug dependency also may reduce the attractiveness of these diversion programs.

Treatment Alternatives to Street Crime. TASC programs identify drug abusers from the population of arrestees, diagnose their drug problems, refer them to appropriate community drug treatment programs, monitor their progress in the programs, and report this information back to criminal justice system officials. TASC originally was designed as a pretrial diversion program, but the reluctance of criminal justice system officials to permit the TASC diversion of any but the most youthful and situational user of "soft" drugs led to a modification of the initial approach. Today very few of TASC's clients are pretrial divertees.[37]

This change in program focus is not unique to the TASC program. Diversion programs that are unable to generate sufficient referrals from the criminal justice system may accept pretrial releasees, probationers, and even parolees into their programs. Some observers view these steps as necessary to ensure that all persons who need assistance will receive it. Other observers view these practices as self-serving efforts to keep afloat programs that would otherwise lose their funding. These steps are criticized because they are considered to turn programs designed to divert clients out of the criminal justice system into programs that are simply new components of the criminal justice system.

In most communities, eligibility criteria for TASC diversion are strict; participation is generally limited to the first-time user of nonnarcotic drugs. In one jurisdiction, marijuana offenses are the only crimes the prosecutor is willing to divert.[38] In those jurisdictions in which eligibility criteria are less rigid, project staff routinely prepare extensive defendant evaluations; nevertheless, the courts refuse diversion to most such offenders.[39]

The Charlotte, North Carolina, TASC project is unlike many others currently in operation in that a high proportion of its clients enters the program prior to trial. Although clients may be referred to TASC while on probation or parole, over 50 percent of the participants enter the program after being released from custody following arrest.[40] Eligible defendants are drug users with no significant arrests for the sale or distribution of drugs, no significant history of violent crime, and no psychiatric history.[41] Potentially eligible defendants are contacted by a TASC screener within hours after arrest and informed of the TASC alternative. Interested persons are interviewed, and the defendant's case is discussed with the defendant's attorney and the arresting officer. If the defendant wants to participate in TASC and is viewed as a suitable client, he is accepted into the program. A TASC staff person will accompany the defendant to each subsequent judicial hearing and routinely inform the court of the individual's status in the program.

This TASC project does not provide for the deferred prosecution of defendants. Program participation occurs during the normal period of pretrial proceedings. Defendants enter TASC without the prior consent of the prosecutor. Although it is clearly the hope of TASC clients that successful program participation will lead to a dismissal of the charges or other favorable consideration by the prosecutor, the prosecutor is in no way obligated even to acknowledge TASC participation. The defendant has no guarantee of either diversion or leniency. The fact that prosecutor approval is not required for program participation may well account for the high percentage of Charlotte TASC clients who enter the program prior to trial. Unfortunately, no information on the outcome of TASC client prosecutions has been reported; so it is not known how prosecutors evaluate and respond to defendant success or failure in TASC programs.

Like most TASC programs, the Charlotte project has a variety of treatment programs available for referrals (figure 2-2). Full-time TASC "trackers" receive monthly written reports on the treatment of clients in these programs and weekly contact is maintained by telephone. To avoid termination from TASC, a participant must avoid a new conviction, attend counseling sessions regularly, and gradually reduce to zero the number of "dirty" urines (urinalyses that reveal current drug use) during the period of treatment.[42]

An evaluation of the TASC project revealed that, of the 406 persons admitted to treatment during the first two years of the project's operation, slightly more than one-half were successfully terminated or were still in treatment at the end of the research period.[43] This figure includes TASC participants on probation and parole, as well as pretrial referrals.

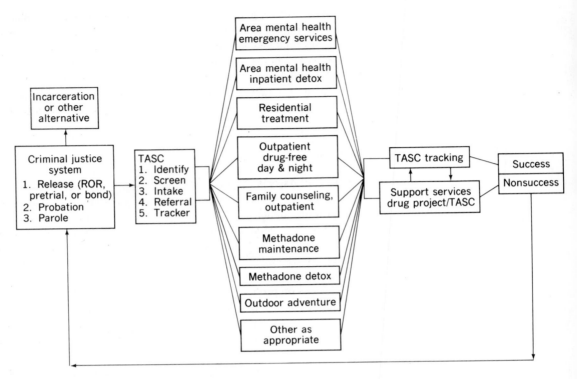

FIGURE 2-2 Simplified Client Flowchart: Charlotte TASC Program
SOURCE: TASC, Mecklenburg County, Application for Federal Assistance, LEAA (Charlotte, N.C., 1977).

The results of national evaluation of TASC programs were reported in 1982.[44] This study of TASC clients in six cities revealed that, when compared to other drug users in treatment, TASC clients are more likely to be young, male, and nonwhite. They more frequently reported recent arrest, incarceration, and reliance on illegal sources of income than did other drug abuse clients. Criminal justice system involvement per se was associated with treatment retention rates; persons involved with the criminal justice system remained in treatment longer than other clients. Finally, TASC clients were doing as well in treatment as other clients after six months of participation. More lengthy follow-up studies of TASC clients are currently underway.

❏ Community Dispute-Resolution Programs

Dispute-resolution programs have grown dramatically during the last fifteen years. These programs focus on settling informally (i.e., without court action) the hassles that arise from everyday life.[45] Dispute-resolution programs use techniques such as conciliation, arbitration, mediation, and fact finding as alternatives to formal court action. These programs serve to speed up the justice process, are low cost (as compared to going to court), and are within the reach of most citizens.

Over three hundred dispute-resolution programs have been developed in the United States since 1970. The underlying assumption of these programs is that there is a need for an informal mechanism to resolve disputes and these mechanisms may be more effective and efficient as a means of resolving disputes than reliance on a formal court process. Citizen dispute-resolution programs directly address the problems associated with using the courts to resolve problems, they avoid the long delays, the high costs associated with litigation, and citizen dissatisfaction with the judicial process.

❏ Neighborhood Justice Centers

The American Bar Association defines Neighborhood Justice Centers (NJCs) as "Facilities . . . designed to make available a variety of methods of processing disputes, including arbitration, mediation, referral to small claims courts as well as referral to courts of general jurisdiction."[46] Many such programs provide additional services as well; they may conduct fact-finding hearings, offer various forms of counseling, or provide referrals to social service agencies. Virtually all these programs developed during the 1970s.

Most NJCs focus on problems between people with ongoing relationships; such programs frequently handle disputes among neighbors. Quarrels between strangers are difficult to mediate because there is little incentive for the parties involved to work out some sort of mutually satisfactory agreement. All programs studied handle both civil and criminal matters. They usually focus on relatively nonserious crimes, although some programs mediate felonies; in at least one program, crimes as serious as rape, burglary, and kidnapping have been mediated.

Complainants are referred to NJC programs from a variety of sources, such as friends, co-workers, police, prosecutors, and judges. Some persons need no referral because the NJC is well established and has become generally known within their community.

Some NJC programs pursue complainants and attempt to maintain their participation in the program after the initial complaint has been made. Others view attrition as a sign that the disputes may have been informally resolved and encourage informal settlements by requiring a cooling off period prior to a hearing.

Several programs request both complainants and respondents to sign agreements to participate in the hearings. Although the agreements are voluntary, they may encourage disputants to recognize the seriousness of NJC proceedings. A few "threaten" respondents with prosecution if they fail to appear for hearings. However, NJCs cannot force respondents to agree to an informal dispute settlement; in fact, no program that deals with criminal matters attempts to utilize compulsory arbitration.

Mediation is the principal method of resolving disputes involving criminal matters. It begins with the provision of an opportunity for each disputant to air his or her grievance; in some cases, solutions can be negotiated at this time. If no agreement is reached, the mediator then assumes the role of a neutral third party and questions the participants to clarify the issues and identify areas of agreement and disagreement. The mediator may introduce potential solutions, either in individual

Case Example

An example of a specific case may help illustrate dispute resolution at work. This particular hearing occurred at the San Francisco Community Board project, but the type of dispute is representative of those seen at many projects across the country. The case involved two next-door neighbors.

The presenting complaint was an assault and battery. The complainant (let's call him Mr. Janaslav) had been in a fight with the respondent (Mr. Valdez), and Mr. Valdez had seized a board from Mr. Janaslav's hands and swung it, breaking Mr. Janaslav's arm. Both men were in their 40s. When Mr. Janaslav went to the district attorney's office to swear out a complaint, he told the prosecutor about the dispute's complex history. The prosecutor immediately referred the case to the local mediation program having found such cases to be inappropriate for adjudication in the past. The project scheduled a hearing a few days later. The hearing was held in the evening at a day care center, and both extended families attended. Both the complainant and the respondent presented their views to the mediators, and it became clear that the core of the dispute was really over the complainant's driveway being blocked repeatedly. The Valdez family had five cars, and one of them seemed to be always blocking the Janaslav drive-

way. Mr. Janaslav's mother lived with him and had to be rushed to the hospital often on short notice for a lung condition. A previous fight over the driveway blocking had resulted in Mr. Janaslav being punched in the nose and retreating to his garage. Since that time Mr. Janaslav reports that the neighboring Valdez children always gave him the "evil eye" as if he were a coward. The Valdez family retorted that Mr. Janaslav was a belligerent person who was always pointlessly harassing them.

The five-person mediation panel guided the discussion of the controversy and attempted to help define the issues at hand. In the early phase of the discussion, the potential for future escalation of the dispute became very clear. Mr. Janaslav (sitting there with his arm in a cast and sling) noted that he had a knife at home, and if he was threatened again, he didn't know what he would do. As the discussion continued, a comment was made which seemed to be a turning point: Mr. Janaslav and Mr. Valdez were both arguing, and Mr. Janaslav said, "Look, I'm afraid of you people. You have more men in your household. I'm scared." The Valdez family members seemed genuinely taken aback that they frightened Mr. Janaslav, since they thought that he was an ogre. The idea that he was actually feeling on the

sessions or with all participants present. Sometimes private sessions are very effective. Concessions often are more easily made out of the presence of other disputants, where face-saving requirements might inhibit any action that has the appearance of giving in.

NJCs have utilized a variety of personnel, including lay citizens with special training in mediation, law students, lawyers, and professional mediators. There are advantages and disadvantages to each type of employee. Citizens may be difficult to recruit and train, but they can be expected to know and understand their communities. Law students may be plentiful and can be trained within the academic setting, but they may lack the maturity to handle difficult negotiations. Lawyers and professional mediators may be highly skilled and experienced, but they are also very costly.

❑ Night Prosecutor Program

The Columbus, Ohio, Night Prosecutor Program is one of the oldest and best known dispute settlement programs in the United States. It was established in 1971 as a joint effort by the Capital University Law School and the city attorney's office.[47]

defensive and that he had the courage to say so was somehow a turning point. The Valdez family members began to cautiously apologize at that point, and conversation began to turn toward possible solutions to the controversy. Mr. Valdez offered to paint the curb a foot and a half on either side of the driveway. If a Valdez car ever extended over that point, then Mr. Janaslav was to tell Mr. Valdez, and the car would be moved. Mr. Valdez said the communication should be between the two heads of the households, because "men understand these things better." The women of the two families agreed. The mediation panelists swallowed hard—they clearly did not share the views of the two families that "men understand these things better," yet they remained nonjudgmental to make the agreement work. The project reports that the agreement was successful; the families report that they are not having problems.

It is useful to picture what would have happened had the prosecutor accepted this particular case. Either it would have been dismissed (perhaps due to the complainant's frustration with continuances) or it would have reached trial and a verdict. The trial would have dealt with the narrow issue of the assault and battery. The other issues that animated the dispute would have been irrelevant and inadmissable for the most part. Communication would have taken place through professional intermediaries, and the court could either find innocence (angering Janaslav further) or guilt (enraging the Valdez family). The kids would still give Janaslav the "evil eye," making his daily life miserable; the driveway would still be intermittently blocked; the two families would continue to live an uncomfortable existence. And the dispute might escalate. Only a few weeks before this fight occurred, a person was shot by his neighbor in San Francisco over a recurrent blocked-driveway controversy.

A brief look at crime data indicates the magnitude of the problem. The vast majority of American homicides are not television's stereotyped stranger-to-stranger offenses. They are husbands killing wives, relatives killing relatives, neighbors shooting neighbors. The issues involved are rarely more glorious than a blocked driveway. The Vera Institute of Justice's recent study of felonies in New York notes that, "because our society has not found adequate alternatives to arrest and adjudication for coping with interpersonal anger publicly expressed, we pay a price." The price includes court congestion, high dismissal rates, and ineffective dispute resolution. The Vera researchers recommended experimentation with mediation projects to handle many types of cases.

SOURCE: Daniel McGillis, *Community Dispute Resolution Programs and Public Policy* (Washington, D.C.: U.S. Department of Justice, 1986).

Complainants are referred to the program by the prosecutor's office or may be seen on a walk-in basis. They are interviewed by legal interns, who determine if the dispute is amenable to mediation. If it is, a form describing the nature of the complaint is prepared and a date is set for a hearing. The respondent is mailed a request to appear at the hearing and informed that "failure to appear may bring further legal action."[48]

Hearings are held from 6 P.M. to 10 P.M. on weekdays and on Saturday mornings; the average hearing lasts about an hour. During the hearing, the program is explained to participants and each party is offered an opportunity to speak. The hearing officer encourages disputants to explore underlying issues. Witnesses may be presented and they too may offer potential solutions. If participants cannot reach an agreement, the hearing officer will suggest a solution. He or she also informs participants of legal issues and criminal penalties that may apply.

Social work graduate students are available for counseling and referrals; groups for battered women and problem drinkers have been established to provide intensive counseling. Field workers are available to handle invalids' complaints. They frequently assist senior citizens complaining of harassment by neighborhood youths; after the interview, the worker locates the youths and attempts to resolve the problem.

Illustrative Cases: The Columbus Night Prosecutor Program

Case A—Mr. M. and Mr. R. were neighbors. Mr. M's complaint involved two dogs, owned by Mr. R., which allegedly were keeping the neighborhood awake every night with their continued barking. Mr. M. was almost apologetic as he explained to the hearing officer that he had no personal grudge against Mr. R.; he just wanted to get some sleep at night. Mr. R. admitted that his dogs barked an excessive amount at night but said that he needed them as watchdogs. The hearing officer pointed out to Mr. R. the existence of a Columbus city ordinance carrying a criminal penalty that prohibits the keeping or harboring of any animal that creates noises that are unreasonably loud or disturbing or of such a character, intensity, or duration as to disturb the peace and quiet of the neighborhood or be detrimental to the life and health of any individual.

Mr. R. seemed impressed by the existence of the ordinance and said that he would keep the dogs in the house at night and if that did not solve the problem he would get rid of the dogs. The hearing officer reminded Mr. R. that a record of the hearing and his agreement would be kept on file at the prosecutor's office, where possible further action would be considered.

Case B—A more familiar situation that results in a hearing involves an assault and battery by a husband on his wife. Frequently the woman will arrive in the night prosecutor's office soon after the battle has ended, complete with a black eye and torn clothing. She usually wants to have her husband arrested right away and put in jail. Unless there is a very real danger that the husband is going to attack her or others again in the immediate future, the clerk usually explains the futility of an arrest. In Columbus the bail for assault and battery is normally low enough so that anyone arrested on that charge will very likely be out on the street again in less than an hour after he is arrested. Through experience the staff has learned that rather than providing a solution to the wife's problem, the fact that he has been arrested frequently infuriates the husband so much that he goes right back home and beats his wife again. Experience has also shown that it is generally the wife who later comes in and posts the bail money! The clerk explains the hearing procedure, suggesting to the wife that the night prosecutor's program offers the husband and wife a chance to discuss their problems in a calm, controlled setting with an unbiased third party to mediate. The clerk points out that the hearing process may be a much more positive step, which offers the possibility of long-term gains as opposed to the questionable value of having the husband thrown in jail.

The hearings are conducted by lawyers, law students, and others who have received forty hours of training in mediation and conflict resolution techniques. Role playing and nonverbal behavior are emphasized during the course of training. Students normally co-mediate disputes with experienced hearing officers prior to undertaking the task on their own.

In a recent survey, the program received approximately 50,000 referrals and conducted 27,000 hearings—40 percent of these cases involved bad checks.[49] The remaining cases were interpersonal disputes; complainants in almost half of these cases failed to appear for their scheduled hearings. Only 9 percent of the total number of cases scheduled led to criminal complaints being issued; the remaining cases may be considered to have been diverted out of the criminal justice system. It is unclear, however, how many of these disputes would normally have been prosecuted. Nevertheless, nine out of ten participants reported being satisfied with the program's results, which seem to have been achieved at minimal expense.[50]

Evaluation of NJCs.   In 1980, the Institute for Social Analysis reported the results of a lengthy study of three experimental NJCs. The evaluation of these programs, established in Atlanta, Los Angeles, and Kansas City, was designed to answer

When the husband and wife appear for the hearing, the hearing officer allows them to express their hostilities, then talks with them about possible solutions. Usually the hearing officer will ask the couple if they want to continue the marriage or get a divorce. Most often neither party wants a divorce. The wife does not want her husband arrested; she simply wants him to stop beating her. The hearing officer points out to the husband the problems he will encounter if he is arrested on an assault and battery charge, including the possibility of losing his job, obtaining a criminal arrest record, and suffering all the social stigmas that accompany such a record. If there are children, the hearing officer points out that the couple have the responsibility to give them as good an environment as possible in which to live. He may refer the couple to a counseling service or to other community agencies established to help citizens with whatever personal problems they are encountering.

Frequently in such a hearing one partner will reveal problems in the marriage or feelings of which the other partner was not aware. The couples leave the night prosecutor's office in various frames of mind. Some of them are still hostile and threatening but agree not to file charges at that time. Others admit to each other their shortcomings and leave with an agreement to try to work things out. Whatever their attitude, however, they have been given an opportunity to talk over the problems that caused the confrontation, an opportunity that seldom is presented when the parties go directly to court.

Case C—Two children, next door neighbors, became involved in a street fight. Their mothers broke up the fight and after a flurry of name calling, were soon rolling around on the ground while their children, and other neighbor children, stood watching. Both were soon in the police station wanting to file assault and battery charges against the other.

During the subsequent hearing before the night prosecutor, the mutual recriminations began escalating until both women were on their feet yelling at each other. Finally, 20 minutes into the hearing, one woman shouted: "You son-of-a-bitch, that's the same attitude when you wouldn't let me borrow that cup of sugar two years ago!" The other woman replied, shouting: "You bastard, that's the day I learned that my father had cancer!" The first woman suddenly quieted, and said: "Ah, honey, I didn't know that—why don't you come over tomorrow and have a cup of coffee, and we'll get this ironed out." On that note, the hearing ended.

SOURCE: From the files of the Columbus Ohio Night Prosecutor Program, Columbus, Ohio.

several critical questions concerning community dispute settlement programs. Researchers wanted to know if they resolved problems better, quicker, and/or more inexpensively than the court system.

The study reported that the programs handled almost 4,000 cases during their first 15 months of operation.[51] Almost half the complaints were not resolved by the NJCs because respondents refused to participate, could not be contacted, or one or both of the disputants failed to appear for hearings. About one-third of the cases were resolved through mediation; the remaining cases were settled by the disputants prior to a hearing. The resolution rate was comparable to that achieved by courts handling similar cases.[52]

Disputants whose complaints were resolved by the NJCs were overwhelmingly satisfied with their experiences and reported that the agreements reached through mediation were still in force six months after the hearings. It appears that NJCs do resolve complaints more quickly than the courts; in Kansas City, for example, dispute settlement typically was accomplished in less than one-fourth the time required for court settlement.

Although judges in all three cities supported the NJCs, they reported no significant decline in their caseloads. At an average cost of $150 per case, the NJCs were competitive with current court costs. The research team recommended increased public awareness and use of NJCs as a means of lowering case management costs.

Problems and Issues in Diversion

❑ Problems in Deferred Prosecution and Pretrial Intervention Programs

The most significant problems facing diversion programs today are of particular relevance to deferred prosecution and pretrial intervention programs. Diversion programs institutionalize and expand the informal use of discretion by providing new mechanisms for selecting defendants for diversion and providing new or additional treatment alternatives. This development in itself is not necessarily troublesome, but diversion programs often provide no new mechanism for reviewing or monitoring the increased use of discretion by criminal justice officials or diversion project staff. All the potential abuses of the routine inherent in the informal use of discretion are magnified and extended to additional decision makers.

There are many ways to misuse this informal discretion. A legally innocent person can be pressured into diversion by persons, friendly or otherwise, who convince him of the inevitability of a conviction and describe diversion as a less painful alternative to conviction and punishment. Similarly, a defendant may be "sold" a treatment program, coerced into believing that it will solve his personal problem(s).

Once diversion has been accepted, the defendant is required to cooperate and participate in treatment, whether or not he feels it is valuable. Failure to show signs of progress may lead to a reinstatement of charges; yet such failures only establish that he is not amenable to a particular form of treatment, not that he is guilty or innocent or needs punishment. The coercive nature of these efforts is unmistakable and uavoidable; yet within the criminal justice system, such coercions would be permitted only if a defendant had been convicted of a crime.

Diversion programs can be used to force treatment upon people who have committed no crime and coerce treatment when a crime has been committed but evidence is insufficient to obtain a conviction. Diversion may thus be used to cover up inappropriate or careless police procedures that produce evidence that is inadmissible in court.

A defendant who accepts diversion gives up a number of rights designed to protect him from arbitrary proceedings during a criminal prosecution, including

1. The right to plead not guilty
2. The right to a speedy trial
3. The right to a trial by jury
4. The right to confront his accusers
5. The privilege against self-incrimination

Without the benefit of these protections, the defendant may be placed in a rehabilitation program that in some instances has included residence in a treatment facility for up to two years; he also may be required to make restitution. If he fails to make progress during the diversion period, he has none of the protections offered to probation or parole violators, who are often released under conditions much like those of diversion. Frequently, the only protections the defendant in a diversion program has are the decision makers' good intentions.

❏ The Rehabilitative Ideal

Much has been written about the failure of correctional treatment programs. Diversion proponents assume that changing the context of treatment will provide more effective results. One has only to review studies of the effectiveness of counseling, education, vocational training, and other rehabilitative programs applied to noncriminal disadvantaged persons (and in the case of counseling programs, to middle- and upper-class persons as well) to learn that "people changing" is at best an imperfect art. Diversion programs have yet to demonstrate otherwise.

The pros and cons of diversion have received considerable attention and discussion in recent years. There is general agreement that the criminal justice system has failed to achieve its diverse goals, but there is less agreement on the desirability of various alternatives to its use. The future will no doubt bring us many new proposals for change, all of which must be subjected to repeated critical examination. We cannot simply accept what is new because we naively assume that it couldn't be any worse than what we've got.

❏ Diversion and the Victims of Crime

The criminal justice system frequently has been criticized because it focuses too much attention on criminals and too little on victims. Many diversion programs are open to this same criticism. The decision not to prosecute a defendant may be made with little or no consideration of the victim's feelings about the crime. The decision to divert usually focuses solely on offender problems and needs.

Such disregard for the victim's perspective is unnecessary. Diversion programs may involve victims in decision making in a variety of ways, including requiring them to approve the decision to divert before a defendant may enter the diversion program. Research has indicated that victims tend to approve diversion decisions when: (1) the offense is a property crime, (2) the defendant does not have an extensive prior record, (3) restitution is a condition of diversion, and (4) the diversion program staff shows concern for the victim's feelings.[53] This apparent regard for the victim's perspective, accompanied by opportunities for the victim and defendant to meet, discuss the offense, its cause and consequences, and the potential impact of diversion, have been found to soften victims' resistance to diversion and diminish their desire for punishment.

Although involving the victim in diversion decision making may cause the programs to lose some eligible candidates for diversion, the benefits may outweigh the disadvantages. Victims may learn about the workings of the criminal justice system and offender problems and needs. They also may be able to regain some of the self-respect, composure, compassion, and objectivity that is often lost after a victimization. Because many diversion programs focus on the types of offenders that victims are most willing to divert, it seems pointless and potentially damaging to the long-term goals of diversion to ignore the victims of crimes.

The Overreach of the Criminal Law

The present "overreach" of the criminal law contributes to the crime problem in the following ways:

1. Where the supply of goods or services is concerned, such as narcotics, gambling, and prostitution, the criminal law operates as a "crime tariff" which makes the supply of such goods and services profitable for the criminal by driving up prices and at the same time discourages competition by those who might enter the market were it legal.

2. This leads to the development of large-scale organized criminal groups which, as in the field of legitimate business, tend to extend and diversify their operations, thus financing and promoting other criminal activity.

3. The high prices which criminal prohibition and law enforcement help to maintain have a secondary criminogenic effect in cases where demand is inelastic, as for narcotics, by causing persons to resort to crime in order to obtain the money to pay those prices.

4. The proscription of a particular form of behavior (for example, homosexuality, prostitution, drug addiction) by the criminal law drives those who engage or participate in it into association with those engaged in other criminal activities and leads to the growth of an extensive criminal subculture which is subversive of social order generally. It also leads, in the case of drug addic-

tion, to endowing that pathological condition with the romantic glamour of a rebellion against authority or of some sort of elitist enterprise.

5. The expenditure of police and criminal justice resources involved in attempting to enforce statutes in relation to sexual behavior, drug taking, gambling, and other matters of private morality seriously depletes the time, energy, and manpower available for dealing with the types of crime involving violence and stealing which are the primary concern of the criminal justice system. This diversion and overextension of resources results both in failure to deal adequately with current serious crime and, because of the increased chances of impunity, in encouraging further crime.

6. These crimes lack victims, in the sense of complainants asking for the protection of the criminal law. Where such complaints are absent it is particularly difficult for the police to enforce the law. Bribery tends to flourish; political corruption of the police is invited. It is peculiarly with reference to these victimless crimes that the police are led to employ illegal means of law enforcement.

Alternatives to Diversion

Efforts to remove certain acts from the jurisdiction of the criminal justice system or to remove the prohibitions and sanctions against those acts from the criminal law are referred to as decriminalization. The acts generally proposed for decriminalization are commonly referred to as victimless crimes—public drunkenness, drug abuse, gambling, disorderly conduct and vagrancy, abortion, prostitution, and consensual sex acts. Diversion programs usually focus on offenders from only two of these crime categories—public drunkenness and drug abuse—because there is greater agreement on such offenders' need for treatment and the inappropriateness of punishing them for their "conditions." It should be noted, however, that the scope of the decriminalization argument encompasses a great variety of controversial behaviors, ranging from drug use to homosexuality.

The proponents of decriminalization ask why an act that is appropriate for diversion should remain prohibited by the criminal law. Why set up an elaborate mechanism for offender identification, evaluation, and treatment to supplement the criminal justice system if it is agreed that it is more desirable to handle the offender in a noncoercive manner? Why not divert these offenses once and for all from the criminal justice system and find appropriate community agencies to provide services for individuals whose behavior indicates a need for treatment?

Although a persuasive case can be made for decriminalization, few states have moved to decriminalize even the most minor drug offenses or public intoxication. Much of what has been labeled the decriminalization of marijuana use has in fact been only a reduction of penalties (for example, eliminating jail and prison sentences) and a substitution of citations for the arrest and detention of marijuana users (see table 2-1).

There are many reasons for this reluctance to decriminalize public inebriation and drug abuse, but three of them are particularly significant. First, Americans have grown accustomed to using the criminal law to designate what is evil or harmful and relying on the criminal justice system to apply the appropriate response to such behaviors. An examination of any state's penal code will convince even the most casual observer that, throughout our history, what has been viewed as "bad" has been made illegal, without too much regard for the appropriateness or desirability of enforcing such laws. Many people still feel that to decriminalize an act is to con-

TABLE 2-1 Characteristics of Marijuana Laws in States That Have Decriminalized Possession of Marijuana, as of July 1, 1986

State	Maximum fine imposed	Maximum amount possessed	Classification of offense	Effective date
Alaska	$100	Any amount in private for personal use or 1 ounce in public[a]	Civil	Sept. 2, 1975
California	100	1 ounce	Misdemeanor—no permanent criminal record	Jan. 1, 1976
Colorado	100	1 ounce	Class 2 petty offense—no criminal record	July 1, 1975
Maine	200	Any amount[b] for personal use	Civil	Mar. 1, 1976
Minnesota	100	1 1/2 ounces	Civil	Apr. 10, 1976
Mississippi	250	1 ounce	Civil	July 1, 1977
Nebraska	100	1 ounce	Civil	July 1, 1978
New York	100	25 grams (approximately 7/8 ounce)	Violation—no criminal record	July 29, 1977
North Carolina	100	1 ounce	Minor misdemeanor	July 1, 1977
Ohio	100	100 grams (approximately 3 1/2 ounces)	Minor misdemeanor—no criminal record	Nov. 22, 1975
Oregon	100	1 ounce	Civil	Oct. 5, 1973

Note: Distribution of marijuana by gift or for no remuneration is treated as simple possession in California, Colorado, Minnesota, and Ohio (for up to 20 grams). Mississippi has mandatory minimum fines of $100 for first offense and $250 for second offense within a two-year period, but state judges can suspend payment of these fines. Subsequent offenses are subject to increased penalties in Minnesota, Mississippi, New York, and North Carolina.

[a]The Supreme Court of Alaska ruled in 1975 that the constitutional right of privacy protects the possession of marijuana for personal use in the home by adults. This decision invalidates the $100 fine for simple possession in the home.

[b]There is a rebuttable presumption that possession of less than 1 1/2 ounces is for personal use and possession of more than 1 1/2 ounces indicates an intent to distribute.

SOURCE: T. Flangan & K. M. Jamieson, *Sourcebook of Criminal Justice Statistics 1987* (Washington, D.C.: Bureau of Justice Statistics, 1987), p. 115.

done it. Regardless of the effectiveness of the penal sanction, such perceived tolerance of undesirable behaviors is considered unacceptable.

Second, there is widespread belief that decriminalization will encourage many individuals to adopt the previously illicit behavior. The feeling here is that the threat of punishment is a deterrent to crime. Although there is evidence that victimless crimes flourish or decrease based on social factors rather than in relation to the threat of punishment and that the punishment offered by the criminal justice system is neither swift nor certain enough to provide a deterrent effect, this belief in the deterrent capabilities of the criminal justice system is deeply entrenched in our society.

Finally, there is the reality of the social problem that remains after decriminalization. Drunks sprawled on city streets and sidewalks, the uncertain impact of narcotics addiction, and the chronic use of less serious drugs all pose problems with which this society does not seem fully prepared or willing to deal. At this time, diversion programs may offer a "means of testing and demonstrating the feasibility and implications of decriminalization."[54] If diversion programs prove successful, carefully planned decriminalization efforts may become the next priority.

The alternatives to traditional criminal justice processing are not limited to diversion or decriminalization. A variety of strategies may be employed to address the specific difficulties experienced by particular categories of offenders or individual defendants. These additional strategies include:

1. Various procedures for speeding up court processing
2. Measures to expunge criminal conviction records
3. Expansion of policies forbidding discrimination against persons solely on the basis of an arrest record
4. Improved pretrial release and detention services
5. Expansion and enrichment of probation programs[55]

Every state has adopted at least one of these strategies to improve criminal justice system operation. For example, forty-seven states have adopted strategies to reduce pretrial delay.[56] All these efforts can work to promote the general objectives of speedy, fair, and effective treatment of criminal offenders.

New Directions in Diversion Programs

❑ Need for Alternatives

Although many questions have been raised about the appropriateness and effectiveness of various diversion strategies, it seems unlikely that the concept of diversion and its principal objectives will decline in appeal in the future. The chronic overburdening of our correctional and judicial resources and the fact that so many offenders seem "divertable" speak for the increased use and the anticipated endurance of diversion efforts. A study by Galvin indicated that about 45 percent of arrests are "probably divertable" (table 2-2). Although few, if any, serious violent crimes and offenses in which firearms are used may be diverted, as many as 60 percent of drug, traffic, and manslaughter offenses and 90 percent of public intoxication arrests may be appropriately handled outside the criminal justice system.

TABLE 2-2 Arrests, Percent "Prosecutable," and Percent Probably "Divertable" (hypothetical jurisdiction)

Type of arrest	Totals		Probably prosecutable		Probably divertable	
Violent and firearms	7.0%	(840)	75%	(630)	—	—
Other "interpersonal"	15.4%	(1,848)	80%	(1,478)	20%[b]	(370)
Property	17.3%	(2,076)	85%	(1,765)	20%[b]	(415)
Drugs	7.2%	(864)	75%	(648)	60%[c]	(518)
Public intoxication	18.9%	(2,495)[a]	95%	(2,370)	90%[d]	(2,245)
Traffic and manslaughter	17.0%	(2,040)	90%	(1,836)	60%[e]	(1,224)
All other	17.0%	(2,040)	85%	(1,734)	30%	(612)
Drug dependents	3.0%[e]	(360)	80%	(288)	30%	(1,081)
TOTAL	100.0%	(12,203)	85.7%	(10,461)	45.0%	(5,492)[e]

[a]Public intoxication arrests would total 2,268. We added 10 percent on assumption this might represent the frequency, nationwide, with which such persons are taken by police to detox centers instead of to jail. The total in parentheses is adjusted to accommodate this addition. Percentages for various crime categories in the arrest column are of the 12,000 total.

[b]Diversion of the majority of these might be achieved through "adjustments" and referral service at the police and/or prosecutor level (for example, "dispute settlement" programs).

[c]Half to two-thirds of these would be for possession of marijuana, usually in small quantities. Decriminalization would be more economical and probably about as effective as diversion.

[d]Diversion, in this instance, is primarily by police to detox centers.

[e]If we exclude public inebriates from all calculations, we arrive at the following: 9,708 arrests; 8,091 "prosecutable" (83.3 percent); 3,247 "divertible" (33.4 percent).

SOURCE: John J. Galvin et al., *Alternatives to Prosecution: Instead of Jail,* vol. 3 (Washington, D.C.: U.S. Government Printing Office, 1977), p. 42.

As diversion programs expand, they may be increasingly linked organizationally with pretrial release agencies (see chapter 3). Pretrial service agencies, locally operated or state administered, may be expected to provide both alternatives to criminal prosecution for selected defendants (diversion) and alternatives to jail detention (pretrial release) for persons who will be processed through the criminal justice system. Uniform and consistent eligibility criteria, referral, and treatment services may be expected to characterize these new pretrial service agencies.

Summary

Diversion programs developed from a dissatisfaction with the limited and often arbitrary use of discretion by police and prosecutors and concern about the ineffectiveness of criminal prosecutions. It was felt that alternative proceedings would not only avoid the psychological, social, and financial repercussions of an arrest, prosecution, and conviction, but also provide a more therapeutic environment for offender rehabilitation.

Today there is a great variety of diversion strategies available. Some serve as alternatives to arrest and focus on family crisis intervention or the treatment of public drunks. Others provide alternatives to prosecution and address the problems and needs of drug offenders, the vocationally disadvantaged, youthful and multiple offenders, and citizens with grievances against their neighbors.

Each type of diversion program has its own unique history, objectives, and success rate. Programs for the vocationally disadvantaged have been the most extensively researched; findings indicate that they can reduce offender recidivism and enhance the employment status of their clients. Most forms of diversion vary considerably in their effectiveness, depending on the criteria for success. Generally, however, the earlier the diversion occurs, the greater its financial benefits.

Diversion programs face a number of challenges; these challenges are most critical for deferred prosecution and pretrial intervention programs. These programs assume defendant guilt and provide treatment that is often similar to that available to probationers and parolees. Clients in these programs have virtually no due process protections and lose many rights that would apply during a criminal prosecution. In the future, some accommodation between informal decision making and constitutional guarantees may be expected to develop in many diversion programs.

Other expected developments in diversion include the establishment of pretrial service agencies that combine both pretrial release and diversion services and experimentation with alternatives to diversion. The future of diversion inevitably will depend on societal attitudes toward crime, as well as criminal and victim expectations of the criminal justice system.

KEY WORDS AND CONCEPTS

alcohol detoxification
  programs
arrest-stage diversion
conditional diversion
criminal justice system
  objectives
decriminalization
deferred prosecution
discretion
diversion

family crisis
  intervention
mediation
minimization of
  penetration
neighborhood justice
  centers
offender change
  objectives
pretrial diversion

pretrial intervention
prevention
speed and quality
  of justice
Treatment Alternatives to Street
  Crime (TASC)
unconditional
  diversion

NOTES

1. President's Commission on Law Enforcement and Administration of Justice, *The Challenge of Crime in a Free Society* (Washington, D.C.: U.S. Government Printing Office, 1967), p. 134.
2. James Austin and Barry Krisberg, "Wider, Stronger and Different Nets: The Dialectics of Criminal Justice Reform," *Journal of Research on Crime and Delinquency*, January 1981, p. 170.
3. National Advisory Commission on Criminal Justice Standards and Goals, *Report on Corrections* (Washington, D.C.: Government Printing Office, 1973), p. 73.
4. Austin and Krisberg, "Wider, Stronger and Different Nets," p. 171.
5. Ibid.
6. Edwin M. Lemert, "Diversion in Juvenile Justice: What Hath Been Wrought," *Journal of Research in Crime and Delinquency,* January 1981, p. 40.
7. Joan Potter, "The Pitfalls of Diversion," *Corrections Magazine* 7(1), 1981: 5.
8. Austin and Krisberg, "Wider, Stronger and Different Nets," p. 170.

9. Potter, "The Pitfalls," p. 6.
10. Letter cited by Eliot Richardson to Harold E. Hughes, chairman, Sub-Committee on Alcoholism and Narcotics, Uniform Alcoholism and Intoxication Treatment Act (Washington, D.C.: U.S. Government Printing Office, 1973).
11. Peter Finn, "Decriminalization of Public Drunkenness: Response of the Healthcare System," *Journal of Studies on Alcohol* 46(1), 1989: 7.
12. Personal communication with Jim Kelly, social research assistant, Seventh Street Alcohol Detoxification Center, Charlotte, North Carolina.
13. Morton Bard, *Training Police as Specialists in Family Crisis Intervention* (Washington, D.C.: Government Printing Office, 1971).
14. Raymond Nimmer, *Diversion: The Search for Alternative Forms of Prosecution* (Chicago: American Bar Foundation, 1974), p. 76.
15. Vera Institute of Justice, *The Manhattan Court Employment Project: Final Report* (New York: Vera Institute of Justice, 1970), p. 3.
16. Potter, "The Pitfalls," p. 10.
17. Vera Institute of Justice, *The Manhattan Court Employment Project,* p. 4.
18. Potter, "The Pitfalls," p. 10.
19. Ibid., p. 36.
20. Joan Potter, "Advocates for Change," *Corrections Magazine* 7(1), 1981: 8–9.
21. Joan Mullen, *The Dilemma of Diversion* (Washington, D.C.: U.S. Government Printing Office, 1974), pp. 91–92.
22. Ibid.
23. Robert Balch, "The Juvenilization of the Criminal Justice System," *Federal Probation* 38(2), 1974: 46–50.
24. Robert Leonard, "Deferred Prosecution Program," *The Prosecutor* 8(4), 1972: 316–317.
25. John J. Galvin et al., *Alternatives to Prosecution: Instead of Jail,* vol. 3 (Washington, D.C.: U.S. Government Printing Office, 1977), p. 71.
26. Ibid.
27. Nimmer, *Diversion,* pp. 67–74.
28. Ibid., pp. 69–70.
29. Ibid., p. 71.
30. Ibid., pp. 71–72.
31. Ibid., pp. 72–73.
32. Potter, "The Pitfalls," p. 10.
33. Galvin et al., *Alternatives,* pp. 75–76.
34. Ibid., p. 77.
35. Ibid., p. 81.
36. Nimmer, *Diversion,* p. 87.
37. System Sciences, Inc., *Evaluation of the Treatment Alternatives to Street Crime Program, Phase II: Final Report* (Bethesda, Md.: System Sciences, Inc., 1978), p. viii.
38. Ibid., p. 6.
39. Ibid.
40. Hayes and Associates, Inc., *TASC Second Annual Evaluation Report* (Winston-Salem, N.C.: 1979), p. 5.
41. TASC, Mecklenburg County, Application for Federal Assistance, LEAA (Charlotte, N.C., 1977), insert 14.
42. Ibid., p. 39.
43. Hayes and Associates, Inc., *TASC,* pp. 4, 8.
44. James Collins et al., *Criminal Justice Clients in Drug Treatment* (Draft Copy) (Research Triangle Park, N.C.: Research Triangle Institute, 1982), pp. 92, 93.
45. McGillis, *Community Dispute-Resolution Programs and Public Policy: Issues and Practices* (Washington, D.C.: National Institute of Justice, U.S. Department of Justice, December 1986), p. ix.
46. American Bar Association, *Report of the Pound Conference Follow-up Task Force,* American Bar Association, August 1976, p. 1.
47. Ibid., p. 108.

48. Ibid., p. 113.
49. McGillis, *Community Dispute-Resolution Programs,* p. 127.
50. Abt Associates, *Neighborhood Justice Centers* (Washington, D.C.: U.S. Government Printing Office, 1977), p. 120.
51. Roger Cook, Janice Roehl, and David Shephard, *Neighborhood Justice Centers Field Test* (Washington, D.C.: National Institute of Justice, 1980), p. 8.
52. Ibid.
53. J. C. Stillwell, *Victim-Defendant Relationships in an Adult Division Program* (Rockville, Md.: NCJRS Microfiche Program, 1977).
54. Galvin et al., *Alternatives,* p. 6.
55. Ibid., pp. 7, 8.
56. P. A. Ebener, *Court Efforts to Reduce Pretrial Delay—A National Inventory* (Santa Monica, Calif.: Rand Corporation, 1981).

FOR FURTHER READING

Abt Associates, *Neighborhood Justice Centers* (Washington, D.C.: U.S. Government Printing Office, 1977).
Galvin, John J., et al., *Alternatives to Prosecution: Instead of Jail,* vol. 3 (Washington, D.C.: U.S. Government Printing Office, 1977).
McGillis, Daniel, *Community Dispute-Resolution Programs and Public Policy: Issues and Practices* (Washington, D.C.: U.S. Department of Justice, 1986).
Nimmer, Raymond, *Diversion: The Search for Alternative Forms of Prosecution* (Chicago: American Bar Foundation, 1974).

3: Pretrial Release Programs

Historical Development of Pretrial Release Programs
   The Beginning of Pretrial Release Programs
   Bail Reform in the Federal Judicial System
   Emergence of Supervised Pretrial Release
   Pretrial Service Agencies
   The Federal Bail Reform Act of 1984
Continuing Problems of Jail and Bail
   Local Jails
   Use and Administration of Bail
   Deposit Bail
Nonfinancial Pretrial Release Programs
   Prebooking Releases
   Postbooking Releases
   Objectives
   Basic Services of Postbooking Programs
   Release on Recognizance Programs
Supervised Pretrial Release
Problems and Issues in Pretrial Release
   Preventive Detention and Pretrial Crime
   Restrictions on and Conditions of Pretrial Release Conduct
   The Use of Bail Guidelines
Evaluations of Pretrial Release Programs
   The Des Moines Supervised Pretrial Release Project
   Federal Pretrial Service Agencies
   Pretrial Release Programs
   Assessing the Economic Costs
Future Directions in Pretrial Release
   Development of Statewide Pretrial Release Systems
   Replicating a Model Pretrial Release Program
Summary

IN THE PRECEDING CHAPTER, we examined a variety of community-based programs designed to remove accused offenders from the criminal justice system. In this chapter, we consider programs with a different objective. Pretrial release programs serve as alternatives to the pretrial detention or jailing of accused offenders. Individuals who have not qualified for diversion, or for whom no diversion program is available, may be candidates for pretrial release. Although they remain within the jurisdiction of the criminal justice system, pretrial releasees are permitted to stay in the community while they await adjudication. In the 1980s pretrial release programs emerged as a major strategy to reduce jail crowding by decreasing the number of offenders detained in jail awaiting trial.

Pretrial release programs may be classified along two dimensions. The first focuses on the time at which the release decision is made. Prebooking releases may occur in the field or at the police station immediately after the accused is brought in. Postbooking releases occur, as the term implies, after the accused has been booked or admitted into the jail.

The second dimension that may be used to distinguish the various pretrial release programs is the financial requirement of the release. Some forms of pretrial release require only that the offender give his word that he will appear for his court hearing. These releases may be considered nonfinancial. Pretrial release alternatives that require offenders to "back up" their promises to appear with a monetary or financial pledge may be considered financial forms of pretrial release.

Within each general category of pretrial release alternative, there are various program options available (see table 3-1). Generally speaking, each major form of pretrial release devloped in response to problems encountered in the administration of justice. Bail was a response to the problems of pretrial detention; nonfinancial forms of release were a response to the problems of bail and the commercial bondsmen; and supervised pretrial release programs were a response to the limitations of release on recognizance programs. Before looking at the contemporary form of each of the programs, all of which coexist today, we look at the historical development of the release alternatives. In this way, we may better understand how each program was originally viewed as a reform and how disenchantment with the reform led to the search for new alternatives.

TABLE 3-1 Pretrial Release Programs: Timing and Requirements of Release

	Prebooking	Postbooking
Financial	Stationhouse bail	Bail (commercial bondsman)
		Deposit bail
Nonfinancial	Summons	Release on recognizance
	Citation	Conditional release
		Supervised pretrial
		Third-party release
		Pretrial work release

Historical Development of Pretrial Release Programs

The history of pretrial release programs can be traced back to medieval England, when those accused of crimes were detained in local jails until a traveling magistrate arrived in their jurisdiction. These individuals were often detained for months at a time in unsanitary and disease-ridden dungeons. The local sheriff was responsible for these defendants. Because these early jails were not designed to hold offenders securely for long periods of time, many escaped. Local sheriffs, who did not enjoy the role of jailer, were anxious to see these individuals removed from their custody. To accomplish this, they frequently turned a defendant over to a willing friend, relative, or employer of the accused. This third party would offer himself or money as surety, a person who is legally liable for the conduct of another, for the accused person's appearance before the magistrate.[1] If the defendant failed to appear in court, the surety could be imprisoned or forced to pay the sum of money to the sheriff.

This practice of releasing a defendant prior to trial with a personal or financial guarantee of court appearance became known as release on bail. Although the origin of the term is uncertain, it appears to come from the French word *bailer,* which means "to hand over or deliver."[2]

The practice of bail was much abused almost from its inception. Working with no guidance and often motivated by personal gain, many sheriffs simply released anyone who could provide surety and jailed the rest. To remedy this problem, in 1275, specific offenses were established as "bailable" (persons accused of these acts could be released on bail) and other crimes were designated "not bailable." Eventually, the authority to set bail was removed from the sheriff and vested in justices of the peace.

In an attempt to discourage the setting of unreasonably high bails, the English Bill of Rights in 1689 stated that excessive bail should not be required. It did not indicate, however, how to determine the appropriate amount of bail in any specific case.

Amendment VIII

"Excessive bail shall not be required, nor excessive fines imposed, nor cruel and unusual punishments inflicted."

SOURCE: U. S. Constitution.

The United States Constitution incorporated the prohibition against excessive bail. By the end of the 18th century, bail was provided for in all noncapital offenses throughout most of the United States. Because a great many serious offenses were punishable by death, relatively few accused persons were released prior to trial. During the next 100 years, however, legislation sharply restricted the number of crimes punishable by death and judges assumed considerable discretion in setting bail. They tended to use their discretion rather conservatively; when determining bail, they often considered the defendant's likelihood of future criminal conduct as well as the probability of his appearing at trial. Because of this practice, bail amounts tended to be high.

As the population grew and became more mobile, other changes in the American bail system occurred. Because it was no longer always possible for a defendant to provide a friend or relative to act as surety, commercial bondsmen developed to provide this service. Although they did not offer the supervision of defendants that friends and employers might offer, they could post the required amount of bond and assume financial liability if the defendant fled. They provided this service in return for a nonrefundable fee.

The introduction of the commercial bondsmen significantly altered the practice of bond from its original form. Defendants could now "buy" their freedom from the commercial bondsman prior to trial. The importance of personal ties within the community through friendship and employment diminished, if they did not disappear.

It soon became apparent that the practice of commercial bonding created as many problems as it solved. No longer was a judge responsible for the "jail or bail" decision. Commercial bondsmen, free to select or refuse clients based upon their own self-interested judgments, held the keys to the jailhouse door.

During the 1920s, a number of studies were conducted on the operation of the criminal justice systems in Ohio, Missouri, Illinois, and Oregon.[3] These studies revealed the following:

1. The conditions in local jails were appalling. Legally innocent persons were frequently held for unreasonably long periods of time and alongside convicted criminals in decaying, unsanitary, and overcrowded facilities. Persons without funds were given virtually no opportunity to obtain pretrial release.
2. No standards were utilized in setting bail and discriminatory treatment was common.
3. Generally less than 5 percent of the defendants who were released failed to appear for their scheduled court proceeding(s).
4. One-third of all defendants jailed prior to trial were never convicted. Pretrial detainees were more likely to be indicted and convicted and to receive prison sentences after conviction than defendants freed prior to trial.
5. Bail bondsmen were found to pose significant problems for the administration of justice. In addition to the discriminatory treatment of potential clients, many of them were unreliable and posted bond when they had insufficient funds.

Later research by Caleb Foote in Philadelphia and New York City documented these findings and provided additional evidence of the continuing problems of jail and bail.[4] Although the need for alternative methods for providing pretrial release was clear, no signficant efforts were made in this direction until the 1960s. However, it was not simply the research findings of Foote and others that led to the initiation of bail reform and the beginning of pretrial release programs. The first pretrial release program was the result of one man's very personal examination of our criminal justice system and his subsequent revulsion at what he saw.

❏ The Beginning of Pretrial Release Programs

In 1960, Louis Schweitzer, a wealthy retired chemical engineer, visited the Brooklyn House of Detention at the suggestion of a friend, who learned that Schweitzer, as an immigrant Russian boy, had once lived a few blocks from where the jail now stood. Schweitzer reported:

> I'd never been in a criminal court and hardly knew anybody who had. . . . I visited the prison and was appalled. The youngsters were treated like already convicted criminals, despite our treasured principle that people are presumed innocent until proven guilty. The only crime we knew they committed was the crime of being too poor for bail. I found out later that most of them were eventually given suspended sentences or acquitted after an average wait in jail of more than a month each.[5]

After discussions with a variety of criminal justice professionals, Schweitzer established and funded the Vera Foundation (which he named for his mother) and its Manhattan Bail Project. The original purpose of the Vera Foundation (which is now known as the Vera Institute of Justice) was to assist judges in their efforts to identify individuals who could be released on their own recognizance, or promise to appear, prior to trial. New York judges, like magistrates in most jurisdictions, already had the authority to release persons accused of crimes without bail when they gave their word that they would appear at trial. What judges needed, however, was a method of gathering and verifying information about defendants—their family, employment, and community ties—in order to determine when release on recognizance was appropriate. Without this information, judges were understandably reluctant to release defendants only on the basis of their promise to appear.

The staff of the Manhattan Bail Project solved this problem. They interviewed defendants and contacted their references in order to verify the interview statements. They provided the judges with this information and with recommendations regarding the accused person's suitability for an on recognizance (OR) release.

The Manhattan Bail Project was originally designed as an experimental program. Because its impact on the criminal justice system was potentially far-reaching, every effort was made to monitor program operations closely so that its effectiveness could be measured.[6] After careful evaluation, it was judged an unqualified success.

The results of the Manhattan Bail Project encouraged jurisdictions across the country to replicate the Vera Foundation's effort. These new projects showed similar positive results. By the 1980s, over 200 cities had developed similar programs.

❏ Bail Reform in the Federal Judicial System

As data supporting the effectiveness of pretrial release programs continued to develop, there was growing evidence that bail administration in the federal judicial system was plagued by all the problems previously found in the state court systems. Research studies indicated that high bail was often set for purposes of preventive detention or to give the defendant "a taste of jail" rather than to ensure court appearance. Commercial bondsmen were found to discriminate in their selection of clients, often refusing to provide their services because defendants were members of minority groups or because the amount of bail required was too low to make the case worth their while. These problems led to the passage of the Federal Bail Reform Act in 1966. Its purpose was "to revise the practices relating to bail to assure that all persons, regardless of their financial status, shall not needlessly be detained . . . when detention serves neither the ends of justice or the public interest."[7]

The 1966 Federal Bail Reform Act was significant for three reasons:

1. It created a presumption in favor of pretrial release instead of detention.
2. It specified that the least restrictive form of pretrial release that would assure court appearance must be imposed.
3. It identified the factors the judge was to consider in his or her determination of the appropriate release option: the nature and circumstances of the offense charged, the weight of the evidence against the accused, the defendant's family ties, employment, financial resources, character, and mental condition, the length of his residence in the community, his criminal record, and his record of court appearances.[8]

❏ Emergence of Supervised Pretrial Release

The late 1960s and early 1970s witnessed a number of changes in pretrial release programs. There was a slowing in the growth of traditional release programs as judges became more willing to release defendants on their own recognizance without the special services of a pretrial release agency. The initial funding of many original pretrial release programs elapsed. Many of these programs were originally funded by federal dollars, and state and local governments were reluctant to provide sufficient operating expenses. During this same time period, however, supervised pretrial release (SPTR) programs were developed and soon expanded nationwide. These projects enabled individuals considered to be poor risks for release on recognizance (ROR) to be released under community supervision prior to trial. Growth in the number of persons released without supervision began to decline, until, in some jurisdictions, most defendants released were required to accept some form of supervision.

❏ Pretrial Service Agencies

The concept of the pretrial service agency was also born during the 1970s. These agencies provide comprehensive pretrial services, including supervision of persons released by the court, provision of recommendations for specific conditions for release, development and monitoring of support, rehabilitative and crisis intervention services for defendants, and coordination of relations between the courts and law enforcement agencies related to the identification and apprehension of persons who fail to appear.

❏ The Federal Bail Reform Act of 1984

This act significantly modified the 1966 act by expanding the criteria to be used for the release decision to include protection of the community through a prediction

The Bail Reform Act of 1984

Persons charged with Federal offenses may be released or detained prior to trial. The determination is typically made by a judge or magistrate at a hearing shortly after arrest. Specifically, the defendant may be:

- released on nonfinancial conditions (generally, personal recognizance, unsecured bond, or compliance with other conditions relating to travel, custody, or treatment);
- released on condition that the individual meet financial bail conditions (deposit, surety, or collateral bond), possibly in conjunction with other nonfinancial conditions;
- detained for failure to meet bail conditions; or
- detained without bail (pretrial detention).

Under the Bail Reform Act of 1966, the judicial officer was generally required to impose the minimal conditions of release necessary to assure only that the defendant appear in court. Further, while an individual might be held for failure to post bail, detention without bail was permitted only in cases involving capital crimes.

The Bail Reform Act of 1984 materially changed these provisions. In particular, the Act provides that, in reaching decisions on bail and release, the court shall give consideration not only to ensuring the defendant's appearance in court but also to protecting the safety of individuals and the community.

The pretrial detention provisions of the Act make special reference to particular categories of offenses and offenders. The Act authorizes pretrial detention for defendants charged with crimes of violence, offenses with possible life (or death) penalties, major drug offenses, and felonies where the defendant has a specified serious criminal record.

Additionally, the Act creates a rebuttable presumption that no conditions of release will assure the appearance of the defendant and the safety of the community under the following circumstances: the defendant committed a drug felony with a 10-year maximum sentence; the defendant used a firearm during the commission of a violent or drug trafficking offense; or the defendant was convicted of specified serious crimes within the preceding 5 years while on pretrial release.

The Act does not require that prosecutors request pretrial detention for all defendants in these groups.

The Act also provides for temporary detention (up to 10 working days) of illegal aliens or persons under pre- or posttrial release, probation, or parole at the time of the current offense. This provision was added for the purpose of allowing time for other law enforcement or immigration officials to take appropriate action.

SOURCE: *Pretrial Release and Detention: The Bail Reform Act of 1984*, Bureau of Justice Statistics Special Report (Washington, D.C.: U.S. Government Printing Office, February 1988).

of dangerousness. This act permitted judicial officials, following a hearing, to detain individuals on the basis of the threat they pose to the community. The boxed essay above explains the major components of the act.

Continuing Problems of Jail and Bail

Currently, pretrial release programs operate in over 200 jurisdictions. Many of these programs' basic objectives have been incorporated into routine court practices even when no specialized pretrial release services are available. The need to detain as few persons as possible prior to trial and to release appropriate defendants under nonfinancial conditions of release has achieved considerable acceptance within the criminal justice system and the general community. This acceptance is a product of continuing crowding problems in local jails, the administration of bail, and the high costs associated with confinement.

❏ Local Jails

Six major problems plague contemporary jails.

1. *Inadequate facilities.* Jails are usually the last public buildings to be renovated or replaced. Many jails in use today are over 50 years old; some are over 100 years old. As a result, many jails are decaying structures that possess few modern amenities. They are poorly ventilated, smelly, unhealthy, and depressing. Electrical wiring is often dangerously in need of repair. Lavatory sinks and toilet facilities may work poorly or not at all. Even in new jails, showers and laundry facilities are in short supply, so many inmates have little opportunity to bathe or wash their clothing. Clothing also is often in short supply, and inmates sometimes have to wear whatever they wear into the jail for the duration of their stay. Housekeeping duties are usually the responsibility of inmate workers, and many cleanup jobs are left undone. Jails are frequently considered a low-budget priority item for city and county governments.

2. *Staff.* Jails are frequently staffed by law enforcement personnel with no experience and virtually no training in corrections. The jail employees' sympathies are with police rather than defendants and convicted offenders. Even when jail staff are interested in inmates' problems and needs, they are often unable to assist them because of limited skills and a lack of resources.

3. *Violence.* Physical assaults and homosexual attacks are not uncommon in local jails. Because of the crowded conditions and the inadequate numbers of jail staff, security is a problem. Many different types of inmates with a variety of drug, alcohol, psychological, and medical problems are detained together with only limited opportunities to identify and segregate potentially dangerous individuals.

4. *Medical care.* Because most jails have no physicians or nurses or duty, sick and infirm inmates are sometimes confined for days, weeks, or months at a time without assistance. The training of custodial workers is generally limited to simple first aid; there are few provisions for medical emergencies.

5. *Work, recreational, and rehabilitative programs.* Most jails have no employment opportunities, recreational facilities, or rehabilitative programs for inmates. Card games and radios provide limited diversion from the boredom of confinement. Rehabilitation programs are also notably lacking. It is not uncommon to find jails that employ no professional educational or counseling staff and instead rely on volunteers to generate whatever rehabilitative programming is offered. Time spent in jail is usually referred to as *dead time.*

6. *Overcrowding.* Jail populations have skyrocketed in the 1980s. According to the National Institute of Justice Census of Local Jails, 1988, jail populations have increased 117 percent from 1978 to 1988. As the community's "dumping ground," jails have always been overcrowded. Today many jails are additionally forced to house inmates who belong in state prisons until the state institutions can find available beds. Inmates are sometimes placed with three or more other defendants in cells built for one offender. "Bullpens" or "tanks" may hold as many as 30 inmates.

Confining a convicted offender under the preceding circumstances is bad enough. The results of confining persons who are theoretically presumed to be innocent may be, as one judge described, awesome:

. . . it costs the taxpayers tremendous sums of money; it deprives the affected individual of his most precious freedom, liberty; it deprives him of the ability to support himself and his family; it quite possibly costs him his job; it restricts his ability to participate in his own defense; it subjects him to the dehumanization of prison; it separates him from his family; and without trial, it casts over him an aura of criminality and guilt.[9]

Research on the effects of pretrial detention indicates that persons who are detained prior to trial are generally more likely to be indicted, convicted, and sentenced to incarceration after conviction than persons who are released prior to trial. Pretrial detention may therefore be seen as a double punishment: The defendant is punished by incarceration prior to a finding of guilt and punished again because the likelihood of his eventually being found innocent or receiving a community-based sentence is significantly reduced by pretrial confinement.

❏ Use and Administration of Bail

The problems that plague bail systems today are the same problems that developed soon after bail was established as an alternative to pretrial detention. They result from the assumptions upon which the bail system is based and the difficulties of administering the system in a fair and equitable manner.

Underlying Assumptions. Pretrial release on bail is based on two aspects of the defendant's circumstances: the severity of the charges and his financial commitment. The logical assumptions underlying bail are as follows:

1. Defendants who face relatively serious charges are more likely to abscond than defendants facing less serious charges.
2. Defendants accused of serious charges must make a stronger showing of good faith in order to obtain pretrial release than defendants confronting less serious charges.
3. The fear of financial loss is the most powerful available deterrent to would-be absconders.
4. The strongest showing of good faith that a defendant can make is a financial commitment.
5. Defendants facing serious charges should be required to make greater financial commitments (bail) to obtain release than defendants accused of less serious crimes.

Although the preceding propositions are not in themselves unreasonable, several important facts are missing from the deductions. First, all persons are not equally able to make financial commitments. Less financially able individuals will always be at a disadvantage under this system and less likely to obtain release. A recent study revealed the widespread nature of this problem: The median amount of bail set for pretrial detainees was 83 percent of the total annual income of over half the inmates of local jails.[10]

Second, one would expect the effectiveness of financial commitments as a deterrent to absconding to vary according to the defendant's financial status. The well-to-do defendant would be less likely to feel the deterrent impact of bail than the low-income defendant. Finally, many factors other than financial commitments, including such extralegal considerations as family ties, length of residence in the community, and employment, may be expected to influence a defendant's decision to appear for his hearings.

Bail Administration.   There are two major problems underlying bail administration. The first involves the setting of bail; the second concerns the role of the commercial bondsman in bail administration.

There are no constitutional guidelines for setting the appropriate amount of bail for any specific defendant. It is therefore difficult to determine when a bail amount is excessive—that is, when the amount is greater than that necessary to ensure court appearance. Because of this ambiguity, judges may unknowingly set needlessly high bails simply because they overestimate the amount required to ensure court appearance. Judges may also knowingly set high bails for a variety of purposes, such as punishment, deterrence from future criminal activity, encouraging a plea of guilty, encouraging a defendant to avoid delay in bringing the case to trial, and preventive detention. Unless a bail amount is patently outrageous (and here the burden of proof is on the defendant), it is impossible to prove that the bail system has been inappropriately used. The "hidden" nature of bail decision making opens the door to much abuse.

"Making bail" in the United States typically involves the services of a commercial bondsman. There are over 5,000 professional bondsmen. Although many bondsmen are respected and hardworking businessmen, others are not. Unscrupulous bondsmen have discriminated against poor, minority and less serious offenders, provided kickbacks to court and jail employees to ensure client referrals, and bribed judges to ensure that bail forfeitures would be forgiven.[11]

Although it has been some years since the most recent national study of commercial bail, it appears that money bail is still the most widely used form of pretrial release. There are, however, tremendous variations in release practices. The National Bail Study, which reported on the release and detention rates of twenty major cities, revealed that some jurisdictions released only slightly more than one out of ten defendants on bail.[12] Other cities relied on bail as a form of pretrial release for over two-thirds of all defendants. On the average, slightly less than half of all defendants were released on bail; 33 percent were detained prior to trial; and the remainder were released under nonfinancial conditions. Five states (Nebraska, Wisconsin, Kentucky, Oregon, and Illinois) have eliminated or greatly reduced the practice of providing bail for a profit.

❑ Deposit Bail

In recent years, a method of administering bail that sidesteps the need for bondsmen has gained considerable acceptance. Under these programs, known as deposit bail plans, the court assumes the bondsman's traditional role. Defendants for whom bail has been set are released when they deposit with the court a specified percentage of the bond (usually 5 to 10 percent). Unlike in commercial bonding arrangements, the deposit is returned to the defendant when he appears in court. Most jurisdictions require that a small sum (usually 1 percent of the total bail amount) be retained by the court to cover the cost of administering the deposit bail system; in other jurisdictions, a fee is retained only when a defendant is found guilty. The court

Current Facts about Bail and Pretrial Detention

Any decisions to alter current policies governing bail and pretrial detention must take account of the following facts about who is detained prior to the trial, how those who are released behave, and the quality of the decisionmaking process about bail.

Who Is Detained?

The majority of defendants today, over 85 percent, are released in some manner before trial; some 70 percent of those released are freed nonfinancially.

A large number of jails in the country are extremely crowded, with many under court orders because their crowded conditions violate constitutional standards governing the custody of prisoners.

A large minority of those detained in jail are people who are charged with minor offenses; many apparently lack the resources to raise even the low bail imposed.

The Conduct of Those Who Are Released

Among those who are released, seven of every eight return for trial or other disposition of their cases. On average, one of every six released defendants is arrested for an offense committed during the period of pretrial release. These new offenses, as a group, are slightly more serious than the initial charges in these defendants' cases and result in a rate of conviction equal to that in the pending cases.

Some 30 percent of those defendants who are rearrested while on pretrial release are rearrested more than once. In jurisdictions that emphasize appearance for trial as the ony legitimate basis for setting release conditions, rearrested defendants are often (as many as two-thirds) rereleased with *no change* being made in their existing, usually nonfinancial, conditions of release. In fact, in such jurisdictions judges are usually not aware that defendants seeking release are already released in a pending case or are out on probation or parole.

One estimate is that pretrial offenses account for about one-fifth of all crimes resulting in arrests in the United States.

Bail Decision Making

There is great variation in the pattern of pretrial criminality from jurisdiction to jurisdiction. Moreover, there is tremendous variation in the release conditions and bail amounts set by different judges within a single jurisdiction.

There is continuing confusion about whether and how society's interest in preventing crimes committed by people on bail should be accommodated within bail policies and decision making.

SOURCE: Martin Sorin, "Out on Bail," *Crime File Study Guide, National Institute of Justice* (Washington, D.C.: U.S. Government Printing Office, n.d.).

may impound the deposit if the defendant is sentenced to pay a fine or to cover attorney costs.

Deposit bail plans have been successful and have increased the number of individuals who are able to make bail. Friends and relatives seem to be more willing to loan the defendant the money to post bond when they know their loan can be repaid when the deposit is refunded.

Deposit bail plans generally produce the same rate of court appearance as commercial bond, and at virtually no additional cost to the taxpayer. Traditionally, courts handle bonds for defendants and commercial bondsmen and receive no fee for their administrative costs; the courts rarely collect bond forfeitures under commercial bonding arrangements. Under deposit bail plans, the court uses the retained fee to cover administrative costs and bond forfeitures are more easily collected because there are no middlemen (bondsmen) to discourage collection. Deposit bail plans may actually generate revenues. This is apparently what occurred when Philadelphia

implemented a deposit bail plan. Based on the project's first seven months of operation, it was estimated that between $500,000 and $1,000,000 per year could be
generated.[13]

Nonfinancial Pretrial Release Programs

Today there are a number of alternatives to the traditional practices of jail or bail.
Prebooking alternatives include summons and citations. Postbooking alternatives
may be generally classified as on recognizance releases or conditional, supervised
releases.

❏ Prebooking Releases

Summons are similar to arrest warrants, but they do not require the defendant to
be taken into custody. A summons is a request that an individual appear at a future
court proceeding. Summons are issued by magistrates (judicial officers with limited
jurisdiction) and are usually served by law enforcement officers, although in some
jurisdictions private citizens may be used as well.

Citations are "tickets" issued by police. Like summons, they request that an
individual appear at a future court proceeding. The person receiving a citation must
sign it, the signature constituting a promise to appear in court. Citations issued by
the arresting officer at the point of apprehension are known as field citations; when
the requests to appear are issued at the police station prior to or following the defendant's booking, they are referred to as station house citations. Prebooking releases
are normally used with traffic offenders for such offenses as speeding or with misdemeanants charged with victimless or property crimes. Summons and citations
impose no conditions on the released person's behavior and require no financial
payment to guarantee court appearance. Little is known about the defendant when
the summons or citation is issued; in the case of field citations, the defendant's identity may be the only verifiable item of information. For these reasons, summons
and citations are rarely used in cases of felony or violent crime. Most jurisdictions
do not make extensive use of summons and citation procedures; those that do, use
them in less than 25 percent of their misdemeanant arrests.[14]

Many proponents of pretrial release alternatives to detention and bail favor
expanding the use of summons and citations to more misdemeanant defendants
and to selected felons as well. These release measures are the fastest and least
expensive forms of pretrial release. Booking and detention costs can be avoided and
the defendant can be released almost immediately after contact with law enforcement officials.

❏ Postbooking Releases

Recognizance Releases.   On recognizance releases are known as personal
recognizance, pretrial parole, promise to appear (PTA), and release on recognizance
(ROR). All these measures provide for the release of a defendant prior to trial based

on his signed promise to appear for all scheduled court proceedings. No restrictions are placed on the defendant's pretrial conduct and no financial payments are required.

Judges are responsible for the final ROR decision. Pretrial release program staff provide information and recommendations to the court regarding individual defendants' eligibility and their appropriateness for release. Suitable defendants are usually released at their initial appearance. In some jurisdictions, however, the pretrial release agency is authorized to release persons charged with minor offenses without judicial involvement, and defendants can be released prior to initial appearance.

In the federal judicial system and a number of state programs, OR releases are accompanied by the execution of an unsecured appearance bond. This form of bond, also known as personal recognizance bond, requires defendants to pay the full amount of the bond *only* if they fail to appear in court. The unsecured appearance bond therefore serves as a fine to be paid if the defendant fails to appear.

Conditional and Supervised Pretrial Release.   These are nonfinancial forms of release that impose restrictions on a defendant's conduct as a prerequisite for his release. Such conditions may require him to report regularly to the pretrial release agency, to restrict travel out of the jurisdiction, or to obtain counseling or vocational training. Some method of monitoring the defendant's compliance with pretrial release conditions is usually authorized. Conditional release generally refers to release under minimal or moderately restrictive conditions with little monitoring of compliance. Supervised pretrial release refers to a release that imposes more restrictive conditions, often including the defendant's participation in therapeutic or rehabilitative programs, and that entails considerable supervision.

Third-party release is a form of supervised pretrial release under which an appropriate third party assumes responsibility for the defendant's court appearance. The third party may be the accused's friend, relative, employer, attorney, or clergyman, a volunteer, or a social services agency. The third party may arrange for or provide specialized therapeutic or helping services in addition to supervisory ones.

Supervised pretrial work release is in reality a form of pretrial detention; defendants are, however, freed during working hours so they may continue employment during incarceration.

Conditional and supervised pretrial releases are usually obtained at the defendant's initial appearance. In some jurisdictions, however, supervised pretrial release is seen as a means of providing release for individuals who fail to obtain ROR and who are jailed following initial appearance. Conditions imposed on release usually are nonfinancial, although in some jurisdictions deposit bail is occasionally used as a condition of release.

Figure 3-1 is a sequential illustration of pretrial release alternatives to detention as they might be available to prospective defendants. The earliest and least restrictive form of release is the summons; pretrial work release is normally the defendant's last hope of release. Although all alternatives are generally not available in every community, a combination of approaches is normally employed.

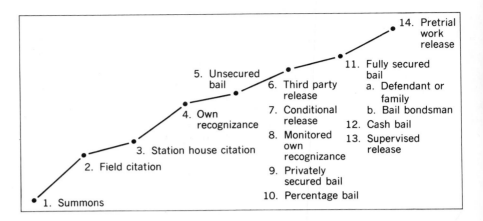

FIGURE 3-1 Pretrial Alternatives to Detention

Source: *Instead of Jail: Pre- and Post-Trial Alternatives to Jail Incarceration: Volume I* (Washington, D.C.: U.S. Government Printing Office, 1977), p. 8.

❏ Objectives

Pretrial release programs share basic goals as well as basic functions. The National Center for State Courts has identified six basic objectives of pretrial release.[15]

Increased Release Rates. One of the primary aims of pretrial release programs is to increase the proportion of individuals released under nonfinancial conditions. Ideally, defendants will be released on their own recognizance. If a defendant is considered inappropriate for an OR release, then restrictions on pretrial conduct as well as supervision of the defendant to ensure compliance with those restrictions may be required. The accomplishment of this objective serves both to benefit individual defendants and to reduce jail overcrowding.

Speedy Operations. A second program objective is to release defendants from custody as soon as possible; in many instances, custody can be avoided entirely. One measure of the effectiveness of a pretrial release program is the length of time defendants are detained prior to release. Figure 3-2 provides estimates of the average detention time under different types of pretrial release.

Equal Justice. Pretrial release programs attempt to minimize discriminatory treatment of defendants on the basis of wealth and other factors unrelated to the likelihood of court appearance. This is generally accomplished by ensuring that poor defendants have the same opportunity for obtaining pretrial release that more financially able persons have. Beyond this, the objective of equal justice also requires that all persons have equal opportunities for speedy release and for release under the least restrictive conditions necessary to ensure court appearance.

Low Failure-to-Appear Rates. Pretrial release programs originally established their usefulness through the achievement of failure-to-appear rates that were equal to or lower than those achieved by the traditional bail system. This objective

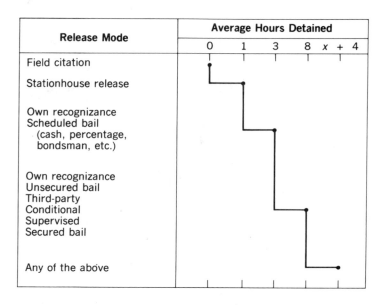

Release Mode	Average Hours Detained				
	0	1	3	8	x + 4
Field citation					
Stationhouse release					
Own recognizance Scheduled bail (cash, percentage, bondsman, etc.)					
Own recognizance Unsecured bail Third-party Conditional Supervised Secured bail					
Any of the above					

FIGURE 3-2 Detention Time and Method of Release
Source: *Instead of Jail: Pre- and Post-Trial Alternatives to Jail Incarceration: Volume I* (Washington, D.C.: U.S. Government Printing Office, 1977), p. 9.

is still a primary aim today. An effective pretrial release program must be able to ensure that defendants released prior to trial will appear at their scheduled court proceeding.

Protection of the Community. In 1987, the U.S. Supreme Court ruled in *U.S.* v. *Salerno,* 1987, that pretrial detention based on dangerousness was constitutional. This ruling upheld key provisions of the Bail Reform Act of 1984. Most pretrial release programs, directly or indirectly, attempt to prevent or reduced the incidence of pretrial crime. This is often accomplished through the imposition of conditions on the defendant's behavior during release and the supervision of his conduct during the release period. Because pretrial release is an alternative to pretrial detention, which provides a fail-safe method of protecting the community, pretrial release programs are necessarily expected to produce low rates of pretrial crime.

Minimum Economic Costs with Maximum Benefit. Although pretrial release programs may be easily justified on the basis of their societal benefits and contributions to the fair and equitable administration of justice, their financial costs and economic benefits are increasingly important. On the benefit side, there are savings to the community whenever a defendant who would have been detained is released. On the cost side, the expenses of pretrial release program operations must be deducted from the savings. The costs of pretrial crime must be weighed against the costs of lost jobs and welfare payments to families of pretrial detainees. These costs are difficult to calculate and troublesome to evaluate, because problems arise whenever we attempt to put a price tag on justice.

Guidelines for Interviewing Defendants Prior to Release and Verifying Interview Response

The interviewer should explain to the defendant (1) who he is, (2) that the purpose of the interview is to help him obtain pretrial release, (3) that the information he gives will be held in confidence and used only for the purpose of setting bail, and (4) that the interview is optional. The interviewer should not discuss the defendant's guilt or innocence or provide him with any legal advice. The interviewer should serve as an impartial agent of the court and not as an advocate of the defense or prosecution. If asked, the interviewer may explain the different forms of release available in the jurisdiction.

Every significant detail related to the defendant's probability of appearing should be obtained. All facts should be recorded and verification should begin immediately after the interview is completed.

When verifying the defendant's statements, the interviewer should never suggest the answers he expects from a reference. Instead of asking "Has he lived at 19 Pleasant Street for two years?" ask "Where does he live?" and "How long has he lived there?" When comparing the defendant's statements with those made by his references, remember that minor discrepancies don't necessarily mean that the defendant lied; they may indicate only that the reference has a limited knowledge of the defendant's residence or family ties. Beware of the defendant who says he has no phone or that he can't remember or locate in a telephone directory the name or number of his employer, relatives, or friends. Check with the reference facts about the defendant that an imposter would not know.

Without misrepresenting his intent or purpose, the interviewer should obtain the reference's confidence by indicating that the interviewer is trying to help the defendant. Often the reference will reveal information not disclosed by the defendant.

Don't contact the defendant's employer without the defendant's written consent and don't volunteer information that might cause the defendant to lose his job. If the employer requests information, however, don't refuse to provide it.

Adapted from: John J. Galvin et al., *Instead of Jail: Pre- and Post-Trial Alternatives to Jail Incarceration: Volume 2; Alternatives to Pretrial Detention* (Washington, D.C.: U.S. Government Printing Office, 1977), Appendix, pp. 4–7.

❏ Basic Services of Postbooking Programs

In determining the appropriate form of release, judges frequently rely upon the services of pretrial release programs and their staff. The National Evaluation Program (NEP) Phase I assessment of pretrial release programs surveyed 115 pretrial release programs in 1975. The NEP study, summarized here, identified and described five basic services provided by pretrial release agencies.[16] In some jurisdictions, these services may also be provided to law enforcement officers to assist them in selecting defendants for station house citation release.

Interviewing. Pretrial release programs interview defendants to obtain information about their backgrounds and community ties. Defendants may be interviewed prior to being booked, after booking but before their initial appearance, or following their initial appearance. The time at which an individual is interviewed determines the time at which he can be released and how much detention time he must serve. Individuals interviewed prior to or immediately following booking may be released after spending less than a few hours in custody; individuals interviewed only after initial appearance may spend a number of days in jail.

The selection of defendants for pretrial release interviews varies from program to program. Most pretrial release programs exclude some defendants from consideration. Persons charged with violent crimes or being held on a warrant or detainer from another jurisdiction usually are not eligible for program participation. Persons who are charged with narcotic violations, lack a local address, have a record of prior failures to appear in court, or are arrested while on probation or parole are also frequently excluded from consideration.

Verification.   Verification of the information received from a defendant is one of the most important functions of pretrial release programs. Although judges can interview defendants at the bail setting hearing about their backgrounds, employment histories, and community ties, they cannot reliably determine the accuracy of the defendant's statements. Pretrial release agencies check the accuracy of defendants' statements by contacting persons named as references and asking them for information about the defendant.

Most pretrial release programs contact friends, relatives, or the defendant's employer in an attempt to verify the information provided. Much of the verification work is accomplished by telephone, although at least one program uses a mobile field unit so staff can visit persons in the community when necessary. Most programs require two sources of verification for each item of information. When the defendant is charged with a minor offense, however, verification is sometimes omitted.

Screening for Release Eligibility.   All pretrial release programs use some criteria for determining if an interviewed defendant is a good candidate for release. Most programs use the same standards for release originally developed by the Manhattan Bail Project; these criteria focus on the defendant's community ties (measured by employment status, length of residence, and family contacts), prior record, and current charge. The defendant's appropriateness for release is then measured against these criteria on either a predetermined point scale or may be considered subjectively and individually by program staff. Some programs employ a combination of these approaches. According to the NEP study, the subjective or combination approach is used in three out of four pretrial release agencies.

Release Recommendations.   According to NEP statistics, 91 percent of all pretrial release programs attempt to make recommendations to the court instead of simply supplying the judge with the information that has been gathered. Most programs will recommend against pretrial release in situations where release seems unsuitable; other programs simply provide the court with available information and make no recommendation where release is considered inadvisable.

The early pretrial release programs generally made recommendations only on the appropriateness of OR releases. Now two-thirds of all programs make recommendations for conditional or supervised pretrial release. Usually, the judge will determine the specific conditions to impose, although, in at least one jurisdiction, the pretrial release agency sets the conditions after the judge has authorized conditional release. Specific bail amounts are recommended in appropriate circumstances by one-third of the pretrial release programs, and 23 percent make recommendations for deposit bail.

Follow-up Procedures.   Most pretrial release programs take some steps to ensure that persons released prior to trial appear at their scheduled court proceeding. Generally, the defendant is mailed a reminder of the date, time, and place of his court

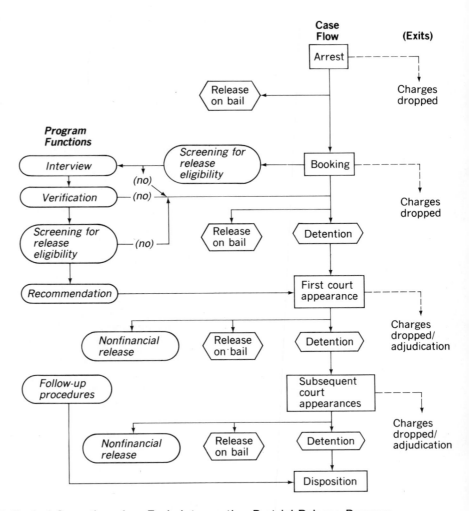

FIGURE 3-3 Typical Operation of an Early Intervention Pretrial Release Program
SOURCE: Wayne H. Thomas et al., *National Evaluation Program Phase I Report: Pretrial Release Programs* (Washington, D.C.: U.S. Government Printing Office, 1977), p. 85.

proceeding; some programs contact the defendant by phone. Most programs require the defendant to check in with them within 24 hours of release or, more often, to report at regular intervals throughout the duration of the release period.

Pretrial release programs usually attempt to locate defendants who fail to appear and attempt to persuade them to return voluntarily. Over half the programs provide information to the police when defendants fail to appear. Although this authority is rarely utilized, the staff of about 25 percent of the pretrial release programs are empowered to arrest defendants who fail to appear.

Figure 3-3 is a flow diagram of a typical early intervention pretrial release program (a program that interviews defendants before initial court appearance). It indicates the functions served by the pretrial release program and their relationship to the flow of a case through the criminal justice system.

❏ Release on Recognizance Programs

The most critical decision made in ROR programs is the selection of appropriate defendants for release. The difficulty of this decision becomes apparent whenever one attempts to develop and apply appropriate criteria for release. For example, consider the following defendants who appeared before a Los Angeles court.[17] Which ones would you recommend for release on their own recognizance? How can you justify your decisions?

Own Recognizance Case I

Name:	Manuel P. Montoya
Age:	19
Address:	3267 Valley View Road, Duarte, California no phone
Charge:	Kidnap for ransom and armed robbery
Bail set:	$10,000
Represented by:	Self
Race:	Mexican-American
Occupation:	Construction worker
Employment:	Self-employed for 2½ years; earns $660 per month
Residence:	As above
Marital status:	Married 3 years; two children; wife pregnant
Parents:	Manuel Montoya and Luisa Montoya (Def. does not know address or telephone number)
References:	None
Education:	11th grade
Criminal record:	
Arrests:	Runaway
	4 juv. burglary
	Drunk
	Burglary
	Possess. of marijuana: no disposition
Convictions:	2 juvenile petty theft: probation
	Drunk/obstructing officer: jail
	Juvenile burglary: probation
	Drunk: probation
Agency comments:	Pomona Police Department Robbery Detective states def. uses many aliases, has no known permanent address or ties. Detective is strongly opposed to OR release.
	San Gabriel Valley Department of Probation Office states def. is wanted by other jurisdictions, demonstrated poor probation adjustment with a history of camp escapes, was runaway from home. Probation officer recommends against OR release.

Own Recognizance Case 2

Name:	Nancy C. Redding
Age:	29
Address:	16754 Sunset Place, Venice. Mother's phone 821-5362
Charge:	Possession of dangerous drugs

Bail set: $500
Represented by: Self
Race: White
Occupation: Not known
Employment: Unemployed at time of arrest; employed 2 years as
                           secretary, N.C.R. Company; supervisor: William Robinson;
                           receives $131 a month from County Welfare
Residence: 1406 W. 4th Street, L.A., at time of arrest
Marital status: Not known
Parents: Arthur & Freda Redding, 16754 Sunset Place, Venice
References: Mother; William Robinson
Education: Not known
Criminal record:
  Arrests: LAPD—records no prior arrests
                           Def. states: (prior) possession dangerous drugs, released
  Convictions: none
Agency comments: Detective, LAPD, states not opposed to OR release if other
                           factors favorable.

Own Recognizance Case 3

Name: Manuel J. Dominguez
Age: 22
Address: 6774 Oak Street, Delano, California
Charge: Burglary
Bail set: $2000
Represented by: Self
Race: Mexican-American
Occupation: Not known
Employment: Was not employed at time of arrest; former job: Bleeker
                           Tools, Perry Street, Brea; employed about 4 mos.; Ralph
                           Blank, supervisor; has application in at National Airways
Residence: As above, lives with mother, 2 brothers, 2 sisters; father
                           deceased
Marital status: Single
Parents: Esther Dominguez, mother
References: Ralph Blank, Bleeker Tools; mother; brother at National
                           Airways
Education: 11th grade
Criminal record:
  Arrests: Burglary: dismissed
  Convictions: Loitering: 1 year suspended sent. $100 fine
                           Marijuana: suspended sent.
                           Petty theft: 22 days in jail
                           Resisting arrest: 30 days in jail
                           Possession dangerous drugs: CYA (currently on parole)
Agency comments: Delano Burglary Detective states due to def's. involvement
                           with 2 co-defs. who are prime police problems opposes OR
                           release. CYA Parole Officer states prior record has been
                           excessive but believes due to neighborhood influence and
                           associates. No police or community problems past 1 year.
                           Doing well on parole. Recommends OR release.

Own Recognizance Case 4

Name: Stanley W. Karnow
Age: 38
Address: 1438 E. 30th Street, Los Angeles, phone: 241-0676

Charge:	Sales of narcotics
Bail set:	$5000
Represented by:	Public defender
Race:	Negro
Occupation:	Disc jockey
Employment:	Jockey Club, Wesley Parks, owner; earns $400 per month; employer states can continue
Residence:	As above; lived at same address 27 years with brother and cousin
Marital status:	Single
Parents:	Deceased
References:	John Karnow, brother; Frank Moore, cousin
Education:	11th grade
Criminal record:	
Arrests:	Robbery
	Traffic
	Gambling
	5 theft/burglary
	3 poss. marijuana/dangerous drugs
	6 sales marijuana/dangerous drugs
Convictions:	2 gambling: fine
	2 theft: fine/jail
	2 possession/sale narcotics: jail/fine
	2 traffic/drunk: jail
	forgery: jail/probation
Agency comments:	Narcotic Detective, LAPD states opposed to OR release. Def. had quantity of narcotics in possession when arrested; sales involved; has extensive criminal record.

The Los Angeles Court denied ROR to Montoya and Karnow and released defendants Redding and Dominguez. Arrest charge and prior record seem to have played an important role in the decision making. What about family ties, employment, and residence? Were these factors given much weight in the decision making? Should they have received greater attention?

Utilizing pretrial release criteria is a difficult task because specific characteristics of the offenses and the offender are often contradictory. For example, habitual offenders may have strong family ties. Criteria must be applied consistently if all defendants are to be treated equally, but at times, fair and just criteria can lead to unfair individual judgments. However, individualized decision making can lead to discriminatory treatment. At best, we can strive to achieve a balance between the objectives of individualization and equality.

The Des Moines Project.   The Des Moines Project, which we refer to in several chapters of this text, consists of a number of community-based correctional services integrated into one program. In 1972, the Law Enforcement Assistance Administration (LEAA) designated the Des Moines program an exemplary project. It has since been replicated in cities in Utah, Minnesota, Florida, California, Louisiana, and Washington. Because it is a model program and because its pretrial services unit separates the ROR and SPTR components of release services into two clearly distinguishable organizational components, we use the Des Moines Project to provide examples of both OR and SPTR programs.

The operating philosophy of the Des Moines OR Project is simply stated: The major purpose of pretrial detention is to ensure court appearance. Similarly, the only purpose of posting bond is to ensure court appearance. Any individual who cannot afford to post bond but who has sufficient community and family ties to guarantee court appearance should be released on his own recognizance.

Four part-time interviewers, who are law students attending a local university, two full-time interviewers, and one full-time project supervisor conduct all pretrial release interviews. The interviews are conducted in city and county jails from 8 A.M. to midnight during weekdays. On weekends, interviews are conducted following arraignment or as needed. All persons arrested and formally charged are interviewed, except for those charged with intoxication, failure to appear, federal offenses, and nonindictable traffic offenses; juveniles; and persons held on detainers.

During the pretrial release interview, defendants are questioned about their residence, family ties, employment, and prior criminal record. The names of persons well acquainted with the defendant are obtained for verification purposes. Usually, the interviewer contacts only one or two persons the accused identifies. More persons are contacted when there is some question about the accuracy of the defendant's statements. Records of prior arrests and convictions, bench warrants, and holds are also obtained.

The release decision is based upon the number of points a defendant obtains in the pretrial release point schedule (see figure 3-4). All defendants who achieve five or more points are recommended for release. The only service provided to persons released on OR is notification of the time and place of their court proceeding.

Over 7,000 defendants were released on OR during the project's first nine years of operation. This number represents 58 percent of all defendants interviewed. The court accepted project recommendations for release in 97 percent of all cases. During this period, only 1.8 percent of the defendants released on OR failed to appear.

Supervised Pretrial Release

Supervised pretrial release programs are designed to permit the release of defendants who do not qualify for OR release. SPTR involves (1) imposition of conditions for release and (2) supervision of defendants to ensure that they comply with release conditions. In addition to the normal conditions of release, electronic monitoring, house arrest, and urine testing can be used to assure that the community is protected from the alleged offender. The NEP survey of pretrial release programs revealed that, in 1975, 64 percent of the programs made recommendations for conditional release and 36 percent made recommendations for supervised release.[18]

The court usually sets conditions for release, although in some jurisdictions the release agency determines the appropriate conditions after the court has approved the defendant for release. Release conditions are usually a combination of standard conditions imposed on all defendants and individualized requirements designed to meet individual defendants' particular problems and needs. Standard conditions generally include:

PRETRIAL RELEASE POINT SCHEDULE

Confidential: For staff only
Des Moines Pretrial Release Project
Point Schedule

To be recommended for release on his own bond, a defendant needs:
1. A Polk County address where he can be reached,
2. A total of five (5) points from the following categories:

Int [interview]	Ver [verified]	
		Residence
3	3	Present residence one year or more
2	2	Present residence 6 months, or present and prior 1 year
1	1	Present residence 4 months, or present and prior 6 months
		Family Ties
3	3	Lives with wife* AND had contact** with other family members
2	2	Lives with wife or parents
1	1	Lives with family person whom he gives as reference

*If common-law, must have been living together for 2 years to qualify as "wife"
**Must see the person at least once a week

		Time in Des Moines or Polk County
1	1	Ten years or more
		Employment
4*	4*	Present job one year or more
3*	3*	Present job four months, or present and prior 6 months
2*	2*	Present job one month
1*	1*	Current job or unemployed 3 months or less with 9 months or more on prior job or supported by family or receiving unemployment compensation or welfare

*Deduct one point from first three categories if job is not steady, or if not salaried, if defendant has no investment in it.

		Prior Criminal Record
2	2	No convictions
1	1	No convictions within the past year
0	0	One felony conviction, or misdemeanor conviction(s) within the past year
−1	−1	Two or more felony convictions
		Total Points Toward Recommendation

Sample illustration: Joe Smith has lived with his parents and his common-law wife (with whom he has been living for three years) at his present address for six months. He moved to Des Moines six months ago and has been working at his present unsalaried job for 4½ months. He had two felony convictions within the last year. Joe receives the following points:

Residence: 2	Employment: 2
Family ties: 3	Prior criminal record: −1
Time in Des Moines: 0	Total points toward recommendation: 6

FIGURE 3-4 The Des Moines Project Pretrial Release Point Schedule

SOURCE: *A Handbook on Community Corrections in Des Moines: An Exemplary Project* (Washington, D.C.: U.S. Government Printing Office, n.d.), pp. 79–80.

1. *Reporting.* The defendant is required to report to the pretrial agency on a regular (usually weekly) basis. The contacts may be made in person or by phone.
2. *Residence.* If the defendant has no stable place of residence, he may be required to obtain a residence that can be reached by phone in the local area.
3. *Employment.* The unemployed defendant may be required to obtain a job within a specified number of days following release or to enroll in a school or job training program. If the defendant has a job, he may be required to maintain his present employment during the pretrial period.
4. *Third-party release.* If the defendant has a relative or friend willing to supervise him during the release period or if an organization, such as a training or rehabilitation program, is willing to accept custody of the defendant, then a third-party release may be granted.
5. *Probationary conditions.* Several conditions frequently imposed on probationers are often imposed on pretrial releasees as well. The defendant may be required to obey a curfew, stay away from the complaining witnesses, refrain from criminal activity, and report for alcohol, drug, or mental health related treatment.
6. *Cash bonds or deposit bonds.* Minimal financial bonds may be used to supplement and reinforce the nonfinancial conditions of release.

Supervision of most pretrial releasees is not intensive. When released defendants report to the pretrial release project, information about their program status is collected. Often only defendants' statements are used to assess their compliance with release conditions. Additional checks are usually made only in the case of high-risk defendants, who may be visited in their home or place of employment. Their friends, relatives, or employers may be contacted to ensure compliance with release conditions. When defendants are released to third parties or receive treatment or assistance from social service organizations, these agencies are expected to report regularly to the pretrial program. The paperwork this reporting requires can quickly become unmanageable, so many social service organizations provide only minimal and informal reports on the status of defendants in their programs.

The Des Moines ROR program releases only those individuals who have significant family and community ties. The supervised pretrial release program was established in 1970 to provide defendants denied ROR with a nonfinancial release opportunity.[19] Today this program is known as Release With Services (RWS). The purpose of the RWS program is to obtain a defendant's release and to assist in correcting his problems prior to trial so that, if convicted, he may be placed on probation.

The program is staffed by a full-time director, an assistant director, a jail interviewer, a case load supervisor, and four counselors. A psychiatrist interviews clients on a weekly basis and provides consultation to the counselors.

Defendants rejected for ROR are referred to the RWS program and interviewed by the jail counselor, who attempts to develop detailed information on the defendant's history, type(s) of offenses allegedly committed, relationships with family and friends, and residence and employment history.

The decision to recommend a defendant for RWS is made subjectively. The question to be answered here is this: "Can the program help the potential client

A Scene from the Polk County Des Moines Jail

Sitting next to one young prisoner, who is barefoot in faded blue "POLK COUNTY JAIL" overalls, counselor Lew Busch tells him he has been rejected for pretrial release. "You've got no job, no residence," he says, "That's not much to go on."

"I know," answers the inmate. "But I do have a job now . . ." explaining that he has just been hired, and will stay with a former inmate who was recently released. Busch raises his eyebrows—it is a dubious arrangement.

"I'll think about it," he says. "But I've gone out on a limb before, and got screwed."

"I understand," says the young man. "I know it's not much to go on. . . ."

"No, it isn't." Busch smiles.

"I'm not booking on this," says the inmate.

"I wouldn't want you to," Busch says, and the interview ends, as the two shake hands.

The inmate will not be released, Busch explains, as he lives in another state and "waited until he was in jail to find a job and a place to live. I'm looking for community ties"—one of the key requirements for pretrial release.

Another inmate enters, and the quiet discussion resumes. His case is similar to the other, except he is a local resident, has a job with a manpower agency, and plans to hire his own attorney. Busch explains that, if he is released, the program guarantees his appearance at trial. He asks some probing questions to satisfy himself that this man will show up in court.

"I'm not gonna run," says the inmate. "I got too much to lose."

"What?" says Busch.

"Uh . . . I don't want no warrant out on me," the inmate answers.

Busch studies the man's face for several seconds, then makes up his mind. "I'll get you out," he says.

The fine line between who stays in jail and who gets out is the domain of Lew Busch, the RWS counselor who makes the decisions on borderline cases. For hundreds of Polk County prisoners, Busch holds the key to the jailhouse door.

Busch does not talk about "rehabilitating" criminals, but prefers the concept of "turnaround." His life is a good example: he's an ex-convict, hired by his parole officer for his current job, where he has become a celebrity on both sides of the bars. While he maintains his rapport "on the street," he also serves on the Metropolitan Justice Commission with one judge and goes fishing with another.

Busch goes beyond the "objective criteria for release," drawing on his own experience to determine if an offender is going to make that "turnaround." His recommendations are almost automatically approved by judges. Inmates know that, and whenever Busch walks past the cells he is besieged with pleas for help. "I'll do what I can," he tells them. "Sometimes I have to hide when I come in here," he confides.

SOURCE: "Replicating LEAA's First Exemplary Project," by R. Wilson. Copyright 1976, by *Corrections Magazine* and Criminal Justice Publications, Inc., 116 W. 32 Street, New York, NY 10001.

receive probation if convicted and will the client cooperate with the program?"[20] If the project recommends the defendant for release and the court accepts the recommendation, a release contract is prepared and the defendant signs it (see figure 3-5).

After the defendant is accepted by the program, the casework supervisor examines the available information on the defendant and assigns him to the counselor who can provide the greatest assistance. Shortly after his release, the defendant is administered a series of psychological tests to assist the counselor in diagnosing his needs. Both client and counselor then develop an individualized program for the defendant.

The plan's initial focus is on the defendant's immediate needs, such as food, clothing, and shelter. The plan also identifies long-term problems and attempts to resolve them through referrals to drug or alcohol therapy; psychiatric, family, or

SPTR PROJECT RELEASE CONTRACT

    I, _____, having read the order of the Court of this date releasing me from custody to the Des Moines Model Neighborhood Corrections Project, hereby agree to the following conditions of release established by the Des Moines Model Neighborhood Corrections Project:

1. I will appear in Court when required or be subject to bond forfeiture, imprisonment in the penitentiary for a term of not more than Five Years, or fined not to exceed $5,000.00.
2. I will not violate any laws of the State of Iowa, or any ordinance of any City of said State.
3. I will not violate the laws of any State of the United States.
4. I will make a report in person to the Des Moines Model Neighborhood Corrections Project at least three times weekly or as often as the latter may require.
5. I will maintain suitable residence and employment throughout the period of the time under the project's supervision and shall not change either residence or employment without prior approval from the supervising authority.
6. I will appear for any meetings that the project feels are to my benefit, and also agree to testing at the project and interviewing by the Staff Psychiatrist.
7. I will not leave the territorial limits of Polk County, Iowa, without written consent of the supervising authority.
8. I will abstain from the excessive use of intoxicants, or any use of drugs unless prescribed for me by my Doctor, and I agree to submit to toxicology testing upon the request of my Counselor.
9. I will not engage in any antisocial conduct which would furnish good cause to the Court to believe that the release order should be revoked in the public interest.
10. I will actively cooperate and participate in any program established for me by the Des Moines Model Neighborhood Corrections Project.

Special conditions: _____

_____

_____

_____

_____

    I have carefully read and do clearly understand the provisions of my release and do hereby agree to abide by and accept the said terms and conditions. I further understand that any violation of the above conditions is a violation of my release which could cause my release to be revoked by the Court and could result in the issuance of a warrant for my arrest.

Dated this _____ day of _____, 19_____ .

_____   _____
            Witness   Client

FIGURE 3-5 The Des Moines SPTR Project Release Program
SOURCE: *A Handbook on Community Corrections in Des Moines: An Exemplary Project* (Washington, D.C.: U.S. Government Printing Office, n.d.), pp. 94–95.

financial counseling; remedial education programs; and medical treatment. The program has also provided direct services to clients; evening courses have included instruction in community services and the management of educational problems. Because many of the RWS clients have employment problems, counselors attempt to identify the factors that contributed to these problems. Absenteeism, conflicts with work supervisors, and ineffective job performance are met with referrals to employment counseling, job training, and vocational rehabilitation. About 150 community agencies provide services to RWS clients. Although long-term planning is difficult because of the defendant's short-term involvement with the program (usually about three to four months), the plan provides guidance for the client and serves as a measuring stick by which to assess his performance in the program.

Prior to sentencing, the defendant's counselor makes a recommendation to the court in which she or he describes the defendant's progress in the program and informs the court of improvements in the areas of family, employment, and community ties. If significant progress has been made, the counselor recommends a deferred or suspended sentence. If the court accepts this recommendation, the defendant is placed on probation.

As in the ROR project, the defendant's release is revoked if he fails to appear for trial or if he is arrested during the release period. Although release may be revoked if he fails to make progress in the program, this rarely occurs.

The program provides staff members with intensive in-service training, which consists of both formal lectures and informal discussion. At the training meetings, counselors learn problem-solving skills and are provided with current information about community resources.

Problems and Issues in Pretrial Release

Several legal issues are repeatedly raised in discussions of pretrial release practices and programs. The most significant are the general issue of preventive detention—the practice of detaining defendants prior to trial because they are believed to pose a threat to the community—and several related issues regarding the appropriateness of restrictions or conditions placed on a defendant's conduct during pretrial release.[21]

❑ Preventive Detention and Pretrial Crime

During the 1980s, thirty-two states and the federal government passed laws that permitted dangerousness to be considered in the pretrial release decision.[22]

The use of preventive detention presents some of the most difficult questions raised in the field of criminal justice. Legal scholars, humanitarians, and criminal justice researchers and practitioners have debated the subject for decades without resolution.

Proponents of preventive detention argue that some persons accused of crimes present a danger to the community. They believe that these persons should be jailed prior to trial to protect the community from potential crime. Proponents of preventive detention argue that much of our crime problem could be resolved if potential offenders were removed from the streets as soon as they were arrested. They reason that, because most defendants are guilty of their charges, few innocent persons would suffer because of this practice. The pro-preventive detention view seems to be gaining considerable popularity and political support. In 1981, the Reagan administration made the pretrial incarceration of defendants identified as dangerous a priority on its justice system agenda, and many states seem to be following suit.

Those who oppose preventive detention do so on a number of grounds. It has been argued that preventive detention violates the Eighth Amendment right to reasonable bail in noncapital cases; it imprisons for unproved, anticipated crime; and it violates the presumption of innocence.[23] The American Bar Foundation has suggested that preventive detention contributes to the creation of a class of hardened criminals because it increases the number of individuals who suffer the hardships of local jails and serves only to embitter defendants.

Preventive detention also aggravates the problem of jail overcrowding by further swelling the ranks of the detained. To those who fear pretrial crime, opponents of preventive detention respond that, because most pretrial crime is committed only after the defendant has spent weeks or months in the community awaiting trial, it would be far easier and less costly to release the defendants and reduce delay in court proceedings, rather than incarcerating defendants for the entire pretrial period.

Perhaps the most significant argument against preventive detention is that it is unworkable. No method of prediction has thus far been capable of identifying the potential offender with any meaningful degree of accuracy. In most cases, only about 30 percent of the predictions will be correct. This means that, for every ten persons jailed to prevent them from criminal conduct, seven will have been needlessly detained because they pose no actual threat to the community.[24]

❑ Restrictions on and Conditions of Pretrial Release Conduct

Restrictions placed on a defendant's pretrial release conduct should be reasonably related to the aim of ensuring the defendant's appearance in court. Conditions unrelated to this aim are of questionable constitutionality. In some cases, such conditions may violate specific constitutional guarantees. For example, in 1977, Russell Means, a leader of the American Indian Movement (AIM), was placed on pretrial release on the condition that he refrain from participating in AIM activities. His release was revoked when he gave a speech at an AIM meeting. The U.S. District Court for South Dakota found that Means's First Amendment rights were violated when the release conditions restricted his freedom of speech.

When pretrial release is conditioned on a defendant's participation in therapeutic, educational, or vocational programs, questions of coercion may be raised. The jailed defendant is in a poor position to weigh the merits of such programs; true voluntary acceptance of these services is unlikely to be achieved in a situation when the alternative to acceptance is detention. Requiring participation in rehabilitative programs also appears to violate the presumption of innocence. Because participation in these same programs may be required as a condition of probation, the line between pre- and post-conviction community supervision can easily become blurred.

In some jurisdictions, the number of conditional and supervised releases has steadily grown and the frequency of OR releases has declined. There is some feeling that these releases are being overused and that defendants' liberties are being unnecessarily restricted. At this time, the precise amount of supervision required to ensure court appearance is unknown. To provide little or no supervision of persons placed on conditional or supervised pretrial release seems to make a mockery of the conditions and restrictions imposed. But supervision can be overdone. For example, consider this individual and his supervision by a Federal Pretrial Service Agency (PSA):

> A 40-year-old defendant was charged with filing false tax returns. PSA classified the defendant as a maximum risk. He had no prior record and no drug or alcohol problems but had strong community and employment ties. During the thirty-one days before the defendant was sentenced, the PSA made a total of twenty-three contacts with the defendant, his employer, and others.[25]

Unwarranted supervision not only interferes, without reason, with the defendant's freedom, but is costly and time-consuming. Until we know how much is enough, the need to respect individual liberties while ensuring that released defendants are sufficiently supervised to guarantee their future appearance in court represents a continuing dilemma.

❏ The Use of Bail Guidelines

An innovative action research project conducted in the city of Philadelphia pioneered the use of bail guidelines to assist judges with making the pretrial release decision.[26] The intent of these guidelines was to structure the discretion of judges, and to ensure equity and consistency across the jurisdiction regarding the pretrial release decision.

Evaluations of Pretrial Release Programs

At this time, evaluations of pretrial release programs leave much to be desired. Although there have been some improvements in the quality of pretrial release research, the conclusions formed by the National Center for State Courts in 1975 continue to hold true.

> Many (studies) failed to discuss critical issue areas such as scope of the project's coverage, the effectiveness of the project in minimizing the time between arrest and pretrial release, or the extent to which persons released by the project subsequently became involved in criminal activity while awaiting disposition of the original charges. And, even when these issues were addressed, there were usually grave weaknesses in the research methodology employed.[27]

These weaknesses in evaluative research are particularly surprising when one considers that the first pretrial release program, the Manhattan Bail Project, was established under an experimental research design that permitted a rigorous evaluation of the project's effectiveness. Since that time, relatively few efforts have been made to evaluate pretrial release programs under controlled conditions.

❑ The Des Moines Supervised Pretrial Release Project

One of the best single evaluation efforts was conducted by the National Council on Crime and Delinquency (NCCD).[28] The program under examination was the supervised pretrial release program for high-risk defendants in Des Moines, Iowa, which we described earlier in this chapter. The program was evaluated over a three-year period, ending in 1974. Defendants supervised by the program were compared with individuals released on bail (who were thought to be slightly better pretrial release risks than program clients) and to defendants who were not recommended for release by the program but who were released anyway. The research produced the following findings:

1. Client selection. Defendants who were not recommended for release by the project, but who were nevertheless released by the court, had higher rates of pretrial crime than SPTR clients: 34 percent versus 23 percent. Thus, the SPTR project was able to identify appropriate candidates for supervised pretrial release.

2. FTA rates and pretrial crime. SPTR clients were no more likely to miss scheduled court proceedings or engage in pretrial crime than defendants released on bail. Approximately 2 percent of each group failed to appear and 20 percent of each group was charged with pretrial crimes.

3. Pretrial jail time. NCCD calculated that 25,681 days' detention time were avoided because of the project's efforts. Over 10,000 of these days would have been served in detention by individuals who were not convicted of the crimes of which they were accused.

4. Pretrial employment and income. During the pretrial release period, the SPTR clients earned a total of $374,205.

5. Court outcome. SPTR clients received more favorable dispositions of their charges than defendants jailed prior to trial. They were slightly less likely to be convicted, and upon conviction received prison sentences less frequently than pretrial detainees.

6. Economic benefits. During the research period, the cost of operating the SPTR program was $518,235. NCCD calculated that, in addition to the 25,681 jail days, an estimated 40,000 prison days (which SPTR clients would have received if they had been sentenced similarly to pretrial detainees) were avoided. When these savings were added to the income generated by SPTR clients, the total financial benefit to the community was estimated at $716,929.

❑ Federal Pretrial Service Agencies

In 1978, the General Accounting Office (GAO) reported their findings from an evaluation of the federal pretrial service agencies.[29] This study focused not only on project impact or outcome, but on the process by which services were provided to the courts and to defendants.

The GAO found that pretrial service officers varied considerably in their recommendations for pretrial release and that there were substantial variations in the amount of supervision provided to defendants in different districts. For example, persons defined as maximum risks in one district received four personal contacts during pretrial release; in another district, similarly defined defendants received only one personal contact. One district supervised all defendants prior to trial, but another supervised only selected individuals.

The pretrial service agencies provided social services to relatively few individuals. Of the over 400 defendants in the research sample, only 11 were required to receive social services as a condition of release. Several judges indicated that they were reluctant to require a defendant to receive social services because they felt such conditions may violate a defendant's presumption of innocence.

❑ Pretrial Release Programs

One of the most extensive evaluations of pretrial release programs was conducted by the Lazar Institute.[30] The study examined pretrial release programs in eight jurisdictions. The sites were not randomly selected; the jurisdictions were chosen to reflect geographic dispersion, a wide range of release types, and broad eligibility for program participation. A willingness to cooperate with the research effort, accurate record keeping, and a population large enough to permit analysis were also prerequisites to site selection. The jurisdictions examined included Maryland, Florida, Kentucky, Arizona, California, and the District of Columbia. The results of the study, reported in 1981, may be grouped into four sections:

1. *Release rates.* Of the approximately 3,500 defendants processed through the eight court jurisdictions, 85 percent were released prior to trial. Most of these persons were released on nonfinancial conditions. Few defendants were supervised during the pretrial period. Nevertheless, about 20 percent of the defendants *were* detained at some point prior to trial for three months or longer.

2. *Court appearance.* Eighty-seven percent of the defendants made every court appearance required of them. Slightly more than one in ten persons failed to make one or more court appearances, but only 2 percent were fugitives at the conclusion of the study. Most persons who missed an appearance voluntarily returned or had simply forgotten to appear. The average defendant was required to make between two and three court appearances. The study found no significant differences in the failure-to-appear rates of persons released under financial and nonfinancial conditions.

3. *Pretrial crime.* Almost one of every six defendants released was arrested during the pretrial period. Thirty percent of those persons arrested were arrested more than once. Generally, pretrial crimes were less serious than the original charges. About half those arrested for pretrial offenses were convicted of those crimes.

4. *Program impact.* The assessment of program impact focused on persons who were *not* processed by the pretrial release programs in an attempt to discover what would have occurred if the programs had not existed. Only four jurisdictions were able to provide data for this assessment, and even these sites presented methodological problems that limited the analysis. Generally, this assessment showed little positive program impact. Using the criteria of release rate, speed of release, type of release, and equity of release procedures, only one of the programs demonstrated greater effectiveness in all four dimensions; the remaining pretrial release programs showed mixed results.

The Lazar Institute concluded its research report with a series of recommendations for courts and law enforcement officials and for pretrial release program policy and operation. The following are thirteen of the most significant suggestions:

Recommendations for courts and law enforcement:

1. Implement systematic follow-up procedures to identify and apprehend fugitives.
2. Promote speedier trials, perhaps 30 to 60 days following arrest, to reduce pretrial crime by as much as 55 percent.
3. Take action to ensure that persons rearrested during the pretrial period are detained.
4. Consider implementing consecutive sentences for persons convicted of pretrial crime and scheduling "high-risk" offenders for early trials.
5. Seek ways, such as broadening release criteria, to release more defendants prior to trial. This can be accomplished without increasing rates of failure to appear or pretrial crime.
6. Increase use of prebooking releases.
7. Consider the use of halfway houses and other placement alternatives to jail detention.

Recommendations for program policy and operations:

8. Programs should provide specific release recommendations for all interviewed defendants (the absence of a recommendation conveys a negative rather than a neutral evaluation).
9. Programs should evaluate their postrelease follow-up activities.
10. Programs that process only misdemeanors should consider expanding their operations to include felony defendants in order to increase cost-effectiveness.
11. Programs should implement multistage screening mechanisms so that more attention can be devoted to cases involving more difficult release decisions.
12. Programs should screen detained populations after release decisions are made and recommend reconsideration of release conditions to the court when appropriate.
13. Programs should consider broadening release criteria to permit greater numbers of defendants to be released. This can be done without increasing failure-to-appear rates or pretrial crime.

❑ Assessing the Economic Costs

Costs and Benefits.   Calculating the costs of pretrial release programs is not easy. Although the funding required to operate the program can be easily identified by referring to the program's annual budget, the expenses resulting from efforts to apprehend defendants who fail to appear are more difficult to measure. Additionally, the costs of pretrial crime, the dollars lost through property crime, and the indirect costs of violent crime must also be considered.

Because pretrial release programs release defendants who would otherwise have been detained, the savings in jail administration costs are generally viewed as one of the programs' greatest economic benefits. However, the precise amount of this savings is not easy to determine. Many pretrial programs release defendants who could and would have avoided detention by posting bail. In an effort to reduce the financial hardships these persons may suffer, the programs make possible their conditional, supervised pretrial release or release on recognizance. An assessment of the actual savings made possible by a pretrial release program must exclude these persons from consideration.

Detention costs are troublesome to calculate, even when only persons who would have been detained are considered. Jail administration costs are composed of both fixed costs—those incurred regardless of the number of inmates in the facility—and variable costs—those that increase or decrease based upon the number of inmates detained. Building maintenance costs and administrative staff salaries are examples of fixed costs; food and clothing for inmates are examples of variable costs. When a pretrial release program decreases the number of defendants detained prior to trial, generally only the variable costs of jail administration are reduced; fixed costs remain the same regardless of the number of detainees. These calculations are made more complex because many jails are overcrowded. Reducing the number of persons detained often does little to reduce jail administration costs because the end product is a jail operating at normal capacity, not a detention facility with empty cells.

Pretrial release programs may provide savings in addition to those that can result from the detention of fewer defendants. Released defendants can earn money to support their families, pay attorneys, make restitution, and pay fines that may be imposed by the court. Detained defendants can do none of these things—their families may have to rely on public assistance; court-appointed attorneys or public defenders may have to be used; restitution or the payment of fines may be impossible; and, of course, unemployed inmates pay no taxes.

Cost-Effectiveness. Are pretrial release programs cost-effective? Do they provide a reasonable return for the costs they incur? Some critics of pretrial release programs argue that many defendants could be released on their own recognizance without the services of pretrial release programs. These critics maintain that judges today are more willing to release defendants without bond than they were when pretrial release programs were first established. The findings of the Lazar Institute study seem to support this view. Because of increased judicial acceptance of ROR, the interviewing, verification, and recommendation functions of pretrial release agencies may be needed only when judges are unwilling to grant OR releases independently.

Today there are still many jurisdictions lacking pretrial release programs and where judges rarely grant on recognizance releases. In such communities, attempts to establish a pretrial release program often confront both judicial and law enforcement opposition. The paradox is that the programs are most needed where they have little chance of support. Where there is support, pretrial programs may be unnecessary because of judicial willingness to release defendants on recognizance without special program services.

Future Directions in Pretrial Release

A variety of factors will influence the future of pretrial release programs. The findings of the Lazar Institute study suggest that nonfinancial forms of pretrial release should be encouraged, but that stricter controls are needed to minimize the time defendants spend in the community and to respond to the problem of pretrial crime. The current political climate suggests that preventive detention is gaining support, although the problem of jail overcrowding will probably make its widespread implementation impractical, if not undesirable as well. Two additional developments, the establishment of statewide pretrial release systems and efforts to replicate the Des Moines Project may also influence the future prospects of pretrial release programs.

❑ Development of Statewide Pretrial Release Systems

The original pretrial release programs were relatively small projects that operated in single jurisdictions. Their principal aim was to assist defendants in obtaining release on recognizance and to ensure that released defendants appeared in court. Over the years, there has been a growing trend toward the expansion of pretrial release program goals and services. The federal pretrial services agencies, the Des Moines Project, and the D.C. Bail Agency are examples of programs that not only assist accused persons in obtaining ROR, but also assist high-risk defendants in securing conditional and supervised release. They supervise defendants and provide counseling, educational, and vocational services either directly or through referrals to community resources.

The increasing complexity of pretrial services and the continued success of pretrial release programs has prompted the growth of statewide pretrial release programs. For example, Kentucky initiated a locally operated statewide and state-funded pretrial release program. Release services are available on a 24-hour, 7-day-a-week basis. Pretrial release officers do not make specific release recommendations to the court, but present and interpret information gathered from defendants using a formal point system. Defendants are eligible for release on recognizance, conditional release, unsecured bail bond, deposit, or full cash bail.

Oregon has provided for similar release services to be made available in each of its counties. The presiding judge in each circuit court can appoint pretrial release officers. Unlike the Kentucky system, Oregon's pretrial release officers are authorized to make certain release decisions. Senior correctional officers in local jails may make release decisions in the absence of a judge or pretrial release officer.

Connecticut passed a pretrial reform bill that authorizes statewide pretrial services. Other states are making studies of the need for coordinated statewide pretrial release programs.

All the efforts we have described illustrate a growing trend in the field of pretrial release—the integration and coordination of pretrial release services into a comprehensive statewide pretrial release system. The desirability of this trend is unquestionable. States can assist localities in the planning of local programs, provide guidelines or standards for program operation, and, most important, provide the funding necessary to establish and maintain effective pretrial release services.

❏ Replicating a Model Pretrial Release Program

The failure of a model program to work in any environment could discourage communities from trying to implement change if they take these studies to indicate that even the best is not always good enough. This would be a misreading of the findings. The attempt to replicate the Des Moines project has in fact produced confirmation of some of the basic tenets of community-based corrections. There is no substitute for local planning and participation in program development. There is no single model for success. Community-based correctional programs must be accepted and supported by the community if they are going to survive.

Summary

Centuries ago, the problems created by the pretrial jailing of defendants led to the development of pretrial release procedures. The first form of release was bail; friends or relatives of the accused would supervise the defendant in the community to ensure his appearance in court.

As the population grew and became too mobile for this informal system to work, commercial bondsmen appeared to fill the void. They provided no supervision to defendants, but would post bond for virtually anyone who could afford their fee.

Because the problems of local jails worsened with time and because the commercial bail system created more difficulties than it solved, alternative nonfinancial methods of pretrial release were developed. The first organized pretrial release program was the Manhattan Bail Project, which was established in the early 1960s. This release on recognizance program proved so successful that it was quickly replicated throughout the country. The U.S. Congress soon legislated a presumption in favor of release on recognizance for federal defendants that has been adopted by over one-third of the states.

Today pretrial release programs are in operation throughout the United States. Pretrial release programs have been developed in most states and the federal judicial system. Contemporary alternatives to jail or bail include law enforcement administered summons and citations; deposit bail; and recognizance, conditional, and supervised releases. Pretrial release programs generally attempt to secure nonfinancial releases for defendants at their initial appearance. Pretrial release staff interview defendants about their community ties and offense history and verify statements made during the interviews by contacting references identified by defendants. The programs select appropriate candidates for release and make release recommendations to the court. The programs also take steps to ensure that defendants appear in court. Defendants released on recognizance may receive only mailed reminders of the time and place of their court proceeding. Persons placed on conditional or supervised pretrial release will have restrictions placed on their pretrial conduct and will receive some degree of supervision to ensure compliance with these restrictions. They may also be required to participate in therapeutic, educational, or vocational programs during the pretrial period.

Pretrial release programs appear to be meeting their basic objectives. They increase the number of persons released prior to trial and reduce the amount of time defendants spend in custody. Their failure to appear and pretrial crime rates are as low or lower than those achieved under bail. Their economic costs and benefits are difficult to evaluate, however, not only because of the complexity of the financial calculations, but because social and human costs cannot be excluded from the equation.

Pretrial release programs play an important role in our criminal justice system, particularly in dealing with jail crowding issues. In the future, we will probably see an expansion of pretrial release services and increased state involvement in the planning and administration of pretrial release programs. Increasing efforts to assess and refine pretrial release program objectives will undoubtedly benefit all community-based correctional programs.

KEY WORDS AND CONCEPTS

bail
citations
commercial bondsmen
conditional release
costs and benefits
deposit bail
equal justice
failure-to-appear rates
fixed costs
follow-up procedures
forfeiture
interviewing

magistrates
on recognizance (OR)
pretrial crime
preventive detention
release on
    recognizance (ROR)
release rates
release
    recommendations
screening for
    release eligibility
speed of operations

supervised pretrial
    release
supervised pretrial
    work release
summons
surety
third-party release
unsecured appearance
    bond
variable costs
verification

NOTES

1. National Center for State Courts, *An Evaluation of Policy-Related Research on the Effectiveness of Pretrial Release Programs* (Denver, Colo.: National Center for State Courts, 1975), p. 5.
2. Ibid., p. 6.
3. Roscoe Pound and Felix Frankfurter (eds.), *Criminal Justice in Cleveland* (Cleveland, Ohio: Cleveland Foundation, 1922); Arthur L. Beeley. *The Bail System in Chicago* (Chicago: University of Chicago Press, 1927); Missouri Association for Criminal Justice, *The Missouri Crime Survey* (New York: Macmillan, 1926); Wayne L. Morse and Ronald H. Beatties, "Survey of the Administration of Criminal Justice in Oregon, Report No. 1: Final Report in 1971 Felony Cases in Multnomah County," *Oregon Law Review* 11 (June 1932): supplement.
4. Caleb Foote, "Compelling Appearance in Court: Administration of Bail in Philadelphia," *University of Pennsylvania Law Review* 102 (1954): 1031–1079; "The Administration of Bail in New York City," *University of Pennsylvania Law Review* 106 (1958): 693–730.
5. Don Oberdorfer, "The Bail-Bond Scandal," *Saturday Evening Post,* June 20, 1964, p. 66.
6. Charles Ares, Anne Rankin, and Herbert Sturz, "The Manhattan Bail Project: An Interim Report on the Use of Pretrial Parole," *New York University Law Review* 38 (1963): 67.
7. Bail Reform Act of 1966, 18. U.S.C. 3146 *et seq.*
8. Ibid.

9. Mark Place and David A. Sands, "Incarcerating the Innocent," in *Jails and Justice,* Paul F. Cromwell, Jr., and Joseph H. Schryver (eds.) (Springfield, Ill.: Thomas, 1975), p. 37.

10. John Goldkamp, "American Jails: Characteristics and Legal Predicaments of Inmates," *Criminal Law Bulletin* 15 (May–June 1979): 223–231.

11. "Bail," *The Pretrial Reporter* 2 (January 1978): 7.

12. Wayne H. Thomas, Jr., *Bail Reform in America* (Berkeley, Calif.: University of California Press, 1976), p. 12.

13. Ibid., p. 196.

14. Wayne H. Thomas, *National Evaluation Program Phase I Summary Report: Pretrial Release Programs* (Washington, D.C.: U.S. Government Printing Office, 1977), pp. 18–27.

15. National Center for State Courts, *An Evaluation of Policy-Related Research,* p. 59.

16. Thomas, *National Evaluation Program,* pp. 18–27.

17. "An O.R. Hearing," *Bill of Rights Newsletter* 8 (Spring 1974): 16, 17, 23.

18. Thomas, *National Evaluation Program,* p. 78.

19. Peter S. Venezia et al., *Pretrial Release with Supportive Services for "High Risk" Defendants* (Davis, Calif.: National Council on Crime and Delinquency, 1973).

20. Rob Wilson, "Replicating LEAA's First Exemplary Project—Plaudits in Des Moines, But Problems in Salt Lake," *Corrections Magazine* 11 (September 1976): 14.

21. David E. Aaronson et al., *The New Justice: Alternatives to Conventional Criminal Adjudication* (Washington, D.C.: U.S. Government Printing Office, 1977).

22. Andy Hall, with Elizabeth Gaynes, D. Allen Henry, and Walter F. Smith, *Pretrial Release Options* (U.S. Government Printing Office, 1984), p. 117.

23. "Preventive Detention: An Empirical Analysis," *Harvard Civil Rights/Civil Liberties Law Review* 6 (March 1971): 298.

24. Ibid., p. 296.

25. General Accounting Office, *The Federal Bail Process* (Washington, D.C.: U.S. Government Printing Office, 1978), p. 25.

26. John S. Goldkamp and Michael R. Gottfredson, *Judicial Guidelines for Bail: The Philadelphia Experiment* (U.S. Government Printing Office, July 1984).

27. National Center for State Courts, *An Evaluation of Policy-Related Research,* p. viii.

28. Venezia et al., *Pretrial Release with Supportive Services.*

29. General Accounting Office, *The Federal Bail Process.*

30. Lazar Institute, *Pretrial Release: A National Evaluation of Practices and Outcomes* (Washington, D.C.: Lazar Institute, 1981).

FOR FURTHER READING

Fleming, Roy B., *Punishment Before Trial: An Organizational Perspective of Felony Bail Process* (New York: Longman, 1982).

Goldfarb, Ronald, *Ransom* (New York: Harper & Row, 1965).

Goldfarb, Ronald, *Jails, the Ultimate Ghetto* (Garden City, N.Y.: Anchor Press, 1975).

Goldkamp, John S., *Two Classes of Accused: A Study of Bail and Detention in American Justice* (Cambridge, Mass.: Ballinger, 1979).

Thomas, Wayne H., *Bail Reform in America* (Berkeley, Calif.: University of California Press, 1976).

Wice, Paul B., *Freedom for Sale* (Lexington, Mass.: Lexington Books, 1974).

4: Probation

PROBATION HAS LONG BEEN one of the most popular forms of correctional disposition. About four times as many offenders are placed on probation as are sent to prison. As a sentencing alternative, probation embodies the essential elements of the reintegrative philosophy of corrections. It is designed to keep the offender in the community under supervision and provide him with resources drawn from his immediate community environment. Today, probation is especially important as a less costly alternative to incarceration in crowded prisons. The challenge is to adapt probation to the diverse needs of the offender while protecting the community from further criminal activity. In this chapter, we examine the development of probation, identify contemporary objectives, and discuss signficant issues in the probation process.

Probation can be defined in various ways. The National Advisory Commission on Standards and Goals maintains that probation can be defined as (1) a form of sentencing disposition, (2) the legal status of an offender, (3) a subsystem of corrections, and (4) a process.[1]

In considering probation as a form of sentence, the American Correctional Association provides us with a useful definition: "Probation is a judicial disposition (sentencing alternative) that establishes the defendant's legal status under which his freedom in the community is continued subject to the supervision by a probation organization and subject to conditions imposed by the court."[2] This definition identifies four essential elements of probation. First, probation is a form of sentence and is judicially imposed. Second, the offender is permitted to remain in the community while serving his sentence. Third, although the offender remains in the community, his freedom is conditional and he is subject to court-imposed conditions that restrict his behavior. Fourth, the offender's behavior while under sentence is supervised by a representative of a probation organization that serves the court. The probation agency's responsibility is to ensure that the probationer follows the conditions the judge sets forth. If the offender violates those conditions, the probation organization is responsible for initiating the revocation of probation.

When probation is viewed as the offender's legal status, it focuses attention on the restricted nature of the offender's liberty. Although he remains free in the community, the conditions placed on his freedom, as well as the ever-present threat of revocation and subsequent incarceration, distinguish him from the average free citizen. For example, he may be required to obtain employment, attend drug counseling programs, and pay restitution.

As a subsystem of corrections, probation is referred to as one of three major components—probation, prison, and parole. This view considers probation as interrelated and interdependent with the larger system of corrections.

When probation is examined as a process, its two main functions—the preparation of presentence investigation reports, which are ordered by the court or prescribed by law, and the supervision of persons placed on probation—are emphasized.[3]

Contemporary Objectives

A national study of adult probation services has identified four major objectives of probation:

1. Protect the community from antisocial behavior
2. Reintegrate the criminal offender
3. Further justice
4. Provide the requisite services in an effective and efficient manner[4]

Community protection is an objective that probation shares with all other forms of correctional programs. One of the basic purposes of corrections is to provide public protection by aiding in the prevention of crime.[5] Probation addresses this goal by preparing the presentence investigation (PSI) report and supervising offenders. The PSI permits the probation agency to screen offenders according to the risk or danger they may pose to the community. Those viewed as posing a threat to the community can be identified and referred to noncommunity and more secure placements, usually involving incarceration. The supervision functions of probation also protect the community by monitoring probationers' behavior and removing them from the community when they violate the conditions of their probation.

In pursuit of the objective of reintegration, probation also serves two important functions. First, it attempts to determine the offender's special needs. Second, it attempts to meet them with community resources.

To satisfy the objective of furthering justice, the probation agency must meet reponsibilities to the offender, the community, and the criminal justice system. The probation agency must perform all the roles society has designated for it and protect the sometimes conflicting rights and liberties of the community and probation clients.

Provision of probation services refers to the administrative features of the probation organization. This objective calls for the effective and efficient delivery of services that include reporting to the court and supervising offenders.

Court Use of Probation

An understanding of the probation process requires an understanding of how offenders are placed on probation. Judges can sentence individuals to terms of probation in several ways, depending upon state legislative provisions.[6]

First, a judge can sentence an offender directly to probation. Second, a judge can impose a prison sentence on an offender and then suspend it and place the offender under probation supervision. Under both procedures, the offender's continued presence in the community is contingent upon his good behavior. If probation is revoked under the first procedure, the court must set a prison sentence if incarceration is required. Under the second procedure, the probationer who is revoked serves the original prison sentence. Depending upon the jurisdiction, time spent in the community may or may not be subtracted from the length of sentence.

A third alternative permits the judge to defer formal sentencing and place the offender on probation. If the offender remains law abiding during the prescribed term, the original charges are usually dropped. This procedure is comparable to postconviction diversion. In some jurisdictions, there is a fourth variation, which involves the judge's sentencing the offender to a short jail or prison term or placement in a "boot camp" prior to commencing a term of probation. This practice is often referred to as a split sentence or shock incarceration.

Historical Perspective

❏ The English Tradition

Probation, like many of our other major correctional reforms (such as the penitentiary, the indeterminate sentence, and parole) took form in the United States, but it was essentially an outgrowth of several practices found in English common law. Probation developed as a variation of the English practice of the conditional suspension of punishment pending the offender's good behavior. Probation was not the result of a deliberate legislative or judicial act; instead, it was the result of the gradual growth and modification of existing legal practices.[7] These practices were designed to lessen or avoid the imposition of severe penalties on certain offenders. The widespread use of severe punishments in the past, including executions for relatively minor crimes, led judges and prosecutors to search for ways to soften the harshness of legal penalties.[8] Probation developed as a solution to excessively harsh punishment.

The early procedures used to circumvent the mechanical application of the criminal justice process include the benefit of clergy, judicial reprieve, release on recognizance (with and without surety), and the pardon.[9] Each of these practices enabled judicial officials to consider the individual factors of each case, thus avoiding the automatic application of prescribed punishments.

The benefit of clergy permitted religious officials to have the privilege of avoiding secular forms of punishment (usually execution) by having their cases transferred to a religious or ecclesiastical court. The prescribed penalties were generally less severe in these nonsecular courts. To receive benefit of clergy, a defendant was required to prove his literacy, generally by reading a passage from the Bible. The benefit of clergy proved to be so popular that it was later extended to all persons who could demonstrate literacy. Not surprisingly, abuses set in when illiterates began memorizing the required biblical passage. The practice continued in England until the mid 1800s but was never formally adopted in the United States.

The judicial reprieve was another legal technique judges used. It involved the temporary suspension of either the sentencing decision or the execution of sentence. During the period of suspension, the defendant could appeal the conviction by seeking a pardon. In some cases, the temporary suspension of punishment was followed by the dropping of criminal proceedings against the individual. In other cases, judges used the reprieve when they were not satisfied with the end result of the criminal proceeding and decided to take independent and contrary action.

The recognizance, with and without surety, provided for the release of an individual from custody during the criminal proceeding.[10] Initially, this release took place prior to trial, but, in some cases, it was extended to other stages, including the postconviction period. The recognizance was used to ensure that the offender would show up for his trial and also as a type of sentence for certain offenders.[11] During the 1800s, the recognizance was used in the United States with juvenile offenders when the court felt that imprisonment was inappropriate. In 1836, Massachusetts passed a law that officially provided for the release of minor offenders on recognizance with sureties at any stage of the criminal proceeding.[12]

In the United States, the court's power to suspend sentences became a source of controversy. The issue was essentially an argument over the separation of powers. Those supporting the judiciary's position maintained that the precedent of judicial reprieve permitted the courts to suspend sentences indefinitely. Persons supporting the legislative position argued that the courts had the authority to suspend sentences only temporarily, not indefinitely. This view held that, by indefinitely suspending sentences, the courts were usurping legislative prerogative.

This controversy reached a conclusion in 1916, when the U.S. Supreme Court decided in *United States* v. *Killets* that the federal courts could not indefinitely suspend the imprisonment or execution of a sentence; this was a legislative right.[13] The Court did suggest, however, that Congress had the authority legislatively to provide the courts with the discretion to suspend sentences temporarily or indefinitely. Congress enacted legislation authorizing the suspension of prison sentences, and probation was eventually adopted as a formal sentencing option.

❑ Early U.S. Practices

The evolution of probation practices in the United States can be traced to the lower courts of Boston, Massachusetts. In 1841, John Augustus, a shoemaker by trade, became interested in helping minor offenders. With judicial approval, Augustus was permitted to stand bail for petty offenders, usually drunkards, and to receive them into his custody. Action against these offenders was deferred until after a specified period of time, when the offender would be ordered to reappear before the presiding judge and account for himself. Augustus appeared alongside the defendant and gave testimony regarding the offender's conduct in the community. If the defendant had been law abiding and industrious, the charges against him were dropped; if he had failed to rehabilitate himself, prosecution continued. During Augustus's time of service, he was credited with helping over 2,000 persons, very few of whom returned to the courts as failures. John Augustus was credited with devising rudimentary forms of investigative and screening procedures, supervision practices, and the delivery of social services to offenders.[14] These early accomplishments provided the foundation for modern probation.

Two points regarding Augustus's activities must be emphasized if we are to put his work into proper perspective. John Augustus was unpaid and, as such, was probably the first volunteer in probation. His involvement with the offender was a result of a deeply felt personal commitment, and he was free of the bureaucratic trappings of modern probation. But his efforts were not universally hailed. He encountered considerable resistance from local criminal justice officials, particularly those who received fees based on the conviction and sentencing of offenders.[15] These officials had a vested interest in processing and convicting as many offenders as possible, and Augustus's activities threatened their source of income. Fortunately, Augustus had enough supporters among the lower court judges to permit his experiment to continue.

John Augustus and the Beginnings of Probation

"In the month of August, 1841, I was in court one morning, when the door communicating with the lock-room was opened and an officer entered, followed by a ragged and wretched looking man, who took his seat upon the bench allotted to prisoners. I imagined from the man's appearance, that his offense was that of yielding to his appetite for intoxicating drinks, and in a few moments I found that my suspicions were correct, for the clerk read the complaint, in which the man was charged with being a common drunkard. The case was clearly made out, but before sentence had been passed, I conversed with him for a few moments, and found that he was not yet past all hope for reformation. . . . He told me that if he could be saved from the House of Correction, he never again would taste intoxicating liquors, there was such an earnestness in that tone, and a look of firm resolve, that I determined to aid him, I bailed him, by permission of the Court. He was ordered to appear for sentence in three weeks from that time. He signed the pledge and became a sober man; at the expiration of this period of probation, I accompanied him into the court room. . . . The Judge expressed himself much pleased with the account we gave of the man, and instead of the usual penalty—imprisonment in the House of Correction—he fined him one cent and costs amounting in all to $3.76, which was immediately paid. The man continued industrious and sober, and without doubt has been by his treatment, saved from a drunkard's grave."

SOURCE: John Augustus, *A Report of the Labors of John Augustus, for the Last Ten Years, in Aid of the Unfortunate* (Boston: Wright & Hasty, 1852). Reprinted as *John Augustus, First Probation Officer* (New York: Probation Association, 1939), pp. 4–5.

After Augustus, the practice of having volunteers working with the courts to divert and assist certain minor offenders continued. In 1878, Massachusetts authorized the first formal probation statute, which provided the mayor of Boston with the authority to appoint a probation officer who would report to the chief of police. Subsequently, several other states adopted similar programs.

It was not until the early 1900s that the probation movement gained real momentum as a social reform and became widely accepted. In 1900, only six states provided for probation. By 1920, this situation had changed drastically: every state permitted juvenile probation, and thirty-three states permitted adult probation.[16]

The rapid growth of probation in the early 1900s has been attributed by some to the Killits case, which laid the groundwork for probation legislation. Other observers link probation's growth to its association with the juvenile court movement, which began in 1899 and spread rapidly in the early 1900s. A third explanation attributes the rapid growth of probation to the efforts of the Progressives, a social reform movement of the era.[17] As a social movement, the Progressives were essentially anti-institutional and were in favor of less restrictive forms of social control. They also supported an individualized, case-by-case approach to justice that stressed the informal and flexible rehabilitation of the offender.[18] Probation appeared to be a reform that fit the bill. By 1954, every state had adopted it as a form of correctional disposition.

Today, probation is the single most widely utilized correctional disposition. One-quarter of all felony arrests end in probation. The number of probation officers has failed to keep pace with the number of offenders, leading to a "probation crowding" problem that rivals institutional crowding.

Probation Crowding

- Almost two-thirds of all convicted adult offenders are placed on probation, yet probation receives less than one-third of the correctional resources.
- The probation population doubled in the past decade, with no significant capacity increases.
- Probation populations are increasing at a slightly higher rate than prison, jail, and parole populations: The adult imprisoned population increased by 47.7 percent between 1979 and 1984, while the adult probation population increased by 57.75 percent.
- Nationwide, about 15 percent of new probationers are committed to prison within one year due to technical violations, rearrest, or reconviction. However, there is much interstate variation in the subsequent-imprisonment rate for probationers.
- A subgroup of high-risk probationers can be identified who fail at very high rates (over 60 percent rearrested in the first year on probation).
- The increased use of split sentencing is transforming probation into a parole agency.

- Changes in sentencing statutes have directly and indirectly affected probation via (1) the increased rate of probation (i.e., net widening), (2) the use of split sentences, and (3) the need to use probation as an alternative to prison.
- Changes in age composition have placed more offenders "at risk" for probation.
- In general, states with higher reported crime rates and higher arrest rates also have higher rates of all forms of correctional control, including probation.
- Prison crowding leads to the use of back-door early release strategies.
- When these offenders fail (i.e., are reconvicted), they are placed on probation as a front-door diversionary strategy. The cycle continues unabated as prison failures become probation failures who get returned to prison.

SOURCE: James M. Byrne, Arthur Lurigio, and Christopher Baird, "The Effectiveness of the New Intensive Supervision Programs," *Research in Corrections*, 2(2) (1989).

Administrative Issues

The administrative structure of U.S. probation services reflects the decentralized and fragmented character of contemporary corrections. As with other forms of corrections, there does not appear to be a single model or standard for organizing or operating a probation agency. Two issues appear to underlie the variegated structure of probation services.[19] The first issue concerns the level of government—city, county, or state—responsible for administering the probation agency. The second issue addresses the appropriate location of probation agencies in the governmental structure. Should they be a part of the judiciary or the executive branch?

Regarding the first issue, studies of governmental responsibility for probation services have identified three basic administrative models: the state-administered, locally administered, and "mixed" models.[20] In the state-administered model, a state-level agency is responsible for coordinating staffing and funding of probation services statewide. The locally administered model places the responsibility for probation services in the hands of a city or county government. The mixed model of administration involves the state and local forms of government sharing the responsibility for providing probation services. In the mixed model, the state agency is generally responsible for setting standards and monitoring the provision of services to probationers, and localities (usually counties) are given responsibility for day-to-day system operation. Table 4-1 presents a state-by-state breakdown of probation administration by level of government.

TABLE 4-1 Probation Administration, by Government Level

State Probation Only

Alaska	Maryland	South Dakota
Connecticut	Montana	Tennessee
Delaware	Nevada	Utah
Hawaii	New Mexico	Vermont
Idaho	North Carolina	Virginia
Iowa	North Dakota	Washington
Louisiana	Rhode Island	West Virginia
Maine	South Carolina	Wisconsin

Local Probation Only

County only	County and city
Arizona	Indiana
California	
Illinois	
Massachusetts	
New Jersey	
Texas	

State and Local Probation

State, county, and city	State and county	State and city
Arkansas	Florida	Alabama
Colorado	Georgia	Kansas
Michigan	Mississippi	Kentucky
Minnesota	Oregon	New Hampshire
Missouri	Pennsylvania	Oklahoma
Nebraska		
New York		
Ohio		
Wyoming		

SOURCE: National Council on Crime and Delinquency, "Probation in the United States" 1979, *National Probation Reports* (San Francisco: National Council on Crime and Delinquency, 1981), p. 33.

After a considered review of the issue, the National Advisory Commission on Standards and Goals in Corrections concluded that the state-administered probation system is superior to the locally controlled model.[21] The principal advantages of this approach are that it ensures uniformity in the quality and delivery of services provided throughout the state and maximizes the efficient use of increasingly scarce resources. Proponents of the alternative models argue that the benefits of local control outweigh the disadvantages resulting from limited resources.

The second major issue focuses on the branch of government that is best suited to administer probation services. Arguments in favor of placing probation under the authority of the courts include:

1. Probation would be more responsive to court direction.
2. This arrangement would provide the judiciary with an automatic feedback mechanism on effectiveness of dispositions through reports filed by probation staff.
3. Courts have a greater awareness of needed resources and may become advocates for their staffs in obtaining better services.

    4. Increased use of pretrial diversion may be furthered by placing probation in the judicial branch.[22]

This approach has been criticized because of the lack of judicial expertise in the area of administration and management and because it is feared that court administration would lead to a reordering of probation priorities in such a way that more emphasis would be given to services to the court than to probationers. Probation staff could easily be misused in this model and be required to perform nonprobation tasks.

There are several reasons for placing probation services in the executive branch of government:

    1. All other subsystems for carrying out court disposition of offenders are in the executive branch. Closer coordination and functional integration with other corrections personnel could be achieved by a common organizational placement, particularly as community-based correction programs increase. Furthermore, job mobility would be enhanced if related functions are administratively tied.

    2. The executive branch contains the allied human services agencies, including social and rehabilitation services, medical services, employment services, education, and housing. Where probation also is in the executive branch, opportunities are increased for coordination, cooperative endeavors, and comprehensive planning.

    3. Decisions involving resource allocations and establishment of priorities are made by the executive branch. It initiates requests to the legislative bodies for appropriation of funds, and by doing so sets priorities for allocating limited tax dollars. When probation is included in the total corrections system, more rational decisions about the best distribution of resources can be made.

    4. Probation administrators are in position to negotiate and present their case more strongly if they are in the executive branch.[23]

In general, evaluations of the desirability of executive versus judicial administration of probation services conclude that the executive branch is better suited for administrative tasks. Table 4-2 presents the distribution of responsibility for adult probation by level and branch of government. In slightly more than half the states reporting, probation was administered by a state agency, although, in many jurisdictions, state and local levels of government shared this function. Apparently, state involvement in probation administration is extensive.

TABLE 4-2 Responsibility for Adult Probation, by Level and Branch of Government

Branch of government	Level of government			
	State	Local	State and local	Total
Executive	22	0	1	23
Judicial	1	3	3	7
Executive and judicial	3	0	18	21
Total states	26	3	22	51

In the most recent national census, approximately 3 million persons were found to be under some form of community supervision. In 1987, more than two-thirds of all sentenced offenders and 86 percent of all persons under community supervision were probationers.[24] This number is almost four times the number of persons serving prison sentences.

Probation is clearly the most frequently used form of correctional disposition. However, in examining the use of probation by the individual states, there appears to be a great deal of variation among the states. Table 4-3 provides a state-by-state breakdown of the total number of persons on probation as of December 31, 1987, the number of persons who entered or exited probation case loads during 1987, and the rate of probation per 100,000 adults in the population. California leads the nation with the largest number of cases supervised (239,851); North Dakota supervised the least (1,616). When population variations and probation entries are taken into account, the distribution among the states changes. Georgia placed the largest proportion of offenders on probation during 1987; Kentucky utilized probation less frequently than any other state. These variations may be attributed to a number of factors, but two that are certainly important are differences in sentencing philosophies and the availability of probation resources within the states. We examine these issues in the next section.

Granting Probation

The decision to sentence an offender to probation is an important one for both the offender and the community. From the offender's perspective, it is the difference between freedom and confinement. For the community, it is a question of protection from criminal behavior. The responsibility for this decision rests with the court, and a number of factors can influence the sentencing judge.[25] Legislative provisions regarding who may be placed on probation vary considerably from state to state. Some states statutorily prohibit certain types of offenders from receiving probation.[26] For example, California statutorily excludes certain types of persons convicted of violent crimes; in Illinois, offenders convicted of rape are ineligible for probation. States that prohibit the use of probation for offenders convicted of certain crimes limit judges' discretion in sentencing those offenders by restricting the range of sentencing options.

From an organizational perspective, the availability of probation services and the judge's perception of the quality of those services can also influence judicial decisions. For example, in a particular state, probation may exist by statute, but some localities may not have probation services available. In other communities, probation case loads may be so high that the ratio of probationers to probation officers renders probation supervision simply a form of suspended sentence. Judges who are aware of this problem may choose to impose alternative dispositions that require intensive supervision of the offenders.

A third factor is the offender's willingness to accept probation. Unlike being sentenced to a jail or prison term, the defendant does have some say in the matter.

TABLE 4-3 Movement and Rate of the Probation Population under State and Federal Jurisdiction, by Region and Jurisdiction, 1987

Region and jurisdiction	Probation population on Jan. 1, 1987	Movement during 1987		Probation population on Dec. 31, 1987	Rate (per 100,000 adult residents) of persons under probation supervision
		Entries	Exits		
United States, total	2,114,821	1,376,244	1,249,012	2,242,053	1,247
Federal	57,337	23,077	20,428	59,986	33
State, total	2,057,484	1,353,167	1,228,584	2,182,067	1,213
Northeast	395,836	215,530	193,093	418,273	1,095
Connecticut	41,304	30,841	28,486	43,659	1,779
Maine	4,620	3,281	3,296	4,605	521
Massachusetts	94,945	56,390	53,274	98,061	2,170
New Hampshire	3,583	3,001	2,434	4,150	525
New Jersey	51,359	27,817	23,389	55,787	955
New York	107,337	42,724	36,908	113,153	840
Pennsylvania	78,985	43,977	37,878	85,084	937
Rhode Island	8,174	4,915	4,908	8,181	1,081
Vermont	5,529	2,584	2,520	5,593	1,371
Midwest	444,241	349,004	310,189	483,056	1,101
Illinois	76,203	51,319	45,190	82,332	963
Indiana	50,806	51,410	45,238	56,978	1,403
Iowa	12,584	11,756	11,595	12,745	606
Kansas	17,125	8,666	7,602	18,189	997
Michigan	102,653	82,928	71,585	113,996	1,691
Minnesota[a]	38,901	40,397	34,935	44,363	1,415[b]
Missouri	33,819	28,700	21,451	41,068	1,082
Nebraska	11,265	11,514	11,268	11,511	983
North Dakota	1,544	788	716	1,616	333
Ohio	72,339	45,316	46,163	71,492	900
South Dakota	2,354	4,416	4,176	2,594	506
Wisconsin	24,648	11,794	10,270	26,172	740
South	854,043	559,828	527,589	886,282	1,441
Alabama	21,371	10,502	8,467	23,406	789
Arkansas[b]	12,700	2,981	2,206	13,475	774[b]
Delaware	7,985	5,544	4,241	9,288	1,927
District of Columbia	12,307	9,370	10,880	10,797	2,222
Florida	139,859	173,888	160,537	153,210	1,644
Georgia	109,485	61,235	60,236	110,484	2,463
Kentucky	6,841	4,579	4,239	7,181	263
Louisiana	27,677	10,134	7,498	30,313	964
Maryland	69,134	43,700	40,018	72,816	2,135
Mississippi	6,458	2,930	2,636	6,752	368
North Carolina	58,644	33,519	29,223	62,940	1,315
Oklahoma	22,740	12,571	11,758	23,553	990
South Carolina	21,110	13,406	10,908	23,608	950
Tennessee	26,291	18,944	18,832	26,403	733
Texas	290,074	146,810	147,194	289,690	2,454
Virginia	17,126	7,418	6,599	17,945	404
West Virginia	4,241	2,297	2,117	4,421	314

TABLE 4-3 (continued)

Region and jurisdiction	Probation population on Jan. 1, 1987	Movement during 1987		Probation population on Dec. 31, 1987	Rate (per 100,000 adult residents) of persons under probation supervision
		Entries	Exits		
West	363,364	228,805	197,713	394,456	1,087
Alaska	2,885	1,251	1,195	2,941	831
Arizona	20,283	10,082	7,767	22,598	916
California	218,526	139,110	117,785	239,851	1,178
Colorado	16,335	8,298	10,177	14,456	597
Hawaii	8,404	5,983	5,505	8,882	1,114
Idaho	3,770	2,197	1,821	4,146	598
Montana	2,943	1,091	866	3,168	542
Nevada[b]	5,518	2,904	3,084	5,338	707[b]
New Mexico	4,175	3,948	4,113	4,010	381
Oregon	23,402	10,402	10,833	22,971	1,127
Utah	5,620	3,738	3,525	5,833	555
Washington	49,663	38,740	29,982	58,421	1,734
Wyoming	1,840	1,061	1,060	1,841	538

[a]Estimated 1987 exit data.
[b]Estimated all data.
SOURCE: Adapted from *Sourcebook on Criminal Justice Statistics* (Washington, D.C.: U.S. Government Printing Office, 1989), pp. 590, 591.

He is given the choice of either agreeing to the conditions of probation or rejecting them and receiving an alternative punishment, generally imprisonment.

The final major factor influencing the sentencing decision is the judge's perception of the appropriateness of probation for a particular offender. The judge may be assisted in this determination by the presentence investigation report (PSI) and the probation officer's recommendation. We discuss the significance of the PSI in a subsequent section.

The American Bar Association has provided guidelines to assist sentencing judges with the probation decision. They recommend that probation should be the preferred sentence except in the following cases:

1. Confinement is necessary to protect the public from further criminal activity by the offender.
2. The offender is in need of correctional treatment that can most effectively be provided if he is confined.
3. It would unduly deprecate the seriousness of the offense if a sentence of probation were imposed.[27]

The bar association also recommends that the court consider "the nature and circumstances of the crime, the history and character of the offender, and the available institutional and community resources.[28] In effect, it is suggesting that the judge consider three sets of factors: the offense, the offender's personal characteristics and background, and community correctional resources.

Some research has been conducted to determine what factors most heavily influence a judge's decision to grant probation. One study of 277 cases in a federal district court in California found that probation officers' recommendations have a significant impact on the decision. In 95 percent of the cases studied, the court followed the probation officer's recommendations. Subsequent studies of probation decision making in California state courts and in ten other federal judicial circuits confirmed the importance of the probation officer's recommendation.[29] In the vast majority of cases, the sentencing judge followed the probation officer's recommendation.

A look at the factors influencing probation officers' judgments helps explain why their recommendations are so important. A federally funded study known as the San Francisco Project found that the probation recommendation was positively related to the following offender characteristics: educational level, monthly income, occupation level, marital and employment stability, participation in religious activities, and military record.[30] Recommendations against probation and for imprisonment were more likely when offenders exhibited any of the following characteristics: homosexuality, alcohol involvement, weapon use, violence associated with the present offense, family criminality, and drug abuse.[31]

The San Francisco study also attempted to determine whether probation officers and judges agreed or differed in their ranking of the factors considered most important in the probation decision. Probation officers and judges participating in the study were asked to rank in terms of their significance the factors they believed influenced their decision regarding the dispositions of offenders. Table 4-4 presents their responses. In terms of the relative importance placed on each factor, it appears that the judges and probation officers share similar perspectives, although they differ in terms of the relative emphasis placed on each item. Both groups ranked prior record, confinement status, number of arrests, offense, and longest term of employment as the most significant factors in the sentencing decision. There is considerable agreement on the factors that "qualify" a defendant for probation. When

TABLE 4-4 Rank of Demographic Factors Used by Probation Officers and District Court Judges for Sentencing Alternatives

Demographic factors	Probation officers' ranking	District court judges' ranking
Prior record	1	3
Confinement status	2	2
Number of arrests	3	4
Offense	4	1
Longest employment	5	5
Occupation	6	8
Number of months employed	7	6
Income	8	10
Longest residence	9	7
Military history	10	9

Source: Joseph D. Lohman, Albert Wahl, and Robert Carter, *San Francisco Project Report 5* (Berkeley, Calif.: February 1966), p. 68.

probation officers work with judges over extended periods of time, they are probably influenced by the judges' perspectives. Probation officers may make recommendations that "second guess" the judges' views and are therefore very likely to be followed.

□ Sentencing Guidelines

Sentence guidelines are now used to assist judges with their decision making in many jurisdictions.[32] These guidelines are standardized instruments designed to provide clear and explicit direction to the court in determining the appropriate punishments. Their purpose is to reduce the incidence of arbitrary decision making and to encourage consistency in sentencing within a jurisdiction.

□ Standardized Sentencing Instruments

Figures 4-1 and 4-2 present examples of standardized sentencing instruments. To utilize the guidelines, a crime score and offender score must first be computed for each offender. The second step requires the user to refer to the sentencing grid and identify the appropriate disposition. To illustrate the use of this instrument, consider an offender who committed a crime that involved use of a weapon and resulted in an injury. His crime score would be 3. If his background involved one prior adult felony conviction and one prior incarceration, his offender score would be 3. Using the sentencing grid, we can determine that a sentence of between 4 and 6 years is appropriate.

□ Presentence Investigation Report

One of the primary functions of probation organizations is the preparation of the presentence investigation report. The PSI report serves at least five purposes in the sentencing and correction phases of criminal justice.[33] Its primary purpose is to assist the judge in making an appropriate sentencing decision by providing supplemental information not revealed at the trial regarding the offender's personal and social circumstances. Utilizing this information, the judge can tailor a punishment that satisfies the purposes of justice and meets the offender's needs.

A second PSI objective is to provide a basis for an offender's probation plan. Treatment and supervision needs are identified so that appropriate services can be provided. Another function of the PSI is to assist institutional correctional officials if the offender is sentenced to a prison term. The PSI provides information that facilitates the classification of the offender for custody, work, education, and other prison programs. A fourth purpose of the PSI is to provide information about the offender to the parole board for use in release decision making. Finally, the PSI plays a very important role as a source of information for research in the field of corrections. The PSI represents a primary source document regarding offenders' background characteristics and personal attributes.

PSI Preparation.   In most jurisdictions, probation officers prepare the PSI report. However, there is no single procedure or set of guidelines governing the

Offender: _____ Docket number: _____

Judge: _____ Date: _____

Offense(s) convicted of: _____

_____

Crime score:
A. Injury
    0 = No injury
    1 = Injury
    2 = Death   _____ +
B. Weapon
    0 = No weapon
    1 = Weapon
    2 = Weapon present and used   _____ +
C. Drugs
    0 = No sale of drugs
    1 = Sale of drugs   _____ =

Crime score

Offender score:
A. Current legal status
    0 = Not on probation/parole, escape
    1 = On probation/parole, escape   _____ +
B. Prior adult misdemeanor convictions
    0 = No convictions
    1 = One conviction
    2 = Two or more convictions   _____ +
C. Prior adult felony convictions
    0 = No convictions
    2 = One conviction
    4 = Two or more convictions   _____ +
D. Prior adult probation parole revocations
    0 = None
    1 = One or more revocations   _____ +
E. Prior adult incarcerations (over 60 days)
    0 = None
    1 = One incarceration
    2 = Two or more incarcerations   _____ =

Offender score

Guideline sentence: _____

Actual sentence: _____

Reasons (if actual sentence does not fall within guideline range): _____

_____

FIGURE 4-1 Crime and Offender Score Calculations
SOURCE: Jack Kress et al., *Developing Sentencing Guidelines: Trainers Handbook* (Washington, D.C.: National Institute of Law Enforcement and Criminal Justice, 1978), p. 78.

Crime score

4–5	4–6 years	5–7 years	6–8 years	8–10 years
3	3–5 years	4–6 years	6–8 years	6–8 years
2	2–4 years	3–5 years	3–5 years	4–6 years
1	Probation	Probation	2–4 years	3–5 years
0	Probation	Probation	Probation	2–4 years
	0–1	2–4	5–7	8–10

Offender score

FIGURE 4-2 Felony Sentencing Grid
SOURCE: Jack Kress et al., *Developing Sentencing Guidelines: Trainers Handbook* (Washington, D.C.: National Institute of Law Enforcement and Criminal Justice, 1978), p. 79.

preparation of the document and the identification of the items of information appropriate for inclusion in the report. Practices vary from jurisdiction to jurisdiction according to whether the report is required by statute or is optional at the judge's discretion. A recent study found that, in 22 states and the federal government, the PSI was mandatory for virtually all felony cases; the PSI was required in 19 states when probation was being considered as a sentence.[34] In the remaining states and Washington, D.C., the PSI was discretionary. PSI's are rarely prepared for misdemeanants.

Report Purpose and Content. The PSI is usually prepared after conviction and before sentencing, although some states leave the timing of the report up to the individual judge. Timing is somewhat controversial because the amount of information gathered is influenced by the amount of time available for preparation. One view maintains that a lengthy and detailed investigation should be initiated as soon as possible so that the report will be ready when needed. However, beginning the report before conviction presupposes the offender's guilt and may damage his reputation when the field investigation is conducted. Also, if the defendant is found not guilty, the probation agency's resources would have been wasted.

In most jurisdictions, probation officers are aided in their investigation by standardized forms that are usually referred to as either short or long forms. Their purpose is to guide the probation officer in collecting information regarding certain characteristics of the offender. The long form provides for a more in-depth investigation of a person's social and personal background, motivations, and characteristics. The short form is utilized when less detailed information is required or when probation resources are too limited to permit lengthy, in-depth investigations.

PSI preparation and utilization varies with the type of information collected. The primary purpose of this report is to assist the sentencing judge in determining an appropriate sentence for a convicted offender. Although the PSI plays a critical role in the entire criminal justice process, the type of information collected reflects a principal concern with factors considered relevant to the purposes of punishment.

To illustrate the range of factors included in the PSI, consider the information federal probation officers include: offense, defendant's version of the offense, prior record, family history, marital history, home and neighborhood, education, religion, interest/leisure activities, health, employment, military service, and financial condition.[35] The information is summarized at the conclusion of the report and a recommendation regarding disposition is offered. In some jurisdictions, the recommendation is offered only when the sentencing judge specifically requests it. As noted earlier, research suggests that there is a high rate of agreement beween the probation officer's recommendation and the judge's final decision.

Privately Prepared Presentence Reports.   Privately prepared presentence reports appeared on the scene in the late 1960s.[36] These reports are commissioned by defense counsel in an attempt to develop alternatives to confinement in cases where incarceration seems likely. A variety of individuals and organizations are involved in such efforts. Former probation officers may offer such a service for a fee as a profit-making venture.

Not-for-profit organizations are also involved, as part of their advocacy for alternatives to confinement. The largest such organization is the National Center on Institutions and Alternatives. NCIA developed in Washington, D.C., and now has branches in California, New York, North Carolina, Florida, and Nebraska. NCIA refers to its reports as Client Specific Plans (CSP's). CSP's are individualized sentence recommendations that address defendant, victim, and criminal justice system concerns through a combination of treatments and conditions. Provisions are usually made for counseling, education, community service, restitution, employment, and some form of supervision. Since the program deals primarily with felonies, short periods of confinement—such as jail, weekend jail, and work release—are often advocated. CSP's generally arrange for treatment prior to sentencing, and provide a more complete diagnostic approach to the offender's criminality than the more descriptive PSI.

Research indicates that although there is variation from jurisdiction to jurisdiction, CSP recommendations tend to be accepted in full or in part by the sentencing judge. Comments from judges rejecting CSP's indicate that failure to accept the plan is generally the result of differing perceptions of the severity of the offender's prior record and/or current offense (figure 4-3).

Probation Supervision

Probation agencies' second major function is supervising offenders placed on probation. In this section, we review several significant issues associated with the supervision process, including styles of supervision adopted by probation officers, strategies underlying the supervision process, case load management, conditions of probation, and the revocation process.[37]

❏ Supervisory Styles

The supervision of offenders is influenced by two sometimes conflicting duties: controlling the offender and providing social services. The first function places probation officers in a law enforcement role. They monitor the probationer's activities and ensure that the conditions of probation set forth by the court are met. When these conditions are violated, probation officers must take the offender into custody

---

Focus on the Offender's Prior Record

A good plan, but probation has been violated.

The defendant obviously has had no changes in attitude.

The client is obviously not interested in alternatives or the client would have tried them before.

The client's background and attitude mitigate use of the plan.

The client was given chances in the past.

Prior performance indicates that nothing works for this person.

Society needs retribution; this is a repeat offender, so it would not be fair to the community to act otherwise.

A good plan, very impressive, but the defendant must be sentenced to prison because of a parole violation.

Focus on the Nature of the Offense

The plan is not punitive or enough of a deterrent.

Program and plan were wonderful, but the crime is too serious to follow plan.

Incarceration is necessary for this serious offense.

The crime was serious enough to warrant some type of incarceration.

This was a violent crime with drug use; the defendant also pleaded down to a lesser offense.

FIGURE 4-3 Selected Comments from Judges Rejecting CSP's

SOURCE: William Clements,"Judicial Use of Private Presentence Reports. The Case of Client-Specific Planning." Presented at the Annual Meeting of the Academy of Criminal Justice Sciences, Orlando, Fla., March 1986.

and initiate a revocation proceeding. In actuality, very little proactive monitoring takes place because of the massive caseloads for which individual probation officers are responsible. Most of the monitoring is reactive—probation officers respond to official and unofficial reports of misconduct.

The provision of social services by probation officers is essentially a helping function. They attempt to deal with the offender's problems directly, by providing such services as counseling, or indirectly, by serving as a referral source. Individual probation officers vary in terms of their relative commitment to both the duties of control and service provision. Some officers prefer the law enforcement approach, others view themselves more as social workers.

Research on the subject of probation supervision indicates that probation officers choose one of several adaptive orientations to the supervision function.[38] One study suggests that probation officers' working philosophy could be differentiated into four styles defined by the officer's self-image.[39] The "law enforcers" stress their role's law enforcement and police functions. Their primary concerns focus on compliance with court orders, the authority delegated to them by the court, their decision-making powers, their responsibility to ensure public safety, and police work.

Individuals identified as "time servers" view their task as "just a job." They have few career aspirations and little professional orientation. Officers who view

Federal Probation Officer Wins by Using 'Tough Love'

by Frances Spotswood

"Tough love" is what John O'Callaghan practices, and it is what he preaches to his clients and their families.

A federal probation officer in the Northern District of Alabama, O'Callaghan spends his working hours trying to help convicted criminals get back on the right track. Many of them are alcoholics.

A young woman who told about her family session with O'Callaghan said he didn't fit her image of a probation officer.

O'Callaghan stopped by to see her and her husband just before the brother got out of prison. He said he was going to try to help Bobby straighten up and asked the sister to call him if they had problems when the prisoner came home.

"He was in a jogging outfit when he came by. I guess he was going to run. That's one of the things he does with Bobby, runs with him," said the sister.

Bobby got out of prison, came to his sister's apartment, and got very drunk. The sister called O'Callaghan. He came and calmed her down, then convinced his client that he should go to a treatment facility. O'Callaghan took him there.

"He is young, casual and he cares. He doesn't let awkward situations be awkward. He's a nice guy, but he won't put up with any nonsense," the sister said.

O'Callaghan's co-workers say he is just what a probation officer is supposed to be. They nominated him for the Ezra Nash Award which goes each year to the outstanding federal probation officer in the Southeast. Friday, in a ceremony at the Birmingham federal building, he received that award for 1981.

Also present were some of the people O'Callaghan calls "my treasures." They are the people who give his clients jobs and will take a chance on another one even if some don't work out.

One of the employers said, "I've got two of John's boys and they give me less trouble than most of the other employees. One of them walks to work every day, and I know he has to leave home by a quarter to five (a.m.) to make it."

He said O'Callaghan checks on the men, counsels with them and is ready to come to the plant any time he is needed.

"I haven't needed to call him. If I have a little trouble with one of the men, I just remind him that if he messes

themselves as "therapeutic agents" undertake responsibility for providing treatment. Many of these officers view themselves as social workers and seek professional status. "Synthetic officers" attempt to combine the law enforcement and treatment aspects of probation. They try to balance a concern with the offender's problem and treatment with the community's needs for public protection.

❑ Service Delivery Strategies

Two service delivery strategies are currently utilized in probation supervision: the caseworker model and the resource broker model.[40]

The caseworker approach utilizes a social work orientation that stresses a one-to-one relationship between the probation officer and the offender. The establishment of rapport leads to the development of a meaningful relationship between the officer and the client. That relationship is used as a leverage in changing the offender's behavior. This model has long been associated with probation and can probably be traced back to John Augustus's early humanitarian efforts. However, in recent years, this approach has come under attack for being unrealistic. As Allen states, "large caseloads, staff shortages, and endless report writing leave the probation officer unable to perform all the tasks called for by casework."[41]

up he will mess up John too and lose the faith John has in him. That works," the employer said.

O'Callaghan has a caseload that most of his fellow officers don't envy, but he volunteered for it. About half of his clients are not only ex-convicts but uncured alcoholics.

"I inherited my first alcoholic from another probation officer when I came to work here in 1976. It was a bad case. The man had hit bottom. He'd lost his profession, his family, his home and his liberty, but he managed to pull out of it. He's doing well now. We still keep in touch," he said.

O'Callaghan said working with that man got him interested in working with alcoholics. "I enjoy it. They're all different, but most of them are talented, interesting people—when they are sober. Maybe I enjoy it because it is so rewarding to see one of them make it."

One of his clients is a man of 60 who has been drinking hard since he was a boy and has a long record of bank robberies, but his last binge was almost fatal.

Doctors said the man would have died if O'Callaghan hadn't gotten him to the emergency room when he did. For the last six months the man has been sober and working.

"I think that's a success story and I believe it will keep on being one," O'Callaghan said.

Just before his award ceremony, however, he had to deal with a failure. He had to recommend revoking a client's probation, sending him back to prison.

"Maybe I'm too soft, but I don't want to send a person back unless he is a danger to the community. I don't believe a person gets much rehabilitation staring at cell walls," he said.

The man he revoked Friday was a danger. He wouldn't stop drinking, and his family was terrified by his violence.

O'Callaghan's working hours are uncertain, to say the least. To drive a client to work on time, he got up at 5 a.m. every morning for a week until other transportation arrangements could be made.

It's not unusual for him to get a call at midnight from the family of a woman who has been drinking and is trying to attack them.

Although O'Callaghan works some odd hours and some long ones, he said he makes time for his church, Trussville First Baptist, and his family—his wife, Linda, and their two girls, Christy and Carrie.

"They are my first priorities," he said.

SOURCE: *Birmingham News*, April 18, 1982, p. A1.

Today an alternative to the caseworker approach is available. Under the resource brokerage model, the probation officer is no longer required to have the time or skills necessary to help all offenders with every problem. Instead, the probation officer refers clients to appropriate community resources. Serving as a broker, the probation officer attempts to identify the offender's unique needs and match them with available community resources. The probation officer continues to supervise the offender and monitor his progress in community programs. (See figure 4-4.)

Generally, an eight-step plan is followed in resource brokerage. Probation officers are required to perform the following steps:

1. Inventory resources
2. Develop resource banks
3. Prepare the community
4. Develop client contracts
5. Develop plans
6. Refer to community resources
7. Purchase services
8. Follow up and evaluate[42]

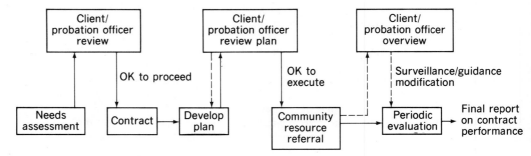

FIGURE 4-4 Resource Brokerage Client Contact

SOURCE: James J. Dahl and Michael Chapman, *Improved Probation Strategies: Trainers Handbook* (Washington, D.C.: U.S. Government Printing Office, 1980), p. 177.

The strategy of resource brokerage is more consistent with the aims of reintegration than the casework approach. Reintegration stresses the development of strong community ties and the linkage of the offender to community, educational, and social services (see figure 4-5). Resource brokerage can accomplish these aims.

A variation of the casework and resource brokerage approaches involves the establishment of teams of probation officers who are jointly responsible for managing case loads.[43] Each probation officer is expected to have specialized skills. The team brings together the precise skills individual offenders need. Supervision teams can therefore provide multiple services to probationers.

❑ Case Load Management

Case load management refers to the strategies probation organizations use to assign cases or clients to probation officers in a manner that ensures the efficient and effective use of probation resources.[44] Several interrelated concerns are involved in case load management, including the degree of supervision required to monitor probationers and the nature and extent of services to be provided. Probation agencies currently employ a variety of techniques to assign case loads. Offenders can be assigned to case loads randomly, alphabetically, by certain personal traits or offense characteristics, or simply by the geographic area of the probationer's residence.

The level of supervision provided to individual offenders varies. Some offenders require intensive supervision and assistance; others require minimal supervision. In some agencies, special intensive supervision case loads are utilized; in others, an attempt is made to assign each probation officer some clients who require minimum intervention and others who need intensive supervision in order to achieve a balanced case load.

The choice between a generalized and specialized case load system requires a probation agency to determine whether it has the resources to assign probationers to case loads on the basis of some particular trait and to permit a probation officer to specialize with a certain type of offender or whether undifferentiated case loads must be maintained. When probation officers are especially skilled in some area of assistance (for example, drug or employment counseling) and when a significant

FIGURE 4-5 Resource Brokerage

Source: James J. Dahl and Michael Chapman, *Improved Probation Strategies: Trainers Handbook* (Washington, D.C.: U.S. Government Printing Office, 1980), p. 176.

number of clients that need assistance, specialized case loads consisting of similarly troubled offenders are often utilized. When staff resources are limited or when there is greater diversity in client needs, generalized case loads that include offenders with varying needs are utilized.

◻ Conditions of Probation

Offenders placed on probation must agree to abide by certain rules and regulations prescribed by the sentencing court. This set of rules and regulations is generally referred to as the "conditions of probation." In some states, these conditions are established by the legislature and written into law. In other states, judges have the discretion to impose specific conditions on a case-by-case basis. In still other jurisdictions, the discretion to impose conditions is left to the probation organization. In most communities probationers must comply with both general and individualized conditions of probation.

The National Advisory Commission on Standards and Goals recommends against applying standard conditions to all offenders. Instead, they suggest a more flexible approach involving three considerations: first, that the conditions be tailored to fit the unique needs of the offender; second, that the conditions imposed be reasonably related to the offender's correctional program; and third, that the conditions imposed not be unduly restrictive or conflict with the offender's constitutional rights.[45]

The American Bar Association supports the advisory commission's recommendations. Additionally, they suggest that the conditions imposed by the court should not be vague and ambiguous, but specific and understandable. The following is a list of the conditions suggested by the American Bar Association:

1. Cooperating with a program of supervision
2. Meeting family responsibilities

Court Limits Woman's Right to Male Guests in Her Home

PROVIDENCE, R.I., March 11 — The State Supreme Court has upheld an order prohibiting a divorced woman from having an unrelated man stay overnight with her in her home when her children are present.

The 1986 order by Judge William Goldberg of the Family Court, upheld Tuesday, said that if the woman, Carla J. Parrillo, violated his decree, she risked being found guilty of a misdemeanor, jailed for a year and fined $500.

Ms. Parrillo, 33 years old, of Johnston, said in an interview that she no longer kept company with Joseph DiPippo, who was staying with her a few nights a week at the time of Judge Goldberg's order. But she said she now had a new companion, who sometimes spent the night with her while her children were there. And she said that despite the high court's ruling she did not intend to change her habits, even if it meant going to jail.

Live 'My Own Life'

"I'm going to go on living my life in my own home according to my moral judgment," Ms. Parrillo said after the Supreme Court decision. "I think it's a very unjust decision by the Supreme Court, and my lawyer and I intend to appeal it to the U.S. Supreme Court."

In his decision modifying the divorce decree of Carla and Justin Parrillo, Judge Goldberg said it was clear that Ms. Parrillo was "taking good care" of her three children, whose ages are now 15, 13 and 10. But he said "the court must infer" that her companion's staying with them overnight "is not conducive to the welfare of the children," at least psychologically.

"If she married this man, he's the stepfather; nothing could be done about" their having sexual relations while the children were staying in the same house, Judge Goldberg said. "But under the situation," he said, "the court doesn't feel that it is a suitable arrangement for the children to be put into."

A few months after their divorce in May 1986, Mr. Parrillo, a construction worker, went to his former wife's home and smashed the windows of her companion's automobile. Mr. Parrillo said he was upset that the man was staying overnight there while the Parrillo children were present. Mr. Parrillo also cut the amount of money he was giving Ms. Parrillo for groceries because he said he did not want to support another man.

In response Ms. Parrillo asked Judge Goldberg to cite her former husband for contempt in cutting back his payments. The judge refused and instead granted Mr. Parrillo's request barring Ms. Parrillo from having any men stay overnight with the children present.

Patricia A. Hurst, a lawyer for the Rhode Island affiliate of the American Civil Liberties Union, contended in representing Ms. Parrillo on appeal that Judge Goldberg's decision violated her client's constitutional rights to privacy, due process and freedom of association.

The lawyer urged the high court to adopt the position that, when an unmarried woman has her children living with her and is considered to be a fit mother, a court "may not infer" that a sexual relationship with a companion "is not in the children's best interests" unless there is evidence that the relationship has "an identifiable adverse effect upon her minor children."

Ms. Parrillo testified before Judge Goldberg that she and her companion slept together "behind closed doors" in her home, and that she saw no risk for her children because they had separate bedrooms.

In upholding Judge Goldberg, Justice Thomas F. Kelleher said in the ruling, "We see no great constitutional issue in this controversy."

SOURCE: *New York Times*, March 12, 1989, p. 16. Copyright © 1989 by The New York Times Company. Reprinted by permission.

3. Maintaining steady employment or engaging or refraining from involvement in a specific employment or reciprocation
4. Pursuing prescribed educational or vocational training
5. Undergoing available medical or psychiatric treatment
6. Maintaining residence in a prescribed area or in a special facility established for or available to persons on probation
7. Refraining from consorting with certain types of people or frequenting certain types of places

8. Making restitution of the fruits of the crime or reparation for loss or damage caused thereby. (It is suggested that repayment schedules be formulated with the probationer's ability to pay in mind.)[46]

Probation conditions imposed on offenders tend to fall into two categories. They are oriented toward either reforming the offender or controlling his behavior.[47] Reform-oriented conditions might require the offender to attend school, receive drug treatment, or undergo psychiatric treatment. Control-oriented conditions might include reporting requirements, restrictions on geographic mobility, and prohibitions from hanging around with certain types of persons or frequenting inappropriate places.

About two-thirds of probation agencies now collect supervision fees as a condition of probation.[48] These fees account for as much as 60 percent of probation budgets in some jurisdictions. Fees generally range between $10 and $40 per month. Although the fees have received some criticism, there is general agreement that they represent an important source of revenue and can be used to help teach offenders to pay their own way.

In summary, most professionals in the field of probation services seem to agree that a flexible approach should be taken with regard to probation conditions. The conditions should be clear and specific. The offender must also be capable of following and obeying them. Conditions that are vague, ambiguous, or unenforceable should be discouraged.

The probation officer plays a very important role in ensuring that the offender understands and follows the conditions of probation. The probation officer generally has the responsibility for explaining the conditions to the offender to ensure that he or she understands them and to inform the offender of the consequences— that is, revocation of probation—of violating them.

❏ Revocation

Two sets of decision makers are involved in the probation revocation process. The probation officer has the authority to initiate the revocation process, but the actual decision to revoke an offender's probation rests with the sentencing judge.

Considerable flexibility exists throughout the revocation proceeding and revocation is not automatic. Generally, there are two types of violations: legal violations, which involve the commission of a new crime, and technical violations, which involve no criminal conduct, but a violation of the conditions of probation. When a violation occurs, the probation officer has the discretion either to take formal action and report the violation or to ignore or tolerate minor misbehavior. If the decision is made to invoke the formal revocation process, certain guidelines provided by case law must be followed.

Two Supreme Court cases have shaped the revocation proceeding. The first is *Morrissey* v. *Brewer,* 408 U.S. 471 (1972), which directly addressed parole revocation proceedings. The due process protections established for parolees were subsequently extended to probationers in *Gagnon* v. *Scarpelli,* 411 U.S. 778 (1973). These cases provided probationers with the right to a two-stage hearing that includes minimum due process protection during a revocation proceeding. In the first, preliminary hearing, a determination is made as to whether probable cause exists to revoke probation. The rights provided at this stage of the proceeding include:

1. Prior notice of the hearing
2. Written notice of the charges
3. The right to be present at the hearing
4. The right to present evidence and witnesses
5. The right to a hearing before a detached and neutral hearing officer

These same rights apply at the second stage of the revocation proceeding, where the actual revocation decision is made. In certain special circumstances, such as when a probationer is incapable of speaking effectively for himself and has requested counsel, the advice of counsel may also be provided.

Research on Probation

❑ Limitations

Before looking at the available research studies on probation, it is important to consider their limitations. Although no correctional strategy is easy to evaluate, probation (and parole) evaluation poses some special difficulties because of ambiguity surrounding the appropriate measures of success.

The effectiveness of most correctional programs is measured by recidivism. For probation, recidivism can be defined in at least five different ways:

1. Violations of the conditions of probation known to the probation officer
2. Arrests for violations of the conditions of probation
3. Arrests for new offenses committed by probationers
4. Convictions for new offenses committed by probationers
5. Revocations of probation

An offender may fall into the first category and not the second; he may fall into any of the first four categories and still not have probation revoked. Nevertheless, probation violation and revocation are frequently used as measures of probation success.

As previously noted, probation officers have considerable discretion regarding their responses to violations of a probation condition. If an officer feels that continued community supervision is preferable to an arrest, he or she may choose to reprimand and warn the offender, but to take no formal action. Similarly, revocation is an administrative decision. Within the bounds of due process, probation supervisors are permitted to individualize their judgments regarding the offender's need for incarceration. If a probationer is making substantial progress in the community and does not seem to warrant imprisonment, he may be continued in the community. Because probation staff may differ in their willingness to initiate the revocation process and because official and informal policy may vary from jurisdiction to jurisdiction, it is difficult to determine whether probation is "working" or if probation supervisors are tolerating violations and minor offenses in a special effort to maintain offenders in the community.

The first major assessment of probation effectiveness was undertaken little more than a decade ago. In 1979 the National Institute of Law Enforcement and Criminal

Justice (NILECJ) reported the results of a review of the probation evaluation literature.[49] For analytical purposes, the literature was divided into three groups: studies that compared the effectiveness of probation with that of alternative sentencing options, studies that measured probation outcome without any form of comparison, and studies that attempted to isolate the factors that enhance the likelihood of probation success.

Surprisingly, only five methodologically sound studies attempted to compare the effectiveness of probation with that of other sanctions. Three of the evaluations compared probation with incarceration by examining the experiences of probationers and similar offenders who had been incarcerated and were subsequently paroled. All three studies defined recidivism as a new offense or a technical violation. Two of the evaluations, one of which included a mixed group of offenders and one of which included only burglars, found that probation did produce lower recidivism rates except for mixed offenders with two or more prior felony convictions. The third study, which focused on female offenders, found no differences between probation and incarceration. Because probationers were actually compared to parolees, the benefits of parole might be expected to mitigate some of the negative effects of imprisonment, thus muddying the comparison of probation and prison.

A fourth study compared probationers, persons sentenced to probation following a jail term, and persons sentenced only to jail. Each group was followed for one full year in the community. The probation group produced the lowest rate of recidivism; almost two-thirds of the probationers had no subsequent arrests for technical violations or new offenses. Half of the shock probationers and 47 percent of those sentenced only to jail had no further violations during their year in the community.

The final comparison of probation supervision with an alternative sanction examined misdemeanant probationers. The subjects were randomly assigned to experimental and control groups. The probationers in the experimental group received supervision; those in the control group did not. Considering only a conviction for a new offense as the criterion for success, 22 percent of the supervised probationers and 24 percent of the nonsupervised probationers recidivated.

One can conclude little from the preceding findings. No two studies examined the same types of offenders under similar circumstances. At present, we can state only that, except for those persons with several prior felony convictions, probation seems to be at least as effective as alternative dispositions for persons normally jailed or imprisoned

The NILECJ study examined a number of studies that reported recidivism rates for probation.[50] This assessment also produced no general conclusions about probation effectiveness because the studies examined diverse groups of offenders and employed varying definitions of success and follow-up periods. From an examination of the individual researcher's conclusions, it appeared that a failure rate of 30 percent or less was generally viewed as demonstrating the effectiveness of probation.[51]

Attempts to identify factors that enhance probation effectiveness are limited by the same methodological difficulties that plagued the preceding studies. Nevertheless, of the ten studies just reviewed, over half produced significant correlations between recidivism and the following offender characteristics: previous criminal history, youth, status other than married, unemployment, low income, education below fourth grade, abuse of alcohol or drugs, and property offender.[52] Previous criminal history was most frequently found to be a significant factor influencing recidivism. This finding supports the previously reported conclusion that persons with several prior felony convictions were less successful on probation than other offenders.

❏ Evaluations of Specific Treatment Strategies

The NILECJ study identified approximately 20 studies of particular probation strategies and categorized them according to their principal focus: vocational counseling and/or employment, group and/or individual counseling, and drug treatment.[53]

In regard to employment, only tentative evidence was found to support the proposition that employment counseling, including diagnostic services, vocational evaluation, referral services, job coaching, and stipends, can lower recidivism. Although there is no doubt that employment and probation success are related and that these services can enhance the offender's employment status, employment counseling *alone* seems insufficient to reduce recidivism.

Support for the effectiveness of individual and group counseling is similarly mixed. Some success has been reported in treating sexual offenders and mixed offender groups whose participants actively engage in group activities, jointly develop treatment strategies with staff, and provide help and support to fellow group members. Other programs have shown no significant differences between counseled and noncounseled probationers. Poor research methodology is especially problematic in this area. In addition to all the previously mentioned difficulties, most evaluations have failed to define and describe adequately the treatments being offered, making a test of their effectiveness virtually meaningless.

Probation staff may treat drug addiction in various ways. It can be viewed as a disease requiring methadone maintenance; it can be approached using casework techniques and referrals to appropriate social services; or it can be attacked using behavior modification strategies. There is data to support the positive impact of each of these strategies. Dole and Joseph have reported findings of dramatic reductions in arrest rates of probationers receiving methadone.[54] Comparing pretreatment and posttreatment arrest rates, subjects receiving methadone experienced a reduction from 120 to 55 arrests; a comparison group experienced 134 arrests.

A Philadelphia study randomly assigned drug-using probationers to regular supervision and drug counseling, which included intensive supervision, education, referrals, and rehabilitative treatment. The experimental group demonstrated lower recidivism rates than the drug users assigned to regular supervision *and* nondrug users under regular supervision.[55]

A behavior modification program that provided verbal encouragement and reductions in time on probation to drug users who performed specific behavioral tasks has also shown positive results. Not only did the number of arrests and probation violations decrease as a result of this strategy, but this group also demonstrated a higher rate of employment and attendance at group meetings than a control group.[56]

These studies show that probation can have a demonstratively positive impact on certain groups of offenders. When the offender's problem is well defined and the rehabilitative strategy is clearly articulated, comprehensive, and directly related to criminal behavior, the results can be impressive.

❑ The Rand Study

In 1985 the Rand Corporation reported the results of a study, sponsored by the National Institute of Justice, of felony probation.[57] The Rand study used data from more than 16,000 offenders convicted of felonies in California, and recidivism data on probationed felons in Los Angeles and Alameda counties. The purpose of the research was to answer the following questions:

> What criteria are used by the courts to determine which offenders will be imprisoned and which will be granted probation?
> How many of these probationers are ultimately rearrested, reconvicted, and reimprisoned?
> How accurately can one predict which felons will recidivate and which will not?[58]

The examination of sentencing criteria indicated that, within each crime category, prior record, being a drug addict, being on community supervision at the time of the arrest, being armed, using a weapon, and seriously injuring a victim were all associated with being sent to prison rather than being placed on probation. The manner in which the case was processed was also a significant factor. In general, offenders with private attorneys, those who had obtained pretrial release, and those who pleaded guilty were more likely to receive probation.

Although the preceding criteria were highly correlated with the nature of the sentence, about 25 percent of sentences were not predicted by these factors, indicating that many probationers were indistinguishable from prisoners, in terms of their crimes and prior record. Not surprisingly, those probationers with histories and offenses comparable to prisoners were about 50 percent more likely to be rearrested than were other probationers.

The research concluded that felony probation in the jurisdictions studied presented a significant threat to public safety. Two-thirds of the probationers were rearrested during the 3½-year follow-up. More than half of the total number of probationers were reconvicted, and 34 percent were reincarcerated. The vast majority of the criminal charges against these offenders involved burglary/theft, robbery, or other violent crimes.

Predictions regarding reconviction based on type of crime, prior record, and substance abuse were found to be accurate in about two out of three cases. Interestingly enough, the nature of the presentence investigation recommendation was of little value in predicting recidivism. About two-thirds of those recommended for probation and two-thirds of those recommended for prison were subsequently rearrested. Using factors associated with probation success, the study found that only about 3 percent of prisoners could have been safely placed on probation as now administered.

The study concluded with a call for expanded use of risk/needs assessment scales, to improve case management, and the development of intermediate sanctions and new strategies to better supervise and control offenders in the community. Although it is unclear whether felony probation in California accurately reflects felony probation elsewhere, the Rand study provided further impetus to efforts already under way to improve offender classification and to tailor community supervision to particular characteristics of offenders.

Innovations in Probation

❑ Probation Classification Systems

Classification systems became widely used in the 1980s as probation departments were confronted with the need to allocate increasingly scarce resources while client populations had begun to include more and more serious offenders. Research had indicated that clinical judgments alone often produced inconsistent decisions. The use of a structured instrument yielded better and more consistent judgments.

Risk/needs classification systems assess items of information proven to be related to the level of risk posed by offenders' release to the community, and their particular needs during supervision (figure 4-6). Offenders with high levels of risk and needs are provided with more intensive levels of supervision and service. Cases are normally reassessed at regular intervals, and levels of supervision are modified as appropriate.

❑ Intensive Supervision Programs (ISP)

Intensive supervision programs meet a variety of needs. There is general agreement that many offenders deserve and require more punishment and control than are provided by standard probation, but less than are provided by incarceration. As an intermediate sanction, intensive supervision programs represent an attempt to better fit the punishment and control aspects of dispositions to the crime and the criminal. Intensive supervision programs are also viewed as a less costly alternative to incarceration. To the extent that ISP's serve prison-bound offenders, prison overcrowding can be addressed without incurring the costs of new construction. In addition, as the Rand study indicates, many persons currently on probation could benefit from increased monitoring and supervision. ISP's may increase community safety. Finally, such programs better identify and serve offender needs as a by-product of better assessment and closer contact with clients.

Obviously, some of these goals are in conflict. A program that provides more supervision to clients currently on probation is not going to reduce prison overcrowding or save money. A program that diverts offenders from prison may well save money, but at some cost to community protection. Like supporters of many other correctional innovations, proponents of ISP's tend to minimize these conflicts while emphasizing program benefits.

Almost all states have implemented or are in the process of implementing ISP's. Still, relatively few offenders are participating in the projects, which is not surprising, given the costs of such efforts relative to standard probation. While the average probation caseload is over one hundred offenders, ISP caseloads have fewer than twenty-five offenders. Most states have fewer than twenty officers managing ISP caseloads.[59]

All ISP programs share certain common elements.[60] They provide supervision that is more extensive, more focused, and more ubiquitous than standard supervision. Each week, multiple personal contacts and collateral contacts with family and friends are employed to regulate the offender's travel, employment, curfews, drug use, and other relevant behaviors. Success means that levels of supervision generally decline until the offender is placed on a standard caseload. There are swift and

DEPARTMENT OF CORRECTIONS
DIVISION OF PROBATION & PAROLE

Client No. _____   Client Name: _____   Officer No. _____

CLIENT RISK ASSESSMENT
Instructions: Enter numerical rating in box at right.

1. **TOTAL NUMBER OF PRIOR FELONY CONVICTIONS:**
   (include juvenile ajudications, if known):
   a. None .... Enter 0
   b. One .... Enter 2
   c. Two or more .... Enter 4

2. **PRIOR NUMBER OF PROBATION/PAROLE SUPERVISION PERIODS:**
   (include juvenile, if known):
   a. None .... Enter 0
   b. One or more .... Enter 4

3. **PRIOR PROBATION/PAROLE REVOCATIONS:**
   (adult only):
   a. None .... Enter 0
   b. One or more .... Enter 4

4. **AGE AT FIRST KNOWN CONVICTION OR ADJUDICATION:**
   (include juvenile, if known)
   a. 24 years or older .... Enter 0
   b. 20 through 23 years .... Enter 2
   c. 19 years or younger .... Enter 4

5. **HISTORY OF ALCOHOL ABUSE:**
   a. No history of abuse .... Enter 0
   b. Occasional or prior abuse .... Enter 2
   c. Frequent current abuse .... Enter 4

6. **HISTORY OF OTHER SUBSTANCE ABUSE:**
   (prior to incarceration for parolees):
   a. No history of abuse .... Enter 0
   b. Occasional or prior abuse .... Enter 1
   c. Frequent current abuse .... Enter 2

7. **AMOUNT OF TIME EMPLOYED IN LAST 12 MONTHS:**
   (prior to incarceration for parolees; based on 35 hr. week)
   a. 7 months or more .... Enter 0
   b. 4 months through 6 months .... Enter 1
   c. Less than 4 months .... Enter 2
   d. Not applicable .... Enter 0

8. **AGENT IMPRESSION OF OFFENDER'S ATTITUDE:**
   a. Motivated to change; receptive to assistance ..... Enter 0
   b. Dependent or unwilling to accept responsibility .. Enter 3
   c. Rationalizes behavior; negative, not motivated to change ..... Enter 5

9. **RECORD OF CONVICTION FOR SELECTED OFFENSES:**
   (include current offense, add categories and enter total)
   a. None of the following .... Enter 0
   b. Burglary, Theft, Auto Theft, Robbery .... Add 2
   c. Forgery, Deceptive Practices (Fraud, Bad Check, Drugs) .... Add 3

10. **ASSAULTIVE OFFENSES:**
    a. Crimes against persons which include use of weapon, physical force, threat of force, all sex crimes, and vehicular homicide.

    ☐ Yes   ☐ No

Total Score (Range 0-34) ☐☐

CLIENT NEED ASSESSMENT
Instructions: Enter numerical rating in box at right.

1. **ACADEMIC/VOCATIONAL SKILLS:**
   a. High school or above skill level .... Enter 0
   b. Has vocational training, additional not needed/desired ...... Enter 1
   c. Has some skills; additional needed/desired ...... Enter 3
   d. No skills, training needed .... Enter 5

2. **EMPLOYMENT:**
   a. Satisfactory employment for 1 year or longer .... Enter 0
   b. Employed; no difficulties reported; or homemaker, student, retired, or disabled and unable to work ..... Enter 1
   c. Part-time, seasonal, unstable employment or needs additional employment; unemployed, but has a skill ..... Enter 4
   d. Unemployed & virtually unemployable; needs training ..... Enter 7

3. **FINANCIAL STATUS:**
   a. Longstanding pattern of self-sufficiency .... Enter 0
   b. No current difficulties .... Enter 1
   c. Situational or minor difficulties .... Enter 4
   d. Severe difficulties .... Enter 6

4. **LIVING ARRANGEMENTS (Within last six months):**
   a. Stable and supportive relationships with family or others in living group ..... Enter 0
   b. Client lives alone or independently within another household ..... Enter 1
   c. Client experiencing occasional, moderate interpersonal problems within living group .... Enter 4
   d. Client experiencing frequent and serious interpersonal problems within living group ...... Enter 6

5. **EMOTIONAL STABILITY:**
   a. No symptoms of instability .... Enter 1
   b. Symptoms limit, but do not prohibit adequate functioning ..... Enter 5
   c. Symptoms prohibit adequate functioning .... Enter 8

6. **ALCOHOL USAGE (Current):**
   a. No interference with functioning .... Enter 1
   b. Occasional abuse, some disruption of functioning, may need treatment ..... Enter 4
   c. Frequent abuse, serious disruption; needs treatment ..... Enter 7

7. **OTHER SUBSTANCE USAGE (Current):**
   a. No interference with functioning .... Enter 1
   b. Occasional substance abuse, some disruption of functioning, may need treatment ..... Enter 4
   c. Frequent substance abuse, serious disruption, needs treatment ...... Enter 6

8. **REASONING/INTELLECTUAL ABILITY:**
   a. Able to function independently .... Enter 1
   b. Some need for assistance, potential for adequate adjustment ..... Enter 4
   c. Deficiencies suggest limited ability to function independently ..... Enter 7

9. **HEALTH:**
   a. Sound physical health; seldom ill .... Enter 1
   b. Handicap or illness interferes with functioning on a recurring basis ..... Enter 2
   c. Serious handicap or chronic illness, needs frequent medical care ..... Enter 3

10. **AGENT'S IMPRESSION OF CLIENT'S NEEDS:**
    a. None .... Enter 0
    b. Low .... Enter 1
    c. Moderate .... Enter 4
    d. High .... Enter 6

Total Score (Range 5-61) ☐☐

SCORING AND OVERRIDE
Instruction: Check appropriate block
SCORE BASED SUPERVISION LEVEL: ☐ Maximum ☐ Medium ☐ Minimum

Check if there is an override ☐ Override Explanation: _____

_____

FINAL CATEGORY OF SUPERVISION: ☐ Maximum ☐ Medium ☐ Minimum

Date Supervision Level Assigned
MONTH   DAY   YEAR
☐☐ ☐☐ ☐☐☐☐

APPROVED (Supervisor Signature and Date)   Agent

FIGURE 4-6 Risk/Needs Assessment Instrument

SOURCE: Anthony Walsh, *Understanding, Assessing, and Counseling the Criminal Justice Client* (Pacific Grove, Calif.: Brooks/Cole, 1988), p. 110.

severe penalties for failure. Table 4-5 identifies key features of ISP programs in thirty-one states.

Georgia's ISP is probably the best known.[61] It began in 1982 as a means of providing punishment that was less costly than incarceration. By 1985, the program had supervised over 2,300 probationers. The program has strict requirements:

- 5 face-to-face contacts per week
- 132 hours of mandatory community service
- mandatory curfew
- mandatory employment
- weekly check of local arrest records
- automatic notification of arrest elsewhere via the State Crime Information Network Listing
- routine and unannounced alcohol and drug testing.[62]

Most of the offenders chosen for the program are nonviolent property offenders already sentenced to prison. A five-year follow-up study indicates that 36 percent are subsequently sentenced to prison, against 42 percent of a comparison group sentenced to prison.[63] An evaluation of the project concluded that prison overcrowding was relieved by the introduction of the ISP, with no substantial risk to the community.

Questions have been raised about the reported effectiveness of Georgia's program, with some indication that the results achieved were the product of the generally nonserious offenders placed on intensive supervision in Georgia. A subsequent study of three ISP's in California considered program impact when more serious offenders are intensively supervised.[64] The research indicated that while the programs may be successful in rapidly identifying offenders who violate probation conditions, they are no more effective in deterring criminal behavior than is standard probation. This indicates that the increased cost of ISP may not be worth the benefit. One significant limitation of the California study should be noted. The programs' failure to provide drug treatment to needy offenders may well have made any enhancement of supervision levels irrelevant.

TABLE 4-5 Key Features of Selected ISP Programs in Thirty-one States

Program feature	Number	Percentage
1. Curfew/house arrest	25	80.6%
2. Electronic monitoring	6	19.3
3. Mandatory (high needs) referrals/special conditions	22	70.9
4. Team supervision	18	58.1
5. Drug monitoring	27	87.1
6. Alcohol monitoring	27	87.1
7. Community service	21	67.7
8. Probation fees	13	41.9
9. Split sentence/shock incarceration	22	70.9
10. Community sponsors	4	12.9
11. Restitution	21	67.7
12. Objective risk assessment	30	96.7
13. Objective needs assessment	29	93.5

SOURCE: James M. Byrne, Arthur J. Lurigio, and Christopher Baird, "The Effectiveness of the New Intensive Supervision Programs, *Research in Corrections,* 2 (2) (Washington, D.C.: U.S. Department of Justice, 1989).

❑ House Arrest

House arrest programs require offenders to obey a curfew and remain within the confines of their residence during specified hours. House arrest can be used as a stand-alone sanction or in conjunction with intensive probation supervision. Generally the programs are viewed as an alternative to incarceration, as a means of easing prison overcrowding. With little emphasis on the quality or nature of supervision, the programs are generally considered more punitive than ISP. At present, a number of states are employing house arrest as a sanction, with the largest programs operating in Florida, Oklahoma, Kentucky, Oregon, and California.[65] The largest program is that operating in Florida.

Like many other house arrest programs, Florida's Community Control Program (FCCP) was established to divert offenders from prison.[66] Since its inception in the early 1980s, it has supervised over 25,000 offenders. As expected, the persons in the program represent a more serious group of offenders than those normally placed on probation or jailed, and less serious than those sent to prison (table 4-6).

All offenders are placed on caseloads of no more than twenty persons. All FCCP participants are under house arrest, which in this program means that they are allowed to leave home only for necessities, such as employment and grocery shopping.[67] There are twenty-eight case contacts each month. Some offenders are also monitored electronically. Community service and restitution are also part of the program.

Evaluation of the program is made more difficult by the fact that FCCP was established at the same time that the state enacted more stringent sentencing criteria. It appears that many of the FCCP offenders would have been incarcerated in the absence of its development, but, on the whole, incarceration rates in Florida have increased since the program began.[68]

❑ Electronic Monitoring

The purpose of electronic monitoring is to provide greater community control. Electronic monitoring provides technological verification of an offender's whereabouts. Two types of devices are currently in use. Continuously signaling devices provide

TABLE 4-6 Comparison of Offenders in Florida's Community Control Program with Those on Probation and in Jail or Prison

Offense categories	Probation	Jail	FCCP	Prison
1. Murder/manslaughter	0.3%	0.3%	0.7%	4.4%
2. Sexual offenses	1.4%	0.7%	5.7%	4.1%
3. Robbery	1.2%	1.7%	4.3%	11.1%
4. Violent personal	9.4%	7.3%	14.4%	8.1%
5. Burglary	13.2%	15.8%	14.3%	19.7%
6. Theft, forgery, fraud	28.6%	23.3%	22.6%	19.9%
7. Drug offenses	36.5%	43.5%	31.3%	24.4%
8. Weapon offenses	4.1%	4.4%	3.5%	3.9%
9. All others	5.3%	3.0%	3.2%	4.4%

SOURCE: S. Christopher Baird and Dennis Wagner, "Measuring Diversion: The Florida Community Control Program," *Crime and Delinquency* 36(1) (1990): 121.

Electronic Ankle Bracelet Keeps Crooks Confined without Bars

by J. E. Ferrell

As you read this, Milton Avol, 63, a Beverly Hills neurosurgeon, is confined to a prison of his own making—a run-down Hollywood apartment building he owns, complete with roaches, rats and squalor.

No guards at the door are keeping the slumlord there for 30 days to serve a sentence handed down by Los Angeles Municipal Judge Veronica Simmons McBeth two weeks ago.

Avol is wearing an electronic bracelet around his ankle. He was sentenced two years ago to live in one of his buildings for a probation violation stemming from his conviction on health, fire, building and safety code violations.

Since 1977, he has been charged with hundreds of code violations. He also has been sued by his building's tenants.

The electronic bracelet Avol is wearing around his ankle is set so that if he strays more than 150 feet from a point within the apartment, an alarm will go off in the offices of Trax Monitoring in Auburn, a small town northeast of Sacramento in the foothills of the Sierras.

Trax Monitoring President Jack Wood and his crew will relay any alarm to the offices of the Los Angeles County city attorney, which will notify the judge.

The system, manufactured by B.I. Inc. in Boulder, Colo., is a crook's version of an answering machine: it tells the cops that he is always home.

A small transmitter, attached to the plastic strap worn around Avol's ankle and encoded with information about him (name, identifying number), sends a signal to a receiver in a small box.

The box, containing a field monitoring device that tracks and records Avol's movements, is plugged into a wall socket to keep its battery pack charged, and is also connected to a telephone line with a jack.

The field monitoring device is programmed to call the Trax Monitoring computer at intervals determined by the city attorney's office. It sends the information about Avol's movements to the computer, which keeps a 24-hour record.

The system is fairly tamper-proof. If Avol tries to disconnect the box, if he tries to cut off the strap or slide

active monitoring—a device strapped to the offender sends out an alert if the offender should leave his home. Passive systems require offenders to respond to a computer-generated telephone call by placing a wristlet in a verifier box or by repeating a series of words for voice verification. The calls may be placed randomly or according to a fixed schedule.

As of 1988, more than 2,000 offenders in thirty-three states were being supervised electronically.[69] Almost half of all such offenders live in just two states, Florida and Michigan (figure 4-7). About one-quarter of these persons are traffic offenders and another 35 percent are property or drug offenders. Approximately 10 percent are convicted of violent crimes.

In most programs, offenders pay for their own supervision.[70] The fee is determined according to a sliding scale, up to a maximum of $15 per day. There is variation in the degree to which equipment is monitored. Some programs monitor the technology only during work hours; others provide continuous coverage. There is also variation in program success rates—programs that can control intake tend to be more successful than those that must accept all referred clients.

Problems in program operations range from the technological to the familial.[71] Locations close to radio stations, poor telephone lines and wiring, and call-waiting feature can interfere with the technology, as can power surges and computer downtime. Family members must adjust to increased contact with the offenders, as they do in house arrest programs, and to limitations on phone time.

it off his leg, an alarm will go off at the Trax offices. If he unplugs the telephone or leaves it off the hook so that the field monitoring device cannot make its call, the Trax computer will sound an alarm, because it is programmed to expect calls at certain intervals.

The electronic tether, also known as a high-tech ball and chain, has been in use about three years in a few test programs around the country as a potential method to relieve overcrowding in prisons and to keep closer tabs on probationers or parolees.

Success in fitting an electronic tether to Avol may force other slumlords to take notice, said Deputy City Attorney Stephanie Sautner, supervising attorney for Los Angeles County's Slum Housing Task Force. The organization targets the buildings that have the worst safety, health and fire code violations.

"We have 100 cases pending in Los Angeles," Ms. Sautner said. "Usually, these people get fines and probation the first time, and jail the second time around. We're interested in how this will work. I can't think of a more fitting punishment for the crime."

A handful of companies make electronic tethering systems, which are being used by approximately 1,000 probationers and parolees in several states, including Oregon, New Jersey, Utah, Michigan, Indiana and Florida.

The costs range from $7 to $13 a person a day. Work release programs, in which a criminal is incarcerated at night and let out to work during the day, cost from $20 to $28 a person a day, said John Hinebauch, vice president of B.I. Inc.

Prisons cost $50,000 to $75,000 a bed to build and $40 to $60 a day per person to manage.

It was Jack Love, a former district court judge in Albuquerque, N.M., who came up with the idea for the devices in 1977 when he read a Spiderman comic book in which the villain put a bracelet on Spiderman to monitor his whereabouts.

Electronics engineer Michael Goss put together a prototype system for Love, and founded a company to manufacture the devices. That company has gone through a couple of management changes, and is now B.I. Inc.

SOURCE: *Birmingham Post Herald*, July 24, 1987, 3C. Reprinted with permission from The San Francisco Examiner. © 1987 San Francisco Examiner.

Electronic monitoring is likely to continue to grow as the search continues for meaningful alternatives to imprisonment and standard probation. There is evidence, however, that technology may not offer significant improvement over the human factor. Electronic monitoring was implemented as an adjunct to Georgia's ISP in 1987. Staff reported no widespread gains in curfew infractions discovered; the technology was unable to deter drinking or the use or selling of drugs from home.[72] While it was useful in identifying violations, it provided little of new value.

❑ Split Sentences, Shock Incarceration, and Boot Camp

Split sentences require offenders to serve a brief period of confinement prior to placement on probation. While such sentences are nothing new, their use is on the increase. In several states, nearly one-third of those placed on probation receive some sentence to confinement.[73] Almost a dozen states are now employing correctional boot camps as a means of achieving "shock incarceration," and a similar number have such programs in the planning stage.[74] The purpose of all such efforts is the same—to deter offenders from further crime by giving them a brief, severe period of incarceration.

While the evidence on program effectiveness is mixed, it is clear that the programs have considerable public appeal. The notion of confinement in a military-style environment is especially appealing to those who feel that standard confinement

*Programs exist, but no offenders were being monitored on this date.
**No response.
Note: There are no programs in Alaska.

FIGURE 4-7 Number of Offenders Being Electronically Monitored on February 14, 1988

SOURCE: Annesley Schmidt, "Electronic Monitoring of Offenders Increases," *NIJ Reports* (Washington, D.C.: U.S. Government Printing Office, 1989), p. 2.

may be too easy on offenders. Boot camps also appeal to those who believe that discipline is a key component of rehabilitation.

Louisiana's Shock Incarceration Program, established in 1987, illustrates the contemporary boot camp experience.[75] The program consists of two phases: 90–180 days in a rigid military-training atmosphere followed by intensive community supervision. To be eligible for the program, one must be a first-time felon with a sentence of seven years or less and recommended by the Division of Probation and Parole, the sentencing court, and a designee of the Louisiana Department of Public Safety and Corrections. Offenders are recommended for the program after being sentenced to a regular prison term. The program is strictly voluntary, and the offender may withdraw at any time. Persons who choose to leave the program, or who are removed for insufficient progress or misbehavior, complete their sentences in a regular prison.

In addition to military training, drill, and physical exercise, the boot camp experience includes treatment programs, such as ventilation therapy, reeducative therapy, substance-abuse education, and prerelease education.[76] The staff "drill instructors" are expected to act as role models, counselors, and agents of behavior change through positive reinforcement and support. The program requires offenders to earn their way out of the program, moving through stages until they are judged ready for graduation.

Preliminary research indicates that offenders leaving the program may be more positive about their experiences than inmates incarcerated in regular prison.[77] It is unclear to what extent this perception results from self-selection into the program, or to what extent it lingers long after release. The program's therapeutic emphasis may also be a factor in encouraging positive inmate evaluations.

The Future of Probation

At present, the vast majority of offenders is sentenced to probation rather than prison. There is no reason to believe that this pattern will change in the future. In recent years, we have witnessed an increased acceptance of retribution as a correctional objective and determinate sentencing as the method by which to achieve equal punishment. These factors may reduce probation populations in some jurisdictions. However, the economic and human costs of incarceration are so great and so widely acknowledged that it is doubtful these population reductions will be more than temporary. It is more likely that the search for more efficient and effective probation strategies will continue. To date, no alternative sentence seems to offer as much flexibility and potential for both offender control and offender change.

Perhaps the greatest challenge to probation is the challenge to implement effective change. This is no easy task, as indicated by the results of an effort funded by the Bureau of Justice Assistance (BJA) to expand the use of intensive probation supervision.

BJA funded eleven jurisdictions to field-test a model ISP based on the Georgia program.[78] Sites were instructed to implement the Georgia model but to tailor it to local needs. At this writing, the evaluation was still under way. Some programs are thriving, while others have terminated or drastically curtailed their efforts. What accounts for the ability to implement a new program in a successful fashion?

Joan Petersilia, principal investigator of the study, identifies the following factors as necessary for accomplishing change.

1. The project addresses a pressing local problem.
2. The project has clearly articulated goals that reflect the needs and desires of the "customer."
3. The project has a receptive environment in both the "parent" organization and the larger system.
4. The organization has a leader who is vitally committed to the objectives, values, and implications of the project and who can devise practical strategies to motivate and effect change.
5. The project has a director who shares the leader's ideas and values and uses them to guide the implementation process and ongoing operation of the project.
6. Practitioners made the project their own, rather than being coerced into it; that is, they "buy into" it, participate in its development, and have incentives to maintain its integrity during the change process.

Boot Camp: Some States Rehabilitate Prisoners the Military Way

by Larry Green

FREESOIL, MI — Camp Sauble is nestled deep in a frosty Michigan forest where chirping birds dart freely from one leafless tree to another. Smells of autumn fill the air: Pine and pollen, decaying leaves and dying grasses.

Thomas Russell and John Waters came to this bucolic place in the back seat of a sheriff's squad car wearing bright county orange jail jumpsuits. Their journey did not end peacefully.

Russell and Waters were yanked from the car by five big, shouting men in dark blue uniforms who slammed them up hard against the back fender.

"Maggots," one of the uniforms yelled in an angry, booming voice.

"Scumbag," screamed another.

"Parasite," hollered a third in a seemingly uncontrolled rage.

Russell, 18, and Waters, 19, were patted down, forced to keep their legs wide and their trembling fingers curled as the staccato harangue continued.

"Here you control nothing," bellowed one of the uniformed men, his face flushed, his mouth an inch from Russell's ear, his broad rimmed hat pushing up against the man's quivering head. "We don't care what you have to say. We don't care what you think. You're a parasite. You feed off society."

"All I'm going to give you for 90 days is a bunch of hell and hard time," another shouts into Waters' left ear.

Welcome to "shock incarceration"—a new concept in prison-based behavior modification rapidly gaining popularity with corrections departments across the country.

Known as "boot camps," these minimum security facilities are modeled on rugged military basic training. They are used as short-term alternatives to longer stays in overcrowded, undisciplined prisons for young criminals who are sentenced to prison for the first time.

Georgia pioneered the paramilitary concept in 1983. Today there are at least 15 camps operating in 11 states. Up to 30 more states either have camps on the drawing boards or under construction.

All for Show?

Critics say boot camps are better theater than corrections policy.

"There is no evidence that so-called therapeutic programs based on threat and coercion ever worked," said Jerome G. Miller, founder of the National Center on Institutions and Alternatives and the former director of youth corrections programs in Pennsylvania and Massachusetts. "You can coerce people into conformity while you've got them, when there's enough brute force around. But to suggest that that somehow or other changes them is nonsense."

Proponents say they are at least as effective as prisons and may cost taxpayers less.

New York State, for example, estimates that it saves $1.5 million for each 100 successful shock releases because the prisoners spend fewer days behind bars.

Fans of the programs range from urban mayors like Detroit's Coleman Young to U.S. drug policy chief William Bennett.

New York's shock program is considered a model. Lasting six months—twice as long as most—it provides intensive therapeutic treatment of drug and alcohol addiction and includes a year of post-release monitoring and assistance.

Rigid Discipline

But Michigan's Camp Sauble, beginning its second year of full operation, is more typical of shock incarceration programs. Although here it is called Special Alternative Incarceration and inmates are called "probationers" to help them escape the stigma of being an ex-convict.

Located in the west central part of the state near Lake Michigan, Camp Sauble is home to 120 men between 17 and 25 years old who live rigidly disciplined lives under the omnipresent, watchful eyes of drill

7. The project has clear lines of authority; there is no ambiguity about "who is in charge."
8. The change and its implementation are not complex and sweeping.
9. The organization has secure administrators, low staff turnover, and plentiful resources.[79]

instructor-like guards who greet every infraction with humiliating shouts and punishing exercises.

Unlike prisons, corrections officers are in total control here. So much in control that once inside, official visitors wander around the entire fenced camp unescorted and without fear.

Virtually every aspect of the prisoners' lives is monitored. Do they brush their teeth? Do they change their underwear daily? Are they overweight? Do they eat everything they pick up in the chow line?

"Armstrong, who dressed you this morning?" shrieks corrections officer John Charette shortly after he stormed through the dormitory housing new camp admissions with their 5 a.m. wake-up—the crashing together of two trash can lids.

"You wear that shirt yesterday?" he shouts at an inmate. "We change clothes every day. We don't live like pigs. That's something you did on the streets. We're not on the streets anymore. UNDERSTAND?"

Prisoners march silently from one task to another. Smoking is forbidden. If inmates are not eating—in silence—they are working, exercising, studying or in counseling.

Most of the work is teamwork. "They have antisocial behavior patterns and don't want to help anybody and don't want anybody to help them," said Bruce L. Curtis, the camp commander. "We teach that to accomplish things (requires) a team effort. They have to work as teams, even to make beds."

Inmates must keep their heads shaved, a requirement that robs them of their identity and leaves them looking more like benign space creatures than the hardened street-smart men many of them are.

Commands are answered "yes, sir," and "no, sir." Nobody dares to speak without permission. Ever.

The silence is important said Lt. Fred Blaauw. "All they're going to talk about is what they did on the streets. Prisons are just training centers to be better criminals."

"Here you do what we say. We don't want to hear what you say. You had your say on the streets," said Inspector William Ray, the deputy director of Camp Sauble.

Inmates have but one hour a day to themselves and they must spend it silently reading or writing or just sitting. Beds and footlockers are kept military neat. Visitors are forbidden and inmates are permitted only one 10-minute phone call a week and only after they have served the first six weeks of their 13-week stay.

Life in the camps is so tough that in some states more than half of those who begin shock incarceration drop out, choosing instead to spend up to three years in less rigid, mainstream prisons. In New York, 56 percent have dropped out. Here in Michigan about one-third either quit or are kicked out.

But even quitting a shock camp is not easy. In Michigan, would-be quitters are subjected to ridicule and threats, they are reasoned with, they are given time for reflection and they are given a hearing during which their decision is questioned and reviewed.

"If we can hold them here for three weeks, our chances for success are good," says Lt. Jerry Howell. "But it bewilders me. I've seen 500 quit. It seems like their history is so bleak that they don't see a future."

Once a inmate does quit, he must spend a day or more dressed in yellow on a yellow cot in the camp's main hall where everybody can see him. Quitters eat last and are served their meals on yellow trays by kitchen workers—other inmates—who turn their backs.

Camp corrections officers are screened and go through four weeks of special training. "We tell them the first thing that can destroy this program is a staff member abusing his authority," said Curtis, a former U.S. Marine and Army Ranger. "What we look for (in staff) is a real good stable mind. I don't care if they have military experience."

"There is no reward to working in a prison," said veteran corrections officer Howell. "You're just there and (inmates) hate you automatically. Here you actually see change. In 90 days it's astounding. Here we believe what we're doing counts, that we're not just putting in eight hours watching convicted felons."

SOURCE: *Birmingham Post Herald*, December 16, 1989, pp. 1, 2B. Copyright, 1989, Los Angeles Times. Reprinted by permission.

We can expect that probation will continue to be the most widely used correctional disposition because it is less costly, more humane, and no less effective for most offenders than incarceration. These are certainly good reasons for using probation, but, in a sense, probation strategies seem to win over existing alternatives by default: No better option is currently available. If we want something more than this from probation, we will have to study current practices, think seriously about what probation should be achieving, and attempt to implement the changes necessary to make probation an effective strategy in its own right.

Summary

Probation is currently the most widely utilized postconviction correctional disposition. In the United States, it originated in the altruistic efforts of a shoemaker who felt that friendly supervision would do more to rehabilitate offenders than a jail sentence. Today probation is our most useful reintegrative strategy because it permits offenders to remain in the community while they receive counseling and assistance. At the same time, probation attempts to ensure community protection through the monitoring of offender behavior.

Although most observers have concluded that probation can be most effectively administered as an executive branch of state government, probation granting is a judicial function. The sentencing judge grants probation after determining that an individual offender is suitable for community supervision. This judgment is reached by referring to statutory eligibility requirements and by assessing the offender's background report, known as the presentence report. The preparation of presentence reports is one of the major responsibilities of probation officers, whose other major function is supervising offenders.

Preparing presentence reports is difficult, sometimes involving gathering and verifying information on the offender's crime, prior record, attitude toward his offense, family life, employment and educational history, and early years. When probation officers are asked to make recommendations for or against the granting of probation, judges usually follow these recommendations.

Probation supervision typically involves a synthesis of law enforcement and counseling activities. Because of their large case loads, which make individual casework virtually impossible, and the need to assist the offender in establishing long-term community ties, probation officers serve as resource brokers. These brokers of community services assess inmate needs, refer offenders to appropriate agencies, and monitor their progress in the community.

Probation conditions serve both reform and control objectives. They should reflect individual needs and capabilities rather than standardized rules. The violation of probation conditions may or may not lead to the revocation of probation and the incarceration of the offender. Before revocation can occur, either following a technical violation (of a condition) or a new crime, a two-stage revocation proceeding must be conducted to assess (1) probable cause that a violation occurred and (2) the desirability of revocation. This two-stage proceeding is designed to protect the offender from arbitrary and unnecessary incarceration.

Research on probation indicates that probation programs can be improved through the use of risk/needs assessments. Such classification schemes tailor supervision levels to the particular characteristics of individual offenders. At present, indications are that many persons on probation may require more supervision than they are getting. Yet these persons may not require incarceration. The benefits of intermediate punishments seem apparent.

Intensive supervision programs, house arrest, electronic monitoring, and shock incarceration are all means of addressing the need for mid-range options in the correctional continuum. While they may serve as more punitive dispositions than standard probation, they may also provide the increased contact and guidance necessary to make probation a truly reintegrative strategy.

KEY WORDS AND CONCEPTS

benefit of clergy	intermediate punishments	revocation
boot camp	judicial reprieve	sentencing guidelines
case load management	presentence investigation	shock incarceration
casework	privately prepared presentence reports	split sentence
conditions of probation	probation fees	supervision styles
electronic monitoring	probation termination	
house arrest	resource broker	
intensive supervision programs (ISP)		

NOTES

1. National Advisory Commission on Criminal Justice Standards and Goals, *Corrections* (Washington, D.C.: U.S. Government Printing Office, 1973), p. 1.
2. American Correctional Association, *Manual of Correctional Standards* (College Park, Md.: 1975), pp. 7–8.
3. Robert Carter and Leslie Wilkins (eds.), *Probation, Parole and Community Corrections* (New York: Wiley, 1976).
4. Harry Allen, Eric Carlson, and Evalyn Parks, *Critical Issues in Adult Probation: Summary* (Washington, D.C.: National Institute of Law Enforcement and Criminal Justice, 1979), p. 23.
5. American Correctional Association, *Manual of Correctional Standards*, p. 1.
6. Donald J. Newman, *Introduction to Criminal Justice* (New York: Lippincott, 1978), p. 281.
7. Carter and Wilkins, *Probation, Parole and Community Corrections*, p. 82.
8. George Killenger, Hazel Kerper, and Paul Cromwell, *Probation and Parole in the Criminal Justice System* (St. Paul, Minn.: West Publishing, 1976), p. 29.
9. United Nations Department of Social Affairs, *Probation and Related Measures, 1951,* as cited in Carter and Wilkins (eds.), *Probation, Parole and Community Corrections*, pp. 81–88.
10. Ibid., p. 84.
11. Carter and Wilkins, *Probation, Parole and Community Corrections*, p. 82.
12. Ibid., p. 84.
13. Ibid., p. 87.
14. Killenger, Kerper, and Cromwell, *Probation and Parole*, p. 3.
15. Ibid., p. 23.
16. David Rothman, *Conscience and Convenience: The Asylum and Its Alternatives in Progressive America* (Boston: Little, Brown, 1980), p. 44.
17. Ibid., p. 6.
18. Ibid., p. 44.
19. National Advisory Commission on Criminal Justice Standards and Goals, *Corrections*, p. 313.

20. President's Commission on Law Enforcement and Administration of Justice, *Task Force Report on Corrections* (Washington, D.C.: U.S. Government Printing Office, 1967), pp. 35–37.
21. National Advisory Commission on Criminal Justice Standards and Goals, *Corrections*, p. 316.
22. Ibid., p. 313.
23. Ibid., p. 314.
24. Bureau of Justice Statistics, "Probation and Parole 1987" (Washington, D.C.: U.S. Government Printing Office, 1988), p. 1.
25. Killenger, Kerper, and Cromwell, *Probation and Parole*, ch. 3.
26. Ibid., p. 39.
27. American Bar Association Project on Minimum Standards for Criminal Justice, *Standards Relating to Probation* (New York: American Bar Association, 1970).
28. Ibid., p. 160.
29. Robert Carter and Leslie Wilkins, "Some Factors in Sentencing Policy," in Carter and Wilkins, *Probation, Parole, and Community Corrections*, pp. 211–235.
30. Ibid.
31. Ibid.
32. Jack Kress et al., *Developing Sentencing Guidelines: Trainers Handbook* (Washington, D.C.: National Institute of Law Enforcement and Criminal Justice, 1978).
33. Administrative Office of the U.S. Courts, *The Presentence Investigation Report* (Washington, D.C.: U.S. Government Printing Office), p. 1.
34. Allen, Carlson, and Parks, *Critical Issues*, pp. 106–107.
35. "The Selective Presentence Investigation Report," *Federal Probation* 38, 1974, p. 48.
36. William Clements, "Judicial Use of Private Presentence Reports: The Case of Client Specific Planning." Presented at the Annual Meeting of the Academy of Criminal Justice Sciences, Orlando, Fla., 1986.
37. Allen, Carlson, and Parks, *Critical Issues*, p. 62.
38. Ibid., p. 63.
39. Ibid., p. 58.
40. Ibid., p. 65.
41. Ibid., p. 160.
42. James J. Dahl and Michael Chapman, *Improved Probation Strategies: Trainers Handbook* (Washington, D.C.: U.S. Government Printing Office, 1980).
43. Ibid., p. 66.
44. Ibid., p. 65.
45. National Advisory Commission on Criminal Justice Standards and Goals, *Corrections*, p. 159–160.
46. American Bar Association Project on Standards for Criminal Justice, *Standards Relating to Probation*, p. 45.
47. William Parker, *Parole: Origins, Development, Current Practices, and Statutes* (College Park, Md.: American Correctional Association, 1976), p. 37.
48. Gerald Wheeler et al., "The Effects of Probation Service Fees on Case Management Strategy and Sanctions," *Journal of Criminal Justice* 17 (1989): 15–24.
49. Allen, Carlson, and Parks, *Critical Issues*, pp. 29–33.
50. Ibid., pp. 34–36.
51. Ibid., p. 36.
52. Ibid., p. 37.
53. Ibid., pp. 144–159.
54. Vincent P. Dole and Herman Joseph, "Methadone Patients on Probation and Parole," *Federal Probation* 34 (June 1970), pp. 42–58.
55. Seymour Rosenthal, "Report on the Evaluation of Philadelphia County Probation Department Adult Probation Drug Unit" (Philadelphia: Temple University, 1974).
56. Robert L. Polakow and Ronald M. Doctor, "A Behavior Modification Program for Adult Drug Offenders," *Journal of Research in Crime and Delinquency* 11 (January 1974), pp. 63–69.

57. Joan Petersilia et al., *Granting Felons Probation* (Santa Monica, Calif.: Rand Corp., 1985).

58. Ibid., p. v.

59. James M. Byrne, Arthur J. Lurigio, and Christopher Baird, "The Effectiveness of the New Intensive Supervision Programs, *Research in Corrections,* 2(2) (1989).

60. Ibid., p. 11.

61. Billie Erwin and Lawrence A. Bennett, "New Dimensions in Probation: Georgia's Experience with Intensive Probation Supervision (IPS)," *Research in Brief* (Washington, D.C.: U.S. Government Printing Office, 1987).

62. Ibid., p. 2.

63. Billie S. Erwin, "Tools for the Modern Probation Officer," *Crime and Delinquency* 36(1) (1990): 61–74.

64. Joan Petersilia and Susan Turner, "Comparing Intensive and Regular Supervision for High-Risk Probationers: Early Results from an Experiment in California," *Crime and Delinquency* 36(1) (1990): 87–111.

65. Byrne, Lurigio, and Baird, "The Effectiveness of the New Intensive Supervision Programs," p. 16.

66. S. Christopher Baird and Dennis Wagner, "Measuring Diversion: The Florida Community Control Program," *Crime and Delinquency* 36(1) (1990): 112–125.

67. Ibid.

68. Ibid.

69. Annesley Schmidt, "Electronic Monitoring of Offenders Increases," *NIJ Reports* (Washington, D.C.: U.S. Government Printing Office, 1989), pp. 2–5.

70. Ibid., p. 4.

71. Ibid., p. 5.

72. Erwin, "Tools for the Modern Probation Officer."

73. Byrne, Lurigio, and Baird, "The Effectiveness of the New Intensive Supervision Programs."

74. Doris L. MacKenzie and James W. Shaw, "Inmate Adjustment and Change During Shock Incarceration." Presented at the annual meeting of the American Society of Criminology, Chicago, 1988.

75. Ibid.

76. Ibid.

77. Ibid.

78. Joan Petersilia, "Conditions That Permit Intensive Supervision Programs to Survive," *Crime and Delinquency* 36(1) (1990): 126–145.

79. Ibid., p. 130.

FOR FURTHER READING

Allen, Harry, Eric Carlson, and Evalyn Parks, *Critical Issues in Adult Probation: Summary* (Washington, D.C.: U.S. Government Printing Office, 1979).

Carter, Robert, and Leslie Wilkins (eds.), *Probation, Parole and Community Corrections* (New York: Wiley, 1976).

National Advisory Commission on Criminal Justice Standards and Goals, *Corrections* (Washington, D.C.: U.S. Government Printing Office, 1973).

5: Restitution and Community Service Programs

Contemporary Applications of Restitution and Community Service
Offense Categories
Criminal Justice System Stages
Extent of Use
Historical Perspective
Objectives
Just Punishment
Offender Treatment
Benefits to Victims
Benefits to the Community
The Restitution/Community Service Process
Eligibility Criteria
Amount of Restitution/Community Service
Victim/Offender Relations
Enforcement
Program Models: Community Supervision and Residential Alternatives
Win-Onus Restitution Program
Minnesota Restitution Center
Georgia's Experiment
Problems and Issues
Restitution versus Victim Compensation
Rehabilitation, Restitution, and Community Service
Enforcement of Restitution Conditions
The Future of Restitution and Community Service Programs
Emphasis on Work/Employment
Universal Appeal
Economic Benefits
Victim Assistance
Summary

THE PROGRAMS DISCUSSED in this chapter provide some of the criminal justice system's most innovative and creative responses to crime available in the criminal justice system. Crime victims, offenders, the general community, and criminal justice professionals tend to support these measures strongly because they truly provide something for everyone. In many ways, restitution and community service programs may foretell the future of community-based corrections. In the following sections, we examine their weaknesses and their strengths in an effort to understand the complex nature of these increasingly popular programs.

Webster's Dictionary defines restitution as "the act of restoring; especially the restoration of something to its original owner."[1] In contemporary correctional usage, restitution has been defined as "a requirement, either imposed by agents of the criminal justice system or undertaken voluntarily by the wrongdoer but with the consent of the criminal justice system, by which the offender engages in acts designed to make reparation for the harm resulting from the criminal offense."[2]

Restitution Is an Ancient Principle

"If anyone sins and commits a breach of faith . . . through robbery, . . . he shall restore it in full, and shall add a fifth to it, and give it to him to whom it belongs."

Leviticus 6

"If a man has stolen an ox . . . if (it belongs) to a god (or) a palace, he shall pay thirtyfold; if of a villein . . . tenfold. If the thief has not the means of payment, he shall be put to death."

Code of Hammurabi, 2100 BC

Galaway has developed a typology of restitution based on the nature of the offender's payment, which may be in the form of money or service, and the nature of the recipient who may be either the individual victim or the community as a whole (table 5-1).[3] In the United States, monetary payments from the offender to the victim and service provided by the offender to the community are the most common forms of restitution. This latter form is often referred to as symbolic restitution because restoration for the harm done is made in the form of good works benefiting the entire community rather than the particular individual harmed. In this chapter, we refer to symbolic restitution as community service and use the term *restitution* to describe the monetary payments offenders make to individual victims.

Restitution programs can be distinguished from victim compensation projects. Although both plans provide financial reimbursement to crime victims, only restitution requires that the payments be made by the individual who committed the offense. Victim compensation programs normally draw upon funds raised by taxation; the particular offender is not involved in the transaction and may not even have been identified. An independent victim compensation board or committee assesses the extent of the victim's losses and determines his or her eligibility for payment. We examine the relative advantages and disadvantages of this plan and consider offender restitution later in this chapter.

TABLE 5-1 Typology of Restitution

	Form of restitution	
Recipient of restitution	Monetary	Service
Victim	Type I: monetary-victim	Type III: service-victim
Community organization	Type II: monetary-community	Type IV: service-community

SOURCE: Burt Galaway, "The Use of Restitution," *Crime and Delinquency 23*(1), 1977: 63.

Contemporary Applications of Restitution and Community Service

❑ Offense Categories

Restitution is almost invariably limited to use in economic offenses. The money or goods taken from victims and the damage done to their property is restored through financial payment. Restitution can be used in response to violent crimes, but the difficulty of putting a price tag on physical injury, which must include estimates of hospital fees, loss of income, and the financial effects of pyschological trauma, limit its use even as a supplement to incarceration for violent offenders.

Community service is normally utilized for property offenders as well, although the various forms that service may take make it adaptable to a broad range of minor offenses. For example, a person convicted of cruelty to animals may be required to work a specific number of hours in an animal shelter. An individual found to have been driving while intoxicated may be required to work in treatment programs for alcoholics or a hospital emergency ward. However, the nature of the work required in service to the community does not have to be designed to instruct the offender in the error of his ways; the offender's characteristics and the nature of the "good works" may be totally unrelated. Because it is not always feasible or even desirable to place offenders in situations related to their criminal activity, the emphasis in community service is usually on the symbolic nature of the reparation—"doing good" in the community after having caused harm through crime.

❑ Criminal Justice System Stages

Restitution and community service may be required of offenders at various stages of the criminal justice system. Restitution is also frequently used as an informal disposition prior to an arrest or criminal prosecution. Police or prosecutors, with the agreement of the victim(s), may permit shoplifters to return stolen merchandise or allow check offenders to pay off their debts in lieu of criminal proceedings. Similarly, restitution and community service frequently serve as formal conditions of pretrial diversion. Prosecution can be avoided if the defendant is willing to repay the crime victim or perform a specific number of hours of community service. Neighborhood justice centers frequently rely on restitution as a resolution for citizen disputes.

Restitution and community service are often employed as conditions of probation. Statutes in many states permit courts to order payment of restitution as a requirement of probation; in other areas, courts use this sanction by virtue of their general power to establish probation conditions.[4] Courts are also experimenting with community service as a condition of probation, especially for juveniles, youthful offenders, first offenders, and misdemeanants.

Community service is rarely utilized for offenders who receive prison sentences or even persons required to live in halfway houses as a condition of diversion, probation, or parole. Restitution is commonly used for these individuals. Georgia operates a number of community restitution centers (now known as diversion centers), where probationers live as they complete court-ordered restitution. In North Carolina, inmates on work release are often required to use some of their earnings to make restitution as they serve out their sentences. In the early 1970s, Minnesota established a restitution center to which selected offenders were paroled after negotiating a restitution agreement in collaboration with the victim and a restitution center staff member.[5]

❑ Extent of Use

A recent government publication reported there are several hundred restitution programs in operation throughout the United States at the adult and juvenile level.[6] While restitution and community service have experienced phenomenal growth, these programs have still not been widely accepted by the criminal justice community as a standard sanction. A number of factors appear to be responsible for the tremendous growth of these programs, including a growing recognition of the need to address the losses suffered by the victim, the need to make offenders more accountable for their crimes, and the need to provide effective alternatives (from a punishment perspective) to the use of overcrowded prisons and jails.

Historical Perspective

The history of restitution is extremely long and can be traced back to pretribal man. Hudson has described the development and modification of the concept of restitution as encompassing three broad stages.[7] Initially, each person acted individually to define the law and administer punishment. As human beings began living in tribes and kinship groups, the idea of collective social responsibility began to emerge, and with it came the development of blood feuds between kinship groups for the purpose of resolving individual grievances. Then a system of mitigating and resolving blood feuds emerged—victims and/or their families were compensated by the offending family group for deaths or injuries inflicted. The next stage witnessed the displacement of the family's central role in criminal matters. By the end of the twelfth century, the state (the king) was defined as the offended party whenever a crime was committed. It became the right and responsibility of the state (rather than the individual victim or his family) to punish offenders and collect damages (fines). The state thus came to represent the victim in criminal proceedings. The practice of offender restitution came to play a very insignificant role in criminal justice.

Although it has received only limited use as a penal sanction, the concept of restitution has remained alive and well throughout the years. In the sixteenth century, Sir Thomas More suggested that offenders be required to make restitution to

Restitution in Alabama: Crime Doesn't Pay, but Criminals Do, with Restitution

Almost four years ago, a 35-year-old Birmingham woman was arrested on charges of stealing $4338 from the gas station where she worked by falsifying bank deposit slips.

After an indictment by a Jefferson County Grand Jury, she pleaded guilty in Circuit Court to four counts of embezzlement.

"My husband had been out of work for four years and had back surgery four times. We had gone head over heels in debt," she said in a statement in the court.

Under state law, she could have received a fine and a jail sentence. Instead, (the judge) opted for restitution.

So the woman—who dropped out of school after the 8th grade to get married and was a $175-a-week waitress at a local restaurant at the time of her trial—was sentenced to five years probation and ordered to pay $50 a week to pay off what she took.

What happened to that woman is not unique. In fact, judges across the state have, for years, been ordering convicts to repay the victims of their crimes.

But restitution—the idea of making a criminal pay his victim—is getting more popular. . . .

Restitution arrangements are usually popular with victims of crimes because restitution is viewed as good, old-fashioned justice. "I think it's beautiful that they've got something like this (restitution)," said the manager of a Homewood health club, whose business was the target of an employee's $8000 embezzlement scheme

in 1978. "I'd rather the man pay the money back than go to jail. He's paying on time, and he's paying his debt. He's doing fine," said the manager. . . .

Judges say they like it, too, because they say fines and simple probation are often thought to be too lenient. (One judge) calls restitution "earned probation," without which many repeat offenders would wander away and "laugh at the system."

The remaining alternative, imprisonment, often turns nonviolent offenders into violent ones and is an expensive burden on taxpayers besides. A typical order of restitution is worked out by a probation officer for the judge's approval. If the offender fails to make his payments, which may be weekly or monthly installments, he will be summoned before a judge to explain the problem. Depending on the judge's decision, the offender then may be given a short extension to meet the terms of the restitution order, or he may be ordered to pay a fine. Otherwise, he must go to jail.

One 35-year-old woman who was charged with stealing more than $12,000 worth of jewelry from the home of an elderly Birmingham woman pleaded guilty before (the judge), was sentenced to three years probation, and then was ordered to pay $255 a month until her debt was paid. She is currently making payments on schedule and will complete her sentence in 1983.

But a 40-year-old Birmingham man who was arrested on charges of pocketing thousands of dollars from forged

the victims of their crimes and labor on public work projects. Two hundred years later, Jeremy Bentham described monetary restitution and the replacement of stolen goods as essential to efforts to fit the punishment to the crime. Another perspective was provided by Herbert Spencer, who viewed prison labor as a way for the offender to make restitution and contribute to the payment of the cost of incarceration. The length of an inmate's prison sentence, he argued, should be based on the amount of damage done and the offender's ability to work off his debt to his victim.[8]

In 1891, the International Penal Association Congress considered recommendations for the abolition of short prison sentences and the introduction of court-ordered restitution as a correctional alternative, but the proposal drew only limited attention. Almost fifty years later, the British penal reformer, Margaret Fry, resurrected the restitution concept and gave it a new twist—offender rehabilitation: "repayment is the best first step toward reformation that a dishonest person can take. It is often the ideal solution."[9] Although her work contributed to the later development of victim compensation programs in several countries, a 1958 survey of twenty-nine nations revealed that restitution to crime victims was still almost nonexistent.[10]

refund tickets at the auto parts store where he worked was thrown in jail after he skipped a few $100-a-month payments. Jefferson County officals ultimately gave him a second chance when his attorney brought in a $1900 check to cover the missed payments.

The Jefferson County Circuit Clerk said most defendants eventually pay what they owe because, "If they don't, they'll end up in jail."

Not all convicts on restitution programs are ordered to pay money, however. The Lauderdale County District Judge said she often orders poor or youthful offenders to perform community service instead of paying monetary restitution. A Jefferson County Family Court judge said he often orders juveniles who can't afford to repay their victims to rake leaves or pick up trash in a public place like a park, for example, as a "symbolic restitution." And in Mobile, a Juvenile Judge requires youthful offenders to pay back their victims and perform community service. "If someone steals a $25 dollar item that is in good enough condition to be returned to the shelf, I multiply its value by three," this judge said. "Then I require the youth to work until he earns $75." He said he makes the thief repay the victim and then give what is left to charity. The judge named several charities which have benefited. More than $2500 has gone to the University of South Alabama's cancer research program, he said. . . .

Despite the success of restitution arrangements, citizens and lawmen say they have concerns about how restitution programs work. For example, the family of an elderly Birmingham woman who was run down and critically injured by a teenage drunken driver wanted the judge to send the offender to jail rather than order him to pay the hospital bills. On June 10, 1980, the 74-year-old (woman) was taking her evening walk in Wylam when she was injured by a hit-and-run driver. (She) suffered compound fractures in her legs, two broken ribs, and a fractured pelvis. Her hospital bills quickly mounted into the thousands of dollars, and they're still increasing. A 22-year-old man, who already had a burglary conviction and seven traffic offenses on his record, was convicted of leaving the scene of an accident. The driver was put on probation and ordered to pay $100 a month as restitution. But the grandson of the victim said the offender was getting off too easy. "He bought his freedom. And at $100 a month, that's pretty cheap" (he said), adding that the family preferred the judge send the defendant to prison.

(The judge in the case) said his decision to put the driver on probation was based on his review "of all the facts. And I still stand by my decision." Since the defendant was convicted in the spring of 1981, (the victim's) doctor bills and related expenses have reached about $40,000, (the grandson) said. At the rate he is paying, the driver will have repaid about $6000 to the victim by 1986. (The grandson) is worried that his grandmother will have to foot the bills herself at the end of the defendant's five-year probationary period.

SOURCE: Dean Burgess, "Crime doesn't pay, but criminals do, with restitution," *The Birmingham News*, 8 August 1982, pp. 1–2B.

Restitution programs gradually gained support throughout the 1960s. In 1962, the Model Penal Code developed by the American Law Institute proposed that a defendant placed on probation may be required to "make restitution of the fruits of his crime or to make reparation, in an amount he can afford to pay, for the loss or damage caused thereby."[11] The American Bar Association (ABA) later recommended that decisions regarding fines and their amount should take into account whether the imposition of the fine will interfere with the offender's ability to make restitution.[12] Both the ABA and the National Council on Crime and Delinquency (NCCD) supported the use of restitution as a condition of probation; NCCD's recommendation provided for restitution to victims and dependents of victims killed "for any money or property loss or compensation for injury directly resulting from the crime."[13] The 1973 report of the National Advisory Commission on Criminal Justice Standards and Goals viewed offender restitution as a factor mitigating the imposition of a prison sentence.[14]

Legislation providing for the use of restitution as a component of sentencing and/or an objective of specific correctional programs was developed and implemented in many states throughout the 1970s. During that same period, Law Enforcement Assistance Administration (LEAA) grants provided funds to programs in eleven states and the Office of Juvenile Justice and Delinquency Prevention funded over forty restitution programs. Today most states have implemented restitution procedures, and many jurisdictions have subsequently experimented with community service as an alternative to confinement or monetary restitution.

Objectives

Restitution and community service can serve the correctional objectives of just punishment and rehabilitation for the offenders and may provide benefits to the victims and the general community. In addition, the humanitarian aims of corrections are served whenever restitution or community service is substituted for further processing through the criminal justice system (conditional diversion) or serves as an alternative to initial or continued confinement. Permitting offenders to attempt to undo their wrongs seem much more appropriate for many offenders than subjecting them to the effects of a criminal prosecution or incarceration. Restitution and community service have also been viewed as making punishment a more humane undertaking by making it a more meaningful process. Requiring offenders to work off their crimes in proportion to the damage done may be more merciful and more fair than requiring periods of incarceration or community supervision unrelated to the injury or the offense.

❑ Just Punishment

One of the oldest justifications for punishment is retribution, or *lex talionis,* "an eye for an eye." Restitution represents a contemporary version of this biblical statement. With restitution, offenders repay their debt to the victims and/or society in a manner that is proportional to the offense. For much of the nineteenth and twentieth centuries the prevailing correctional punishment ideology calculated the criminals' debt repayment (for their transgression to society) in terms of years of confinement in a jail or prison. With restitution and community service as punishments, judges may be more creative in determining how offenders repay the community for their crimes.

❑ Offender Treatment

The humanitarian benefits of restitution and community service are closely linked to their rehabilitative objectives. Both forms of sanction can be directly or indirectly related to the offense committed, thus personalizing justice in a manner impossible when only imprisonment or community supervision is imposed. Making punishment more meaningful should promote the goals of rehabilitation because the offender comes to view the criminal justice system as responding to his particular behavior.

Fulfilling the conditions of restitution or community service orders may provide the offender with an enhanced feeling of self-worth. Paying off his debt and providing volunteer services to the community may give the individual a sense of

Participant Views of Community Service Programs

"I actually enjoyed the work. In fact, I am seriously considering to continue with volunteer work. . . . It gave me a higher opinion of our judicial system. I know that if I would have been given a fine or some other punishment, I would have gone away bitter toward the system and the law. Instead, the program turns the punishment into useful energy and gives one the pride of knowing you've helped another person."

"I think they should use this volunteer work more often cause I think a person can get a lot more out of it than a fine. Cause money can hurt your pocket for a while but you can't remember it as well as a learning experience."

"I came to respect the courts and realize that the law is made for people and that the courts aren't out to get you but are there to help you."

"I am aware now more than ever in my life as having been sheltered. . . . Certainly most persons privileged as I have not stood before a judge nor have they had to face themselves as possible outcasts in the eyes of members of our society. . . . In such a situation it is hard to find the resources that will help one see oneself as a valuable human being. . . . I want to say how valuable the program to which I was assigned was and is in my life. To be able to spend time with people, help each other, to be able to feel like I am constructively working out my debt to society and helping children become better citizens, is a debt beyond words."

SOURCE: James Beha et al., *Sentencing to Community Service* (Washington, D.C.: U.S. Government Printing Office, 1977), p. 58.

accomplishment; his time has not been wasted, but has been put to good use. For many persons, it may be the first time they have worked in a volunteer service capacity. This new learning experience could promote attitudinal changes in many offenders as they come to understand themselves and others better through their efforts. If nothing else, a well-designed community service project may broaden the offender's horizons. Restitution may provide a sense of achievement as the offender steadily approaches and meets his payment goal. Both restitution and community service should increase the participant's self-respect rather than denigrate it with meaningless punishment.

Restitution and community service may promote rehabilitation in other ways as well. Both procedures provide offenders with a means of expressing guilt for their conduct. Such feelings may become more manageable because the offender is able to do something constructive following his offense, rather than repressing whatever remorse he may feel and attempting to rationalize his behavior. He may be able to express, accept, and resolve his personal conflicts about his actions. Some therapists view the acknowledgment of responsibility that is required in restitution as a prerequisite for offender change.

Finally, restitution and community service programs may contribute to the development of personal discipline and good work habits among offenders. Because restoration payments are made and specific hours of work must be completed, offenders are required to maintain good relations with supervisors and co-workers and achieve an acceptable level of job performance. To make restitution payments, personal income must be budgeted and saved. It is hoped these skills can be maintained and extended to other areas of offender behavior after restitution and community service requirements have been fulfilled.

❑ Benefits to Victims

The victims of crime are the most direct beneficiaries of restitution efforts. Because many crime victims are, like offenders, financially disadvantaged, they are poorly equipped to manage the economic loss and related financial difficulties of crime. Reimbursement may be essential to the victim's financial recovery from criminal attack. Regardless of social status, most victims tend to rank the economic effects of crime as serious problems (table 5-2).

Financial aid also may facilitate the victim's psychological recovery from victimization. Of critical importance is the concept of equity—restoring what has been lost, attempting to undo the damage done. Restitution offically recognizes the injury done to the victim and promotes restoration. It brings victims into the criminal justice system as active participants; their concerns do not fall on deaf ears but are heard, evaluated, and provide the basis for sanctioning the offender. Such experiences should promote victims' feelings of self-worth, feelings that often receive low priority in contemporary criminal proceedings.

Restitution also facilitates victims' development of a realistic view of the attacker; they may learn about the offender's background, circumstances, and motivation for the offense. Seeing the criminal as a human being with problems and needs, as a person willing to make amends for his actions, may encourage victims to adopt a less punitive approach toward the immediate criminal proceedings. Victims come to view the offender as less of a predator and to see themselves consequently as less vulnerable to attack; they may thus be willing to accept a more moderate disposition for the offender. Restitution encourages victims to look toward the the future and the financial payments they will receive, rather than to the past and the vengeance they may desire.

❑ Benefits to the Community

The community may benefit from restitution and community services programs in several ways. Community service obviously provides a direct benefit in the volunteer

TABLE 5-2 Summary of Crime-Related Victim Problems

Problem	Victims experiencing problems		Victims rating problem as "very serious"	
	Number	Percentage	Number	Percentage
Physical injury	470	27%	240	51%
Property loss	768	45	432	56
Property damage	658	39	355	54
Lost time	835	49	389	47
Lost income	446	26	278	62
Lost job	39	2	35	90
Insurance canceled	13	1	9	69
Mental or emotional suffering	1,001	57	495	49
Reputation damaged	251	12	110	44
Problems with family	358	25	182	51
Problems with friends	215	12	83	39

SOURCE: Center for Criminal Justice and Social Policy, *A Guide for Community Service* (Milwaukee, Wis.: Marquette University Press, 1976).

If You Want a Second Chance, Earn It

Raymond is 21 years old. After high school, he worked sporadically as a roofer in a business with his cousin. Last fall, he was driving a friend's Volkswagen while high on Quaaludes. When the police finally stopped the car after a seven-mile chase, five police cruisers were damaged, as well as the Volkswagen. The cost: $4,500.

"I should have done a lot more damage, as jammed as I was," Raymond says. "I was on three Quaaludes."

Raymond had a record; he had been arrested eight times as a juvenile. This time he received a year in the House of Correction, with eleven months suspended. But instead of going to jail, Raymond spent the active month of his sentence working as a janitor in the South Shore Day Care Center earning money so that he could pay back his victims. He was given a chance to take part in an innovative restitution program called "Earn It," which operates out of the East Norfolk District Court in the township of Quincy near Boston, Massachusetts.

The money Raymond earned—about $350—went to pay for the damage to his friend's car. To make up the damage done to the cruisers, he had to work this summer at the District Court building doing general maintenance work.

"This is about the most decent program you'll ever find," Raymond now says. "It learns you a lesson. They're pretty decent here, but they don't want to hear any bullshit. I can pay whatever I can afford and I have a year to pay it all back. I'm getting my old job back this fall, and I don't want to get in any more trouble. I'm going to my girl's house to watch T.V. No more hanging out on corners drinking."

SOURCE: Jon Ciner, "If You Want a Second Chance, 'Earn It,'" *Corrections Magazine* 4(4), 1978: 64. Copyright 1978 by *Corrections Magazine* and Criminal Justice Publications, Inc., 116 West 32 Street, New York, NY 10001.

work performed in public and private agencies. The hours of service offenders contribute may make new service projects possible, supplement existing resources, and permit community activities to be accomplished more efficiently or with greater care.

Utilizing restitution and community service as an alternative or addition to penal sanctions may mitigate the public's desire for vengeance much as it affects the victim's perspective. Criminals can be viewed as citizens who have offended community standards and are therefore required to pay their debt to the community. Persons who have fulfilled the conditions of restitution or community service can then be accepted back into the fabric of society without the lingering feeling that justice was not done, that the punishment was not enough. The label of having completed restitution or community service is clearly preferable from all perspectives to the stigma of having completed a prison sentence.

Finally, community attitudes toward the criminal justice system may improve with the increased use of restitution and community service. A survey of citizens' views regarding creative restitution, which includes the use of monetary payments, service to victims, and service to the community as alternative dispositions, indicated that program support is overwhelmingly strong.[15] Similar findings were reported by a study of the views of judges, solicitors, and practicing attorneys.[16] Nine out of ten persons questioned favored using creative restitution for various property crimes, drunk driving, and income tax evasion. These programs received considerably greater support than victim compensation plans. Restitution and community service may not only better serve the general public's view of what the criminal justice system should be doing, but may also facilitate greater agreement among the justice system, its personnel, and the community regarding the system's functions and goals.

The Restitution/Community Service Process

❑ Eligibility Criteria

Eligibility criteria for participation in restitution or community service programs vary from jurisdiction to jurisdiction. (See boxes on pages 145 and 147 for examples of juvenile restitution criteria and target population.) Normally, participants are first offenders who have committed relatively minor economic crimes, offenses against the public order, or traffic violations. However, judges and parole boards generally have considerable discretion to use the sanctions whenever they consider the offender an appropriate candidate. The only additional factor that invariably enters into the selection of offenders for restitution is the defendant's ability to afford financial payments to the victim. This consideration is of particular importance when decision makers view only full restitution—payment for *all* victim losses—as an appropriate requirement. Some jurisdictions avoid the all or nothing question by awarding partial restitution to victims based on the offender's ability to pay.

The length of time required to complete restitution payments is an important related concern. A low-income offender could pay off even a large sum of money if the payments were stretched out over twenty to thirty years. Most persons feel that a more reasonable time frame should be selected to evaluate an offender's ability to fulfill restitution requirements. Otherwise the payments may be so small as to be of little value to the victim but may represent a seemingly endless burden to the offender. In such cases, the entire procedure can easily become little more than a record-keeping nuisance. Additionally, those victims who are covered by insurance may prefer to recover their loss from the insurance company and be done with the matter.

❑ Amount of Restitution/Community Service

The amount of restitution to be made is normally based solely upon the amount of financial loss the victim suffers as a direct result of the crime—the money taken or the monetary value of the stolen goods or damaged property. Additional indirect injuries, however, can also be calculated; the income lost through unemployment and the costs of hospitalization, medical and psychological treatment, and vocational rehabilitation may be considered whenever the victim is in some way debilitated by the criminal attack. Income lost because of time spent in court also may be considered. The final restitution order may be determined by any of these factors, viewed in the context of the offender's ability to pay.

There are two methods for calculating the number of hours an offender is expected to contribute to community service. The first approach specifies the fine an offender would normally be expected to pay or the potential loss associated with an attempted theft. It places a dollar value on volunteer work (for example, $10 a day) and requires the offender to work the number of days and hours necessary to "earn" the fine or make symbolic restitution for what was stolen. The second approach directly specifies the number of hours of work an offender should complete as penalty for his crime; for example, twenty-four hours might be required for possession of a small amount of marijuana.[17] The second method permits greater flexibility in the development of community service requirements because it is not

Examples of Eligibility Criteria for Juvenile Restitution Programs

The Following Criteria Will Be Considered Prior to the Development of a Plan of Restitution:

1. Males and females between the ages of 10 and 18 years may be considered. The tender age child with limited ability to make monetary payments may be inappropriate for full monetary restitution.
2. Community Service Restitution should not be considered for children involved in aggravated offenses, unless first staffed with the Restitution Program Manager.
3. The child and parents should be in agreement with any and all restitution plans.
4. Restitution is to be used to enhance normal diversionary or probationary processes by making the child more aware of the harm to others caused by their acts.
5. The child should be able to complete the Plan of Restitution within the term of probation or by their 18th birthday.
6. Consideration must be given to the fairness of the amount to ensure that this is a beneficial therapeutic program.
7. Restitution may be sought in cases which involve property loss, property damage, and personal injury.

Dallas County, Texas

. . . There are limitations to the type of referrals that the Restitution Program will accept. The program is not designed to provide services to offenders with a history of violent behavior, untreated drug/alcohol problems, severe emotional problems, or unstable living situations. Second-time referrals are eligible for services with special conditions. No third-time referrals are accepted.

Dane County (Madison), Wisconsin

Eligibility Criteria

1. The youth has been adjudicated as delinquent for committing a crime against person or property;
2. Commitment to Department of Human Services (DHS) may be a realistic disposition in this case;
3. The youth must have been convicted of a felony offense or have had two prior convictions;
4. The youth has a place to live in the community;
5. The youth is not being revoked for violation of probation.

Washington, D.C.

For Acceptance of a Juvenile into the Restitution Program:

Nonviolent offender, resident of St. Tammany Parish, between the ages of 10 and 16, recommended by the. . . Court . . . Division of Youth Services, District Attorney, or Law Enforcement Agencies.

Covington, Louisiana

Target Population for Court-Ordered Probation Plus

Juveniles between the ages of 13–17 who have committed and been adjudicated for property theft, property damage, regulatory offenses and violations of city ordinances are eligible. All other types of referrals will be screened and accepted on the condition of space availability.

Probation Plus, Macon County, Illinois

Selection Criteria

A. The individual must be between 10 and 17 years old and a resident of Lee County, N.C.
B. The Juvenile must be adjudicated for the offense(s) for which he or she was charged and must be on probation unless otherwise specified.
C. The offense(s) committed will be for property crimes and physical damage crime.
D. The juvenile must be deemed physically, mentally, and emotionally able to fulfill a restitution requirement.
E. The juvenile and his [sic] parent or legal guardian must be willing to sign a contractual agreement which will stipulate the number of hours of work to be performed and the date for completion as determined by the Lee County Restitution Program.
F. The juvenile's home situation must be stable and structured to a degree which would enable completion of the obligation.

Lee County (Sanford), North Carolina

SOURCE: Anne L. Schneider (ed.), *Guide to Juvenile Restitution* (Washington, D.C.: U.S. Government Printing Office, July 1985), p. 23.

Target Population for Restitution Programs

Restitution programs typically begin by taking only the "safest" juvenile offenders—minor property offenders, sometimes even status offenders (for whom it is difficult to develop meaningful restitution orders since there has been no "harm" done). Over time, judges develop confidence in the ability of the program to deal with more serious offenders. One of the most complex issues that will be faced by any program, however, is the definition of an "eligible" client.

Serious Offenders

Programs that take serious offenders face the risk of a repeated serious offense that could damage the credibility of the program. On the other hand, programs that take only minor offenders will not make as much of a contribution to the juvenile justice system, since they will be dealing with a smaller portion of the delinquent population.

Burglaries and arson with loss below $10; other property offenses with losses $11 to $250	89	15
Any property offense with losses less than $11 except burglaries and arson	87	15
Personal offenses		
Rape, armed robbery, aggravated assault; unarmed robbery with losses less than $250	85	18
Unarmed robberies and aggravated assaults with losses less than $250	85	18
Other personal offenses (obstructing an officer, hazing, coercion, threat)	85	16

How Well Do Serious Offenders Do in Restitution Programs?

	Successful completion (percent)	Reoffense rate at 12 mo. (percent)
No. of Cases	13,589	15,009
Property offenses		
Burglaries and arson with loss/damage more than $250	82%	14%
Burglaries and arson with loss less than $250; other property offenses with losses more than $250	85	14

How Well Do Chronic Offenders Do in Restitution Programs?

No. of prior referrals	Successful completion (percent)	12-month recidivism (percent)	No. of cases
None	90%	10%	5,936
One	87	13	2,844
Two	84	17	1,614
Three	81	20	976
Four	80	22	578
Five	77	25	352
Six or More	77	24	797

SOURCE: Anne L. Schneider (ed.), *Guide to Juvenile Restitution* (Washington, D.C.: U.S. Government Printing Office, 1985), p. 16.

tied to existing penal sanctions (fines) or the value of what was stolen if the crime attempted had not been completed. It may, however, appear somewhat arbitrary because there is no objective link between the crime and the number of hours that must be served.

❏ Victim-Offender Relations

Victim involvement in community service projects is rare; generally, community service is required when no specific victim can be identified or when the offense falls

Victim Mediation: The Hit-and-Run Driver

This is the case of a 65-year-old man, a concertmaster for the Shubert Theatre, who was on his way home from work on a cold, snowy, winter night, when he became the victim of a hit and run driver. This gentleman was trapped in his car for over three hours until help arrived.

During the face-to-face meeting, the older man spoke quietly, describing his experience. As he related more and more about the case, his voice grew stronger and his anger and frustration during what happened to him were clearly coming through.

During this time, the offender (a young man, 17 years of age) stared at the ground, had little eye contact with the victim, and said very little. He didn't speak until the victim directly addressed the offender and said, "You know, I have a grandson about your age. I don't understand how anyone could leave someone in the way you left me. What if I were seriously hurt or dying? As it was, I banged by head and was very confused for a few minutes. Do you realize how awful it was for me to be alone and have to wait such a long time for help?"

At this point, the offender, a strong, muscular fellow, looked up at his victim. There were tears in his eyes as he said, "Believe me, I haven't stopped thinking about that night. I haven't been able to sleep through a night since then. I thought I really hurt you very badly.

Did you know that I got out of my car and ran to see you, but you were dead! There was a big bang on the side of your head. I panicked and ran away. I'm sorry. I should have stayed to help or at least called someone from a phone booth. I'll pay you whatever you say. Whatever you want. I'm glad you're alive."

The older man stared at the offender a few seconds. He stood up and extended his arm to shake hands with his offender saying, "It's O.K., son, we all make mistakes. You just have to learn to be responsible for them. I don't want anything from you except for what it actually cost me. Two hundred dollars is what I had to pay so that's what I think is fair. What do you think?

One week later the victim called to thank me for the two hundred dollar check he had received from the offender. He said, "I really didn't expect anything like what happened during that meeting. I was so mad at that kid, I could have killed him. Now I feel that he made up for what he did. You people are on the right track up there."

—Loraine Rosenblatt, Earn-It
Quincy, Massachusetts

Source: Anne L. Schneider (ed.), *Guide to Juvenile Restitution* (Washington, D.C.: U.S. Government Printing Office, 1985), p. 54.

into the category of victimless crimes, such as drug or alcohol offenses. Restitution programs present a different picture; victim involvement may be extensive and include active participation in decision making regarding the offender's appropriateness for restitution, the amount of restitution to be required, and the scheduling of payments. Personal contact between the offender and the victim may also be extensive during the payment period. Some victims may not desire to play such an active role in restitution efforts; they may fear a reprisal from the offender or view such activities as merely bothersome and inconvenient. Other persons may prefer to trust a third party to negotiate the restitution agreement. Some victims share culpability for the criminal act and are reluctant to seek restitution; others view punishment as preferable to restitution and refuse to involve themselves in negotiations designed to provide restitution as an alternative to imprisonment.

Although most research indicates that correctional administrators and probation and parole officers support direct victim/offender involvement in the restitution process, actual victim involvement is extremely limited. One study found that only 6 of 525 cases of restitution involved the face-to-face contact of victims and offenders.[18] Although victims often have input into the decision-making process regarding the extent of their financial loss, the court or restitution project staff members normally formulate the restitution order. Sometimes victims are not even adequately informed when restitution has been required of their offender.[19]

Research on victim participation in restitution reveals that insurance companies and large businesses are awarded a large percentage of all restitution payments.[20] These victims would be expected to show less interest in active participation in restitution negotiations than individual victims; their predominance among restitution victims may partially explain victims' limited roles in the restitution process.

❏ Enforcement

Some offenders required to complete community service orders are virtually on their honor to fulfill their agreements. Others are supervised by staff at the agencies at which they work; diversion project staff and probation and parole officers may also share in the monitoring of offender compliance with the service order. Failure to fulfill the terms of the agreement may result in the reinstatement of prosecution, revocation of probation or parole, and/or imposition of a fine.

Compliance with restitution orders is monitored and enforced in the same manner as community service, but additional alternative responses are available. Contempt citations or attachments of the offender's salary are sometimes utilized when the failure to make payments appears willful. When unemployment, income reduction, or increase in financial responsibilities seems to have caused the problem, the restitution order may be modified to reflect the offender's changed circumstances. A grace period of three months is normally allowed before any action, punitive or otherwise, is taken.

Program Models: Community Supervision and Residential Alternatives

❏ Win-Onus Restitution Program

Win means to fight, endure, struggle, to desire to gain victory. *Onus* is responsibility for a wrong. *Restitution* means to give back to the rightful owner something that has been lost or taken away. In 1972, Winona County, Minnesota, initiated an experimental program to serve as an alternative to fines, probation, or jail for nonviolent adult misdemeanants. The program objective was to impose sentences that would benefit the offender, the victim, and the community. The program's philosophy is simple: "If you've wronged someone, it is your responsibility to make it right with the person you have wronged or to the community as a whole, and at the same time do constructive things for yourself to improve your self-esteem and social position."[21]

The program is founded on the belief that most offenders view themselves as losers, isolated from the general community. Involvement with the criminal justice system normally increases the offender's sense of isolation; the system's punitive approach to crime often encourages hostile and immature responses from offenders.

Program Operation.　Persons convicted of such crimes as disorderly conduct, theft, simple assault, shoplifting, driving while intoxicated, reckless driving or vandalism are eligible for Win-Onus; this group comprises about 10 percent of all misdemeanants and traffic offenders.[22] Following conviction, offenders are questioned by the judge to determine their suitability for the program; appropriate candidates are referred to court service officers (CSOs), who describe Win-Onus. If the crime directly involved a specific victim, the option of monetary or service restitution is explored with the offender and the victim; if no victim can be identified, community service is considered. The offender's problems and needs are also examined—alcohol and drug abuse and marital and employment difficulties are common among program participants. A list of possible sentencing alternatives (table 5-3)

TABLE 5-3 Win-Onus Program Sentencing Alternatives

An offender may request to donate his time or his services to any charitable or governmental agency. Many offenders have come up with their own ideas. The following have been accepted.

Alternatives That Help Others

Work at YMCA	Work in Watkins Memorial Home
Work at YWCA	Work in group homes
Work for American Red Cross	Pick up litter on highways
Work for Boy Scouts	Clean litter from lakes and streams
Work for Girl Scouts	Donate blood
Work for church organizations	Become a volunteer probation officer
Help a victim of vandalism	Work for historical society
Shovel sidewalks or do yard work	Work in day-care centers
for invalid persons or senior	Work in Big Brother program
citizens	Work in mental health center
Paint and repair government buildings	Work in children's homes
Clean streets or parks	Work for Minnesota Society for Crippled
Work in high schools	Children
Work in colleges	Work for sportsmen's club projects
Work in vocational schools	for wildlife
Work in Winona volunteer services	Work in Winona County Fairgrounds
Work in St. Anne's Hospice	Erase graffiti from public buildings
Work in Sauer Memorial Home	Work in special projects or organizations
Work in Tri-County poverty	Work for Winona Art Center
program	Repair vandalism done by others

Alternatives That Help the Offender

Personal counseling	Legal counseling
Alcohol education clinic	Alcoholics Anonymous
Driver's improvement clinic	Alcohol and drug abuse programs
Vocational education classes	Mental health center treatment
High school or college	State hospital treatment
Family services	Marriage counseling
Vocational rehabilitation center	Group counseling
Medical treatment	Employment counseling
Surrender driver's license	Stay out of a certain bar (disorderly
Sell or junk automobile	conduct)
Refrain from owning an automobile for a	Stay out of a certain store (shop-
given time	lifting)
Stay away from ex-wives, ex-husbands,	Sell, surrender, or destroy weapons
and/or relatives and certain individuals	

SOURCE: Dennis A. Challeen and James H. Heinlen, "The Win-Onus Restitution Program," in *Offender Restitution in Theory and Action,* Burt Galaway and Joe Hudson (eds.) (Lexington, Mass.: Lexington Books, D. C. Heath and Company, 1978), pp. 157, 158. Copyright 1978, D. C. Heath and Company.

is then reviewed, and together the offender and the CSO develop a sentence to propose to the judge. The judge can accept, reject, or modify this proposal; judges generally accept and impose the sentences because the CSO is able to discourage inappropriate ones.

The Winona County Court Services Department supervises the sentences and verifies the offender's fulfillment of his agreement. Credit for community service is earned at a rate of $2.50 per hour; $10 of work equals one day that could have been served in the county jail. Completion of a counseling, education, or training program may equal $100 or more. When the sentence is completed, the case is closed, but offenders are encouraged to continue their self-improvement efforts and return to the Court Services Department for counseling if new problems arise. Failure to fulfill the terms of the agreement results in imposition of the fine or jail sentence that would normally have been employed.

In addition to restitution payments, offenders have provided a wide range of services to the community. Little league hockey teams have received coaches; church carpeting has been cleaned; and junior high school students have received tutoring. Some projects have involved the joint efforts of a number of offenders—twenty persons developed an ecology project and cleaned miles of ditches along a county highway; other groups painted park benches or worked for the bicentennial committee. Day-care centers, the Parks Department, churches, the local historical society, programs for retarded children, and various government agencies have benefited from offender community service.

Evaluation.   A four-year evaluation of Win-Onus found that, of the 815 offenders who had participated in the program, only 22 (2.7 percent) were repeaters.[23] Most of the new offenses involved driving while intoxicated, disorderly conduct, or shoplifting. Thousands of dollars in restitution payments were made to victims and thousands of hours were devoted to community service projects.

❑ Minnesota Restitution Center

The Minnesota Restitution Center (MRC) provided the original model for the contemporary use of restitution and community service in a residential center. Established in 1972, the program was designed to serve as an alternative to incarceration for property offenders from the Minneapolis–St. Paul area who were sentenced to two years or less.[24]

To be eligible for the program, an offender must have served four months in prison and have the earning power to make restitution within the time remaining on his sentence. Chronic recidivists, professional criminals, and dangerous offenders were not accepted into the program; middle-class persons who could make restitution without the center's assistance were also excluded. The program's director described MRC residents in the following way: "We end up with a pretty homogeneous kind of client, by and large relatively passive . . . inadequate type of guys who can't cope with more than three things going wrong on the same day, rather than the aggressive, angry sort of guy."[25]

Program involvement begins with an orientation meeting between MRC staff and potential participants who are still in prison. Suitable candidates who volunteer for the program then negotiate individualized restitution contracts with the victims of their crime and MRC and Minnesota Corrections Authority staff members. The contract specifies the amount, form, and schedule of payment. The amount of restitution is determined by a discussion with the victim and the offender and a review of police records, presentence investigations, and court transcripts. If the victim is unwilling to meet with the offender (as many are), a parole counselor negotiates the amount of the settlement. An account for restitution payments is then established in a local bank. When the contract is fulfilled, a check and a letter of explanation are sent to the victim.

Although it was generally considered a success, the Minnesota Restitution Center was closed in 1976 because the implementation of the state's Community Correction Act reduced the number of property offenders who were being sent to prison. The program's director summarized its achievements:

> We've had some guys go through who didn't look like model citizens at the end, who still have a set of values different from yours and mine. But, if they've squared up with the original victim . . . and gained a little knowledge about themselves and about the world that will keep 'em out of jail the next time (then that's okay with us). That's as far as we want to go or ever are going to be able to go. If you can learn how to keep out of jail, that's a tall order and we'll be satisfied with that.[26]

❑ Georgia's Experiment

The Georgia Department of Corrections has developed both residential and non-residential restitution and community service programs. The programs were originally funded by LEAA in the mid 1970s, but the residential program proved to be so popular with citizens and criminal justice personnel that the state assumed funding responsibility after two years of program operations.[27] In 1989, there were eighteen residential facilities in operation.

The residential programs, known as community diversion centers, serve both probationers and parolees; restitution is normally used as a condition of community supervision, although it may also serve as an alternative to probation or parole revocation. Nonviolent property offenders of average intelligence who can make restitution within a reasonable time period are eligible for the program. Each center houses twenty to forty offenders for up to five months. Program staff usually number between eight and thirteen, supplemented by volunteers and student interns. Individual plans are developed; counseling is provided by center staff; and referrals are made to community resources for educational, vocational, medical, and legal services.

Probationers are generally required to make full or partial financial restitution as determined by the judge in cooperation with defense and prosecuting attorneys. The offender normally resides at the center until payments are completed, although he may eventually be transferred to community supervision. Parolees are normally required to live at the center for a specified time period, to maintain regular employment, and to provide community service after work and on weekends. Community service has included "work in mental hospitals, repairing houses of elderly pensioners, working with children in church and youth group recreational programs, charity work, and community cleanup projects."[28]

A 1975 study of the centers revealed that 84 percent of the residents served were probationers; most of the residents had been convicted of burglary, forgery, or theft.[29] Of the 113 offenders terminated from the program, 57 had been fully released or released to community supervision, and 56 had absconded or had been revoked from probation or parole. In 1978, it was reported that about 85 percent of the program participants are rearrested within eighteen months of release.[30]

Although the program may not be producing great reductions in recidivism, the economic benefits are considerable. During a one-year period, the residents earned a total of $128,437 in restitution payments; 8,372 hours of community service were provided. Over $150,000 was paid in state and federal taxes, and over $200,000 was spent in the local communities for clothing, transportation, recreation, and personal items.[31] In addition, the total cost of care per individual has been much less for restitution center residents than prison inmates.

Georgia's efforts to implement restitution and community service alternatives to incarceration have met with considerable success, as indicated by the support of citizens, criminal justice personnel, and legislators. This support seems to be based on the program's financial benefits to the victims and the community, the community service projects made possible by joint offender/citizen efforts, and the belief that restitution/community service is a more appropriate response to crime than most traditional dispositions.

Problems and Issues

❑ Restitution versus Victim Compensation

Restitution and victim compensation programs are the two major forms of financial assistance available to crime victims. Although both programs have similar basic objectives, they differ considerably in philosophy, procedures, and practical implications. In recent years, considerable attention has been focused on these programs' relative merits as local and state governments have attempted to develop more appropriate responses to crime and its victims.

Philosophy and Goals. Restitution programs hold individual offenders responsible for their crimes, but compensation programs attribute that responsibility to the state. They view the state as having failed to fulfill its obligation to protect the citizen from harm, and therefore compensate victims for their injuries. In compensation programs, crime victims' interests override all other factors; financial assistance is determined by victim needs, not by the ability of the criminal justice system to identify, arrest, and convict the offender, determine his ability to make restitution, and enforce a restitution agreement. It is generally argued that, if the predominant concern is victim assistance, compensation programs provide a more comprehensive means of providing financial aid. Restitution programs necessitate offender involvement because they require the offender to assume responsibility for his behavior; the state's role is limited to bringing the offender to justice, negotiating, and enforcing a settlement.

Victim Compensation Program Operations. Most compensation projects follow the same basic procedures: (1) Victim claims are screened to determine eligibility. (2) Supporting documentation is requested from claimants. (3) The case is

Victim Compensation in New York

Mr. and Mrs. Walker were shopping at their local grocery store in Brooklyn on December 14, 1974. Suddenly, a 30-year-old man entered the store, pulled out a revolver, and demanded that Mr. Walker "give it over." He then shot Mr. Walker in the stomach; Walker died before reaching the hospital.

At the time of his murder, Mr. Walker, a construction worker, was earning $1,000 a month. His life insurance policy benefits and small savings left his 44-year-old widow and 9-year-old daughter only $11,000.

Almost two years later, the New York State Crime Victims Compensation Board awarded Mrs. Walker $15,000 for the loss of her husband's earnings and as reimbursement for the funeral expenses, which amounted to $1,626.50. Mrs. Walker would receive no further crime-related benefits, and her $200-a-month

Social Security benefits from the federal government barely covered her rent. She worked as a practical nurse to supplement that income.

The defendant was tried and convicted of manslaughter. He was sentenced to serve 20 years to life in a state prison. By the time of his release, the murderer would have cost the state of New York a minimum of $220,000, based on the 1976–1977 cost of $10,537 to imprison each of the 10,020 incarcerated felons in New York State. The state corrections budget for 1976–77 was $240 million. In that same year, the crime compensation board was appropriated $3 million to give to victims.

SOURCE: J. L. Barkas, from *Victims: Violence and Its Aftermath*, 1978. Copyright © 1978 by J. L. Barkas. Reprinted with the permission of Charles Scribner's Sons.

investigated and the information provided is verified. (4) A recommendation is made to the program's award committee. (5) The final award/no award decision is made.

A 1975 study of victim compensation programs revealed that all programs in operation at that time provided compensation only to victims of violent crimes.[32] Most programs also made awards to a member of the victim's immediate family in the case of victim death. Claims normally had to be filed within one year after the crime; only injuries resulting from crimes reported to police were eligible for aid in most programs. Medical expenses and loss of support or income qualified for reimbursement in all programs; funeral expenses and pain and suffering were less frequently eligible for compensation; property loss was not a legitimate claim in any state. Most programs required the victim to have suffered a minimum financial loss before qualifying for an award; the maximum award possible was generally $10,000. The programs differed widely in the number of claims they had received, processed, and awarded. During a year's operation, claims received ranged from 50 in one state (Alaska) to 2,341 in another (New York). Awards varied from about one-third to 95 percent of all claims received.

Program Costs and Benefits. One of the most critical issues in an evaluation of the merits of victim compensation and restitution programs is the economic costs and benefits the programs incurred. Compensation programs invariably operate at a cost to the taxpayer. The 1975 survey revealed yearly costs of between $88,000 and $3,100,000, depending upon program size.[33] Restitution projects may involve financial savings to the taxpayer because they can provide community supervision or community residential alternatives to costly incarceration. Restitution payments do not necessarily involve special costs to the taxpayer because payments are made by offenders, and criminal justice officials (probation and parole officers), who would be supervising the offender even if restitution had not been required, generally supervise payment.

It is difficult to determine the relative economic benefits of restitution and compensation programs to victims. Theoretically, compensation programs could serve all crime victims; restitution programs are inherently limited to cases where offenders can be identified and required to make restitution. However, no state had yet committed itself to the enormous cost of compensating all crime victims. It is not clear whether victims today receive greater payments from compensation or restitution programs.

Resolution of the restitution versus victim compensation debate is not yet in sight. Restitution programs are currently more popular than compensation programs because of their cost benefits, the focus on offender responsibility, and fears that victims or alleged victims who inflate their losses to attain large awards may misuse compensation programs. However, compensation programs still receive considerable support; in 1977, they were operating in almost half of all the states.[34] Given the current focus of restitution programs on nonviolent property offenders and the emphasis on violent crime in compensation projects, the programs may well continue to serve complementary goals and objectives for victim assistance and offender rehabilitation.

❑ Rehabilitation, Restitution, and Community Service

Much of the recent interest in restitution and community service programs focuses upon their rehabilitative potential. Yet program implementation is not always consistent with rehabilitative goals. In most communities, restitution seems to be used not as a sole sanction or alternative to imprisonment, but as an add-on to routine punishments. Although there is some evidence that victims prefer to see restitution used in conjunction with other sanctions, this practice may make offenders feel that they are receiving double punishments. A 1980 survey of victims and offenders from 19 adult restitution programs found that offenders who were required to make restitution in addition to serving a prison sentence felt that such judgments were especially unfair.[35] Offenders viewed sole sanction or restitution plus probation as more appropriate dispositions.

Although voluntariness is viewed as essential if restitution is to exert a rehabilitative effect, it is difficult to make restitution truly voluntary. It is either used as an alternative to a more punitive disposition or added to a traditional sanction such as probation, incarceration, or parole. In both situations, restitution is at least somewhat coerced and its rehabilitative value may decline to the extent that the offender comes to view restitution as just a fine paid to a different party. When restitution becomes part of the plea bargaining process, this perspective seems inevitable.

There is also some question about the use of partial restitution as a disposition for offenders unable to make complete reimbursement within a reasonable time period. If an offender is permitted to pay back one-half or one-third of the money he stole or a small proportion of the value of goods stolen, restitution may encourage rather than discourage crime. It has been argued that such plans merely tax the criminal for his acts of thefts; the reparations not only do not restore equity, but they mock the ideal of restitution.

The confrontation of the offender and victim and their negotiations regarding the restitution agreement are designed to facilitate mutual understanding and to encourage the offender to think twice before committing another crime. In reality, such occurrences are unlikely. Victim/offender contact is extremely limited, often by victim choice. Most victims fail to fit an image likely to discourage further crime—department stores, insurance corporations, and other businesses that are awarded restitution payments may well encourage the criminal's view that the rich get richer and the poor must manage any way they can.

The rehabilitative impact of community service sentencing also merits closer examination. After studying the current use of community service sentences, Harland concluded that they are generally

> neither an alternative to incarceration nor a truly voluntary endeavor on the part of most offenders. In addition, there is doubt about the role, if any, that the possible rehabilitative effects of community service may play in sentencing decisions, and about the merit behind rehabilitative claims for service penalties. Rather, stripped of its euphemistic terminology, the "voluntary service alternative" bears a striking resemblance to the Thirteenth Amendment concept of involuntary penal servitude as a punishment for crime.[36]

The rehabilitative impact of community service sentences may be especially dubious when the nature of the service is unrelated to the offender's crime. When the offender convicted of driving while intoxicated is sentenced to pick up litter in a park, he may have difficulty understanding the symbolic nature of his actions and may view his disposition simply as forced labor. This situation is not unlikely, because volunteer work clearly related to the offender's crime is not always available or desirable. The focus is often understandably on community needs, not offender rehabilitation.

The preceding concerns indicate that neither restitution nor community service programs are inherently rehabilitative. To achieve the goal of offender change, the programs have to be designed and implemented with constant attention to therapeutic objectives. These objectives often conflict with other program aims because, like most correctional programs, restitution and community service do not provide simple solutions to the problem of crime.

☐ Enforcement of Restitution Conditions

Because restitution is frequently a condition of probation or parole, the enforcement of restitution conditions through revocation proceedings is a common problem. Imprisonment for debt is a violation of the U.S. Constitution; so probation and parole officers are extremely reluctant to consider initiating revocation proceedings unless it is clear that the offender is able, but unwilling, to make restitution payments.

Most jurisdictions permit a three-month grace period to elapse before considering enforcement efforts. Income and expenses must then be verified to ensure that the offender is financially able to meet his payment schedule. If it appears that he is economically unable to maintain his agreement, attempts are usually made formally (through a modification of probation conditions) or informally (through an agreement negotiated between the offender and the victim) to reduce the amount of restitution payments. In such cases, the payments may be spread out over a longer period or partial restitution may be allowed.

A Look at Community Service Sentences

Joseph Morris, a 29-year-old man with a long record of arrests, was using a shovel to chop up a pile of concrete and dirt that used to be a sidewalk on 116th Street in New York City's Harlem. Several other men were shoveling the debris into a battered green dumpster, to clear the way for a new sidewalk.

Down the street, standing in front of a scarred, boarded-up building, were several clusters of men, swigging seven-ounce Budweisers in the deadening summer heat. Presumably, they were carrying on 116th Street's main commercial enterprise, which is the sale of illicit drugs.

After a while, one of them strolled by, singing a song with a disco beat, apparently composed for the delectation of the workers: "Breakin' up that r-r-r-ock on the chain gang. . . ."

"What's that?" asked Morris, lifting his head to watch the stranger pass.

"Breakin' up the r-r-r-ock on the chain gang," the man sang again. He gave a big grin and waved as he left. Morris watched him, unable to speak for a moment.

"Oh, so you know about it, huh?" he finally said. Then he started shoveling again.

It was not exactly the chain gang; there were no armed guards watching Morris and his co-workers, and no chains. But Morris was wielding a shovel because he had been convicted of a crime—two police officers had found him sitting in a stolen car. Morris was serving a sentence of unpaid community service, an idea that has grown steadily more popular in recent years.

That popularity reflects something of a turnabout. The original advocates of community service, who founded dozens of programs in the late 1970s, saw it as a benign reform in the corrections system; now, the growth in community service reflects the public's demand that minor offenders who used to get off on probation receive some further punishment. "The most common political problem during the early life of community service and restitution was that it was driven by a social premise, that work was good for the offender," said Mark Corrigan, director of Brandeis University's National Institute for Sentencing Alternatives. "That was a liability, because there's been a disenchantment with doing things for the offender. . . . Now we're seeing a second wave in the growth of programs, because it's looked upon as a good way to punish. That makes it ideologically attractive to many people."

"Community service is the ideal middle ground between probation and prison," said Andrew Klein, chief probation officer of the Quincy, Mass., criminal court,

Even when the offender's financial status has been verified and his failure to make restitution is clearly a result of a reluctance to make payments and not of a limited income, probation and parole officers may still attempt to avoid revocation. If the offender has committed no crimes or other violations of community supervision, revocation may not serve the objectives of offender rehabilitation, reintegration, or community protection, the traditional purposes of probation and parole. Such proceedings place the probation or parole staff in the role of agents for a debt collection agency. Imprisonment does not result in the payment of restitution, only punishment for an offender who may otherwise be making a positive adjustment to the community. To avoid such situations, probation and parole officers have been known to juggle the books to hide an offender's failure to meet his restitution schedule.

The enforcement of restitution conditions can place the staff of supervising agencies in a difficult position. Permitting a pattern of nonpayment is clearly not desirable, but the available alternatives often provide no suitable remedy. The problems of determining offender ability and intent, the desire to encourage whatever positive adjustment has been made, and staff members' discomfort as they attempt to operate as debt collectors limit the effectiveness of enforcement strategies.

which runs one of the nation's largest community service programs. "It's satisfying to the public because they see the offenders out there doing something, and it's good for the offenders because they feel justice is being done." Joseph Morris liked doing community service for another reason. "What I like is, at night we get to go home," he said.

At first, community service programs were thought of as alternatives to jail sentences. To the dismay of some, however, it now appears that community service is not lightening the load on other parts of the criminal justice system. Though there are some exceptions, so far judges have used community service mainly to add a further sanction to probation—not to cut down on the case loads of overworked probation officers, nor to lessen the number of sentences to desperately crowded jails. And there are questions about fairness; with few exceptions, community service programs are populated by white, middle-class, first-time offenders who have committed traffic violations or petty property offenses. Often, the only poor people doing community service are there because they cannot afford to pay a fine.

This has provoked a sharp debate about the value of the community service programs now in existence. "You talk to all these nicey-nice people who think they're doing something quite decent by letting all these thousands of petty offenders do work for the community. What they're doing is actually indecent," said Jerome Miller, director of the National Center for Institutions and Alternatives (NCIA), an organization that lobbies for and helps start community corrections programs. "It's closing the door to that sanction for the people who are being sent to institutions."

Arthur Hopkins, director of the Maryland Division of Adult Probation and Parole, disagreed. "Community service has a value in itself in that offenders are giving something back to the community," he said. "There's no harm in doing that. The people going to jail now are not the Boy Scouts and virgins."

"It may be possible to expand in both directions," says Michael Smith, director of the Vera Institute of Justice, which runs the New York City program in which Joseph Morris worked. "The available consequences [of crime]—prison or probation—are often either too draconian or too soft. What we're trying to build is a new sanction. Whether that can be done, I have no idea."

SOURCE: Kevin Krajick, "Community Service: The Work Ethic Approach to Punishment," *Corrections Magazine* 8(5), 1982: 7, 8. Copyright 1982 by *Corrections Magazine* and Criminal Justice Publications, Inc., 116 West 32 Street, New York, NY 10001.

The Future of Restitution and Community Service Programs

Restitution and community service programs may be expected to continue to grow in popularity and increase in number throughout the next decade. Both seem to suit the interests and concerns of citizens and corrections professionals regarding contemporary criminal justice system objectives.

❑ Emphasis on Work/Employment

Many of today's correctional efforts seem to focus on offender employment and labor. Work is an essential element of an independent noncriminal existence; it is therapeutic and a constructive means of occupying one's time. Work benefits the individual, his family, and the community. Any correctional program that utilizes work as a central element is likely to achieve considerable support because program participation is viewed as time well spent and the aftereffects of a positive work experience may generalize to postcorrectional employment efforts.

The Vera Institute's Community Service Sentencing Project

In New York City, an assortment of thieves, pickpockets, burglars, and drug dealers are repairing apartment buildings, schools, parks, and nursing homes in an unusual community service program. The program, run by the private, nonprofit Vera Institute of Justice, is one of a handful in the country that deals with offenders who probably would otherwise go to jail.

Unlike most other programs, "We're not interested in white, middle-class offenders with fine community ties," said Michael Smith, director of the Vera Institute. "We're interested in a socially disabled population that is chronically involved in crime."

The program's participants are almost all black and Hispanic. Each has an average of seven arrests behind him, mostly for petty property crimes, and almost half have already served jail time, usually for theft, possession of stolen property, criminal trespass, or unauthorized use of a vehicle.

Vera researchers estimate that most offenders in the program would normally be sentenced to serve one to six months in jail. Few would get sentences of a year or more in a state prison because most of those who go to prison in New York have committed very serious or violent crimes, and the program does not yet accept such offenders.

A small-scale version of the program was begun in the Bronx in 1979 with a grant from the Edna McConnell Clark Foundation. Counterparts of the Bronx project opened in Brooklyn in 1980 and in Manhattan in 1981. The three programs are now funded by the city and state as part of an effort to reduce overcrowding in the city's jails. The projects will supervise about 1,000 offenders this year.

The community service sentence is not a condition of probation, nor are offenders required to go into any treatment programs. "We have begun trying to set this forth as a distinct disposition and as a punishment," said Judith Greene, director of the Manhattan program. "We don't want it to be seen as giving the guy a break, or slapping the wrist."

All offenders do a standard sentence of seventy hours, usually completed in two weeks of full-time work. "We're trying to establish a consensus of what seventy hours means," said Michael Smith. "If we're going to have a sentence that is an alternative to jail, then it's got to be one that we can enforce. . . . Right now, this is our limit."

"Ten days is a long time for our clients," said Judith Greene. "It may be the first time they've ever had to get up in the morning and be somewhere, and that in itself is onerous to them. . . . Most of them don't look past this afternoon. Time horizons for them are very short." Of the one-size-fits-all sentence, Greene said, "We've tried to build a streamlined model of the community service sentence that makes it easy for judges to use in a high-volume urban court."

Offenders who are sentenced to the program have to show up at nine o'clock the next morning. More than half of them do so without any prodding, and work every day until their sentences are over. The rest need the encouragement of warning phone calls and visits from Vera staff members. If an offender is absent from work for four days without an excuse, his name is turned over to the police warrant squad for arrest. If the police catch the offender, the judge usually resentences him to jail.

"The people we get are used to sentences that don't mean anything," said Judith Greene. "If they didn't come to see their probation officer in the past, nothing happened to them. When they realize that we are actually going to track them down, they usually just give up and do the seventy hours."

Unlike most community service projects, which farm out individual offenders to social service agencies that provide their own supervision, Vera participants all work in crews run by the project's own staff. "The people we get can be difficult to deal with," said William Rodriguez, one of the work supervisors. "It's better to have them all in one spot with someone who's used to dealing with them. . . . We have to make sure they're not running

☐ Universal Appeal

Restitution and community service can be all things to all persons. The work (and financial payments) may be considered punishment by those who view punishment as the criminal justice system's appropriate response to crime. It may be viewed as rehabilitative by individuals who support treatment as a correctional objective. In restitution and community service projects, the offender is neither let off nor into the office next door and stealing a typewriter, or wandering off to get high."

The work is hard. On a typical day, a Vera work crew may have to paint part of a building, or clean out heaps of garbage and debris from an alley, or carry pieces of sheetrock up four or five flights of stairs. In Manhattan, the crews work mainly with the West Harlem Group Assistance Corporation, a nonprofit organization that buys and rehabilitates some of the devastated tenements that occupy much of upper Manhattan. The organization employs carpenters, plumbers, and electricians to do the skilled work, while Vera participants supply the heavy labor. "It's the disgusting, hard jobs that have to be done that nobody has the money to pay for," said Lauren Pete, director of the Bronx project.

It is uncertain whether community service or the services offered by the program cut down recidivism. A recent study by Vera researchers indicated that 44 percent of the offenders who go through the program are rearrested within four months, almost all of them for petty theft. Similar offenders who serve time in jail are arrested at a slightly higher rate, but the difference is so small that it could be statistically insignificant. . . .

The average cost of the seventy-hour community service sentence is about $760—much less than it would cost to send the offender to jail, according to Vera staff researchers. The researchers estimate that offenders would serve an average of 45 days of jail time were it not for the program, and that at any one time, the program frees 95 of the city's jail cells.

In addition, the offenders do hundreds of thousands of dollars worth of work each year. (Given the inexperience of most offenders, not all the work is of the highest quality. One woman began painting a wall in a community center with a hand broom she had found, until a supervisor pointed out that it was better used for sweeping. "Oh, I thought it was a paintbrush," the woman said.) Nevertheless, the program is popular with the community groups and institutions that receive the free labor. "I wish I was articulate enough to describe what these people have done for our community," said Maurice Callender, executive director of the West

Harlem Group Assistance Corporation. Callender estimated that offenders did $85,000 worth of renovation work in the first nine months of 1982—work, he said, that has speeded up the renovation of desperately needed apartment housing to liveable conditions.

Offenders in the program are almost universally enthusiastic about it, mainly because most of them know what it is like at Rikers Island, the city's rotting, overcrowded jail. "I don't like working without pay, but when you compare ten days of this with 90 days at Rikers—whew, there's no choice," said one man who asked not to be identified. He and several others had just emerged from the basement of an abandoned tenement where they had been removing piles of trash. The basement turned out to be infested with fleas, and everyone was scratching and sweating—it was summer, and 95 degrees out—but no one was complaining. "I don't care how bad this is, it's like a reward," said another man. "This is work, but it's freedom, and I like freedom." Many offenders expressed surprise at the fact that such a program existed for them. "This community service program, this used to be for the Kennedy kids, when they got in trouble, not for blacks," said one man.

Not everyone is happy with the program. Least satisfied is the Manhattan district attorney's office, which runs a special project designed to lock up exactly the same population that Vera targets for community service. The office's Misdemeanor Trial Program is aimed at putting chronic property offenders in jail for up to a year.

"You are not punishing them by letting them loose and giving them a job," said Robert Holmes, an assistant district attorney in charge of the program. "If we can postpone another victim of crime for nine months instead of this ridiculous seventy hours, then we're doing our jobs."

SOURCE: Kevin Krajick, "This Is Work, But It's Freedom," *Corrections Magazine* 8(5), 1982: 17–19. Copyright 1982 by *Corrections Magazine* and Criminal Justice Publications, Inc., 116 West 32 Street, New York, NY 10001.

subjected to meaningless punishment, a balance that is difficult to obtain under more traditional sanctions.

❏ Economic Benefits

Correctional programs must increasingly be sold on the basis of their financial benefits. Restitution and community service are normally less costly than imprisonment, often even when residence in a community facility is a program component. Victims benefit from the restitution and the community benefits from the labor performed in service projects. Offenders and their families benefit from the offender's opportunity to obtain or maintain employment and contribute to the family's support. All these factors argue for the continued expansion of restitution and community service projects.

❑ Victim Assistance

Our concern with victims has grown considerably in recent years. Research has attempted to determine the characteristics that identify persons as vulnerable to victimization and the influence of such factors as age, race, sex, socioeconomic group, and geographic area on the patterns of victimization. Victim assistance projects have been established across the United States to provide temporary shelter, food, clothing, legal services, counseling, and financial assistance. Victims of such crimes as rape, child abuse, and wife beating have received particular attention, as have elderly crime victims.

Restitution programs provide a means of redressing victims' financial losses. They are less costly than victim compensation programs and have the added appeal of requiring the offender to accept responsibility for the reparations effort. Like community service programs, they seem ideally suited to the contemporary view of offender, victim, community, and criminal justice system relations.

The extent of support for restitution programs is illustrated by Alabama's 1980 passage of a law making restitution mandatory for certain categories of offenders. Although many judges already used restitution, the law was intended to unify its application throughout the state. The law also permits a crime victim to sue an offender in civil court for damages and to use a judge's restitution order as full proof of liability, permits a victim to make a restitution claim against an offender earning a salary in a prison work-release program, and makes restitution an absolute condition for parole in cases where the judge orders it.[37]

In the future, we may expect a growth in legal challenges to and restrictions on restitution and community service programs. Questions of fairness and equity will increasingly be raised as we attempt to serve the competing interests of offenders, victims, and the community. These and other challenges should be viewed as positive developments, for they indicate an effort to refine and improve upon ancient concepts and practices that are only now receiving the attention they deserve.

Summary

Restitution and community service programs are designed to restore what has been lost as a result of a crime. Monetary restitution programs provide financial payments from the offender to the crime victim; community service programs make symbolic restoration by requiring the offender to work in programs or on projects designed to enhance the public welfare. Both programs are normally utilized for economic offenders or persons convicted of minor crimes, who may be required to make restitution or provide community service as a condition of their probation or parole agreement.

Although the concept of restitution has been with us for centuries, until recently, it played an insignificant role in the criminal justice system. Traditionally, the state has been viewed as the injured party in a criminal offense. Only civil suits and insurance policies have served as a means of recovering victim losses. During the middle of this century, however, it was proposed that restitution might prove therapeutic to the offender as well as financially beneficial to the victim. This possibility, plus a growing concern with the problems and needs of crime victims, enabled restitution programs to gain considerable support. Community service programs were later developed in an attempt to provide creative alternatives to monetary payments. Today, restitution and community service programs are common alternatives or supplements to traditional offender dispositions because they combine benefits to the offender, the victim, and the community.

Although restitution and community service programs may appear to be relatively simple responses to the problem of crime, they are not. Various issues, including the desirability of full versus partial restitution, the low-income or unemployed offender's ability to make financial payments, the voluntariness of restitution agreements and their enforcement, and victim/offender relations in restitution projects must be addressed in any program attempting to use restitution systematically. Community service projects require the consideration of different but related problems, such as the amount of service required to pay back the community for various types of offenses and the desirability and feasibility of placing the offender in service roles related to his prior criminal activity.

Both restitution and community service programs seem to have achieved the support of the community and criminal justice professionals on the basis of their economic benefits to the victim and service benefits to the community. Although future research efforts may prove otherwise, neither program has yet been demonstrated to be an effective measure to reduce offender recidivism. However, because the programs meet contemporary views of criminal justice system objectives, they may be expected to increase in popularity and in number in future years.

KEY WORDS AND CONCEPTS			
	community restitution	equity	restitution
	centers	full restitution	symbolic restitution
	community service	partial restitution	victim compensation

NOTES

1. *Merriam-Webster Dictionary* (New York: Simon & Schuster, 1974), p. 597.
2. Burt Galaway, "The Use of Restitution," *Crime and Delinquency* 23(1), 1977: 57.
3. Ibid., p. 63.
4. Ibid., p. 60.
5. Harry E. Allen et al., *Halfway Houses* (Washington, D.C.: U.S. Government Printing Office, 1978), pp. 98–107.
6. Douglas C. Mcdonald, *Restitution and Community Service* (Washington, D.C.: U.S. Government Printing Office, 1988).
7. Joe Judson and Burt Galaway, *Considering the Victim* (Springfield, Ill.: Thomas, 1975), p. xix.

8. Ibid., p. xx.
9. Margaret Fry, *Arms of the Law* (London: Victor Gollancz, 1951), p. 126.
10. Ibid., p. xxiii.
11. American Bar Association Commission on Correctional Facilities and Services and Council of State Governments, *Compendium of Model Correction Legislation and Standards*, 2nd ed. (Washington, D.C.: American Bar Association, 1975), pp. III–48.
12. Ibid., pp. II–19.
13. Ibid., pp. II–57.
14. Ibid., pp. VIII–58.
15. John T. Gandy, "Community Attitudes Toward Creative Restitution and Punishment" (unpublished doctoral dissertation, University of Denver, 1975).
16. Robin S. Bluestein et al., "Attitudes of the Legal Community Toward Creating Restitution, Victim Compensation and Related Social Work Involvement" (unpublished master's thesis, University of South Carolina, 1977).
17. James Beha et al., *Sentencing to Community Service* (Washington, D.C.: U.S. Government Printing Office, 1977), p. 14.
18. Joe Hudson and Steven Chesney, "Research on Restitution," in *Offender Restitution in Theory and Action,* Burt Galaway and Joe Hudson (eds.) (Lexington, Mass.: Lexington Books, 1978), p. 136.
19. Ibid., p. 137.
20. Ibid.
21. Dennis A. Challeen and James H. Heinlen, "The Win-Onus Restitution Program," in *Offender Restitution in Theory and Action,* Burt Galaway and Joe Hudson (eds.) (Lexington, Mass.: Lexington Books, 1978), p. 151.
22. Ibid., p. 152.
23. Ibid., p. 155.
24. Allen et al., *Halfway Houses,* pp. 98–103.
25. Michael S. Serrill, "The Minnesota Restitution Center," *Corrections Magazine* 1(3), 1975: 16.
26. Ibid., p. 20.
27. Anne Newton, "Sentencing to Community Service and Restitution," *Criminal Justice Abstracts* 11(3), 1979: 463.
28. Ibid., p. 464.
29. Ibid.
30. Hudson and Chesney, "Research on Restitution," p. 145.
31. Anne Newton, "Sentencing to Community Service," p. 465.
32. Anne Newton, "Aid to the Victim," *Crime and Delinquency Literature* 8(3), 1976: 374–375.
33. Ibid., pp. 376–377.
34. J. L. Barkas, *Victims* (New York: Scribner, 1978), p. 185.
35. Steve Novack, *National Assessment of Adult Restitution Programs, Preliminary Report III* (Duluth: University of Minnesota Press, 1980).
36. Alan T. Harland, "Court-Ordered Community Service in Criminal Law: The Continuing Tyranny of Benevolence?" *Buffalo Law Review* 29(3), 1980: 425–486, as cited in *Criminal Justice Abstracts,* December 1980, p. 78.
37. Dean Burgess, "Crime doesn't pay, but criminals do with restitution," *The Birmingham News,* 8 August 1982, pp. 1–2B.

FOR FURTHER READING

Galaway, Burt, and Joe Hudson (eds.), *Offender Restitution in Theory and Action* (Lexington, Mass.: Lexington Books, 1978).
Hudson, Joe, and Burt Galaway, *Considering the Victim* (Springfield, Ill.: Thomas, 1975).
Newton, Anne, "Sentencing to Community Service and Restitution," *Criminal Justice Abstracts* 11(3), 1979: 463.
Schneider, Anne L., (ed.), *Guide to Juvenile Restitution* (Washington, D.C.: U.S. Government Printing Office, 1985).

6: Temporary Release Programs

Contemporary Programs
  Work Release
  Study Release
  Furloughs
Objectives
  Offender Reintegration
  Management
  Humanitarianism
  Evaluation
Historical Perspective
  Work-Release Programs: The Early Years
  Furlough Programs: The Early Years
  From Reform to Reintegration
  The Need for Prerelease Exposure to the Community
  The Development of Study Release
  Federal Prisoner Rehabilitation Act of 1965
Program Administration
  Administrative Models
  Selecting Inmates
A Closer Look at Work Release
  Specific Objectives
  Staffing the Programs
  Inmate Employment
  Economic Benefits
  Research
A Closer Look at Study Release
  Specific Objectives
  Status of Study-Release Programs
  Types of Programs Available
  Case Studies
  Effectiveness
A Closer Look at Furloughs
  Specific Objectives
  Prerelease Furloughs and Home Furloughs
  Evaluation
Problems and Issues in Temporary Release
  Violation of Regulations
  Absconding
  Crime
New Directions in Temporary Release
Summary

THE PROBLEMS CAUSED by prolonged incarceration are diverse. Vocational and social skills deteriorate; independence and self-esteem decline; family and community support systems disappear. This chapter examines some of the methods of dealing with these problems so that inmates can better adjust to the community following imprisonment. Temporary release programs permit inmates to work or study in the community prior to release or to visit the community for a specified number of days for any of a number of purposes. The primary objective of temporary release programs is to combat the effects of institutionalization and to prepare inmates for reintegration into society.

Although all the programs we discuss are designed to prepare inmates for final release from prison, each can serve additional or alternate functions as well. For example, work release is sometimes used as a sentencing disposition; inmates receiving such sentences are placed on work release immediately after imprisonment, instead of during the last part of their sentences. Furlough programs can be used as alternatives to conjugal visiting; study release can be used to supplement institutional educational programs.

Each form of temporary release can also be part of halfway house programming. An offender can live in a community correctional facility and work or study in the community during the week and visit his family (on furlough) on weekends. Incarceration in a traditional prison is obviously not a prerequisite for work release, study release, or furlough. But an offender's residence in a traditional prison, and the problems it causes, link these diverse programs as they attempt to meet a common objective. Temporary release programs provide a critical link between the imprisoned offender and the community. They are the primary means of bridging the confinement/community gap.

> The suspicion that unrelieved confinement cannot adequately prepare prisoners to function as responsible citizens after their release has been nagging serious men for at least 100 years. Yet, those whose business it is to confine society's offenders seldom seem able to acquire the strength of conviction, muster the courage, or mobilize the public support required to abandon or modify what they widely suspect to be sterile practice and, instead of pursuing courses of action more in keeping with their suppositions, these administrators tend to complacently repeat the errors of the past. At the base of this lies the average man's deep-seated and largely unresolved conflict concerning the proper means and ends of criminal justice.
>
> *Walter H. Busher*

Contemporary Programs

Temporary release programs are designed to prepare inmates for their eventual return to the community by releasing them for specified periods of time. During the release period, the inmate may work, attend school, visit with his family, or make other preparations for final release.

❑ Work Release

Work-release programs have been referred to by many names—work furlough, day parole, day pass, and community work. Regardless of the specific term employed, any program that provides for (1) the labor of prison or jail inmates in the community,

(2) under conditions of relaxed supervision, (3) for which inmates are paid prevailing free-world wages may be defined as work release. During nonworking hours, inmates on work release serve time like any other offenders. While at work, however, they labor under conditions similar (and in many cases, identical) to those of free persons. They must meet the same job requirements set for other employees, and they work with and are supervised by civilians.

As of June 30, 1988, there were almost 15,000 state inmates on work release.[1] Table 6-1 shows that some states make much greater use of work release than others. Alabama, Florida, and North Carolina each has over 1,000 inmates on work release, but many states have relatively few inmates on work release. The differences in the size of work-release populations are not simply a function of the total number of inmates in a correctional system. For example, Alabama had only 12,196 inmates in correctional institutions, but had 1,131 work releasees. Pennsylvania had 17,268 inmates in correctional institutions, but only 15 work releasees.[2] Factors such as prison overcrowding and historical events, as well as commitment to offender reintegration, have affected work-release utilization across the nation. There is every reason to believe that work-release programs will continue to expand during the 1990s.

In most jurisdictions, work-release inmates labor under conditions identical to those experienced by free men. The inmates must locate their own job and must arrange for transportation to and from employment on a daily basis. In such programs, correctional authorities may have little or no involvement with the inmate's employer. In other settings, the correctional agency or institution may employ a work-release coordinator to identify potential jobs for offenders, negotiate official agreements or informal relationships with prospective employers, and arrange for employment interviews for carefully selected inmates. In some jurisdictions, longstanding agreements between correctional authorities and large-scale employers make employment interviews unnecessary; any inmate that correctional authorities screen and recommend for the work-release program is accepted without question. Corrections employees provide inmates with transportation to and from the work place; in some instances, the employer may transport a large number of inmates to industrial or agricultural jobs.

The type of institution and its location are important influences on work-release programs. Those located near urban areas generally have access to a wide variety of employment opportunities. A rural setting may not only restrict job opportunities, but may make it more difficult for inmates to blend unnoticed into the work force of a small and tightly knit community.

Inmates confined in maximum security institutions may be expected to experience considerable conflict as they attempt to reconcile two drastically different roles— inmate and free man. Additionally, because few inmates in maximum security institutions are likely to be eligible for work release, institutional security demands and limited resources may well restrict the use of the program. Medium or minimum security institutions are more likely to provide the staff and other resources necessary to operate a smooth functioning work-release program. Custody concerns are less important in these settings and more inmates are eligible for work release; more institutional resources can therefore be diverted to work-release programs. These resources may include work-release coordinators and special counseling and security staff.

In most jurisdictions, inmates are paid directly by their employers but are required to turn their checks over to correctional authorities. Correctional officials

TABLE 6-1 Adult Inmate Population as of June 30, 1988

State	Inmate population	Number on work release	Number on furlough/ supervised release
AL	12,196	1,131	637
AK	2,497		214
AZ	11,690		
AR	5,361	279	2
CA	72,121	1,115	
CO	5,103		
CT	7,376	272	1,775
DE	3,101	180	144
FL	33,801	2,889	
GA	18,701	466	
HI	2,055	123	
ID	1,475	95	
IL	20,554	687	
IN	11,187	798	
LA	3,157		
ME	1,259	110	58
MD	13,881		
MA	6,265	494	1,389
MI	22,143		
MN	2,822	81	12
MS	6,047		
MO	12,038	483	76
MT	1,210		5
NE	2,096	230	61
NV	4,547	117	
NH	954	57	
NJ	14,413	515	
NM	2,767	101	4
NY	42,251		
NC	17,487	1,851	1,420
ND	508	7	6
OH	24,750		281
OK	9,401	119	516
OR	4,629		1,037
PA	17,268	15	419
RI	1,684	154	
SC	11,860	895	
SD	967		1,246
TN	7,381	65	16
TX	39,652		45
UT	2,010		
VA	11,953	132	
VT	770	80	
WA	6,113	660	
WV	1,138	209	10
WI	6,004		
WY	893		
Total	536,009	14,910	9,373

SOURCE: American Correctional Association, *Directory of Juvenile and Adult Correctional Departments, Institutions, Agencies and Paroling Authorities* (College Park, Md.: American Correctional Association, 1989, p. xxi). Reprinted with permission.

make deductions from the inmate's wages to cover the cost of confinement. Usually 5 to 10 percent of the inmate's pay is used to reimburse the state for room and board. Deductions may also be made to repay welfare agencies for the cost of supporting the inmate's family during his absence, to pay his debts, to make restitution, or to cover the costs of his transportation to and from employment. The remainder of the inmate's check is then deposited into his savings account. Offenders are usually required to save a specific percentage of their earnings for final release. Limited withdrawals, however, can be made during incarceration, usually to purchase cigarettes, toiletries, radios, and other personal items.

❑ Study Release

Study-release programs are very similar to work-release programs; differences are a result of the type of placement inmates receive. Study-release inmates are students rather than workers and employees. Like work-release inmates, however, they fulfill two roles—student by day and inmate by night.

Inmates on study release can attend a variety of instructional programs, including vocational and technical schools, high school, high school equivalency classes, adult basic education courses, colleges, and universities. Like other students, study-release candidates must meet the entrance requirements of their chosen educational program and must maintain the same academic standards set for all students.

Study-release program operation is influenced by the same factors that influence work-release programs. The institution's location determines the availability of educational programs. Urban environments generally offer programs for students who share common cultural backgrounds with offenders; educational programs in rural areas generally have a more restricted student body. Because few of their residents are generally eligible for study release, maximum security institutions are generally unable to devote significant resources to the programs. Needed resources include physical facilities, such as quiet areas for late night study, and counseling and support services.

The major distinction between work and study release appears to be a product of the economic issues surrounding temporary release. Work-release programs can reduce the costs of incarceration and provide inmates with funds. Study-release programs create expenses because student tuition generally must be paid for each course undertaken. Unless inmate students can obtain financial aid or have their own personal financial resources, study release seems a financial liability when compared to work release.

Financial aid, including veteran's benefits, vocational rehabilitation funds, and basic opportunity grants, is often available to prospective study-release participants. A few states, such as South Carolina, permit inmates to earn the necessary educational funds through part-time work programs.

In most jurisdictions, funding for study-release programs is limited, so study release is not extensively utilized. Educational programs operated within institutional walls are made to serve the needs of inmate students. But financial restrictions are not the only factors limiting inmate participation in community study. Given a choice between work and study release, most inmates would probably select the employment option. Work provides an immediate financial return. Study can provide only long-term and uncertain benefits. In addition, many states require an inmate to have a job lined up to be considered for parole. Inmate students who do not have sufficient resources for self-support will find that they will be encouraged to find employment in order to be considered for release on parole. Work may provide a feeling of personal satisfaction and self-worth; for most inmates, the educational process has provided only feelings of incompetence and failure. Thus, inmate demand as well as program costs may be expected to restrict the establishment and utilization of study-release programs.

In 1988, thirty-three correctional agencies provided approximately 900 inmates with access to study-release programs.[3] This low figure, in comparison to the total inmate population, may be attributed at least partially to punitive public attitudes toward the treatment of prisoners as well as to the reluctance of prison administrators to stir up controversy within their state by offering convicted felons the opportunity to attend class with free citizens.

❑ Furloughs

Furloughs are authorized, unescorted leaves from confinement granted for specific purposes and for designated time periods. Most furloughs are for twenty-four to seventy-two hours, although they may be as short as only a few hours or as long as several weeks. Inmates are usually eligible for furloughs at regular intervals. Furloughs may be as frequent as every one or two weeks or as rare as once or twice a year. Statutes, administrative regulations, and the inmate's custody status and individual need usually determine furlough duration and frequency. Virtually all overnight furloughs are to the inmate's home or to that of a family member.

Furloughs may be granted for a variety of purposes, the most common being the following:

1. To maintain or reestablish family ties
2. To solve family problems
3. To prepare for final release, to attend employment interviews, to search for housing, to obtain a driver's license, and so forth
4. To attend a short-term educational or vocational program
5. To attend a special event in the community (for example, to speak to a civic or student group)

Underlying all these specific purposes of furlough is the reintegrative function that these temporary leaves serve. Furloughs allow inmates to "wet their feet before plunging into the mainstream of society."[4]

In some jurisdictions, the inmate and his counselor conscientiously plan furloughs in detail. They outline specific objectives for the leave and the inmate is expected to complete each one. These structured furloughs are frequently used in prerelease planning. In other jurisdictions, furloughs are not planned or structured at all. Inmates are permitted to visit their families in the community and to relax and enjoy their freedom from incarceration. These home furloughs permit an inmate to become reacquainted with family and friends, to resolve potential conflicts, and to demonstrate to himself and others that he can make it "this time."

Like work-release and study-release inmates, furloughees face transportation problems. Inmates returning to homes many miles from prison often have difficulty negotiating and financing travel arrangements. Some institutions provide funds to hardship cases, but, in many instances, the inmate must work out his own solution to the problem. Such difficulties are minor compared to those of the inmates who have no family to visit on furlough. Friends are rarely permitted to receive furloughees as temporary guests. For more than a few inmates, no friends are available in any event.

In order to permit inmates with no community ties an opportunity to spend some time in the community prior to release, volunteers are sometimes permitted to provide housing for inmates on furlough. A furlough volunteer may be a person who has visited, counseled, or tutored the inmate on a regular basis during his confinement or a representative of a civic or social group that wants to sponsor an inmate. Social service and charitable organizations are also sometimes permitted to receive inmates on furlough. For example, in New York, female inmates who have no family are often furloughed to a convent outside of New York City.

During the 1970s and 1980s, home furlough programs experienced considerable growth. In 1971, only twenty-five state correctional systems operated home furlough programs. At that time, almost 250,000 furloughs were granted annually.[5] By 1989, all of the state prison systems reported operating furlough programs.[6]

It is more difficult to determine the actual number of inmates who receive furloughs because some correctional systems maintain statistics only on the number of furloughs granted per year and not on the number of inmates released. Because many eligible inmates receive furloughs as frequently as three to six times a year, these statistics overrepresent the number of inmate furloughees. Nevertheless, the fact that thousands of furloughs are granted annually indicates that many inmates are regularly receiving temporary leaves from confinement. Generally speaking, there is one inmate participating in a furlough program for every three inmates on work release.

Willie Horton and the Presidential Election of 1988

Willie Horton, a convicted murderer serving a life term in the state prison system of Massachusetts was released on a furlough from which he did not return. His escape and subsequent crimes became a major campaign issue in the 1988 presidential election. Horton was released on a pass from prison, escaped and went on a crime spree. While on the run, he kidnapped and raped a Maryland woman and assaulted her fiance. Shortly thereafter he was arrested and tried for the attacks.

In a series of print and video ads, President Bush's campaign suggested the responsibility for Horton's crime spree lay with the liberal prison release policies, supported by Michael Dukakis, the governor of Massachusetts and the Democratic nominee for president. These liberal release policies, it was alleged, permitted dangerous offenders (like Horton) serving life sentences in prison an opportunity for temporary release to taste the fruits of freedom by visiting the community. Bush's campaign published photographs of Horton, a black, along with information about his rape victim, a white female. At the time, campaign watchers pointed out that the ad was racist and preyed upon the fears of white women. The Willie Horton issue dogged Dukakis and his supporters during the remainder of the campaign, and many observers believed that this issue was at least partially responsible for Dukakis's defeat in the presidential election.

Objectives

❏ Offender Reintegration

The primary objective of temporary release programs is to prepare the inmate for final release and to facilitate his adjustment to the community. Temporary release programs attempt to accomplish this aim by briefly exposing the offender to the demands and responsibilities of freedom while he is still within the custody of correctional authorities. The inmate may work or study in the community, renew ties with family and friends, and make specific preparations for final release. At night or after a few days of release on furlough, the inmate returns to the confines of the institution. Support services and counseling available within the institution can help him deal with role conflicts and family problems and assist him in managing increasing amounts of trust and responsibility.

Temporary release programs can be employed regardless of the offender's proximity to release. In the early stages of incarceration, participation in temporary release programs may help inmates maintain contact with the free world and minimize the effects of institutionalization. As the offender nears final release, temporary release programs can more directly focus on postrelease realities and demands. All methods of employing temporary release programs serve the same basic objectives of offender reintegration. Inmates who maintain family ties and community contact throughout incarceration face a less difficult adjustment when they are finally released.

❏ Management

Participation in temporary release programs is one of the most highly desired privileges available within prison. For this reason, work- and study-release assignments and home furloughs are often used for management purposes in correctional institutions. Good inmate behavior can be rewarded with temporary release opportunities. Violations of institutional regulations, failure to make a positive adjustment to institutional routine, an uncooperative attitude, or unwillingness to participate in institutional programs can be met with a denial of temporary release privileges. In this way, the incentive of an approval for temporary release can be used to control and manage inmate behavior.

❏ Humanitarianism

Temporary release programs serve humanitarian purposes. Offenders are provided with respites from the pains of imprisonment and are given opportunities to regain their feelings of self-worth through involvement in the normal human pursuits of work, study, and family interaction. Temporary release programs acknowledge the prisoner's basic human dignity and the essentially brutalizing effects of imprisonment.

❏ Evaluation

Temporary release programs also serve evaluative functions. An inmate placed on temporary release is provided with an opportunity to demonstrate to parole authorities that he can conduct himself responsibly in the community. After evaluating an offender's behavior on temporary release, parole officials are better able to assess his readiness for release. Without opportunities to evaluate offender behavior in free-world settings, parole authorities must rely on an inmate's institutional adjustment as a measure of appropriateness for release. Obviously, there is no necessary association between an ability to adjust to prison routine and a capacity to live responsibly in the community.

Each form of temporary release has its own objectives in addition to those already mentioned. We discuss these aims later when we consider the specific nature of work-release, study-release, and furlough programs.

Historical Perspective

Work-release, study-release, and furlough programs were not widely utilized in American correctional systems until the 1960s. However, both work-release and furlough programs were first established in U.S. prisons in the early 1900s and were available in other countries even prior to the turn of the century. These early U.S. programs operated in only a few states. Even though their operation proved successful in each jurisdiction where they were implemented, work-release and furlough programs did not spread beyond a few prison systems. Prevailing penal philosophy supported the reform of inmates within prison walls rather than in the community.

During the post–World War II years, a series of events led to increasing concern for prisoners' postrelease adjustment to the free world. Correctional efforts began to include offender reintegration as well as inmate rehabilitation. This change in emphasis led to a reemergence of work-release and furlough programs and the development of study-release programs.

❑ Work-Release Programs: The Early Years

Background.   Neither prisoner labor nor the practice of permitting inmates to work outside prison walls is a new development in U.S. corrections. Since the construction of the first correctional institutions in this country, inmates have been required to work on public projects in the community. As early as 1786, correctional reformers experimented with using public labor as a form of punishment.[7] Both the harshness of the labor and the humiliation of the public display was expected to discourage future criminality. In later years, many correctional systems used inmates to build and maintain highways, drain swamps for flood control, and fight fires. These inmates worked under armed guard and close supervision. The image of the southern chain gang is probably the most familiar version of this practice.

In the 1800s, inmates were frequently leased to private contractors for work in agriculture, industry, and construction. The contractors were expected to provide the inmates' basic needs and in return receive the offenders' labor. The lease system was especially popular in the South, although it was well accepted throughout the United States. Both businessmen and correctional officials benefited from the system. Contractors received cheap labor and the state was spared the expense of feeding and housing offenders.

The Irish System.   True work release, which pays inmates for community labor performed under relaxed supervision, probably originated in the Irish penal system. In 1854, Sir Walter Crofton, who was then chairman of the board of directors of the Irish prisons, introduced a series of reforms designed to train men " 'naturally' to a state of reformation that would justify public acceptance of the released prisoner."[8] Flogging was abolished and three stages of penal servitude were established.

The first stage consisted of at least eight months of harsh prison discipline. Inmates were placed on restricted diets and provided with little work. No vocational training was offered, but one hour of each day was devoted to instruction in and orientation to the prison system, expectations for inmate behavior during incarceration, and the futility of continuing in a life of crime.

Inmates who advanced to the second stage were transferred to another prison, where work was required. Inmates earned marks for good behavior, participation in school activities, and industriousness. These marks could be used to reduce the inmate's sentence. In addition, convicts were paid modest wages for their labor.

In the final stage, inmates were transferred to small prisons that housed fewer than one hundred men. The work required from the residents of these institutions closely resembled that engaged in by free men. Only a few unarmed guards supervised offenders as they worked in the community. These final units served as filters between imprisonment and release on parole.[9] Trust was placed in the convict, giving him a chance to prove his ability to handle responsibility and permitting the community to witness the offender's trustworthiness. To ensure that reform was accomplished, lectures in morality and the benefits of regular employment were provided.

Although British penologists considered the Irish system a success, the practices Crofton introduced received only limited use. Then, as now, public demand for more severe punishment of offenders tended to overshadow the proposals of reform-minded citizens.

Work Release in the United States.   Work release first appeared in the United States in Vermont in 1906.[10] Vermont sheriffs had previously been authorized to assign inmates to various forms of work. A few enterprising law enforcement officials used their authority to permit carefully selected inmates to work in the community.

Seven years later, the first formal work-release program was developed in Wisconsin. The program was created by the Huber Law, which was named for the state senator who introduced the legislation. This law established a county-administered correctional program known as day parole for misdemeanants. With the permission of the sentencing judge, inmates serving terms of one year or less could be "paroled" during working hours to labor in the community. These inmates were paid generally acceptable wages for their work. In return for this opportunity, offenders were expected to pay for their own room and board during incarceration and to provide (to the best of their ability) for the support of their families. The inmates' earnings were collected by the county sheriff, who was responsible for making the appropriate deductions and administering the program.

A number of factors led to the establishment of Wisconsin's work-release program. Many of its proponents were concerned about inmate idleness and the opportunities for vice and corruption generated by the absence of meaningful activity in local jails.[11] Work release was viewed as economically desirable because it could offset jail costs and the expenses required to maintain an inmate's family. The program's most immediate objective, however, was to free up a large number of able-bodied men for the labor market. Wisconsin was experiencing a labor shortage and it was hoped that work release could meet some of the employment demand.[12]

Although Wisconsin's work-release program was generally considered to be a success, there was virtually no further development of work-release programs for almost fifty years. Then, in 1957, North Carolina implemented a work-release program similar to Wisconsin's. Although it was originally restricted to misdemeanants in local institutions, the program was soon expanded statewide, and the eligibility criteria for participation was broadened to include felons. This move represented a significant development in the history of work release. The extensive development of work release in North Carolina was probably influenced more by the existing organizational structure of that state's prison system than by a commitment to offender reintegration.[13]

Prior to the 1950s, North Carolina's prison system had been a division of the state's Department of Transportation. Inmates were the principal source of labor for highway construction and maintenance. To accommodate this labor force, a large number of small, minimum to medium security prisons had been constructed throughout the state. These facilities were intended to house inmates only during their nonworking hours; little or no education, training, or counseling was provided. When the Department of Corrections was made an independent agency and inmate labor on public highways was severely restricted, North Carolina prison officials were left with a large number of institutions that were ill suited to rehabilitative programs. Work release seemed to provide the most promising solution to the problem. Inmates could be provided with on-the-job skills, and the state, the offender, and his family could benefit financially from the program. At the same time, inmates would not be required to spend more than a few of their waking hours within the institution.

North Carolina's legislature was apparently convinced of the value of work release. The number of eligible inmates increased every year between 1957 and 1967, until North Carolina was operating the largest institutional work-release program in the United States.[14]

□ Furlough Programs: The Early Years

The first organized furlough program implemented in the United States was established in Mississippi in 1918.[15] Ten-day holiday leaves were permitted to prison farm inmates who had served at least two years of sentences of three or more years. Selected offenders were generally allowed to spend the Christmas period with their families. Four years later, Arkansas established a similar program for inmates who were eligible for parole. To be approved for furlough, an inmate had to be a good security risk and must have made a positive adjustment to prison life.[16] In both states, relatively few inmates were actually released on furloughs.

These early furlough programs were designed to serve a mixture of humanitarian and control purposes.[17] Home furloughs were viewed as a means of providing the inmate with a respite from the pains of imprisonment while enabling him to maintain family ties. Furloughs were also one of the most highly desired privileges available to inmates and thus were expected to serve as powerful incentives to good behavior.

Like work-release programs, furlough programs developed slowly in the United States. Although furloughs were widely utilized in Europe and Latin America to assist the inmate's maintenance of family ties, no additional furlough programs were established in the United States for over forty years.

❑ From Reform to Reintegration

Correctional administrators' reluctance to establish work-release and furlough programs can be attributed to the reform philosophy that dominated correctional thinking in the early 1900s.[18] At that time, the generally accepted aim of incarceration was to remove the offender from the evil influences found in the community. Correctional efforts were to reform the inmate through educational programs and emphasize good work habits and moral values. The offender was to be released only when he was strong enough to withstand the temptations of the free world. In reality, most prisoners received more punishment than reformation.

The isolationist approach to corrections began to lose support shortly after World War II. Correctional workers who had recently passed through separation centers during the demobilization of the armed forces became aware of the need for similar programs to facilitate inmates' transition from prison to the community.[19] Institutional prerelease programs developed as a result of this concern, providing inmates with basic information about employment opportunities, obtaining and keeping a job, and parole regulations.

❑ The Need for Prerelease Exposure to the Community

Although institutional prerelease programs benefited the individuals who completed the instruction, they were necessarily limited in their effectiveness. One of the greatest problems in prerelease preparation was the difficulty of maintaining inmate interest in lecture and discussion groups and in creating a realistic focus on potential problems in community adjustment.[20] Because the inmates were institutionalized during instruction and had frequently spent several years without substantial community contact, it was easy for them to underestimate the problems they might encounter. A means of briefly exposing inmates to the demands of the free world was required so that they could more readily perceive and understand the problems that might develop in their transition to freedom. At the same time, it was necessary to maintain control over offenders during the prerelease period so that they would not be overwhelmed and so that counseling and advice could be offered.

Work-release and furlough programs seemed to be the ideal means of preparing inmates for final release. Inmates placed on work release could learn good work habits and earn money for use after release while they gradually adjusted to the free world. Furloughed offenders could renew family ties and seek employment and housing during their brief community visit. More important, they could walk the streets, eat in restaurants, travel on buses, shop in department stores, and engage in all other forms of endeavor that would soon be available to them as free men. Such simple activities could serve to reduce the culture shock they might otherwise experience.

□ The Development of Study Release

It was recognized that not all offenders were ready for employment in the community. Some inmates would need to improve their academic or vocational skills prior to work; others might be able to increase their employment potential substantially by completing high school or college. Study-release programs were created for these individuals. Study-release programs were identical to work-release projects except for the nature of the inmate's community placement. Rather than working in the community, selected inmates became students in vocational and technical schools, basic and adult education programs, and colleges and universities.

□ Federal Prisoner Rehabilitation Act of 1965

The greatest impetus for the development and expansion of work-release, study-release, and furlough programs came from the federal government. In 1965, Congress passed legislation that provided for work release, study release, and furloughs for inmates in the Federal Bureau of Prisons. This legislation authorized the attorney general to "extend the limits of the place of confinement of a prisoner to whom there is reasonable cause to believe he will honor his trust," by authorizing him, under prescribed conditions, to

> (1) visit a specifically designated place or places for a period not to exceed thirty days and return to the same or another institution or facility. An extension of limits may be granted . . . for any . . . compelling reason consistent with the public interest; or
> (2) work at paid employment or participate in a training program in the community on a voluntary basis while continuing as a prisoner of the institution or facility to which he is committed.[21]

In this act, Congress linked work-release, study-release, and furlough programs both operationally and conceptually. It became federal correctional authorities' responsibility to develop the eligibility criteria and screening process necessary to select appropriate inmates for an extension of the limits of confinement. Because of the temporary nature of these extensions, the three programs came to be known as temporary release programs. The linking of these programs with the information and counseling services recently developed for inmates approaching final release from incarceration was referred to as graduated release.

Today, temporary release programs are authorized in almost every state. They offer the best strategies currently available to assist incarcerated offenders in their transition to freedom.

Program Administration

❑ Administrative Models

In most correctional institutions and systems, a single organizational unit is charged with the responsibility of administering all temporary release programs. This linking of work-release, study-release, and furlough programs simplifies program operation. Each form of release requires the selection of appropriate candidates for release and the development and approval of suitable community assignments or furlough residences. These activities are most easily carried out by a single organizational unit.

Three models for temporary release program administration are currently employed in the United States: the local, state, and mixed administration models.[22]

Local.   The local model is patterned after Wisconsin's first work-release program. The sheriff or other criminal justice official responsible for the county or city jail usually administers temporary release at the county level. Under this model, judges are authorized to place convicted misdemeanants on work or study release as a condition of their sentence. Furloughs are infrequently granted under this model because sentences are usually short and inmates of local jails are generally confined within their own community. They are therefore less likely to feel the effects of institutionalization and loss of family ties than felons imprisoned in remote areas of their state.

The sheriff is responsible for implementing the judge's orders on a day-to-day basis. Generally, his temporary release responsibilities are limited because the programs are small. Judges tend to be conservative in their use of work- and study-release dispositions. In some jurisdictions, only persons already working or attending school in the community are sentenced to work or study release.

A more significant influence on the size of locally administered temporary release programs is the availability of pretrial diversion programs and intensive probation services.[23] Pretrial diversion programs remove the best risks—the first offenders with strong community ties—from the criminal justice system. Those not diverted, who continue through the system, are most frequently placed on probation. Where intensive services are available for high-risk offenders, many of those misdemeanants who would otherwise have been jailed are placed on special probation case loads. These programs tend to take the offenders who would qualify for work or study release. The growth of community-based corrections has thus in many ways reduced the demand for work- and study-release programs in local jails.

State.   Under the state model, the responsibility for operating temporary release programs is vested in the state corrections department; offenders placed on temporary release are inmates of state correctional facilities. State parole authorities are sometimes authorized to participate in the screening of eligible inmates for temporary release approval, but the corrections department retains primary responsibility for the routine functioning of work-release, study-release, and furlough programs. A temporary release unit is generally established with the state correctional agency. Its task is to interpret and develop administrative guidelines for program operations throughout the state, including specific procedures for screening eligible inmates for temporary release and formal approval of release requests.

In most states, complex decision-making networks are established to screen candidates for temporary release. Inmate requests for temporary release are first reviewed at the institutional level and then referred to the central office. A typical request might be sequentially reviewed by an inmates' counselor, an institutional temporary release committee composed of representatives of both custody and program staff, the warden or superintendent or his designee, a central office temporary release committee, and, in some states, the commissioner of corrections. At each level of review, the inmate's risk to the community, need for a temporary release assignment, institutional adjustment and behavior, and the recommendations of institutional staff members who know the inmate well may be considered. The system is designed to ensure that only the most deserving and trustworthy offenders are granted temporary release. Department guidelines and procedures often restrict program participation far beyond statutory provisions.

State-operated temporary release programs frequently employ specialized staff members to develop jobs for inmates placed on work release, to establish contacts with educational institutions, and to arrange for the transportation of all temporary releasees. Special clerical staff may handle the massive amounts of paperwork that temporary release programs can generate. Counselors who focus their efforts on temporary releasees' problems may also be available, although such services are usually rather limited.

Mixed.   The mixed model attempts to ensure that state-administered temporary release programs consider community interests regarding the placement of offenders on temporary release. Although state correctional agencies are responsible for the routine operation of temporary release programs, state and local authorities share the responsibility for recommending and/or approving inmates for temporary release. At the time of sentencing, judges may recommend a temporary release placement for an offender sentenced to imprisonment in a state correctional institution. Prior to granting temporary release to an inmate not recommended for such a placement by the sentencing judge, that same judge may be contacted by state authorities and asked for his assessment of the appropriateness of a temporary release assignment. If the sentencing judge recommends against placing the inmate on temporary release, he would generally not be released. Even if the sentencing judge initially makes a recommendation for temporary release, correctional authorities can deny the privilege.

This model is somewhat cumbersome and can produce delays in the processing of temporary release requests. Problems may arise when sentencing judges are asked to reflect on the suitability for release of inmates sentenced years earlier. This model has the advantage of ensuring that temporary release placements do not conflict with the original aim of the inmate's sentence. Potential community response to the offender's release can also be assessed, which is especially important when the inmate will be returning to the community in which his offense was committed.

❑ Selecting Inmates

The selection of inmates for temporary release programs is generally a product of the application of statutory and administrative eligiblity criteria and individualized evaluations of the appropriateness of specific inmates for release. Resource availability also restricts program participation. If no work or educational placements are available or if no arrangement can be made for an offender's residence on furlough, program participation is not possible.

In the local model, statutory requirements and judicial evaluations determine inmate selection. Few jailers place additional restrictions on offender participation beyond those imposed by inadequate resources. Statutes generally permit the sentencing of certain categories of offenders, such as misdemeanants, to work or study release. Judges have broad discretion to select from among eligible offenders the persons they consider most appropriate for temporary release. Although the factors considered in making these judgments depend upon individual sentencing philosophies, potential community reaction, the need to ensure community protection, and the potential benefit of the sentence to the offender will invariably be considered.

In the state and mixed models of temporary release, state department of correction policies will significantly influence inmate selection for temporary release. As in the local model, statutory restrictions on eligibility are generally limited and correctional authorities have broad discretion in developing their own administrative guidelines. In most jurisdictions, these administrative directives restrict program participation beyond statutory requirements. For example, in North Carolina, all inmates who have sentences of less than five years are eligible by statute for work release. (Inmates serving longer terms must receive special approval by the parole commission.) North Carolina employs a mixed administrative model, and judicial recommendations are considered prior to placing an offender on work release. Inmates who were not recommended for work release at the time of sentencing must meet the following departmental conditions:

1. The inmate must have served a minimum of 10 percent of his sentence.
2. The inmate must have attained minimum custody by the date he is to begin participating in work release.
3. The inmate must not have had an escape within six months of the approval.
4. The inmate must not have had a major infraction within three months of approval.
5. If the inmate is serving a sentence for a serious sexual or assaultive crime (or has such a history), the approving authority for minimum custody is the director's review committee.[24]

North Carolina inmates who are recommended for work release by the court are excluded from program participation if they fail to meet the third and fourth departmental requirements.

North Carolina's temporary release policy is fairly representative of program eligibility requirements. Eligibility requirements in most states specify that time served, custody status, escape risk, institutional adjustment, offense, and offense history must be considered prior to temporary release approval. These requirements are established to ensure that released inmates earn their assignments through good institutional behavior and that the community will not be endangered by the release of an offender who is likely to abscond and/or commit a serious crime while on temporary release.

Not all inmates who are eligible for temporary release under statute or administrative directive are placed on work or study release or approved for furloughs. Each inmate's application for temporary release is rigorously examined and screened, generally by both institutional and departmental correctional authorities. Special approval by top-level parole or corrections officials may be required for offenders convicted of dangerous crimes. At each level, the offender's potential threat to the community is reevaluated and inappropriate candidates are rejected.

The degree of subjectivity that enters into the decision-making process varies from jurisdiction to jurisdiction. In most states, administrative guidelines identify the offenders who should be excluded. Institutional authorities thus have considerable discretion to determine who from among the remaining inmates should be granted temporary release. Virtually all statutes and departmental regulations contain statements indicating that temporary release is, under all circumstances, to be considered a privilege rather than a right.

A few states have attempted to develop temporary release point systems similar to those employed in pretrial release programs. The Vera Institute of Justice, which initiated the first pretrial release program in the United States, was instrumental in developing a point system for the New York Department of Correctional Services' temporary release program. Such innovations usually encounter considerable resistance from institutional staff, who argue that the temporary release approval process requires individualized decision making, not uniformity. The use of objective criteria is said to be insufficient to exclude potentially dangerous offenders from temporary release program participation. Correctional staff often argue that discretion is needed so that temporary release can be used as an incentive to encourage inmates into institutional programs and desirable behavior patterns. If temporary release is made automatic upon the accumulation of a specific number of points, some of the ability to fit eligibility requirements to inmate needs will be lost. A less frequently voiced, but underlying, criticism is the loss of personal power that a point system would introduce into correctional systems. Staff members responsible for temporary release approval understandably resist a significant loss of authority.

A Closer Look at Work Release

❏ Specific Objectives

In many ways, work release appears to be a program that is all things to all people. Depending upon the philosophy and position of the person questioned, immediate economic conditions, and prevailing correctional policy, a variety of specific aims are revealed. One observer recently remarked that work-release programs are usually established first and justified later.[25]

A national survey of correctional adminstrators conducted in the late 1960s identified the following objectives of work-release programs:

1. Ease the inmate's transition to the community
2. Provide the inmate with a job
3. Help the inmate support himself
4. Help the inmate support his dependents

James Brown, Social Worker with Soul
by Jon Pareles

AIKEN, S.C., May 1—The Godfather of Soul is glad to have a day job. Two days away from his 57th birthday, James Brown is working here as a spokesman for the Aiken/Barnwell Counties Community Action Commission, a nonprofit agency serving the poor and elderly. The job keeps him out of jail under a work-release program, and for the moment he is speaking more like a social worker than a rock star.

"We're working with the kids, we're working with the homeless, we're trying to train young people for jobs," Mr. Brown says. "I go to schools, we go to different organizations, seminars, addressing the young people, and we try to keep a focus on what we're about here. Hopefully, we'll get across to someone that needs help and someone who also can support the organization. There's not enough money to go around. It's like the story of Christ, two little fish and five loaves of bread to feed oh so many."

In Jail Since 1988

But Mr. Brown has been off the scene for about a year and a half. In December 1988, he began serving a six-year sentence at the State Park Correctional Center for failing to stop his pickup truck for a police officer, and for aggravated assault. The sentence was the result of a high-speed chase that began after Mr. Brown carried a shotgun into an insurance seminar that was taking place next to his office in Augusta, Ga. Fleeing the seminar, he got into his truck, was pursued by the police and drove across the nearby South Carolina border, where he was arrested.

In Georgia, the same chase resulted in a six-year sentence (which he is serving concurrently in South Carolina) on charges including carrying a deadly weapon at a public gathering, attempting to flee a police officer and driving under the influence of drugs. Mr. Brown was already on probation in Georgia after being convicted of assault and battery in an incident involving a policeman.

For the last two weeks, Mr. Brown has been in the state's work-release program, confined to the minimum security Lower Savannah Work Center here when he's not on the job. Yet at the moment, he doesn't look like an inmate.

SOURCE: *New York Times,* May 3, 1990. Copyright © 1990 by The New York Times Company. Reprinted by permission.

5. Help determine the inmate's readiness for release
6. Preserve the inmate's family ties
7. Enhance the inmate's sense of self-worth and responsibility
8. Build good work habits[26]

All temporary release programs share several of these objectives. The primary distinctions lie in the areas of economic benefits and the development of good work habits. Only through work release can an offender earn money for himself, his family, the state (through payments to offset the costs of incarceration), and the victim (when the sentencing judge orders or recommends restitution). Only through gainful employment under normal working conditions can an inmate develop and practice the skills required to maintain and excel in a job.

A more recent survey of eighty county work-release administrators was reported in 1979.[27] It revealed a broad range of perceived objectives (table 6-2). The aim of transition received relatively little emphasis, primarily because inmates in county jails generally serve short sentences in their own communities. The transition to freedom following release is not very demanding. In other areas, the specific objectives identified are similar to those revealed in the earlier study—offender rehabilitation, economic benefits, and family stability.

Witte conducted one of the more interesting studies of the goals of work-release programs in North Carolina in 1973.[28] Prior to evaluating the effectiveness of a work-release program in one region of the state, a team of researchers interviewed institutional staff members to obtain their perceptions of program objectives. The study revealed the following aims:

1. Provide inmates with a stable work record and job experience
2. Permit inmates to keep their families together and support their dependents
3. Provide inmates with new job skills
4. Provide inmates with jobs upon release
5. Influence inmate contact with the community in a positive way[29]

In an attempt to determine if the work-release program was accomplishing these specific objectives, the researchers interviewed a sample of released inmates who had been placed on work release during incarceration and a control group of released inmates who had served their entire sentences under total confinement. A comparison of the two groups revealed that:

1. Inmates who had been placed on work release had greater work stability and lower unemployment rates and received higher wages following release than the control group.
2. Participation in work release had little effect on family stability.
3. Work-release inmates learned few job skills during their temporary release assignments because they were generally placed in unskilled jobs.
4. Inmates on work release frequently had jobs awaiting them upon final release, but were more likely to switch jobs soon after release than the control groups.[30]

TABLE 6-2 Work-Release Program Goals Identified by County Work-Release Administrators

Goal references	Number and percentage of administrators mentioning the goal at least once	
	Number	Percentage
Alternative to total confinement	23	29%
Reshape conceptions of the prisoner	8	10
Economic benefits	54	68
Maintenance of labor force	26	33
Vocational	25	31
Transition	16	20
Family stability	42	53
Reformation of inmate	71	89
Attitudinal	21	26
Behavioral	52	65
General	47	59
Punitive	2	3
Specific deterrence	18	23
General deterrence	2	3
Program improvement	28	35

SOURCE: John Moore and Stanley Grupp, "Work-Release Administrators' Views of Work Release," *Offender Rehabilitation* 3 (1979): 196. Reprinted with permission.

The number of inmates in each sample was small; some aspects of the research methods raise questions about the validity and generalizability of the findings to other work-release programs. Nevertheless, perceived work-release objectives may not accurately reflect program impact.

Two years later, the research team returned and once again interviewed staff members about the aims of work release.[31] The interviewers found that the perceptions of objectives had changed considerably. Now the purposes of work release were described as:

1. Reducing inmate recidivism
2. Reducing the tax burden by requiring inmates to reimburse the state for incarceration costs
3. Providing inmates with the personal satisfaction of gainful employment in order to further rehabilitation efforts
4. Controlling inmate behavior through the use of work release as a reward for appropriate institutional conduct[32]

The reasons for these changes in viewpoint were not fully explained. It is apparent, however, that the preceding objectives indicate a greater concern with the problems of crime, institutional management, and the costs of incarceration than the earlier, more optimistic objectives that focused on family and employment needs.

More recently, work-release programs have been used to reduce overcrowding in major institutions. According to a survey conducted by the Corrections Compendium, eighteen states reported the use of these programs to relieve overcrowding in major institutions.[33]

❑ Staffing the Programs

The number and type of staff assigned to a work-release program are influenced by the administrative model in use, the correctional agency's penal philosophy, and its commitment to work-release programs. Generally, one of two staffing patterns is employed.

The first approach is a "make do" procedure. The work-release program is authorized, and existing staff members are assigned various responsibilities for program operation. These new and additional responsibilities often place considerable burdens on staff members and require them to choose between competing (and sometimes conflicting) demands on their time. Because work-release duties are the new and less familiar assignment, the employee's original job is likely to receive a greater commitment. The work-release program may suffer because staff priorities favor competing assignments.

The second approach requires hiring new staff members, who may be recruited and trained to serve as work-release specialists in the areas of job development, security, and counseling. These specialists direct most of their efforts toward work-release responsibilities and are given few unrelated institutional assignments.

When resources permit, the second approach is obviously preferable to the first. The development of a quality work-release program is enhanced when program administrators can improve their job performance through training and specialization. But when no additional funding is available, some interested and dedicated staff members have been able to operate valuable programs even under difficult conditions. The motivation of staff members who are assigned to new programs is clearly a critical factor.

❑ Inmate Employment

Limitations.   The availability of employment opportunities is a major factor in the success of a work-release program. If opportunities are limited, even the most eligible and appropriate candidate for temporary release will be unable to participate in the program. When jobs are plentiful, many eligible inmates can be placed on work release; offenders may be able to find meaningful jobs that will be available for them even after final release.

Three factors limit inmate employment opportunities. The location of the institution is of paramount importance. Unfortunately, many of our major correctional institutions were built before the aims of community-based corrections achieved general acceptance. These prisons were built when the "out of sight, out of mind" philosophy prevailed and are thus frequently located in remote areas. Isolated and rural settings rarely offer numerous meaningful job opportunities for urban offenders.

The incidence of unemployment in the local labor force exerts considerable influence on inmate employment opportunities. When unemployment rates increase, the number of jobs available to inmates shrinks. This curtailment is partly a result of a reduction in the actual number of jobs; it also reflects the widespread belief that inmates should not displace noncriminal citizens from the employment market. In many states, this belief has been incorporated into laws governing the operation of work-release programs. The Federal Prisoner Rehabilitation Act also requires the consideration of local employment conditions prior to the granting of work-release privileges. According to the act, federal inmates cannot be placed on work release unless:

1. Representatives of local union central bodies or similar labor union organizations are consulted.
2. Such paid employment will not result in the displacement of employed workers, be applied in skills, crafts, or trades in which there is a surplus of available gainful labor in the locality, or impair existing contracts or services.
3. The rates of pay and other conditions of employment will not be less than those paid or provided for work of similar nature in the locality in which the work is to be performed. (See Public Law 89–176, 1965.)

The last requirement indicates a concern that inmates might unfairly compete with citizens by accepting lower wages or less satisfactory working conditions than free persons. Inmates might well prefer low wages and poor working conditions to total confinement; so this requirement ensures that inmates have no unfair advantage over other prospective employees. It also protects inmates against exploitation by employers seeking cheap labor for difficult or unpleasant work.

Employer willingness to hire inmates significantly affects work-release program operations. As we discuss more fully in chapter 12, many employers are reluctant to hire ex-cons. The idea of hiring a con who is not yet an ex may be even more unappealing. The prospective employer may fear the offender, thinking he is dangerous and likely to steal. Some employers argue that inmates have little to lose when they commit a crime while on work release because they will only get more of the same punishment—prison—if they are caught. Other employers are unwilling to reward inmates with jobs. These attitudes seem to be changing as more and more people realize that crime rates for inmates on temporary release are extremely low and that inmates have a great deal to lose if they commit a crime during release— the chance of ever being placed on temporary release again. They may also face a penalty for the new crime committed and/or for absconding. Additionally, the public is gradually accepting the fact that work release provides not a reward for previous offenses, but a chance to avoid a future of crime.

Finding a Job. Assuming that employment is available in the local community, the inmate is faced with the task of finding a job. For most inmates, this was no easy matter when they were free. While confined, inmates may find the difficulties insurmountable.

One of the best ways to obtain a job is through personal contacts.[34] If the inmate has friends or family in the surrounding community, they can identify prospective jobs. When this approach is not available or does not work, other procedures must be tried. Some progressive correctional systems permit inmates to explore local job opportunities in short-term (3–6-hour) furloughs. During the leaves, they knock on doors and visit public employment services. If furloughs are not permitted for job hunting, inmates must resort to letter writing and sometimes telephone calls to potential employers. The telephone book and newspaper want ads are the principal sources of job information for these applicants.

Some work-release programs employ specialized staff members as job developers. Their primary task is to seek out job opportunities from local employers. This is not always an easy task. Job developers must be part salesman and part employment counselor. They must sell the idea of work release to the business community, identify the right inmate for the job, and make sure that both inmate and

---

The Problems of Finding a Job

A counselor in the Duval Adjustment center for female offenders (Jacksonville, Florida):

A lot of places, they say sure they agree with the program and all but they don't want to be the first one to hire a woman from the center, yet the ones who do hire say ours are the best, always there and always on time. I have girls here with key punch experience, dental experience, and I can't get them a job. I can sit there and tell the employer, "I've known this woman for three months. She's clean and cooperative." Yet they'll hire someone off the street they know nothing about.

A job counselor in a correctional center for men (Jacksonville, Florida):

Job placement this time of year is extremely difficult. There are fewer jobs and we're in constant competi-

tion with free people. Some men are cooks or welders or doing warehouse work. Most are unskilled and work as laborers. Forty percent make the minimum wage. I try to get it up around $3 an hour, and I try to be sure that the inmate makes no less than the other workers.

An inmate, on informing prospective employers of his status:

Some people are real nasty off the bat. Some are cordial at first but when they find out where you're from they get indignant. I think when you go in and try to be honest it doesn't work.

SOURCE: Joan Potter, "The Dilemma of Being Half In and Half Out," *Corrections Magazine*, June 1979, p. 67. Copyright 1979 by *Corrections Magazine* and Criminal Justice Publications, Inc., 116 West 32 Street, New York, N.Y. 10001.

employer live up to their employment agreements. If significant problems arise from either the inmate's or the employer's perspective, the entire work-release program will suffer, and the job developer will often be held responsible.

Obtaining Job Approval. Once the inmate has secured a job, his path is still not clear; his employment must be approved by the correctional agency. Statutes or administrative regulations in many states prohibit inmates from employment in certain jobs that might bring them into contact with undesirable elements. For example, employment in legalized gambling establishments, such as race tracks, casinos, or jai alai games, may not be permitted.

In evaluating the suitability of a job, correctional agencies may utilize formal or informal criteria. North Carolina's requirements are both explicit and representative. Inmate job plans are reviewed to ensure that:

1. The job is within the inmate's capability.
2. The job pays the prevailing wage.
3. The employer is legitimate.
4. There is a possibility of continued employment after release.
5. There are no other criminal elements present.
6. Transportation to the job site is available.
7. The job provides some type of supervision.[35]

If an inmate's prospective job meets these requirements, he is recommended for work release. If his employment plan fails to meet these criteria, he must find another job.

Types of Jobs Held. Inmates preparing for work release can anticipate filling a need for unskilled and low-paying labor. Very few are able to secure jobs that are skilled or semiskilled; few work-release jobs pay more than the minimum wage. Although a small number of inmates enter incarceration with marketable and well-paid skills, enabling them to obtain work-release employment within their areas of expertise, these persons provide the exception to the rule. A lack of resources prohibits the development of extensive and up-to-date vocational training programs in most correctional institutions; so inmates are generally ill prepared for all but the most menial labor.

An illustration of typical work-release positions and earnings is provided in table 6-3, which describes jobs secured and wages paid to work releasees in North Carolina.

❏ Economic Benefits

Some of the most attractive features of work release are the economic benfits to be derived from inmate earnings. The inmate is able to put some money aside for his final release and can withdraw small amounts from his savings for personal expenses during incarceration. City, county, state, and federal governments can increase their revenues because inmates pay taxes on their earnings. The department of corrections reduces operating costs because deductions are made from the inmate's wages to cover room and board; transportation costs to and from the inmate's place of employment are also deducted. The inmate's family is provided for because

TABLE 6-3 Typical Job Placements of Work Release in North Carolina

Female inmates	*Male inmates*
Job	*Job*
Waitress	Barber
Seamstress	Floorman
Nursing assistant	Stockroom clerk
Kitchen aide	Laborer (construction)
Salad preparer	Machine operator
Cleaner	Laborer
Machine operator	Mechanic's helper
Carpenter's helper	Cook's helper
Secretary	Cook
Receptionist	Helper
Technician	Laborer (moving)

SOURCE: Work-release employment data provided by North Carolina Dept. of Corrections, Division of Prisons (June 20, 1979).

part of the inmate's earnings are contributed to family support. And finally, the victims of crime may receive some financial compensation because offenders placed on work release can make restitution for their crimes.

The amount of money that can be made, saved, and paid out by work releasees is high. The financial benefits of work release have rarely gone unnoticed by correctional authorities. The State of Florida reports that inmates have earned over $150 million in its work-release program. In addition, prisoners on work release have paid over $1 million in court costs and fines, over $22 million in taxes and social security, $55 million in subsistence and transportation costs, and over $11 million toward the support of their dependents.[36] In Alabama, where the state operates ten work-release facilities, inmates earned over $2 million in 1989.[37] Of that amount $552,951 went to the state in the form of payments for room and board, an additional $103,124 was paid to the state for transportation reimbursement, $97,703 was collected in restitution, and over $200,000 was paid in income taxes.

Clearly, work-release programs provide considerable economic benefits. Although most calculations of these benefits fail to take into account the costs of operating work-release programs, program financial assets undoubtedly far outweigh liabilities. No other single correctional program provides such a large return for a relatively small investment.

❏ Research

Studies of the effectiveness of work-release programs generally attempt to measure program success in terms of one or more of the following criteria: (1) economic benefits, (2) postrelease recidivism, (3) attitudinal change, and (4) postrelease employment patterns. The only real consensus regarding the effectiveness of work-release programs is found in the area of economic benefits. Virtually all studies that have

An Inmate's Perspective on Work Release

"I've been a burglar all my life," said Edward Cohran, a genial 42-year-old with thinning blond hair. Cohran, who had been in and out of prison many times since he started breaking into pay phones when he was a teenager, sat at ease in an office of a building supply company where he was employed as a shipping supervisor. Nights and weekends, Cohran lived at the community work-release center in Jacksonville, Florida.

"The first paycheck I got here was the first I ever drew in my life," Cohran said. "It was for $140. I'll never forget it. When I got to the center, Mr. Evans (the job developer) talked to me about getting a job and asked me what I wanted. I said, 'This is going to be real strange for me because I've never worked before.' I went to three or four places. They'd say, 'What is your previous work record?' And I'd say, 'None.' It was looking bad for a few weeks there." Then Evans found Cohran a job as a warehouse worker. "It was not a real good experience at first," Cohran recalled. "I didn't like getting up at 5 A.M. and getting over here and taking orders from people. Being a burglar I could get up when I wanted and do what I wanted." An employee at the warehouse who was a former prisoner from New York encouraged Cohran to stick with it, and so did Evans, and Cohran was eventually promoted to a supervisory job.

"I have thirty-six days until parole," he said, "and I plan to stay here. It makes me feel good, and my wife and father are real happy, too."

SOURCE: Joan Potter, "The Dilemma of Being Half In and Half Out," *Corrections Magazine*, June 1979, p. 66. Copyright 1979 by *Corrections Magazine* and Criminal Justice Publications, Inc., 116 West 32 Street, New York, NY 10001.

examined the financial aspects of work release have found that substantial economic benefits can be derived from the programs. Although the amount of financial gain varies from program to program, no research has yet revealed an unprofitable work-release program.

Recidivism. Evaluations of the postincarceration performance of work releasees in terms of their rearrest, reconviction, or reincarceration are not uniform in their findings. Most studies of work releasees' recidivism suffer from a number of methodological problems, one of the most significant being the lack of an appropriate control group with which to compare the work-release participants. Ideally, an experimental research design would be employed. Inmates would be randomly assigned to an experimental group and placed on work release or to a control group, where they would be denied the privilege of temporary release. Following final release, the recidivism of both groups would be studied and the rates of postrelease criminal activity compared. Unfortunately, this rarely occurs.

Judges and state correctional authorities are extremely reluctant to place inmates on work release by random assignment. At present, many inmates are ineligible for program participation by statute or administrative requirements. Even those not automatically excluded from consideration are rigorously screened before recommendations are made. Only the best risks and most trustworthy offenders are approved for work release. Random assignments presumably would not provide much protection for the community.

One could, however, focus on inmates who are approved for work release; some of these persons could be randomly assigned to work release and the others could serve as a control group. This approach would have the advantage of generating two comparable samples of offenders. But inmates assigned to the control group would by chance be denied a privilege they had earned. This option clearly has its drawbacks.

In most situations, researchers have been forced to utilize less than satisfactory control groups, composed of persons incarcerated but not approved for work release or individuals placed on probation. When the recidivism rates of work releasees are compared to those of probationers, the work releasees tend to have higher postrelease crime rates. Probationers are usually less serious and less chronic offenders than persons who are imprisoned; so this finding is understandable.

When work releasees are compared to inmates not approved for work release, the work releasees tend to have lower postrelease rates of crime. This finding is also expected because work releasees are, after all, better risks than inmates denied the privilege of temporary release. An interesting variation on this finding was obtained in Witte's study of work release in North Carolina.[38] Random samples of 297 work releasees and 344 non-work releasees were selected. The inmates were followed up for an average of 37 months after final release. No significant difference in the rate of return to criminal activity was found. Work releasees tended to commit new offenses within a shorter period of time following release, but their crimes were generally less serious than those committed by non-work-release participants.

The most methodologically sophisticated study of work-release recidivism was reported by Waldo and Chiricos in 1977.[39] Inmates eligible for work release within the Florida Department of Corrections were randomly assigned to work release or total confinement. Eighteen measures of recidivism were examined. The study found no appreciable difference between the two groups' postrelease criminal activity. Work-release participation failed to influence postrelease recidivism regardless of prior record, employment since release, or the offender's demographic characteristics.

Attitudinal Change.   An earlier report by Waldo, Chiricos, and Dobrin describes an attempt to measure attitudinal changes resulting from work-release participation.[40] The same Florida inmates who later participated in the recidivism study were administered attitude questionnaires six months prior to release and again immediately prior to release. For the work-release sample, the first testing occurred immediately prior to placement on work release. The researchers had hypothesized that inmates who participated in work release would experience:

1. An expanded perception of legitimate opportunity
2. An increase in achievement motivation
3. An increased expectation that future difficulties with the law could be avoided
4. An increase in self-esteem or improved self-image
5. A shift toward middle-class orientations[41]

The research revealed that inmates on work release experienced no significant improvement in any of these areas. In fact, inmates on work release experienced a decrease in self-esteem during program participation. The authors concluded that the experience of being part free man and part convict might have had a demoralizing impact on the work-release participants. Being an inmate among inmates might not do much for one's self-concept, but being an inmate among free men could actually damage one's feelings of self-worth.

Postrelease Employment.   As previously noted, Witte's North Carolina study found that work releasees were more likely to have secured jobs upon release than non-work-release participants. Although the work releasees frequently changed jobs shortly after release, the movement was generally toward higher paying jobs. In general, the work releasees showed greater postrelease job stability than other inmates.

These findings tend to confirm the results of an earlier study by Johnson.[42] He found that former work releasees secured better jobs after release than offenders who had not participated in work-release programs.

Summarizing the preceding findings, one may conclude that there are definite economic benefits from work release and that work release seems to assist inmates in developing good work habits that may pay off following release. Attitudinal changes and recidivism rates provide less evidence of work-release success.

When assessing these findings, one must remember that most work-release programs have received less than the ideal amount of resources and staffing required to implement and maintain a quality program. Job placements tend to be in unskilled and low-paying positions. Unless special counseling and assistance are provided to work releasees, it seems unlikely that their contacts with the free world will prove much more successful than those of most ex-inmates in their first postprison jobs. But even if work release fails to reduce the likelihood of postrelease crime, it can provide many inmates with a chance they might otherwise not have.

> "I was eligible for parole but I requested work-release. . . . I've been locked up over ten years and I have nobody out there. It would have been impossible for me to go straight to the street. How could I pay my rent and get everything else I need with the little they give you when you leave? With the money I make on this job, I've already bought clothes, dishes, towels, a can opener and a coffee pot. If a man has someone to help him, and he can handle it, parole is better. But for me, I wouldn't have known where to go or what to do. Work-release is better."—*A ten-year veteran of Florida prisons.*[43]

A Closer Look at Study Release

❑ Specific Objectives

Study-release programs have one distinct and important objective in addition to those shared with other temporary release programs—the education of imprisoned offenders. The rationale for inmate educational programs is twofold. First, there is a strong belief in this country that all persons have a right to a basic education. This right is not forfeited upon conviction for a crime; it applies to all individuals, free or imprisoned. Many arguments for inmate educational programs are based upon these humanitarian beliefs. Second, inmate educational programs serve practical aims as well. It has been suggested that a primary objective of prisoner education is to provide offenders with the means of gaining access or removing obstacles to the opportunity structure of society.[44] Instructional programs that develop such basic skills as reading and writing or vocational skills for specific jobs or that provide high school and college-level course work may help the individual obtain the legitimate employment he needs if his return to the community is to be successful.

Study-release programs have two distinct advantages over instructional programs conducted within institutional walls:

First, the policy (study release) provides the potential for a richer educational experience, that is, the offender, by being placed in the community, is more likely to be exposed to quality education, updated equipment, and current technology as well as a positive spin off effect from socializing with free-world classmates and instructors. Second, it is probable that such a policy can alleviate many administrative problems, such as the staffing and equipping of duplicative facilities inside correctional institutions.[45]

❑ Status of Study-Release Programs

Very few descriptive studies of educational release programs have been conducted. Virtually all that is generally known about study-release programs in the United States is reported in four nationwide surveys conducted in 1971, 1974, 1977, and 1981. Each of these studies included the District of Columbia, the fifty state departments of correction, and the Federal Bureau of Prisons. The objective of the first research project was to determine the nature and extent of study-release programs in American correctional institutions, the perceived effectiveness of the programs, and the direction of future program expansion.[46] The second and third surveys were designed as follow-up examinations of trends in program development and change.[47] The final survey was part of a larger study of inmate participation in prison education programs.[48]

The surveys reported that study-release programs varied considerably from state to state. The types of programs available were influenced by the statutory authority under which study release was authorized, the educational philosophy of the correctional agency, the availability of educational placements in the community, and the amount of financial aid available for inmate students. Changes in any one of these factors could be expected to affect the operation of study-release programs significantly.

The first survey found that forty states, the Federal Bureau of Prisons, and the D.C. Department of Corrections were operating study-release programs. A total of 3,087 inmates were placed on study release in 1971. Approximately 2 percent of this number absconded (ran, walked, or otherwise escaped from custody).

The Federal Prisoner Rehabilitation Act appeared to be the single most important catalyst to study-release program development. Most of the states had established their programs after the federal system had implemented the enabling legislation, and many of them modeled their programs after federal procedures.

❑ Types of Programs Available

Four types of educational activities are typically available in study-release programs: adult basic education (ABE), high school or high school equivalency (HSE), technical or vocational education (VOKE), and postsecondary education (college). The first survey reported that thirty-eight states permitted inmates to attend local colleges, thirty-two states authorized vocational training, eight states permitted inmates to attend high school in the community, and seven states authorized inmates to attend community ABE programs. Most inmates on study release participated in the vocational training programs.

The subsequent surveys reported growth in the number of programs followed by stabilization and decline. In 1977 there were forty-three study-release programs in operation and 3,717 inmates on study release.[49] As before, inmates were attending a wide variety of community-based educational programs. Despite the increase in program participation, the absconder rate declined to a low of 1 percent in 1977. By 1981 fewer than two-thirds of the states were operating a study-release program. Several of these states reported minimal participation. In addition to meeting general temporary release criteria, many states also required offenders to meet educational criteria such as having already completed a certain number of credit hours.[50]

The absolute number of inmates participating in study-release programs is still quite small, and it is unlikely that inmate students will ever equal inmate workers in number. However, community educational programs will no doubt continue to supplement institutional programs. Study release can be a valuable means of facilitating inmate reintegration into the community when the programs are carefully planned and conscientiously administered. Unfortunately, not all of them are.

❑ Case Studies

Study Release in New York State. The New York State Department of Correctional Services operated one of the most attractive study-release programs in the nation. Selected inmates were provided with tuition (up to $1,000 per year), clothing, a meals and transportation allowance, and petty cash. No research had been conducted on program effectiveness. In 1975, however, a staff member in one of the correctional facilities decided to investigate the program. She conducted a case study of the inmates participating in study release at her institution.[51]

The research revealed that, during one fall semester, slightly more than half of the forty-eight inmates enrolled in the program dropped out; during the following semester, almost half of the remaining twenty-three men failed to complete the program. An examination of the postrelease experiences of inmates who had been enrolled in the program one year earlier indicated that all but one had been financially unable to continue their education following release.

The high number of program dropouts was attributed to the fact that many of the inmates were transferred to work release or paroled. A powerful incentive for inmates to drop out of study release was the requirement that they have a job plan and a verifiable means of support as a precondition to consideration for parole. Little effort was made to ensure that inmates placed on study release had the resources to continue their education or training following release. Thus, a program that appeared exemplary at first glance was found to provide little if any benefit to offenders. In fact, the experience of beginning community study only to terminate it after a few brief months might well have damaged inmate hopes and expectations of ever completing an educational program.

Several approaches could be used to remedy the problems identified in the New York program. Inmates could be placed on combined work/study release, where they could work part-time and attend school part-time. Individualized attention to each inmate's financial needs and resources could facilitate the identification of financial aid opportunities available after release. Selection procedures for study-release programs, transfer policies to work release, and parole decision making could be coordinated to ensure that no student who wished to remain would be abruptly removed from a community educational program. Unfortunately, New York's temporary release program has been severely cut back due to public criticism, and few of these improvements have been implemented.

Project Newgate. A major stimulus to the development of postsecondary educational programs for inmates was provided by Project Newgate.[52] This program, which can now be found in a number of state correctional institutions, addresses some of the very problems that plagued New York's study-release effort. Designed to offer a continuum of services to inmates both prior to and following release, it serves as both an inside and outside educational program. While incarcerated, inmates may receive both social and academic preparation for college attendance. After release, participating colleges and universities work to ensure that ex-offender students benefit from continued college attendance. Study release serves as a transitional stage linking the inside and the outside. The overall objective of these services is to increase the inmate's potential for successful community adjustment.

An evaluation of the Newgate program revealed a number of factors that were associated with successful educational programs:

1. An active outreach and remedial program designed to assist inmates
2. The existence of extracurricular activities that enhance and supplement the educational environment
3. A sequence of transitional components that provide support services to the inmates being released
4. The involvement of independent colleges and universities in program operation[53]

❑ Effectiveness

To date, no significant research designed to measure the impact of study-release programs on inmate attitudes or behavior has been reported. We do not yet know whether study release can increase an offender's employment opportunities or reduce the likelihood of his return to crime. Given the small number of inmates participating in most educational release programs, it is unlikely that we will have such information in the near future. At this time, we can only note that merely providing the initial opportunity for community study is rarely enough to ensure that offenders benefit from education release. Inmates require preparation and assistance academically, financially, and emotionally if study-release programs are to succeed.

A Free Prisoner and an Odd Way to Live

Going to jail is a trip. Being half in and half out of jail is stranger yet. That's where I'm at. I'm in the (study) furlough program for the City Jail Farm at Elmwood which means that I'm in jail, but I get out to school on certain days and within certain hours. . . . It is sort of like being a free prisoner. Well, no, it is more like being a highly restricted citizen . . . I'm not sure which it is, but I'm sure it is an odd way to live.

Source: Anonymous, *Spartan Daily,* San Jose State University, November 12, 1971.

A Closer Look at Furloughs

❑ Specific Objectives

In addition to the facilitation of inmate reintegration into the community, the assessment of offender readiness for release, and the management and humanitarian aims achieved by temporary release, furloughs can serve therapeutic purposes. It has been proposed that even a brief period of freedom may restore an inmate's feelings of dignity and self-worth. Furloughs may thus be a useful tool in stimulating an inmate's growth and development.[54] Furloughs can help inmates feel better about themselves and their future prospects. For those inmates for whom total and uninterrupted imprisonment may lead to emotional disturbance and even suicide, furloughs may offer a relief unattainable within an institutional environment.[55]

Furloughs can also supplement institutional rehabilitative efforts. Inmates may participate in various brief educational and vocational training programs not available within the institution. When inmates are permitted furloughs to search for jobs in the local community, their experiences may demonstrate their need for additional education and training in a way that no amount of advice or lectures by correctional counselors can. This enhanced awareness of the need for employment skills may encourage inmates to participate in instructional programs during confinement. Additionally, knowledge of an inmate's experiences during community release and the effectiveness of his efforts to deal with conflict and potential problems may assist correctional staff in their development of individualized treatment plans.

Many proponents of furlough programs argue that home furloughs are a preferable and more feasible alternative to conjugal visiting programs, which bring offenders' wives into designated areas of the institution for overnight visiting. Throughout the years, efforts to establish and administer conjugal visiting programs have encountered considerable difficulty. Few correctional institutions have adequate facilities for conjugal visiting. Security problems are difficult to overcome. The potential for degradation of prisoners' wives is always present. Because many inmates have common-law marriages there are questions about the appropriate definition of marriage for conjugal visiting purposes. Regardless of the definition employed, single inmates will be ineligible for participation. Furlough programs can accomplish the same objectives as conjugal visiting programs without the disadvantages.

❑ Prerelease Furloughs and Home Furloughs

We have already noted that furloughs may be granted for a wide variety of specific purposes—to participate in community events, receive short-term educational or vocational training, prepare for final release, maintain family ties, and so on. Most furloughs however, are granted for one of two purposes—to allow the inmate to prepare for his final return to the community or to provide him with an opportunity to reestablish family ties. In 1977, all but eight states, the Federal Bureau of Prisons, and the District of Columbia authorized furloughs for these purposes.[56]

In most cases, inmates furloughed for either purpose will reside with family members during temporary release because they are expected to provide some supervision or guidance to the inmate during his stay in the community. Inmates who stay alone in apartments or hotels or reside with friends during release might face increased temptations to "stray from the straight and narrow path." Because few community facilities (such as halfway houses) can provide short-term accommodations to visiting inmates, an inmate's family home is often the only residence available. Although most furloughs are to the home of a family member, for the purposes of our discussion, we will refer to furloughs for the purpose of making release preparation as prerelease furloughs; temporary leaves designed to improve or maintain inmate/family relations will be referred to as home furloughs.

Prerelease Furloughs.   The California Department of Corrections established a model furlough program in 1969 as a direct result of findings indicating that California's institutional prerelease program was having little positive impact on participants.[57] It was reasoned that, because bringing community resources into the institutions had failed, the most logical alternative was to send the inmate to the community.

The prerelease furlough program was designed to permit the temporary release of a large number of inmates awaiting final release, rather than only a select few. All inmates who were within ninety days of release were eligible by statute for no more than two prerelease furloughs. Each correctional institution developed its own procedures for selecting inmates. After six months of operation, approximately 1 percent of the total population of California's correctional institutions was being furloughed each month. One institution released as many as 5 percent of its inmate population every thirty days.

An evaluation of the prerelease furlough program was reported two years after it began.[58] The study focused on the experiences of inmates in the Southern Conservation Center, which furloughed the largest number of inmates. To apply for temporary release, inmates in that institution were required to develop a furlough plan outlining their proposed activities in the community. The inmate's counselor evaluated the plan and suggested additions or deletions. Appropriate plans were then referred to the casework supervisor and subsequently to the prerelease furlough program administrator for final approval. The superintendent of the facility had the authority to deny furloughs in exceptional cases.

The data for the study were based on the furlough application forms of 165 inmates, interviews conducted with these offenders following temporary release, and a questionnaire sent to each inmate's family or sponsor asking for their reaction to his furlough. One-fourth of the inmates who received furloughs had been locked up for four or more years; the average time served was thirty-four months. The average inmate was furloughed forty-eight days prior to release. Most of the inmates stayed with parents or wives during their temporary release.

Table 6-4 indicates the plans inmates developed for their prerelease furloughs and their success in completing them. Most plans involved a search for employment. Although over half the inmates began this search with no job offer in sight, eighty-seven inmates secured employment while on furlough. Eighty-six percent of all furloughees planned to apply for or obtain a driver's license; almost two-thirds of them were successful. Seventy-two inmates planned to contact their parole officers during temporary release; five *additional* inmates achieved this aim. Fifty-four inmates wanted to reestablish family ties; a total of seventy-four inmates accomplished

TABLE 6-4 Inmate Prerelease Furlough Plans and Success Rates

Plan	Number of inmates		Success on first or second furlough	
	Number	Percentage	Number	Percentage
Look for a job (no offer on file)	85	53%	40	47%
Confirm an existing job offer	63	39	47	75
Obtain or apply for a driver's license	137	86	86	63
Contact parole agent	72	45	77	107[a]
Get reacquainted with family	54	34	72	133[a]
Contact some social agency	7	4	5	71
Other	33	21	37	112[a]
Total number of cases 160[b]				

[a]As a percentage of those who had such plans for the first furlough.
[b]No information on five furloughees.
SOURCE: Norman Holt, "Temporary Prison Release," *Crime and Delinquency* 17 (October 1971): 414–430).

this goal. Inmates were surprisingly successful in accomplishing their proposed objectives. Many inmates who did not reach their goals made considerable effort and were unable to succeed through no fault of their own.

Inmates and their families viewed the prerelease furloughs as extremely worthwhile. Inmates enjoyed being with family or friends and simply being free. Many noted that having worked out their postrelease plans made it easier for them to finish serving their time. Families were pleased with their husbands' or sons' return and hopeful for the future, as indicated by the following remarks:

"We were very happy to have him home after six years. I do hope LeRoy will do good. I'll try my best and do everything I can to help him. My husband and him get along fine, and (he) thinks this time LeRoy has to try and do good and he will also help in everything he can."

"He has a home with his mother and father as long as he wants to stay with us."

"It gave him back his faith to know his family and friends still have faith in him and want to give him a helping hand."

"The visit was better than I expected because everybody pitched in to help him. I thought there was going to be regrets because of what happened (his being in prison) but there were none. All the family were very nice to him."

"I am his mother. My home is his too. I hope he comes home soon. He worked all of the time he was home—came home went to bed early. He did real good—he is a good boy—just did wrong."

"Seeing his family's happiness at his presence and our desire to make his visit pleasant seemed to restore his confidence and self-assurance."[59]

Of the 165 men released, only 14 encountered difficulties on furlough. Nine returned late and 2 returned under the influence of drugs or alcohol. Only 1 individual was charged with a crime—a misdemeanor—committed during temporary release; only 2 persons absconded. Without question, the program was a benefit to virtually all participants.

Home Furloughs.   Virtually all research on home furloughs has revealed the same general pattern of inmate experiences.[60] Generally, the home furlough experience may be thought of as consisting of three basic stages: prefurlough, community release, and postfurlough.

The prefurlough stage begins when the inmate is approved for temporary release. Most inmates understandably are excited about the prospect of release. Time seems to drag as the furlough date approaches. Any delay or difficulty in the arrangements for release may cause considerable irritation. For some inmates, the prefurlough stage is accompanied by anxiety and tension as the offender contemplates his family's reception and his ability to adapt to freedom after what may have been a long period of confinement. In most cases, inmates await their furloughs in a manner not unlike awaiting parole. They fantasize about freedom but try not to raise their expectations too high. Many inmates have had disappointing release experiences before.

While in the community, inmates usually spend considerable time with family members. They attend entertainment events, eat in restaurants, and visit friends and relatives. Inmates take care of personal matters, shop for clothes, and so on. Much time is often spent simply relaxing at home.

Generally, inmates appear to fit back into a normal, routine existence with little difficulty. There is scant evidence that inmates experience severe culture shock as a result of their return to freedom, even when they have spent many years in prison. This is not too surprising when one considers that few demands are placed on inmates whose furloughs are designed primarily to reacquaint them with family members. Relatives tend to do what they can to ensure that no difficulties arise; their interaction with the inmate often takes on a honeymoon quality. For many inmates, home furloughs serve as a needed but brief vacation from confinement.

Prior to their return to incarceration, some inmates face a moment of truth during which they consider not returning to prison. This thought usually passes very quickly; most inmates guard against its development by psychologically preparing for the inevitability of return even prior to temporary release. Such preparations are apparently quite successful because very few furloughees fail to return to confinement.[61]

Once they have returned to prison, there is a tendency for some inmates to become slightly depressed; they may withdraw from institutional routine and interaction with other inmates. The loss of family, friends, and freedom and the unpleasant confrontation of isolation, deprivation, and confinement with what one offender termed "all these undesirables" is the source of such adjustment problems. These feelings usually pass in a few hours and rarely last more than a few days. Inmates often demonstrate a remarkable capacity to make the prison/freedom/prison transition with relative ease.

Inmates almost invariably report that furloughs help them maintain family ties. The following remarks illustrate the extent of this feeling. In response to the question, "What would you say was the best part of the furlough for you?" three female furloughees replied:

> "Being with my mother, I think, and my baby. Because I think my mother is really something. She hurt just about as much as I did about me being in here. Because I know she was happy those days I was home, when she came home she knew I'd be there."

"Being with my son and talking to him. I just feel closer to him. Each time I go out I feel a lot more closer to him than I did before. We go someplace out to eat, McDonald's or something like that and it was nice."

"I think that late Monday afternoon my husband and I went to my parents' house and stayed by ourselves. I thought that was great. We went for a long walk and we went out on the boat and talked. It's hard to say things in letters. But to ask questions that are in your head, you find out exactly how you are going to react."[62]

❑ Evaluation

Most studies of furlough programs have examined inmates' responses as they describe their experiences prior to, during, and following temporary release. The research has also focused on reported interactions with family and friends and inmate activities in the community. Only one reported study has attempted to go beyond this somewhat limited focus. That research was conducted by LeClair, in his evaluation of the Massachusetts home furlough program.[63]

LeClair attempted to determine whether inmates who received furloughs were less likely to be reincarcerated following release than inmates who did not participate in the furlough program. The study population consisted of all men released from state correctional institutions during 1973 and 1974. Recidivism was defined as any parole violation or new conviction that led to a return or new commitment to incarceration. Recidivism rates were compared for inmates who had received one or more furloughs and inmates who had never received furloughs.

Recidivism was significantly lower for inmates who had received furloughs than for inmates who had not. Statistical analysis revealed that this finding was attributable to the impact of the furlough program, rather than the types of inmates selected for temporary release. These findings indicate that home furloughs may be a valuable means of assisting inmates in their return to the community. At this time, however, it would be naive as well as premature to assume that a few furloughs can make a difference between success or failure in the community for every inmate. Nevertheless, for many inmates in the marginal risk category, the provision of opportunities for graduating the release process may significantly enhance their chances for successful reintegration.

Problems and Issues in Temporary Release

All temporary release programs are subject to the same three basic problems: violations of program rules and regulations, absconding, and temporary release crime. Although none of these difficulties is severe in terms of the numbers of inmates involved, the community response to these problems may be of tremendous importance. Citizen outrage is particularly vehement when crimes are committed by inmates assigned to work or study release or released on furlough. As we shall see, the acts of a handful of men may result in the almost complete loss of temporary release opportunties for many inmates.

❑ Violation of Regulations

Late returns from work, school, or furloughs, excessive use of alcohol, and use of illicit drugs are generally the most common serious temporary release rule violations. Work releasees may stop at a bar between work and prison; inmate students may use marijuana, narcotics, or barbiturates after school; and furloughees may try to spend a few extra hours with family members. The official reaction to these violations is generally to withdraw temporary release privileges from the inmate; in some instances, the inmate may lose good time or may be placed in administrative segregation as punishment. The particular correctional response will reflect institutional and departmental policy and the circumstances of the violations. Inmates may have transportation difficulties that cause them to return late to the prison through no fault of their own. In some prisons, these circumstances would be viewed as mitigating; in others, the inmate would be charged with absconding. Some institutions are not concerned with whether a man drinks on furlough as long as he does not return to the prison intoxicated.

The prison officials' only means of determining drug or alcohol use is to require urinalysis, breathalyzer, or other tests; but these tests are of limited utility unless the drug or alcohol intake has been fairly recent. Enterprising furloughees have been known to schedule their narcotics use so that no trace of the substance is left in their system on their return to prison.

The extent of temporary release rule violations is difficult to assess. Most drug and alcohol violations are probably not discovered. Late returns may be ignored, moderately disciplined, or charged as abscondings. There is some evidence that the extent of rule violation may be fairly high when strict rule enforcement is the norm. In one jurisdiction, as many as 30 percent of the inmates placed on temporary release were removed for administrative reasons.[64] This rate, however, includes removals for minor as well as serious violations. Even if the proportion of rule violations is high, many proponents of temporary release programs would argue that late returns and alcohol use are manageable problems. Inmates are responding to the difficulties of being half prisoner and half free citizen.

❑ Absconding

In most jurisdictions, inmates who abscond from temporary release are classified as escapees; if convicted of escaping, they frequently receive lengthy prison sentences in addition to their original terms. The severity of the penalty for absconding and the rigorousness of the temporary release selection process have worked to keep absconder rates low. An average of approximately 5 percent of inmates on temporary release will abscond; this number includes inmates who return voluntarily after a short absence as well as offenders who are never found.

Research has indicated that a temporary release program's escape rate is influenced by the following:

1. Criteria and care used in case selection
2. Constraints as to work sites (for work-release programs)
3. Transportation arrangements

4. Nature and extent of services, such as surveillance and supportive counseling
5. Level and consistency of rule enforcement[65]

One other factor may influence the escape rate in work- and study-release programs. Inmates who enter the community on a regular basis to work or attend school may be sorely tempted to visit family or friends when they are supposed to be attending their placement. If home furlough opportunities are not frequently available, this natural temptation may unfortunately prove to be overpowering.

The State of Florida reported that in 1989 only one inmate out of 5,658 released on furlough failed to return.[66] The State of Massachusetts has been releasing inmates on various forms of furlough since 1972.[67] Since that time over 124,000 prisoners have been released on this program, with only 652 recorded escapes. This works out to a success rate of 99.5% of all furloughs.

❑ Crime

The most significant problem in the area of temporary release is crime. When an inmate commits a crime while visiting the community on work or study release or on a furlough, citizens are invariably outraged. Political pressure is brought to bear, and, not infrequently, the entire temporary release program is held accountable for the acts of a few men. For example, consider the Washington, D.C., experience:

On June 11, 1971, Calvin F. Smith and Joseph M. Joyner broke into the northeast Washington home and laundromat of John R. Turner in search of money. When Turner discovered them, one of the men shot him in the groin. He died later from the wound.

In January 1973, Smith and Joyner were each sentenced to twenty years to life in prison for first-degree murder, plus five to fifteen years for armed robbery and burglary.

On September 25, 1974, Calvin Smith was arrested by FBI agents at Washington's Union Station. He had a one-way Metroliner ticket to New York and a box under his arm containing a sawed-off shotgun.

But Smith had not escaped from prison. He had been released on furlough by officials at the D.C. Correctional Complex in Lorton, Virginia. In fact, he had been making frequent unescorted trips into the District of Columbia for several months. Smith had been acting as "entertainment coordinator" for the Lorton prison complex. His job was to arrange visits to the D.C. prisons by outside speakers, singing groups, and other community organizations.[68]

In the words of one commentator, Smith's arrest "brought the roof down on the Department of Corrections furlough program."[69] The program was already plagued with problems, but Smith's arrest may have been a critical factor in the drastic curtailment of what was once the most extensive and liberal furlough program in the country.

The preceding series of events has been reenacted in cities across the nation. When a citizen is victimized by a temporary releasee, facts become almost irrelevant. People forget that the incidence of temporary release crime is usually extremely low, that probationers and parolees generally are more likely to engage in crime than inmates on temporary release, and that the inmates placed on work or study release or approved for home furloughs will soon be returning to the community on a permanent basis. We have not yet found a way to ensure that cooler heads prevail when a temporary release program comes under fire. Unfortunately, it is inevitable that at least one temporary releasee in almost every program will at some time engage in some criminal activity. This means that the future of temporary release programs can never be secure.

The preceding problems are not the only important issues in temporary release; they are only the most threatening ones. Three critical needs still remain. Appropriate eligibility criteria and selection procedures for participation must be developed. Cooperative relationships between prisons and employers and schools must be established. Supportive services for inmates who live in both the prison and the free world must be provided if temporary release is to aid an offender's reentry into the community.

Perhaps the most critical issue here is the community's willingness to accept offenders back. Such acceptance requires that inmates be given every chance to prepare themselves for final release. It requires a willingness to permit inmates to work and study and visit with their families prior to final release and a readiness to go behind prison walls to help prepare the remaining offenders for their eventual return to society.

New Directions in Temporary Release

Two trends may be expected to influence the future of temporary release programs. The first is the movement toward determinant sentencing. More and more states seem to be evaluating their sentencing practices and concluding that problems resulting from disparity of sentencing and the perceived failure of parole require a change. In a number of states, the changes have included an adoption of determinant sentencing in which the nature of the offender's crime determines the sentence he will receive and relatively little emphasis is placed on the offender's background or the specific circumstances of the offense. Once the offender is incarcerated, his institutional behavior has relatively little influence on the length of time he serves. In some states, parole has also been abolished or greatly curtailed; the inmate must then serve his time with sharply reduced opportunities for early release.

Under such conditions, the released offender may receive little assistance in his efforts to adjust to freedom; whatever aid parole officers formerly provided will be lost. Correctional officials wishing to facilitate inmate reintegration may choose to employ temporary release programs as a means of filling in the gaps left by the shrinkage of parole opportunities. Temporary releases may be granted so that inmates can achieve the graduated release that parole was once designed to provide.

The abolition of some parole programs may also encourage correctional authorities to use temporary release programs in a different way. Because parole will no longer be available as an incentive for good inmate behavior, temporary release programs may come to play an even greater role in institutional management. Temporary release privileges may be granted to deserving inmates and denied to offenders who manifest a poor institutional adjustment.

A second trend is the development and use of work-release facilities as a means of defusing overcrowding in major institutions. Some prison systems have developed work-release centers as a low-cost alternative to the expanding of major correctional institutions. In a survey conducted in 1989, maximum security cells cost approximately $78,000 per cell to construct, while minimum security cells (work-release centers) cost $28,000 to build.[70] The development of these program facilities permits prison administrators to transfer the less dangerous offenders, or those nearing the end of their prison terms, to these less secure programs, thereby freeing up bed space for more serious offenders.

Summary

Temporary release programs were established in American prisons to meet a critical correctional need—preparing the incarcerated offender for final release or parole to the community. Although the programs had diverse origins, the 1960s witnessed their linking both conceptually and administratively. The growing acceptance of the goals of community-based corrections was responsible for this new direction, as prison officials began to address postrelease realities in their development of correctional programs. Temporary release programs accomplish this aim by providing inmates with brief exposures to the community prior to final release.

Perhaps the most critical stage in temporary release programming is the selection of inmates for work or study release or furloughs. Eligibility criteria and selection procedures should be broad enough to allow inmates who may benefit from the programs to participate, while ensuring that no offender who poses a threat to the community is released. This is a difficult task; most programs tend to be cautious in their selection process because the criminal activities of a few men may severely damage an entire program. Another factor that may also restrict temporary release program participation is that temporary release is viewed as a privilege; so only inmates who show a positive institutional adjustment are generally approved for it.

Work-release programs have a number of advantages; the most obvious asset is the economic benefit to inmates, their families, the victim, and the state. However, potential inmate employees face a number of problems as well—lack of jobs, reluctant employers, low pay, and generally unskilled, unrewarding work. Study-release programs can provide offenders with needed education in a normal, community setting—high school, vocational school, or college. When well-planned programs are available, inmates may benefit from study release in nonacademic as well as academic ways. Furloughs help offenders maintain family and community ties. When they are used to permit inmates nearing final release or parole to obtain jobs or arrange housing in the community, inmates can experience both the practical and psychological benefits resulting from successful accomplishment of a task.

The future outlook for temporary release programs is mixed. Determinant sentencing, temporary release crime, and administrative problems will have competing influences on temporary release programs. Because virtually all inmates are eventually released, it can only be hoped that prerelease preparation of a useful nature will be made available to all needy offenders.

KEY WORDS AND CONCEPTS

absconding
community labor
conjugal visiting
  programs
determinant
  sentencing
discretion
economic benefits
eligibility requirements
employment
  opportunities
evaluative objectives

extension of the limits
  of confinement
home furloughs
Huber Law
humanitarian
  objectives
job suitability
management
  objectives
mandatory release
prerelease furloughs
prevailing wages

Project Newgate
reintegration,
relaxed supervision
stages of penal
  servitude
stalled reform
temporary release
  crime
therapeutic objectives
transition
unescorted leaves

NOTES

1. American Correctional Association, *Directory of Juvenile and Adult Correctional Departments, Institutions, Agencies and Paroling Authorities* (College Park, Md.: American Correctional Association, 1989), p. xxii.
2. Ibid., pp. xxii, xxiii.
3. "Survey Education Release: 1989," *Corrections Compendium,* vol. XIV, no. 8 (November 1989).
4. Connecticut Department of Corrections, *Good Corrections,* CDC & 7423 (Hartford: Connecticut Department of Corrections, n.d.).
5. Michael S. Serrill, "Prison Furloughs in America," *Corrections Magazine* 1 (July–August, 1975): 5.
6. "Survey Education Release: 1989."
7. Walter Busher, *Ordering Time to Serve Prisoners* (Washington, D.C.: U.S. Government Printing Office, 1973), p. 2.
8. Elmer H. Johnson, *Crime, Correction, and Society* (Homewood, Ill.: Dorsey Press, 1978), p. 363.
9. Ibid., p. 364.
10. Busher, *Ordering Time to Serve Prisoners,* p. 3.
11. Alvin Rudolf, *Work Furlough and the County Jail* (Springfield, Ill.: Thomas, 1975), p. 123.
12. Ronald Goldfarb and Linda Singer, *After Conviction* (New York: Simon & Schuster, 1973), p. 528.
13. Vernon Fox, *Community-Based Corrections* (Englewood Cliffs, N.J.: Prentice-Hall, 1977), p. 80.
14. Ann D. Witte, *Work Release in North Carolina: The Program and the Process* (Chapel Hill, N.C.: Institute of Government, 1973), p. 2.
15. C. W. Marley, "Furlough Programs and Conjugal Visiting in Adult Correctional Institutions," *Federal Probation* 37 (1973): 19–25.
16. Ibid., p. 19.
17. Richard Ely, "The Development of Temporary Release Programs" (unpublished manuscript, 1975).
18. Ibid.
19. H. G. Moeller, "Community-Based Correctional Services," in *Handbook of Criminology,* Daniel Glaser (ed.) (Chicago: Rand McNally, 1974), p. 895.
20. A. M. Kirkpatrick, "The Human Problem of After Care," *Federal Probation* 21 (1957): 22–25.
21. Public Law 89–176, September 10, 1965.

22. Correctional Research Associates, "Community Work: Alternatives to Imprisonment—Principles and Guidelines" (Washington, D.C.: Correctional Research Associates, 1967).
23. John Galvin et al., *Instead of Jail: Pre- and Post-Trial Alternatives to Jail Incarceration: Sentencing the Misdemeanant* (Washington, D.C.: U.S. Government Printing Office, 1977), p. 85.
24. Witte, *Work Release in North Carolina: The Program.*
25. Busher, *Ordering Time to Serve Prisoners.*
26. Eugene Doleschal and Gilbert Geis, *Graduated Release* (Washington, D.C.: Government Printing Office, 1971), p. 9.
27. John Moore and Stanley Grupp, "Work Release Administrators' Views of Work Release," *Offender Rehabilitation* 3 (Spring 1979): 193.
28. Witte, *Work Release in North Carolina: The Program.*
29. Ibid.
30. Ibid.
31. Ann Witte, *Work Release in North Carolina: An Evaluation of Its Post Release Effects* (Chapel Hill, N.C.: Institute of Research in Social Science, 1975).
32. Ibid.
33. "Work Release 1989, Summary," *Corrections Compendium,* vol. XIV, no. 5 (June 1989), pp. 13–21.
34. Mason J. Sacks, "Making Work Release Work: Convincing the Employer," *Crime and Delinquency,* July 1973, p. 255.
35. Witte, *Work Release in North Carolina: The Program.*
36. Florida Department of Corrections, *Legislative Manual,* February 1989: 12.
37. State of Alabama, *Monthly Statistical Report,* December 1989/January 1990: 8.
38. Witte, *Work Release in North Carolina: An Evaluation.*
39. Gordon Waldo and Theodore Chiricos, "Work Release and Recidivism: An Empirical Evaluation of a Social Policy," *Evaluation Quarterly* 1(1977): 87–108.
40. Gordon Waldo, Theodore Chiricos, and Leonard Dobrin, "Community Contact and Inmate Attitudes," *Criminology* 11(1973): 345–381.
41. Ibid., pp. 351–352.
42. Elmer Johnson, "Work Release—A Study of Correctional Reform," *Crime and Delinquency* 13(October 1967): 521–530.
43. Joan Potter, "The Dilemma of Being Half In and Half Out," *Corrections Magazine* (June 1979): 68.
44. Marjorie Seashore and Steven Haberfeld, *Prisoner Education: Project Newgate and Other College Programs* (Chicago: Praeger, 1976), p. 20.
45. R. Smith, J. McKee, and M. Milan, "Study Release Policies of American Correctional Agencies," *Journal of Criminal Justice* 2(1974): 358.
46. Ibid., p. 358.
47. David Shichor and Harry Allen, "Study Release: A Correctional Alternative," *Offender Rehabilitation* 2(June 1977): 7–17. Smith and Petko, "An Updated Survey."
48. Contact, Inc., "Education Programs," *Corrections Compendium* 6(11), 1982, pp. 5–11.
49. Ibid.
50. Ibid., p. 5.
51. This study was reported by Bernard McCarthy in *Bay View Correctional Facility: An Operational Overview* (Albany: New York Department of Correctional Services, 1976), p. 5.
52. Seashore and Haberfeld, *Prisoner Education.*
53. Ibid., p. 185.
54. Paul Clark, "The End of Misery," *The Atlantian* 120 (Spring–Summer 1963): 11–13.
55. American Prison Association Committee on Classification and Casework, *Handbook on the Inmate's Relationships with Prisons from Outside the Adult Correctional Institution* (New York: American Prison Association, 1953).
56. Smith and Petko, "An Updated Survey," p. 124.
57. Norman Holt, "Temporary Prison Release," in *Correctional Institutions,* 2nd ed., Robert Carter, Daniel Glaser, and Leslie T. Wilkins (eds.) (Philadelphia: Lippincott, 1972).

58. Ibid.
59. Ibid., pp. 437–438.
60. For a review of the literature, see Belinda McCarthy, *Easy Time: Female Inmates on Temporary Release* (Lexington, Mass.: Lexington Books, 1979), pp. 9–12.
61. Smith and Petko, "An Updated Survey," p. 124.
62. McCarthy, *Easy Time,* pp. 49–50.
63. Daniel LeClair, "Home Furlough Program Effects on Rates of Recidivism," *Criminal Justice and Behavior* 5(September 1978): 249–258.
64. William Ayer, "Work Release Programs in the United States: Some Difficulty Encountered," *Federal Probation* 34(March 1970): 53–56.
65. Galvin et al., *Instead of Jail,* p. 84.
66. Florida Department of Corrections, *Legislative Information Manual,* February 1989: 9.
67. Michael White, *Massachusetts Department of Correction Review of Current Research 1989,* Massachusetts Department of Corrections, March 1990: 12.
68. Michael Serrill, "Furloughs in D.C.—A Tense Issue," *Corrections Magazine,* March–April 1975, pp. 53–54.
69. Ibid.
70. David Camp and Camille Camp, *The Corrections Yearbook,* 1989: 25.

FOR FURTHER READING

Busher, Walter, *Ordering Time to Serve Prisoners: A Manual for the Planning and Administering of Work Release* (Washington, D.C.: U.S. Government Printing Office, 1973).

Doleschal, Eugene, and Gilbert Geis, *Graduated Release* (Washington, D.C.: National Institute of Mental Health, 1971).

Galvin, John, et al., *Instead of Jail: Pre- and Post-trial Alternatives to Jail Incarceration: Sentencing the Misdemeanant* (Washington, D.C.: Department of Justice, 1977).

McCarthy, Belinda, *Easy Time: Female Inmates on Temporary Release* (Lexington, Mass.: Lexington Books, 1979).

7: | Halfway Houses

Objectives
   Benefits to the Offender
   Benefits to the Community
   Benefits to the Justice System
Historical Perspective
Program Models
   Referral
   Intake
   Programming
   Program Illustrations
Program Planning and Operations
   Target Population Selection
   Location and Site Selection
   Personnel and Training
   Treatment Services
   Resident Security and Community Protection
   An LEAA Exemplary Project
Problems and Issues in Halfway Houses
   The Dilemma of Being Half In and Half Out
   Halfway House/Community Relations
Program Evaluation
   National Evaluation Program
   NEP Recommendations
   GAO Survey
   Minnesota Evaluation
The Future of Halfway Houses
   Management by Objectives
   Management Information System
   Mutual Agreement Programming
Summary

HALFWAY HOUSES ARE DESIGNED to help ex-offenders negotiate the critical transition from confinement to the community. They may also be used to aid other offenders in need of short-term supervision in a community residential setting. The provision of a supportive environment, the basic necessities of food and shelter, and assistance in securing employment, education, and counseling services facilitates adjustment to the community and thus promotes the correctional goal of reintegration.

A great variety of correctional facilities and programs has claimed the title of "halfway house." Some of these facilities are actually small, secure, community-based institutions that provide a full range of correctional programs; others are loosely structured programs that provide shelter but little else to ex-offenders who live in the house on a voluntary basis.[1] Most halfway houses lie somewhere between these two extremes—they provide moderate levels of supervision and programming for various categories of offenders.

Today's halfway houses typically serve prereleasees, persons who are being permitted to serve the last portion of their prison sentence in the community, or parolees (see figure 7-1). In some jurisdictions, however, halfway houses serve other offenders as well. For example, defendants selected for diversion, pretrial release, or probation may be required to live in a halfway house as a condition of supervision. Inmates on probation or parole may also be placed in a halfway house as an alternative to probation revocation when it appears that they are in danger of failing in the community.

The type of population served varies from community to community and from halfway house to halfway house, depending upon the characteristics of the specific program and the services the halfway house provides. Some halfway houses are administered by correctional agencies and accept only offenders as residents. Others, especially those that provide special treatment programs for alcoholics, drug abusers, or persons with mental health problems, accept individuals referred from social service agencies and self-referrals as well as offenders. Still others focus the majority of their efforts on nonoffenders and accept criminal justice clients only occasionally. Programs that accept both offenders and nonoffenders are often administered by public health or welfare agencies or by private organizations.

A national survey of correctional agencies reported that, in 1989, there were more than 900 halfway houses operating across the United States.[2] Over 90 percent of the programs are privately administered. Most programs have an average capacity of about twenty-five residents, although they vary in size from 140 to only 6 beds. The average length of stay in a halfway house ranges from eight to sixteen weeks.

At least thirty-eight jurisdictions use halfway houses or community treatment centers for prereleasees or parolees. Almost 15,000 inmates were released to halfway houses in 1978. Halfway houses are used as an alternative to imprisonment by at least nineteen jurisdictions and have a total nationwide capacity exceeding several thousand beds.

Objectives

A National Evaluation Program (NEP) survey of halfway houses reported by the U.S. Department of Justice in 1978 concluded that the principal goal of halfway houses for prereleasees and parolees was

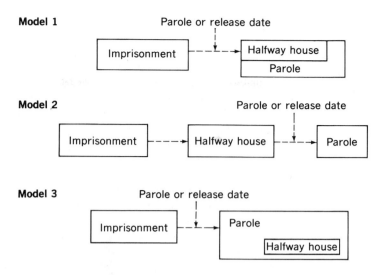

FIGURE 7-1 Three Models of Release or Transfer from Prison to Halfway House

SOURCE: "Halfway Houses and Parole: A National Assessment," by E. Latessa and H. Allen, *Journal of Criminal Justice*, 10, 1982: 156. Copyright 1982, Pergamon Press, Ltd. Reprinted with permission.

> To assist in the reintegration of ex-offenders by increasing their ability to function in a socially acceptable manner and reducing their reliance on criminal behavior.
>
> To accomplish this objective, the halfway house accepts ex-offenders released from prison, provides the basic necessities of room and board, and attempts to determine each individual's reintegration problems, plan a program to remedy these problems, and provide supportive staff to assist the resident in resolving problems and returning to society as a law-abiding citizen.[3]

By facilitating community adjustment, halfway houses can benefit both the offender and the community.

❑ Benefits to the Offender

Providing the ex-offender with the basic necessities of food, clothing, and shelter is undoubtedly more humane than returning him to the community with no thought to his ability to locate a job or a place to live. Although parolees are required to have a residence and employment plan prior to release, these plans are often less than ideal and sometimes unrealistic. The housing plan often identifies the ex-offender's family home as his parole residence. Preexisting problems with family members may make these living arrangements difficult to maintain; the additional stress of readjustment can make them untenable. Similarly, the jobs identified by persons hoping to "make" parole frequently consist of low-paying, monotonous employment under poor working conditions simply because the would-be parolee is willing to accept any job to facilitate his release. Once freed, the unattractive aspects of the work and the parolee's reactions to these conditions may lead to early termination. Halfway houses can help avoid these problems by providing ex-offenders with the basic necessities while they locate housing and employment suitable to their needs and resources.

Halfway houses also provide the emotional support offenders need to manage the demands and pressures of readjustment. Informal counseling is available and staff members are willing to listen to and discuss residents' personal dilemmas. Perhaps more important, the offender is in a setting where those who share his predicament are at hand to provide understanding and support. For individuals who require more intensive interventions, halfway houses can offer more structured therapeutic programs; drug, alcohol, or family counseling can enable the offender to develop his skills and resources to meet community demands while still in the semisheltered program environment.

Finally, halfway houses can help ex-inmates find and obtain community services. The halfway house staff can act as advocates for ex-offenders, providing them with support, security, and direct assistance while plans for education, training, employment services, financial assistance, and counseling from community agencies are being developed and implemented. Because community programs may have waiting lists or delays in service delivery, halfway house personnel can work to facilitate the bureaucratic process while the halfway house meets the individual's most immediate needs. Halfway house programs for those offenders who have not served a prison term provide an alternative to incarceration. Like programs for prereleasees and parolees, they provide a humane and supportive environment for meeting basic offender needs. Community resources are used to facilitate the adjustment of those persons who do not require imprisonment, but who need more assistance and supervision than a nonresidential program can provide.

❑ Benefits to the Community

Halfway houses can serve the community in two ways. First, they provide a sufficiently secure environment to protect the community. Residents' activities and associations are monitored and support services, staff role models, and recreational pursuits are available. Persons supervised under these conditions should be less likely to engage in criminal behavior than offenders with less assistance and fewer opportunities.

Second, facilitating inmate adjustment to the community is expected to reduce recidivism following residence in the halfway house. The opportunity provided to get firmly on his feet, to achieve some success in negotiating the routine distresses and temptations of living and working, and to develop and implement realistic plans for the future should reduce postrelease criminal behavior.

❑ Benefits to the Justice System

Halfway houses, community treatment centers, and other minimum security facilities provide a low-cost housing alternative to prison systems for handling nondangerous offenders. With many correctional systems experiencing unprecedented overcrowding in their prisons, combined with the active intervention of federal courts to force state correctional systems either to reduce their prison population to within constitutional (i.e., manageable) limits or to expand capacity, halfway houses have been viewed as a reasonable and cost-effective way to expand the capacity of a prison system rapidly and at less cost than constructing more secure facilities.

Historical Perspective

The precise origin of halfway houses is unknown. Some writers suggest that they grew out of early acts of Christian charity. For example, St. Leonard established a monastery during the middle of the first century that provided room and board for convicts whose release he had been able to obtain from the king.[4] From the time of this early effort to the present, religious communities have frequently provided ex-convicts with food and shelter upon their release from prison.

Sir Walter Crofton's Irish system, described in the previous chapter, may also be responsible for the development of the halfway house. This system of penal servitude provided for incarceration in a maximum security prison followed by work in the free community and residence in an intermediate institution. This intermediate institution, with its emphasis on work in the community and preparing the offender for release, seems to be the most direct forerunner of the contemporary halfway house. Undoubtedly, it was the first attempt by correctional officials to create a special residence designed to facilitate the offender's transition from prison to freedom.

The first formal recommendation for the establishment of a halfway house in the United States was made in 1817. During the preceding year, a riot in a Pennsylvania prison prompted the legislature to establish a commission to study prison problems and suggest reforms. One of the most interesting of the commission's many recommendations reflected a concern for the ex-convict's well-being. The commission proposed a building to be

> erected of wood, at a small expense, as it is only recommended by way of experiment. The convicts who are discharged are often entirely destitute. The natural prejudice against them is so strong, that they find great difficulty in obtaining employment. They are forced to seek shelter in the lowest receptacles; and if they wish to lead a new course of life, are easily persuaded out of it, and perhaps driven by necessity to the commission of fresh crimes. It is intended to afford a temporary shelter in this building, if they choose to accept it, to such discharged convicts as may have conducted themselves well in prison, subject to such regulations as the directors may see fit to provide. They will have a lodging, rations from the prison at a cheap rate, and have a chance to occupy themselves in their trade, until some opportunity offers of placing themselves where they can gain an honest livelihood in society. A refuge of this kind, to this destitute class, would be found, perhaps, humane and politic.[5]

This proposal was never implemented because many persons feared criminal contamination. It was believed that, if ex-inmates lived together, they would spread their criminality from one to another like a disease. Solitary confinement within the halfway house was thought to be necessary to inhibit the spread of criminality. Because ex-offenders, as free persons, would probably be unwilling to accept such living conditions, halfway houses seemed impractical.

Opposition to halfway houses continued in corrections for many years. Even normally progressive prison reform organizations and proponents of parole rejected the idea that ex-prisoners could benefit from a transitional group residence prior to complete freedom.

For the remainder of the century, private citizens made virtually all subsequent efforts to provide halfway houses for ex-offenders in the United States. In 1845, the Quakers established the Isaac T. Hopper Home in New York City. It is still in operation today. Almost twenty years later, a group of reform-minded Bostonians established a home for Massachusetts women released from prison or jail. Their Temporary Asylum for Discharged Female Prisoners provided "shelter, instruction, and employment for discharged female prisoners who are either homeless or whose homes are only scenes of temptation" for almost twenty years.[6]

In 1889, the Philadelphia House of Industry was created; it is still receiving parolees from Pennsylvania prisons today. During the next decade, Maud Booth and her husband established Hope Hall for ex-inmates in Manhattan. Although police opposition repeatedly threatened the program, it survived, and similar facilities were subsequently established in Illinois, California, Louisiana, Iowa, Ohio, Texas, and Florida. All these shelters met considerable opposition from parole authorities because association with former prisoners was forbidden by parole regulations.

Little growth in halfway house development occurred during the next half century. A few mission-type homes were established, and the Salvation Army and the Volunteers of America continued to provide lodging for ex-offenders, as they did for other homeless men. The halfway house movement was not revived until the 1950s, when St. Leonard's and Dismas House, founded by clergymen, and other facilities established by private citizens began to appear. Most observers seem to agree that "growing dissatisfaction with high recidivism rates, combined with a new awareness of the problems facing the released prisoner" sparked the renewal of interest in halfway houses.[7]

In 1961, Attorney General Robert F. Kennedy added his support for the growing halfway house movement and explained his objectives:

> We wanted to develop a center where in addition to the basic needs of food and a room, the released inmate would be helped to find a job where he would be given the support and guidance to enable him to live with his emotional problems, and where he might make the transition from the institution to community life less abruptly, less like slamming into a brick wall. We wanted a center which would be his sponsor in the "free world," introducing him to community life gradually and withdrawing when the process was completed. Ex-prisoners in all age groups need this kind of assistance.[8]

His concerns persuaded Congress to appropriate funds to establish three experimental prerelease guidance centers for juvenile offenders. Following the success of these centers, the Federal Prisoner Rehabilitation Act of 1965 (discussed in chapter 6) authorized the establishment of halfway houses for adult offenders as well as other community corrections programs.

During the late 1960s, halfway houses began to expand their functions to include halfway-in services for persons placed on probation and other offenders. For these individuals, halfway houses serve as an alternative to incarceration. Since that time, halfway houses have been serving persons in a variety of criminal justice statuses, offering halfway-in programming for persons diverted from the criminal justice system, placed on pretrial release, or sentenced to probation. At the same time, most halfway houses continue to function as halfway-out houses, providing counseling and other forms of assistance to prereleasees and parolees.

The growth of halfway house programs was strongly influenced by the organization of the International Halfway House Association (IHHA) in 1964. The

IHHA was organized to promote the establishment of halfway houses, encourage the development of high standards in their operations and management, and serve as a professional forum for the exchange of ideas. Since that time, interest in halfway houses has continued to grow, and the developing characteristics of halfway houses have reflected the diversity of public and professional interest. Halfway houses have become increasingly sophisticated in recent years. Although most continue to focus on the needs of the ex- or soon to be ex-offender, they provide an expanded range of services and their ties to correctional agencies and community resources have significantly improved.

Program Models

Although halfway houses vary considerably, there appears to be a continuum of program objectives and services along which most may be measured. The two opposing end points of the continuum are the supportive and the intervention programs; most halfway houses fall somewhere between these two models.[9]

Generally, supportive programs tend to have few professional staff members, offer few, if any, counseling services, and be geared toward resource identification for offenders. Supportive programs are based on the assumption that "the offender possesses sufficient motivation to utilize those community resources that meet his or her particular needs."[10] In these programs, staff functions primarily as an information service that refers offenders to appropriate community services. Program personnel assume that residents will take advantage of these services once they become aware of them and possess enough self-control to require only limited supervision.

Intervention programs have relatively large numbers of professionals and offer extensive counseling services. Intervention programs assume that offenders possess neither the motivation nor the personal resources to use the community services they require. The program's professional staff is responsible for remedying the deficiencies that inhibit utilization of needed community resources by providing prevocational, vocational, and psychological counseling on both an individual and group basis.

Regardless of the nature of the program, all halfway houses perform three basic functions: referral, intake, and programming.[11]

❑ Referral

Referral is the directing of potential residents to the halfway house. It does not guarantee acceptance into the program, but instead implies only "an interest in the program for a particular offender on the part of the offender himself, the halfway house or institutional staff, or an interested party."[12]

The halfway house's ties to the correctional institution(s) from which offenders are released is of critical importance to the referral process. A facility with close ties to a prison, such as those that serve as work-release or prerelease correctional centers, often has no control over the referral process—only the availability of bed space limits correctional referrals. Although such programs cannot pick and choose their residents, they avoid the necessity of recruiting.

Halfway houses that have no direct ties to the correctional system must depend upon informal relations with correctional authorities and social service agencies to recruit clients. Good relations are essential if the halfway house is to operate near capacity; numerous referrals also permit the facility to select those individuals most suited to the program.

❑ Intake

Intake begins when halfway house staff members initiate their assessment of an individual referred to the program. The process includes the decision to accept or reject the candidate and all orientation efforts designed to acquaint newly accepted residents with the "rules, regulations, goals, and philosophy of the house program."[13] During this period, which ranges from two to thirty days, new residents are usually restricted to the house.

The intake process varies, depending upon the program's supportive or intervention focus. In supportive halfway houses, the focus is on determining if the offender can benefit from the services the program offers. An assessment is made of the individual's

1. Family and community ties
2. Potential for employment and/or skill development
3. Mental health
4. Physical condition
5. Level of motivation to seek and hold employment
6. Desire to succeed in the community
7. Level of savings[14]

Persons with few resources in these areas are usually considered unsuitable for supportive programs.

Intake in intervention programs utilizes clinical, diagnostic, and classification procedures to assess the individual deficiencies of personality and social adjustment. Depending upon the particular treatment program the halfway house offers, various techniques of personality, attitude, and behavior assessment may be employed to identify offender problems and needs. Persons found to be in need of the intervention the halfway house offers are generally accepted into the program.

❑ Programming

The programming process consists of five overlapping phases: plan development, service provision and resident participation, review of participation and progress, release decision and process, and follow-up.[15]

Plan Development.   The first step in halfway house programming is usually the development of a plan of action for the resident. This plan identifies objectives the offender should accomplish during his residence in the program and often specifies how much time it may take. Usually both the resident and his halfway house counselor develop the plan. Working together, they discuss the offender's problems and attempt to achieve a mutual agreement regarding objectives and the best means to accomplish them. The plan is sometimes prepared in the form of a contract that specifies both offender and staff responsibilities; in other programs, the agreement is more informal. Most programs attempt to develop individualized treatment plans; some halfway houses, however, attempt to select similar residents and utilize one house plan for all residents.

Service Provision and Resident Participation.   The halfway house or the community may provide services to residents. Interpersonal counseling is the service most frequently offered by the halfway house. Employment counseling and job placement are also frequently provided, but these services and other educational programs are more often provided by community agencies.

All halfway houses require clients to meet certain expectations for continued residency, often including:

1. Observe at least minimum security requirements (checking in and out is generally required)
2. Keep rooms and belongings in good condition
3. Perform household duties
4. Attend counseling sessions
5. Secure and maintain employment
6. Demonstrate appropriate attitude and behavior[16]

Review of Program Participation and Progress.   In most halfway houses, residents are reviewed on a regular basis. Reviews focus on program participation and progress and occur between one and four times per month. At such reviews, staff and employer reports of resident behavior are generally discussed; the residents' self-evaluation and information from social service agencies and schools that deal with them are also sometimes considered. The resident's future in the program depends upon the results of the evaluation and his criminal justice status. The unsuccessful resident may be evicted from the house and suffer the collateral consequences of renewed prosecution, jailing, or imprisonment. Residents with less serious problems may be punished by a reduction of privileges. Residents making satisfactory progress may have their programs modified or continued as before. Persons who have received as much benefit as possible from the program may be terminated.

Release Decision and Process.   When the offender has accomplished what he was expected to achieve, he is ready for release. Consideration for release is usually initiated by the client's attainment of specific program goals or by his exceeding the average length of stay in the program. A final criterion for release is the client's ability to prepare for leaving the program. These preparations include locating appropriate housing and employment and developing financial plans for the future.

Follow-up.   Follow-up activities may include both services to the former resident and data-gathering efforts for the purpose of program evaluation. Efforts are made to prevent the offender from encountering further legal difficulties and to assist him if it appears that he was released too soon. Information about resident adjustment to the community, usually including employment status and subsequent criminal behavior, is gathered for periods ranging from three months to two years. Follow-up activities generally receive little emphasis in most halfway house programs because the limited staff and resources available are directed toward serving in-house residents.

❑ Program Illustrations

Massachusetts Prerelease Centers. Massachusetts provides a good example of a state committed to community residential assistance for ex-offenders.[17] In 1972, a correctional reform law requiring the establishment of community correctional programs was passed. The reform law permits transfer to prerelease facilities during the last eighteen months preceding an inmate's parole eligibility. One month after the law was passed, the first prerelease unit was established in a vacant building on the grounds of the Boston State Hospital.

Most inmates are transferred to prerelease programs when they are eight months from parole eligibility. They are given two weeks to find a job, after which they pay the state for their room and board, depending upon how much they earn. The men progress through the programs through a series of five phases. Entry to a phase depends upon appropriate behavior; with each phase comes additional furlough time, ranging from ten hours a week in phase I to forty-eight hours in phase V.

The inmates in the programs are usually older offenders who have spent three to four years in prison. They have little difficulty in locating jobs, although many of these jobs are menial and low paying. Employment coordinators assist the men in obtaining employment, sometimes making as many as seventy-five attempts before a job is secured. Although it is against Massachusetts law to discriminate against offenders, many employers are not interested in hiring inmates on prerelease.

Minnesota PORT Programs. Minnesota's statewide PORT (Probational Offenders Rehabilitation and Training) programs began with a tricounty program in Rochester, Minnesota.[18] That program serves both adult and juvenile males referred from local courts. Their offenses range from truancy to armed robbery.

Entrance into the program is voluntary. Candidates undergo a three-week, live-in evaluation at the PORT facility prior to acceptance. During this time the candidate and the screening committee, comprised of a psychiatrist, a probation officer, a lay person from the community, the executive director, and representatives from both the resident and counselor groups, determine if PORT is the choice of both parties.[19] Candidates must identify and describe to the committee their reasons for wanting to enter PORT; this practice is designed to encourage the resident's desire to be helped by the PORT program. The executive director of the PORT program described the core of the program as

> a combination of group treatment and behavior modification. The residents meet as a group Sunday, Wednesday, and Friday evenings with the program director and the two trainees. Confrontation, frankness, honesty, trust, care, reality-testing, and decision making are the ingredients of the group process. The quality of the culture at PORT is primarily affected by the success of this phase of the program. The behavior modification feature was added after a year of operation when we found that the group alone was insufficient. Group sessions were spending too much time on individual's problems in school and job performance, inconsistencies developed in ascertaining acceptable levels of performance, and the newcomer's association with outside groups and their often varying value systems confused him. Also, the fact that the program was experiencing some failures led to the addition. A point system is used to mete out levels of freedom systematically, based upon measured performance in tangible areas. These include weekly school and work reports, building cleanup, managing a budget, planning and carrying out social activities successfully, and similar accomplishments.

Operationally the newcomer starts off at the bottom rung of a group-evolved classification system which has categories ranging from 1 (minimum freedom) to 5 (freedom commensurate with that of an individual of the same age in the community). Working up the ladder is accomplished through a combination of earning points and group decision. Through the process of demonstrating performance to the group and earnings on the point system, the resident gradually weans himself from PORT, increasingly gaining the freedom and responsibilities accorded the "normal" person of his age.[20]

PORT is sometimes used as an alternative to revocation for persons on probation or parole. The case of Roger, a 15-year-old with a chronic history of assault, illustrates the program's work with just such an offender:

Roger had been out of a state institution for three months when he again became involved in a number of fights and assaults. This, plus poor adjustment to home, school, and parole supervision, would have resulted in his return to an institution had PORT not been available.

During the initial several months at PORT his adjustment was poor. When frustrated, he cried, when collected, he "conned" the therapy group, which they pointed out to him. The fighting continued, culminating in his being expelled from school. When that occurred, instead of returning to PORT, he ran off, which he had done on two other occasions. Some days later, through the help of other PORT residents, he was picked up by the police and jailed.

The "group" and staff recognized that Roger's associates were the strongest force in his life, much stronger than PORT, and if we were going to interrupt this progression of negative behavior, it would be necessary to alter the nature of their influence. His associates were informed that Roger would not be released from jail until he met with the PORT program director, Jay Lindgren, and members of the group at the jail and unless they promised that they would support only responsible behavior on his part. They appeared at the appointed time but the setting created so much tension that another session was scheduled for the next day at PORT. Results were beyond expectation. For example, the leader of the group of friends turned to Roger during the meeting and said that Jay wasn't as bad a guy as he, Roger, had made him out to be.

At this writing some five months later, Roger is in class 5 and asking the group to leave PORT. He has been maintaining a "C" average in school where his adjustment has been satisfactory; he works part-time at a service station. A month ago he was picked up drinking with his friends. However, after they explored the behavior with him, the group concluded that the incident was more a learning experience than a regression. He spends less and less time at PORT and probably will be released soon. The question of PORT's being able to afford the necessary controls and help for Roger was raised several times during the course of his stay. If the special school operated by the public schools at Rochester State Hospital had not been available to take the boy when he was expelled, institutionalization would have occurred, because he was of school age. Each time he had a problem, help, care, pressure, and loss of freedoms emanated from the group and the program, and he emerged stronger after every experience.[21]

Program Planning and Operations

Planning and operating a halfway house is no simple task; yet most in existence today developed with relatively little guidance. Subsequently, many programs have suffered from poor or incautious planning and administration. To remedy this problem, the National Institute of Law Enforcement and Criminal Justice (NILECJ) funded a study of halfway house program models. The project's objective was to identify critical issues in halfway house planning and operation and offer guidelines for addressing these issues. The final report was published in 1978; today it serves as one of the best sources of information available on such issues as target population selection, location and site selection, personnel and training, treatment services, and security.[22] The following sections focus on the issues the NILECJ report addressed and provide a profile of contemporary halfway houses as reported by the NEP survey of approximately 200 halfway house programs.

❏ Target Population Selection

One of the most critical questions in halfway house planning is who is to be served. Much of the success depends on the planners' ability to identify persons in need of halfway house services and to develop a program to meet those needs. Any planning effort should begin with a needs assessment designed to identify the number of offenders within a particular jurisdiction who might benefit from halfway house services and the types of problems they would require assistance in resolving.

The National Council on Crime and Delinquency has identified six factors that can be used to assist in the selection of a target population.[23]

1. *Geographic location.* If the program aim is to reintegrate offenders into the community, then only persons who are residents of that community or who are willing to relocate to that community should be selected as residents.

2. *Age.* Residents should be able to utilize all services provided by the halfway house, so persons selected for the program should normally be between the ages of 17½ and 60. Younger individuals might be expected to have difficulty entering the work force; older persons may be too close to retirement age for gainful employment. Currently, over half of all halfway house residents are between the ages of 21 and 30.[24]

3. *Sex.* Sex is an important consideration only because it is necessary to ensure that there are enough people in the target population to merit a halfway house. A halfway house may be single sex or coed, although resistance to a coed facility may be encountered in some communities. Most halfway houses are for males only; about 10 percent serve only females and almost one-fourth are coed.[25]

4. *Length of stay.* The length of the client's sentence must be matched to the halfway house program. Individuals placed on community prerelease status for the last three months of their prison sentence cannot be expected to take full advantage of a program that requires six months to a year of residency. The model policy statement developed by the United States Bureau of Prisons for their community residential centers recommends that client selection should anticipate the following minimum lengths of stay for specific program services:

Work release employment placement only	30 days
Work release to accumulate savings	90 days
Preparole and prerelease testing in the community	90 days
Marital and family counseling	30–60 days
Aftercare treatment for alcoholism	60 days

Vocational and special training   Open
Aftercare treatment for drug addiction   90 days[26]

As noted earlier, the average length of a residence in a halfway house is between eight and sixteen weeks.

5. *Offender characteristics.* Dangerous, hostile, and emotionally disturbed offenders should probably be excluded from minimum security programs such as halfway houses. Any individual likely to jeopardize the other residents, the program, or the community should also be excluded. Most halfway houses exclude persons with mental and emotional problems; persons with physical disabilities and sexual deviancy are also frequently prohibited from participation.[27]

6. *Drug dependent and alcoholic offenders.* The NCCD recommends that these persons should be admitted to the program only if professional staff are available to work with them. Perhaps as a result of a lack of trained staff, many programs bar offenders with drug and alcohol problems.[28] However, about one-third of all halfway house programs are specifically designed for such offenders.[29]

❏ Location and Site Selection

If halfway houses are to facilitate offender reintegration into the community, they must be located in the community. The critical question is which community and what neighborhood. Citizen attitudes are one of the most important considerations in the selection of location—many houses have been forced to close or relocate because of unfavorable community response. Neighborhood residents are often concerned about danger to persons or property from halfway house residents or about a decline in real estate values following the opening of a home for ex-offenders. Although research in a number of states indicates that crime rates do not increase and property values do not decline when a halfway house enters the neighborhood, public attitudes continue to be fearful and neighborhood problems rank as one of the most serious difficulties reported by halfway houses.[30]

The type of neighborhood suitable for the establishment of a halfway house is the subject of some debate. The American Correctional Association suggests that halfway houses should be located in as good a neighborhood as the community will permit.[31] Other observers suggest that the environment should be similar to the areas to which residents will be returning, which usually suggests a low socioeconomic neighborhood. "Commercial locations or those undergoing transition or redevelopment, marked by little neighborhood cohesiveness and a resultant anonymity" are sites favored by such advisors, who feel that halfway house residents need to be able to blend into the community and feel a part of it, "rather than being identified and stigmatized as being from a correctional center."[32] There is considerable opposition to locating the halfway house in a deteriorating area, but a "racially, culturally, and economically diverse community" is generally viewed as desirable.[33]

At present, halfway houses appear to be an urban phenomenon—nine out of ten are located in urban areas and two-thirds are in counties with populations of 500,000 or more. The programs are usually located in areas zoned for multiple-family housing; only one in five has been established in a neighborhood restricted to single-family dwellings. Most of the facilities are in multiracial, lower-middle socioeconomic areas. The halfway house's approach to community relations is generally to keep a low profile, although some programs provide special services to the community, such as chaperoning senior citizens and sponsoring cleanup projects and social events.[34]

The final question pertaining to halfway house geographic location is accessibility to essential community resources. Although the program may be established in virtually any type of community, it must be located near public transportation, employment, and educational opportunities. Other community resources, such as medical and social services and recreational activities, must also be conveniently located.

A critical issue that may influence or supersede questions of geographic location is the type of facility desired and available for use as a halfway house. Old homes or unused public buildings are sometimes donated or made available virtually rent-free to halfway house administrators; such actions often constitute unrefusable offers. Halfway houses have been located in abandoned military barracks, old hotels, newly constructed, specially designed correctional centers—every imaginable structure capable of serving as a communal residence.

Three-fourths of the halfway houses in operation today are relatively new, having developed during the 1970s. Former homes and hotels serve as the site of about half of the halfway houses; about 10 percent of the halfway houses utilize space rented from YMCAs, the Salvation Army, or apartment buildings. The remaining structures are so diverse as to resist classification. Most facilities require residents to share a bedroom with another participant; in 40 percent of the programs, three or more persons share rooms.[35]

❏ Personnel and Training

Halfway houses originated with virtually all-volunteer staffs, but today they utilize a variety of personnel, including professionals, paraprofessionals, student interns, and ex-offenders, as well as volunteers. Ideally, professional people with graduate degrees or college plus experience are employed to fill the central roles of program director and treatment staff. Paraprofessionals, persons with a combination of background, education, and experience appropriate to halfway house employment, can supplement professional staff. Specially trained paraprofessionals can "provide links with community resources, . . . work with special problems, such as drug abuse and alcohol, or facilitate group or individual counseling."[36] Volunteers can serve in a great variety of capacities. Those persons from backgrounds similar to the residents may serve as role models for the ex-offenders; volunteers from middle-class backgrounds can facilitate clients' entry into jobs and educational opportunities that might otherwise be closed to them. Student interns may be utilized similarly to volunteers or paraprofessionals, depending upon the involvement of their educational institutions in preparing them for their halfway house responsibilities. Ex-offenders can be employed in any of the preceding capacities, depending upon their education and work experiences. Ex-offenders can contribute much to the halfway house program; they may bring a special knowledge and understanding of offender problems and needs that can facilitate many aspects of program operation.

The average halfway house program today has between four and seven full-time employees; one or two persons may serve as administrators and two to five staff members may function in treatment capacities.[37] Almost half the programs employ between one and three part-time staff. Two-thirds of the halfway houses use volunteer services; as many as 200 volunteers may be serving a single program. Volunteers are used in many capacities—leading group sessions, raising funds, transporting residents, organizing community events with residents, and substituting for evening staff. Relatively few programs employ ex-offenders; those that do are more often private rather than publicly administered facilities.

The NEP survey indicated that three-fourths of halfway house administrators, but only half of treatment personnel, hold college degrees.[38] Their degrees are often in areas unrelated to their roles and responsibilities as treatment staff. Less than 40 percent of the program administrators and fewer than one in six treatment personnel hold graduate degrees.

A recent survey of halfway house administrators revealed that high staff turnover is one of their most significant problems. A variety of causes was said to underlie problems in staff retention: "low pay levels, few opportunities for advancement, and *burnout* due to frequent and intensive contact with residents" were the most frequently mentioned sources of employee distress.[39]

Although not all these problems can be resolved through careful staffing, they can be at least partially addressed by several measures. Increasing staff salaries is one obvious, if sometimes unfeasible, approach. Ensuring that the halfway house has an adequate number of staff members is another; it can reduce unnecessary burdens on employees. Good recruitment and selection practices can weed out persons especially prone to burnout. Comprehensive and realistic job descriptions that specify needed skills and personality attributes can facilitate this process. Finally, providing career ladders for paraprofessionalism and tying promotions to specific performance criteria can really pay off; these efforts can stimulate good employee morale and create a challenging atmosphere that offers meaningful rewards as well as serious responsibilities.

❑ Treatment Services

Halfway houses may provide a great many services to their clients, either directly or through referral to community resources. The types of services the house offers should reflect resident needs and generally should complement rather than duplicate existing community resources. Some services, of course, such as interpersonal counseling, must be available within the halfway house regardless of community offerings —interpersonal counseling provides the core of the special support and understanding necessary to facilitate the ex-offender's adjustment to freedom. Basic employment and educational counseling can usually be offered to residents, depending upon the availability of qualified staff. More professional assistance in the areas of vocational and educational testing and placement may be obtained from community resources. In-house drug and alcohol counseling are essential if residents have substance abuse problems, but such services may be complemented by specialized community services.

Many halfway houses develop some sort of individual plan for each resident.[40] Most of the plans indicate specific objectives to be achieved and time frames for their accomplishment. Resident counseling receives the greatest emphasis in today's halfway house treatment efforts—one-third of the program is usually devoted to interpersonal counseling. Three out of four halfway houses offer family counseling, but considerably less program time is devoted to this form of service.

Employment and education are viewed as principal goals for halfway house residents. Nine out of ten programs offer some employment counseling within the house, and many facilities refer residents to community employment services. Half the programs provide educational counseling and placement and almost one-third offer in-house instruction.

Financial assistance and counseling are available in most halfway house programs. Drug and alcohol counseling is the central focus of a number of programs and a major emphasis in many others; between one-half and two-thirds of all facilities provide special treatment and counseling for residents with drug and alcohol abuse problems.

Table 7-1 lists major program services provided by contemporary halfway houses. Interpersonal and employment counseling and services account for over half of all treatment efforts; 40 percent of all halfway house residents also receive

Table 7-1 Summary of Treatment Services Data, by Percentages

Service	Average percentage of house program effort devoted to service	Average percentage of residents receiving service from community agencies	Percentage of houses offering service to ex-residents
Interpersonal counseling	31.0%	17.0%	54.8%
Family counseling	6.6	6.5	49.3
Vocational testing/ Assessment	2.9	26.9	25.0
Vocational skill training	1.8	20.8	23.1
Employment counseling	18.3	18.8	45.4
Educational testing	1.9	16.4	25.6
Education	2.2	16.9	32.6
Educational counseling	5.3	12.5	35.7
Financial assistance/ Counseling	8.4	15.9	35.7
Physical rehabilitation	0.4	5.8	0
Alcohol abuse	6.0	15.9	17.6
Drug addiction/ Dependency	5.3	17.4	35.9
Recreation	6.0	19.4	36.4
Psychological testing	1.7	13.8	21.4
Psychological/Psychiatric services	2.6	15.5	19.8
Total	100.4%		

Note: Total exceeds 100% due to the variance (from 125 to 152) in total number of houses reporting on each service.

Source: R. P. Seiter et al., *Residential Inmate Aftercare: The State of the Art, Supplement A—Survey of Residential Inmate Aftercare Facilities, National Evaluation Program Phase I* (Columbus: Ohio State University, 1976), p. 43.

employment services from the community. Follow-up program services are routinely offered to many former halfway house residents; interpersonal family and employment counseling are the most frequently offered services to ex-clients.

❑ Resident Security and Community Protection

Although halfway houses are minimum security facilities and are designed to approximate normal community living conditions, they are expected to offer sufficient program structure. This does not mean that halfway houses should be run like mini-institutions located in community settings—bars, locks, and constant surveillance are wholly inappropriate for halfway houses. However, the period of transition from prison to the community is a stressful phase of adjustment, often complicated by temptations to return to the companionship of former associates and previous behavior patterns. A halfway house program that provides some external controls over resident behavior can protect residents from injuring (in one way or another) themselves, each other, and the community.

Basic controls that most halfway houses can employ include:

1. House rules of behavior
2. Curfews, night security, and supervision
3. Logs of resident activities, sometimes subject to verification[41]

The rationale behind each of these controls is the development of personal responsibility. House rules should be similar to the rules that govern conduct in the general society.[42] Informal discussions with staff members should help residents conform to house rules. Residents should receive positive feedback for appropriate behavior, but they should also be frankly informed of failure to meet their responsibilities. All rules should be clearly specified to each resident when he enters the program; both residents and staff should review rules and their enforcement whenever it appears that particular regulations are problematic or are being enforced in a selective or arbitrary fashion.

Limiting the resident's time spent in the community during the evening hours and providing special security and supervision during this period is designed to reduce the residents' unstructured leisure time in the community, when temptations of various types may become particularly powerful. Such controls also provide the neighboring community with a feeling of safety and protection. Similarly, requiring residents to account for their time and efforts to verify the accuracy of resident activity reports are designed to ensure that residents do not find themselves in the wrong place at the wrong time.

The United States Bureau of Prisons recommends that the development and implementation of controls should be guided by two considerations.[43] First, controls should be relaxed as residents demonstrate responsible behavior; the objective of the external controls is only to provide sufficient structure until the resident is able to develop and successfully utilize his inner behavioral controls. Second, controls do not have to be applied equally to all residents; persons with particular problems, such as alcoholism, may be reasonably restricted from certain activities not off limits to other residents. Similarly, some persons may be required to meet special program requirements designed to help them manage specific personal difficulties;

for example, residents who are chronically in debt may be required to limit their cash on hand and increase their savings to levels beyond that expected for the average resident.

☐ An LEAA Exemplary Project

The Montgomery County Work-Release/Pre-Release Center represents a successful blending of treatment and control objectives in a release preparation program.[44] The program principally serves offenders sentenced to jail terms of eighteen months or less, although about 10 percent of the residents are state or federal inmates. All persons referred to the program are screened for suitability; only inmates within six months of release or a parole hearing are accepted for admission. As of 1978, about half the offenders were felons and 88 percent were male.

Treatment.   The treatment program includes both work release and education release; all residents are expected to secure employment within the first three weeks of their stay. They are assisted in this task by a full-time work-release coordinator, who tests them for vocational aptitude and arranges interviews with potential employers. The residents receive counseling on a weekly basis. Twice a week they attend "social awareness" classes, where such topics as money mangement, housing, and family planning are discussed. These classes are designed to improve the residents' problem-solving and decision-making abilities, as well as to better their communication skills. Community resources are frequently utilized by offenders; drug and alcohol counseling, family and group therapy are typically provided to residents by community agencies.

Control.   All residents must sign a contractual agreement with program staff prior to entry into the program (see box, page 225). A pre-release agreement, which specifies the house rules all program residents must follow, is also signed. The program uses periodic, unannounced counts to determine all residents' whereabouts and to encourage offender accountability. Residents' employers and community service agencies are also contacted on occasion to verify the clients' employment and participation in treatment programs. Residents are permitted furloughs in a closely supervised temporary release program. The penalties for rule violation are explicit and range from counseling to removal from the program.

Residents move through a series of three phases as they progress through the program; each offers the participant increased privileges. The individual's performance is scored on an 18-point scale that focuses upon such behaviors as money management, interpersonal relations, job performance, and program participation.

Each offender has 20 percent of his pay deducted for room and board; a maximum of $200 may be deducted each month. An additional 10 percent is put into reserve for savings. Many residents also make support payments to their families or pay restitution to their crime victims.

Cost and Benefits.   In 1977, the cost of maintaining an offender in the program for one year was about $9,000; the comparable cost of jail incarceration was $12,000. Between 1972 and 1975, program participants paid $73,000 in taxes, $3,000

Montgomery County Pre-Release Agreement

**As a Voluntary Participant in the Pre-Release Program,
I Agree to Follow the Program's Rules:**

1. I agree to industriously work at my employment, training or educational program. I will go to and from its location by the most direct route in the least amount of time. After each day's approved activities I will immediately return to the Pre-Release Center. If any situation occurs which prevents me from returning at the prescribed time, I will immediately call the Pre-Release Center for instructions. I will not be absent from the approved day's activities without approval of a Center staff member.

2. I will not act as a strike breaker, or participate in any strikes, demonstrations, or similar activities and I will report any similar situations to the Pre-Release Center staff.

3. I agree to buy the necessary materials, clothing and/or equipment essential to my employment.

4. Prior to making any move to change my employment I will inform the staff of the Pre-Release Program and obtain their approval.

5. I agree to deposit with the Work Release Supervisor my earnings less payroll deductions and I further agree to pay the County 20% of my income for room/board, etc. while working and at the Pre-Release Center. I also agree to pay my valid debts. Prior to borrowing money, incurring debts, opening bank or charge accounts, etc., I will obtain approval from Center staff.

6. I will arrange my own transportation to and from work. I understand that before operating a motor vehicle I must have a valid driver's license, automobile registration, and proper insurance coverage as required by Maryland law.

7. I agree not to leave the Pre-Release Center premises without prior authorization from Center staff.

8. It is, of course, understood that I will obey all laws of the State of Maryland. Should I have any contact with the police I will immediately notify a Center staff member.

9. I agree not to use, possess or introduce into the Pre-Release Center any weapons, alcoholic beverages, narcotics or drugs (unless under doctor's orders).

10. I agree to resolve the problems I confront in non-violent ways and I will not verbally or physically abuse another person.

11. I agree to submit to urinalysis or alcolyser tests when requested by Pre-Release Center staff.

12. I agree to participate in the Center's Social Awareness Program, in the group counseling program and (or) other community programs (i.e., alcohol or drug groups) dependent upon my problems, needs and goals.

13. If I earn home visitation privileges while in this program, I agree to spend my time at prearranged activities with my family or friends as approved by the Center staff, and I will conduct myself properly, obeying all laws as well as the rules of the program during my release into the community.

14. I have read the Pre-Release Center Guidebook and agree to follow the program activities and procedures of the Pre-Release Center.

I am *committed* to making those personal changes necessary for me to remain crime free. Thus, I am ready to become meaningfully *involved* in this program and the treatment opportunities made available to me. I am prepared to honestly accept responsibility for my own behavior and will demonstrate *responsibility* through my actions.

I realize that if I violate my part of this agreement I can be immediately removed from the program and placed in security confinement, and I will be subject to the penalties provided by law.

_____   _____
Resident's Signature   Date

_____   _____
Signature of Staff Member   Date

SOURCE: Robert Rosenblum and Deby Whitcomb, *Montgomery County Work Release/Pre-Release Program, Montgomery County, Maryland* (Washington, D.C.: Government Printing Office, 1978), p. 127.

in fines, and $500 in restitution and legal fees. Families of residents received approximately $100,000 in support payments.

Effectiveness.   Almost 300 residents were released from the Montgomery County program between 1972 and 1975; virtually all had jobs, housing, and employment at the time of release. Only 5 percent of the participants absconded from the program; 1 percent were arrested for new crimes during their residency. On the basis of a one-year follow-up, only one out of five clients was rearrested after completing the program.

Problems and Issues in Halfway Houses

❏ The Dilemma of Being Half In and Half Out

There are few inmates who would choose prison over life in a halfway house; yet living in a halfway house presents certain problems. Although it is agreed that halfway houses should offer inmates as much freedom as they can reasonably handle, there is disagreement about the amount of structure and security necessary to ensure that the transition from prison to the community is gradual. From the inmate's perspective, it sometimes appears that the halfway house offers no more freedom or responsibility than prison. During incarceration, such restrictions might be more easily tolerated, but when they exist side by side with eight or more hours of freedom during work in the community, they are difficult to manage. Halfway house residents have frequently objected to being treated like children and required to obey "petty" regulations. In an effort to demonstrate to wary citizens that appropriate security measures are being enforced, some programs have developed and implemented rules and regulations more strict than those in most contemporary institutions. The necessary balance between security and resident responsibility is often difficult to obtain.

Furloughs.   One of the greatest sources of conflict is the granting of furlough privileges. Many programs permit inmates to travel to and from their jobs independently and function freely in the community for up to ten hours per day, only to restrict them to the facility on evenings and most weekends. Such restrictions can be frustrating. The temptations of freedom are within reach but unattainable. Because many programs require all residents to spend a specific period of time in the program before furloughs are permitted, inmates who can handle freedom responsibly are sometimes unnecessarily restricted to quarters. The dilemma, of course, appears whenever attempts are made to separate the responsible from the less responsible residents; no scale has yet been devised to make such decision making foolproof. Unfortunately, the program's desire to err on the side of caution can place unnecessary pressures on halfway house residents.

Employment Problems.   The problems of securing and maintaining employment plague many halfway house residents. Offenders sometimes spend months in the community without finding a job. Such delays often lead to the offender's return to prison; if offenders are permitted to remain in the community, the effects of continued unemployment can be exceedingly demoralizing. Some programs restrict

Freedom: Halfway House Style

About 50 . . . inmates live in the Tallahassee Community Correctional Center, a U-shaped concrete building in a business section of the city and just next door to a fenced-in state "road prison" in a similar design.

Residents of the work-release center work as masons, cooks, plumbers, carpet installers, painters, demolition workers, roofers, septic tank cleaners, and warehouse loaders. Many make the minimum wage, but those with skills earn more. Residents pay for room and board on a sliding scale depending on their income, and must buy clothing, sheets, pillowcases, blankets, and all personal supplies. They pay $1.50 a day for transportation to and from work.

Some residents said it was difficult, after all the deductions were made from their paychecks, to save very much money. "It's not possible to save enough to get out and buy a car and put a down payment on an apartment," one man said. But most said they preferred the community center to the prison they had left behind. "We have screens on the windows instead of bars," said one, "and they're not searching you all the time."

Many inmates, the men said, are returned to prison for breaking rules, and they blamed this on the frustration caused by the lack of furloughs. (Furlough eligibility is strict in Florida, but rules seem to vary from center to center.) Work releasees, one inmate said, sometimes "try to get away with things. They leave their job, change their job, smoke pot, and drink. They get into trouble with women, like being with a woman in a car. If they'd let you go home on furlough every once in a while, you wouldn't have to do these things." Another resident added: "I don't see why I can be out there for eight hours a day among people and can't go out for a few hours on a Saturday. When you start going out and working, at first you're so happy, and then after a month or so you don't get a furlough and eventually you say, 'I owe this to myself,' and you end up in trouble."

Source: Joan Potter, "The Dilemma of Being Half In and Half Out," *Corrections Magazine* 5(2) (1979): 67, 68. Copyright 1979 by Corrections Magazine and Criminal Justice Publications, Inc., 116 West 32 Street, New York, NY 10001.

persons to the halfway house unless a job interview is scheduled in an effort to keep residents from roaming the streets. Such regulations led one halfway house resident to report: "It's a trick . . . I can't get a social pass (permission to leave the center) because I don't have a job and I can't get a job because I am unskilled."[45] The jobs that are secured are often below the offenders' level of ability. Another inmate remarked: "Everybody knows that when they've got hard work to do and want cheap labor, they call here and we have to take it."[46] The low wages provided by such employment often make saving for final release difficult.

Halfway House Facilities. The facilities in which halfway house programs operate often cause additional problems. The structures are sometimes dilapidated buildings in decaying parts of the community simply because no other facilities could be readily secured. Small dismal rooms, peeling paint, dirty torn carpeting, or floors smelling of disinfectant are typical of such programs. One female halfway house resident remarked: "This place projects an image, a dope-fiendish image. The neighborhood is kind of bad. By being in this kind of area the men around here know who we are and they'll stand in the doorway waiting for us to come out."[47] Another inmate noted: "It's depressing enough going out every day and filling out applications . . . and hearing them say, 'We're not hiring,' or, 'I'll call you if a job is available,' and then having to come back and sit in an ugly room."[48]

Combating the Inmate Code. A 1978 study of an East Los Angeles halfway house revealed that the inmate code was alive and well in that community-based

The Inmate Code in a Halfway House:
A Source of Resistance to Constructive Reintegration

1. Above all else, do not snitch. Informing was regarded as an act directed not simply against an individual, but against the whole collection of deviant colleagues. Snitching would permanently jeopardize a resident's standing with other types, residents, and inmates. His reputation would be spread throughout the whole deviant community, and he would find that he could no longer operate with other deviants. . . .

2. Do not cop out. That is, do not admit that you have done something illegal or illegitimate. Someone who turned himself in willingly would be regarded as strange, "not like us," dumb, and probably not trustworthy, because to "cop out" was a form of defecting to the other side. To turn oneself in could be viewed as a form of defection, because it implied agreement with the standards that one had violated. To turn oneself in to a parole agent when one was about to be caught anyway or when one was "tired of running" and likely to get caught by the police, however, was not talked about as "copping out."

3. Do not take advantage of other residents. This maxim was principally directed against thievery among residents. However, if a resident had something stolen

from him, it was his own responsibility to take care of the thief. Unlike the case of the snitch, a resident could not count on others to negatively sanction the thief. Residents were prohibited by the code from appealing to staff for assistance in locating the stolen goods.

4. Share what you have. A regular resident should be relatively generous with other residents in terms of his money, clothes, and wine. If he used drugs, he should offer a "taste" to others that were around when he "geezed". He should share drugs with his closest friends and sell drugs to others, if he had more than he needed. He should share his "fix" (syringe and spoon) with others and "score" (purchase drugs) for those who could not find a connection (source of drugs).

5. Help other residents. This maxim was principally a directive to help one's fellows avoid detection and punishment. It included "standing point" for them (being a lookout for staff or the police when the other was involved in a compromising activity, such as injecting drugs), warning them about suspicions that staff had, telling staff that they were ignorant about the activities of other residents, so as not to help staff indirectly investigate another guy, arguing with staff on the behalf of

facility (see box above). The inmate code, which encourages loyalty to residents and distrust of staff, appeared to act as a significant barrier to reintegration. Keeping offenders who could have been imprisoned in the community or moving inmates into the community from jail or prison does not necessarily make them receptive to rehabilitation.

Although inmates may be anxious to transfer to a halfway house and noninstitutionalized offenders may view a halfway house commitment as preferable to imprisonment, it would be unreasonable to expect the new resident's initial positive reaction to his placement to be retained throughout his stay at the facility. Some offenders may be less than pleased with halfway house placements. If halfway houses are widely utilized as prerelease centers, inmates may view such transfers as a right, not a privilege, and arrive disgruntled about delays. Other offenders may view halfway houses as a more severe disposition than they expected, having hoped for no more than probation supervision.

Many inmates may settle in to the halfway house as they would adjust to prison—adopting a "do your own time" ethic that resists any outside intervention. Staff must work to demonstrate that the resident can try new behaviors without fear of failure, that there is real support for the resident's efforts to change, and that meaningful guidance and assistance are available. Here the halfway house staff another resident, providing cover stories for other residents, helping another resident sneak into the house after curfew, etc.

6. Do not mess with other residents' interests. A resident should not prevent others from enjoying their deviance, should not disapprove of it, and should not in any way draw staff's attention to it. This includes not "bringing the heat" by engaging in suspicious actions or by getting into an unnecessary altercation with staff. For example, one could "bring the heat" by leaving evidence of drug use around the house which would lead staff to suspect everybody.

7. Do not trust staff—staff is heat. This maxim simply says that in the final analysis staff cannot be trusted, because one of staff's principal occupational duties is to detect deviance. Anything a resident might let them know about himself or others could, in some presently unknown fashion, be used by them to send him or some-one else back to the joint. So, if a resident has anything deviant going for him at all (like having a common-law wife, occasionally using heroin, having user friends in his house, or even using marijuana), he is well advised not to let his agent know his real residence and to give his mother's address instead. In this way he avoids letting his agent know anything that might lead to the discovery of his deviant doings. This advice holds even if a resident is on the best of terms with his agent.

8. Show your loyalty to the residents. Staff, in fact, is "the enemy," and a resident's actions should show that he recognizes this. He should not "kiss ass," do favors for staff, be friendly to staff, take their side in an argu-ment, or accept the legitimacy of their rules. Any of these acts can be understood as a defection to their side, and makes a resident suspect of being the kind of "guy" that would snitch. It is not that being friendly to staff or com-plying with staff's regulations is intrinsically illegitimate, but these matters indicate what kind of person one is and that one, thereby, may not be trustworthy in pro-tecting residents and their interests. If a resident makes it clear in other ways (as, for example, in his private deal-ings with other residents) that he indeed is on the residents' side, these signalizing activities may then be understood in other ways by the other residents. They may be understood as efforts to manipulate staff in some concrete way, e.g., a resident wants them to give him the best jobs they have, or wants to make the kind of impression on his parole agent that will lead the agent away from suspecting him when he otherwise might.

SOURCE: From "The Inmate Code in a Halfway House, by D. L. Wieder. In N. Johnston and L. Savitz (Eds.), *Justice and Correc-tions* (The Hague: Mouton, 1974), pp. 520–523.

can draw upon the armory of community resources and services to encourage the resident who is unsure of where his loyalties lie. Staff can also tailor desired privileges to individual efforts at responsible behavior. By using its substantial resources, the halfway house is much better prepared to overcome inmate resistance than the tradi-tional prison.

❑ Halfway House/Community Relations

Although no research has indicated that the establishment of a halfway house in any way reduces neighborhood security or leads to higher crime rates, the public's fear of such occurrences is real and pervasive. It appears that most citizens are ex-tremely reluctant to have a halfway house established in their own residential area. Many programs have failed simply because they were unable to overcome com-munity resistance. Considering the very real problems that ex-offenders confront when they attempt to reestablish themselves in the community, citizen hostility is doubly damaging—it hurts the program and confirms offender suspicions about the good will of the community.

Although a certain amount of community resistance seems inevitable, halfway house program administrators can attempt to keep it at a manageable level, using

The Mariana (Florida) Community Center

The community center in Mariana is in a flat, monotonous rural area out of sight of houses or businesses. It consists of a cluster of old white frame buildings which are expected to soon be replaced by a one-story concrete structure that had been built on the same grounds. The wooden buildings were constructed as a "road prison" in 1934; so people who live and around Mariana are used to seeing prisoners working on the roads. The facility was closed as a road prison in 1964 and reopened seven years later as a "study-release" center, with inmates attending classes at a local community college. The center was turned into a work-release facility about three years ago.

Residents work at a Coca Cola bottling plant, a window shade factory, a furniture plant, and on construction jobs. They range in age from 18 to 64, and are serving sentences of from one year to life. Only 25 percent come from the area. Most earn the minimum wage and do manual labor. "They have a real good relationship with the community," said Herbert Melvin, a counselor. "People say they'd rather hire them than anyone else. They're on time and they show up every day." With a good record, men are usually paroled after six months, Melvin said.

Source: Joan Potter, "The Dilemma of Being Half In and Half Out," *Corrections Magazine* 5(2) (1979): 67, 68. Copyright 1979 by *Corrections Magazine* and Criminal Justice Publications, Inc., 116 West 32 Street, New York, NY 10001.

various strategies to minimize public hostility and promote community acceptance. Many of these efforts must be initiated in the program planning stage; this period is of critical importance in all attempts to establish a stable and enduring program.

The following sequence of activities is recommended in developing sound community relations:

1. Meet individually with local government leaders (planning boards; private and public social, health, and welfare agencies; fraternal, church, and neighborhood improvement groups). Local police support is essential. If school-age populations are involved, school authorities should be contacted. This list is not inclusive and is only suggestive of the many important groups to contact.

2. Form a steering committee of local leaders. It is helpful to have this group meet regularly to permit recognition and assurance of its mutual interest and support for the program.

3. Explain the program honestly. It is inadvisable and mistaken not to discuss the program in all its ramifications—this means difficulties and problems expected, as well as benefits and advantages.

4. The assistance of neighborhood leaders, whose support has been enlisted previously, will do much to temper community antagonism and help keep negative opposition forces from polarizing.

5. Regularly scheduled meetings should be held both during the planning stages and after the program opens. It is helpful to hold annual or semiannual community meetings (open houses) to which all who are interested may come to visit, meet staff, and learn of the progress, problems, and needs of the halfway house.[49]

Positive halfway house/community relations require the program to bring something to the community, rather than simply drawing upon its services and resources. The program's facility can be used as a meeting place for community organizations. Halfway house residents can provide services to local residents; social events can be sponsored by the program. There is virtually no limit to what the halfway house can contribute if it views itself as an integral part of its community. This self-perception is imperative if the community is to adopt that same viewpoint.

Program Evaluation

In 1982, Latessa and Allen summarized the efforts of ten correctional systems to evaluate their halfway houses (table 7-2). Prior to their assessment, the most comprehensive study of halfway houses had been conducted by the National Evaluation Program. This in-depth investigation of halfway houses merits a closer examination.

❑ National Evaluation Program

In 1977, NEP reported the results of an extensive evaluation of prior research studies of halfway houses.[50] A total of fifty-five evaluative reports were reviewed. Despite numerous methodological problems in many, if not most, of the research efforts, the following general conclusions were reached.

TABLE 7-2 Evaluation Study Outcomes and Comments

Jurisdiction	Outcome/Comments
Alabama	LEAA grant; higher risk clients can be contained at half the cost.
California	In-house study; private houses are economically and operationally more feasible than state-operated houses.
Connecticut	In progress.
Iowa	Done by parole board a year ago; found no significant difference in outcome between halfway house residents and those released to the community directly, but did not consider differences among clients. The parole agency does not necessarily agree with the findings of the study.
Massachusetts	Informal assessment; showed halfway houses to be good for transition period.
Michigan	Found halfway houses to be effective for screening for parole release.
Mississippi	In progress.
Missouri	Compared halfway house and non-halfway house clients; no difference in number of later violations or problems, but halfway house clients had more severe problems to begin with.
District of Columbia	Evaluation in 1977–78; found that halfway houses run by ex-convicts had a better track record than the others.
Federal	Found that halfway houses had no effect on recidivism, but did improve employment.

SOURCE: "Halfway Houses and Parole: A National Assessment," by E. Latessa and H. Allen, *Journal of Criminal Justice* 10(2) (1982):161. Copyright 1982, Pergamon Press, Ltd. Reprinted with permission.

Recidivism.   Almost two-thirds of the studies attempted to measure resident recidivism. Generally, residents' postrelease behavior was followed up for between twelve and eighteen months. Evidence on program impact is divided. About half the studies found lower recidivism rates for halfway house residents when they were compared with institutional parolees; the remaining studies found no differences between former halfway house residents and the comparison group.

Efficiency.   Twelve of the fifty-five reports examined the efficiency with which services are provided to halfway house residents. These studies usually took the form of a cost analysis. Because halfway houses differ so greatly in the amount and quality of services they provide, it is difficult to generalize about program costs. Existing evidence indicates that halfway houses can operate at a cost below, equal to, or greater than institutional costs. Halfway house services almost invariably cost more than probation or parole.

One problem that repeatedly seemed to raise program costs was low utilization. Halfway houses operated at between 21 percent and 76 percent capacity; ideal occupancy was reported to be 85 percent. Per diem costs (cost per resident per day) ranged from $13.19 to $70.50 (a program with 21 percent occupancy).

Treatment Services.   Halfway houses appear able to help ex-offenders locate and maintain employment during the period of their residency in the program; there is evidence, however, that this employment is short-lived after the individual leaves the program. There is little evidence that educational services influence residents' postrelease behavior. Surprisingly, virtually no research on the impact of interpersonal, drug, or alcohol counseling was found, even though these services provide the major focus of many halfway house treatment programs. The effects of family counseling, financial and housing assistance, and leisure time activities are similarly uncertain.

Program Security.   Only one measure of the impact of in-house security efforts was available—program noncompletion rates, which ranged from 30 percent to 50 percent. But they are difficult to evaluate because they include persons terminated because of failure to adjust to the program and job loss as well as residents evicted because of misbehavior. Studies of residents' in-program criminal behavior indicate that between 2 percent and 17 percent of all residents are charged or convicted of new offenses during their program stay. About one-fourth of these offenses involve attacks on the person; another 25 percent involve property crimes; and the remainder generally consist of drug-related or public order offenses. There is no indication that actual or perceived crime rates increase or that the public perceives a decline in neighborhood security following the establishment of a halfway house.

❏ NEP Recommendations

The NEP recommended that future research efforts focus on providing "systematic evaluative research that utilizes good design, randomization, control groups, adequately operationalized variables, and consideration of intervening variables."[51] It was also proposed that research on halfway houses should not be limited to measures of client recidivism, but should focus on broader issues of ex-offender adjustment to

Assigned score	Adjustment criteria
+1	Employed, enrolled in school, or participating in a training program for more than 50 percent of the follow-up period.
+1	Held any one job (or continued in educational or vocational program) for more than a six-month period during the follow-up.
+1	Attained vertical mobility in employment, educational, or vocational program. This could be a raise in pay, promotion of status, movement to a better job, or continuous progression through educational or vocational program.
+1	For the last half of follow-up period, individual was self-supporting and supported any immediate family.
+1	Individual shows stability in residency. Either lived in the same residence for more than six months or moved at suggestion or with the agreement of supervising officer.
+1	Individual has avoided any critical incidents that show instability, immaturity, or inability to solve problems acceptably.
+1	Attainment of financial stability. This is indicated by the individual living within his means, opening bank accounts, or meeting debt payments.
+1	Participation in self-improvement programs. These could be vocational, educational, group counseling, or alcohol or drug maintenance programs.
+1	Individual making satisfactory progress through probation or parole periods. This could be moving downward in levels of supervision or obtaining final release within period.
+1	No illegal activities on any available records during the follow-up period.

FIGURE 7-2 Adjustment Criteria Index

SOURCE: Harry E. Allen, *Halfway Houses* (Washington, D.C.: U.S. Government Printing Office, 1978), p. 75.

the community. One method of broadening the research focus is to use the Relative Adjustment Scale to measure program effectiveness in facilitating offender reintegration. The Relative Adjustment Scale consists of an index of the severity of nonresident criminal behavior used in conjunction with an index of social adjustment (figure 7-2) to measure program impact. The scale was formulated in the belief that reintegration is not "a sudden change in behavior, but movement toward acceptable societal norms." It is therefore important to assess various aspects of adjustment in order to gauge the true extent of an offender's movement toward appropriate behavior.[52]

The adjustment index emphasizes work and educational stability, self-improvement efforts, financial responsibility, probation or parole progress, and the absence of critical incidents or illegal activities. Used along with the index of criminal severity, it allows calculation of the offenders' relative adjustment. Persons may be considered to have made relatively positive adjustments even though they have been involved in minor deliquent acts; but individuals with no criminal activity but with no evidence of positive adjustment in other areas of life will not qualify as complete successes. The information this scale provides should be more realistic than efforts to classify offenders as successes or failures based upon only one aspect of adjustment.

❑ G.A.O. Survey

The General Accounting Office conducted a different type of evaluation when they studied fifteen halfway houses in Florida, Missouri, Pennsylvania, and Texas to determine "whether the states had developed coordinated effective strategies for integrating halfway houses with their overall correction efforts."[53] The research concluded that halfway houses had considerably increased in number and could either become a valuable alternative for many offenders or could die out for lack of funds and public support. The states lacked well-organized systems for coordinating state and locally operated programs; no single agency had information about all halfway houses in any state. The states had no way of ensuring that halfway houses were located in the communities that had the greatest offender populations and that were not already served by existing programs. They also had no means of determining if a community had sufficient resources to meet offender needs if a halfway house was established. Finally, it appeared that the states had failed to coordinate halfway houses with other parts of their correctional systems—prisons and probation and parole agencies had no plans for determining the extent to which halfway houses could or should be used. These findings indicate that extensive planning and coordination of information is drastically needed if halfway houses are to reach their objectives; otherwise, haphazard program development and isolation from the agencies charged with primary responsibility for offender rehabilitation may prove their undoing.

❑ Minnesota Evaluation

One state has attempted to conduct a systematic evaluation of halfway houses established by both its Department of Corrections and local units of government. Minnesota evaluated all halfway houses for released offenders established in that state during a four-year period.[54] Their findings, reported in 1976, were less than encouraging—only about one-third of the halfway house residents were successfully terminated from their programs. Forty-five percent of the residents failed to complete the project because of absconding, failing to cooperate, or similar difficulties. The remaining residents generally withdrew from the programs voluntarily, were withdrawn by their referring agency, or transferred to another program. The research concluded that halfway houses were an inappropriate form of rehabilitation for most of the clients sent to them. Most of the clients in the PORT-type programs studied would have been placed on straight probation if the halfway houses had not been available. Although persons who successfully completed the halfway house programs demonstrated higher levels of postrelease success than residents unsatisfactorily terminated, there were so few successes that program impact was severely limited. The Minnesota study examined factors related to low program completion rates and proposed the following recommendations for halfway house development, integration, and administration:

1. No new halfway house programs should be established unless they are to be evaluated under strict research conditions.
2. A high priority should be placed on cost benefit analysis.
3. Efforts should be made to increase resident program completion rates.

4. An investigation should be made to into new nonresidential community correctional programs and institutional programs.
5. The training of halfway house staff should be improved.
6. Funds should be made available to replace halfway house staff members while they attend training programs.
7. Career ladders should be developed for halfway house paraprofessionals.
8. Continued efforts should be made to obtain the referral of felons to community residential programs as an alternative to incarceration.[55]

The Future of Halfway Houses

The future of halfway houses will inevitably be determined by the ability of the programs to improve the coordination of their services with correctional systems and community resources. The enhancement of halfway house internal organization and management strategies will be essential to this effort and will provide increased cost efficiency as well. Three valuable administrative strategies are management by objectives, managment information systems, and mutual agreement programming.

❑ Management by Objectives

Management by objectives (MBO) is a relatively simple technique designed to improve administration. It requires "the establishment and communication of agency goals and objectives, the setting of individual staff job targets supporting those goals and objectives, and periodic reviewing and evaluating of staff performance related to those job targets and the results achieved in light of the agency's goals and objectives."[56]

MBO permits program activities to be organized around specific goals and objectives. Three types of goals are normally developed: long range, short term, and job targets. Each type of goal is developed in each of the agency's key result areas, such as program delivery; staff training and development, community relations, and communication; records, reports, and research; facilities, equipment, and supplies; and finances.[57] For example, if it is determined that a large number of repeat felony youthful offenders are not completing the halfway house program, the following plan might be developed for the key result area of program delivery:

Long-Range Goal—To have in operation . . . a residential treatment program from which 80 percent of the "hard core" young adult offenders successfully graduate.

Short-Range Objective—To have written . . . a residential treatment program for the "hard core" young adult offender.

Staff Job Target—. . . To have written the first draft of a residential treatment program for the "hard core" young adult offender.[58]

All goals are developed in terms of measurable activities to be accomplished within specific time frames. Staff job targets are ranked to permit efficient organization of tasks. Generally speaking MBO permits the halfway house (or any other program) to know where it is going, where it has been, and with considerable precision, the current status of program operations.

❏ Management Information System

The management information system (MIS) developed by Massachusetts Halfway House, Inc., "functions as a communication mechanism, a tracking and monitoring system, and a vehicle used as an aid in the evaluation of employee job performance."[59] Utilizing a series of forms especially developed for halfway house administration, virtually all program activities are recorded on a continuing basis. At any given time, the halfway house is thus able to identify what information is being communicated within the organization, the status of task accomplishment, and each employee's job performance level. Such information is clearly an invaluable tool to program administration and evaluation.

❏ Mutual Agreement Programming

Mutual agreement programming (MAP) involves the development of individualized contracts by halfway house staff, parole authorities, and prospective halfway house residents. Each party agrees to honor certain commitments:

Residents must assume responsibility for planning (along with program staff) and successfully completing an individually tailored rehabilitative program in order to obtain release on parole on a mutually agreed upon date.

Parole board members must establish a firm parole date and honor it if the resident fulfills the explicit objectives and mutually agreed upon criteria stated in the MAP contract.

Program staff must provide the services and training sources required by the resident, as explicitly guaranteed in the contract, and must fairly assess their own performance in the program.[60]

MAP programs provide several advantages over more traditional parole plans: A specific release date and the conditions for release are clearly established for the offender; parole and halfway house obligations are made explicit; and any individualized treatment plan for the parolee is formulated and implemented.

Such developments seem imperative if halfway houses are to realize their potential for offender assistance. Although these new strategies may generate additional paperwork and somewhat "bureaucratize" the reintegration programs, their payoff may be considerable—particularly if the goals of the contract are achieved.

Summary

Today's halfway houses are as varied as the offenders they serve. The programs originally created by dedicated citizens and volunteers in an attempt to meet the basic needs of the ex-prisoner returning to the community now provide food, shelter, counseling, and employment assistance to persons diverted from the criminal justice system, defendants awaiting trial, and convicted offenders, as well as ex-inmates. Halfway houses offer their residents services ranging from sophisticated diagnostic and clinical treatment programs to the identification, referral and securing of community resources.

Halfway houses continue to serve principally the ex-offender; their objective is to facilitate his reintegration into the community. By easing the inmate's transition to the free world, halfway houses serve both offenders and the community. The ex-offender is given a chance to adjust gradually in a supportive environment in which his basic needs can be met; the community receives both short- and long-term benefits from the supervision and assistance provided to ex-inmates returning from prison.

To accomplish their goals, halfway houses must carefully select their residents, facilities, and location. Treatment and control strategies must match the offender's needs and resources and must reflect his capacity for responsible behavior. Staffing and training activities can make or break the program; so recruitment and selection procedures must be comprehensive and clearly linked to job descriptions. Orientation and in-service and academic educational experiences need to be used to ensure that capable employees grow and develop with their responsibilities.

Research indicates that halfway houses can reduce recidivism and serve as cost efficient alternatives to incarceration. Halfway houses are not always successful, however. Poor planning and coordination with community resources and correctional agencies, programming difficulties, public fears and hostility, and dilemmas inherent in the halfway in/halfway out predicament of residents often prove the downfall of these facilities. In the future, some of these problems may be overcome by more comprehensive planning efforts and the introduction of various management strategies.

KEY WORDS AND CONCEPTS

basic necessities
burnout
community protection
community services
criminal contamination
direct services
emotional support
gradual transition
halfway house/ community relations

humanitarian benefits
intake
intervention programs
Management by Objectives (MBO)
Management Information System (MIS)
Mutual Agreement Programming (MAP)

per diem costs
programming
recidivism
referral
Relative Adjustment Scale
supportive programs
target population

NOTES

1. Edward Latessa and Harry E. Allen, "Halfway Houses and Parole: A National Assessment," *Journal of Criminal Justice* 10(2), 1982: 153–163.
2. David Camp and Camille Camp, *The Corrections Yearbook,* 1989: 38.
3. Harry E. Allen et al. *Halfway Houses* (Washington, D.C.: Government Printing Office, 1978), pp. 2, 6.
4. J. T. L. James, "The Halfway House Movement," in *Alternatives to Prison,* Gary R. Perlstein and Thomas R. Phelps (eds.) (Pacific Palisades, Calif.: Goodyear, 1975), p. 148.
5. Edwin Powers, "Halfway Houses: An Historical Perspective," *American Journal of Correction* 21 (July–August 1959): 35. Reprinted with permission from the American Correctional Association.
6. Ibid.

7. Oliver J. Keller and Benedict S. Alper, *Halfway Houses: Community-Centered Correction and Treatment* (Lexington, Mass.: Lexington Books, 1970), p. 8.
8. Robert F. Kennedy, "Halfway Houses Pay Off," *Crime and Delinquency* 21(1) (1964): 3.
9. Edward M. Koslin et al., "Classification, Evaluation, and Treatment Models in Community Ex-Offender Residency Programs," *Proceedings of the 103rd Annual Congress of Correction of the American Correctional Association* (College Park, Md.: American Correctional Association, 1974), pp. 134–136.
10. Ibid., p. 135.
11. Richard P. Seiter et al., *National Evaluation Program Phase 1 Summary Report: Halfway Houses* (Washington, D.C.: U.S. Government Printing Office, 1977), pp. 9–13.
12. Ibid., p. 9.
13. Ibid., p. 10.
14. Ibid.
15. Ibid.
16. Ibid., p. 12.
17. Michael S. Serrill, "Profile: Massachusetts Adult Correctional System," *Corrections Magazine* 2(2) (1975): 48.
18. Kenneth Schoen, "PORT: A New Concept of Community-Based Correction," *Federal Probation* 36 (September 1972): 35–40.
19. Ibid., p. 36.
20. Ibid., pp. 36–37. Reprinted with permission from *Federal Probation* (1972).
21. Ibid., p. 37. Reprinted with permission from *Federal Probation* (1972).
22. Allen et al., *Halfway Houses*, pp. 5–22.
23. Ann Parker et al., *So You Want to Start a Community Corrections Project* (Hackensack, N.J.: National Council on Crime and Delinquency, 1974), pp. 3–4.
24. Richard P. Seiter et al., *Residential Inmate Aftercare: The State of the Art—Supplement A—Survey of Residential Inmate Aftercare Facilities* (Columbus: Ohio State University, 1976).
25. Ibid.
26. U.S. Bureau of Prisons, *The Residential Center—Corrections in the Community* (Washington, D.C.: U.S. Government Printing Office, 1973), p. 14.
27. Seiter et al., *Residential Inmate Aftercare*.
28. Ibid.
29. Ibid.
30. Ibid.
31. American Correctional Association, *Manual of Correctional Standards* (College Park, Md., 1966), p. 137.
32. Keller and Alper, *Halfway Houses*, p. 107.
33. Richard L. Rachin, "So You Want to Open a Halfway House," *Federal Probation* 36(1) (1972): 34–36.
34. Seiter et al., *Residential Inmate Aftercare*.
35. Ibid.
36. Allen et al., *Halfway Houses*, p. 16.
37. Seiter et al., *Residential Inmate Aftercare*.
38. Ibid.
39. Allen et al., *Halfway Houses*, p. 17.
40. Seiter et al., *Residential Inmate Aftercare*.
41. Allen et al., *Halfway Houses*, pp. 7–8.
42. U.S. Bureau of Prisons, *The Residential Center*, p. 20.
43. Ibid., pp. 20–21.
44. Robert Rosenblum and Debra Whitcomb, *Montgomery County Work Release/Pre-Release Program, Montgomery County Maryland* (Washington, D.C.: U.S. Government Printing Office, 1978), pp. 1–6.
45. Joan Potter, "The Dilemma of Being Half In and Half Out," *Corrections Magazine* 5(2) (1979): 69.
46. Ibid., p. 68.

47. Ibid., p. 69.
48. Ibid.
49. Rachin, "So You Want to Open a Halfway House," p. 171.
50. Richard P. Seiter et al., *NEP Phase 1 Summary Report: Halfway Houses,* pp. 25–33.
51. Ibid., p. 19.
52. Allen et al., *Halfway Houses,* p. 74.
53. General Accounting Office, *Federal Guidance Needed If Halfway Houses Are to Be a Viable Alternative to Prison* (Rockville, Md.: NCJRS Microfiche Collection, 1975), p. i.
54. Governor's Commission on Crime Prevention and Control, *Residential Community Corrections Programs in Minnesota: An Evaluation Report* (Rockville, Md.: NCJRS Microfiche Collection, 1976).
55. Ibid., pp. 288–296.
56. Allen et al., *Halfway Houses,* p. 80.
57. Ibid.
58. Ibid.
59. Ibid., p. 85.
60. Ibid., p. 98.

FOR FURTHER READING

Allen, Harry E., et al., *Halfway Houses* (Washington, D.C.: U.S. Government Printing Office, 1978).

Keller, Oliver J., and Benedict S. Alper, *Halfway Houses: Community-Centered Correction and Treatment* (Lexington, Mass.: Lexington Books, 1970).

Parker, Ann, et al., *So You Want to Start a Community Corrections Project* (Hackensack, N.J.: National Council on Crime and Delinquency, 1974).

United States Bureau of Prisons, *The Residential Center—Corrections in the Community* (Washington, D.C.: U.S. Government Printing Office, 1973).

8: Parole

PAROLE IS ONE OF THE MOST CONTROVERSIAL CORRECTIONAL PROGRAMS. It was once viewed as a necessary transition phase between prison and freedom, a period when correctional authorities could supervise newly released offenders and offer the assistance they need to get back on their feet. Parole supervision was expected to serve both control and rehabilitative objectives. The parole decision-making process was also established both to encourage rehabilitation and to ensure community protection. It was purposely designed to be an informal and subjective administrative process, in which qualified professionals could review an inmate's criminal offense, his personal background, and his prison record in an effort to determine his readiness for release. It was assumed that incarceration was essentially a rehabilitating experience. By releasing the offender when the prison experience had achieved its maximum benefit, and when the offender was no longer a threat to the community, parole could facilitate the offender's adjustment to freedom.

In recent years, this view of parole has been repeatedly challenged. Critics of parole have argued that it simply does not work, that its underlying assumption of offender rehabilitation during incarceration is fallacious, that the parole release decision-making process is arbitrary, and that the surveillance and supervision of offenders in many jurisdictions is dangerously inadequate.[1]

While the debate over the fairness and effectiveness of parole practices continues, parole is still evolving. Indicative of its changing role in contemporary corrections is the current trend toward limiting judges' and parole authorities' discretion. Today more than three-quarters of the states have enacted determinate or mandatory sentencing laws that provide fixed prison terms for offenders. Eighteen other states have begun using parole guidelines that limit parole boards' decision-making authority.[2]

These developments represent major changes in the sentencing and parole decision-making processes. Parole has traditionally been linked to an indeterminate sentencing model—that is, sentences that include a maximum and minimum term of confinement set by a judge. Parole authorities made their release decision within these court-determined boundaries. States placed only very general restrictions on parole decision making, such as requiring offenders to serve the minimum of an indeterminate sentence. Good-time statutes, which permit offenders to have time deducted from their sentences for good behavior, often reduced the actual time served even beyond these limitations. This reduction of judicially imposed sentences by correctional officials is only one of the concerns of parole critics. In this chapter, we discuss the full range of critical issues in parole.

Definition

Parole has been defined as the "release of an offender from a penal or correctional institution, after he has served a portion of his sentence under the continued custody of the state and under conditions that permit his reincarceration in the event of misbehavior."[3] Today parole is the primary mechanism by which inmates are released from prison. Over two-thirds of all adult felons are placed on parole as a condition of their release from prison.[4]

Inmates who are not granted parole may be released in one of two other ways. First, they may receive a conditional or mandatory release. This form of release is based on the accumulation of good-time credits, which are deducted from the sentence because the inmate has conformed to institutional rules and regulations (statutory good time) or because he has performed some outstanding service during incarceration (meritorious good time). A second type of release is unconditional; it occurs through the maximum expiration of sentence. Inmates who "max out" serve their entire prison terms without benefit of parole or the accumulation of good-time credits. Most inmates sentenced to relatively short terms in county or city jails serve out their entire sentences because early release procedures are unavailable or underutilized. Parole release is generally available only to felons serving time in state or federal prisons. It is ironic that society provides the opportunity for early release principally to more serious, long-term offenders.

To complicate matters, parole is frequently confused with probation in the eyes of the general public. This confusion probably stems from the similarities between the two: both require the offender to adhere to specific conditions of release and to accept community supervision. In some states, probationers and parolees are supervised by the same agency. However, the differences between the two client statuses are significant. Parole represents a form of release from prison; probation is a form of sentence that does not include incarceration. Split sentences, which provide for a short period of incarceration followed by probation, are an exception to this rule. An administrative agency, usually referred to as the parole board, makes parole decisions. In contrast, the probation decision is a judicial function and is made by a sentencing judge. Probationers and parolees also face different problems of adjustment. Probationers are not removed from the community, but parolees may have been isolated from the free world for many years before their release from prison. As a result, parolees often confront many serious difficulties during their transition from prison to the community.

As an organizational component of corrections, parole represents the final stage of the criminal justice system. By the time an offender is eligible for parole, his status has changed several times since his initial contact with the criminal justice system. He has been defined and treated as a free citizen, a suspect, an arrestee, a detainee, a defendant, a convict, and an inmate. If he is released on parole, he is placed under correctional supervision in the community and is referred to as a parolee. The community regards the individual who has "done his time" not as a free citizen, but as an ex-offender. Although he has paid for his crime through punishment, a person convicted of a felony loses many of his privileges as a citizen. He may be denied the right to vote, hold public office, obtain license for an occupation, or enter into civil contracts. These losses are generally referred to as the collateral consequences of conviction or civil disabilities. Some of these rights may be restored, but only if the offender applies to the appropriate state or federal authority.

The inmate returning to the community faces more than a loss of rights. His most immediate need is to survive—to find housing and feed and clothe himself while he searches for a job. If an offender has no family or friends to assist him and no money to tide him over until he obtains employment, his search for self-sufficiency may become desperate. Most offenders leave prison with the same problems with which they entered: drug, alcohol, emotional, interpersonal, educational, and employment problems that may stand as obstacles to law-abiding independence. Parole is expected somehow to help the newly released offender manage all these difficulties while protecting the community from ex-offenders who may be tempted to return to crime.

Objectives

The changing nature of parole makes the identification of systemwide parole objectives difficult. Because many parole systems are in a state of flux, the objectives vary from jurisdiction to jurisdiction. However, the National Commission on Criminal Justice Standards and Goals attempted to identify basic objectives that most parole agencies appear to support. Their effort yielded the following list of goals: reduction of recidivism, achievement of fairness and propriety, imposition of appropriate sanctions reflecting public expectations, and maintenance of the justice system.[5]

Most, if not all, correctional systems share the first objective, the reduction of recidivism. The possibility that an offender might return to a life of crime is addressed by the parole release decision-making process, which is expected to screen out dangerous offenders, and by parole supervision. This supervision consists of two components: controlling the offender's behavior and providing social services and assistance.

The objective of ensuring fairness and propriety reflects a number of concerns, ranging from providing procedural rights to parolees to equalizing some of the perceived injustices associated with sentencing disparity (for example, when two offenders are convicted of similar crimes but receive vastly different sentences). Parole boards can minimize such disparities.

The use of appropriate sanctions reflecting public expectations requires parole authorities to be responsive to the community. The impact of the perceived community demands or pressures can be considerable. Community reaction may lead to reductions in the release rate or to the removal of a particular offender from parole consideration because of the notoriety of his crime or the status of his victim(s). Another side of public reaction is the community's role in welcoming the parolee upon his return to freedom. Community hostility and outright rejection can make the provision of services and assistance difficult at best.

The final major objective of parole is the maintenance of the justice system. The National Advisory Commission on Standards and Goals concluded that parole boards act as a kind of "system regulator."[6] Because parole boards control the flow of ex-inmates into the community, they influence all other parts of the justice system, from police to prison. Within the correctional institution itself, parole's impact is extensive. Parole board policy not only influences the length of time inmates will serve; parole board actions also influence the types of programs inmates will participate in. If parole boards look favorably upon prisoners who acquire educational credentials, this concern will rapidly spread to the inmate population and participation in educational programs will significantly increase. Parole board actions may also affect morale. Especially if the decision making appears arbitrary, prisoner morale may be negatively affected.

Historical Development

The word *parole* comes from the French term *parole d'honneur,* which means "word of honor." Parole can be traced back to our English heritage. Three British correctional practices played an especially important role in the emergence of parole in the United States in 1876: the policy of transportation, the use of the conditional pardon, and the ticket of leave.[7]

The transportation of criminals by the British, which has its roots in the ancient practice of banishment, began in the 1600s.[8] The English experiment with transportation was designed to deal with some troubling socioeconomic problems that plagued England at the time. The country was experiencing high levels of unemployment along with the related social problems of crime and poverty. At the same time, the English were suffering a shortage of manpower in their American colonies. Transportation directly addressed all these social problems.

Initially, criminals were granted reprieves or stays of execution if they were ablebodied and fit for work. Those persons granted reprieves were subsequently transported to the colonies for work. Because the transported felons sometimes surreptitiously returned to their homeland, restrictions were eventually placed on the transportees, prohibiting them from returning to England. This practice became known as the conditional parole. A prisoner who violated his conditions would have his reprieve or pardon withdrawn and his original sentence imposed; offenders who remained in the colonies had their sentences suspended.

The mechanics involved in transporting criminals were relatively simple:

> When transportation was just beginning, the Government paid a fee to the contractor for each prisoner transported. However, in 1717, a new law was enacted and this procedure was discontinued. Under the new procedure the contractor or shipmaster was given "property in service" of the prisoner until the expiration of his full term. After a prisoner was delivered to the contractor or shipmaster, the Government took no interest in his welfare or behavior unless he violated the conditions of the pardon by returning to England prior to the expiration of his sentence.
>
> When the pardoned felons arrived in the Colonies, their services were sold to the highest bidder and the shipmaster then transferred the "property in service" agreement to the new master. The felon was no longer referred to as a convicted criminal but became an indentured servant.[9]

The American Revolution ended the transportation of criminals to the British colonies in North America. However, the English crime problem did not abate, nor did the English find they had adequate resources to deal with their prisoner population at home. A search for solutions resulted in the transportation of convicted felons to Australia. This practice began in 1787 and continued until 1867, when the Australians' strenuous objections ended this penal practice.

The mechanics of transporting criminals to Australia differed somewhat from those of transporting them to America. The government met all the expenses incurred in transportation. The offenders did not become indentured servants, but remained prisoners under the control of the British, who assumed responsibility for their behavior and welfare.[10]

In Australia, the colonial governor was responsible for the felons and had the authority to assign convicts to free settlers. Convicts assigned to settlers were expected to serve out their sentences, performing various tasks for their civilian supervisors. After a period of so-called "penal servitude," the transportees were granted pardons, which released them from their enforced labor. These pardons became known as "tickets of leave." The ticket of leave generally read as follows:

> It is his Excellency, the Governor's pleasure to dispense with the government work of _____ tried at _____ convicted of _____ and to permit _____ to employ (off government stores) in any lawful occupation within the district of _____ for his own advantage during good behavior or until his Excellency's further pleasure shall be made known.[11]

The method by which tickets of leave were granted underwent several changes. In the beginning, they were awarded to inmates for a variety of reasons, including good behavior, meritorious service, or marriage.[12] Later, the ticket of leave was granted only after the inmate had served a specific portion of his sentence. This practice was put into law with the English Penal Servitude Act of 1853. From that point on, prisoners sentenced to terms of fifteen years or more were required to serve a minimum of six years before they could be considered for release. This practice is very similar to our contemporary practice of specifying minimum terms of imprisonment to be served prior to release on parole.

In 1854, Sir Walter Crofton introduced three stages of penal servitude into the Irish convict system.[13] Crofton's work was influenced by Captain Alexander Machonochie, who had experimented with these penal practices in New South Wales. Underlying these experiments was the objective of providing offenders with a graduated release experience. In Crofton's Irish system, offenders passed through three stages of confinement. After an initial stage of hard labor in isolation, the offender was provided with an opportunity to perform congregate labor. When he progressed to the third stage of penal servitude, the offender was placed in a transitional setting where he lived and worked under relaxed security conditions. If the offender successfully reached the third penal stage, he was granted a ticket of leave, which permitted him to return to the community. His freedom, however, was conditional. If he misbehaved, he would be returned to prison to serve out his unexpired term.

In the United States, these correctional reforms came to the attention of Zebulon Brockway. Brockway, who became superintendent of the Elmira Reformatory in 1876, incorporated the concepts of the indeterminate sentence, parole, and the earning of good-time credits into his program for youthful offenders at Elmira.[14] He also persuaded the New York State legislature to pass an indeterminate sentencing law, which shifted the authority for determining the time prisoners actually served from the judiciary to correctional officials. Correctional authorities were to evaluate inmate behavior and conformity to institutional discipline. When officials believed that an inmate was fit for freedom, he was released for a six-month period of parole supervision by a volunteer-based guardian. These guardians were ordinary citizens who contributed their time and energies freely. Later, supervision was also provided by volunteer-based prison societies, which were concerned with the social welfare of newly released offenders. By 1900, parole was available in some form to inmates in twenty states. Less than twenty-five years later, only a few states had failed to adopt parole procedures.

Another correctional innovation of the 1800s was good-time credits, which attempted to provide inmates with incentives to improve themselves while under correctional custody. It was believed that there was no better way of achieving inmate commitment to institutional objectives than to provide credits for sentence reduction for good behavior. The first good-time statute was passed in 1817 in New York State; by 1916 every state had authorized a good-time law.[15] Release based on the accumulation of good-time credits is referred to as *supervised mandatory release*. The releasees are supervised by parole officers.

Good-time practices have continued to the present. Today, institutional administrators are among the strongest proponents of good time because it gives inmates incentives to obey prison rules and regulations. It also helps them make the most of their incarceration experience. This type of release also provides prison administrators another mechanism by which to reduce crowding in correctional facilities.

TABLE 8-1 Adults on Parole, 1988

Jurisdiction	Parole population 1/1/88	Entries in 1988	Exits in 1988	Parole population 12/31/88	Percent change in parole population during 1988	Number on parole on 12/31/88 per 100,000 adult residents
U.S. Total	**362,748**	**263,798**	**219,116**	**407,977**	**12.5%**	**224**
Federal	18,846	13,288	11,647	20,487	8.7	11
State	343,902	250,510	207,469	387,490	12.7	213
Northeast	**90,879**	**55,384**	**41,583**	**104,680**	**15.2%**	**272**
Connecticut	466	130	225	371	− 20.4	15
Maine*	0	0	0	0		0
Massachusetts	4,018	4,300	3,985	4,333	7.8	95
New Hampshire	421	213	173	461	9.5	57
New Jersey	15,709	9,943	7,189	18,463	17.5	314
New York	31,244	17,130	14,412	33,962	8.7	251
Pennsylvania	38,398	23,157	15,089	46,466	21.0	508
Rhode Island	423	403	384	442	4.5	58
Vermont	200	108	126	182	− 9.0	44
Midwest	**46,747**	**38,237**	**33,896**	**51,088**	**9.3%**	**115**
Illinois	13,744	10,153	9,528	14,369	4.5	167
Indiana	3,071	3,792	3,452	3,411	11.1	83
Iowa	1,966	1,479	1,500	1,945	− 1.1	92
Kansas	2,676	2,405	1,584	3,497	30.7	190
Michigan	6,342	5,886	4,551	7,677	21.1	113
Minnesota	1,444	1,799	1,604	1,639	13.5	51
Missouri	6,423	4,225	3,422	7,226	12.5	189
Nebraska	459	676	688	447	− 2.6	38
North Dakota	133	139	109	163	22.6	34
Ohio	5,988	4,494	4,491	5,991	0.1	75
South Dakota	492	776	651	617	25.4	120
Wisconsin	4,009	2,413	2,316	4,106	2.4	115
South	**141,609**	**79,581**	**64,251**	**157,486**	**11.2%**	**253**
Alabama	3,456	2,361	1,116	4,701	36.0	157
Arkansas	3,932	1,757	1,849	3,840	− 2.3	220
Delaware	1,100	456	463	1,093	− 0.6	221
Dist. of Col.	3,659	2,801	2,511	3,949	7.9	824

Contemporary Parole

The Uniform Parole Reports collected by the National Council on Crime and Delinquency and published by the U.S. Department of Justice reported that, as of December 31, 1988, there were 407,977 persons under the correctional supervision of parole agencies.[16] In addition to parolees, this figure includes other offenders, defined as mandatory or conditional releasees, who were under parole agency supervision.

The number of persons on parole varies considerably from state to state (see table 8-1). Factors influencing parole release include the state's parole law, eligibility criteria, formal and informal practices of the parole board, the community's attitude toward parole practices, and various problems affecting institutional

TABLE 8-1 (continued)

Jurisdiction	Parole population 1/1/88	Entries in 1988	Exits in 1988	Parole population 12/31/88	Percent change in parole population during 1988	Number on parole on 12/31/88 per 100,000 adult residents
Florida	2,873	2,214	2,525	2,562	– 10.8	27
Georgia	10,917	6,970	6,579	11,308	3.6	248
Kentucky	3,338	2,614	2,509	3,443	3.1	125
Louisiana	7,243	—	—	8,097	11.8	260
Maryland	8,063	5,256	4,094	9,225	14.4	265
Mississippi	3,456	1,315	1,594	3,177	– 8.1	173
North Carolina	4,646	8,009	6,464	6,191	33.3	128
Oklahoma	1,762	—	—	1,455	– 17.4	62
South Carolina	3,469	1,247	1,044	3,672	5.9	146
Tennessee	9,263	4,374	4,108	9,529	2.9	262
Texas	67,308	32,901	22,382	77,827	15.6	657
Virginia	6,283	6,811	6,484	6,610	5.2	145
West Virginia	841	495	529	807	– 4.0	58
West	**64,667**	**77,308**	**67,739**	**74,236**	**14.8%**	**201**
Alaska	435	593	539	489	12.4	137
Arizona	2,224	3,425	3,239	2,410	8.4	95
California	41,333	62,773	54,742	49,364	19.4	237
Colorado	1,680	1,643	1,580	1,743	3.8	72
Hawaii	1,012	716	620	1,108	9.5	137
Idaho	865	273	345	793	– 8.3	113
Montana	624	269	222	671	7.5	115
Nevada	1,598	1,556	1,438	1,716	7.4	218
New Mexico	1,194	1,281	1,395	1,080	– 9.5	102
Oregon	1,988	2,248	1,626	2,610	31.3	125
Utah	1,137	832	751	1,218	7.1	115
Washington	10,211	1,585	1,051	10,745	5.2	311
Wyoming	366	114	191	289	– 21.0	86

Note: Nine states estimated numbers in one or more categories.
—Not reported.
*Maine eliminated parole in 1976.
SOURCE: Bureau of Justice Statistics, "Probation and Parole 1988" (U.S. Department of Justice, November 1989), p. 3.

corrections (for example, prison riots, overcrowding, and court orders). From a system perspective, such factors as the political environment, law enforcement policies, and judicial behavior all influence the use of parole within a particular state.[17]

An examination of national parole population trends suggests that more and more offenders are being released to parole supervision every year. Although the shift toward limiting sentencing judges' and parole authorities' discretion may have an impact on this trend, it appears that, as prisons become more overcrowded, correctional authorities searching for relief will increasingly utilize parole and/or other early release procedures.

More than 80 percent of inmates released from prison in the United States are subjected to some form of parole supervision. A major shift, however, has occurred in the method of releasing inmates from prison to correctional supervision in the community. As table 8-2 shows, the overall rate of inmates released by parole boards has declined from 72 percent of all inmates released from prison in 1977 to 40 percent in 1988, and the percentage of inmates released via mandatory or conditional release (based on the accumulation of good-time credits) increased from 6 percent of all releasees in 1977 to over 30 percent of inmates released from prison in 1988.[18]

Any increased use of parole would strain the resources of already over-burdened parole agencies. If additional resources are not provided, we can expect parole agencies to come under new criticism for not supervising offenders adequately. In the past, such criticism has led to a "lock 'em up" approach to crime control, which only exacerbates prison overcrowding. Taken together, the preceding steps produce what some observers have called "the revolving door of justice."

TABLE 8-2 State Prison Releases, by Method, 1977–1988

			Percent of prison releases						
			Conditional releases				Unconditional releases		
Year	Total releases from prisons	All	Discretionary parole	Supervised mandatory release	Probation	Other	Expiration of sentence	Commutation	Other
1977	115,213	100%	71.9%	5.9%	3.6%	1.0%	16.1%	1.1%	0.4%
1978	119,796	100	70.4	5.8	3.3	2.3	17.0	0.7	0.5
1979	128,954	100	60.2	16.9	3.3	2.4	16.3	0.4	0.6
1980	136,968	100	57.4	19.5	3.6	3.2	14.9	0.5	0.8
1981	142,489	100	54.6	21.4	3.7	3.1	13.9	2.4	1.0
1982	157,144	100	51.9	24.4	4.8	3.6	14.4	0.3	0.6
1983	191,237	100%	48.1%	26.9%	5.2%	2.5%	16.1%	0.5%	0.6%
1984	191,499	100	46.0	28.7	4.9	2.7	16.3	0.5	0.9
1985	203,895	100	43.2	30.8	4.5	3.0	16.9	0.4	1.2
1986	230,672	100	43.2	31.1	4.5	4.6	14.8	0.3	1.4
1987	270,506	100	40.6	31.2	4.4	5.7	16.2	1.0	0.9
1988	301,378	100	40.3	30.6	4.1	6.0	16.8	1.0	1.2

Note: The data are from the National Prisoner Statistics reporting program. The total releases from state prison are those for which the method of release was reported. Deaths, unspecified releases, transfers, and escapes were not included. Altogether, 320,805 persons were released or removed from state prisons in 1988.
Source: Bureau of Justice Statistics, "Probation and Parole 1988" (U.S. Department of Justice, November 1989).

Administrative Structure

Over the years, three organizational models for the administration of parole services have emerged. They are referred to as the institutional, the autonomous, and the consolidated models.[19]

The institutional model invests institutional officials with the paroling decision. The rationale for this practice rests on the belief that, because prison officials are in day-to-day contact with the offender, they are the most knowledgeable regarding the offender's fitness or readiness for release. This model has been criticized because it is feared that the parole decision might be compromised and affected by factors unrelated to the offender's fitness for parole (for example, prison overcrowding). The institutional model has not gained much of a foothold at the adult level of corrections, but it appears to be the preferred method for placing juveniles on aftercare services (the equivalent of adult parole).

The autonomous model places the authority for parole decisions in the hands of a separate agency that is independent from the organization that administers the prison. Supporters of this model argue that the parole decision process will be more objective under this strategy than under the institutional model. It is suggested that the independent agency is less likely to be influenced by issues related to prison management. Critics of the autonomous approach argue that it interferes with the concept of a unified and consistent correctional process—that is, parole decisions may not be consistent with institutional treatment objectives and may even be at odds with prison programming.

The consolidated model represents a compromise between the institutional and autonomous models. It combines the best features of both strategies. A quasi-autonomous parole board is created within a larger corrections department. Institutional officials provide input into decision making but do not have the authority to release inmates early. This appears to be the preferred model in adult corrections today.

Essential Elements of Parole

In the following sections, we discuss the essential characteristics of an effective and efficient parole system as outlined by the American Correctional Association. An examination of some of the elements they label essential provides an overview of contemporary parole operations:

1. Flexibility in the sentencing and parole laws
2. A qualified parole board
3. A qualified parole staff
4. Freedom from political or improper influences
5. Parole assigned to a workable position in the governmental administrative structure
6. Proper parole procedures
7. Prerelease preparation within the institution
8. Parole search
9. A proper attitude by the public toward the parolee[20]

❑ Sentencing Flexibility

The structure and function of parole is inextricably tied to the sentencing model used within a particular jurisdiction. The structure of the sentencing laws determines to what extent the parole board is empowered to release inmates from prison prior to the expiration of their court-imposed sentences. The National Advisory Commission on Standards and Goals acknowledged the significance of sentencing models when it stated:

> All parole systems, no matter how autonomous, are part of a larger process—not only of corrections generally, but also of a complex sentencing structure involving trial courts and legislative mandates. The structure and functions of parole systems and their relative importance in the jurisdiction's total criminal justice picture all depend largely on the sources of sentencing authority and limits on sentencing alternatives and lengths.[21]

Table 8-3 provides an overview of the various sentencing models in use today and their implications for parole.

As we discussed earlier, the intermediate sentence has been linked with parole since its inception and appears to be the model most consistent with the objectives of parole. Under this model, the legislature is responsible for setting the minimum and maximum prison sentence for a particular offense; the judge specifies a prison term within the parameters provided by the legislature; the parole board determines the actual time to be served. Under this model, three sources of authority—the legislature, the court, and the parole board—influence the sentencing and paroling practices of a particular jurisdiction.

The range of discretion provided to the parole board under the indeterminate sentencing model varies across jurisdictions. If the parole board is provided with total discretion regarding the release decision, then actual time served could range from one day to life. Such a policy would invest the parole board with almost total responsibility for the release decision. Political realities have prevented the widespread adoption of this practice; today its use appears to be on the decline. Judges and legislators are extremely reluctant to give up their authority and place total discretion in the hands of parole board members, who are generally the governor's appointees.

As an alternative, the American Correctional Association recommends a sentencing model that is consistent with the objectives of parole but provides some limits on discretion. Under this model, the sentencing judge specifies a maximum sentence but sets no minimum term, thereby empowering parole authorities to release inmates at any point up to the maximum term set.

In contrast to the position of the American Correctional Association, which generally encourages flexibility in the sentencing process, there have been significant steps taken in many jurisdictions to reduce the discretion available to judges and parole authorities. As previously noted, nearly every state has some sort of mandatory sentencing for certain offenses, and thirteen states and the federal government have adopted sentencing guidelines.[22]

Although there are many explanations for this trend toward reduced flexibility in the sentencing process, one important consideration is the disparity that can result from the wide latitude given to judges and parole decision makers. Parole was

TABLE 8-3 Sentencing Practices in the United States

Mandatory Sentencing

Law requires the judge to impose a sentence of incarceration, often of specified length, for certain crimes or certain categories of offenders. There is no option of probation or a suspended sentence.

Mandatory sentencing laws are in force in forty-six states (all except maine, Minnesota, Nebraska, and Rhode Island) and the District of Columbia. In twenty-five states imprisonment is mandatory for certain repeat felony offenders. In thirty states imprisonment is mandatory if a firearm was involved in the commission of a crime. In forty-five states conviction for certain offenses or classes of offenses leads to mandatory imprisonment; most such offenses are serious, violent crimes, and drug trafficking is included in eighteen of the states. Many states have recently made drunk driving an offense for which incarceration is mandated (usually for relatively short periods in a local jail rather than a state prison).

Presumptive Sentencing

The discretion of a judge who imposes a prison sentence is constrained by a specific sentence length set by law for each offense or class of offense. That sentence must be imposed in all unexceptional cases. In response to mitigating or aggravating circumstances, the judge may shorten or lengthen the sentence within specified boundaries, usually with written justification being required.

Presumptive sentencing is used, at least to some degree, in about twelve states.

Sentencing Guidelines

Explicit policies and procedures are specified for deciding on individual sentences. The decision is usually based on the nature of the offense and the offender's criminal record. For example, the prescribed sentence for a certain offense might be probation if the offender has no previous felony convictions, a short term of incarceration if the offender has one prior conviction, and progressively longer prison terms if the offender's criminal history is more extensive.

Sentencing guidelines came into use in the late 1970s. They are:

- used in thirteen states and the federal criminal justice system.
- written into statute in the federal system and in Florida, Louisiana, Maryland, Minnesota, New Jersey, Ohio, Pennsylvania, and Tennessee.
- used systemwide, but not mandated by law, in Utah.
- applied selectively in Massachusetts, Michigan, Rhode Island, and Wisconsin.
- being considered for adoption in other states and the District of Columbia.

Sentence Enhancements

In nearly all states, the judge may lengthen the prison term for an offender with prior felony convictions. The lengths of such enhancements and the criteria for imposing them vary among the states.

In some states that group felonies according to their seriousness, the repeat offender may be given a sentence ordinarily imposed for a higher seriousness category. Some states prescribe lengthening the sentences of habitual offenders by specified amounts or imposing a mandatory minimum term that must be served before parole can be considered. In other states the guidelines provide for sentences that reflect the offender's criminal history as well as the seriousness of the offense. Many states prescribe conditions under which parole eligibility is limited or eliminated. For example, a person with three or more prior felony convictions, if convicted of a serious violent offense, might be sentenced to life imprisonment without parole.

SOURCE: Bureau of Justice Statistics, "Report to the Nation on Crime and Justice," 2nd ed. (U.S. Department of Justice, March 1988), p. 91.

originally viewed as a means of reducing sentencing disparity, but many observers of the correctional process think that parole often falls far short of this goal and instead may introduce greater disparity into release decision making. Ideally, a parole system must be flexible enough to permit individualization of judgments but equitable and consistent enough to promote confidence in the fairness of the process.

A second significant concern is the extent of sentence reduction achieved through parole and good-time procedures. There is considerable feeling among the general public that parole has gone too far and that sentences need to be made more definite, both for punitive and deterrent purposes.

❑ Qualified Parole Board

Given the responsibilities of their office, the need for qualified parole board members appears obvious. As will be seen, few states have bothered to set up guidelines that would ensure the selection and appointment of qualified individuals to these very important positions.

In order to address the qualifications of parole board members, we need to know something of what they do. Their responsibilities lie in two areas: general policymaking and individual decision making regarding specific cases. Policymaking includes interpreting parole to the public and promoting sound parole legislation as well as formulating regulations and guidelines on all matters related to the work of the parole board. Parole decision-making functions include reviewing cases to fix parole eligibility dates, granting and revoking paroles, discharging offenders from parole when supervision is no longer required, and determining the conditions of parole. Where the work load is heavy, many agencies appoint a full-time administrator who is responsible for the details of day-to-day parole agency management.

The American Correctional Association suggests that prospective candidates for appointment should not be political officials and should have the following qualifications: good character, academic training in corrections or a closely related discipline (criminology, sociology, social work, or law), and experience with and an understanding of the offenders and their problems.[23] The National Advisory Commission on Criminal Justice Standards and Goals suggests that members should also have a high degree of skill in comprehending legal issues and statistical information.[24]

A critical factor in selecting individuals for the parole board is the process by which members are appointed. In a majority of these states, the governor has the power to appoint members to the parole board. Most appointments are for terms of six years or less. One survey of the appointment process reported that at least two-thirds of the states had either no criteria or standards so vague as to render them meaningless.[25]

❑ Qualified Parole Staff

The quality of parole services will only be as good as the quality of employees working in the field of parole. In addition to the members of the parole board, there are several types of parole employees: administrators, field parole officers, and clerical workers. In some agencies, paraprofessionals (often ex-offenders) may also be employed as parole aides.

The National Manpower Survey of the Criminal Justice System identified several tasks that are the responsibility of parole officers.[26] These include periodically meeting and communicating parole policy to offenders, counseling, advising and assisting inmates regarding a variety of issues ranging from personal problems to employment needs, handling paperwork associated with parole casework, and making decisions regarding the offender's status on parole—that is, is he making a successful adjustment or should parole be revoked?

The selection of individuals for parole fieldwork should be based on merit. There seems to be some consensus that the qualifications for a professional position should include graduation from an accredited university with a concentration in a corrections-related area. In addition, one year of supervised experience with a social service agency or one year of graduate study also seems desirable. At present, most states require a college degree but do not require any particular field of educational study.

The National Advisory Commission suggests that there should be some provision for hiring non-college educated persons (for example, ex-offenders) who might be very skillful in dealing with certain offender-related problems.[27] Career opportunities would have to be expanded to meet the needs of qualified individuals who enter parole work through nontraditional channels so they may rise through the ranks to professional positions. It has also been suggested that an attempt should be made to recruit a professional parole staff that reflects the ethnic makeup of the offender population. Hiring persons who share background and other important characteristics with offenders may enhance communication and understanding between parole staff and parolees.

❏ Freedom from Influence

Many important correctional decisions involve discretion. In terms of impact, these decisions can have serious implications for the offender (continued incarceration) and for the community (in terms of crime control). The control and exercise of discretion can also have a major impact on the organization and function of corrections. It is therefore imperative that the decisions made not be influenced by partisan politics or considerations of personal gain. For example, the distribution of corrections jobs as rewards for political loyalty is not an uncommon practice, but it impedes professionalization in corrections. Political officials have also attempted to intervene in release decision making to obtain favorable treatment for specific offenders or to bar the release of inmates perceived as threats to the community. These actions undermine staff, inmate, and community commitment to the goals of corrections and can have disastrous consequences for parole system operation.

❏ Effective Parole Administration

There are currently four organizational structures used to administer parole in the United States.[28] In most states, the parole board administers the combined probation and parole system. Under the second model, probation and parole are not unified; the parole board administers only parole services. In other states, parole and institutional corrections are unified. The fourth administrative structure unites probation, parole, and institutional corrections in one superstructure. Table 8-4 presents the results of a national survey of the organizational structure of parole.

The ideal structure for parole services administration is a subject of debate. Service continuity and coordination is enhanced by combining services under one organizational umbrella. But separating probation and parole from institutional corrections may permit these services to be more responsive to the orders of the courts and parole board, respectively. The problems of institutional corrections may divert administrative attention and subsequent funding from community-based services to prisons in a unified structure. The objective is to coordinate services without sacrificing recognition of the unique and sometimes conflicting problems of probation, prison, and parole administration.

❏ Proper Parole Procedures

Providing a comprehensive and effective parole system requires considering several interrelated components. The American Correctional Association maintains that minimum procedural requirements for a complete parole system include the following: providing offenders with information concerning parole purposes, requirements, and expectations; preparing preparole reports for subsequent parole hearings; conducting various types of parole-related hearings; assisting inmates with developing satisfactory parole plans; providing graduated release experiences for inmates preparing for release; and providing services to parolees in the community.[29] In addition, an adequate parole system is responsible for the parole revocation process and for the discharge of parolees no longer in need of supervision. These activities reflect the three basic functions of the parole process: preparole preparation, parole-related hearings, and postrelease services and responsibilities.

Preparole Activities. Preparole activities include education, planning, and preparation.[30] Education involves informing the inmate of how he can earn parole and what will be expected of him. Planning and preparation for parole involves both staff and inmates. Inmates, usually with the assistance of staff, attempt to set up an institutional program designed to prepare them for parole release. Ideally, this program begins the day the offender enters the institution, but practice suggests otherwise. Institutional administrators and personnel are frequently preoccupied with the present rather than the future; their primary concern is to encourage the offender to adjust to prison living rather than to begin preparation for release. Because of this problem, many correctional agencies have adopted short-term, intensive, institutional prerelease or preparole programs. These programs are usually sixty to ninety days in length and are provided to offenders as they near their release dates. They are often designed as much to undo the effects of incarceration as to prepare the inmate for his return to society.

Another important task involved in the preparole planning process is the preparation of a case file on the inmate by the institutional parole officer or other institutional personnel. This file, usually referred to as the preparole report, is given

TABLE 8-4 Characteristics of Adult Paroling Authorities, 1989

State	Name of agency	Independent	Number of board members	Fulltime board	Administration of field parole services
AL	Bd of Pardons & Paroles	Yes	3	Yes	Bd of Pardons & Paroles
AK	Bd of Parole	Yes	5	No	Dept of Corrections
AZ	Bd of Pardons & Paroles	Yes	5	Yes	Dept of Corrections
AR	Bd of Pardons & Paroles	Yes	5	No	Dept of Corrections
CA	Bd of Prison Terms	Yes	9	Yes	Dept of Corrections
CO	Bd of Parole	Yes	5	Yes	Div of Comm Svcs/DOC[e]
CT	Bd of Parole	Yes	11	No[a]	Dept of Corrections/Div of Parole
DE	Bd of Parole	Yes	5	No[a]	Dept of Corrections/Div of Comm Svcs
DC	Bd of Parole	Yes	3	Yes	Bd of Parole
FL	Parole Bd	Yes	7	Yes	Dept of Corrections
GA	Bd of Pardons & Parole	Yes	5	Yes	Dept of Corrections
HI	Paroling Authority	Yes	3	No[a]	Parole Auth
ID	Commission for Pardons & Parole	Yes	5	No	Dept of Corrections
IL	Prisoner Review Bd	Yes	10	Yes	Dept of Corrections
IN	Parole Bd	Yes	5	Yes	Dept of Corrections/Parole Svcs
IA	Bd of Parole	Yes	7	No	Dept of Corrections/Parole Svcs
KS	Parole Bd	Yes	5	Yes	Dept of Corrections
KY	Parole Bd	Yes	5	Yes	Corrections Cabinet
LA	Bd of Parole	Yes	5	Yes	Dept of Public Safety
ME	Parole Board[f]	Yes	5	No	Dept of Corrections
MD	Parole Commission	No	7	Yes	Dept of Public Safety & Corrections Svcs
MA	Parole Bd	Yes	7	Yes	Parole Bd
MI	Parole Bd	No	7	Yes	Dept of Corrections
MN	DOC, Office of Adult Release	No	4	No[a]	Dept of Corrections
MS	Parole Bd	Yes	5	No[a]	Dept of Corrections
MO	Bd of Probation & Parole	Yes	3	Yes	Bd of Probation & Parole
MT	Bd of Pardons	Yes	3	No	Corrections Dept/Comm Corrections Bd
NE	Bd of Parole	No	5	No[b]	Dept of Correctional Svcs
NV	Bd of Parole Commissioners	Yes	3	Yes	Dept of Parole & Probation
NH	Bd of Parole	Yes	3	No	Dept of Corrections
NJ	Parole Bd	Yes	7	Yes	Dept of Corrections
NM	Parole Bd	Yes	3	Yes	Dept of Corrections
NY	Bd of Parole	Yes	12	Yes	Division of Parole
NC	Parole Commission	Yes	5	Yes	Dept of Corrections
ND	Parole Bd	Yes	3	No	Parole & Probation Dept
OH	Adult Parole Authority	No	7	Yes	Dept of Rehab & Corrections
OK	Pardon & Parole Bd	Yes	5	No	Dept of Corrections
OR	Bd of Parole	Yes	5	Yes	Corrections Division
PA	Bd of Probation & Parole	Yes	5	Yes	Bd of Probation & Parole
RI	Parole Bd	Yes	5	No	Dept of Corrections
SC	Bd of Probation, Paroles & Pardon Svcs	Yes	7	No	Dept of Probation, Pardon Svcs
SD	Bd of Pardons & Paroles	Yes	3	No	Office of Correctional Svcs
TN	Bd of Paroles	Yes	5	Yes	Bd of Paroles
TX	Bd of Pardons & Paroles	Yes	3[d]	Yes	Bd of Pardons & Paroles

(continued)

TABLE 8-4 Characteristics of Adult Paroling Authorities, 1989 (*continued*)

State	Name of agency	Independent	Number of board members	Fulltime board	Administration of field parole services
UT	Bd of Pardon & Parole	No	5	No	Div of Corrections
VT	Bd of Parole	Yes	5	No	Dept of Corrections
VA	Parole Bd	Yes	5	Yes	Dept of Corrections
WA	Indeterminate Sentence Review	Yes	7	Yes	Dept of Corrections
WV	Bd of Probation & Parole	Yes	3	Yes	Dept of Corrections
WI	Parole Bd	No	9	Yes	Dept of Corrections
WY	Bd of Parole	Yes	3	No	Dept of Probation & Parole
US	Parole Commission	Yes	9	Yes	U.S. District Courts

[a]The chairman serves full-time; members serve part-time.
[b]The chairman and two members serve full-time; two members serve part-time.
[c]MN Corrections Bd legislatively abolished June 30, 1982.
[d]Plus nine-member Parole Commission.
[e]DOC = Department of Corrections.
[f]Parole abolished; hears only pre-1976 cases.
SOURCE: *Directory: Juvenile and Adult Correctional Departments, Institutions, Agencies and Paroling Authorities* (College Park, Md.: American Correctional Association, 1981 and 1989). Reprinted by permission.

to the parole board prior to the offender's hearing and should provide adequate information to allow the board to reach a reasonable decision regarding the inmate's prospects for parole. In many cases, this document is the sole basis for the parole decision; as a result, it must include relevant and pertinent information regarding the offender, his past, and his future plans.

In practice, the quality and comprehensiveness of parole reports vary from one system to another, but most contain several basic elements:

1. Information regarding the offender's present offense, including arrest and conviction
2. Information regarding the offender's individual and social characteristics
3. A copy of the offender's presentence investigation report
4. Institutional reports regarding the offender's adjustment to prison, participation in programs, institutional disciplinary infractions, and any recommendations by the institutional staff
5. The offender's parole plan (Usually, this must include the residence in which the offender will be staying upon release and a job. Most states require either a confirmed employment offer [job in hand] or a letter of assurance from an employer that the prospective parolee will be provided a job once he is released on parole.)[31]

In addition to these items, some parole boards permit statements or recommendations from the offender's sentencing judge and/or prosecutor or information regarding the victim's attitude toward the offender's release to be included in the parole report.

Parole Hearings.   There are several types of parole-related hearings. In some states where indeterminate sentences are used, the parole board sets the offender's minimum parole eligibility date. In other jurisdictions, the parole eligibility date is set by statute or by court order. After the eligibility date has been fixed, the parole board may conduct additional hearings to review cases on an annual basis to assess inmate progress.

Parole boards are responsible for presiding over hearings in which they determine prisoners' readiness for release. Although these hearings determine the actual time to be served by inmates, legal counsel and the presentation of witnesses are not permitted and hearings are often less formal than a judicial proceeding. They normally involve an interview with the inmate as well as a review of the preparole report. Although the intent of the interview is to gain insight into the inmate's character, these interviews often last only a short time and can become very superficial and routine.

Most states require the parole board to determine to the best of its ability that the prisoner will not violate the law again. A survey of U.S. parole boards revealed that the items listed in table 8-5 are the most crucial elements in release decision making.

The Model Penal Code, drafted by the American Law Institute, recommends consideration of the following factors:

1. The prisoner's personality, including his maturity, stability, sense of responsibility, and any apparent development in his personality that may promote or hinder his conformity to law
2. The adequacy of the prisoner's parole plan
3. The prisoner's ability and readiness to assume obligations and undertake responsibilities
4. The prisoner's intelligence and training
5. The prisoner's family status and whether he has relatives who display an interest in him or whether he has other close and constructive associations in the community
6. The prisoner's employment history, his occupational skills, and the stability of his past employment

TABLE 8-5 Items Parole Board Members Consider Most Important in Parole Decisions

Item	Percent including item as one of five most important
1. My estimate of the chances that the prisoner would or would not commit a serious crime if paroled	92.8%
2. My judgment that the prisoner would benefit from further experience in the institution program or, at any rate, would become a better risk if confined longer	87.1
3. My judgment that the prisoner would become a worse risk if confined longer	71.9
4. My judgment that the prisoner had already been punished enough to "pay" for this crime	43.2
5. The probability that the prisoner would be a misdemeanant and a burden to his parole supervisors, even if he did not commit any serious offenses on parole	34.3
6. My feelings about how my decision in this case would affect the feelings or welfare of the prisoner's relatives or dependents	33.8
7. What I thought the reaction of the judge might be if the prisoner were granted parole	20.9

SOURCE: National Advisory Commission on Criminal Justice Standards and Goals, *Corrections* (Washington, D.C.: U.S. Department of Justice, 1973), p. 394, from National Parole Institutes, *Selection for Parole* (New York: National Council on Crime and Delinquency, 1966).

7. The type of residence, neighborhood, or community in which the prisoner plans to live

8. The prisoner's past use of narcotics or past habitual and excessive use of alcohol

9. The prisoner's mental or physical makeup, including any disability or handicap that may affect his conformity to law

10. The prisoner's prior criminal record, including the nature, circumstances, and frequency of previous offenses

11. The prisoner's attitude toward law and authority

12. The prisoner's conduct in the institution, including particularly whether he has taken advantage of the opportunities for self-improvement afforded by the institutional program, whether he has been punished for misconduct within six months prior to his hearing or reconsideration for parole release, whether he has forfeited any reductions of term during his period of imprisonment, and whether such reductions have been restored at the time of hearing or reconsideration

13. The prisoner's conduct and attitude during any previous experience of probation or parole and the recency of such experience.[32]

In addition to these prisoner characteristics, a consideration of the community's readiness for the offender's return is often regarded as an important component of the release decision-making process. A decision not to release an inmate should be fully explained to the offender so that he can make the necessary improvements to gain release at a subsequent date.

In some states, the parole board does not physically preside over the parole hearings; instead, parole examiners, who are employees of the board, conduct the hearings. They hear the cases and make recommendations to the board. In some states, the board is still responsible for all release decisions; in others, the board reviews only those cases in which the inmate or the correctional authority is dissatisfied with the hearing examiner's decision (see figure 8-1). The use of parole examiners can be a very effective means of reducing the parole board's work load. Properly recruited and trained, examiners can conduct in-depth professional investigations and interviews, freeing parole board members to devote more time to issues of policymaking.

The parole board is also responsible for parole revocation procedures and must approve the revocation of an offender's parole. Similarly, the parole board is responsible for determining discharge procedures for offenders who no longer need parole supervision and issuing final discharges to deserving parolees.

Postrelease Services. The final major activity of parole is the provision of postrelease services. The principal activity of this phase of the parole process is the supervision of parolees. As with the probation function, the supervision process includes two components: providing social services and monitoring the parolee's behavior. The service-delivery systems for probationers and parolees are similar; in some jurisdictions, the same agency deals with both types of offenders. However, parolees' adjustment problems are usually significantly greater than those of probationers. The person placed on probation usually remains in the community, and ties to family, job, or school remain essentially intact. This is not the case for the parolee,

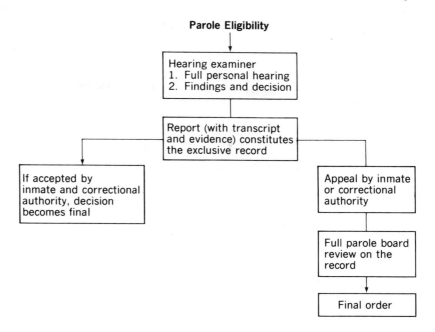

FIGURE 8-1 The Hearing Examiner Model

SOURCE: National Advisory Commission on Standards and Goals: *Corrections* (Washington, D.C.: U.S. Government Printing Office, 1977), p. 404.

who must establish or reestablish ties to a community from which he has been forcibly removed for several months or several years. The longer the offender has been in prison, the less likely he will be to have a support group waiting for him in the community. Figure 8-2 presents the form used by the Wisconsin Division of Corrections to assess offender strengths and weaknesses and facilitate parole supervision planning.

The conditions of parole the parole board establishes are very important tools in the supervision process. Like probation conditions, parole conditions help the offender when he needs reform (an offender might be required to undergo drug treatment or counseling or to continue his education). They also assist parole officers in their attempt to monitor and control the parolee's behavior by requiring the offender to report to them regularly, inform them about changes in residence or employment, refrain from associating with known offenders, and so on. Prior to parole, the offender is required to agree in writing to abide by all parole conditions. Should he fail to fulfill this agreement, parole can be revoked and he can be returned to prison.

The conditions placed on the offender vary from state to state. The Model Penal Code provides guidelines for states considering a review and possible revision of parole conditions. It recommends the following conditions for parole:

When a prisoner is released on parole, the Board of Parole shall require as a condition of his parole that he refrain from engaging in criminal conduct. The Board of Parole may also require, either at the time of his release on parole or at any time and from

BUREAU OF PROBATION AND PAROLE

Client Profile Check List For _____
Name of Client

Explanation of Categories:

Strength: (An item that might exert a positive influence on the client's adjustment.)

Neutral: (An item that is not related to the case, not applicable, or unknown.)

Problem: (An item that might exert a negative influence on the client's adjustment.)

The significant information necessary to complete this *Check List* should be available from the Social History or Preparole Investigation. Consider carefully all of these items below (they follow the general sequence of the Social History Investigation Outline) and check those which should be considered in the case of supervision planning for this client.

Strength	Neutral	Problem	
			1. Use of aliases
			2. Appearance
			3. Area of residence
			4. Court-ordered conditions/obligations
			5. Prior record
			6. Relationship with parents
			7. Marital history of parents
			8. Relationship with other family members
			9. Family criminal history
			10. Client sexual behavior
			11. Educational attainment
			12. School adjustment
			13. Abuse of drugs/alcohol
			14. Physical health
			15. Emotional stability
			16. Financial management—debts
			17. Present job adjustment
			18. Employment history
			19. Marketable skills
			20. Use of leisure time
			21. Associates/companions
			22. Attitude of spouse
			23. Relationship with spouse
			24. Marital history of client
			25. Present marital status of client
			26. Emotional climate of home
			27. Community acceptance
			28. Ability to communicate
			29. Self-concept
			30. Acceptance of responsibility
			31. Response to supervision
			32. Previous performance on supervision
			33. Motivation to change
			34. Relationships with police
			35. Resource availability
			36. Gang involvement
			37. Absconder—risk
			38. Crime against person—risk
			39. Crime against property—risk
			40. Other

FIGURE 8-2 Wisconsin Division of Corrections Client Profile Check List

SOURCE: L. H. Blair et al., *Monitoring the Impact of Prison and Parole Services* (Washington, D.C.: U.S. Department of Justice, 1977), p. 56.

time to time while he remains under parole, that he conform to any of the following conditions of parole:

    a. Meet his specified family responsibilities;

    b. Devote himself to an approved employment or occupation;

    c. Remain within the geographic limits fixed in his Certificate of Parole, unless granted written permission to leave such limits;

    d. Report, as directed, in person and within thirty-six hours of his release, to his parole officer;

    e. Report in person to his parole officer at such regular intervals as may be required;

    f. Reside at the place fixed in his Certificate of Parole and notify his parole officer of any change in his address or employment;

    g. Have in his possession no firearm or other dangerous weapon unless granted written permission;

    h. Submit himself to available medical or pyschiatric treatment, if the Board shall so require;

    i. Refrain from associating with persons known to him to be engaged in criminal activities or, without permission of his parole officer, with persons known to him to have been convicted of a crime;

    j. Satisfy any other conditions specifically related to the cause of his offense and not unduly restrictive of his liberty or incompatible with his freedom of conscience.[33]

Revocation.   There are two types of parole violations: a legal violation, which consists of a new crime committed by the parolee, and a technical violation, which is a violation of one of the parole conditions. Revocation is not automatic upon the commission of a violation; the parole officer has the discretion to initiate the revocation proceeding. The officer may overlook isolated technical violations. If the violation involves a new offense, the revocation proceeding is generally begun, but the return of the parole violator to prison is still not automatic.

As with the probation revocation process, the parole revocation proceeding must provide certain due process protections to the parolee. These protections include a two-stage hearing procedure. At the first stage, a preliminary hearing is held before an uninvolved person or impartial officer—not necessarily a judicial official—who determines if there is reasonable cause to believe that parole conditions were violated. The offender is provided notice of the hearing and a full description of the charges. At the second stage, the formal revocation proceeding takes place before the parole board or its representative. Minimum due process protection provided to the offender at this stage includes:

1. Written notice of the charge
2. Disclosure of evidence against him
3. The right to be heard in person and present witnesses and evidence in his own behalf
4. A right to confront and cross-examine adverse witnesses (unless good cause is found for not permitting the interaction)
5. A neutral and detached hearing body (such as a parole board)
6. A written statement by the fact finders explaining the decision[34]

Promising Parole Strategies

Parole has undergone many changes in the past few years. Many states have modified or are in the process of modifying the paroling process. Several general observations may be made regarding the current status of parole (and probation) services.[35] First, despite extensive criticism, the rehabilitation ethic is not dead; many of today's parole programs are still designed to change and assist the offender. Second, the problems created by the conflicting roles assumed by parole officers, who must act as both police officers and social workers, remain unresolved. Third, there is an increasingly pervasive public perception of the threat of crime. This is often translated into a demand that parole agencies emphasize their control function. Fourth, during the past years, parole populations have increased dramatically. The number of staff assigned to parole agencies, however, has not kept pace with the rapid increase in case loads. Thus, parole resources are seriously overburdened. Fifth, there has been considerable growth in private sector involvement in the provision of services to parolees. At the same time, some parole agencies have been experimenting with the use of volunteers in parole. Finally, there has been continued growth in the use of halfway houses and work-release centers for parolees. All these trends affect the formulation and delivery of parole services. Innovations in parole may be grouped according to their principal focus: improving parole decision making or improving parole supervision.

❑ Parole Decision Making

Guidelines.   In terms of decision making, one of the most significant innovations is the development and use of parole guidelines, which structure the discretion of parole decision making and ensure that the decisions reached are fair and just. The advantage of guidelines, as one study suggests, is that they facilitate the attempt "to achieve a balance between the evils of completely unstructured discretion and those of a totally fixed and mechanical approach."[36]

The U.S. Parole Commission developed an actuarial tool known as the Salient Factor Score.[37] Designed to facilitate the parole decision-making process, it also illustrates the use of parole guidelines. This device helps the commission determine the period of confinement offenders should serve on the basis of two factors: offense severity and parole prognosis (based on the offender's personal characteristics). Fourteen states, the District of Columbia, and the federal system have adopted similar instruments.

The Salient Factor Score is based on the points assigned to an offender on seven items. When these points are totaled, a composite score ranging from 0 to 11 is obtained. Parole researchers have found that persons with high scores are generally good risks for parole. Figures 8-3 and 8-4 illustrate the Salient Factor Scoring device and the guidelines in determining parole release. Whenever the board decides not to follow the guidelines, it must justify this action in writing. The case of John Wilkes illustrates the use of the Salient Factor Score and Parole Guidelines:

At age 32, John Wilkes was convicted of illegally transporting Mexican citizens across the border into Texas. At the time of the offense, he had been employed for ten of the previous twenty-four months and had no history of drug or alcohol abuse. His prior record consisted of a conviction for burglary at age 22. He was committed for that offense and then successfully paroled.

Using the Salient Factor Score and Parole Guidelines, it is determined that John is a good risk for parole. His score is 8, and he would normally be paroled after fourteen to eighteen months of incarceration.

		John Wilkes' Score
Register Number _____ Name _____		
Item A		(2)
No prior convictions (adult or juvenile) = 3		
One prior conviction = 2		
Two or three convictions = 1		
Four or more prior convictions = 0		
Item B		(1)
No prior commitments (adult or juvenile) = 2		
One or two prior commitments = 1		
Three or more prior commitments = 0		
Item C		(1)
Age at behavior leading to first commitment (adult or juvenile):		
26 or older = 2		
18–25 = 1		
17 or younger = 0		
*Item D		(1)
Commitment offense did not involve auto theft or check(s) (forgery/larceny) = 1		
Commitment offense involved auto theft [X], or check(s) [Y], or both [Z] = 0		
*Item E		(1)
Never had parole revoked or been committed for a new offense while on parole, and not a probation violator this time = 1		
Has had parole revoked or been committed for a new offense while on parole [X], or is a probation violator this time [Y], or both [Z] = 0		
Item F		(1)
No history of heroin or opiate dependence = 1		
Otherwise = 0		
Item G		(1)
Verified employment (or full-time school attendance) for a total of at least 6 months during the last 2 years in the community = 1		
Otherwise = 0		
TOTAL SCORE		(8)

Note:
   For purposes of the Salient Factor Score, an instance of criminal behavior resulting in a judicial determination of guilt or an admission of guilt before a judicial body shall be treated as if a conviction, even if a conviction is not formally entered.

*Note to Examiners:
   If Item D and/or E is scored 0, place the appropriate letter (X, Y or Z) on the line to the right of the box.

FIGURE 8-3 Salient Factor Score
   SOURCE: P. B. Hoffman and S. Adelberg, "The Salient Factor-Score: A Non-Technical Overview," *Federal Probation* 44 (1980): 50–52. Reprinted with permission from Federal Probation, 1980.

FIGURE 8-4 Adult Guidelines for Decision Making

Severity of offense behavior (Examples)	Parole prognosis (salient factor score)			
	Very good (11 to 9)	Good (8 to 6)	Fair (5 to 4)	Poor (3 to 0)
Low Alcohol or Cigarette Law violations, including tax evasion (amount of tax evaded less than $2,000) Gambling law violations (no managerial or proprietary interest) Illicit drugs, simple possession marijuana/hashish, possession with intent to distribute/sale [very small scale (e.g., less than 10 lbs. of marijuana/less than 1 lb. of hashish/less than .01 liter of hash oil)] Property offenses (theft, income tax evasion, or simple possession of stolen property) less than $2,000	6 months	6–9 months	9–12 months	12–16 months
Low/Moderate Counterfeit currency or other medium of exchange [(passing/possession) less than $2,000] Drugs (other than specifically categorized), possession with intent to distribute/sale [very small scale (e.g., less than 200 doses)] Marijuana/hashish, possession with intent to distribute/sale [small scale (e.g., 10–49 lbs. of marijuana/1–4.9 lbs. of hashish/.01–.04 liters of hash oil)] Cocaine, possession with intent to distribute/sale [very small scale (e.g., less than 1 gram of 100% purity, or equivalent amount)] Gambling law violation—managerial or proprietary interest in small scale operation [e.g., Sports books (estimated daily gross less than $5,000); Horse books (estimated daily gross less than $1,500); Numbers bankers (estimated daily gross less than $750)] Immigration law violations Property offenses (forgery/fraud/theft from mail/embezzlement/interstate transportation of stolen or forged securities/receiving stolen property with intent to resell) less than $2,000	8 months	8–12 months	12–16 months	16–22 months
Moderate Automobile theft (3 cars or less involved and total value does not exceed $19,999) Counterfeit currency or other medium of exchange [(passing/possession) $2,000–$19,999] Drugs (other than specifically categorized), possession with intent to distribute/sale [small scale (e.g., 200–999 doses)] Marijuana/hashish, possession with intent to distribute/sale [medium sale (e.g., 50–199 lbs. of marijuana/5–19.9 lbs. of hashish/.05–.19 liters of hash oil)] Cocaine, possession with intent to distribute/sale [small scale (e.g., 1.0–4.9 grams of 100% purity, or equivalent amount)]	10–14 months	14–18 months	18–24 months	24–32 months

FIGURE 8-4 Adult Guidelines for Decision Making *(continued)*

Severity of offense behavior (Examples)	Parole prognosis (salient factor score)			
	Very good *(11 to 9)*	*Good* *(8 to 6)*	*Fair* *(5 to 4)*	*Poor* *(3 to 0)*

Moderate (continued)

Opiates, possession with intent to distribute/sale [evidence of opiate addiction and very small scale (e.g., less than 1.0 grams of 100% pure heroin, or equivalent amount)]

Firearms Act, possession/purchase/sale (single weapon: not sawed-off shotgun or machine gun)

Gambling law violations–managerial or proprietary interest in medium scale operations [e.g., Sports books (estimated daily gross $5,000–$15,000); Horse books (estimated daily gross $1,500–$4,000); Numbers bankers (estimated daily gross $750–$2,000)]

Property offenses (theft/forgery/fraud/embezzlement/interstate transportation of stolen or forged securities/income tax evasion/receiving stolen property) $2,000–$19,999

Smuggling/transporting of alien(s)

High	11–20 months	20–26 months	26–34 months	34–44 months

Carnal knowledge

Counterfeit currency or other medium of exchange [(passing/possession) $20,000–$100,000]

Counterfeiting [manufacturing (amount of counterfeit currency or other medium of exchange involved not exceeding $100,000)]

Drugs (other than specifically listed), possession with intent to distribute/sale [medium scale (e.g., 1,000–19,999 doses)]

Marijuana/hashish, possession with intent to distribute sale [large scale (e.g., 200–1,999 lbs. of marijuana/20–199 lbs. of hashish/.20–1.99 liters of hash oil)]

Cocaine, possession with intent to distribute/sell [medium scale (e.g., 5–99 grams of 100% purity or equivalent amount)]

Opiates, possession with intent to distribute sale [small scale (e.g., less than 5 grams of 100% pure heroin, or equivalent amount) except as described in moderate]

Firearms Act, possession/purchase/sale (sawed-off shotgun(s), machine gun(s), or multiple weapons)

Gambling law violations—managerial or proprietary interest in large scale operation (e.g., Sports books (estimated daily gross more than $15,000); Horse books (estimated daily gross more than $4,000); Numbers bankers (estimated daily gross more than $2,000)]

Involuntary manslaughter (e.g., negligent homicide)

Mann Act (no force—commercial purposes)

(continued)

FIGURE 8-4 Adult Guidelines for Decision Making (*continued*)

Severity of offense behavior (Examples)	Parole prognosis (salient factor score)			
	Very good (11 to 9)	Good (8 to 6)	Fair (5 to 4)	Poor (3 to 0)

High (continued)

Property offenses (theft/forgery/fraud/embezzlement/interstate transportation of stolen or forged securities/income tax evasion/receiving stolen property) $20,000–$100,000

Threatening communications (e.g., mail/phone)—not for purposes of extortion and no other overt act

Very High — 24–36 months | 36–48 months | 48–60 months | 60–72 months

Robbery (1 or 2 instances)

Breaking and entering—armory with intent to steal weapons

Breaking and entering/burglary—residence; or breaking and entering of other premises with hostile confrontation with victim

Counterfeit currency or other medium of exchange [(passing/possession)—more than $100,000 but not exceeding $500,000]

Drugs (other than specifically listed), possession with intent to distribute/sale [large scale (e.g., 20,000 more doses) except as described in Greatest I]

Marijuana/hashish, possession with intent to distribute/sale [very large scale (e.g., 2,000 lbs. or more of marijuana/200 lbs. or more of hashish/2 liters or more of hash oil)]

Cocaine, possession with intent to distribute/sale [large scale (e.g., 100 grams or more of 100% purity, or equivalent amount) except as described in Greatest I]

Opiates, possession with intent to distribute/sale [medium scale or more (e.g., 5 grams or more of 100% pure heroin, or equivalent amount) except as described in Greatest I]

Extortion [threat of physical harm (to person or property)]

Explosives, possession/transportation

Property offenses (theft/forgery/fraud/embezzlement/interstate transportation of stolen or forged securities/income tax evasion/receiving stolen property) more than $100,000 but not exceeding $500,000

Greatest I — 40–52 months | 52–64 months | 64–78 months | 78–100 months

Aggravated felony (e.g., robbery; weapon fired or injury of a type normally requiring medical attention)

Arson or explosive detonation [involving potential risk of physical injury to person(s) (e.g., premises occupied or likely to be occupied)—no serious injury occurred]

Drugs (other than specifically listed), possession with intent to distribute/sale [managerial or proprietary interest and very large scale (e.g., offense involving more than 200,000 doses)]

Cocaine, possession with intent to distribute/sale [managerial or proprietary interest and very large scale (e.g., offense involving more than 1 kilogram of 100% purity, or equivalent amount)]

FIGURE 8-4 Adult Guidelines for Decision Making (*continued*)

Severity of offense behavior (Examples)	Parole prognosis (salient factor score)			
	Very good (11 to 9)	Good (8 to 6)	Fair (5 to 4)	Poor (3 to 0)
Greatest I (continued)				
Opiates, possession with intent to distribute/sale [managerial or proprietary interest and very large scale (e.g., offense involving more than 50 grams of 100% pure heroin, or equivalent amount)]				
Kidnaping [other than listed in Greatest II; limited duration; and no harm to victim (e.g., kidnaping the driver of a truck during a hijacking, driving to a secluded location, and releasing victim unharmed)]				
Robbery (3 or 4 instances)				
Sex act—force [e.g., forcible rape or Mann Act (force)]				
Voluntary manslaughter (unlawful killing of a human being without malice; sudden quarrel or heat of passion)				
Greatest II	52+ months	64+ months	78+ months	100+ months
Murder				
Aggravated felony—serious injury (e.g., robbery: injury involving substantial risk of death, or protracted disability, or disfigurement) or extreme cruelty/brutality toward victim				
Aircraft hijacking				
Espionage				
Kidnaping (for ransom or terrorism: as hostage; or harm to victim)				
Treason				

Notes: There is a separate guideline chart for Youth Nara cases not shown. Specific upper limits are not provided due to the limited number of cases and the extreme variation possible within category. This revision is effective June 1979.
SOURCE: P. B. Hoffman and S. Adelberg, "The Salient Factor-Score: A Non-technical Overview," *Federal Probation* 44 (1980): pp. 50–52.

Mutual Agreement Programming. Mutual agreement programming (MAP) is essentially a contract between the state and the offender regarding his date of release from prison.[38] It requires the cooperation and involvement of the offender, prison officials, and parole authorities. The offender agrees, usually at the beginning of his prison term, to participate in specific programs that are designed either to change his behavior (for example, Alcoholics Anonymous) or to provide him with new skills (for example, vocational training). The prison's role in this contract is to provide the mutually agreed upon resources. The parole authority in turn agrees to release the offender if he successfully completes his program obligations (see figure 8-5).

The release date is a critical factor in the contract. The parole board's full cooperation is required if the MAP concept is to be realized. This cooperation is not always easily achieved because parole boards are reluctant to give up any of their discretion.

The actual mechanics of the MAP process begin with a statement of expectations signed by the three parties early in the offender's prison career (usually at prison reception).[39] The agreement reached specifies a program designed to meet

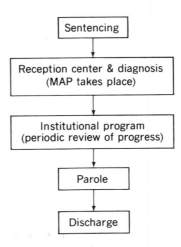

FIGURE 8-5 The Mutual Agreement Programming (MAP) Process

the offender's needs with objectives identified in incremental steps. Two strategies are utilized to induce the offender's participation and commitment to the change process. First, the offender is actively involved in the planning process for his program and, second, rewards are used to reinforce his behavior. The ultimate reward is release from prison on parole.

It is important to recognize that the rewards are not automatically provided to the inmate; he must earn them. At regular intervals during his prison term, the offender's progress is reviewed to determine if he is continuing to fulfill his part of the agreement. When a MAP program is adopted, the parole decision-making process becomes an individualized and therapeutic process whereby the release decision is totally based on the offender's progress toward self-improvement. If he does not take affirmative action to change his behavior, he is not released.

Although mutual agreement programming appears to be a rational process that permits an offender to use his time in prison profitably, few states have embraced the concept, and none currently use it. The reasons are varied.[40] Several obstacles are the result of a lack of cooperation between parole boards (particularly autonomous ones) and corrections departments. Frequently, the parole board views MAP as usurping its release decision-making authority because prison officials are given a more significant role in the parole release process. Another impediment to successful MAP adoption is correctional system failure to deliver the resources or programs that it agreed to provide. The prison system can usually point to legitimate reasons why programs cannot be provided, such as budget cuts, prison overcrowding, and so on. However, the result is that the inmate works to meet his commitment, but the state fails to fulfill its side of the bargain.

A final obstacle to the introduction of MAP programming concerns its effectiveness in terms of reducing recidivism. Evaluations of MAP in Wisconsin, a state that pioneered its use, and Michigan have revealed that, when MAP was compared with traditional forms of parole release, significant differences in recidivism were not apparent.[41]

❑ Parole Supervision

Classification. One of the most challenging problems in both probation and parole is the classification of offenders regarding their need for services and supervision. Without an effective classification scheme, scarce resources can be wasted. Some clients will be underserved; others will be overmonitored; and staff will be chronically overworked. Wisconsin's case management and classification system represents one state's apparently effective approach to this problem.

The Wisconsin system has four basic components:

1. Risk and needs assessment. This evaluation involves the use of a risk scale that discriminates between high-, moderate-, and low-risk individuals and a needs assessment instrument that focuses on academic/vocational needs, employment, financial management, marital/family problems, companions, emotional stability, alcohol usage, other drug usage, mental ability, health, and sexual behavior. Risk and needs assessments are used to assist staff in determining the level of supervision an offender requires.

2. Case management classification. This component involves the use of an interview guide to assist the staff in determining the type of supervision an offender requires. Four supervision strategies commonly utilized are selective intervention, casework/control, environmental structuring, and limit setting.

3. Management information system. This system provides for the routine collection and systematic organanization of information obtained on offenders at admission, reevaluation, and termination. This data provides a "before, during, and after" record for each client and can be used to identify trends, project populations, examine usage of community resources, plan future purchase of services priorities, and answer special requests for information.

4. Work load deployment and budget procedure. This procedure provides information on each supervising staff member's work load. This information facilitates the deployment of staff and the budgeting of new positions.[42]

A two-year follow-up of the implementation of Wisconsin's classification system yielded the following results:

Assignment to different levels of supervision based on assessments of needs and risk appears to have had a significant impact on probation and parole outcomes in Wisconsin. Increased contacts with high need/high risk cases resulted in fewer new convictions, rule violations, absconsions, and revocations. At the same time, decreasing contacts with low risk clients had no perceivable adverse effects.

The Wisconsin Risk Assessment Scale has demonstrated effectiveness in predicting success or failure in completing probation or parole terms. In a sample of 8,250 clients, the percentage of individuals rated low risk and later revoked was 3 percent, while 37 percent of the cases rated high risk were subsequently revoked.

Maximum supervision clients in Wisconsin require an average of three hours of agent time per month; medium supervision clients take 1.25 hours per month, while minimum supervision cases require only 0.5 hours per month of agent time. Hence, an agent can supervise about six low risk/low need clients in the time required to supervise a single high risk/high need individual.

Emphasis on proper implementation of the classification process and controls on paperwork and information flow were essential to the success of the Wisconsin system.[43]

The Safer Foundation

"A year and a half ago," said David Willer, the Safer Foundation's director of employment services, "things were a lot better than they are today. Then, we could find jobs that had potential, some that (gave workers) a possibility of moving up into a trade or making more money. Now, we're focusing on fast food, gas stations, really dead-end jobs, and still telling guys it's a way of getting started." The previous week, Willer said, "one of my best job developers went to see thirty-one companies, mostly light manufacturing. Eleven had people on layoff, three were in the process of declaring brankruptcy, and the rest weren't hiring."

Unemployment is high in Chicago, as it is in most Midwest industrial cities. Officially, unemployment hovered near 11 percent in Chicago early this year. Among black and Hispanic youths, it was nearly five times greater. Businesses all over the city have been laying off employees, and even closing their doors for good.

In fiscal 1982, the Safer Foundation, operating with a $2.5 million annual budget, found jobs for 2,350 ex-offenders, and placed 1,500 others in counseling or educational programs. But that was before the twin blows of recession and government funding cutbacks struck. In fiscal 1982, state, county, and city funding made up more than 80 percent of the Safer Foundation's budget; much of that funding has been cut back. The directors of the foundation, two former Jesuit priests, are politically astute; they have the ear of Chicago Mayor Jane Byrne and the support of the Illinois Department of Corrections. As long as the state and city have some employment funds to disburse, the Safer Foundation can be expected to be at the head of the list. . . .

The Safer Foundation, which takes its name from that safer streets theme, occupies three floors of a building on South Wabash Avenue in Chicago's downtown business district. The day begins for the foundation's clients at 8:30 A.M., as they get off the elevator on the ninth floor of the building and are greeted by two men working behind a desk in the lobby. The clients include recent parolees from Illinois state prisons, misdemeanants released from county jails, and probationers. Some were referred by their parole agents; some were sent by friends; and others had heard about Safer and just walked in.

Most are neatly dressed and appear both eager and apprehensive. There are few whites and women; almost all the clients are young black men. Ninety-two percent of Safer's clients in 1981 were men and 8 percent were women. Fifty-four percent had no high school diploma; 50 percent had been convicted of crimes against people; 85 percent had been arrested more than twice; and 95 percent had incomes below the poverty level.

Beyond the reception area, in a room at one end of a long corridor, about a dozen of Safer's clients, participants in the basic skills training program, are studying the daily edition of the *Chicago Tribune*. At the other end of the hallway, in a bright, spacious room, students in the job readiness program are seated at desks, each with a telephone and a phone book in front of him, making call after call to prospective employers, while counselors listen and give advice.

The basic skills and job readiness programs are part of the Safer Foundation's innovative approach to preparing clients for the workaday world. The clients in the basic program are learning to read, write, and do simple arithmetic on a nine-week schedule. The job readiness program teaches clients how to look for work. Clients in both programs receive the minimum wage and must punch a time clock, do a specified amount of homework, and follow strict rules of behavior.

One of the job readiness program's job developers, Yusef Balderos, has been with Safer for four years. He is one of the many ex-offenders employed by Safer. In the job readiness program, he said, "we're not just taking somebody and shoving him out there. We're working with him, trying to stabilize his behavior, helping him see what he wants, why he got fired from his last job. We stress punctuality, responsibility, and participation."

A supervisor in the job readiness program is Shaka Jackson, who has been with the Safer Foundation since his release from prison eight years ago. A basic problem with the employment of ex-offenders, he said, is that "too much is expected of the ex-offender. He's expected to get on the street, get a job, and everything is supposed to be all right. Here's a dude with no experience with the work ethic, and we expect him not to make any mistakes." A goal of the job readiness program, Jackson said, is to "get cats familiar with the expectations of the middle-class work ethic. We try to get him used to the rigidity of working life."

Jackson said he realizes that many of his clients are still working outside the law. "With what's going on today we can't realistically tell a guy not to hustle," he added. "We try to tell him to create as little pain as possible in the world while he's trying to survive. Most of the people who come in here aren't professional criminals. Most cats know how to do something legitimate. A car thief knows all about cars; most burglars are very creative; most guys know how to paint. . . . Many who come in here don't talk. We try to get them verbal. In our society, if you're not verbal you're invisible. . . ."

Safer began to find jobs for ex-offenders in manufacturing as well as construction. But some of the ex-offenders were not working out on the job. "Guys were quitting," Wilhelmy Curran said. "Employers would call and say, 'You sent me another of those s.o.b.s.' I would say, 'This is part of the guy's rehabilitation. We call it structured job-hopping.' " But, said Wilhelmy, "I began to see the problem. Most of these guys had never worked before, and certainly not a 40-hour week, under supervision."

As government funding for the Safer Foundation increased, the educational and counseling programs that have become its hallmark were added. The results have been impressive. According to Safer's 1981 annual report, only 10.9 percent of the foundation's clients return to prison over a two-year-period, and 93 percent were still in the community one year after release.

About a dozen job readiness clients were gathered for a group session. The discussion was focused on one participant, Fred, who complained that he was having trouble finding the kind of job he wanted. Fred was an attractive, well-spoken young man, neatly and conservatively dressed.

"What kind of a job do you want?" a group member asked him, Fred said he could not take a job paying only the minimum wage because he had a wife and two children to support. After questioning him further, the group discovered that Fred had no income at all. "Isn't it better to earn the minimum wage than nothing?" they asked. Then, at the suggestion of the group leader, the members listed all of Fred's assets and had him list all of the things he knew how to do. Then everyone suggested jobs that Fred might be able to fill. As they talked, Fred looked increasingly hopeful, and the other young men seemed energized by the discussion. Throughout the entire session, the feeling was one of mutual support. A serious effort was being made to take a realistic look at each man's situation.

Despite such encouragement, however, most clients are having a hard time finding work. Lester, who, at 33 is older than the average client, was sentenced to one year in prison and one year on parole for the crime of grand theft. He was released after nine and one-half months and came to the Safer Foundation for help. He spent two weeks in the job readiness program where, he said, he learned "how to fill out applications, what to look for in a job, how to decide on goals, how to talk to employers." Although he went to job interviews, he said, "they weren't hiring." Because he does not have a high school diploma, Lester enrolled in the basic skills and education program and is now working to get a high school equivalency degree. After he reaches that goal, he said, "my object is to come here every day and work with a job developer. I really need a job real bad. But GM and Ford are laying off; the steel mills are laying off. It's hard even to get a restaurant job." Lester lives with his girlfriend, who works as a data processor. He would also like to get some training in the computer field, he said, "but first I need a job to survive."

As the economy worsens, Shaka Jackson said, so does the ex-offender's level of despair. "Dudes getting out of the penitentiary now, their rage is too high; the pace is too much for them; they're being backed into a corner. But the bottom line is—you got to do what you got to do to stay out of jail. You've got to stay out of the madhouse. And the most dangerous person is the one who has no support on the outside."

Raymond Curran sounded a similar warning as he discussed his fears of the consequences of unemployment rising at a time when the Illinois corrections department had combined a new early release policy with suggestions that it might close many work-release centers. "With no gradual process of de-escalation from the violence of prison," Curran said, "these people are like sticks of dynamite being released from prisons. I think if the Safer Foundation does nothing but talk to people, it helps defuse these bombs."

SOURCE: Joan Potter, "The Safer Foundation: 'Find Them a Job or They'll Do a Job' " *Corrections Magazine* 8(3) (1982): 18–19. Copyright 1982 by *Corrections Magazine* and Criminal Publications, Inc., 116 West 32 Street, New York, N.Y. 10001.

Employment Programs for Ex-offenders. One correctional strategy that has received considerable support in the past several years is programming designed to provide employment services to parolees and other ex-offenders. These programs are based on the assumption that a relationship exists between unemployment and crime. It is commonly believed that a person who is able to support himself and his dependents by working is less likely to engage in criminal activity than one who is not working. This assumption permeates our crime control efforts; as a result, we find that a great many employment-related programs have been established at various stages of the criminal justice and juvenile justice systems.

This emphasis on employment is not new—work has always been an important aspect of the correctional endeavor. Offenders have been required to work as a condition of probation and parole; inmates have been assigned to work projects both as punishment and for therapy; and offenders are being assigned in increasing numbers to community-based work-release programs.

A number of programs currently exist to assist parolees in upgrading their postrelease employment prospects, including:

1. Institutional preparation, in which the offender is provided training and other related services prior to release
2. Postrelease community readjustment services, which provide supportive assistance (housing, food, clothing, and transportation to work)
3. Preplacement job preparation, which stresses job readiness skills
4. Job development, which involves generating job opportunities for offenders
5. Job placement, which attempts to match the offender with appropriate employment
6. Postplacement support for both the employer and the offender, which is designed to facilitate the adjustment of both to the new work relationship.[44]

A national survey was conducted for the National Institute of Justice to determine the status of employment services for ex-offenders. This survey identified six intervention strategy models for ex-offender employment programs: job development and placement, residential services, supported work experiences, skill training, job readiness, and financial assistance.[45]

Job development programs involve the location and/or creation of job opportunities in the private sector for ex-offenders and the matching (through a screening process) of persons with jobs. Halfway houses (residential services) provide shelter and social support to the offender. Supported work experiences place offenders in subsidized jobs where they are closely supervised. As a result, the offender works in a highly supportive environment that is expected to ease his transition into the world of work. Skill training deals directly with deficiencies in employment-related skills. These programs provide basic training to offenders to enable them to obtain jobs. Job readiness programs teach offenders how to find jobs. They introduce offenders to the process of seeking employment, reading classified advertisements, obtaining and succeeding on interviews, and so on. The final approach involves direct financial assistance. These programs provide recently released offenders with cash assistance for a short time, ranging from one to three months. These programs are designed to reduce financial pressure on newly released inmates.

The Plight of Ex-offender Job Programs

It was a grey morning on New York City's Upper West Side. A chill wind blew in from the Hudson River. A slender young man huddled in a dark blue sweatshirt made his way down the block and entered a two-story, red-brick building. On the front of the building was a plaque that read "N.A.A.C.P. Project Rebound, Inc."

The young man had been released from state prison a week earlier. He was a high school dropout, and his only job had been as a janitor's helper. As his parole date approached, he had written to Project Rebound and had received a letter saying the agency would help him get job training and find work after his release.

When he arrived at the Project Rebound offices, however, he found no help available to him. The receptionist was polite but firm with him. "I'm sorry," he was told. "We can't take anyone in for job orientation for a month. But if you'll fill out this application, we'll put it on file and contact you as soon as the freeze is over." The young man filled it out and returned to the street, where icy pellets of snow had begun to fall.

Project Rebound was forced to defer its promise because it, and scores of other ex-offender employment programs across the country, have had their federal funding slashed. Project Rebound runs its on-the-job training on Comprehensive Employment and Training Act (CETA) funds administered by the U.S. Department of Labor and funneled through the New York City Department of Employment (DOE). Since August 1981, CETA funds to DOE have been cut by 50 percent. When the parolee showed up at Project Rebound, DOE had slapped a one-month freeze on program funds because of these cuts.

"Right now," said Angelique Martin Davis, Project Rebound's director, "even if you're middle class and white it's hard to find a job. If you're black, poor, and an ex-offender, you're in the worst place. When they come to us, they're frustrated, angry, and scared. I can't tell them about DOE. They don't give a damn about DOE."

Project Rebound has been operating since 1971, making it one of the oldest ex-offender employment programs in the city. Much of its stability comes from its connection with the mid-Manhattan branch of the NAACP. Out of the dozens of community-based organizations that once offered help to ex-offenders in New York City, it is one of the handful that remains. And even Project Rebound, which has already cut its staff by more than half, might not exist past September, when Department of Labor allocations for the 1982 fiscal year come to an end. "I think we'll get through until August," Davis said, "I don't know what will happen after that."

What is happening to Project Rebound is happening to ex-offender employment programs all over the United States. In 1976, a study done by the National Institute of Law Enforcement and Criminal Justice identified more than 250 projects around the country designed to help inmates make the transition from prison to employment. No one knows how many there are today, but there is little question that the number is dwindling rapidly. The experience in a few cities shows the trend.

In New York City, there were at one time more than fifty ex-offender job programs, says Bill Diaz, the job developer for the special defender services section of the Legal Aid Society, which is the local public defender's office. Now, he says, "they have dwindled down to a precious few."

In 1980, the National Alliance of Business and the U.S. Probation Service launched a joint ex-offender employment effort called the Community Alliance Program for Ex-offenders (CAPE). Today, CAPE is struggling to survive because of funding losses and high unemployment rates in two of the three cities in which it operates.

Project Jove, a San Diego, California, ex-offender employment program thought by some experts to be one of the best in the nation, has been forced to close four of seven offices and reduce its staff from 135 to 75 in recent months. "When we need this kind of program the most," said the program's director, Tom Wornham, "(government agencies) are cutting back."

Source: Joan Potter, "Can Ex-Offender Job Programs Survive Reaganomics?" *Corrections* Magazine 8(3) (1982): 15–16. Copyright 1982 by *Corrections Magazine* and Criminal Justice Publications, Inc., 116 West 32 Street, New York, N.Y. 10001.

Today, ex-offender employment programs are in serious trouble. Funding cutbacks, high unemployment rates, and growing conservatism in correctional policymaking have led to the demise of many programs. In addition, research has shown that the programs have often fallen far short of their goals. The NIJ survey of ex-offenders' employment strategies revealed that, although these programs place thousands of persons in unsubsidized jobs and effectively recruit employers, 40 to 60 percent of the ex-offenders who seek assistance do not receive it.[46] Planned reentry services that are initiated before release from prison or jail, substance abuse treatment, and postplacement services—all of which are essential to job retention, employment adjustment, and eventual reintegration—were virtually ignored by most of the programs. Once an ex-offender was placed in a job, service and assistance to him were generally terminated.[47] Although the programs had a positive impact on postrelease employment, they were not designed to achieve maximum impact on the long-term ex-offender problem of unemployment, underemployment, and recidivism.[48] The NIJ researchers concluded their report with a recommendation for the implementation of a six-step program (figure 8-6) designed to achieve the long-range goals of increased job retention, increased earnings, increased career mobility, and reduced recidivism rates.

Parole Officer Aide Programs. During the 1970s, several states experimented with the use of ex-parolees as assistants for professional parole officers. We discuss the general problems and issues surrounding the use of ex-offenders in correctional programs in chapter 12. Here we examine the special benefits of such programs for parolees, who can be assisted by persons who have experienced and overcome the same problems they are currently encountering. The Ohio Parole Officer Aide Program represents a model achievement in the use of ex-parolees to assist parolees. The program was developed in 1972 in an attempt to benefit the parolee, the ex-offender, and the Adult Parole Authority, the agency responsible for administering parole services in Ohio.[49]

The Parole Officer Aide (POA) Program attempted to recruit interested ex-offenders who had previously worked in ex-offender programs and possessed the necessary interpersonal skills to provide counseling and support to parolees. Most of the persons selected for the program were former parolees who had been off parole and steadily employed for at least six months. Applicants were carefully screened through evaluation of their prior criminal, personal, and parole records and a series of interviews with parole officers and POA staff.

All POAs received the same training as new Ohio parole officers; they also had to have completed a six-month probationary period during which in-service training was informally provided. Parole officer aides carried out basically the same functioning as parole officers, although they were restricted by statute from owning or carrying a gun, making arrests, or transporting arrested offenders. Additionally, the POA program did not permit aides to sign technical parole violation reports; this restriction was designed to limit the aide's involvement in the investigatory aspects of parole supervision, although aides might still assist in drafting the report.

Parole officers and aides worked as a team; generally, they were more likely to receive multiple-problem offenders in their case loads than officers who worked alone. POAs devoted most of their efforts to case-load supervision and support activ-

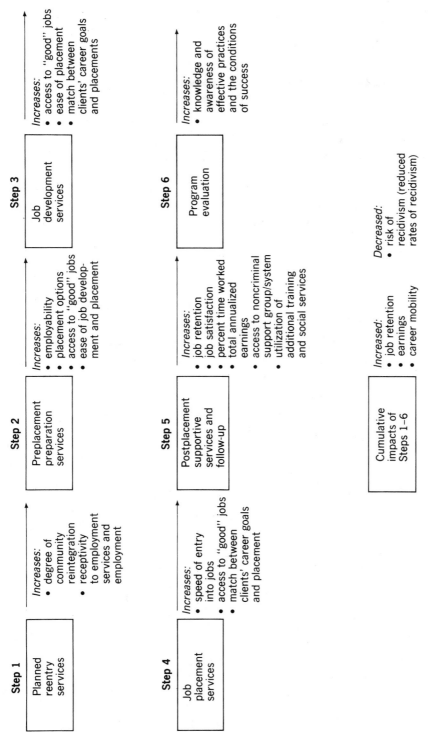

FIGURE 8-6 Intended Impacts of the Intervention System on Ex-offender Clients and Employment Recidivism Outcomes

SOURCE: Cicero Wilson, Kenneth J. Lenihan, and Gail Goolkasian, *Employment Services for Ex-Offenders* (Washington, D.C.: U.S. Government Printing Office, 1981), p. 83.

ities; speaking engagements, public relations, and job development activities occupied about one-third of their time.

One of the most significant achievements of the Ohio program was the institutionalization of POA jobs. Although the program was initially established with the assistance of federal funds, the aide positions were assigned a civil service classification to facilitate the transition to state funding after the federal grant expired. POAs could be promoted to parole officers on the basis of their experience and skills in counseling, completing forms, and working within the framework of a governmental organization. Ten hours of paid educational leave are available to all Ohio civil servants; two-thirds of the POAs used this leave to complete high school or attend college or graduate school.[50]

Although the Ohio POA program was generally regarded as a success by program participants and staff, it was terminated in 1976. The program's former director reported that the termination resulted from a shift in correctional philosophy from emphasis on offender programs to a focus on the provision of due process guarantees to offenders.[51]

Public Attitudes

If parole is to be an effective means of reintegrating offenders into the community, then the community must be receptive to the parolee's efforts to establish essential community ties. The general public must be willing and able to view the parolee with fairness and to offer assistance as needed. To accomplish this objective, parole agencies need to evaluate, release, and supervise offenders in a manner that merits the pride and respect of the community. The community in turn must understand the parole process and its function in the correctional system.

Today, public understanding of parole seems to be at a low point. The media draw attention to failed parolees who commit new crimes while ignoring the majority who successfully complete parole. In states where early paroles have been granted to large numbers of inmates to relieve overcrowding, the press has sometimes appeared to fan the flames of community outrage rather than to assess the alternatives and examine the actual impact of such releases on crime rates. Parole too often is portrayed as a giveaway, as freedom granted to the undeserving solely because corrections officials lack the will to do otherwise.

Although current public attitudes toward parole have been influenced by newspaper, television, and radio accounts, the media cannot be singled out as the only guilty party in the misrepresentation of parole. State legislators establish parole criteria and standards, determine parole board member eligibility requirements, and, most important, fund all correctional agencies; but they are rarely heard from when parole is attacked. In most states, parole board members have adopted a low profile, perhaps in an attempt to avoid scrutiny of a decision-making process that all too often falls short of the goals of fairness and impartiality.

Parole agency administrators and parole officers have generally chosen not to bring the parole process to public attention, perhaps in the belief that any attention could only yield negative results. In many ways, the media have simply stepped in to fill an information gap, a gap that could be better filled by those who legislate, administer, and deliver parole services.

The American Correctional Association suggests several strategies for the fostering of better public attitudes.

1. Parole personnel should work with community organizations such as the Salvation Army and other organizations that have an interest in parolees' adjustment problems.
2. An organized public information program is a necessity. Parole personnel should seize every opportunity to address civic organizations, church groups, and other interested bodies.
3. Potential employers, civic leaders, and other responsible citizens should be invited to the prisons to observe the correctional process at work.
4. Law enforcement and business executives should be invited to participate in institutional prerelease programs.
5. The parole board should invite representative law enforcement officials, judges, adult students, interested citizens, and responsible members of the press to attend parole hearings.[52]

These and other efforts to inform the public may create temporary problems for administrators as the public attempts to digest and evaluate new information. There has been too much confusion for too long for any informational program to achieve immediate success. But in the long run, an informed citizenry will be more amenable to correctional innovation and the funding of necessary correctional programs if there is a comprehensive and candid presentation of the issues. Correctional administrators must have confidence in the community's ability to respond justly to correction's needs. Correctional efforts can build this confidence through information dissemination.

The Future of Parole

Parole may well change form in the future, but it can be expected to remain a widely used correctional strategy. While the federal government and some states have abolished parole, they have maintained some form of community supervision of released offenders. North Carolina is a case in point. When parole was abolished, a new program known as PRAC (Pre-Release and After Care) was created. PRAC provides for the supervision of all prisoners for ninety days after release by PRAC officers, many of whom were formerly parole officers. What has been abolished in North Carolina is the parole release decision-making process. Similarly, in the federal system parole has been abolished but supervised release has been maintained. It is this component of parole that is most likely to be rethought and restructured in future years. We know that persons released from prison can benefit from community supervision. Even Robert Martinson, father of the "nothing works" perspective in correctional programming, has acknowledged the need for postrelease community supervision, both to facilitate offender reintegration and to protect the community.[53] The best way to determine the length of time an offender should serve in prison is not yet apparent. At present, the confusion over legislative, judicial, and executive responsibility for sentence determination has mistakenly led to a call for parole abolition. Instead, what is needed is a continued examination of the release decision-making process so we can devise a formula that meets our concerns for fairness, equality, and individualization of case management. The search for such a process will probably continue for years to come.

Summary

Parole is the supervision of offenders granted release from prison by a parole board. Inmates may alternatively be released through the maximum expiration of their sentence or upon the accumulation of good-time credits. Parole may be distinguished from these forms of release by the manner in which it addresses the twin concerns of rehabilitation and control. The parole model assumes that inmates will be released when incarceration has achieved its maximum benefit and that community-based guidance, counseling, and behavior monitoring will both assist the ex-offender in his attempt to avoid future crime and protect the community during the adjustment period.

Like several other contemporary community-based programs, parole can be traced to English origins and to Crofton's stages of penal servitude. Today it is the most widely utilized prisoner release mechanism, although there is still considerable variability in the use of parole from state to state. Prison overcrowding is one factor that has encouraged an increase in the use of parole.

Parole is a controversial correctional program, and it is easy to see why. If parole is to achieve its objectives of rehabilitation and control, sentencing practices must be flexible enough to permit the release of individuals at the optimum point during their prison term. But today there is a trend toward minimizing flexibility in the sentencing process. A qualified parole board is needed to make the difficult decisions called for in evaluating an inmate's readiness for release. Few states, however, have established requirements for parole board members. To serve offenders and protect the community, parole field staff need education in the field of criminal justice and must be able to understand their clients' problems. In most states, case load size has increased far beyond the resources of parole field staff. Parole appointments and release decision making must be free from political influence if it is to maintain credibility; too often parole board memberships are merely political plums.

Parole must be coordinated with other correctional services if it is to function effectively. Parole's essential elements are threefold:

1. Preparing inmates for release and developing preparole reports on prisoners
2. Conducting hearings regarding parole eligibility, granting parole, and revoking parole and terminating parole supervision
3. Supervising parolees in the community

Innovative strategies in parole decision making include the use of parole guidelines and mutual agreement programming to facilitate and clarify the release decision-making process. Parole supervision can be improved through the use of well-validated classification schemes, comprehensive employment services for ex-offenders, and the involvement of ex-parolees in parole supervision through the creation of parole aide positions.

If parole is to meet its difficult objectives, citizen awareness and support of parole is essential. Parole board decisions are too important to be made behind closed doors. Parole supervision is too big a job to be accomplished in a hostile environment in which employers and citizens stigmatize and avoid the ex-offender.

Parole will probably continue to serve as our most widely used form of release, but there is concern that it will become more like the arbitrary opening and closing of floodgates than a meaningful crime control and offender rehabilitation strategy. Legislators and parole and correctional authorities must work diligently to make the best use of parole, a program that is now more essential than at any other time in our history. Crowded prisons must be relieved and the released prisoners must be reintegrated into our society if we are to avoid the creation of prisons with rapidly spinning revolving doors.

KEY WORDS AND CONCEPTS

classification	maximum expiration	parole guidelines
definite sentencing	of sentence	parole hearing
good time	mutual agreement	examiners
indeterminate	programming	prerelease preparation
sentencing	parole aides	supported work
job readiness training	parole board	programs

NOTES

1. Citizen's Inquiry on Parole and Criminal Justice, Inc., *Prison Without Walls, Report on New York Parole* (New York: Praeger, 1975).
2. National Council on Crime and Delinquency, *Parole in the United States: 1979* (Washington, D.C.: U.S. Department of Justice, 1979), p. 10.
3. National Advisory Commission on Criminal Justice Standards and Goals, *Corrections:* (Washington, D.C.: U.S. Government Printing Office, 1973), p. 390.
4. National Council on Crime and Delinquency, *Parole in the United States*, p. 21.
5. National Advisory Commission on Criminal Justice Standards and Goals, *Corrections,* p. 393.
6. Ibid., p. 395.
7. George Killinger, Hazel Kerper, and Paul Cromwell, *Probation and Parole in the Criminal Justice System* (St. Paul, Minn.: West Publishing, 1976), pp. 201–209.
8. William Parker, *Parole: Origins, Development, Current Practices and Statutes* (College Park, Md.: American Correctional Association, 1975), p. 14.
9. Ibid., p. 15.
10. Ibid., p. 16.
11. Ibid., p. 17.
12. Ibid.
13. Harry E. Allen and Clifford E. Simonsen, *Corrections in America: An Introduction* (New York: Macmillan, 1981).
14. Killinger, Kerper, and Cromwell, *Probation and Parole*, p. 209.
15. Allen and Simonsen, *Corrections in America*, p. 191.
16. Bureau of Justice Statistics, "Probation and Parole 1989" (Washington, D.C.: U.S. Department of Justice, 1989), p. 4.
17. National Council on Crime and Delinquency, *Parole in the United States*, p. 1.
18. Bureau of Justice Statistics, "Probation and Parole 1988," p. 4.
19. National Advisory Commission on Criminal Justice Standards and Goals, *Corrections*, p. 395.
20. American Correctional Association, *Manual of Correctional Standards* (Washington, D.C.: American Correctional Association, 1969), pp. 115–116.
21. National Advisory Commission on Criminal Justice Standards and Goals, *Corrections,* p. 392.
22. National Council on Crime and Delinquency, *Parole in the United States*, p. 10.
23. American Correctional Association, *Manual of Correctional Standards*, pp. 29–30.

24. National Advisory Commission on Criminal Justice Standards and Goals, *Corrections,* pp. 420–421.

25. Parker, *Parole,* pp. 29–30.

26. National Institute of Law Enforcement and Criminal Justice, *National Manpower Survey of the Criminal Justice System, Corrections* (Washington, D.C.: U.S. Department of Justice, 1978).

27. National Advisory Commission on Criminal Justice Standards and Goals, *Corrections,* p. 436.

28. American Correctional Association, *Manual of Correctional Standards,* p. 124.

29. National Advisory Commission on Criminal Justice Standards and Goals, *Corrections,* p. 1.

30. American Correctional Association, *Manual of Correctional Standards,* pp. 125–131.

31. David Stanley, *Prisoners Among Us: The Problem of Parole* (Washington, D.C.: Brookings Institution, 1976), pp. 48–50.

32. American Law Institute, "Model Penal Code: 1962" in *American Law Institute Compendium of Model Correctional Legislation and Standards,* vol. 3 (Washington, D.C.: U.S. Department of Justice, 1972), pp. III–56. Copyright 1972 by the American Law Institute. Reprinted with the permission of the American Law Institute.

33. Ibid., pp. 58–59.

34. *Morrissey* v. *Brewer,* 408 U.S. 471, 92 SC 2593, 33 L. Ed. 2d, 484 (1972).

35. E. K. Nelson, H. Ohmart, and N. Harlow, *Promising Strategies in Probation and Parole* (Washington, D.C.: U.S. Department of Justice, 1978), pp. 2–3.

36. D. M. Gottfredson, L. T. Wilkins, and Peter Hoffman, *Guidelines for Parole and Sentencing* (Lexington, Mass.: Heath, 1978), p. 37.

37. Ibid.

38. Parolee Corrections Project, *The Mutual Agreement Program: A Planned Change in Correctional Service Delivery* (College Park, Md.: American Correctional Association, 1973), p. 6.

39. Ibid.

40. Ibid., pp. 21–27.

41. Oscar D. Shade, "The Demise of Wisconsin's Contract Parole Program," *Federal Probation* 45 (1981): 34–43.

42. S. Christopher Baird, "Probation and Parole Classification: The Wisconsin Model," *Corrections Today* 11 (May-June 1981): 36–41. Reprinted with permission from the American Correctional Association.

43. Ibid., p. 41.

44. Cicero Wilson, Kenneth J. Lenihan, and Gail Goolkasian, *Employment Services for Ex-Offenders: Program Models* (Washington, D.C.: U.S. Department of Justice, 1981), pp. 3–4.

45. Ibid., pp. 30–31.

46. Ibid., p. 6.

47. Ibid.

48. Ibid.

49. Carol H. Blew and Kenneth Carlson, *The Ohio Parole Officer Aide Program* (Washington, D.C.: U.S. Government Printing Office, 1976), p. 2.

50. Ibid.

51. Personal communication with Nick Sanborn, August 13, 1982.

52. American Correctional Association, *Manual of Correctional Standards,* pp. 132–133.

53. Robert Martinson, "New Findings, New Views: A Note of Caution Regarding Sentencing Reform," *Hofstra Law Review* 7(2) (1979): 243–258.

FOR FURTHER READING

Ericson, Rosemary, et al., *Paroled but Not Free: Ex-offenders Look at What They Need to Make It Outside* (New York: Behavioral Publications, 1973).

Glaser, Daniel. *The Effectiveness of a Prison and Parole System* (Indianapolis: Bobbs-Merrill, 1964).

Stanley, David, *Prisoners Among Us* (Washington, D.C.: Brookings Institution, 1976).

von Hirsch, Andrew, and Kathleen Hanrahan, *Abolish Parole?* (Washington, D.C.: U.S. Government Printing Office, 1978).

9: Problems and Needs of Female Offenders

ALL THE OFFENDER PROBLEMS discussed throughout this text apply equally to male and female offenders. In addition to previously discussed difficulties, female offenders have some special problems. About half of all female offenders have children. Although it is unfair and unjust that mothers bear more of the responsibility for the physical, financial, and emotional well-being of the children than fathers, it is a fact that they do. Many of these mothers are single or divorced women who are solely responsible for their children's welfare. Too often these mothers are inadequately prepared to offer the guidance and supervision effective parenting requires.

Because of the social roles prescribed for women in contemporary society, the female offender often has special barriers to overcome before she can obtain employment. Jobs that provide an income sufficient to meet her family's needs and achieve independent living are rarely available for the female offender with limited skills. Generally speaking, female offenders must meet special emotional and financial demands in an environment that offers limited economic opportunity and even less psychological support.

Incarceration in jails and prisons inevitably disrupts family ties and creates feelings of dependency. Female offenders suffer the same losses as males in this regard. Community-based programs can maintain and promote constructive relationships between family members, especially between mother and child. They can also prepare women for employment and strengthen feelings of independence and maturity. Community-based programs can treat offenders as responsible adults capable of self-direction. Because community programs provide the opportunity for successful experiences, they encourage offenders to live up to realistic expectations.

Female offenders are more likely to be placed in diversion or pretrial release programs and to be sentenced to probation if convicted than are male offenders. This is not because they receive more lenient treatment, but because the crimes women commit are generally less serious than those men commit. Because of the female offender's need for community-based assistance and the likelihood of her being placed in a community program, her special problems and needs merit a closer examination than could be provided in the preceding chapters.

Special Problems of Female Offenders

❑ Women and Crime

Women generally contribute less to the crime problem than men. Most crimes are committed by men; women account for only about 18 percent of all arrests.[1] However, female involvement in some crimes is higher than in others. Women account for almost three-quarters of all arrests for prostitution and commercialized vice and over one-half of all juvenile runaway arrests (table 9-1). As indicated by arrest statistics, women are rarely involved in such crimes as rape, robbery, burglary, and motor vehicle theft. Generally, females commit about 10 percent of all serious violent crimes and 21 percent of all serious property crimes. In terms of their proportion in the population, women are underrepresented in all but a few crime categories.

In recent years, much has been written about the "new female criminal." It has been suggested that today's female offender is more independent and aggressive

TABLE 9-1 Total Arrests in the United States, by Sex, 1988[a]

Offense charged	Number of persons arrested			Percent male	Percent female	Percent distribution[b]		
	Total	Male	Female			Total	Male	Female
TOTAL	**10,149,896**	**8,340,628**	**1,809,268**	**82.2**	**17.8**	**100.0**	**100.0**	**100.0**
Murder and nonnegligent manslaughter	16,326	14,334	1,992	87.8	12.2	0.2	0.2	0.1
Forcible rape	28,482	28,137	345	98.8	1.2	0.3	0.3	–[e]
Robbery	111,344	101,921	9,423	91.5	8.5	1.1	1.2	0.5
Aggravated assault	304,490	263,619	40,871	86.6	13.4	3.0	3.2	2.3
Burglary	331,758	303,898	27,860	91.6	8.4	3.3	3.6	1.5
Larceny–theft	1,162,752	808,329	354,423	69.5	30.5	11.5	9.7	19.6
Motor vehicle theft	153,016	137,623	15,393	89.9	10.1	1.5	1.7	0.9
Arson	14,505	12,607	1,898	86.9	13.1	0.1	0.2	0.1
Violent crime[d]	460,642	408,011	52,631	88.6	11.4	4.5	4.9	2.9
Property crime[e]	1,662,031	1,262,457	399,574	76.0	24.0	16.4	15.1	22.1
Crime Index total[f]	2,122,673	1,670,468	452,205	78.7	21.3	20.9	20.0	25.0
Other assaults	687,928	582,742	105,186	84.7	15.3	6.8	7.0	5.8
Forgery and counterfeiting	73,465	48,588	24,877	66.1	33.9	0.7	0.6	1.4
Fraud	260,848	143,436	117,412	55.0	45.0	2.6	1.7	6.5
Embezzlement	11,699	7,269	4,430	62.1	37.9	0.1	0.1	0.2
Stolen property; buying, receiving, possessing	125,092	110,271	14,821	88.2	11.8	1.2	1.3	0.8
Vandalism	225,544	201,054	24,490	89.1	10.9	2.2	2.4	1.4
Weapons; carrying, possessing, etc.	163,480	150,851	12,629	92.3	7.7	1.6	1.8	0.7
Prostitution and commercialized vice	78,731	24,845	53,886	31.6	68.4	0.8	0.3	3.0
Sex offenses (except forcible rape and prostitution)	78,239	72,522	5,717	92.7	7.3	0.8	0.9	0.3
Drug abuse violations	850,034	718,229	131,805	84.5	15.5	8.4	8.6	7.3
Gambling	18,106	15,319	2,787	84.6	15.4	0.2	0.2	0.2
Offenses against family and children	51,035	42,199	8,836	82.7	17.3	0.5	0.5	0.5
Driving under the influence	1,293,516	1,139,227	154,289	88.1	11.9	12.7	13.7	8.5
Liquor laws	492,385	402,850	89,535	81.8	18.2	4.9	4.8	4.9
Drunkenness	606,053	549,742	56,311	90.7	9.3	6.0	6.6	3.1
Disorderly conduct	573,580	468,923	104,657	81.8	18.2	5.7	5.6	5.8
Vagrancy	29,270	25,843	3,427	88.3	11.7	0.3	0.3	0.2
All other offenses (except traffic)	2,217,116	1,861,131	355,985	83.9	16.1	21.8	22.3	19.7
Suspicion	11,066	9,370	1,696	84.7	15.3	0.1	0.1	0.1
Curfew and loitering law violations	55,327	40,363	14,964	73.0	27.0	0.5	0.5	0.8
Runaways	124,709	55,386	69,323	44.4	55.6	1.2	0.7	3.8

[a]9,970 agencies; 1988 estimated population 188,928,000.
[b]Because of rounding, the percentages may not add to total.
[c]Less than one-tenth of 1 percent.
[d]Violent crimes are offenses of murder, forcible rape, robbery, and aggravated assault.
[e]Property crimes are offenses of burglary, larceny–theft, motor vehicle theft, and arson.
[f]Includes arson.

Source: U.S. Department of Justice, *Crime in the United States, 1988* (Washington, D.C.: U.S. Government Printing Office, 1988), p. 185.

than her predecessors and more likely to involve herself in white-collar crimes such as embezzlement. Some view the new female criminal as a product of the women's liberation movement; because the fight for equal rights has opened up new social roles for women, both legitimate and illegitimate behavior patterns are expected to reflect the new alternatives available to women.

For better or worse, the new female criminal is largely a myth. Although female crime is increasing, the pattern of increase does not indicate the emergence of a new criminal behavior pattern, but simply more of the same. Table 9-2 indicates that, from 1979 to 1988, female crime increased 37 percent, while crime by males increased 19 percent. Most of the increase in female crime occurred in the related offenses of embezzlement and drug abuse violations. Other areas of significant increases include driving under the influence, prostitution, offenses against the family and children, and forcible rape (due to changes in the law of rape).

Some of these dramatic increases may be misleading. Women still account for only 12 percent of all arrests for driving under the influence and 13 percent of all arrests for arson (table 9-1). Only for the crimes of prostitution, fraud, and forgery and counterfeiting do we find that women are accounting for a significant number of the total arrests made.

It appears that, although female crime is growing, fairly traditional forces may be at work in producing the growth. Much of the growth in fraud includes welfare crimes. Changing economic conditions, an increase in teenage pregnancies, and fathers' abandonment of their children may partially explain the growth in this kind of offense. The new female criminal is the old female criminal with more demands and responsibilities and, relative to the job market, fewer marketable skills.

❑ The Female Offender and the Criminal Justice System

There has been considerable debate over the nature and impact of the treatment women receive from the criminal justice system. Many observers have suggested that female offenders have benefited from special handling by chivalrous authorities. Critics of this position argue that paternalistic attempts to protect women from evil have only led to harsher treatment for the "fallen" woman or those women "in danger of falling." Research suggests that, although there has been a slight tendency in the past to treat female criminals more leniently, the less serious nature of female crime is a more significant determinant of criminal justice processing than sex.

Criminal justice officials have traditionally viewed women as nondangerous offenders who are less in need of treatment and more easily rehabilitated than males.[2] This attitude has encouraged leniency, but white middle- and upper-class women are more likely to benefit from this attitude than the majority of lower-class female offenders. Ironically, most women criminals have been victimized by the view that female offenders do not really need treatment. Because of this attitude, the small number of female offenders (only about 17 percent of all arrests, 16 percent of all persons on probation and parole, and 4 percent of prison inmates), and the relative ease with which they are controlled in prison, correctional administrators have tended to minimize the female offender's special problems and needs.[3] Today, except for isolated cases, lenient treatment has virtually disappeared from criminal justice processing, but the development of special programs for women has just begun.

TABLE 9-2 Total Arrest Trends in the United States, by Sex, 1979-1988ª

Offense charged	Males						Females					
	Total			Under 18			Total			Under 18		
	1979	1988	Percent change	1979	1988	Percent change	1979	1988	Percent change	1979	1988	Percent change
TOTAL	6,097,654	7,251,407	+18.9	1,271,573	1,100,491	-13.5	1,152,229	1,583,426	+37.4	327,998	310,369	-5.4
Murder and nonnegligent manslaughter	12,212	12,865	+5.3	1,247	1,498	+20.1	1,865	1,767	-5.3	139	112	-19.4
Forcible rape	21,755	24,768	+13.8	3,444	3,616	+5.0	161	291	+80.7	39	71	+82.1
Robbery	94,031	93,241	-.8	30,357	20,766	-31.6	7,559	8,735	+15.6	2,200	1,698	-22.8
Aggravated assault	168,911	234,590	+38.9	25,210	28,836	+14.4	23,749	36,391	+53.2	4,133	5,156	+24.8
Burglary	325,355	263,638	-19.0	157,987	88,328	-44.1	22,729	24,726	+8.8	11,164	7,238	-35.2
Larceny-theft	572,507	701,437	+22.5	241,282	221,892	-8.0	251,107	309,177	+23.1	89,763	80,043	-10.8
Motor vehicle theft	103,290	122,698	+18.8	49,399	48,408	-2.0	10,266	13,726	+33.7	5,711	5,528	-3.2
Arson	11,987	10,825	-9.7	6,016	4,807	-20.1	1,534	1,646	+7.3	624	500	-19.9
Violent crimeᵇ	296,909	365,464	+23.1	60,258	54,716	-9.2	33,334	47,184	+41.5	6,511	7,037	+8.1
Property crimeᶜ	1,013,139	1,098,598	+8.4	454,684	363,435	-20.1	285,636	349,275	+22.3	107,262	93,309	-13.0
Crime Index totalᵈ	1,310,048	1,464,062	+11.8	514,942	418,151	-18.8	318,970	396,459	+24.3	113,773	100,346	-11.8
Other assaults	305,844	509,516	+66.6	51,910	66,111	+27.4	48,314	92,348	+91.1	13,314	19,966	+50.0
Forgery and counterfeiting	36,970	41,679	+12.7	5,379	3,562	-33.8	16,554	21,443	+29.5	2,207	1,698	-23.1
Fraud	111,343	129,471	+16.3	5,269	8,747	+66.0	76,182	106,036	+39.2	1,855	2,882	+55.4
Embezzlement	4,906	6,344	+29.3	626	522	-16.6	1,670	3,985	+138.6	173	371	+114.5
Stolen property; buying, receiving, possessing	74,058	97,284	+31.4	25,677	24,812	-3.4	8,944	13,072	+46.2	2,534	2,642	+4.3
Vandalism	167,229	174,192	+4.2	89,610	70,233	-21.6	15,668	21,486	+37.1	7,662	6,770	-11.6
Weapons; carrying, possessing, etc.	110,450	133,333	+20.7	19,014	22,472	+18.2	8,570	11,235	+31.1	1,153	1,607	+39.4
Prostitution and commercialized vice	22,687	23,051	+1.6	995	460	-53.8	47,546	51,238	+7.8	1,711	853	-50.1
Sex offenses (except forcible rape and prostitution)	44,412	64,118	+44.4	8,164	10,250	+25.6	3,515	5,113	+45.5	664	719	+8.3
Drug abuse violations	341,130	632,282	+85.3	71,366	58,283	-18.3	53,502	117,186	+119.0	13,748	8,406	-38.9
Gambling	38,075	13,970	-63.3	1,793	635	-64.6	3,813	2,609	-31.6	73	38	-47.9
Offenses against family and children	35,711	34,975	-2.1	1,174	1,285	+9.5	3,668	7,555	+106.0	653	736	+12.7
Driving under the influence	865,964	965,956	+11.5	20,641	12,668	-38.6	84,913	129,470	+52.5	2,344	1,941	-17.2
Liquor laws	237,507	336,353	+41.6	76,969	74,287	-3.5	40,903	73,813	+80.5	21,478	27,236	+26.8
Drunkenness	738,076	479,411	-35.0	28,760	12,712	-55.8	58,894	49,448	-16.0	4,544	2,360	-48.1
Disorderly conduct	462,663	410,939	-11.2	79,276	63,238	-20.2	87,978	92,520	+5.2	16,220	15,238	-6.1
Vagrancy	23,713	24,918	+5.1	3,368	1,856	-44.9	7,970	3,283	-58.8	781	366	-53.1
All other offenses (except traffic)	1,085,803	1,627,843	+49.9	185,575	168,497	-9.2	186,351	313,020	+68.0	44,807	44,087	-1.6
Suspicion (not included in totals)	8,288	3,692	-55.5	2,319	1,337	-42.3	1,391	735	-47.2	516	309	-40.1
Curfew and loitering law violations	33,632	34,976	+4.0	33,632	34,976	+4.0	11,206	12,870	+14.8	11,206	12,870	+14.8
Runaways	47,433	46,734	-1.5	47,433	46,734	-1.5	67,098	59,237	-11.7	67,098	59,237	-11.7

ª6,808 agencies; 1988 estimated population 160,451,000.

ᵇViolent crimes are offenses of murder, forcible rape, robbery, and aggravated assault.

ᶜProperty crimes are offenses of burglary, larceny-theft, motor vehicle theft, and arson.

ᵈIncludes arson.

SOURCE: U.S. Department of Justice, *Crime in the United States, 1988* (Washington, D.C.: U.S. Government Printing Office, 1988), p. 173.

❑ Social Roles and the Needs of the Female Offender

In regard to their problems and needs, criminal offenders are more alike than different. They need education, job training and placement, and counseling to be self-sufficient and to resolve various personal problems. Female offenders do have special needs, however, simply because the roles they tend to occupy in society are different from those held by males. Because women have children, they have special pressures and responsibilities; the financial demands and the all-encompassing managerial and emotional tasks of child rearing must be met. Regardless of the manner in which these obligations are performed, women with children must find the means to support themselves and their children.

Women, especially those in the extremely disadvantaged segments of society, are rarely encouraged to excel academically or even to complete their basic education. Like many in lower socioeconomic groups, these women view life as offering only an endless procession of menial jobs; rising to semi-skilled or skilled employment can seem to be a mysterious, arduous, and risky undertaking. For these women, achievement may undermine more important interpersonal relationships with males; so they may never learn ambition and discipline. Most female offenders are thus poorly prepared for the world of work, especially for the very positions needed to support a family.

Women today are still learning dependent behavior patterns. This learning is particularly prevalent among the more powerless and disadvantaged groups in society, where an individual's actual ability to change his or her economic and social status is limited. Women in these groups learn to promote a feeling of powerfulness and authority in males by assuming a subservient role. Although this dominant male-submissive female characterization is a stereotyped view of more complex social relations, this general pattern of interaction is common. An unwillingness to give up this behavioral pattern inhibits many women's efforts to assume responsibility for their own lives.

The female offender needs education and employment skills that will enable her to earn a living sufficient to support herself and her children. To obtain skills and employment and to manage her own life and raise her children, she needs confidence and the strength to be independent. There are community-based programs designed to meet these needs; although they are few in number, they demonstrate the potential of special programming for female offenders.

Community-Based Correctional Programs for Female Offenders

Community-based programs for female offenders generally focus on developing economic independence, effective parenting skills, and the managerial or survival skills necessary to achieve independent living.

❑ Economic Assistance

The Center for Women Policy Studies surveyed 200 promising correctional programs for women offenders. They visited 38 programs and identified key features of the most innovative strategies. The basic goal of the programs was to break the cycle of dependency, victimization, and crime so characteristic of the female offender.[4] In the area of economic aid, four forms of assistance were identified: job readiness training, vocational training, job development and placement, and follow-up services.

Job Readiness Training.   Job readiness training is especially important for disadvantaged women. They normally have a very stereotyped view of the types of jobs available to them and little familiarity with the world of work, the discipline it requires, or the mechanics of job seeking.[5] Job readiness training can:

1. Provide vocational testing to determine the types of difficulties women may confront upon entering the employment system
2. Offer such basic instruction as how to use public transportation, prepare a resume, or identify existing employment skills
3. Introduce women to the types of jobs available (especially nontraditional jobs) through informational materials, visits to job sites, discussions with employed women, and exploratory training
4. Teach job-seeking skills, such as how to locate job leads and use the want ads
5. Prepare women for jobs and interviews through role playing and practice interviews
6. Offer the opportunities to build the confidence and self-esteem needed to make and maintain the transition to employee[6]

Vocational Training.   Women offenders have always been offered some form of vocational training, but it has not always been very useful. Prison programs have been the least effective.

> Vocational training programs in women's prisons have tended to reflect both a traditional attitude toward women in the work force and the "proper" sort of work for those with criminal records. Typically, what passes for training is traditional female occupations such as food preparation, garment making, and practical nursing, and lots of low-paid or nonpaid "work experience" programs. The work experience programs are designed more to benefit the budget of the confining institution than they are to rehabiltate the confined individuals. Someone has to cook the food, wash the dishes, and mow the lawn; during much of the day a major proportion of inmate energies are devoted to these in-house chores.[7]

Today, effective vocational training for female offenders is more likely to focus on preparation for nontraditional employment. The reason for this shift is economic; blue-collar jobs traditionally held by males pay higher wages than the "pink-collar" jobs normally filled by women. The programs studied by the Center for Women Policy Studies were diverse in form and content: areas of employment training include such fields as auto mechanics, welding, electrical work, electronic circuit design, and truck driving. Both prison and community programs were examined. The best programs shared two features: they prepared women for jobs with higher than average entry-level pay and focused on segments of the employment market where there was a documented demand for workers.[8]

The need for work- or education-release programming for women was found to be particularly acute. Until recently, the proportion of females participating in work release was considerably below that of male prisoners.[9] Correctional administrators have variously argued that (1) work-release programs for women are not cost-effective due to the small numbers of female inmates, (2) most women do not need to learn to support themselves, (3) women do not respond to such programs as well as men, and (4) practical concerns, such as the difficulty of transporting women to job sites, make work release unfeasible in women's prisons.[10] In many places, female inmates have successfully challenged their exclusion from work release in the courts, but work release remains an underutilized correctional alternative for women offenders.

The center studied community-based vocational training programs in New York, Washington, D.C., and California. Two basic training models emerged. The first offered in-house training in such fields as office skills, carpentry, cabinetmaking, plumbing, and electrical skills and provided job placement services. The second approach offered such support services as a pretraining program for women who will enter nontraditional jobs and follow-up counseling for newly employed offenders. Actual training in such programs was contracted out or provided as on-the-job training by the new employer.[11]

Job Development and Placement. Job development and placement activities are basically the same for males and females. A particularly comprehensive program for women, Job Options, Inc., in Harrisburg, Pennsylvania, offers a series of eight services:

1. Screening
2. Orientation
3. Needs assessment
4. Goal setting
5. Employment-readiness counseling
6. Employment search
7. Placement
8. Follow-up services[12]

Supported work projects serve female offenders in several communities. Atlanta's Project Re-Entry places women in public service jobs at a wage of $3 per hour.[13] Clients stay in the program for one year, during which time they are expected to locate permanent, higher paying jobs. Project Re-Entry pays the offenders' wages and monitors work performance and progress.

Placing women in nontraditional jobs requires special efforts to help employers as well as employees make the adjustment. For example, a Washington, D.C., program prepares and distributes an employers' guide that provides information on affirmative action planning, recruitment, handling harrassment, and management issues, such as employee attrition and internal mobility.[14]

Follow-up Services. Follow-up services are particularly important for female workers because of the diversity of problems they may encounter on or off the job. These services may be offered in a variety of ways. A supported work project in Los Angeles builds follow-up services into the work week. Clients work four days a week and spend the fifth day at program headquarters, where they receive individual counseling on any topic related to job seeking or employment.[15] In other programs, staff act as intermediaries when conflicts with employers develop and provide counseling when female workers have problems with co-workers. These and similar efforts provide the female worker with continuing support after employment and facilitate her success both on and off the job.

Issues in Employment Programming.   There are three requirements of effective employment programming. First, comprehensive employment services must be offered to female offenders. Employment readiness training must be linked to vocational training, which must in turn prepare women for existing jobs; follow-up services must be offered to help the new employee keep her job. These services may be offered by one or a combination of community agencies, but they must all be available. A failure to offer comprehensive services can only result in women with less than enough to succeed: job readiness, but no skills; skills, but no job; or a job, but no support system to fall back on when problems develop.

Second, training and placing women in nontraditional jobs is a complex undertaking. There is some evidence that female offenders prefer more traditional forms of employment over such jobs as truck driving and construction and do not keep jobs in nontraditional settings for very long.[16] This should not be surprising because the independence and "liberation" required to prepare for and maintain these positions has not yet filtered down to the social class in which most female offenders are found.

There is no obvious solution to this dilemma. Training programs could screen out all but the most enthusiastic women, but this leaves the majority of female offenders unemployed or underemployed. Reluctant offenders could be subtly coerced into nontraditional jobs, but this would only result in wasted training for many clients. A comprehensive and concerted effort to alter female offenders' perceived work options is needed, but this must be tempered with an understanding of client feelings and flexibility in providing both traditional and alternative training programs. More important, it should be remembered that providing income sufficient to the offender's needs is the program objective; no type of work is inherently inferior or superior to another.

Finally, throughout the job preparation, training, and placement process, the availability of child care is an important concern. Women with children need reliable day-care services if they are going to prepare for and participate in the world of work.

❏ Programs for Parents

Raising a child is a full-time occupation. Even with a spouse or parent available to help with the task, the responsibilities can be overwhelming. With no reliable assistance, the job can seem almost impossible. It is not surprising that many female offenders with children have at one time or another left their children in the care of family or friends.

The inmate mother has special problems. It may be difficult for her to maintain contact with her children's caregivers; she may be unaware or ill-informed about her children's growth, development, and well-being for significant periods of time.[17] Institutional visits may be few and far between; when they do occur, children may be fearful of the formidable physical structure and atmosphere of the institution. The separation of mother and child may produce emotional barriers; the child may come to see the caregiver(s) as the true parent(s) as the mother begins to assume an ambiguous status. When the mother is freed, the transfer of maternal responsibility from caregiver to biological parent may be difficult and emotionally painful.

Temporary Release Programs.   Temporary release programs offer inmates an excellent opportunity to improve their parenting skills and renew ties with their children. Work-release programs have provided inmates with employment in day-care centers, where they receive the emotional rewards of child care while they learn. Furlough programs permit women to interact with their children on their home ground, where both the mothers and children are most at ease and where both can enjoy the simple pleasures of being together.

Community Programs.   Community-based programs can offer comprehensive child-care instruction and counseling. For example, the New York City Foundling Hospital offers a residential program for mothers who have abused their children. Women are admitted into the program under court order; they receive counseling while their children participate in a playschool staffed by therapists specializing in the treatment of the abused.[18] Mothers learn to care for their children properly in a supervised setting. The Foundling Hospital program is unique:

> Because most of the mothers are quite young (on occasion no more than fourteen years old) and are guilty of neglect as well as abuse, the program emphasizes the mechanics of good parenting and orderly family life. The facility has a kitchen and dining room, and the offenders plan the menus for themselves and the children, shop for food in a nearby supermarket, and prepare and serve it in the dining room. Counselors instruct the mothers in the basics of infant and child behavior, because some have inflicted severe punishment on babies when they soiled their diapers or "talked back and wouldn't mind."[19]

Vocaré House, a halfway house in Oakland, California, provides another example of community-based programming for offender mothers. Children up to the age of 12 may live with their mothers at Vocaré, which primarily serves women with drug problems. Upon entering Vocaré, the mother resides in one unit and the children live in another, one block away. The mothers make daily visits while program staff care for the children. During later stages of the program, mothers move in with their children. Parenting skills and efforts to improve the quality of family life are the focus of Vocaré's supportive therapeutic approach.

❑ Survival Training

Women offenders need both the skills and attitudes necessary for independent living. The female offender must learn how to manage money, rent an apartment, locate and use community resources, maintain her own and her children's health, and administer the many legal and contractual requirements that occur in everyday life.[20]

Survival skills programs are currently being offered in a number of women's correctional institutions and community programs. The most frequently offered courses of instruction include banking, money management and budgeting, housing, and using credit and community resources.[21] Community-based courses have the advantage of being able to draw upon a large pool of outside speakers. Community program instruction can encourage clients to assume active roles in the learning process because the women are often able to use the skills they develop immediately. Clients can prepare budgets, open a bank account, or search for housing with the direct aid of project staff, who provide guidance and encourage their efforts.

One of the most important aspects of survival training is the teaching of problem-solving skills. Learning how to determine objectives, analyze a problem, and identify and select from alternative courses of action permits the offender to meet and resolve new demands as they present themselves. Of even greater signficance is the feeling of self-confidence and personal reliability such education can provide. Knowing that she can work out solutions to her own problems may encourage the offender to take greater responsibility for her life and to be less vulnerable to victimization.

❏ Program Illustrations

Georgia has made a concerted effort to meet the special problems and needs of female offenders through community-based programming. The state currently operates both residential and community supervision programs especially designed for the female offender. The following descriptions of the Women's Diversion Center provided by the Georgia Department of Offender Rehabilitation and the Women's Out-Services Supervision Program illustrate Georgia's effort to serve female probationers with special problems or needs.[22]

Women's Diversion Center.   The Women's Division Center in Atlanta, Georgia, accommodates twenty-three female probationers whose offenses vary in severity, as does the length of time each resident is in the program.

The center's basic premise is to give the probationer a chance to prove, while she is serving her sentence, that she is ready to return to the community as a viable resource. During the program's first three years, 146 women had the opportunity to benefit from the center's program. Most of the women granted the privilege of coming to a community center come directly from the courts throughout the State of Georgia. They are screened according to their offense, street probation record, and readiness for this kind of facility. The average resident is a 26-year-old mother of two with an eleventh-grade education.

The center program is divided into four phases, each characterized by its responsibilities, opportunities to be involved in in-house and volunteer activities, pass and phone privileges, points, and amount of monetary withdrawal allowed weekly. The resident also has individualized requirements to perform in each phase. The resident's movement through the phase is also distinguished by the mature acceptance of more accountability for her behavior. At any point, disciplinary action may return the resident to a previously completed phase.

During phase I (length, thirty days), a resident is to become generally oriented to the Women's Diversion Center, its staff, and, above all, its rules and regulations (figure 9-1).

Promotion into phase II (length, thirty days) is granted by the treatment team to the resident who has satisfactorily completed phase I requirements (figure 9-2). With this step, the resident is permitted to earn pass privileges in the community. By this phase, a resident should be actively employed, and she has to meet financial obligations to the State of Georgia and the community in that she is required

Phase I: (minimum length of stay, 30 days)

A resident is to become generally oriented to the Women's Diversion Center, its staff, and above all the rules and regulations of the center.

Responsibilities of residents in phase I:
 1. A resident must learn all center rules and regulations and abide by them.
 2. Resident must have completed fifteen hours of community service work.
 3. Resident will have room curfew of 10:00 P.M. and lights-out curfew of 11:00 P.M.
 4. Resident must meet all obligations of scheduled life skills groups (be on time, keep counseling appointments, etc.).
 5. Residents will be responsible for maintaining kitchen details.
 6. Resident's family must participate in one Family Group Counseling session.
 7. Full-time employment must be maintained.
 8. Resident will not participate in recreational activities without staff supervision.
 9. Resident will not have any pass privileges.
10. Resident must maintain point sheet.

Privileges extended to phase I residents:
 1. Resident will have phone privileges only on Sunday.
 2. Resident will have laundry room use only on Saturday and Sunday.
 3. Resident will receive a weekly allowance of $7.50 during unemployment and $15 during employment, provided money is in her account.
 4. Resident will have full mail privileges.
 5. Resident will not receive visitors during this phase.

FIGURE 9-1 Women's Diversion Center: Residents' Responsibilities and Privileges: Phase I
SOURCE: Georgia Department of Offender Rehabilitation, "The Women's Diversion Center" (Atlanta: Georgia Department of Offender Rehabilitation). Reprinted by permission.

to pay $5 per day for room and board and start paying back her fine and/or restitution. Also required of the resident is a mandatory savings of $5 per week, which is credited to a savings sheet. This savings cannot be withdrawn until release. Residents are also allowed to carry some of the burden of their family's financial obligations by applying for money to send home.

Toward the end of the thirty-day period of phase II, the treatment team again considers the resident's progress as it relates to phase III (figure 9-3). Phase III (length, thirty days) marks the stage at which a resident has accepted the fullest responsibility for her action that the program allows. She has followed rules and regulations, is steadily employed, and has saved some money.

Phase IV (length, indefinite) marks the stage at which the resident is preparing for release from the center (figure 9-4). She is transferred to the probation officer, who plans and implements postrelease plans. Figure 9-5 presents the average resident's daily schedule while in the program.

Women's Out-Services Program.   The Women's Out-Services Program in Rome, Georgia, was created because local judges were concerned about the lack of community-based correctional alternatives for female offenders and because the Georgia Department of Offender Rehabilitation was willing to experiment with a new approach.[23] Diane Wilson, an experienced counselor and program administrator, was hired to develop the program.

Phase II: (minimum length of stay, 30 days)

Phase II is granted to the resident who satisfactorily completes the requirements of phase I. With this step, the resident is permitted to earn pass privileges in the community. Also by this phase, a resident should be actively employed, and she must meet financial obligations to the State of Georgia and the community.

Responsibilities of residents in phase II:
1. Resident must meet all obligations for scheduled life skill groups, being to work on time, keeping counselor appointments, etc.
2. Resident will set up budget and saving plan after employed.
3. Resident must attend at least one Advisory Board meeting.
4. Resident must not violate any rules and regulations of the center.
5. Resident's family must participate in two Family Group sessions.
6. Resident must maintain point sheet.

Privileges of residents in phase II:
1. Resident can use the phone on Tuesday, Thursday, and Saturday.
2. Resident can be visited by family.
3. Resident has room curfew of 11:00 P.M., lights-out curfew by 12:00 midnight.
4. Resident will be eligible for pass privileges.
5. Resident can have regular mail privileges.
6. Resident can receive $15 weekly allowance if gainfully employed.
7. Resident has laundry room use on Monday and Wednesday.
8. Resident can participate in at least one recreational activity without supervision.

FIGURE 9-2 Women's Diversion Center: Residents' Responsibilities and Privileges: Phase II

SOURCE: Georgia Department of Offender Rehabilitation, "The Women's Diversion Center" (Atlanta: Georgia Department of Offender Rehabilitation). Reprinted by permission.

Phase III (minimum length of stay, 30 days)

This phase marks the stage at which a resident has accepted fullest responsibility for her actions that the program here will allow. She has followed rules and regulations, is steadily employed, and has saved money.

Responsibilities of residents in phase III:
1. Resident will continue with employment.
2. Resident can participate in two recreational activities without staff supervision.
3. Resident must abide by center rules and regulations.
4. Resident must attend all scheduled groups and life skill classes, etc.
5. Resident must maintain point sheet.
6. Resident's family must attend two Family Group sessions.
7. Take GED test, if at this level.

Privileges of residents in phase III:
1. Resident has room curfew at 12:00 midnight, lights out at 1:00 A.M.
2. Resident can have full phone privileges.
3. Resident can continue with pass privileges.
4. Resident can receive weekly allowance of $15 if employed.
5. Resident has use of laundry room on Monday, Wednesday, and Friday.

FIGURE 9-3 Women's Diversion Center: Residents' Responsibilities and Privileges: Phase III

SOURCE: Georgia Department of Offender Rehabilitation, "The Women's Diversion Center" (Atlanta: Georgia Department of Offender Rehabilitation). Reprinted by permission.

Phase IV (length of stay, indefinite)

Phase IV marks the stage at which the resident is preparing for release from the center. She, along with counselor and probation officer, plan, design, and implement postrelease plans.

Responsibilities of residents in phase IV:
1. Resident should continue with employment and/or begin job search in returning hometown.
2. Resident must not violate any center rules and regulations.
3. Resident must meet weekly with probation officer to discuss postrelease plans.
4. Resident's family must attend at least one family session.
5. Resident must complete two details per week and keep living area clean.

Privileges of residents in phase IV:
1. Resident has full phone privileges.
2. Resident can receive weekly allowance of $20.
3. Resident has full pass privileges, however, time will be granted at the discretion of the counselor, if resident needs to go to hometown to seek employment and/or place to live.
4. Resident does not have to maintain point sheet.
5. Resident has room curfew of 1:00 A.M., lights out in respect to roommates.

FIGURE 9-4 Women's Diversion Center: Residents' Responsibilities and Privileges: Phase IV
Source: Georgia Department of Offender Rehabilitation, "The Women's Diversion Center" (Atlanta: Georgia Department of Offender Rehabilitation). Reprinted by permission.

	A.M.	P.M.		
Monday	10:00 Intake Orientation	1:00–4:00 Job readiness	6:30–8:00 Communication	
Tuesday	9:00–11:00 Health center	1:00–4:00 Job readiness	6:30–9:30 ABE/GED	
Wednesday	Free time Individual counseling	1:00–4:00 Job readiness	7:00–8:00 Emp. Grp.	8:00–9:30 Spiritual study
Thursday	10:00–12:00 Job readiness (wrap-up)	1:00–4:00 Job interview	6:30–9:30 ABE/GED	
Friday	8:00–12:00 Job interview	1:00–4:00 Job interview		
Saturday	9:00–12:00 Symbolic	Free time or pass	2:00–3:00 Family group (every other Saturday)	
Sunday	10:30–12:30 Church	1:00–4:00 Visitors pass		

FIGURE 9-5 Resident's Daily Schedule
Source: Georgia Department of Offender Rehabilitation, "The Women's Diversion Center" (Atlanta: Georgia Department of Offender Rehabilitation). Reprinted by permission.

The program served three categories of offenders: (1) women who are directly sentenced to the program as a condition of probation, (2) female probationers with special needs who are transferred to the program from regular probation case loads, and (3) probationers who have violated probation conditions and are assigned to the program as an alternative to revocation. The program accommodated approximately 25 female probationers per year. The average client was white, 25 years of age, had 2.3 children, and had completed the ninth grade, although her grade functioning level was rated at 6.4 years. The most frequent offenses included shoplifting, bad checks, and welfare fraud.

The twelve-month program offered GED courses and made referrals to a wide variety of community resources. In addition, six life coping skills classes, designed by Ms. Wilson, were offered (figure 9-6).

The program also attempted to place unemployed female probationers in jobs, but a factory closing that left 3,500 persons unemployed severely hampered this effort. Diane Wilson reported that "most of our clients commit crimes of need and not greed." She illustrated this point with a case example:

> Jennie (not the client's real name) wrote six bad checks totaling $166. The checks were written to buy groceries, children's clothing, and to pay for automobile repairs. Jennie was fined $3,000 and ordered to pay restitution. Jennie entered the Out-Services program after she began having trouble paying off the fine and adjusting to regular probation. After a few months in the program, her payment record improved but her payment schedule was still poor; revocation proceedings were begun.
>
> The Out-Services Program staff investigated Jennie's case and found that during the preceding months Jennie's husband had left her, her two children were ill, and she was forced to relocate because of an inability to pay her rent. At the same time, she was working and attending junior college part-time. When revocation proceedings were begun, she had paid almost $1600 of the fine. Due to the program's efforts on her behalf, Jennie's probation was not revoked and the remaining fine was canceled. Jennie was able to begin making restitution payments and remain in the community.[24]

Issues in the Treatment of Female Offenders

This assessment of the special needs of female offenders has repeatedly emhasized the problem of dependence and the need to encourage self-trust and personal responsibility in female offenders. Treatment programs often place persons in passive, dependent, "patient" roles; such practices are contrary to treatment goals and can easily subvert the helping process. Programs for women may unconsciously encourage the acceptance of traditional social roles by assigning female offenders "women's work" in coed programs, by emphasizing femininity and a gentle demeanor over responsibility and assertiveness, and by failing to focus on the effects of societal role definition and expectations of the female self-image and behavior. These practices are contrary to treatment objectives and can only reinforce the negative self-perceptions that invariably result from the cycle of dependency, victimization, and crime. "Fallen women" do not need to be put back on a pedestal; they need to learn to stand on their own two feet.

FIGURE 9-6 Outlines for Classes Offered by the Women's Out-Services Program

    I. Self-awareness
      Objective: To inform clients of their history as females and to enhance their understand-
                ing of their feelings and emotions that are uniquely female.
      Course Content: What does it mean to be female?
         A. Different physically
            1. Anatomy, physiology, hormones
            2. Illness, infections, good health
            3. Sexually
         B. Society has treated us differently
            1. Jesus's view of women/religious views
            2. Laws
            3. Legal rights
            4. Society's view
         C. Understanding feelings/mental health
            1. Tensions of life
            2. Responses to life—physical/mental
            3. Good/bad feelings
            4. Exercise/Yoga/activities/dancing
         D. Develop own self-concept/awareness
            1. Journal/dreams
            2. Ten commandments for self-awareness
            3. Wishes
            4. Living book—reflect on life
            5. Sexual/assertiveness in general
   II. Parent effectiveness training
      Objective: To improve parents' ability to relate to children to achieve desired and ap-
                propriate behavior. To teach parents how to stop reacting to provocations,
                but to act deliberately instead.
  III. Problem solving and communications skills
      Objective: To educate the client to the process of problem solving so that she will be
                better equipped to identify and work through existing problems or future
                problems that may arise in her life. To help clients become aware of their
                communicating styles and to show them other ways of communicating.
      Course Content:
         A. Introduction to problem-solving process
            1. Five steps to problem solving (Carkhuff)
         B. Group Process of problem solving
            1. "Quaker meeting," group exercise
         C. Communication skills
            1. Verbal
            2. Nonverbal
         D. Four kinds of people
            1. Your personality/communicating styles
         E. Responses to frustrations and tensions
            1. Group exercise to help clients become aware of their responses.
  IV. Consumer education
      Objective: To provide the clients with knowledge of how, where, and why to purchase
                goods and services.
      Course Content:
         A. Shopping/needs vs. wants
            1. Purchasing for the kitchen
               a. Handouts
                  (1) How to eat better for less
                  (2) Stretching your food dollar

          (3) Good food shopping makes "cents"
          (4) Utilizing leftovers
          (5) Vegetables
       b. Discussion
          (1) Purchasing in a grocery store
          (2) Planning before shopping
          (3) Fewer trips mean less cash
          (4) Nutrition and food storage
    2. Advertising and buying
  B. Money management and budget
    1. Meeting your housing needs
       a. Public housing vs. private housing
       b. Location—schools, shopping, employment
       c. Size
    2. Planning your household budget
    3. Banking services/credit cards (use and abuse) (Guest speaker)
    4. Your local utilities
       a. Ways to cut costs
    5. Public services provided by the government
V. Value clarification
  Objective: To help clients in clarifying, understanding, and developing their own personal values. To assist in facilitating the implementation of these values into their lives.
  Course Content:
  A. Value clarification process
    1. Seven criteria
    2. Value indicators
  B. Relationship of values of society
    1. How do you relate your lives to your surroundings?
    2. Clarity of relationship
  C. Group exercises
    1. Thirteen (13) questions (form)
    2. What do I value in life? (forms) Complete in order the forms to be used in this exercise.
VI. Job readiness/Career development
  Objective: To inform clients of the skills needed to obtain and maintain skillful employment. To expose clients to nontraditional jobs. To help clients set career goals.
  Course Content:
  A. Planning to get a job
    1. Class objectives and their importance
    2. Hand out forms
       a. Abilities checklist
       b. Preemployment consideration
       c. Personal views about work
    3. Job readiness pretest
  B. Job information
    1. Discussion on job readiness pretest
    2. How to get a job and keep it
       a. Finding job information
       b. Knowing the job market
    3. Avenues to job skills
    4. The job hunt
    5. Job sources

(continued)

FIGURE 9-6 Outlines for Classes Offered by the Women's Out-Services Program (*continued*)

    C. How to fill out necessary paperwork
        1. Job application handouts
            a. Summary of work experience
            b. Quiz—following directions
            c. Words used on application forms
            d. Sample applications
    D. Interviewing
        1. Interviewing techniques
            a. Making the job interview
            b. The art of interviewing
            c. Tips
            d. Points to ponder
            e. Negative factors list
            f. Expectations of employers and employees
            g. Common interview questions asked
        2. Selling yourself to an employer
        3. After the interview
    E. Self-directed search
    F. Needle sort

SOURCE: Diane Wilson, "Women's Outservices Program Life Coping Skills Training Manual" (Atlanta: Georgia Department of Offender Rehabilitation, 1981). Reprinted by permission.

Summary

In the past, female offenders have been ignored by correctional administrators because they were relatively few in number and often seen as less in need of treatment than male offenders. Today, women criminals receive more attention but not necessarily better treatment.

A number of innovative programs have been developed to prepare female offenders for the tasks of employment and parenting, as well as to provide them with the skills necessary for independence. Such preparation and training is a difficult and complex process. Most female offenders must overcome the disadvantages of social class and minority status as well as gender in their attempt to achieve self-sufficiency. Often the offender's own negative self-image and limited view of her abilities is the greatest barrier to achievement.

KEY WORDS AND CONCEPTS

cycle of dependency, victimization, and crime
employment follow-up services
job development and placement

job readiness training
new female criminal
nontraditional employment

parenting skills
self-esteem
survival skills

NOTES

1. U.S. Department of Justice, *Crime in the United States, 1988* (Washington, D.C.: U.S. Government Printing Office, 1988), p. 185.
2. Darrell J. Steffensmeir, "Assessing the Impact of the Women's Movement on Sex-Based Differences in the Handling of Adult Criminal Defendants," *Crime and Delinquency* 26(3) (1980): 344–357.
3. U.S. Department of Justice, *Sourcebook of Criminal Justice Statistics, 1979* (Washington, D.C.: U.S. Government Printing Office, 1980), pp. 464, 620, and *Correctional Population in the United States, 1985* (Washington, D.C.: U.S. Government Printing Office, 1987), p. 24.
4. Jane Roberts Chapman, *Economic Realities and the Female Offender* (Lexington, Mass.: Lexington Books, D.C. Heath and Company). Copyright 1980, D. C. Heath and Company. This and all quotations from this source are reprinted with permission.
5. Ibid., p. 104.
6. Ibid., pp. 104–109.
7. David North, "Women Offenders: Breaking the Training Mold," *Manpower*, February 1975.
8. Chapman, *Economic Realities*, p. 112.
9. Ibid., p. 113.
10. Ibid., pp. 113–114.
11. Ibid., pp. 115–116.
12. Ibid., p. 117.
13. Ibid.
14. Ibid., p. 118.
15. Ibid., p. 119.
16. Eddyth P. Fortune and Margaret Balbach, "Project MET: A Community-Based Educational Program for Women" (paper presented at the annual meeting of the Academy of Criminal Justice Sciences, Philadelphia, March 10–14, 1981).
17. Belinda R. McCarthy, "Inmate Mothers: The Problems of Separation and Reintegration," *Journal of Offender Counseling, Services and Rehabilitation* 4(3) (1980): 200.
18. Chapman, *Economic Realities*, p. 129.
19. Ibid., p. 133.
20. Ibid., pp. 133–134.
21. Ibid., p. 134.
22. Georgia Department of Offender Rehabilitation, "The Women's Diversion Center" (Atlanta: Georgia Department of Offender Rehabilitation, n.d.).
23. Personal communication with Diane Wilson, director of the Women's Out-Services Program, Rome, Georgia, August 26, 1982.
24. Ibid.

FOR FURTHER READING

Adler, Frieda, *Sisters in Crime* (New York: McGraw-Hill, 1975).
Chapman, Jane R., *Economic Realities and the Female Offender* (Lexington, Mass.: Lexington Books, 1980).
McCarthy, Belinda R., *Easy Time: Female Inmates on Home Furloughs* (Lexington, Mass.: Lexington Books, 1979).
Miller, Eleanor M., *Street Woman* (Philadelphia: Temple University Press, 1986).
Morash, Merry (ed.), *Teaching About Women in Criminal Justice and Criminology Courses: A Resource Guide* (Columbus, Ohio: Women and Crime Division, American Society of Criminology, 1988).

10: Programs for Juveniles

THE JUVENILE JUSTICE SYSTEM USES COMMUNITY-BASED CORRECTIONAL PROGRAMS to a significantly greater degree than the adult criminal justice system because juveniles, more often than adults, have significant family and community ties that can be enhanced and reinforced in reintegration programs. The widely held belief that most juveniles deserve a second or third chance to remain in the community also facilitates the use of community programs for juveniles. A community's willingness to provide community-based programs for adults often depends upon its experience and success or failure with programs for juveniles. Programs that appear to benefit youthful offenders are often subsequently established to serve the needs of adult first offenders or others who have committed only minor crimes.

Many community-based correctional programs for juveniles are similar to those for adults; others reflect the special problems of the adolescent and preadolescent offender. We examine programs for youths in much the same way that we discussed programs for adults. To avoid repetition, in this chapter we focus on the distinctive aspects of programs for juveniles that are similar to those for adults (such as probation) and devote special attention to programs found only in the juvenile justice system (such as foster care).

Criminal Justice and Juvenile Justice

The similarities between the juvenile justice and the criminal justice systems are greater than the differences. Both attempt to respond to the problems posed by individuals who violate the law. The methods of handling offenders differ somewhat, but both systems carry out similar tasks:

1. Suspected offenders are identified and apprehended.
2. Evidence is examined to determine what laws have been broken.
3. Judgments regarding appropriate dispositions are made and executed.

❑ Overview of the Juvenile Justice System

The most significant difference between the criminal and juvenile justice systems is philosophical. The principal objectives of the criminal justice system are to control crime and punish offenders. The juvenile justice system is also expected to control crime, but it emphasizes helping offenders rather than punishing them.

This philosophy of helping or treating juveniles rather than punishing them has a long history in the United States and springs from two sources. First, there is the belief that the juvenile's immaturity diminishes his responsibility for his behavior under the law. Thus, punishment cannot be justified. Second, there is an equally strong belief that young offenders are more amenable to treatment than their older counterparts. It is felt that "if we can help the boy, we won't have to punish the man." Because juveniles are not held legally responsible for their behavior in the same way that adults are and because the emphasis is on helping the offender receive the assistance he needs rather than punishing him, the juvenile justice system adopted a somewhat informal approach to evaluating an offender's problems and behavior and seeking an appropriate remedy.

Some juvenile justice system critics have argued that this system's objectives are less than benevolent. They suggest that the juvenile justice system is in reality a societal mechanism for encouraging conformity to middle-class norms and otherwise controlling youthful behavior, especially that of lower-class youth. Viewed in this light, its informality has been considered as robbing juveniles of the legal protections provided in criminal proceedings rather than facilitating their rehabilitation.

In the 1970s and 1980s, the preceding charges were answered by efforts to incorporate greater due process guarantees into the juvenile justice system. Observers concerned about rehabilitation feared that such steps would make it harder to help children, but there are few signs that this has occurred.

In recent years, new criticisms of the juvenile justice system have been raised. Rather than questioning its benevolent intentions, some of today's critics argue that the system should be more punitive and that juveniles who commit serious crimes should be held legally reponsible for their actions, just as adults are. In some states, efforts have been made to modify the juvenile justice system so that it more closely resembles criminal proceedings.

Today our juvenile justice system, both in objectives and practice, lies somewhere between the extremes of rehabilitation and punishment, of due process guarantees and informality. We now turn our attention to a description of the contemporary juvenile justice system and let the reader determine what goals are really being served.

❑ The Offenders

One important distinction between the criminal justice and juvenile justice systems lies in the types of persons who fall under the jursidiction of the criminal and juvenile courts. The criminal court has jurisdiction over adults charged with violations of the penal law. The juvenile court, or family court, has jurisdiction over status offenders and dependent and neglected children as well as delinquents, who are defined as juveniles (generally persons under the age of 18) who have violated the criminal law. Status offenders are juveniles who commit acts that are prohibited solely because of the youth's status as a minor; typical status offenses include truancy, running away, and ungovernability. Dependent and neglected children are juveniles who have violated no laws whatsoever. Dependent children are those whose parents are unable to care for them; neglected children have been abandoned or physically, emotionally, or financially neglected by their parents.

❑ Processing Juvenile Offenders

Further differences between the criminal and juvenile justice systems can most easily be identified by considering the processing of a delinquent or status offender through the juvenile justice system (see figure 10-1). Offenders may come to the attention of the family court in a number of ways. Victims, parents, school officials, or other concerned parties, such as social service agencies, refer an offender directly to the juvenile court. In most cases, however, complaints are first made to the police. Once the police have identified the juveniles suspected of committing the offense, they may simply reprimand and release them or release after counseling, contacting their

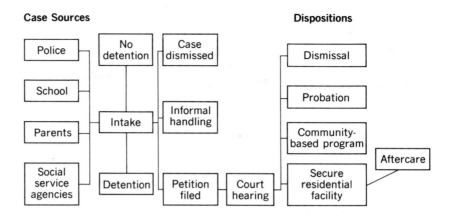

FIGURE 10-1 Processing an Offender through the Juvenile Justice System

parents, or referring them to a community agency for assistance. Alternately, they may choose to take the offenders into custody.

Intake. Once in custody, juveniles are taken directly to family court. If family court offices are closed, the juvenile may be taken to detention until a judge or juvenile probation officer is contacted. All youths referred to the juvenile court undergo a screening process known as intake. During this process, a juvenile court official, usually a juvenile probation officer, interviews the juvenile, his family, the complainant, and other concerned parties to determine the best course of action in dealing with the youth. A variety of alternatives is usually available, but there are basically four options: dismissal of the complaint, informal supervision by juvenile court staff, referral to a community-based program, or formal action initiated by filing a petition that will serve as the formal charge brought before the juvenile court. The initial decision regarding whether to detain a juvenile is also normally made at intake.

Detention. Most juveniles are released to their families after being taken to family court. Those likely to abscond, considered a danger to themselves or others, or who have no place to go, are taken to a detention facility. Federal law prohibits the detention of juveniles in adult jails.

Instead of jail, many communities have established separate secure facilities solely for the temporary care of youthful offenders. Secure detention facilities are physically restrictive, locked environments designed to ensure that the youth will be available to appear in court. Juveniles may be held in detention until the disposition of their offense; the juvenile court judge normally reviews the youth's need for continued detention on a regular basis.

Adjudication. If a petition is filed, the next stage is adjudication, the fact-finding process comparable to an adult offender's trial. Although there are a few notable exceptions, such as the lack of a right to bail, juvenile defendants today are protected by most of the same constitutional rights traditionally guaranteed adults charged with violations of the law. However, the actual process of adjudication frequently differs from the trial model; both prosecutors and defense attorneys often view their task as assisting the judge in determining what action is in the child's best interests.

Disposition.   Following adjudication, an attempt is made to select the disposition that best meets the juvenile's needs and serves community interests. The dispositional alternatives available to the court normally include dismissal, probation, residential and nonresidential community-based programs, and commitment to a secure residential facility, often referred to as a training school. Juveniles released from training schools are generally supervised by juvenile court counselors or juvenile parole officers; this supervision is commonly known as aftercare.

Before examining the variety of community-based programs available for juveniles, we examine the intake process, which serves as a screening process for virtually all juvenile correctional programs.

A Closer Look at Intake

Intake refers to the pretrial investigation and screening of cases referred to juvenile court.[1] Complaints are assessed in terms of the alleged offense, the circumstances surrounding its commission, prior behavior of the youth, and the needs of the youth, his family, and the community.[2] Intake decision making is critical because it determines all future actions by the juvenile court, whether the accusations against the offender will be dismissed or informally or formally handled.

After a complaint has been received, intake staff have three initial decisions to make: (1) whether legal grounds exist for a formal petition of delinquency, (2) whether to dismiss or handle the case formally or informally if there are legal grounds for a petition, and (3) whether to detain alleged offenders if a petition is to be filed.[3] The intake interview with the juvenile and his parents begins with a reading and explanation of the complaint. The youth is questioned about the allegations and given an opportunity to respond. If he denies the offense, the complaint must be dismissed or formally handled. If he admits to the substance of the complaint, additional questions will be asked to determine the circumstances surrounding the offense and to assess the complaint's accuracy. Additional persons, such as teachers, family friends, and social service workers, may subsequently be interviewed. After deliberation, a decision regarding informal or formal processing is made.

If a petition has been filed or if grounds for a petition exist but the final decision on handling has not been made, the intake worker must determine whether the juvenile requires detention. Normally, detention should be considered whenever the youth's behavior presents a danger to himself or others or whenever his behavior indicates that he may abscond prior to his juvenile court hearing.

If a petition is to be filed, the intake worker must next determine how the case should be handled. The best rule of thumb in this area is "the intervention by the court should be proportionate to the severity of the case, that is, the degree of imminent danger the youth poses to self or others."[4]

The preceding description of the intake process represents a model approach to the screening of complaints. The National Assessment of Juvenile Corrections (NAJC) found that the ideal is seldom realized. Less serious offenders frequently receive the greatest attention from intake staff; they are interviewed in greater depth and information about nonoffense behavior is almost invariably sought. More significantly, no relationship was found between the decisions of intake staff and the seriousness of the alleged behavior. Status offenders are as likely to be formally processed as property offenders; they are frequently handled as formally as persons who commit violent crimes.[5] This finding is generally attributed to the fact that status offenders often have problems in the home or other noncriminal behavioral problems that intake staff view as requiring intervention.

When evaluating community-based programs for juveniles, one must keep in mind the type of offender and behavior problems that are appropriate for each program. It is necessary to consider whether it is appropriate to treat status offenders, property offenders, and violent offenders alike because of similar personal problems these youths may share or whether the type of violation should somehow limit the degree of intervention.

In regard to status offenders, the National Advisory Committee for Juvenile Justice and Delinquency Prevention has proposed employing the least restrictive alternative and intervention time period consistent with the nature and circumstances of the youth's conduct, age, interests, and needs, family interests and needs, and the efforts of social service and family court to provide needed services to the youth and his or her family.[6] The committee also states that status offenders should never be confined in a secure detention or correctional facility. Status offenders should be supervised in the community, and, if necessary, placed only in non-secure residential programs.

The following sections describe the variety of community-based programs available for juveniles. Not all programs are available in every jurisdiction. In many communities, juvenile probation is the only community-based dispositional alternative available on a regular basis. In such areas, probation staff must work with community agencies to serve the needs of all offenders who do not require institutionalization.

Other communities can offer one or two group facilities and perhaps a diversion or other community supervision program for children with family, school, alcohol, or drug problems. The full range of programs is generally seen only in large metropolitan areas where the numbers of youths permit increased programming and greater specialization. Even in such environments, however, significant gaps in services may be found.

Juvenile Diversion Programs

There are many strategies for diverting offenders from the juvenile justice process. Some juvenile diversion projects are almost identical to those established for criminal offenders. For example, the Community Arbitration Project (CAP) in Anne Arundel County, Maryland, is a dispute settlement mechanism that mediates juvenile offenses.[7] Police issue citations to juveniles who commit CAP-eligible offenses ranging from vandalism to assault. Offenses are then mediated at a hearing that involves the juvenile, his parents, and often the victim. Community service is routinely utilized as an informal disposition. Other juvenile diversion programs focus on problems that are more specific to juveniles, such as getting along with parents or staying in and completing school.

❏ Youth Service Bureaus

Youth service bureaus (YSBs) are publicly or privately administered agencies developed to address a broad range of youth problems. Their most immediate objective, however, is often diverting delinquents and predelinquents from the juvenile justice system, especially when the bureau is administered by a police or juvenile probation department. The basic functions of YSBs include:

1. Identifying community problems affecting juveniles
2. Developing, monitoring, and strengthening community responses to youth
3. Improving the attitudes and practices of social service and juvenile justice agencies through youth advocacy (system modification)
4. Referring youths to appropriate community resources and monitoring those referrals (service brokerage)
5. Providing direct services
6. Gathering and distributing information

Youth service bureaus accept referrals from any source, including schools, social service agencies, police, and self-referrals. They often operate twenty-four hours a day, seven days a week, and thus can offer immediate assistance without appointment or delay.

The youth service bureaus originated in urban centers in the midwestern United States in the 1950s. The programs generated considerable support; after receiving an enthusiastic endorsement from the 1967 President's Commission on Law Enforcement and Administration of Justice, the bureaus expanded throughout the nation. Although the discontinuation of federal funds in the late 1970s and early 1980s led to the closing of many programs, YSBs still operate across the United States. Their names vary—some are known as Youth Assistance Centers, others as Youth Resource Bureaus—but they all share a single aim: meeting the needs of troubled youth.

The list of youth service bureau activities is almost endless. A survey by the National Advisory Commission on Criminal Justice Standards and Goals identified the following services: 24-hour-a-day counseling, drop-in clinics, family counseling, outpatient medical treatment, crisis intervention, employment assistance, advocacy for youth appearing in juvenile court, temporary shelters and group homes, sponsorship of police-youth dialogues, parent education, self-improvement classes, recreational activities, craft and hobby classes, alternative schools and other education programs, and group discussions with prison inmates.[8] Within the community, a YSB works with various agencies to promote the development of new community resources and to ensure that youths receive the assistance they need from existing programs.

Figure 10-2 illustrates the linkages that a YSB might establish in a typical community. Of course, no youth service bureau offers all these services. Each program is ideally designed to meet the special problems of youth within a particular community. Some programs emphasize direct services; others focus on developing new programs and/or coordinating existing community resources. Programs administered by police or juvenile justice agencies normally emphasize direct services to youth who might otherwise require juvenile court intervention.

Youth service bureau diversion efforts are most frequently found in relatively small communities with populations of 10,000 or less. In 1975, a survey of

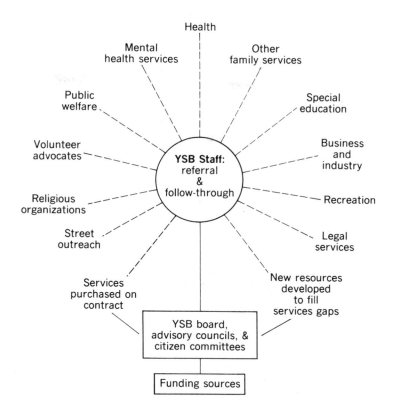

FIGURE 10-2 Typical Community–YSB Linkages

Source: Sherwood Norman, *The Youth Service Bureau: A Key to Delinquency Prevention* (Hackensack, N.J.: National Council on Crime and Delinquency, 1972), p. 15. Reprinted by permission.

YSBs indicated that their clients were predominantly white males; over half had 30 percent or fewer minority clients and 40 percent or fewer had female clients.[9] Not surprisingly, most referrals were found to come from the juvenile justice system.

The Neighborhood Youth Resources Center (NYRC) illustrates YSB services.[10] As one of the nation's largest youth service bureaus, it serves an annual client population of over 1,000 youths with problems ranging from truancy to burglary. Located in a high crime area of Philadelphia, NYRC provides crisis intervention, individual casework, group counseling, educational assistance, referrals to cooperating agencies, and legal representation. In addition, it serves as a recreation, education, and counseling center for all area residents. The program is staffed by individuals whose services are purchased from other community agencies (a lawyer from the Defenders Association, gang workers from the Youth Conservation Services, and so forth). This method of employment enhances the center's ties to other community agencies and ensures that staff are familiar with youth problems and possess the skills to meet their needs effectively.

The YSB in Pleasant Hill, California, operates on a much smaller scale.[11] The program is staffed by three police officers and two civilians and offers a variety of services, including counseling, tutoring, job assistance, and drug education. Much of the emphasis is on reducing truancy and decreasing the number of runaways; police-youth rap sessions are a key component of this effort.

❑ Family-Oriented Diversion Programs

Many juvenile diversion programs attempt to work with the juvenile and his or her family. For example, the Clark County, Washington, Family Crisis Intervention Program offers individual crisis counseling, referral services, and multiple-impact family therapy to status offenders and their families.[12] The program utilizes specially trained teams of volunteers to conduct intensive five- to six-hour counseling sessions.

During counseling, team members attempt to assess the family's ability to function without court intervention and to portray effective communication strategies to family members. The sessions conclude with a discussion of possible referrals to other community resources and suggestions for improving family interaction. The following is a typical case handled by this program.

> Tim, a 13-year-old boy, resided with his natural mother, Jenny, and her boyfriend, Ray, along with two older sisters, Lucy (15), Tina (14), and two younger stepbrothers, Bill (6) and Jim (5). Jenny had been married twice, both marriages ending in divorce. She was employed as a bartender in a tavern. Ray was an unemployed carpenter.
>
> Tim ran away from home for two days, hiding in the woods until he was found by the police. He was brought to juvenile detention because he refused to return home. He stated that Ray drank excessively and abused him physically. Tim stayed in Interim Care pending the impact session one day later. During the session, the family established two goals: (1) to keep Tim from running away and (2) to develop a higher level of trust among family members.
>
> The team focused on some major areas of conflict within the family. Due to Jenny's evening job, she was away from home before the children returned from school. She left Lucy in charge of the children and expected her to prepare meals and take care of the family household. It was apparent that Jenny avoided her family by using work and her free time as an escape. Jenny felt that without her two "good girls," the family would fall apart. Tim had not seen his natural father, who was in prison, for a long time. Bill had been diagnosed as having dyslexia (a learning disability) and did poorly in school. The team discovered that all the children resented Ray and wanted him to leave them alone. Ray and Jenny drank excessively and fought, causing a lot of unrest for the children.
>
> Jenny and Ray admitted that their lives had excluded the children. They agreed to become more involved in family activities and to be home more often. Jenny decided to reduce her working time to three evenings a week. The team recommended that she and Ray seek alcoholic counseling and that they work more closely on managing the family. Tim was returned home and encouraged to communicate his frustration with the family. All the children agreed to talk and reduce their yelling at one another.
>
> Follow-up indicates that Jenny did reduce her working time and is more actively involved in the family. Ray is presently employed. Tim has not returned to the juvenile court and has not run away again.[13]

The Sacramento County Diversion Program offers a more traditional version of family therapy to delinquents, status offenders, and their families.[14] The therapy is provided by trained probation officers, who begin working with the juvenile and his family immediately after the youth is referred to the court. The one- to two-hour sessions may continue for a number of weeks, depending on the nature of the problem confronting the family.

❏ Adolescent Diversion Project

The Adolescent Diversion Project (ADP) established by the University of Illinois offers still another approach to diverting youth from the juvenile justice system.[15] Juveniles are referred to the program by police in lieu of a petition. Youths who choose to participate in the program are assigned to university students, who use behavioral contracting and child advocacy to assist them with their problems. Behavioral contracting involves writing agreements between the youth and his family that detail the behavior expected from the juvenile and the rewards or privileges he will receive if he meets his responsibilities. Child advocacy involves action to assist the youth in managing crisis situations, such as suspension from school, and to ensure that the juvenile receives the services he needs from community agencies and programs.

❏ Youth Courts

An increasingly popular method of diverting juveniles from the justice system involves the use of a youth court. The program originated in Ithaca, New York, in 1962. In 1978, a Youth Forum was established in the village of Horsehead, New York.[16] There, a special youth court staffed entirely by young people between the ages of 10 and 19 considers status offense and misdemeanor charges against juvenile offenders. Before assuming their positions as judges, prosecutors, defense attorneys, and clerks, the youths complete a twenty-hour training course that addresses such topics as the penal law, probation, family court, and the roles played by persons within the criminal justice system. The Youth Forum may hand out dispositions that include up to fifty hours of community service, an essay to be written by the offender, and mandatory attendance at traffic or criminal court. Similar programs are now operating in Canada, Arizona, Minnesota, and Colorado.[17]

In the Denver, Colorado, program, all defendants must admit guilt prior to entering the program; the jury is used only to determine an appropriate disposition for the offender. The disposition often takes the form of a behavioral contract that specifies the areas in which the offender must change his behavior and may include a restitution agreement. The program is unique in that almost half of the jurors are former defendants. These jurors lend special insight to the jury's deliberations.

> In one recent case, a boy who had completed a nine-month contract for assault was consistently the juror most concerned with impressing the defendants with the seriousness of their offense. "Listen," he told a 16-year-old boy who had gone out drinking with some friends and smashed the windows at a rival high school, "you're just laughing through this whole thing. But you can't act cool all the time, or one day you'll be iced. I've been there. You got to be thinking about more than just today. You got to be responsible for yourself."[18]

❑ "Scared Straight" Programs

On March 5, 1979, a documentary film depicting a rap session between representatives of the Lifer's Group at New Jersey's Rahway Prison and juvenile offenders was televised across the country. The rap session was part of New Jersey's Juvenile Awareness Project, a program that had brought over 15,000 youths to Rahway Prison in an attempt to deter them from crime by exploring its consequences. The Lifer's message was clear: criminal careers are unrewarding, getting caught and imprisoned is inevitable, and prison life is brutal. Verbal abuse and physical intimidation were used to get the message across.[19]

Many cities broadcast special programming devoted to discussions of the effectiveness of the New Jersey program and its potential for replication. The television stations that aired the program received a tremendous response from enthusiastic viewers. The broadcast media hailed the program as a panacea, newspaper editorials overwhelmingly endorsed the project and the film won an Emmy as the year's best documentary. Subsequent to the broadcast, thirty-eight states began planning and/or implementing programs modeled after the program depicted by "Scared Straight."[20]

The "Scared Straight" phenomenon represents the darker side of media involvement in corrections. Few attempts were made to accurately describe the program which the film depicted, the juveniles involved or the results of the program.

The Juvenile Awareness Project had been evaluated by New Jersey officials before the documentary was filmed and although it was judged a success, changes were recommended. The inmates' use of false information, threats and intimidation to scare juveniles were to be discontinued.[21]

Further research by the National Center on Institutions and Alternatives (NCIA) revealed that success rates cited in the film were based on letters and testimonials from criminal justice officials, the juveniles and their families, rather than on the results of systematic research. It was also found that, like most of the 15,000 youths who had participated in the New Jersey program, few of the juveniles who appeared in the film had serious criminal records.[22]

Later in 1979, a Rutgers University Professor, James Finckenauer, presented the results of his experimental research on the Juvenile Awareness Project. He found that the rap sessions changed neither the attitudes nor the behavior of program participants, and may have actually made things somewhat worse; a control group of nonparticipants subsequently committed fewer and less serious crimes than the "Scared Straight" subjects.[23]

These findings led many organizations of criminal justice professionals and concerned citizens to urge a reconsideration of the value of "Scared Straight" and similar programs. Organizations such as the National Council on Crime and Delinquency, the American Correctional Association, and the National Advisory Committee for Juvenile Justice and Delinquency Prevention criticized the program(s) for shortsightedness and a lack of attention to social and economic conditions affecting crime, and warned of the potential for psychological harm to some youths.[24]

Subsequent research on the Juvenile Awareness Project and similar programs has produced more of the same: no valid evidence that "Scared Straight" type programs work. It has been suggested that the programs' continued appeal is largely a result of publicity but the underlying ideological message must be credited with part of the programs' perceived effectiveness. That message is that traditional crime prevention and rehabilitation techniques do not work; that crime is a willful act; and that juvenile criminals are near-animals who can be changed only through the use of brutal scare tactics, or, as one television commentator remarked, "whatever it takes to shock the kids into realizing the consequences of their lives of crime."[25]

Realistic, informative discussions of the consequences of crime, visits to correctional institutions and talks with inmates may be useful strategies for working with some juvenile offenders when these techniques are part of a broader effort to deal with the youths' economic, psychological and social problems. However, there seems to be no evidence that scare tactics, including verbal and physical intimidation and threats, are ever effective with any youths.

☐ Diversion and the Juvenile Justice System

The preceding programs are not all the possible juvenile diversion alternatives; in fact, most of the community-based programs we describe later in this chapter may also be utilized to avoid formal juvenile court intervention. The manner in which a community-based program for juveniles is used—that is, as a diversion alternative or a disposition for adjudicated offenders—depends upon the particular treatment or rehabilitative philosophy present within a given community. Programs used only for "divertable" first offenders in one setting may be used for more serious delinquents in others. A single program will often be made to serve both adjudicated and nonadjudicated offenders because there are not sufficient resources to establish specialized programs for all offender groups.

Community Alternatives to Secure Detention

As noted earlier, the vast majority of offenders do not require detention; they await adjudication in their own homes. Those who do require detention do not necessarily need placement in a secure, locked facility. Alternative detention programs may be residential or nonresidential.

☐ Home Detention Programs

The nonresidential programs, often referred to as home detention, are similar to supervised pretrial release programs for adults. Youths are permitted to live at home while they are supervised by juvenile court counselors, who attempt to keep them out of trouble and available to the juvenile court. The juvenile, his parents, teachers, and employers may be contacted on a daily basis. Frequently, the juvenile is required to attend school or work, obey a curfew, keep his parents and/or supervisor informed of his whereabouts, and avoid drugs and unsavory persons and places during supervision. Additional rules may be written into a home detention contract. Counseling and referral services are usually provided to the youth under supervision.

A survey of home detention programs revealed that the average program serves between 200 and 300 youths per year.[26] Between 2 and 13 percent of the juveniles run away or are rearrested during supervision. Failures were found to result from excessive delays in adjudication and attempts to use home detention to test the youth's potential as a probationer.

The San Diego County Home Supervision Program illustrates home detention.[27] Counselors check on the minors in their case load every morning, afternoon, and evening, seven days a week. Personal, unannounced contacts are made every day on a varying schedule; youths thought to be violators may be contacted as many as four times a day. Minors who violate supervision may be taken into custody.

During the first two years of the program's operation, almost 2,500 boys were supervised; about 20 percent were violators, but only thirty-three committed new offenses while in the community. The Home Supervision Program costs less than one-third the amount required to place a youth in secure detention.

Although the emphasis of home supervision is on surveillance, the program does have its lighter moments:

> A Home Supervision officer was chasing a violator who scaled a wall. When the officer also went over the wall, he realized that he had stumbled into a nude swimming party. The quick thinking youth apparently shed his clothes and disguised himself as one of the guests. He was apprehended the following day (fully clothed and grinning ear-to-ear).
>
> Another minor, under house arrest, went to see *Star Wars* and waited in the long line. The probation officer arrived at the theatre just as the boy was buying his ticket. He failed to see his probation officer. The officer, a patient soul, decided he knew where the kid would be, so he checked when the show would let out and returned to make the arrest.[28]

❑ Temporary Shelter Programs

Community-based residential detention programs may utilize foster care or group homes to provide temporary shelter to juveniles who need an out of home placement but do not require confinement in a secure detention facility. The Proctor Program in New Bedford, Massachusetts, and Discovery House in Anaconda, Montana, are representative of foster and group home programs that serve this function.

The Proctor Program is designed to provide temporary foster care to girls between the ages of 12 and 17.[29] Foster care is provided by young women between the ages of 20 and 30. They are normally recruited through referrals from youth-service agencies; so most of the foster parents have had prior experience working with juveniles. In addition, they receive three days of in-service training on such subjects as the juvenile justice system, psychosocial dynamics of adolescence, health needs of young women, and recreational resources.

The foster parents are expected to expose the girls to acceptable lifestyles—normal hours, meals, grooming, and recreational activities. The youths develop close relationships with their proctors, who work with the girls and professional staff in developing long-term plans for the juveniles. The program reports that fewer than 10 percent of the girls run away. There is also some evidence that the juveniles improve their general attitudes toward adults after program participation.[30]

Discovery House is an attention home where youths receive *at*-tention, not *de*-tention.[31] Only serious, violent offenders and prior Discovery House failures are excluded from the program. Most of the youths accepted into the programs are status offenders, but many of them have complicated personal problems that require up to five months' stay.

Problem resolution is the focus of the program; professional services are provided to youths on a contractual basis. Although youths who enter the program are being processed through the juvenile justice system when they arrive at Discovery House, three-fourths of the petitions against the youths are quashed while they are in the program. Like many temporary shelter programs, Discovery House seems to serve as a diversion as well as a detention alternative.[32]

Juvenile Probation Programs

The majority of youths adjudicated by the juvenile court are placed on probation. Many nonadjudicated youths are placed on informal probation, a diversion strategy initiated at intake in which probation staff defer the filing of a petition while the juvenile receives probation counseling and supervision. If the juvenile successfully adjusts to and completes supervision, a petition against the child will not be filed. If the child fails to adjust, a petition is filed. Juvenile probation is clearly the most far-reaching community-based correctional program for juveniles. The nature and scope of its services often determine the types of alternative community programs that will be established within a particular jurisdiction.

Like adult probation, juvenile probation services may be administered by the local court or by a state agency. Within the probation department, activities can normally be divided into intake and supervision duties. Our discussion focuses on probation supervision and specialized programs for juvenile probationers.

The National Assessment of Juvenile Corrections found that the median case load size of juvenile probation officers was 55 youths.[33] Most probationers are contacted once a month; half of the juveniles are seen for less than thirty minutes per visit. Obviously, most of the probation officer's time is not spent in counseling his clients; in fact, less than one-third of his time involves providing direct services to probationers. Officers responsible only for probation supervision (and not intake) spend over half their working hours conducting investigations, attending meetings, appearing in court, and reading and preparing reports.

The counseling that juvenile probationers receive focuses on personal, school, employment, and drug-related problems and probation rules and regulations. Individual and group counseling is the most widely utilized form of treatment, although about one-third of the probation agencies provide employment services, vocational training, or academic education.

Juveniles are normally placed on probation for an indefinite period. The length of time a youth spends on probation is influenced by such factors as his or her age and the end of the school year. The average youth spends 11.5 months on probation.

Although most juveniles on probation receive little counseling, some jurisdictions have developed special programs to meet the needs of serious delinquents or youths for whom assistance might make a difference. Project CREST, Project New Pride, and the Community Advancement Program represent model efforts to assist juvenile probationers.

❏ Project CREST

Project CREST (Clinical Regional Support Teams) in Gainesville, Florida, uses graduate students from the University of Florida's Department of Counselor Education to work with juvenile probationers.[34] The volunteers work in teams of four to six counselors and tutors and are supervised by a doctoral student, who serves as team leader. The ten weeks that the volunteers spend in CREST meet the counselor education program's practicum requirement.

The students receive an intensive twelve-hour orientation and training course before being assigned to a probationer. Using their counselor education, they employ various therapies, including reality therapy and client-centered therapy; individual, group, and family counseling may also be provided. The probationers and their families are seen at least once a week and the youth is also visited at school every two weeks.

CREST staff meetings and team meetings are held several times a month to share information, review cases, discuss problems, and exchange ideas regarding treatment strategies. The students also meet regularly with their client's probation officer, who focuses more on providing structure and limits when clients are working with CREST volunteers. The team members' activities are routinely evaluated by their professors and fellow students; recordings of counseling sessions are submitted for individual and group criticism.

An assessment of Project CREST showed that youths who participated in the program committed fewer offenses than a control group both during and up to two years following treatment.[35] In addition, their grades improved and they were less likely to be suspended from school than juveniles in the comparison group.

❏ Project New Pride

Denver's Project New Pride offers academic education, counseling, employment, and cultural education to serious juvenile offenders.[36] Most of the clients are males between the ages of 14 and 17, have a recent arrest or conviction for burglary, robbery, or assault, and have two prior convictions.

Academic education is provided through one-to-one tutoring from New Pride's Alternative School or the Learning Disabilities Center, which also offers therapy to correct perceptual and cognitive disabilities. The aim of counseling is to improve the youth's self-image and help him cope with his environment. Counselors become involved in all aspects of a youth's life and maintain close contact with family, teachers, and social workers assigned to the juvenile.

A job skills workshop, individual counseling, and on-the-job training in part-time employment are designed to prepare the youth for the working world. Cultural education exposes youth who have known little more than their immediate environment to various activities in the Denver area. Ski trips, wilderness experience weekends, visits to television stations, and restaurant dinners are typical of New Pride's cultural activities.

At its inception, New Pride established a number of basic program objectives: reducing recidivism, job placement, school reintegration, and remediating academic and learning disabilities.[37] The project appears to have met its goals; New Pride clients were rearrested less frequently than a comparison group of youths, and 70 percent of all New Pride youths were placed in full- or part-time jobs. Unexpectedly, 40 percent of the juveniles also decided to return to school after completing the program. This benefit is enhanced by the improvements in academic performance and declines in learning disabilities that New Pride seems to have produced. In 1980, the Office of Juvenile Justice and Delinquency Prevention awarded ten cities a total of over $9 million to establish New Pride Projects in their own communities.

❏ Community Advancement Program

Massachusetts' Community Advancement Program (CAP) is a multisite project that offers intensive supervision to juveniles who have previously failed on probation.[38] CAP youths are counseled by persons with case loads of two to five juveniles. The youths are visited four or five times a week, and their whereabouts are known to the counselor on a 'round-the-clock basis. The counselor's primary objective is to keep the youths out of trouble and employed or attending school. Their responsibilities include monitoring virtually every action and activity in which the youth is involved, ranging from vocational and educational counseling to medical and dental care to recreational activities. Any problem the youth experiences with school, employment, juvenile court, police, or family will receive the counselor's assistance and intervention.

The program has two basic components: tracking and regular supervision. Tracking consists of five hours of supervision per day plus twenty-four-hour-a-day availability for crisis intervention. Tracking is understandably reserved for serious delinquents and costs approximately $97 a week. Juveniles placed on regular supervision receive fifteen hours of monitoring and guidance per week.

Youths remain in the program for six months, during which time they are encouraged to spend some of their time in CAP's storefront drop-in centers, where pool, table tennis, and small libraries are available. The centers are used as staff offices and for recreation and informal youth-staff rap sessions. All youths receive $5 per week for cooperating with their counselors.

Programs for Youths with School-Related Problems

❏ Alternative Schools

Alternative schools provide special education and intensive counseling to juveniles with behavior problems. The juvenile court or the public school in which the student has had difficulty refer youths to these schools. The model for most alternative schools is the Providence Education Center (PEC), established in St. Louis, Missouri.

The Community Advancement Program

Joey is 12 years old. He is a thin, frail-looking youngster, well under five feet tall. He is very shy and doesn't talk much.

Joey lives in the Great Brook Valley public housing project, a sprawling collection of one-story cinder block buildings in the north end of Worcester, Massachusetts. He has twenty-one brothers and sisters, though only six of them still live in the project. Joey's mother is a nervous emaciated woman not much bigger than he is. She is a conscientious mother, rising early every day to wash, clean, and cook. But she has often found it difficult to control her children, most of whom are now in foster homes.

When he was 10, Joey, more for entertainment than personal gain, began stealing cars. He and his friends from the project reportedly stole twenty to twenty-five cars in the course of two years, specializing in Lincoln Continentals. Once they tried to steal an airplane.

Joey was caught several times and placed on probation, but it did no good, and an exasperated judge finally committed him to the state Department of Youth Services (DYS). Five years ago commitment would have meant a stay at the state training school at Oakdale, or perhaps the Lyman School for Boys. But those institutions are closed now, and DYS has had to find more innovative ways of dealing with delinquents like Joey. The guiding principle has been to do everything possible to keep them in their own homes, especially those as young as Joey.

Last summer Joey was placed in the care of the Community Advancement Program (CAP), Massachusetts' largest and, some say, most effective nonresidential treatment and supervision program. As a result, Joey never had to leave home. He has been in no serious trouble since CAP took over his case. . . .

Joey's counselor is Peter Hulett, a 25-year-old former stereo salesman who was born and raised in Worcester, a declining industrial city of about 200,000. When Hulett went to work for CAP in July and Joey was placed in his case load, his most important immediate goal was to keep Joey away from some of his friends who were incorrigible car thieves.

Stealing cars is the principal recreation for most of Worcester's delinquent youth, Hulett says. They will steal anything on wheels. (Massachusetts, according to state officials, has the highest rate of car theft in the nation.) Hulett's routine last summer was to pick Joey up at the project each morning and either drop him at the Worcester storefront or take the boy with him on his visits to the other four youths in his case load.

Hulett says his relationship with Joey is "a big brother thing, a trust thing." Joey's parents have difficulty controlling him, Hulett says, and have now given much responsibility for imposing controls to Hulett. The counselor says, "I don't have much over him except the $5 allowance," which all CAP youth receive every week for cooperating with their counselors. He must therefore rely on a sort of natural rapport with the boy.

In September, when Joey—a chronic truant—returned to school, Hulett dropped him off in the morning and picked him up at night for the first weeks. After negotiating with the school administration, he got him placed in a special education class. As of October, he was doing well in school, Hulett reports, and had not been in any kind of trouble for over six months. Whether Hulett's supervision and counseling will have any lasting impact will not be known until December, when Joey will have been in CAP six months, and must be discharged.

SOURCE: "Community Advancement Program," *Corrections Magazine* 2(2) (1975): 13–17. Copyright 1975 by Corrections Magazine and Criminal Justice Publications, Inc., 116 West 32 Street, New York, NY 10001.

The program originated in the early 1970s and quickly won designation from the Law Enforcement Assistance Administration as an exemplary project.

Providence Educational Center. PEC offers remedial education and counseling services to juveniles who have had difficulty adjusting to public school; PEC students often have delinquent histories as well. Most PEC students are minority youths from large, poor families.[39] They usually enter the program at about age 12 and are several years behind their peers academically. PEC has five service components:

Student Views of an Alternative School: Independence High, Newark, New Jersey

"What other school has field trips every week?" said 19-year-old Marilyn Quinones, who has gone to the school for three years and will graduate this year. She quit public school and admits that she was "difficult to get along with" when she first came to Independence.

"Teachers used to boss me around in (public) school, and I didn't take it from them," she said. At Independence, she feels she is treated "more like a human being." She says she has "changed a lot" since she came.

Steve Brazenas, 15, said, "I like the teachers here. They don't mind joking around with us, and they talk to us like they're talking, not reading something out of a dictionary. They really care about you. Some of them are more like friends. You still have to do the work, but there's nobody driving you."

Many of the students say that the work is not as hard as in public school, but that they feel they are learning more.

"They teach you what you want to learn," said one student who had been arrested several times before he came to Independence. He had quit high school and was "running wild" on the streets, mugging people and stealing cars. (He was never caught for anything serious, he said.) After nearly a year of this life, he heard about Independence from a friend and decided that he didn't want to be on the streets any more.

"When I came here, I calmed down," he said. "I've been learning to deal with people and with reality." He said that he would probably "still be out there knocking people on the head and taking their money" if he had not come back to school. Now, he plans to go to college.

SOURCE: Kevin Krajick, "Independence High: A School for Delinquents," *Corrections Magazine* 3(4) (1977): 47. Copyright 1977 by *Corrections Magazine* and Criminal Justice Publications, Inc., 116 West 32 Street, New York, N.Y. 10001.

1. An Assessment Center that provides extensive diagnostic testing and orientation to referred juveniles
2. The Education Center, responsible for the academic program
3. The Student Work Assistance Program, which provides work-study opportunities for students
4. An aftercare component to help with counseling, alternative placements, and readjustment
5. Two group homes, one for girls and one for boys[40]

PEC relies on a high teacher-student ratio and small classes (average size: fourteen students) to provide individualized attention to the juveniles enrolled in the program. The academic work emphasizes the traditional subjects, such as math and reading, but there is no conventional grading in the school. An attempt is made to take the learning experience out of the classroom and bring it into the students' world. For example, a math class might be taken to a used car lot and a bank in an effort to learn about the financial side of owning a car.[41]

The Providence Educational Center has achieved considerable success in reducing both truancy and delinquent behavior in its students. A 1976 study of 300 PEC students revealed that, although the youths averaged five adjudicated offenses each when they entered the program, only 20 percent had been rearrested following participation.[42] Not surprisingly, the program has earned the confidence and support of local criminal justice officials. As one probation officer noted:

> I think the public school system is failing a lot of kids. It is not developing a curriculum that meets the needs of inner city youth. It takes a different breed of teacher, with patience and understanding, to do that. And I think that is what we have in Providence.[43]

Jacksonville Marine Institute.   Jacksonville Marine Institute offers a different approach to alternative education.[44] Work education and academics are combined with exciting outdoor activity that includes swimming, diving, and cruises on the institute's forty-five-foot sailboat. The program operates from eight locations throughout the State of Florida, and serves approximately 1,200 juveniles annually.

The program is not all fun and games. Entering students sign a contract agreeing to abide by program regulations during an initial thirty-day evaluation period. During this phase of program involvement, they attend short, introductory courses on first aid, health, swimming, and ecology. The next five months offer more intensive instruction in sailing, diving, and marine biology as well as academic and work education classes.

Counseling in the program is informal. Students are expected to behave responsibly and earn points in the token economy for effort and good behavior. They may use the points to purchase long sailing trips, such as a recent cruise to the Bahamas. Shorter, overnight cruises are offered on a regular basis.

Like PEC, this alternative school appears to teach and reach its students successfully. According to reports, only 13 percent of the juveniles favorably terminated from the program are ever convicted of new crimes.[45]

❑ Programs for Juveniles in Traditional Schools

Some programs for youths attempt to work with juveniles who are still able to function within the public school system. For example, the Teacher Probation Officer (TPO) Program provides a reduced teaching load to selected teachers so they may provide probation-like supervision to students attending the school.[46] In-school suspension programs, which currently operate throughout the United States, provide an alternative method for dealing with disruptive and truant children who commit minor offenses. The students attend school but are physically and socially isolated from their peers during the school day. The juveniles spend their time entirely in one room, where they concentrate on remedial work or regular school assignments. The average length of in-school suspension is three days; the youth's parents are frequently asked to attend a parent-teacher conference before the student is returned to the regular classroom.[47]

Other programs in public education use behavior contracts to reduce disruptive behavior. School or community service activities are often assigned to misbehaving youths and those who demonstrate responsible behavior earn special privileges. Special remedial or compensatory educational programs and intensive tutoring are often provided to disruptive students in conjunction with efforts to improve their in-school behavior.

Programs for Runaways

Emergency shelters for runaways have become increasingly common in recent years. These programs provide food and shelter, and often clothing, counseling, and medical care to juveniles who have committed no crime other than being "AWOL" from home. Many times the youth's family has encouraged him to leave or forcibly ejected

"Under 21": Emergency Shelter for Runaways

"At 8 P.M. on a recent night I was sitting in a New York City subway station when a sad-eyed black boy carrying a shopping bag walked over to me and asked where I was going. When I asked him where he was heading, he said that maybe he was going to 'stay down in the subway all night.' Did I know somewhere else he could go 'where I won't get killed?'"

I blurted out the names of the main unofficial shelters in Manhattan for the derelict and homeless: Penn Station, Grand Central, the Port Authority Bus Terminal.

"Will the cops bother me there?" he wondered, and I had no answer. But his mind was racing. "At the bus station could I get a ticket for Atlantic City?" he asked. "How much does it cost for a room there?" This was a pipe dream: The boy had only a dollar and some change.

As a subway train stormed into the station, he picked up his bag and I noticed that it was filled with clothes. It finally dawned on me: This boy was not out for a lark or running away from home for the night. He was, rather, a "bag child," carrying all his belongings in a

sack. He had nowhere to go; perhaps he had no place to return to.

He told me, in a matter-of-fact voice without self-pity, that his name was Eddie Ramsey, that he was 13 years old, and that he had been sent by his mother to a residential school in northern New York State, which ejected him when he ran out of money. His mother had then passed him on to an uncle, who lodged him with the parents of one of Eddie's friends; they charged him $2 a night. Again he ran out of money, and earlier that day they had given him the boot. When he sought sanctuary with his mother and uncle, they turned him away.

Overcoming my impulse not to get involved, I recalled reading about a center for runaways and "throwaways" (the latter clearly applied to Eddie) called Under-21. It was run by a Catholic priest and was located just off Times Square. When I told Eddie that I thought I knew of a place that would take him in, at least for the night, he brightened, but wanted to know, "Do they make you pay?"

(continued)

him. Emergency shelters offer these youthful "throwaways" a way-station while efforts can be made to find them a suitable long-term placement. Whenever possible, however, the goal of counseling efforts is a reconciliation with the family.

Juveniles generally enter emergency shelters through self-referrals or are referred by the police. In addition to providing the basic necessities and attempting to work with the youth and his family, the programs may also provide drug or employment counseling and offer a referral service to community agencies. Because the average length of stay in an emergency shelter is no more than two weeks, the program must focus its primary efforts on meeting the youth's most immediate needs.

A 1980 survey of emergency shelters funded by the former Department of Health, Education and Welfare revealed that 59 percent of the youths served by the programs were female and three-fourths of all residents were white.[48] Most of the juveniles were between the ages of 14 and 16 and had run fewer than 50 miles. Not surprisingly, family problems account for most youths running away from home. After leaving the shelters, most returned to their families or other positive living arrangements; about one-fourth of the juveniles continued running or left without saying where they were going.

Special Approaches in Juvenile Assistance, Inc. (SAJA), Washington, D.C., is fairly typical of programs for runaways. Emergency shelter and crisis intervention is provided for up to 14 youths between the ages of 11 and 17.[49] A staff of four full-time counselors, ten volunteers, and several consultants offer casework, family counseling, court advocacy, and referral services. The average length of stay in SAJA is one week.

"Under 21": Emergency Shelter for Runaways (continued)

When the train stopped at 42nd Street, I called Under-21. A male counselor said, "Bring him right over; we're two blocks away," and thanked me profusely. On the way up Eighth Avenue, we ambled past pushers and pimps bathed in neon light from the dozens of signs advertising sex on celluloid. Eddie said that he'd been through these parts before. "These men," he said, with loathing in his voice, "they say they'll let me stay with them if I do this thing but I don't mess around with that stuff." I marveled at his resolve and wondered how long it would last.

Amid the filth on Eighth Avenue, the lacquered oak facade of Under-21 seemed inviting. The door was locked, but a press on the buzzer brought instant entrance, without prior scrutiny. We entered a large, well-decorated room littered with mattresses and foam rubber pads on which were sprawled two dozen teenagers. On a small balcony in the rear sat another six kids. Several were talking loudly or listening to radios; cacophony reigned.

But there was some order to this chaos; an energetic overseer named Greg seemed to be responsible for that. He asked Eddie his name and age; that was all he wanted to know. I was amazed when he called over another counselor and said, "Eddie here will be staying the night." Obviously it didn't matter why Eddie needed shelter, only that he did need it. As I said goodbye to Eddie, I noticed that he was not so much happy as relieved.

Two weeks later, I asked Father Bruce Ritter, the priest who started Under-21 and its parent shelter, Covenant House, to track Eddie down. A few days later another Covenant House official told me that after two days at the shelter, "Eddie went AWOL. Apparently he wasn't there long enough for anyone to get through to him. But you never know—at least now he knows there's some place he can go. Some kids come and go a half-dozen times."

SOURCE: Greg Mitchell, "For Runaways, a Meal, a Bed—and No Questions Asked," *Corrections Magazine* 6(3) (1980): 29, 30. Copyright 1980 by *Corrections Magazine* and Criminal Justice Publications, Inc., 116 West 32 Street, New York, N.Y. 10001.

Amicus House in Pittsburgh, Pennsylvania, is a program for local runaways.[50] Youths are referred to the shelter by the court or social service agencies as well as through self-referrals. Upon entering the program, youths are restricted to the house for forty-eight hours. They are informed "You're here to think"; counseling is available, but the youth is otherwise forbidden outside contacts. If the youth appears to be trying to resolve his difficulties, the parents may be contacted and a meeting arranged. If the family members are unwilling to work with Amicus House staff to iron out their problems, attempts are made to find an alternative placement for the youth. This measure is normally unnecessary; most juveniles return to their families after two or three weeks.

Wilderness Experience Programs

Outward Bound and similar wilderness experience programs provide youths with the opportunity for a successful experience through wilderness training. Youths who are able to complete their training are expected to feel better about themselves. Because delinquency is viewed as self-destructive behavior engaged in by children with poor self-images, delinquent acts are expected to decline after program participation.

Wilderness training programs did not originate with the aim of reducing youthful recidivism. Instead, they were developed during World War II after observers noted that young British seamen quickly gave up their lives when forced to abandon ship in the North Atlantic. Older, more experienced seamen managed to survive, although they were in poorer physical condition. The first Outward Bound program was established to build muscles and physical stamina in young seamen; more important, it attempted to develop feelings of group pride, personal self-worth, and trust in others among the sailors.[51]

The success of the Outward Bound school led to its replication throughout the world as a program for troubled youth. The first U.S. school was established in the Rocky Mountains of Colorado in 1962. Its curriculum included instruction in mountain walking, backpacking, high altitude camping, solo survival, rappelling, and rock climbing. Similar programs were established in Minnesota, Maine, Oregon, North Carolina, Texas, and Massachusetts. More than 1,000 youths have now participated in the 150 to 200 wilderness programs in the United States.

The original Outward Bound program lasted three weeks and consisted of four basic phases: (1) training in the basic skills, (2) a long expedition, (3) a solo, and (4) a final testing period. This format has been modified in the newer programs to focus on and expand selected program elements. Homeward Bound, established in Massachusetts in 1970, is probably the best known of the second-generation wilderness training schools.

The Homeward Bound school offers six weeks of endurance training and testing to the thirty-two adolescent boys accepted during each program session.[52] Initially, the youths spend their days developing physical fitness, working in community services projects, and developing release plans with their counselors. Evenings are filled with instruction in ecology, survival, search and rescue, and overnight expeditions. After two weeks, the boys begin putting their wilderness training into practice; their activities include a five- to six-hour cross-country "trot," an overnight expedition, a three-day expedition, and a ten-day mobile course across the Appalachian Trail (often in several feet of snow). The exercises culminate with the solo—a three-day, three-night independent journey during which each boy must prove his ability to survive alone in the wilderness.

A comparison of Homeward Bound students with youths committed to a Massachusetts training school indicated that the wilderness experience produces less recidivism institutionalization. Although there is some feeling that the benefits of such programs are short-lived, there is little doubt that wilderness training offers a positive and rewarding experience that is often unavailable in the youthful offender's usual surroundings.

Restitution and Community Service Programs

Restitution and community service programs for juveniles are very much like those for adults; the major distinction reflects the fact that more juveniles are unemployed. Restitution programs for juveniles invariably offer assistance in locating a part-time job so the juvenile can make financial restitution. Community service activities are similar to those for adults, although there is a greater effort to include direct service to the victim as part of the youth's service to the community.

Like those in the criminal justice system, restitution and community service projects for juveniles have become increasingly popular in recent years. The Law Enforcement Assistance Administration greatly facilitated program expansion in the late 1970s when forty-one juvenile restitution programs were established with federal funds. The Jefferson County, Kentucky, Juvenile Restitution Project is typical of these federally funded programs.[53] Youths adjudicated for property offenses or robbery and assault (when medical expenses are involved) are referred to the project by the juvenile court. Work is located for the juveniles, who must pay 75 percent of their wages to the victim. Community service is required when the money or property the youth stole is recovered.

In 1980, a preliminary evaluation of the Jefferson County program reported that most of the participants were white males from low-income families; their average age was 16 years. Most of the juveniles were first or second offenders who were referred to the program because of an adjudication for burglary. The average amount of restitution ordered was $198; about half the total amount ordered was collected. The youths provided over 430 hours of volunteer work during the first seven months of the program's operation; seven victims received direct services from their offenders.

Juvenile Aftercare

Virtually all juveniles who are committed to correctional institutions are released under some type of supervision, which is commonly referred to as juvenile aftercare or juvenile parole. Although juvenile aftercare is in many ways comparable to adult parole, there are also some important differences. Most juveniles receive completely indeterminate commitments to training school. Because they may be released at any time prior to the age of majority, the release decision is of special importance. In most jurisdictions, the total responsibility for release decision making rests with the institutional staff. Although administratively imposed minimum terms and the requirement that the committing judge approve the release decision may influence the decision-making process in some jurisdictions, institutional staff invariably play the most significant role in determining the length of time a youth will be institutionalized.

Permitting institutional staff to have almost complete control over the period of confinement presents a number of problems. Although the staff may be more familiar than anyone else with the youth's problems and his progress during institutionalization, their assessment is necessarily limited to what they have observed during confinement. The youth's ability to function in the community may be difficult to predict from institutional observations. Correctional staff normally have little contact with the youth's family and friends in the community and are generally unfamiliar with the community resources available to assist the youth on his return. The release decision is therefore made with little knowledge of the youth prior to confinement and less information regarding the nature of the free-world environment awaiting him. Additionally, correctional staff may consciously or unconsciously use release as a reward for conformity and the denial of release as a punishment for disobedience. Under such conditions, release decision making ensures the maintenance of institutional order rather than the natural progression of rehabilitated youth into the community.

There is no clear pattern of aftercare service administration. The President's Commission on Law Enforcement and Administration of Justice found that, in most states, the State Department of Corrections or Public Welfare or the State Youth Correction Agency administers juvenile parole. Institutional boards were responsible for this function in ten states.[54] In all but a few jurisdictions, there is no real continuity between the treatment a youth receives in confinement and his aftercare supervision. The educational, vocational, and counseling programs that begin in the training school are not followed up with similar programs in the community. Whatever progress the youth has made is often lost when the institutional support system and programs end.

There are few statistics available on programs for youthful parolees. Although this lack of information is partially the result of variations in the organization and administration of aftercare services, the almost total absence of programs designed specifically for juvenile parolees is a more significant factor. The explanation for this absence is fairly simple: community resources tend to be distributed to programs for juveniles with a greater potential for rehabilitation (that is, probationers); youths who have repeatedly failed in therapeutic programs and are subsequently institutionalized generally return to a community that has given up on and/or forgotten them. At best, they receive limited supervision from counselors who are too overworked to attempt seriously the task of facilitating the youth's reentry into the community.

Juvenile parolees can, of course, enter nonspecialized, community-based programs for youthful offenders, such as group homes. Although the National Assessment of Juvenile Corrections found that previously institutionalized youths can be maintained in residential and nonresidential community programs at virtually no increased risk to the community, few such youths were found in the programs examined.[55] It appears that juveniles on aftercare receive little general or specialized assistance when they return to the community.

The absence of reentry programs for youths is a critical problem in the juvenile justice system. If one considers the difficulties faced by the returning adult parolee and adds to them the special problems of adolescence, it is apparent that returning a child to the community after institutionalization requires special attention and assistance. Far too often, the needed attention and assistance are not forthcoming.

Community-Based Residential Programs for Juveniles

❑ Foster Care

Foster care refers to the placement of a youth in an alternative home in which the adult or adults maintaining the home serve as surrogate or substitute parents. The parental surrogate(s) may care for the child for only a brief period—as short as a few days—or for as long as several years. The length of stay depends upon the youth's need, as determined by his or her legal status, family circumstances, and the success of the child-foster parent(s) arrangement. Foster care may be used for any youth who requires an out-of-home placement. The principal concern in selecting foster care as a placement is that the child has dependency needs and requires parental protection and supervision. Children who demonstrate a strong desire to break free of parental authority and achieve independence are generally poor candidates for foster care. In most cases, youths placed in foster homes require individual attention and are capable of responding to affection; they are normally not serious delinquents and do not have extensive prior records.

The first systematic use of foster care for delinquent children occurred in Massachusetts in 1866. In return for taking youths into their homes, these New England foster parents were paid for the child's board.[56] The use of foster care grew with the juvenile court movement; the placement of a child in an improved family environment seemed to most reformers to be an ideal solution to the problem of a troubled child in a troubled family. That view is still with us today, although it is tempered by a desire to maintain the juvenile in his own home if at all possible. Juvenile probation and aftercare agencies use foster care for juveniles with severe family problems; some jurisdictions are also experimenting with using it as a diversion and temporary detention alternative for such youths.

On an average day, over 7,000 youthful offenders are living with foster parents, more than the number assigned to community-based correctional facilities.[57] Most of these placements are made by social service agencies rather than juvenile correctional authorities, but there is a growing trend for correctional agencies to become more involved in foster care programs. Specialized foster care programs that focus on juveniles with behavior problems are part of this new correctional effort. The low cost of foster care relative to other out-of-home placements, as well as its intrinsic benefits, makes it an appealing correctional alternative.

Unfortunately, there is a shortage of good foster homes. The increased willingness of correctional authorities to place juveniles in foster homes and the growing numbers of throwaway children who are pushed out of their home have created an usually high demand for foster parents. Even under normal circumstances, however, good foster homes are in very limited supply because foster care is a very difficult and demanding undertaking. Children generally enter foster homes after a history of poor relationships with their biological parents and prior parental surrogates. The youths have often been repeatedly moved from one home to another and have learned to anticipate problems that will quickly lead to yet another move. The children develop few behavioral controls; having received little or no affection, they are virtually incapable of giving or accepting it from others. They test each new foster parent by observing his or her response to disruptive or otherwise inappropriate behavior. Even the most sincere and dedicated foster parent may fail these tests. Because the time and emotional investment of foster care is high and the financial compensation is low, it is extremely difficult to secure and maintain good foster parents.

There is no definitive list of the characteristics of good foster parents. However, research has been conducted to predict the success of foster care placements. It appears that certain characteristics of foster parents, children, and social service agency staff tend to produce more successful placements. In general, a placement is more likely to work if the foster mother:

1. Had grown up in a family with a number of brothers and sisters and was an older or the oldest child in her family
2. Had the experience of caring for a child not her own for several weeks, both day and night
3. Showed skill and understanding in handling a number of specific behavior incidents (all typical of school-age children) and in understanding and handling the hypothetical behavior problems shown by a "defiant" and "withdrawn" child
4. Discussed each of her own children (or children she had experience with) as distinct individuals

The placement is likely to be successful if the prospective foster father:

1. Had grown up in a family with a number of siblings (However, his position as the only or oldest child in the family was not a favorable characteristic.)
2. Expressed warmth in talking about his own father and described his father as affectionate toward him
3. Indicated favorable attitudes toward having a social worker visit the home and make definite suggestions regarding the handling of the foster child
4. Showed understanding and skill in responding to specific behavior incidents and in understanding and handling a "defiant" child and a child who is "careless with his clothes and the furniture in his foster home"
5. Focused on the foster child's problems, such as adjusting to a strange situation, in talking about what might be difficult in being a foster parent
6. Reported that he and his wife together made major decisions in the family, rather than either of them having greater authority

In addition, placement is more likely to work out well if:

1. The foster child becomes the youngest child in the family group
2. There are no preschool children in the home (More than one preschooler has even more of a negative effect.)
3. The foster child's natural family retains parental rights, rather than there being a transfer of custody to guardianship
4. The social worker available to make and supervise the placement has had at least several years' experience in the field and is able to have several contacts with the prospective foster parents to prepare them for the placement[58]

☐ Group Homes

Group homes may be known as group centers, group residences, or group foster homes. Like halfway houses for adults, group homes provide supervision and support for persons who can function in a community living situation and do not require institutionalization.

The National Assessment of Juvenile Corrections (NAJC) developed a profile of group homes and the youths who live in them.[59] The average group home houses 11 children; slightly more than half of the youths in the program are white. Three-fourths of the youths are between 16 and 18 years old. Surprisingly, almost two-thirds of the residents can be categorized as middle or upper class, based on their parents' occupation. This finding may be at least partially explained by examining the types of offenses the youths committed: 57 percent were status offenses; 20 percent were property crimes; and only 7 percent were crimes against the person. Many of the status offenses indicated the existence of family problems (such as ungovernability); so the need for an out-of-home placement may have led to assigning the youth to a group home. Additionally, most group home residents had prior experiences with the juvenile court. The average youth had been arrested over six times and had been previously institutionalized.

The NAJC surveyed group home staff members to determine the most popular treatment objectives within the programs. The three objectives most frequently reported were to develop interpersonal relationships, to develop an environment conducive to positive change, and to enhance the youth's self-concept.[60] To accomplish these objectives, eight out of ten programs used individual and/or group counseling. At least half the programs use reality therapy, behavior modification, and family therapy. Educational services normally were obtained from community resources.

Kingsley, Brown, and Gill surveyed group home staffs and residents to assess their perceptions of program strengths and weaknesses.[61] Their findings (table 10-1) indicate that group home staff and residents hold views similar to those expressed by workers and staff in halfway houses: Rules and regulations are described as

TABLE 10-1 Group Home Residents and Staff Perceptions of Strengths and Changes Desired in Rank Order

Staff		Residents	
Strengths	*Desired changes*	*Strengths*	*Desired changes*
Interaction of staff with residents in and outside activities	Too much paperwork	Rules and rewards	Monitoring of behavior; rules systematic
Group counseling	Too large living unit size	Interaction with staff in and outside home (in recreation)	Too much work responsibility is imposed
Open setting encouraging choice and responsibility	Reduce staff-resident ratio	Working back to own home and freedom to stay in community	Nothing
Size of living unit like home	Restrictions on students for inappropriate behavior	Personality (get close to director and house parents)	Curfew too early, needs revision
Management-behavioral	More aftercare agency responsibility while in group home	Group meetings	Too formal group meetings
Involvement with parents and residents	Less houseparent direction for chores	Employment opportunities and pay	More recreation
Opportunities to be creative in operating program	More group meetings	Free time	Jailing as punishment
Time off for staff	Reduce involvement of family	Weekend late curfew	
Nothing outstanding	None	Given leadership in home	

SOURCE: Ronald R. Kingsley, Wesley Brown, and Stewart Gill, "An Analysis of Group Homes," *Juvenile Justice* 26(4) (1975): 23–28. Reprinted with permission from the *Juvenile and Family Court Journal*, published by the National Council of Juvenile and Family Court Judges.

problematic, and both staff and juveniles report that they enjoy the mutual interaction and emphasis on personal responsibility found in the group home.

One of the most popular group home models in use today is the teaching-family model, developed in 1962. First implemented in the Achievement Place group home in Lawrence, Kansas, this approach is now used in over forty homes in over a dozen states. A training and evaluation program has been developed to ensure a consistent level of quality in all programs.

Youth Homes, Inc., in Charlotte, North Carolina, utilizes the teaching-family model.[62] The program serves youths experiencing emotional and behavior problems, delinquents, predelinquents, status offenders, and juveniles referred by human service agencies. The program is staffed by a professionally trained, married couple who provide 'round-the-clock care, supervision, and instruction to assist youths in correcting their behavior problems. The couple also works with the residents' parents or parental surrogates, teachers, and other social service agency staff assigned to work with the youth.

The program attempts to teach social, self-help, and problem-solving skills to residents and to help them accept responsibility for their behavior. Formal and informal individual and group counseling are offered; in addition, the home employs a system of self-government and a token economy to help teach the youths that life's consequences are a direct result of their actions. As the juveniles near the end of their stay in the program, they gradually spend more time in their natural or foster homes. After leaving the program, visits with and support from the teaching parents are still available.

Evaluation is an important program component. Community professionals, parents, and group home residents periodically evaluate Group Homes, Inc. The teaching parents are professionally evaluated on an annual basis. Program effectiveness is assessed through the routine gathering and assessing of information regarding the resident's post-group home adjustment.

Hastings House is a very different type of group home.[63] Located in a middle-class neighborhood in Cambridge, Massachusetts, the program serves twelve to fourteen boys from 14 to 17 years of age. Most of the residents are serious delinquents; many have extensive prior records involving such crimes as burglary and car theft.

The group home is staffed by what the program's director refers to as "a mixture of ex-cons, street people, and professionals."[64] The emphasis is on developing close one-to-one relationships between staff and residents. During an average stay of nine months, the juveniles work their way through four program phases, the last of which is return to the community. Few residents return to their families or to school; instead, they normally obtain employment and become self-sufficient.

Hastings House is apparently successful at developing close staff-resident ties. The program's director reports that the group home's biggest difficulty is getting the youths to leave Hastings House.

❏ Independent Living Programs

One of the most persistent problems in juvenile corrections is the situation of the older adolescent who requires neither institutionalization nor a group home placement, but who is too independent to accept the parental confines of a foster home.

These juveniles are often mature enough to live on their own, but are unable to manage financially or require some guidance and support. Independent living is a relatively new community-based program designed to meet the needs of these youths.

Youths placed on independent living status may live in an apartment, YMCA or YWCA, or other group residence. The supervising agency provides part or all of the juvenile's room, board, and miscellaneous expenses while the youth attends school, receives vocational training, and/or works at a part-time job. Independent living programs are highly individualized and flexible offerings; supervision is provided only to assist the youths in meeting their personal objectives as they progress toward self-sufficiency.

Problems and Issues in Community-Based Correctional Programs for Youths

❑ Treatment versus Control

The most significant issue in community-based correctional programs for youths is neither new nor limited to the juvenile justice system. Since the development of the juvenile court, observers have been debating whether juvenile court intervention is serving treatment or control objectives.

We can summarize the opposing positions as follows. The juvenile court was supposedly established to protect youths from neglecting parents and harmful environments and to offer each child the opportunity required to mature into a physically and emotionally healthy adult. Some observers and workers in the juvenile justice system believe that the juvenile court *does* work, or attempt to work, in the best interests of the child. System critics feel that the expressed concern with the child's interests serves primarily to impose middle-class definitions of health and well-being on the children of lower-class and minority citizens. Those who accept this latter position view court intervention, however well intentioned, principally as an attempt to control nonconforming youth.

Two major problems make resolution of the debate nearly impossible. First, there is little conclusive evidence that any treatment program invariably lowers recidivism or improves a juvenile's chance of growing into a "healthy" adult, however health is defined. This lack of evidence results from the poor quality of research on correctional programs, not the failure of rehabilitation strategies. Although the programs have not been proved effective, they have not been evaluated in sufficient depth to prove them ineffective; in fairness, one may only conclude that further research is needed. Second, the great diversity of youth who appear in juvenile court, ranging from the ungovernable truant to the chronic serious offender, clearly requires different degrees of treatment and control. Even the most dedicated proponents of benevolent juvenile court intervention will generally agree that some treatments, such as those that require institutionalization, are too severe for status offenders. However, most persons who question the true aim of the juvenile court will accept the necessity of controlling chronic property or violent offenders.

It appears that discussion of the treatment versus control issue depends not only on the debaters' ideological positions, but on the nature of the programs they have in mind and the types of youths they are considering. Much of the confusion on this issue no doubt results from a failure to specify the types of problems and the general goals that are seen as appropriate for juvenile justice system intervention.

☐ Restructuring the Juvenile Court

Some critics of the juvenile justice system's treatment orientation have attempted to clarify the goals of the juvenile court by limiting its scope. They argue that the system should have authority over only juvenile criminals, not status offenders. Removing status offenders from court jurisdiction would allow the juvenile justice system to focus on the more serious problems juvenile delinquents pose and eliminate some of the confusion that results when the court tries to act in a parental role. Such suggestions sometimes include recommendations for more punitive dispositions for young criminals, who are viewed as using their youth and the court's good intentions to escape justice.

At present, there is little consensus about the desirability of these changes. Few states have decriminalized status offenses and it is unlikely that many will. Too many people feel that to decriminalize a behavior is to condone it, and, as with victimless crimes, the problem remains after the law has been removed from the books. Although there have been efforts to bring greater uniformity into the juvenile justice process by fitting the disposition to the offense as well as to the offender, few jurisdictions have adopted an openly punitive approach to juvenile justice.

☐ Deinstitutionalization of Juvenile Corrections

Although there is a lack of consensus regarding the appropriate role of the juvenile justice system, there has been no lack of reform-minded activity in juvenile corrections. The most significant reform of the 1970s was the advent of the deinstitutionalization movement. Proponents of deinstititutionalization promote establishing community-based programs for all but the most serious offenders and using closed institutions only as a last resort. The movement originated in Massachusetts during the early 1970s. At that time, Jerome Miller, then director of the state's Department of Youth Services, found it impossible to reform the existing training schools by establishing therapeutic programs for youths or training staff. As a last resort, he closed the existing institutions and gradually assigned the residents to newly developed community programs or simply sent them home.

Today, although the vast majority of Massachusetts youths committed to the Department of Youth Services remain in the community, there are still problems. A recent report on the status of the Massachusetts deinstitutionalization effort indicated that juveniles who proved too difficult to manage in community-based programs were being held in secure detention facilities designed principally for the short-term non-adjudicated offenders.[65] The number of youths in confinement is thus considerably greater than that indicated in official records of the offender population in training schools. The problem of the youth who fails in community-based programs is difficult and is likely to plague efforts to retain youthful offenders in the community.

A different type of problem can arise when deinstitutionalization is accomplished through private agencies contracted to provide services to youthful offenders. Ideally, these private agencies provide more creative, "grassroots" responses to the problems of juvenile offenders than a state bureaucracy could offer. Avoiding civil service requirements and restrictive red tape, new programs can be developed as needed and maintained only if they prove their effectiveness; otherwise an alternative program will be selected to receive state funds.

The preceding ideal is not always realized, however. Over a period of years, private agencies that continue to receive state funds may expand their efforts into many communities and centralize their organizations. These minibureaucracies may develop their own red tape and lose their sensitivity to local problems. Monitoring numerous small programs operated by private agencies throughout a state is a difficult task; most state youth agencies do not yet have the staff or expertise to oversee and evaluate numerous small projects. Without effective monitoring, quality control is impossible to achieve.

A third general problem is that each state desiring to release its incarcerated population must determine the appropriate level of deinstitutionalization; develop a strategy to sell the idea to the community, legislators, police, and juvenile justice personnel; establish procedures for removing children from training schools or restricting their future committment to institutions; and identify and develop appropriate alternatives to incarceration. Defining these goals, processes, and alternative programs is difficult enough; implementing them is a long and arduous task.

Today, too many communities add on community programs without taking the necessary steps to ensure that children who would otherwise have been institutionalized are the beneficiaries of the projects. Such add ons may be valuable treatment programs, but when they serve children who previously would have received little or no intervention (and who did not suffer for the lack of assistance), the treatment programs may function more as control strategies than necessary components of a deinstitutionalization plan. When community-based programs serve to expand the net of social control rather than to provide needed reintegrative services, they become very costly methods of interfering in offenders' lives. Deinstitutionalization efforts must be well conceived and well planned to avoid such a fate.

Research and Evaluation

A comprehensive assessment of community-based programs for juveniles seems like an impossible undertaking, but this is what the National Evaluation Program (NEP) attempted in its 1976 review of programs for youth. It focused on six key issues that affect all community-based efforts. NEP summarized their findings as follows:

Community-Basedness—There are important differences in the extent, quality, and frequency of community linkages in so-called community-based programs.

Control—Treatment is the major concern of community programs, but increased control is often justified by treatment rationales.

Discretion—There is a broad use of discretion in community correctional programs. Ad hoc policymaking often leads to increased duration and degree of control over youthful offenders.

Cost—There is little reliable data on cost. Generally, states spend less on community programs than institutional ones, but the per offender cost of community programs is less than one-half that of institutionalized youth.

Recidivism—There is little evidence that community-based programs are *more* effective in reducing recidivism than incarceration; however, alternative programs are no less successful than institutional ones.

The Role of Community Programs in Juvenile Corrections—There is no relationship between the use of community programs and institutionalization. Generally, states that place more youths in community programs *do not* put fewer youths in institutions; across the states, as the number of community assigned youth increases, the number of institutionalized offenders also increases.[66]

These research findings indicate that community-based correctional programs for juveniles are as effective as institutional programs, which are more costly. At the same time, community correctional programs must be closely monitored; too often they are used to supplement rather than replace institutional efforts and to control rather than therapeutically aid program participants. Finally, these findings point out that "community-based" means more than unlocked doors or a city or suburban location; community-based programs must develop meaningful ties to community resources if they are to warrant their community-based designation.

The Future of Community-Based Correctional Programs for Juveniles

In the coming years, we may anticipate the continued growth of community-based programs for youth. Both residential and nonresidential programs can serve as viable alternatives to institutionalization.

❑ Comprehensive Service Networks

One of the most promising developments in community programs for juveniles is the establishment of comprehensive youth service networks that stretch beyond a single agency. Illinois' Unified Delinquency Intervention Services (UDIS) is such a network. Initiated through a cooperative effort of the Juvenile Court of Cook County, the Illinois Department of Children and Family Services, and the Juvenile Division of the Illinois Department of Corrections, the program is an attempt to promote and coordinate community resources on a countywide scale.

❑ The "Criminalization" of the Juvenile Court

In the future, we may see a "criminalization" of the juvenile court: status offenses decriminalized or status offenders effectively excluded from official intervention by administrative action and more frequent use of definitive sentences for violent and property offenders. For example, Ohio passed a law in 1981 that allows mandatory minimum sentences for serious juvenile offenders.[67] It is unclear how these changes will influence the growth and form of the community programs. Community programs may continue to be considered appropriate for most juveniles even when criminal behavior is involved; if so, the programs will flourish. However, the statutory or de facto removal of status offenders from juvenile court jurisdiction may slow program expansion that resulted only from a concern with the "shallow end" offender. The future of community-based correctional programs for juveniles may be considered a barometer of the acceptance of reintegrative philosophy. If the programs can continue to grow despite a shift in the focus of intervention efforts to a more serious population of juvenile offenders, then we shall have proof positive that the philosophy of reintegration has gained a secure position in correctional policymaking.

Summary

The juvenile justice system makes greater use of community corrections programs than the adult criminal justice system because the philosophy and structure of the juvenile justice system encourage diversion, informal processing and community supervision of offenders, rather than incarceration. Like adult community-based programs, community corrections programs for juveniles serve offenders who have committed crimes. Juveniles who commit crimes are referred to as delinquents. In addition, status offenders, or juveniles who commit such acts as truancy, running away or ungovernability—acts that are prohibited solely because of the youth's status as a minor—are also commonly placed in community-based programs.

Some community-based programs for juveniles, such as probation, aftercare (parole), and group homes (halfway houses) are similar to those for adults. Others, such as youth courts, alternative schools, programs for runaways, wilderness experience programs and foster care are designed to meet the specific problems and needs of adolescent offenders.

There is considerable debate regarding the proper function of the juvenile justice system and the appropriate role of community-based programs in juvenile justice. Some critics feel the system is too lenient with serious juvenile offenders. Other observers have argued that the system over-supervises and over-controls youths whose biggest problem is simply a lack of conformity to middle-class norms.

The great variety of community-based correctional programs for youths should make it possible to appropriately meet the needs of all juveniles, but most communities have established only a few programs. A lack of resources, as well as a lack of agreement regarding program objectives, often results in the misuse of community corrections programs. Much planning and conscientious program implementation are required if the juvenile justice system is to help prevent youthful offenders from becoming adult criminals.

KEY WORDS AND CONCEPTS

adjudication
aftercare
alternative schools
deinstitutionalization
delinquents
dependent and
  neglected children
detention facilities
disposition
emergency shelters

foster care
group homes
home detention
  programs
independent living
in-school suspension
  programs
intake
petition
probation

restitution and com-
  munity service
  programs
status offenders
taking into custody
temporary shelter
wilderness experience
  programs
youth service bureaus

NOTES

1. Mark Creekmore, "Case Processing: Intake, Adjudication, and Disposition," in *Brought to Justice? Juveniles, the Courts and the Law,* Rosemary Sarri and Yeheskel Hasenfeld (eds.) (Ann Arbor, Mich.: National Assessment of Juvenile Corrections, 1976), p. 120.
2. Ibid.
3. Ibid., p. 125.
4. Ibid., p. 136.
5. Ibid., p. 127.
6. National Advisory Committee for Juvenile Justice and Delinquency Prevention, *Standards for the Administration of Juvenile Justice* (Washington, D.C.: U.S. Government Printing Office, 1980), p. 342.
7. Carol H. Blew and Robert Rosenblum, *The Community Arbitration Project: Anne Arundel County, Maryland: An Exemplary Project* (Washington, D.C.: U.S. Government Printing Office, 1979).
8. National Advisory Commission on Criminal Justice Standards and Goals, *Report on Community Crime Prevention* (Washington, D.C.: U.S. Government Printing Office, 1973), pp. 51–69.
9. Phase I Assessment of Youth Service Bureaus, *Summary Report of Youth Service Bureau Research Group for LEAA* (Boston: Boston University Press, 1975), pp. 45, 46.
10. Arthur D. Little, Inc., *Community Alternatives* (Washington, D.C.: U.S. Office of Juvenile Justice and Delinquency Prevention, 1978), p. 4.
11. Clemens Bartollas and Stuart J. Miller, *The Juvenile Offender: Control, Correction and Treatment* (Boston: Holbrook Press, 1978), p. 178.
12. Patricia Anderson et al., *Family Crisis Intervention Program* (Washington, D.C.: Office of Juvenile Justice and Delinquency Prevention, 1979).
13. Ibid., pp. 23, 24.
14. Roger Baron and Floyd Feeny, *Juvenile Diversion Through Family Counseling: An Exemplary Project* (Washington, D.C.: U.S. Government Printing Office, 1976).
15. Richard Ku and Carol H. Blew, *A University's Approach to Delinquency Prevention: The Adolescent Diversion Project* (Washington, D.C.: U.S. Government Printing Office, 1977).
16. Jesse Swackhammer and Curtis Roberts, "Youth Court," *FBI Law Enforcement Bulletin,* March 1980, pp. 17–21.
17. Suzanne Charle, "Young Offenders Face Their Peers," *Corrections Magazine* 6(6) (1980): 34.
18. Ibid., p. 41.
19. Gray Cavender, " 'Scared Straight': Ideology and the Media," *Journal of Criminal Justice* 9(6) (1981): 433.

20. Ibid., pp. 433–434.
21. Ibid., p. 434.
22. Ibid.
23. Ibid.
24. Ibid., p. 435.
25. Ibid., p. 437.
26. Thomas M. Young and Donnell M. Pappenfort, *NEP Phase I Summary Report: Secure Detention of Juveniles and Alternatives to Its Use* (Washington, D.C.: U.S. Government Printing Office, 1977), p. 15.
27. William G. Swank, "Home Supervision: Probation Really Works," *Federal Probation,* 43(4) (1979): 50–52.
28. Ibid., p. 51.
29. John E. McManus, "The Proctor Program for Detention of Delinquent Girls," *Child Welfare* 55(5) (1976): 345–352.
30. Ibid., p. 350.
31. Young and Pappenfort, *NEP Phase I,* p. 20.
32. Ibid.
33. Rosemary Sarri, "Service Technologies: Diversion, Probation, and Detention," in *Brought to Justice? Juveniles, the Courts and the Law,* Rosemary Sari and Yeheskel Hasenfeld (eds.) (Ann Arbor, Mich.: National Assessment of Juvenile Corrections, 1976), p. 158.
34. *Project CREST: Counseling for Juveniles on Probation: An Exemplary Project* (Washington, D.C.: U.S. Government Printing Office, 1980).
35. Ibid., pp. 14, 15.
36. Carol H. Blew et al., *Project New Pride, Denver, Colorado: An Exemplary Project* (Washington, D.C.: U.S. Government Printing Office, 1977).
37. Ibid., p. 8.
38. "Community Advancement Program," *Corrections Magazine* 2(2) (1975): 13–17.
39. Rob Wilson, "Corrections on the Local Level," *Corrections Magazine* 2(6) (1976): 30.
40. Dale Mann, *Intervening with Serious Convicted Juvenile Offenders* (Washington, D.C.: U.S. Government Printing Office, 1976), p. 53.
41. Wilson, "Corrections," p. 30.
42. Ibid.
43. Ibid.
44. R. Stephen Berry and Alan N. Learch, "Victory at Sea: A Marine Approach to Rehabilitation," *Federal Probation* 43(1) (1979): 44–47.
45. Ibid., p. 47.
46. Vernon Fox, *Community-Based Corrections* (Englewood Cliffs, N.J.: Prentice-Hall, 1977), p. 221.
47. Arthur D. Little, Inc., *Alternative Education Options* (Washington, D.C.: U.S. Department of Justice, 1979), p. 6.
48. Greg Mitchell, "Alternatives for Children in Crisis," *Corrections Magazine* 6(3) (1980): 33.
49. Arthur D. Little, *Community Alternatives,* pp. 13, 14.
50. Young and Pappenfort, *NEP Phase I,* pp. 21, 22.
51. Herb C. Willman, Jr., and Ron Y. Chun, "Homeward Bound: An Alternative to the Institutionalization of Adjudicated Juvenile Offenders," in *Alternatives to Imprisonment: Corrections and the Community,* George G. Killinger and Paul F. Cromwell, Jr. (eds.) (St. Paul, Minn.: West Publishing, 1974), p. 102.
52. Ibid.
53. Human Services Department, Louisville/Jefferson County (Kentucky), *Juvenile Restitution Project Preliminary Evaluation: December, 1979* (Louisville, Ken.: 1980).
54. President's Commission on Law Enforcement and Administration of Justice, *Task Force Report: Corrections* (Washington, D.C.: U.S. Government Printing Office, 1967), p. 151.
55. Robert D. Vinter et al., *Time Out: A National Study of Juvenile Correctional Programs* (Ann Arbor, Mich.: National Assessment of Juvenile Corrections, 1976), p. 204.
56. Clifford E. Simonsen and Marshall S. Gordon III, *Juvenile Justice in America* (Encino, Calif.: Glencoe, 1979), p. 230.

57. Bartollas and Miller, *The Juvenile Offender*, p. 156.
58. Arthur D. Little, Inc., *Foster Parenting* (Washington, D.C.: Office of Juvenile Justice and Delinquency Prevention, 1978), pp. 114, 115.
59. Vinter et al., *Time Out*, pp. 1–53.
60. Ibid., p. 128.
61. Ronald F. Kingsley, Wesley Brown, and Stewart Gill, "An Analysis of Group Homes," *Juvenile Justice* 26(4) (1975): 23–28.
62. Youth Homes, Inc., *Group Homes* (Charlotte, N.C.; n.d.).
63. Michael S. Serrill, "Massachusetts: Officials Say Juvenile System Works," *Corrections Magazine* 1(5) (1975): 34.
64. Ibid.
65. *Criminal Justice Newsletter* 11(15) (July, 21, 1980): 5, 6.
66. Andrew Rutherford and Osman Benger, *NEP Phase I Summary Report: Community-Based Alternatives to Juvenile Incarceration* (Washington, D.C.: U.S. Government Printing Office, 1976), pp. 27–31.
67. *Criminal Justice Newsletter* 13(2) (January 18, 1982): 1.

FOR FURTHER READING

Bakal, Yitzhak, and Howard Polsky, *Reforming Corrections for Juvenile Offenders* (Lexington, Mass.: Lexington Books, 1979).

Bartollas, Clemens, and Stuart J. Miller, *The Juvenile Offender: Control, Correction and Treatment* (Boston: Holbrook Press, 1978).

Dunford, F. W., D. W. Osgood, and H. F. Weichselbaum, *National Evaluation of Diversion Projects* (Washington, D.C.: National Institute of Justice, 1981).

Kobrin, S., and M. W. Klein, *National Evaluation of the Deinstitutionalization of Status Offender Programs* (Washington, D.C.: National Institute of Justice, 1982).

Office of Juvenile Justice and Delinquency Prevention, *Prevention of Delinquency Through Alternative Education* (Washington, D.C.: U.S. Department of Justice, 1980).

Sarri, Rosemary, and Yeheskel Hasenfeld (eds.), *Brought to Justice Juveniles, the Courts and the Law* (Ann Arbor, Mich.: National Assessment of Juvenile Corrections, 1976).

Simonsen, Clifford E., and Marshall S. Gordon, *Juvenile Justice in America* (Encino, Calif.: Glencoe, 1979).

Smith, Charles P., et al., Report of the National Juvenile Justice Assessment Centers (Washington, D.C.: U.S. Department of Justice, 1980).

Vinter, Robert D., et al., *Time Out: A National Study of Juvenile Correctional Programs* (Ann Arbor, Mich.: National Assessment of Juvenile Corrections, 1976).

11: Problems and Needs of Drug- and Alcohol-Abusing Offenders

CRIMINAL OFFENDERS OFTEN ABUSE DRUGS OR ALCOHOL, and their drinking or drug-taking problems are usually closely associated with their criminal behavior. It is virtually impossible to promote law-abiding behavior among drug and alcohol abusers unless an effort is also made to help them manage and cope with the problems of substance abuse. Community-based correctional programs are especially important in this effort because effective treatment must prepare drug abusers and problem drinkers to handle the pressures and responsibilities of freedom without resorting to substance abuse. To be meaningful, drug and alcohol treatment must prepare the offender for life in the community. Effective rehabilitation thus requires community-based programming.

In the following sections, we examine the problems of drug and alcohol abuse separately, with special reference to their link to criminal behavior. We assess the characteristics and causes of these problems and discuss both general treatment strategies and specific community-based correctional programs.

Special Problems of Drug Abusers

❏ Drug Abuse and Crime

One of the most significant and difficult problems facing the criminal justice system is the problem of the drug-abusing offender. Both violent and economic crime are linked to illicit substance abuse. Barbiturate and amphetamine use tends to be associated with assaultive behavior; in fact, barbiturate use can produce the same type of violence that often results from alcohol intoxication.[1] Most directly linked to criminal behavior is the problem of narcotics use, which is associated with both violent and nonviolent forms of economic crime. Traditionally, narcotic users have preferred income-producing crimes that require no violent confrontation, such as shoplifting or drug sales; female addicts also engage in prostitution. When necessary to obtain funds, however, addicts have resorted to street robberies (muggings) and crimes that run the risk of victim confrontation (for example, burglary).

There is evidence that addict crime is becoming increasingly violent. One researcher noted after a review of recent studies that "Probably as many as two-thirds of all addicts now engage in crimes against persons (usually muggings and armed robberies) and as many as one-third of all addicts commit these crimes as their primary means of support."[2] The increasingly violent nature of addict crime seems to be the result of the younger addict's opportunistic approach to crime. Unskilled and impulsive, these offenders tend to pursue any activity likely to provide economic gain.

Unlike prior generations of narcotics users, a large proportion of today's addict population engaged in criminal behavior prior to using narcotics.[3] After the onset of addiction, criminality tends to increase and become focused on income-producing activities.[4] One other factor distinguishes contemporary opiate users from previous generations of addicts. Many of today's narcotics addicts are really polydrug users, persons who regularly use more than one controlled substance or who combine alcohol abuse with illicit drug use. Often these individuals can switch to other drugs with relative ease in order to regulate their habits or deal with a temporary reduction in the narcotics supply. This ability to substitute one drug for another (usually methadone and/or barbiturates for heroin) may make the individual's addiction problem more difficult to treat. Polydrug users, when compared with street addicts, engage in criminal behavior at an earlier age and are subsequently more diverse in their criminal activities.[5]

The 1980s also witnessed the emergence of various new illicit drugs, such as crack (cocaine that has been processed into a rocklike substance) and ice (see the accompanying box for a profile of ice).

Fact Sheet: Ice

Ice v. Meth

Methamphetamine originated in Japan in 1919. Ice is a new, smokeable form of methamphetamine. While Ice and "Crystal Meth" are chemically the same, they are structurally different. Ice is a crystalline form of methamphetamine which is high in purity (90–100 percent). It is similar in size and appearance to quartz or rock salt. Crystal Meth, while it is called "crystal," is usually obtained in a powder form and in varying levels of purity. Both Ice and Crystal Meth can be smoked. While the effects of Crystal Meth last two to four hours, the duration of an Ice-high is said to last anywhere from seven to twenty-four hours. Crystal Meth is typically injected, snorted, or ingested orally (in pill form).

Use of any form of methamphetamine results in intense euphoria and tremendous energy. There have been reports of paranoid and violent behavior with prolonged usage. Because the purity of Ice is greater, these effects are intensified. Ice has also been reported to cause nausea, vomiting, rapid respiratory and cardiac rates, increased body temperature, and coma at high dosage levels. Overdoses are common since it is difficult for the users to control the amount of smoke being inhaled. Since 1985, there have been thirty-two deaths attributed to Ice in Honolulu. In the first six months of 1989, there were twelve deaths.

Availability of Ice

Current law enforcement intelligence indicates that Ice is primarily found in Hawaii. Within the last year, Ice has become available on the mainland of the United States. In San Francisco two seizures have been made. While there have been no seizures of Ice in San Diego or Los Angeles, Ice is reportedly available on a limited basis in these cities. The DEA Seattle Division has also made two small seizures of Ice. In October 1989, DEA agents in New York seized 900 grams of Ice from two Korean traffickers, one of whom claimed that he was able to supply ten to twenty kilograms of Ice per month to the United States.

Ice Traffickers

While other forms of methamphetamine are primarily produced domestically, Ice is produced in Hong Kong, Korea, Japan, Taiwan, Thailand, and the Phillipines. There have been no confirmed reports of domestic manufacture of Ice; however, DEA reports suggest that "Asian chemists" have operated a lab in Portland, Oregon, which later moved to the Los Angeles area.

The trafficking of Ice appears to be tightly controlled by a small group of Asians and affiliated gangs. The groups tend to be organized along ethnic lines. The principal trafficking groups are the Vietnamese, Filipinos, and Chinese. For these reasons, intelligence analysts suggest that states having large Asian communities will be among the first to report widespread availability and use. This can be monitored by tracking such indicators as methamphetamine related treatment admissions and emergency room incidents and seizures of the drug by law enforcement agencies. Additionally, the National Institute of Justice–sponsored Drug Use Forecasting (DUF) program, a survey of drug use by arrestees, has added a section to the questionnaire designed to track Ice use.

SOURCE: Bureau of Justice Statistics, *Drugs and Crime Data* (Washington, D.C.: U.S. Department of Justice, 1989).

❏ The Narcotics User: A Portrait in Diversity

The preceding characterization of the criminality of narcotics users pertains only to chronic, habitual users who are *addicted* to narcotics. Drug addiction has been defined as:

> a state of periodic or chronic intoxication produced by the repeated consumption of a drug (natural or synthetic). Its characteristics include: (1) an overpowering desire or need (compulsion) to continue taking the drug and to obtain it by any means; (2) a tendency to increase the dose; (3) a psychic (psychological) and generally a physical dependence on the effects of the drug; (4) an effect detrimental to the individual and to society.[6]

Two additional concepts are often used to define addiction. *Tolerance* refers to the addict's need to increase the dosage of the drug in order to continue to achieve its desired effects. *Withdrawal* refers to the onset of painful physical and psychological symptoms when drug use is discontinued. Addiction produces biological (tolerance and withdrawal), psychological (compulsion and dependence), and social effects (see table 11-1).

There are many misconceptions about addiction. Contrary to popular belief, all narcotics users are not addicts. Many heroin users are only occasional users, referred to as "chippers."[7] Chippers use narcotics in a recreational fashion, on weekends and special occasions, and are able to "regulate their use of heroin in much the way social drinkers regulate their intake of alcohol."[8] Many persons who first used heroin

TABLE 11-1 Sequence of Appearance of Withdrawal Symptoms

	Approximate hours after last dose	
Signs	Heroin and/or morphine	Methadone
Craving for drugs, anxiety	6	24
Yawning, perspiration, running nose, teary eyes	14	34 to 48
Increase in above signs plus pupil dilation, goose bumps (piloerection), tremors (muscle twitches), hot and cold flashes, aching bones and muscles, loss of appetite	16	48 to 72
Increased intensity of above, plus insomnia; raised blood pressure; increased temperature, pulse rate, respiratory rate and depth; restlessness; nausea	24 to 36	
Increased intensity of above, plus curled-up position, vomiting, diarrhea, weight loss, spontaneous ejaculation or orgasm, hemoconcentration, increased blood sugar	36 to 48	

SOURCE: Oakley Ray, *Society and Human Behavior*, 2nd ed. Copyright © 1978 by C. V. Mosby Company. Reprinted by permission.

in Vietnam fit this pattern of use. Today, it is estimated that there are two or three occasional users for each narcotics addict.[9]

Addiction must be viewed as a process, "a sequence of experiences through which an individual acquires a meaningful conception of drug use behavior and its situational contexts."[10] One does not immediately become addicted to heroin after one euphoric experience. In fact, many people experience nausea and considerable discomfort after their initial contact with the drug. Normally, "pre-narcotics addicts" are introduced to heroin by drug users they admire; wishing to gain their respect, they try narcotics. In other cases, individuals who wish to experiment with narcotics seek out known drug users.[11] In either situation, would-be users must prove themselves to be cool and trustworthy to the established heroin users. They must also learn the mechanics of narcotics use, how to recognize and experience the high and, finally, how to maintain a constant supply of narcotics when and if dependence develops. Continued regular use is required in order to achieve addiction.

❏ Characteristics of Narcotics Addicts

Most narcotics addicts live in urban areas characterized by poverty, high crime and delinquency rates, and a high concentration of minority groups.[12] Although heroin use can be found in almost every American city, narcotics addiction tends to be concentrated in the northeastern United States.

The families of heroin addicts tend to be disturbed and severely troubled. Alcoholism and physical and mental illness are frequently present. In such families, children learn few prosocial values or interpersonal skills.[13] Chein et al., who conducted an intensive study of addicts and their families, report:

> In almost all addict families, there was a disturbed relationship between the parents, as evidenced by separation, divorce, open hostility, or lack of warmth and mutual interest. . . .
>
> The families of the addicts did not provide a setting that would facilitate the acceptance of discipline or the development of personal behavioral controls. The standards of conduct offered by the parents were usually vague or inconsistent; the addicts had characteristically been overindulged, overfrustrated, or experienced vacillation between overindulgence and overfrustration.[14]

Although most addicts possess normal intelligence, their educational backgrounds are similarly deficient; most fail to complete high school and many never attend.[15]

❏ The Addict Personality

Although narcotics addicts share certain residential, family, and educational disadvantages, no single addict personality has been identified. Studies of addicts' needs, values, attitudes, and self-concepts have yielded contradictory results. Although most addicts exhibit symptoms of various personality disorders, it is rarely possible to determine whether such personality traits preceded or resulted from addiction. No trait or combination of characteristics has been found to be unique to the addict. Individuals exhibiting personality disorders similar to those of addicts frequently live drug-free lives.

❑ Causes of Drug Addiction

Attempts to identify the causes of narcotics addiction have proven to be more successful than efforts to isolate the causes of crime or to describe the addict's personality. A number of theories have been proposed to explain certain aspects of addiction among certain types of narcotics users, but no single theory can account for every addict's problem. The popular view is that heroin is used for one or more of the following reasons:

1. Its euphoric qualities
2. Ignorance of the effects of long-term use
3. The relief of pain, anxiety, or depression
4. The fact that it allows the user to escape from the demands of the real world
5. Becoming part of the "in" group
6. As a step up from other drugs
7. Peer group pressure[16]

❑ Purposes of Addiction

The idea that narcotics addiction offers anything of value to the heroin user may seem somewhat farfetched, but this is the principal focus of learning theories; drug abuse is a purposeful activity that is designed to achieve specific rewards. The range and complexity of what has been referred to as the purposes of addiction are not readily apparent, however, until one considers the addict as he functions in his world—the street.

Preble and Casey, who have studied not only black and Puerto Rican addicts but Irish, Italian, and Jewish drug users as well, report the following:

> Addicts actively engaged in meaningful activities and relationships seven days a week. The brief moments of euphoria after each administration of a small amount of heroin constitute a small fraction of their daily lives. The rest of the time they are aggressively pursuing a career that is exacting, challenging, adventurous, and rewarding. They are always on the move and must be alert, flexible, and resourceful. The surest way to identify heroin users in a slum neighborhood is to observe the way people walk. The heroin user walks with a fast, purposeful stride, as if he is late for an important appointment—indeed he is. He is hustling (robbing or stealing), trying to sell stolen goods, avoiding the police, looking for a heroin dealer with a good bag (the street detail unit of heroin), coming back from copping (buying heroin), looking for a safe place to take the drug, or looking for someone who beat (cheated) him—among other things. He is, in short, taking care of business, a phrase that is so common with heroin users that they use it in response to words of greeting, such as "how you doing?" and "what's happening?" Taking care of biz is the common abbreviation. Ripping and running is an older phrase that also refers to their busy lives. For them, if not for their middle- and upper-class counterparts (a small minority of opiate addicts), the quest for heroin is the quest for a meaningful life, not an escape from life. And the meaning does not lie, primarily, in the effects of the drug on their minds and bodies; it lies in the gratification of accomplishing a series of challenging, exciting tasks, every day of the week.[17]

Typical of the New York street addict is one who reported:

> "When I'm on the way home with the bag safely in my pocket, and I haven't been caught stealing all day, and I didn't get beat and the cops didn't get me—I feel like a

working man coming home; he's worked hard, but he knows he's done something. . . ." The feeling of hard work rewarded by accomplishment, this addict continued, was strong "even though I know it's not true."[18]

Only when one considers the strong appeal of street life, and the purposeful existence it provides to individuals who otherwise feel that their lives are meaningless, can the difficulty of drug treatment be fully understood. The overwhelming strength of the habit of addiction becomes apparent when this factor is added to other purposes of addiction, such as:

1. Removing the addict from an environment with which he cannot cope
2. Decreasing anxiety and depression resulting from actual or perceived failure to cope with reality
3. Establishing or enhancing self-esteem through membership and acceptance in an esteemed peer group
4. Attempting to cope through the use of heroin as a crutch[19]

❑ Postaddiction Syndrome

A Consumers Union Report on licit and illicit drugs offers a dramatic and explicit description of the discomforting symptoms that continue to plague narcotics addicts long after the physical effects of withdrawal have subsided:

> Most addicts who mainline heroin, when asked what happens when they "kick the habit," describe the classic withdrawal syndrome—nausea, vomiting, aches and pains, yawning, sneezing, and so on. When asked what happens after withdrawal, they describe an equally specific "postaddiction syndrome"—a wavering, unstable composite of anxiety, depression, and craving for the drug. The craving is not continuous but seems to come and go in waves of varying intensity, for months, even years, after withdrawal. It is particularly likely to return in moments of emotional stress. Following an intense wave of craving, drug-seeking behavior is likely to set in, and the ex-addict relapses. When asked how he feels following a return to heroin, he is likely to reply, "It makes me feel normal again"—that is, it relieves the ex-addict's chronic triad of anxiety, depression, and craving.
>
> It is this view—that an addict takes heroin in order to "feel normal"—that is hardest for a nonaddict to understand and to believe. Yet it is consonant with everything else that is known about narcotics addiction—and there is not a scrap of scientific evidence to impugn the addict's own view. The ex-addict who returns to heroin, if this view is accepted, is not a pleasure-craving hedonist but an anxious, depressed patient who desperately craves a return to a normal mood and state of mind.[20]

The ex-addict who seeks a return to normality is very likely to relapse into narcotics use. This likelihood of relapse may be the greatest problem faced in drug treatment programs today. Having achieved the necessary motivation to abstain from narcotics long enough to pass through the withdrawal stage, the addict must then cope with a lingering craving for heroin. This craving may appear days, weeks, or months after the last use of the drug. Because it is unpredictable, it is almost impossible to control.

If long-term abstinence is to be achieved, a drug treatment strategy must contain counseling and support services designed to achieve two related goals: (1) reduce the addict's desire to seek out the purposes of narcotics use and/or to make these purposes seem less appealing and (2) promote the development of the internal controls necessary to withstand a continued desire for narcotics.

Treatment of Drug Abusers

Today there are several thousand drug treatment programs in the United States. The programs are operated by government and nongovernment agencies; some are hospital affiliated, many are not. Further, drug treatment programs can be divided into those that operate for profit and those that are nonprofit. The for-profit programs generally draw insurance-supported referrals, while the nonprofit programs accept a wide variety of clientele. The crack (rock cocaine) epidemic that swept through the United States in the second half of the 1980s overwhelmed the existing capacity of nonprofit programs, and in many cities long waiting lists still exist for admission to those facilities.

There are five major forms of drug treatment currently available: methadone maintenance, therapeutic communities, outpatient drug-free programs, detoxification programs, and correctional programs. We do not examine outpatient drug-free programs, which primarily serve nonaddicts, and detoxification programs, which offer short-term medical assistance to narcotics addicts during the period of withdrawal. Instead, we focus on methadone maintenance and therapeutic community programs, which are the most widely employed narcotics treatment modalities, and on community-based correctional programs designed specifically for narcotics addicts.

❏ Methadone Maintenance

Methadone is a long-acting synthetic narcotic substitute. After the appropriate daily dosage has been established, it blocks the effects of heroin taken by the methadone user. Methadone produces no side effects and can be orally self-administered, thus making its ingestion a simple matter; no needle and syringe that might remind the addict of his former heroin use are required.

Special outpatient clinics provide addicts with methadone. Medical personnel determine each patient's dosage and supervise daily drug administration. Methadone clinics normally consist of a medical unit, with offices for physicians, a common room for group therapy, and several smaller counseling rooms.[21]

Methadone may be used to facilitate detoxification, as a permanent alternative to heroin use, or as a bridge to total drug abstinence. At present, over 75,000 former heroin addicts receive daily doses of methadone.[22] Whether used as a temporary or permanent alternative to heroin, methadone permits the addict to utilize the time previously spent securing drugs in a more constructive fashion. Research indicates that methadone users reduce their criminal behavior and increase their educational and employment achievement. Methadone maintenance appears to be more effective with older narcotics addicts and anxious, compliant, employable individuals from stable families; these persons seem to perform especially well in programs that emphasize middle-class values and productive behavior.[23]

Methadone Maintenance

It was a grey day on a grimy ghetto street in Brooklyn. A light rain began to fall. Hulks of deserted buildings and boarded-up stores offered little shelter to the few pedestrians. What little activity there was on the street took place at the door of a freshly painted, windowless building with an unmarked, steel-reinforced door. A steady stream of people, mostly young, mostly black or Hispanic, passed in and out of the building. Those who loitered too long were chased away by the guard at the door. As it approached two o'clock, the traffic picked up considerably.

"Closing time," explained a New York City drug counselor nodding to the guard as we entered the building, one of the city's 110 methadone maintenance clinics. "We're very strict. If they don't get here on time, they don't get their medication. As you can see, they're highly motivated to get here on time."

Inside the clinic, in a neat, brightly colored waiting room, a number of young men exchanged wisecracks with a woman staff member. Other clients (called "patients" by the staff) thumbed through magazines, read the afternoon paper, or sat quietly waiting their turn to go to the methadone dispensing station. It could have been any hospital out-patient clinic, except for the apparent good health and spirits of the patients and the fact that there were no children and no old people among them. One by one, they approached the glassed-in window, were identified and checked off a list by the nurse on duty, and received a small cupful of pink liquid. After drinking the medication, each patient said a few words to prove to the nurse that the juice was on its way down his throat and not saved to be traded on the street. Some patients also received small bottles containing take-home methadone. (All get take-home doses for Sunday, when the clinic is closed; some have earned the privilege of taking home up to three days' medication.) Others remained to talk to the head nurse about medical problems or to consult with their counselors. The pattern repeated itself until the waiting room was empty and the clinic closed for the day.

SOURCE: John Blackmore, "Once Hailed as a Cure, Methadone Is Now Attacked as Part of the Disease," *Corrections Magazine* 5(4) (1979): 25. Copyright 1979 by *Corrections Magazine* and Criminal Justice Publications, Inc., 116 West 32 Street, New York, NY 10001.

Despite the effectiveness and low cost of methadone maintenance, the treatment has received considerable criticism. Some of this criticism is based on philosophical grounds. Objections have been raised to the concept of "curing" heroin addicts by helping them become addicted to a substitute narcotic. Critics suggest that the goal of treatment should be total abstinence, not "enslavement" to another drug.

Other criticisms of methadone maintenance are prompted by more practical concerns. Observers have noted that addicts often use methadone to regulate their habits. They can decrease their heroin consumption by taking methadone with wine and pills; the wine and pills reduce methadone's ability to block the effects of the heroin.[24] Because most methadone clinics require patients to submit urine specimens for testing for signs of heroin use, addicts wishing to use methadone while continuing their heroin habits must take special measures to avoid detection by program staff. Such addicts often pay nonaddicts for "clean" urine to substitute for their own "dirty" ones.[25] Heroin addicts who participate in methadone programs may also purchase "clean" urine so they can obtain methadone to sell in the street.

The problems created by persons who enter methadone treatment for nontherapeutic purposes are particularly acute in large-scale methadone clinics that inadequately supervise their patients. The solution to these difficulties lies in efforts to screen prospective methadone patients more carefully and to supervise the urine testing and methadone administration more rigorously.

Although it is demonstrably effective in reducing in-treatment criminality, there is evidence that as many as 70 percent of all methadone users eventually return to illicit drug use.[26] Considering the purposes of addiction previously discussed, this finding is not surprising. Methadone maintenance treatment must be combined with supportive therapy if clients are to learn how to use their new found time and energy. Methadone users must establish new personal goals and be offered guidance if they are to learn how to accomplish their newly defined objectives.[27] Without such aid, they may choose to return to the well-defined goals and highly structured life of the heroin addict.

❏ Therapeutic Communities

Therapeutic communities are drug-free communes often staffed by former narcotics addicts. Separate dormitories or suites of rooms are provided for males and females; additional facilities may include a family-oriented kitchen and dining room, recreational areas, and space for individual and group counseling. The average therapeutic community houses thirty to sixty residents and is staffed by one administrator, one secretary, one senior counselor, and eight other counselors.[28] A recent survey indicated that approximately 15,000 persons live in some form of therapeutic community.[29]

In therapeutic communities, drug abuse is normally regarded as a symptom of a deeper personal problem. Confrontational therapy and peer pressure are often employed to change the attitudes, values, and behavior that promote drug dependence.[30] New residents are verbally attacked by fellow residents at group meetings and are criticized for any form of irresponsible behavior. Within the community, drug use is viewed as the height of irresponsibility. The objective of these confrontations is to strip away the drug user's defenses and prohibit the rationalization of irresponsible behavior.

Following the tearing down process, building up begins. After initially performing only menial chores in the community, more important (that is, responsible) tasks are assigned to the resident who has learned to "level" with himself and others. The residents develop self-esteem and feelings of personal worth as they gradually become accepted as functioning members of the community.

The most widely publicized therapeutic communities today are Daytop Village, Odyssey House, Phoenix House, and the Delancey Street Foundation. These programs share the approach to drug treatment we have described, although there are important distinctions between them. Phoenix House and Odyssey House encourage residents to reenter society following treatment and attempt to facilitate reentry during the latter months of treatment. Odyssey House, unlike the other programs, uses professional personnel and has established special programs for adolescent addicts, "gifted" addicts, addict parents, mentally disturbed addicts, and Vietnam veteran addicts.[31] The Delancey Street Foundation requires a two-year commitment from applicants, who must take a vow of poverty before entering the program. The foundation owns and operates several businesses that earn a monthly gross of $30,000. These earnings, coupled with private contributions, enable the program to be largely self-sufficient; no state or federal funds are utilized.[32]

In recent years, with crack sweeping the nation, the demand for the services of therapeutic communities has been considerable. While enjoying a sort of rebirth in the early 1990s, two as-yet-unsolved problems continue to plague virtually all programs. First, only a very small percentage of addicts are appropriate clients for therapeutic communities; it has been estimated that these drug-free/self-help programs reach only 2 percent of all heroin addicts.[33] The vast majority of addicts who enter the programs quickly drop out, unwilling or unable to withstand the harsh regimen, menial tasks, and verbal abuse that are essential elements of treatment.

Second, many of the persons helped by the therapeutic communities seem to become dependent upon the programs; they either never leave the community or become staff members in offshoots of the original program. It is unclear why this dependency develops. Individuals who conquer their drug problem may be unable to find the same level of acceptance and status in the outside world that they find within the therapeutic community. Or they may simply be substituting one dependency for another. Although it may be argued that dependence upon a therapeutic community is preferable to dependence upon heroin, the fact that only a fraction of all addicts can ever achieve even this goal reduces the therapeutic community's utility as a drug abuse treatment strategy.

Therapeutic communities have rarely been subjected to rigorous evaluation. It has been suggested that the paucity of evaluation data is the result of their unwillingness to permit outsiders to learn about their high attrition rates and the difficulty their clients have in achieving a drug-free existence outside the commune. Although therapeutic communities are probably no more reluctant to be evaluated than other types of rehabilitation programs, in the past, the perceived tendency toward secrecy has inhibited research.

It is hoped that future research efforts will meet with greater success. In the realm of drug treatment, no strategy has proved successful in achieving total and permanent abstinence. The evaluation of therapeutic communities, methadone maintenance, and all other rehabilitation strategies can yield valuable insight into the problem of narcotics addiction and facilitate the development of more effective treatment alternatives.

❏ Community-Based Correctional Programs for Narcotics Addicts

The most widely utilized community-based correctional programs for narcotics addicts on probation or parole are specialized supervision programs and halfway houses. In addition, over fifty-five cities have established Treatment Alternatives to Street Crime (TASC) projects that link criminal justice system clients and noncorrectional, community-based drug treatment programs. Over 30,000 addicts have been assisted by TASC referral and monitoring services.[34]

Probation and Parole Programs. Most community supervision programs share a common feature—an attempt to use the coercive force of the criminal justice system to encourage offenders to commit themselves to rehabilitation. Generally, offenders are required to provide urine samples to the supervising agency for testing for drug use; this monitoring effort and the threat of revocation are designed to

Probation Work with Drug Offenders

Since I'm a drug testing officer, all my contacts with clients have to be on a surprise basis. I contact people in the office or their homes or on their jobs. Sometimes we meet at someone's house or a restaurant. I go out quite a bit. My theory is that you don't know what's going on until you get out there on the street and see where it's coming from.

Yesterday, I found that I had two people whose tests showed that they had been using heroin. I have to get these people into the office to find out how much heroin they have taken and what to do about it.

If the drug use is out of control, I'll try to get them into a hospital or a drug program. I'll try to get them off the street one way or another. Somewhere along the line I have to make a decision about what to do with a client.

Naturally, you have to get them drug-free one way or another. This can mean going to jail. But usually there are several choices besides jail. You put them into a hospital. You let the judge know what you're doing. If a person is a threat to other people, you get him into a position where he no longer is a threat.

When I get back from lunch, the office is usually full. I talk to spouses and parents of people in jail. They wonder how their relatives are doing. I study some new cases coming up. A lawyer calls me about what I intend to recommend on a certain case. I write another report and by now it's 3:30 P.M.

The first person whose tests showed he was on heroin comes in. Not only is he back on heroin, but he's gotten arrested in someone's home for burglary. A new offense takes away a lot of your choices. I tell him I can recommend to the judge that he either goes to jail or gets into a drug treatment program. He takes the drug treatment program.

Around four, my clients start coming in. I take urine specimens and do skin tests. The urine test only works if the drug has been used in the last three or four days. But a needle mark stays on for three or four weeks. I have a magnifying flashlight and I look at the veins in their arms. You become very skilled at knowing how a person uses drugs.

Most of the people on probation are just average people. But there are some on probation who are hardcore, repeat offenders. I like to work with this kind—the heavy offender, the one who's been in trouble a long time.

I like crisis. I'm a good problem solver. My work is different, exciting. It gives me a chance to have a lot of contact with people. I was born and raised on the streets. I like the streets and I like the people. I like doing something a lot of people can't do.

SOURCE: Constitutional Rights Foundation, *Criminal Justice* (New York: Scholastic Book Series, 1978), pp. 180–182. Reprinted by permission.

encourage offenders to make a serious attempt at abstinence. In addition, most probation and parole programs for narcotics addicts emphasize the offender's general need to develop a sense of responsibility. Abstaining from narcotics use is one element of responsible behavior; securing employment, supporting one's dependents, and participating in education or vocational training programs are also viewed as essentials of responsible living.

The Narcotic Treatment and Control Unit of the Los Angeles County Probation Department supervises Los Angeles County felons who have narcotics problems.[35] The program's goal is to overcome the probationer's dependence on narcotics and make him responsible for his actions. This aim is pursued through honest and direct counseling efforts that demonstrate respect for the client while showing him that irresponsible behavior will not be tolerated.

Chemical testing for drug use is employed on a regular and surprise basis, and probationers regularly receive skin checks for injection sites. Most offenders are using narcotics when placed on probation; detoxification occurs in the community,

Narcotics Addicts on Parole

Alice is beaming. "I shampooed the rugs this morning," she proclaims proudly, as if she had swum the English Channel.

Sitting across from Alice in the cramped living room of a small apartment in San Bernardino, Calif., Gary Pena glances around at the gleaming ashtrays and uncluttered table tops. "Yeah, and you don't have a pile of dishes and garbage around like you used to," Pena says. "I'm proud of you."

"My old man likes it neat," Alice says.

"You got yourself a nice place, a little money, an old man who comes home every evening—that's where it's at," says Pena. "How long you been in this rat race, anyway?"

"Since '73," Alice sighs. "You know, it gets tiring, running from the law. And the drugs ain't no good anymore, either, they cut them so much."

Pena is a parole officer, and Alice is a narcotics addict under civil commitment. He must make sure that she has not reverted to heroin or, more importantly, crime. Alice, he feels, is doing well. "She needs a lot of structure and support," he says as he drives away. "She calls me twice a week just to say hello. She's on methadone and seeing a psychiatrist. But at any time she can say to hell with things and go back to using."

In his car, Pena carries a pair of handcuffs and a supply of preaddressed, postage-paid bottles for mailing urine samples to a laboratory. These are for surprise tests, given in the field; each addict is also required to come in regularly for scheduled tests. A test will disclose whether a suspect has used heroin (or amphetamines, PCP, cocaine, or codeine) within a three-day period. If Pena is particularly suspicious that an addict is using, he will have the person come in for two tests each week.

"I grew up with hypes," says Pena, 35. His youth was spent in a barrio where drugs were part of the fabric of life. "My neighbors were hypes." He shrugs. "Everybody's chosen a different way to go."

In the afternoon, Pena drives out to visit one of his problem cases. Paul owes $75 a month in child support to his former wife, his current girlfriend is pregnant, and he doesn't have a job.

"You need a job," Pena tells him sternly. "I don't care if it's making a dollar an hour . . ."

"$3.25 is the minimum now," Paul interjects, with the trace of a smirk on his face. This does not go over well with Pena.

"How come you're not motivated?" Pena asks. "You say you don't have a car to look for work. Well, the bus runs every day and it's only 35 cents."

"Sometimes I don't have 35 cents."

"I tell you what, you come down to the office tomorrow. You got thirty days to get you a job. I'm gonna give you written instructions to get a job."

Paul begins to protest. Pena cuts him off. "Don't give me excuses," he says. "Just do it."

Pena is more sympathetic toward another addict, Norman, who is afflicted with a chronic skin disease that keeps him in excruciating pain. His legs are swollen to twice their normal size, and he can barely walk. To top it off, his mother is slowly dying of cancer. Norman uses heroin to kill the pain. Pena says he is satisfied if Norman sticks to alcohol. "He's a broken-down guy," Pena says.

On his other visits, Pena counsels a mother whose son and daughter are both addicts. ("The psychiatrist said I raised him [her son] as a girl," she says mournfully. "It's been a heavy thing.") He gives one of his charges a ride to work, and checks in on an addict-burglar who is taking a welding course. He jokes with a former prostitute who has found a "Sugar Daddy" to keep her, and only protests mildly that she is drunk. "At least it isn't eight o'clock in the morning," he says. Another ex-addict is living in a religious group home, waiting to go to Bible school. "Hey, you've come a long ways," Pena says. "Stay clean two years and get off the program. No way you can't do it." Pena checks his arms anyway and tells him to come in for a urine test.

Jack Steinbrunn, the district administrator in charge of Pena's region, tells his officers that an occasional "dirty" test is not grounds for return to the institution. "The main thing is to curtail criminality," Steinbrunn says. "The easiest thing out here is to find a way to lock 'em up. But you have to be pretty creative to come up with ways to keep them out on the streets." That, Steinbrunn says, is what being a parole officer is all about.

SOURCE: Stephen Gettinger, "For Addicts, Parole Is Tougher," *Corrections Magazine* 6(2) (1980): 48–49. Copyright 1980 by *Corrections Magazine* and Criminal Justice Publications, Inc., 116 West 32 Street, New York, NY 10001.

sometimes at a halfway house that has a "kick pad."[36] Probation officers in the unit are especially knowledgeable about drug abuse patterns and characteristics: "It is typical for the drug-using probationer to try to 'run a game' and lie about his use. Only after he is confronted by someone who can, expertly and firmly, make him look at, and acknowledge his game, does one really get his attention and respect."[37]

Realistic limits are placed on the offender's drug-using behavior; sporadic use may be tolerated, but the reestablishment of a narcotics habit is prohibited. Addicts are encouraged to be truthful about their narcotics use and to contact their probation officers if they violate probation regulations and use narcotics. Acknowledged heroin use results in a confrontation with the probation officer, but not necessarily in probation revocation. An attempt is made to understand the factors that precipitated the incident of use. Only if the probationer fails to report an episode of narcotics use is he immediately returned to court.

The program takes a step-by-step approach to rehabilitation, focusing first on immediate difficulties, such as housing, food, and clothing. Long-term goals, such as family stability, a crime-free lifestyle, and an improved self-image are later addressed using a problem-solving approach.

Staff in the Narcotic Treatment and Control Unit must be capable of becoming intensely involved in their clients' lives. They must be flexible individuals who can treat their clients fairly, based on each individual's strengths and weaknesses. A psychiatrist assists the staff in developing self- and unit-awareness on a monthly basis.[38] These consultations also serve cathartic purposes; staff members are encouraged to ventilate their feelings regarding their extremely demanding and frustrating work.

The Narcotics and Drug Abuse Rehabilitation Program, also in Los Angeles, provides various treatment services on a contract basis to federal probationers and parolees.[39] Approximately 150 persons receive assistance; up to 300 may be accepted into the program. Most of the clients are male minority group members who never finished high school, have at least one prior felony conviction, and have a history of hard drug use.

The program provides individual and group counseling; crisis counseling is available on a twenty-four-hour-a-day basis. Job placement services are also offered. Clients may choose from a range of treatment modalities, including methadone detoxification, methadone maintenance, and the therapeutic community. The program is staffed by professionals, paraprofessionals, and graduate students. As in most drug treatment programs, many of the staff members are former narcotics users.[40]

A three-month evaluation of the program indicated that at least four out of five participants are remaining drug-free. Over half the probationers and parolees are working and/or attending school. Counselor ratings reveal that about two-thirds of the clients are doing well.[41] A two-year program assessment indicated that 12 percent of program participants are convicted of new offenses.

An attempt to explain program successes and failures led its director and associate director to describe a feature of their client population that makes them resistant to treatment—what they refer to as an ingrained, manipulative life-style:

> We have observed time and again that after a considerable amount of time certain of our patients reach a point where they are able to work and earn a satisfactory income,

that interpersonal relationships improve, and significant progress is made in dealing with their drug needs. It then seems as though the life-style characteristics that are so deeply ingrained strike out and the patient is unable to tolerate his new-found stability and success. He may suddenly commit a burglary, or receive stolen goods, or use heroin, even though the gain for any of these activities is extremely small. It is our hypothesis that these individuals become frightened by their stable life-style and the ensuing sense of boredom, which is akin to a depression state, and they feel the need to do something to relieve this *growing tension*. This may reflect an inability to tolerate the negative feelings the person has about himself, which his previous manipulative, hustling life-style enabled him to avoid. This occurs when the addict becomes involved with obtaining drugs, avoiding arrest, and coping with the recurrent illness resulting from withdrawal. His life centers upon his drug-related routine and not upon his own feelings of inadequacy. When those feelings do arise, they can be explained away by the effect of drugs, lack of drugs, or "persecution" by law enforcement. In our experience, individuals who are severly disturbed psychiatrically, or persons who have great difficulty giving up their manipulative, hustling life-style, are most likely to fail in a rehabilitative program.[42]

Today there is a nationwide program of drug treatment services available for federal offenders on community supervision status. The federal program, which began in 1979, contracts with over 200 community drug treatment programs to provide rehabilitative services. In addition, intensive supervision is available within federal probation caseloads and community resources are utilized on a no fee, case-by-case basis. Over 5,000 drug-dependent federal offenders are currently receiving assistance through this program.[43]

Halfway houses for narcotics addicts are similar to the programs described in chapter 7. The houses may be directly administered by criminal justice personnel or they may provide services on a contractual basis. Generally, these programs offer more than simple support services to narcotics addicts because of the seriousness of the addiction problem. Halfway houses typically use a modified version of attack therapy when a confrontational counseling approach is employed. Because client motivation is required if attack therapy is to be successful, the lack of motivation typical of persons coerced into treatment necessitates more encouraging and less demoralizing therapeutic approach.

Working with unmotivated narcotics addicts is extremely demanding. When these offenders share a communal residence, there is a good chance that the least motivated offenders will subvert the treatment of those persons who are considering a commitment to abstinence. This tendency can lead to the development of a thriving drug subculture within the halfway house program. The establishment and maintenance of a rehabilitation ethic in such an environment requires a well-structured and supervised program. In addition, vigilance by staff members who understand themselves and their clients and are strong enough to deal honestly and fairly with persons who often push them to the limit of tolerance is an essential program component. The East Los Angeles Halfway House is an example of what can occur if a halfway house is poorly planned and implemented.

The East Los Angeles Halfway House was designed to provide paroled addict felons with a therapeutic transitional residence prior to release into the community. The National Institute of Mental Health program evaluation indicated that this goal was never achieved.[44] The program's failure was attributed partially to the design of the experiment. Inmates who were expecting to be released directly into the community were randomly selected to enter the halfway house instead of being freed. The members of the experimental group showed considerable resentment at being "helped" in such a coercive manner. When they learned that they were to be charged for their room and board in the halfway house, their fury grew.

The program was located in a Mexican-American barrio with a high incidence of narcotics addiction. The easy availablity of drugs proved too tempting for many halfway house residents, who were confronted on a daily basis with the signs and symbols of heroin use. The site of the program within the barrio caused additional difficulties. Because the building that housed the halfway house also served as the district parole office, the program gradually assumed an authoritarian character. This led to the use of official action in situations that might have better been managed in a more flexible and informal manner.[45]

The program attempted to function as a therapeutic community, but because residents were not motivated to change their behavior, this objective proved impossible to achieve. When residents failed to act responsibly, staff were often indifferent. The staff members viewed the residents as "sick." This angered the residents, but because they were afraid that complaints might negatively affect their parole evaluations, they maintained a resolute silence. This silence extended to group counseling sessions and thus nullified whatever benefits counseling might have achieved.[46]

Such failure of treatment efforts as in Los Angeles is avoidable. The Massachusetts Department of Correction recently began releasing a small number of inmates to drug contract houses. These programs were designed to assist inmates in the transition to total freedom in the community.[47]

A variety of halfway houses, using different treatment strategies, currently serves Massachusetts offenders on a contractual basis. A one-year follow-up of releasees from nine of these programs reported that, of the thirty-four persons released in 1977 and 1978, only three individuals were reinstitutionalized as a result of parole violation or a new conviction.[48] Although the number of subjects included in this evaluation was small, a comparison of the halfway house residents with persons released directly into the community provides a valuable insight. Persons released directly into the community usually recidivate at three times the rate of halfway house residents, thus indicating that halfway houses can effectively reduce recidivism.

New Directions in the Treatment of Narcotics Addicts

Most of the literature on the treatment of narcotics addiction offers little hope for the possibility of a cure. At best, a small proportion of addicts can achieve temporary abstinence, often at a price of addiction to methadone or dependence on a therapeutic community. The most effective treatment is time. Most addicts who survive to middle age gradually reduce their narcotics consumption because of the physical and psychological toll it takes on their lives. (See nearby box). Unfortunately, most narcotics-related crime is committed by youthful addicts, who are capable of many more years of criminality.

I Did Drugs Until They Wore Me Out. Then I Stopped.

by Mike Posey

—San Diego, Calif.

I have to laugh at the debate over what to do about the drug problem. Everyone is running around offering solutions—from making drug use a more serious criminal offense to legalizing it. But there isn't a real solution. I know that. I used and abused drugs, and people, and society, for two decades. Nothing worked to get me to stop all that behavior except just plain being sick and tired. Nothing. No threats, no ten-plus years in prison, not anything that was said to me. I used until I got through. Period. And that's when you'll win the war. When all the dope fiends are done. Not a minute before.

Any real dope freak will continue to use drugs until he has had all the drugs he can take. Meanwhile, he either dies, goes crazy or goes to jail. Those are the options. Every addict knows where he's going. No surprises. But the seduction of the drugs is more powerful than anything that you, someone who has never done it, can ever begin to imagine.

One day, though, if you live, there comes the time when it doesn't work anymore. It just doesn't do it. The feeling is harder to get and harder to keep chasing. You've gotten old.

I was 40. Old and worn out. I used until I just couldn't anymore. Then, I said the only prayer I ever knew: "God, help me . . ."

Unfortunately, most dope addicts never live to do that, and most don't want to. In all the more than twenty years of my insanity, I never once considered anything except where to get off on drugs and how much it might cost.

Obtaining the money wasn't a problem. I could always find the money. I spent many years in prison as a result of that obsessive search for the bread to get off. I spent many days in prison waiting to get out, to get off just that one more time, knowing that, after a few years, it would be really righteous. I didn't once consider the consequences, and even if I had, I would have done what I had to do. Dope is the most potent motivator known to my experience, and it looks like things haven't changed much since I stopped.

There is only a war if everyone is fighting. I don't see the average dope fiend fighting. If a dope fiend can get high without hurting anyone, that's nice. If he has to cut your throat, well, that's fine too. But mostly a dope fiend doesn't want anything except to get high and get by. Nothing more. No place to stay, no job, no kids, no responsibility.

Just say no: What an idea! I wonder why I didn't think of that twenty-five years ago, when I started. I wonder where that thought went. The first time I shot dope and I felt that stuff hit my head and my body convulsed, the best feeling I ever had in my life came over me. I was on top for a couple of hours. No pain. No nothing. That's where the idea went. It went out with all the pain, and the other factors common to addicts.

I started a quarter century ago. I'm old now. I haven't taken a drink of alcohol or used a drug in some years. I had my prayer answered. I'm clean and sober. Sure, I feel better. I look better. I have a wife, and I write, and I am able to be a part of society. But I'm still a dope fiend at heart. And I know full well this "war" is a loser.

You can't expect every dope fiend in the U.S. to quit like I did and never use again. And until all of them quit, there will be a market.

I shot dope until a few years ago, unabated. Even in prison, I managed to stay loaded. Nothing can stop a dope fiend from getting stoned. The dope came in with guys' girls visiting. I saw them fiddle it out from under their dresses in the visiting room. We'd get up in our little cubicles and shoot that wonderful stuff with needles made from light bulb filaments.

When I was on the streets, I did $100 a day, every day. I managed to hustle that C-note every day. I woke up every morning needing to go cop some. Hustling and stealing and conning and boosting and rolling drunks, until I'd make it to the man's house and get the four bags I needed. From there I would go and get high and nod and forget how awful life was.

San Diego, New York City or Davenport, Iowa. A dope fiend is a dope fiend. Nothing changes except the stage. The players will always be there . Good luck on your war. I'm just glad I ain't fighting it anymore.

The Wildcat Project: Typical Clients

Jennifer Rodriguez was pregnant at 13, playing confidence games on New York's West Side at 15, a prostitute at 16, and mainlining heroin at 17. By the time she was in her early twenties, an armed robbery charge brought her three years in prison. Released on parole, anxious to put her past behind her, she began looking for work. Everywhere she went, from the state employment service to private agencies to businesses, she heard the same thing: we have nothing now; come back later, maybe something will open up. Nothing ever did.

Glenn Payne grew up in Harlem on a street that he describes as a hangout for "pimps, whores, pushers, bootleggers, and winos." Unlike some of his friends, Glenn had always liked school and was a voracious reader. But using drugs was the "cool" thing to do, and at the age of 15, he started snorting heroin at weekend parties. Twelve months later he was mainlining. Glenn dropped out of school at 17 and began supporting his habit by purse-snatching and rolling the drunks who fell asleep in midtown movie theaters.

As he grew older, Glenn and his friends graduated to the real thing—armed robbery with sticks, then knives, and then guns. Glenn was arrested four times before he was 19, although he never spent more than two weeks in jail. His mother had him committed to a narcotics rehabilitation center in up-state New York, but while he was there, he refused to participate in the group therapy sessions. He wasn't yet ready to give up the good times and companionship that came with taking drugs.

In 1973, when Glenn was 21, drugs became harder to obtain; pushers found their supplies temporarily cut off and heroin was mixed with flour, talcum powder, or even rat poison. One of Glenn's friends died of an adulterated "fix." For Glenn, using drugs was no longer fun; it was a struggle. He was over 18 and therefore vulnerable to a lengthy prison sentence if caught, and he was increasingly bothered by his parents' and girlfriend's accusations that he would never amount to anything.

The turning point came when Glenn and his friend Fred tried to hold up a grocery store. As Glenn dashed out with the money, he heard a gunshot. Glancing back over his shoulder he saw the shopkeeper holding a rifle and Fred sprawled on the floor, a bullet lodged in his spine. Fred would be a paraplegic for the rest of his life.

A few months later, Glenn enrolled in a methadone treatment program and, after the requisite three months, he signed up for Wildcat.

SOURCE: Lucy N. Friedman, *The Wildcat Experiment: An Early Test of Supported Work in Drug Abuse Rehabilitation* (Washington, D.C.: U.S. Government Printing Office, 1978), pp. 15, 16. Reprinted by permission.

Occasionally, a new approach to the drug problem appears capable of achieving success with some of the many addicts not currently helped by existing programs. Today, supported work programs appear to have great potential for the rehabilitation of narcotics addicts. In 1972, the Vera Institute of Justice established the Wildcat Service Corporation of New York City.[49] Wildcat was designed to assist chronically unemployable individuals, principally heroin addicts and criminal offenders, to secure and maintain employment. By 1976, the program had employed 4,000 ex-addicts and ex-offenders; at that time, 1,000 persons were on its work rolls.

Supported work projects attempt to restructure jobs, rather than individuals, to facilitate long-term employment. Wildcat project clients work in crews of three to seven of their peers (other addicts and ex-offenders), with one member serving as crew chief. Each crew chief is supervised by a person concerned with rehabilitation as well as productivity. The crew's tasks are clearly explained and work rules are clearly defined. Each crew member receives considerable feedback on the quality of his work efforts. Initially, Wildcat clients work in low-stress jobs, where they can gradually develop their work skills and abilities. Frequent rewards of wage increases and bonuses are used to encourage the worker. The project's disciplinary policy attempts to promote good work habits and productivity.[50]

Supported work projects attempt to instill a high regard for the value of work in project clients. Counseling and various support services are provided to assist offenders in meeting their individual needs. The project's focus, however, is on providing work in a setting that supports the worker in such a way that he can learn good work habits on the job without having to suffer the negative consequences (for example, firing) of the learning process. Supported work has been used successfully with alcoholics, welfare clients, and other disadvantaged or handicapped persons.

The Wildcat project assigns its work crews to city agencies and nonprofit organizations. Workers are employed in clerical and paraprofessional positions, on maintenance and construction crews, and in messenger services. To be eligible for the program, an applicant must be (1) a narcotics addict of at least 18 years of age, (2) a welfare recipient for at least six months of the last two years, and (3) currently enrolled in a treatment program. Most persons accepted into the program are referred from treatment and correctional agencies.

A three-year evaluation of the Wildcat experiment revealed that the program significantly increased participants' employment stability and earning capacity. Wildcat employees worked an average of 101 weeks and earned $12,236 during the study period; a control group worked 46 weeks and earned only $4,968. Wildcat employees reduced their dependency on welfare, Medicaid, and food stamps. The arrest rate of Wildcat participants who maintained employment was less than half that of program participants who worked sporadically. The more a person worked, the better his family stability and the greater the reduction in his drug consumption.[51]

The findings of the Wildcat experiment indicate that supported work can help addicts reduce their dependence on narcotics and crime. This result was confirmed by a nationwide study of supported work programs reported in 1980. That study found that ex-addicts in supported work programs did better at finding well-paying jobs and were less likely to commit new crimes than a control group of former addicts.[52] Although there is some evidence that the effects of the project may be short-lived, efforts to make work more meaningful seem to be logical components of the effort to wean addicts from the all-encompassing drug subculture.

Special Problems of Alcohol Abusers

❏ Alcohol and Crime

Alcohol consumption is linked to many forms of criminal behavior. Approximately one-third of all arrests are for alcohol-related crimes such as public drunkenness, disorderly conduct, vagrancy, driving while intoxicated, and liquor law violations. In addition, a significant number of violent crimes involve a drinking victim or offender. Although it is impossible to determine exactly how many murders, robberies, rapes, and assaults involve alcohol abuse, it is clear that drinking influences criminal activity in many ways. A special report to Congress by the former Department of

Health, Education, and Welfare stated: "Alcohol can be involved in forming intent for a crime, in aggravating the course of a criminal event (for example, by triggering excess violence), or in affecting the outcome of a crime already completed (for example, by inhibiting the offender's escape)."[53] Research on the relationship between alcohol and crime has necessarily been limited to studies of the drinking behavior of arrested persons and prison inmates. This research provides us with a general picture of the role of alcohol consumption in particular forms of violence.

❑ Research on Arrested Persons

Studies of alcohol-related violent crime reveal that both offenders and victims of such offenses are often drinking at the time of the offense.[54] The rate of alcohol involvement varies according to the type of crime examined and the particular methodology employed in the research study (figure 11-1). For crimes of robbery, as many as three-fourths of all offenders and 69 percent of the victims may have been drinking. Even higher rates of alcohol involvement are found in research on homicide; some studies have found that more than four out of five homicides involve a drinking offender and/or victim. Assault, rape, marital violence, child abuse and neglect, and child molestation have all been found to involve high numbers of alcohol-consuming offenders. Studies of homicide indicate that nonwhite victims, especially males, are especially likely to have been drinking at the time of the offense. Victim-precipitated homicides, stabbings, and excessively violent murders are all highly associated with alcohol consumption.

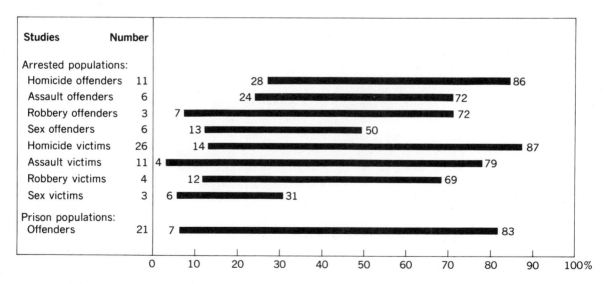

FIGURE 11-1 Alcohol Use by Offenders and Victims

SOURCE: Marc Aarens, Tracy Cameron, Judy Roizen, Ron Roizen, Robin Room, Dan Schneberk, and Deborah Wingard, *Alcohol Casualties and Crime*. Special report prepared for National Institute on Alcohol Abuse and Alcoholism under Contract No. ADM 281-76-0027 (Berkeley, Calif.: Social Research Group, University of California, 1977). Reprinted by permission.

❑ Studies of Prisoners

Studies of prison inmates reveal that drinking often precipitates not only violent crime but property crime as well. Depending upon the measure of alcoholism used and the particular inmate population under study, as many as 83 percent of all prisoners report having a drinking problem.[55] On the average, inmates report a higher rate of drinking problems than is found in the general population.

In order to understand the influence of alcohol on crime, one must consider the effects of alcohol on the human body. While considering these effects, it is important to remember one major distinction between the alcohol and crime and drugs and crime problems. Drug users normally engage in the greatest amount of crime after addiction has occurred; the one-time or occasional user of narcotics poses no special crime problem (other than possession of an illicit substance). However, any person may be influenced by alcohol in such a way that crime results. The social drinker, the problem drinker, and the chronic alcoholic may pose equal crime problems. In fact, most alcohol-related violence probably results not from the outburst of the chronic alcoholic, but from the social drinker or the problem drinker who is still functioning in society and is only moderately disabled by his or her drinking.

The chronic, skid row alcoholic is completely debilitated by his problem; his involvement in crime is often equally divided between offender (public drunkenness) and victim (mugging) roles. This is not to say that the chronic alcoholic is not a serious crime problem. A study of 187 skid row alcoholics indicated that they had been arrested an average of 3.7 times for offenses other than public intoxication. However, by the time an individual's drinking problem has become chronic, most of his nonalcohol-related crime is behind him.[56]

❑ Effects of Alcohol

Alcohol is a depressant; it depresses the functioning of the central nervous system. After a small amount of alcohol has been consumed, the drinker normally becomes relaxed and tranquil. Increased consumption often produces a feeling of stimulation; the drinker becomes more talkative, more active, and often more aggressive.[57] This apparent stimulation results from the depression of the inhibition control center in the brain. It is this loss of normal restraint that may lead to criminal behavior. Alcohol does not provide a motivation for crime (as heroin addiction apparently does); instead, it permits the drinker to act upon preexisting and previously controlled motivations. Without restraint, anger may lead to violence; new found "courage" may lead to the commission of property crimes when inhibitions are diminished.

The effects of alcohol on the drinker and the speed with which they become apparent vary from person to person and depend upon the concentration of alcohol in the blood. Several factors may influence the blood alcohol concentration, including the speed with which alcohol is consumed, the drinker's body weight, the presence of food in the stomach, the individual's drinking history and body chemistry, and the type of beverage consumed.[58] Alcohol may affect the same individual in a different fashion on different occasions. The effects of intoxication are thus somewhat unpredictable; this unpredictability is probably the most dangerous quality of the drug.

The Stages of Alcoholism

Stage One: The Novice. Most people never progress beyond this initial stage. Drinks are usually taken in moderation and then only at social functions. On occasion, the individual at this stage may drink to excess, experiencing a "hangover" the following morning.

Stage Two: Onset of Heavy Drinking and Blackouts. At this stage, the individual begins to drink heavily at bars or at parties and often has trouble later remembering what happened during a drinking bout.

Stage Three: Required Additional Drinking. At this stage, the person finds it increasingly difficult to "get high" and may become self-conscious about his or her drinking. Often the person drinks before going to a party or social event in order to conceal from others the amount of liquor that he or she needs to become intoxicated.

Stage Four: Early Signs of Control Loss. The individual at this stage can no longer control how much he or she will drink on a given occasion. Such a person can, however, control when the first drink will be taken.

Stage Five: Excuse Drinking. At this stage, the drinker may abstain from using alcohol for long periods of time (possibly even months) in an attempt to prove that he or she does not *need* to drink. However, once the drinking behavior is resumed, the individual drinks heavily, which naturally produces feelings of guilt. In order to assuage this guilt, the drinker invents excuses for drinking, claiming, for example, that he or she is celebrating some occasion or has been working too hard and needs a few drinks in order to relax.

Stage Six: Drinking Alone: At this stage, alcohol has become the individual's best friend. The drinker now drinks alone so that excuses for drinking are no longer necessary. The person at this stage gradually moves into a self-imposed dream world which allows him or her to go on drinking without having to face what is actually happening.

Stage Seven: Hostile, Sensitive Drinker. At this stage, the drinker becomes somewhat antisocial. The drinker may provoke unnecessary fights with friends and relatives and begin abusing others—both verbally and physically—without experiencing any apparent remorse.

Stage Eight: Extended Drinking and "Benders." At this stage, the person drinks in the morning to "treat" the hangover from the previous evening's drinking bout. The drinker also begins going on "benders"—that is, extended bouts of drinking. During this period, the drinker has lost most if not all concern for personal welfare as well as that of others.

Stage Nine: "Hitting Bottom." In this final stage, the alcoholic has given up everything for drink. The drinker may remain at this point until continued drinking finally results in death—either directly or indirectly—or he or she may seek treatment. Unfortunately, because the drinker or the drinker's family failed to recognize the problem at an earlier stage, by this point, the drinker may have lost everything he or she had prior to becoming an alcoholic. Had the drinker sought treatment at an earlier stage, much human misery might have been avoided.

SOURCE: Reprinted with permission of Macmillan Publishing Company from *Drug Abuse: A Criminal Justice Primer*, by R. J. Wicks and Jerome J. Platt, pp. 18–19. Copyright © 1977 by Benziger Bruce and Glencoe, Inc.

❑ The Alcoholic and the Problem Drinker

Definition. Distinctions between alcoholics and problem drinkers are a matter of degree; alcoholism is the result of the problem drinker's loss of control and gradual deterioration. Alcoholism is more easily defined simply because its symptoms are more acute. Four basic elements are always present in alcoholism:

1. Compulsive, uncontrollable drinking
2. Chronicity
3. Intoxication
4. Injury to function[59]

Milt has defined alcoholism as "a chronic disorder in which the individual is unable, for psychological or physical reasons, or both, to reform from the frequent consumption of alcohol in quantities sufficient to produce intoxication and, ultimately, injury to health and effective functioning."[60]

Profile of the Alcoholic and Problem Drinker. Research on alcoholics and problem drinkers reveals a very disturbing picture of the effects of alcohol abuse. Problem drinkers are described as "aggressive, attention-seeking, acting out, socially extroverted, lacking impulse control, resentful of authority, lacking feelings for others, power-seeking, and having self-destructive impulses."[61] In the full swing of the disease, alcoholics evidence the following traits:

> an extremely low frustration tolerance, inability to endure anxiety or tension, feelings of isolation, devaluated self-esteem, a tendency to act impulsively, a repetitive "acting out" of conflicts, often an extreme narcissism and exhibitionism, a tendency toward masochistic, self-punitive behavior, sometimes sematic preoccupation and hypochondriasis and often extreme mood swings.
>
> In addition, there is usually marked hostility and rebellion (conscious or unconscious) and repressed grandiose ambitions with little ability to persevere. Most show strong (oral) dependent needs, frustrations of which will lead to depression, guilt, remorse, hostility, and rage.[62]

These characterizations of physical and psychological deterioration reflect the attributes of the alcoholic and problem drinker *after* the effects of alcohol consumption have been felt. There is no specific personality type that is especially prone to alcoholism; rather, alcoholism seems to create a new personality in the problem drinker, often quite different from his or her pre-alcoholic disposition.

❏ Causes of Alcoholism

Explanations of alcoholism are much like attempts to explain narcotics addiction. They focus on such factors as biological predisposition, behavioral conditioning, psychological characteristics and conflicts, and socialization processes. Perhaps the best approach to understanding problem drinking is provided by the multifactor model developed by the Cooperative Commission on the Study of Alcoholism.

> An individual who (1) responds to beverage alcohol in a certain way, perhaps physiologically determined, by experiencing intense relief and relaxation, and who (2) has certain personality characteristics, such as difficulty in dealing with and overcoming depression, frustration, and anxiety, and who (3) is a member of a culture in which there is both pressure to drink and culturally induced guilt and confusion regarding what kinds of drinking behavior are appropriate, is more likely to develop trouble than most other persons. An intermingling of certain factors may be necessary for the development of problem drinking, and the relative importance of the different causal factors no doubt varies from one individual to another.[63]

❏ Diagnosing the Problem

When does alcohol use become alcohol abuse? One of the greatest difficulties in treating alcohol-related problems is making the judgment that, for a specific individual, alcohol consumption has become a problem; it no longer serves merely to reduce tension or facilitate social interaction, but is creating more difficulties than it solves. Because there is no clearly defined line between the social drinker, the problem drinker, and the alcoholic, the diagnosis of alcohol-related problems requires a comprehensive examination of the individual's drinking behavior, the social context in which it occurs, and the consequences of that behavior. The quantity of alcohol consumed, the consumption rate, the frequency of drinking episodes, the effect of drunkenness on self and others, the drinker's visibility to society's labeling agencies, and the drinker's total social matrix must be considered in assessing the extent of the problems producing alcohol consumption.[64]

Treatment of Alcoholics and Problem Drinkers

The treatment of alcohol-related problems is not simply a correctional dilemma. Recent estimates indicate there may be as many as 17 million problem and potential problem drinkers in the United States. Over 3 million of these persons are between the ages of 14 and 17.[65]

Because alcohol-related problems are so prevalent in the general community, an extensive network of programs, many of them federally funded, has developed to meet the needs of alcohol abusers. At present, over 1 million persons are being treated in the community for alcohol-related problems.[66] In most communities, offenders are encouraged to participate in these programs if they have an alcohol-related problem. Specialized programs for drinking offenders are relatively uncommon because they would duplicate projects serving the general public, thus placing an unnecessary drain on correctional resources. Community programs can also be expected to serve reintegrative purposes better than correctional efforts. The offender receives assistance as a citizen who happens to be an alcoholic, not as a criminal with a drinking problem. Additionally, rehabilitation can be continued long after correctional supervision ends.

❑ Goals

Traditionally, the major goal of alcohol abuse treatment has been total abstinence.[67] This viewpoint is based on the belief that alcoholics are incapable of controlling their drinking and that only total abstinence can halt the progression of the disease of alcoholism. Several research studies, including a four-year Rand Corporation examination of over 750 male alcoholics who have participated in various treatment programs, have challenged this view. The Rand study concluded that:

> alcoholism is a chronic, unstable condition. Among persons who come to formal treatment, alcoholism appears to be a continuing condition for the great majority. . . . Data show that remissions are frequent, but are generally intermittent. . . . Remission occurs in two forms: both long-term and nonproblem drinking. . . . These two groups have roughly equivalent levels of social adjustment, mental health, and physical condition.[68]

Supporters of controlled drinking as a treatment goal propose that alcoholics can learn how to drink responsibly. They suggest that alcohol abuse is often the result of an underlying personality disorder; if the disorder can be cured, then controlled drinking is possible.[69] They consider the goal of controlled drinking to be both more realistic and more likely to encourage the reluctant alcoholic to enter treatment than the traditional goal of abstinence.

This position has been most strongly challenged by Alcoholics Anonymous, a self-help group that views abstinence as the only means to recovery for the alcoholic. This organization asserts that anyone who can learn to control his or her drinking was never really an alcoholic.[70]

The proper goal of alcohol abuse treatment is still being debated. Most treatment professionals view the conflicting goals of abstinence and controlled drinking as equally appropriate, but for different types of drinkers. Some alcoholics can never safely take a drink and others can learn to control their problem.[71] In fact, the results of many programs that emphasize total abstinence indicate that most people who complete the programs do not stop drinking, but instead achieve less destructive drinking patterns.[72]

❏ Methods

There is a variety of treatment strategies designed to help alcoholics and problem drinkers overcome their problems. The most widely utilized are prescription drugs, behavioral techniques, family therapy, and Alcoholics Anonymous.

Pharmacological Agents. Although antidepressants are sometimes used in the treatment of alcoholism, disulfiram (Antabuse) is the most widely used chemical treatment method. Antabuse is an alcohol-sensitizing drug that alters the manner in which alcohol is metabolized so that the drinker experiences headache, nausea, vomiting, throbbing in the head and neck, breathing difficulties, and a host of other unpleasant symptoms.[73] Taking Antabuse virtually eliminates the possibility that an alcoholic will impulsively take a drink because an Antabuse user cannot consume alcohol for up to three days without experiencing unpleasant reactions. Although it has been argued that anyone so committed to abstinence that he takes Antabuse on a daily basis probably would not drink under any circumstances, the effectiveness of Antabuse has neither been proved nor disproved.[74] Research is currently being conducted on Antabuse implants, which slowly release the drug into the system and are effective for several weeks. In the future, the alcoholic may need to commit himself to abstinence only once or twice a month to be "protected" from impulsive drinking.

Behavioral Methods. Behavioral approaches are receiving special attention in contemporary alcohol treatment programs. The basic strategy is simple: reverse the sequence in which the alcoholic is rewarded for drinking so that nondrinking brings a reward or avoids a punishment.[75] The approach begins with a careful assessment of drinking behavior, focusing on cues and stimuli, attitudes and thoughts, specific drinking behavior, and the consequences of drinking.[76] Following this assessment, an individually tailored program is developed to modify the behavior. A variety of treatment techniques is employed, including:

1. Aversion therapies, designed to associate the sight, smell, taste, or thought of alcohol with unpleasant experiences such as those produced by Antabuse
2. Assertiveness training designed to teach the drinker how to express inner rage positively

3. Instruction in coping strategies
4. Relaxation techniques
5. Biofeedback and related techniques that assist the individual in recognizing and controlling body states that precipitate or result from alcohol consumption[77]

Family Therapy. Many treatment professionals recommend treating the entire family unit, rather than only the alcoholic patient. A high correlation has been found between marital stability and treatment success.[78] There are many possible explanations for this finding. Family problems often precipitate drinking problems. In many families, alcoholism so severely damages the relationships between family members that special assistance is needed before the family can "get back on its feet," even after the alcoholic has recovered. In other situations, destructive family relations impede the progression of therapy. A comprehensive evaluation of the treatment of alcoholism summarized the benefits of family therapy as follows:

> Involvement of the family in treatment increases the awareness of both the alcoholic and other family members of problems other than alcoholism, such as relationship problems and the way they face reality. It reduces blaming tendencies, teaches new modes of interaction, and permits a focus on a common goal.[79]

Family therapy usually involves only the alcoholic and his or her spouse, although the children, extended family members, and even the problem drinker's friends have participated in various conjoint treatment efforts.

Many positive treatment outcomes have been identified as consequences of family treatment, including improvements in social and marital stability, employment and financial circumstances, quality of child care, and fewer difficulties with the law.[80] Although there is no conclusive evidence that family treatment is invariably effective, there is sufficient evidence to suggest that family treatment alone or in conjunction with other treatments can produce positive outcomes for both alcoholics and their families.[81]

Alcoholics Anonymous. Alcoholics Anonymous (AA) is probably the oldest and best known alcoholic treatment program. It is also one of the largest; AA currently serves over 650,000 participants annually.[82] AA originated in Akron, Ohio, in 1935, when a stockbroker and a surgeon, both alcoholics, utilized an approach developed by Dr. Samuel Shoemaker to help each other and a third alcoholic. Together, these three persons formed Alcoholics Anonymous, a religiously based self-help organization now operating throughout the world.

Although it is primarily a nonresidential program, AA works much like the therapeutic communities for narcotics addicts described earlier in this chapter. An older member takes a new member "under his wing" and fosters an interpersonal dependence that replaces the former dependence on alcohol.[83] The personal satisfaction that the friendship brings and the ability to rely on the established AA member for assistance in self-control permits the new member to begin managing his or her drinking problem. Sobriety is achieved in large part through religion and the Twelve Steps Program (see nearby box), although some AA members also seek professional help.

AA is not the answer for all alcoholics. Lower-middle-class individuals who received religious training in childhood and basically well-adjusted persons who have

Alcoholics Anonymous: The Twelve Steps

We

1. Admitted we were powerless over alcohol—that our lives had become unmanageable.
2. Came to believe that a Power greater than ourselves could restore us to sanity.
3. Made a decision to turn our will and our lives over to the care of God as we understood Him.
4. Made a searching and fearless moral inventory of ourselves.
5. Admitted to God, to ourselves, and to another human being the exact nature of our wrongs.
6. Were entirely ready to have God remove all these defects of character.
7. Humbly asked Him to remove our shortcomings.
8. Made a list of all persons we had harmed, and became willing to make amends to them all.
9. Made direct amends to such people wherever possible, except when to do so would injure them or others.
10. Continued to take personal inventory and when we were wrong promptly admitted it.
11. Sought through prayer and meditation to improve our conscious contact with God as we understood Him, praying only for knowledge of His will for us and the power to carry that out.
12. Having had a spiritual awakening as the result of these steps, we tried to carry this message to alcoholics, and to practice these principles in all our affairs.

SOURCE: *The Twelve Steps*, reprinted with permission of Alcoholics Anonymous World Services, Inc. Copyright © 1939.

experienced recent reverses (for example, loss of job or drinking companions) are the best candidates for the program.[84] Although there is little scientific evaluation of AA's effectiveness, it appears that, for some members, it is at least as successful as alternative methods. In the 1980s, AA became the basis for many drug and alcohol treatment programs.

Community-Based Correctional Programs for Alcoholic Offenders

In has been estimated that as many as 50 to 75 percent of probationers and parolees have some alcohol-related problem.[85] To assist these offenders, many probation and parole offices have established specialized caseloads consisting solely of alcoholic offenders. Officers supervising these caseloads can focus their energies on increasing their knowledge of alcoholism, enhancing their therapeutic skills, and developing and maintaining contacts with community alcoholism treatment projects.

Many probation/parole offices also offer group counseling to alcoholics and problem drinkers. One of the first such programs was established in the Federal Probation Office in the District of Columbia. Offenders were accepted into the program after extensive diagnosis and classification procedures or when treatment was made a condition of probation.

A former supervisor of the Alcoholic Counseling Group described its format:

1. Group discussion is encouraged in reference to alcoholism as a disease, its progressiveness, and many attendant problems, with emphasis on its being arrestable but not curable and that the only solution is complete abstinence.

2. Individuals are urged to select pertinent topics in which they are interested and concerned. These are discussed in depth.

3. Educational films are shown frequently and are selected carefully for their content and value. Usually they depict and discuss the social, psychological, and physical aspects of the problem. Case histories are presented and discussed. Avenues of available help are often the climax of the films.

4. Selected AA speakers discuss their experiences and the help they received through Alcoholics Anonymous. A question-and-answer period follows. All are constantly urged to seek the help available through AA. AA literature is distributed at no cost.

5. Staff members from community resource agencies are invited to discuss their programs and the help their agencies render.[86]

The program attempts to encourage insight and help offenders establish and maintain mature interpersonal relationships. Attitudes are discussed and goals are examined. One offender's success encourages the others to examine their own problems and initiate change.

A typical meeting focuses on such practical matters as the effects of alcoholism on the family, the employer, and the community and the importance of being aware of simple detectable symptoms, including "frequent absenteeism from work (especially on Mondays), personality changes when drinking, reporting while under the influence of alcohol, and arrests for being drunk."[87]

During the one and a half to two-hour meetings, group dynamics are observed carefully; a summary of the significant events of each meeting is recorded for later review and evaluation. Offenders are also encouraged to seek help through AA, which is available on a twenty-four hour basis.

One of the best-known residential programs using AA is Hazelden Rehabilitation Services. The program and services are described in the nearby box.

The Effectiveness of Alcohol Treatment

The effectiveness of alcohol treatment programs may be assessed according to several evaluation criteria. The most widely utilized measures of success are alcohol consumption, behavioral impairment, and social adjustment.[88]

❑ Alcohol Consumption

There is considerable evidence that alcohol treatment programs reduce program participants' alcohol consumption. A nationwide study of programs funded by the National Institute of Alcohol Abuse and Alcoholism revealed that eighteen months after treatment, 46 percent of the male patients and 56 percent of the female patients had abstained from alcohol; one-fourth of the males and over one-third of the females had abstained for at least six months. Alcohol consumption declined to 2.5 ounces (male) and 1.3 ounces (female) per day.[89]

❑ Behavioral Impairment and Adjustment

Patients in alcohol treatment programs generally show signs of social, vocational, and psychological adaptation "related but not parallel" to reductions in alcohol consumption.[90] Job stability seems to be particularly enhanced by alcoholism treatment;

The Hazelden Rehabilitation Program, Center City, Minnesota

Admissions

People come to the Hazelden Rehabilitation Program from all over the world representing all age, social, occupational, and religious backgrounds. People refer themselves, or are referred by concerned persons from the medical, legal, family, mental health, or Alcoholics Anonymous communities. Physically handicapped people capable of self-care (i.e., wheelchair capability) may also participate.

The Hazelden Admissions Office is open twenty-four hours a day, seven days a week. . . . Advance reservations are required.

For a fee, Hazelden provides daily transportation to and from the Twin Cities area, bus terminals, and the Minneapolis–St. Paul International Airport.

Medical Management

Upon arrival at Hazelden, new patients receive a complete physical examination and health assessment. If necessary, the patient undergoes a carefully controlled, individual detoxification plan. A medical evaluation is completed usually within a 48-hour period. Patients move to one of the primary treatment units usually within 24 hours.

Assessment

Because chemical dependency affects all areas of a person's life, each patient's social, emotional, intellectual, spiritual, and physical condition is carefully evaluated, with special attention to the consequences of alcohol and other drug use.

A team of chemical dependency counselors, clergy, psychologists, medical staff, and recreational therapists interviews each patient. These specialists design a highly individualized treatment plan that details specific goals in each area of the patient's life. This plan is the blueprint for the patient's treatment at Hazelden. . . .

Primary Rehabilitation

While the length of stay for patients at Hazelden varies according to individual needs, an average stay is twenty-nine days.

Treatment itself is an absorbing, intensive experience. To learn about their disease, patients attend lectures daily. Psychiatrists, psychologists, physicians, nurses, clergy, and chemical dependency counselors describe chemical dependency from their professional and personal experience.

---

there is also evidence that interpersonal relationships and physical condition improve and arrest rates decline among treated problem drinkers. However, persons who reduce their alcohol consumption do not always show signs of improved adjustment. Conversely, behavioral and social adjustment can improve even when alcohol consumption continues at an unhealthy level.

❑ Patient and Treatment Characteristics

Attempts have been made to identify the most effective treatment strategies and best candidates for rehabilitation. Community-based rehabilitation programs have been found to be as successful as and less expensive than inpatient programs. The 1978 Report to Congress on Alcohol and Health suggested that the least expensive program may well be the preferred treatment option if quality treatment standards are maintained.[91]

Studies of treatment characteristics have revealed that longer, more intensive rehabilitation programs are associated with positive treatment outcome. At present, however, no optimum treatment intensity or length can be specified.[92]

After an exhaustive review of research on differential treatment effectiveness, the 1978 Report to Congress concluded that the client's background and motivation

Daily group therapy helps each patient better understand themselves and their disease. By sharing personal experiences, patients learn—often for the first time—to trust and seek help from friends and loved ones. Group sessions on grief, women's issues, the Steps of Alcoholics Anonymous, and other topics help patients recognize and begin to resolve personal barriers to recovery.

In individual counseling sessions counselor and patient work together to identify personal problems and set specific goals that will lead to a better life. These goals might include overcoming resentment, developing trust in others, or identifying self-defeating behaviors.

The cornerstone of our program is the Steps of Alcoholics Anonymous, with a goal of total abstinence from alcohol and other drugs. Each patient works on adopting the philosophy of Alcoholics Anonymous before leaving treatment. Upon discharge, patients are referred to Alcoholics Anonymous contacts in their home communities.

Care for the family is an important part of our rehabilitation services. Because the disease of chemical dependency directly or indirectly affects the lives of so many people, Hazelden offers a family services program. . . .

Aftercare

Aftercare—counseling that takes place after treatment—eases the transition back to home life. It also prepares the patient to lead a richer, higher quality life of sobriety.

Each patient works with their counselor and the Hazelden aftercare staff to develop an aftercare plan. Typical aftercare plans include participation in Twelve Step groups such as Alcoholics Anonymous or Narcotics Anonymous. Aftercare might also include marital counseling, individual therapy, or family therapy, according to individual situations.

Because many of our patients come from outside of Minnesota, we have developed an extensive network of aftercare providers throughout the country. Through this national network, Hazelden patients living outside the metropolitan area are referred to aftercare facilities in their home communities.

Hazelden also offers special aftercare programs for people who live in the Minneapolis-St. Paul metropolitan area. . . .

SOURCE: From the Hazelden Rehabilitation Program, Center City, Minnesota (1990 brochure). Reprinted by permission.

to seek help may be the most important factors in the treatment process. Research that indicates that many alcoholics experience spontaneous recovery without any formal treatment supports this conclusion. Intensive outpatient treatment increases the problem drinker's chance of recovery, however, perhaps by as much as 25 percent.[93] Taken together, these findings indicate that intensive community-based programs may well provide the best treatment alternative available for the alcoholic offender. However, the problem of motivation remains as a principal barrier to rehabilitation.

❏ Treatment Prerequisites and the Criminal Justice System

Only a small proportion of alcoholics and problem drinkers seek and/or accept treatment. This reluctance to use available assistance is due in part to the belief that alcoholism is a symptom of weakness and that only a strong will is required to conquer the problem. Other persons fail to enter treatment because of an inability or unwillingness to recognize their problem. This denial of alcoholism may be produced by a fear of abstinence as well as a fear of treatment.

Zola has described five timing triggers that must precede a person's decision to accept help in overcoming an alcohol problem.

1. A personal crisis must emerge to cause the patient to dwell on symptoms.
2. The symptoms must begin to threaten a valued social activity.
3. Other people must begin telling him or her to seek care.
4. The consequences of not seeking help must be perceived.
5. The pain, severity, and duration of symptoms must be sufficient to produce action.[94]

The implications of Zola's research are significant. A personal crisis such as arrest may well be sufficient to encourage many alcohol-abusing offenders to consider rehabilitation. If intensive therapy is available to offenders during community supervision, it may be possible to take advantage of the new willingness to accept treatment.

Correctional workers need to learn how to use these timing triggers to increase client motivation. The criminal justice system must develop effective linkages with community alcohol treatment programs and provide incentives and support to the offender who enters treatment. By providing incentives, treatment, and support, the circumstances of crime, arrest, and conviction may be used to promote meaningful behavioral change.

Summary

Narcotics addicts, problem drinkers, and alcoholics present special problems to the criminal justice system. Substance abuse is associated with both violent and property crime; alcohol abuse often produces crimes against the person and narcotics addiction leads to economic crimes.

There are a number of similarities between alcohol and drug abuse and abusers. There is no single addict or alcoholic personality; both alcohol and narcotics can be used on an occasional social basis as well as in a chronic fashion. Both substances offer a similar benefit to their abusers—an escape from reality.

Similar explanations are offered to describe the causes of both problems. Similar treatments are also available, including behavior modification, the use of pharmacological agents, supportive and confrontational therapies, and residential and outpatient programs. Many treatment strategies are criticized for substituting one form of dependency for another. Neither alcohol nor drug abuse is easy to treat; complete and permanent cures are relatively rare.

KEY WORDS AND CONCEPTS

abstinence
Alcoholics Anonymous
alcoholism
Antabuse
chippers
confrontational
  therapy
controlled drinking

drug addiction
methadone
  maintenance
polydrug users
postaddiction
  syndrome
problem drinkers
skid row alcoholics

street life
supported work
  projects
therapeutic
  communities
tolerance
withdrawal

NOTES

1. Jared R. Tinklenberg, "Drugs and Crime," in *Drug Use in America: Problem in Perspective*, Appendix, vol. 1, National Commission on Marijuana and Drug Abuse (Washington, D.C.: U.S. Government Printing Office, 1973), pp. 242–299.
2. C. D. Chambers, "A Review of Recent Sociological and Epidemiological Studies in Substance Abuse" (paper presented at the Neurobiology Seminar, Vanderbilt University, Nashville, Tennessee, May 6, 1977).
3. Robert Gandossy et al., *Drugs and Crime: A Survey and Analysis of the Literature* (Washington, D.C.: U.S. Government Printing Office, 1980), p. xiv.
4. Richard Stevens and Rosalind Ellis, "Narcotic Addicts and Crime: Analysis of Recent Trends," *Criminology* 12 (1975): 474–488.
5. James Inciardi, "The Vilification of Euphoria: Some Perspectives on an Elusive Issue," *Addictive Diseases* 1 (1974): 241–267.
6. Edwin M. Schur, *Crimes Without Victims* (Englewood Cliffs, N.J.: Prentice-Hall, 1965), p. 122.
7. Gandossy et al., *Drugs and Crime*, p. 36.
8. Ibid.
9. Oakley Ray, *Drugs, Society and Human Behavior* (St. Louis, Mo.: C. V. Mosby, 1978), p. 323.
10. Gandossy et al., *Drugs and Crime*, p. 75.
11. Ibid., p. 76.
12. Ibid., p.xii.
13. Jerome J. Platt and Christine Labate, *Heroin Addiction—Theory, Research and Treatment* (New York: Wiley, 1976), p. 319.
14. Isidor Chein et al., *The Road to H: Narcotics, Delinquency and Social Policy* (New York: Basic Books, 1964), pp. 273–274.
15. Gandossy et al., *Drugs and Crime*, p. xii.
16. Robert J. Wicks and Jerome Platt, *Drug Abuse: A Criminal Justice Primer* (Beverly Hills, Calif.: Glencoe Press, 1977), p. 44.
17. Edward A. Preble and John J. Casey, Jr., "Taking Care of Business—The Heroin User's Life in the Street," *International Journal of the Addictions* 4 (1969): 2–3. Reprinted with permission of Marcel Dekker, Inc.
18. Ibid., pp. 21–22.
19. Platt and Labate, *Heroin Addiction*, p. 318.
20. Quoted by permission from "Licit and Illicit Drugs," by Edward M. Brecher and the editors of *Consumer Reports*. Copyright 1972 by Consumers Union of Unites States, Inc.
21. National Drug Abuse Treatment Utilization Survey (NDATUS), *National Drug Abuse Treatment: Insights and Perspectives* (Washington, D.C.: U.S. Government Printing Office, 1977), p. 18.
22. Gandossy et al., *Drugs and Crime*, p. 114.
23. Platt and Labate, *Heroin Addiction*.
24. Edward Preble and Thomas Miller, "Methadone, Wine and Welfare," in *Street Ethnography*, Robert S. Weppner (ed.) (Beverly Hills, Calif.: Sage Publications, 1977), pp. 229–248.
25. Ibid.
26. D. M. Alpern, E. Sciolino, and S. Agrest, "The Methadone Jones," *Newsweek*, February 7, 1977, p. 29.
27. Platt and Labate, *Heroin Addiction*, pp. 320–321.
28. NDATUS, *National Drug Abuse Treatment*, p. 18.
29. George DeLeon and George M. Beschner (eds.), *The Therapeutic Community: Proceedings of Therapeutic Communities of America Planning Conference*, January 29–30, 1976 (Rockville, Md.: National Institute on Drug Abuse, 1977), p. 2.
30. NDATUS, *National Drug Abuse Treatment*, p. 17.
31. Platt and Labate, *Heroin Addiction*, p. 218.
32. Michael S. Serrill, "From Bums to Businessmen: The Delancey Street Foundation," *Corrections Magazine* 1 (1) (1974): 13–28.

33. Platt and Labate, *Heroin Addiction,* p. 220.
34. Charles Winick, "The Drug Offender," in *Psychology of Crime and Criminal Justice,* Hans Toch (ed.) (New York: Holt, Rinehart and Winston, 1979), p. 394.
35. Mildred K. Klein, "Maintaining Drug Abusers in the Community: A New Treatment Concept," *Federal Probation* 36(2) (1972): 18–26.
36. Ibid., p. 22.
37. Ibid., p. 21.
38. Ibid., p. 25.
39. Michael L. Peck and David Klugman, "Rehabilitation of Drug Dependent Offenders: An Alternative Approach," *Federal Probation* 37(3) (1973): 13–23. Reprinted with permission from *Federal Probation* (1973).
40. Ibid., pp. 18–20.
41. Ibid., p. 21.
42. Ibid., pp. 22, 23.
43. Personal communication with Bob Altman, Administrative Office of the U.S. Courts, September 3, 1982.
44. Gilbert Geis, "A Halfway House Is Not a Home: Notes on the Failure of a Narcotic Rehabilitation Project," *Drug Forum* 4(1) (1974): 7–13.
45. Ibid.
46. Ibid.
47. Lawrence T. Williams, *An Analysis of Recidivism Among Residents Released from Drug Contract Houses* (Boston: Massachusetts Department of Correction, 1980).
48. Ibid.
49. Lucy Friedman, *The Wildcat Experiment: An Early Test of Supported Work in Drug Abuse Rehabilitation* (Washington, D.C.: U.S. Government Printing Office, 1978).
50. Ibid.
51. Ibid., p. 3.
52. Manpower Demonstrator Research Corporation, *Summary and Findings of the National Supported Work Demonstration* (Cambridge, Mass.: Ballinger, 1980).
53. U.S. Department of Health, Education and Welfare (HEW), *Third Special Report to the U.S. Congress on Alcohol and Health* (Washington, D.C.: U.S. Government Printing Office, 1978), p. 243.
54. Ibid., p. 242.
55. Ibid., p. 245.
56. David J. Pittman and C. Wayne Gordon, "Criminal Careers of Chronic Drunkenness Offenders," in *Society, Culture and Drinking Patterns,* David Pittman and Charles R. Snyder (eds.) (New York: Wiley, 1962), p. 540.
57. National Institute of Mental Health (NIMH), *Alcohol and Alcoholism: Problems, Programs and Progress* (Washington, D.C.: U.S. Government Printing Office, 1972), p. 3.
58. Ibid., p. 5.
59. Alexander B. Smith and Louis Berlin, *Treating the Criminal Offender* (Dobbs Ferry, N.Y.: Oceana Publications, 1974), pp. 254–265.
60. Harry Milt, *Basic Handbook on Alcoholism* (Fair Haven, N.J.: Scientific Aids Publications, 1967), p. 7.
61. Smith and Berlin, *Treating the Criminal Offender,* p. 255.
62. Ruth Fox, "Alcoholism and Depression," *American Journal of Psychotherapy,* as quoted in Milt, *Basic Handbook on Alcoholism,* p. 40.
63. NIMH, *Alcohol and Alcoholism,* p. 13.
64. Ibid., p. 18.
65. HEW, *Third Special Report,* p. xii.
66. Ibid., p. 273.
67. Ibid., p. 255.
68. J. M. Polich, D. J. Armor, and H. B. Baker, "Patterns of Alcoholism," *Journal of Studies on Alcohol* 41(5) (1980): 414.
69. HEW, *Third Special Report,* pp. 255–256.
70. Ray, *Drugs, Society and Human Behavior,* p. 156.

71. Ibid.
72. Ibid.
73. Ibid., p. 157.
74. Ibid., p. 158.
75. HEW, *Third Special Report*, p. 259.
76. Ibid.
77. Ibid.
78. Curtis Janzen, "Families in the Treatment of Alcoholism," *Journal of Studies on Alcohol* 38(1)(1977): 120.
79. Ibid., p. 122.
80. Ibid.
81. Ibid., p. 124.
82. U.S. Department of Health and Human Services, *4th Special Report to the U.S. Congress on Alcohol and Health* (Washington, D.C.: U.S. Government Printing Office, 1981), p. 137.
83. Eva M. Blum and Richard H. Blum, *Alcoholism* (San Francisco: Jossey-Bass, 1969), p. 162.
84. Ibid., p. 164.
85. Edward W. Soden, "Constructive Coercion and Group Counseling in the Rehabilitation of Alcoholics," *Federal Probation* 30(3)(1966): 56.
86. Ibid., p. 59.
87. Ibid.
88. HEW, *Third Special Report*, p. 264.
89. Ibid., p. 266.
90. Ibid.
91. Ibid., p. 269.
92. Ibid., p. 270.
93. D. J. Armor, J. M. Polich, and H. B. Stambull, *Alcoholism and Treatment* (Santa Monica, Calif.: Rand Corporation, 1976).
94. I. K. Zola, "Illness Behavior of the Working Class," in *Blue Collar World: Studies of the American Worker*, A. B. Shostak and W. Gomberg (eds.) (Englewood Cliffs, N.J.: Prentice-Hall, 1964), pp. 350–361.

FOR FURTHER READING

Brecher, Edward, M., *Licit and Illicit Drugs* (Mount Vernon, N.Y.: Consumers Union, 1972).

Bureau of Justice and Statistics, *Drugs and Crime, Facts, 1989* (Washington, D.C.: U.S. Department of Justice, 1990).

Gropper, Bernard, *Probing the Links Between Drugs and Crime* (Washington, D.C.: U.S. Department of Justice, 1985).

National Institute of Drug Abuse and Alcoholism, *Seventh Special Report to the U.S. Congress on Alcohol and Health* (Washington, D.C.: U.S. Government Printing Office, January 1990).

Ray, Oakley, *Drugs, Society and Human Behavior* (St. Louis, Mo.: C. V. Mosby, 1983).

Wicks, Robert J., and Jerome J. Platt, *Drug Abuse: A Criminal Justice Primer* (Beverly Hills, Calif.: Glencoe Press, 1977).

12: Volunteers, Paraprofessionals, and Ex-offenders

ONE OF THE MOST SERIOUS PROBLEMS facing both public and private correctional agencies is the shortage of personnel required to implement correctional programs. Staff limitations invariably reduce the quality and quantity of services that can be offered to offenders. An otherwise well-designed correctional program may easily fail simply because there is insufficient personnel for successful operation. Fiscal conservatism and reduced funding for special programs makes this problem particularly acute.

This problem may be largely overcome by the focused and careful utilization of unpaid citizens and the employment of paraprofessionals and ex-offenders in various correctional roles. Each of these types of workers can supplement correctional personnel; they can also provide special and often unique assistance to the offenders with whom they work.

To maximize the effectiveness of nontraditional personnel, comprehensive planning, monitoring, and evaluating of programs that rely upon their contributions are essential. In this chapter, we examine these and other issues surrounding citizen participation in corrections and the employment of paraprofessionals and ex-offenders in community corrections. We first focus our attention on volunteer efforts and then turn to a discussion of the special role paraprofessionals and ex-offenders play in corrections.

Citizen Participation in Community Corrections

Few persons would dispute the need for citizen participation in correctional efforts. In a democracy, the nature, quality, and objectives of a correctional system should reflect community sentiments. An involved and informed public is essential for conscientious, intelligent decision making; otherwise, our correctional services will be shaped only by political and bureaucratic interests.[1]

Unfortunately, relations between correctional agencies and the citizens they ultimately serve have not always been good. Correctional administrators have sometimes viewed interested citizens as meddlers in correctional affairs. The majority of citizens has been content to allow public servants to bear the full responsibility for planning and administering penal programs—until a particularly heinous crime or prison riot focuses community outrage on the correctional system. Distrust has characterized what little communication has existed between the community and its criminal justice system.

There is evidence that this undesirable and unwarranted situation is changing. The increasingly vocal victim's rights movement as well as the growing utilization of community alternatives to incarceration have brought correctional issues and programs to the forefront of public attention. Correctional administrators in many jurisdictions are learning that citizen involvement can enhance correctional efforts and that open lines of communication can facilitate, rather than inhibit, the accomplishment of correctional objectives. The realization that community participation is often essential to correctional efforts, such as halfway house implementation and temporary release programming, may have been slow to develop, but it now seems to have gained acceptance in corrections.

Citizens can fulfill many needs in our correctional system. The National Advisory Commission on Criminal Justice Standards and Goals emphasized three distinct aspects of community involvement: policymaking, reform efforts, and direct service roles.[2]

❏ Policymaking

Citizens may serve in a variety of policymaking capacities in corrections. They often work on task forces or participate in study groups and serve in an advisory role to state and local government, criminal justice planners, or correctional administrators. These groups may be comprised of politically influential citizens who serve as "social persuaders," willing to use their influence to promote support for correctional programs. There is also a need to select representatives of a broad cross section of the community in formulating these citizen boards so that no single interest group is allowed to dominate the advisory process. As long as the tasks assigned to these groups are meaningful, with clearly stated objectives and purposes, these organizations are likely to provide valuable assistance. When the groups are developed and implemented merely to promote a facade of citizen involvement, they are destined to result in what may be a bitter failure.

Citizen involvement in policymaking may also be achieved through the development of independent citizen groups established on a voluntary basis. State councils on crime and delinquency affiliated with the National Council on Crime and Delinquency are examples of such organizations. They are frequently comprised of leading citizens capable of facilitating community action. Their membership is drawn from a wide variety of individuals and interest groups who support the councils with voluntary contributions.[3]

❏ Reform Efforts

Citizen involvement in corrections for the purpose of influencing correctional programs and planning is not necessarily initiated from inside the system. Religious, ethnic, and political organizations and associations of ex-offenders may direct their attention to correctional efforts, critiquing current policy and suggesting and promoting reforms. Not surprisingly, correctional administrators often have more difficulty working with representatives of these groups than with members of advisory commissions established under their own direction. Such working relationships are essential, however, not only because of the valuable input they may provide, but because, as public servants, corrections officials need to be responsive to all their constituencies. Open lines of communication can reap considerable benefits in understanding and cooperation.

❏ Direct Service Roles

Most of the citizens who become involved in correctional efforts do so in direct service roles. They serve as volunteers in all forms of correctional programs, institutional as well as community based. Research indicates that the hundreds of thousands of volunteers in corrections outnumber professionals at a rate of four or five to one and that 70 percent of correctional agencies have volunteer programs.[4] The massive use of volunteers in community corrections warrants an in-depth

A Profile of Selected Religious and Reform Organizations and Their Activities in Corrections

Unitarian Universalist Association:
provides financial contributions to the National Moratorium on Prison Construction

Roman Catholic Church:
sponsors halfway houses for offenders, a death penalty study group in Florida, and has published documents on alternatives to incarceration

Society of Friends (Quakers):
sponsors community dispute resolution programs, self-help groups, and community-based centers for prisoner support and prison reform, published *Struggle for Justice* (1970), a critique of the contemporary prison system

United Church of Christ:
sponsors a criminal justice task force within the Commission for Racial Justice. The task force actively opposes prison construction and lobbies for the human rights of prisoners

Church of the Brethren:
funds a "legislative associate" in criminal justice with offices in Washington

Washington Interreligious Staff Council:
a lobbying and advocacy coalition of Catholic, Protestant, and Jewish religious organizations, its efforts are focused on the death penalty, the rights of the confined, prison moratorium, and victim compensation

Interreligious Task Force on Criminal Justice:
a Protestant coalition that was established in the 1960s, it functions as the "think tank" for the National Council of Churches. The task force focuses on broad areas and has recently been especially active in assisting prisoners who are Vietnam veterans

Southern Coalition on Jails and Prisons:
a nine-state coalition that actively opposes prison construction and the death penalty and supports the use of community-based alternatives

SOURCE: Phillip B. Taft, "Religious Reformers Want to Proclaim Liberty to the Captives," *Corrections Magazine* 5(4) (1979): 37–43. Copyright 1979 by *Corrections Magazine* and Criminal Justice Publications, Inc., 116 West 32 Street, New York, NY 10001.

examination of their efforts and experiences. The following sections review the development of volunteer services in community corrections and current patterns of volunteer utilization, focusing on problems and issues in program administration and evaluation.

Volunteers in Community Corrections

❏ Historical Perspective

Although many community correctional programs represent new developments in corrections, the use of volunteers dates back almost 200 years. The first volunteer efforts originated in England in the form of prisoner visiting programs developed by John Howard and Elizabeth Fry. Fry began her volunteer work in the women's section of London's Newgate Prison in 1813. She was so appalled at the state of degradation and misery in the prison—the sight of almost naked babies who had been born in the prison, the lack of clothing and bedding for inmates—that she almost singlehandedly tried to correct the abuses she found.[5] After her death in 1845, a lay visitors group for women was established.

Although the Philadelphia Society for Alleviating the Miseries of Public Prisons has been visiting prisoners since colonial times, little active visitation occurred until the turn of the century.[6] The visiting that did occur was generally informal and merely tolerated by prison officials; visits were most frequently permitted to help long-term prisoners maintain contact with the community. A few organized groups, such as the Salvation Army, engaged in more extensive visitation and were permitted fairly routine access to the inmates.[7]

The first American community corrections volunteer was John Augustus, whose activities led to the development of contemporary probation services. His efforts encouraged other citizens to contribute their energies to assisting criminal offenders, but eventually probation was professionalized and citizen involvement all but disappeared. It was not until 1959 that citizens were again provided the opportunity and encouragement to contribute their time and energies to offender aid. Ironically, the setting was again the criminal court and the offenders were probationers.

Judge Keith J. Leinhouts, a municipal court judge in Royal Oaks, Michigan, is generally credited with reviving the volunteer in corrections movement. He describes the development of the Royal Oaks program for adult misdemeanants:

> In 1959, eight citizens sat around the table on a hot August night discussing the court's problem. All we could do was look at the defendant for a moment or two after he pleaded guilty or was found guilty and was given a fine or a jail term. Completely without any probation program, no presentence investigation or rehabilitative service was possible. What could we do about it? The eight, all expert counselors [a psychiatrist, a psychologist, a social worker, three clergymen, and two junior high school assistant principals] agreed to try to change the system by accepting a case load of five probationers each. In early 1960, the Michigan Corrections Commission appointed one of them chief probation officer and approved the plan to use volunteers. We started assigning probationers to them. . . .
>
> The original eight recruited more volunteers. Soon it was possible to reduce the case load to two or three probationers per volunteer. Eventually, a one-to-one relationship was established. All of the volunteers were experts in some field of counseling. Most of them were educators, ministers, psychologists, and other professionals with at least a master's degree in counseling and guidance.
>
> When we were about nine months old, we had thirty volunteers and some seventy-five probationers. As the judge, I was spending about twenty hours weekly administering the program. This was in addition to my civil, traffic, and criminal judicial duties, which took some forty hours a week. I could not do this indefinitely, for I was the only judge in a city of 90,000 that had many thousand people traveling through it each day. The fact that it is part of the metropolitan area of Detroit further complicated the situation. We needed help and we turned to the volunteer chief probation officer and the community for assistance. We asked two businessmen to each donate $25 a month to the program so we could employ the chief probation officer for forty hours a month to supervise the program. They agreed and we had our first budget and "paid" worker. He met with all of the probationers and volunteers each month. . . .
>
> A few months later, a second part-time professional was added to the staff. He was also one of the original eight volunteers. Two more businessmen contributed funds. The two of them each met with half of the volunteers and probationers monthly.
>
> About this time I was reaching the point of exhaustion. I called a friend of many years, Harry Hassberger. Now retired from his job as an executive with a plumbing and heating company, he was working about three hours a day as a school street-crossing guard. He readily agreed to work fifteen hours a week as a volunteer to administer the program, thus relieving the part-time professionals from burdensome details so they could spend nearly all of their time counseling and supervising the volunteers.

A few months later the school year ended and Mr. Hassberger agreed to work full time for the amount he could receive under Social Security regulations, about 50 cents an hour. Four businessmen contributed $25 each a month to "pay" for his services.

It would be difficult to overestimate his contribution. The young program took on a new dimension of pride and self-assurance. Mr. Hassberger's concern, interest, and dedication became a key part of the program. We were so proud of what he was doing that we became more proud and confident of ourselves. He soon earned the name Harry "The Horse" Hassberger as he ran from room to room almost with the enthusiasm of a youngster chasing a ball.

We learned about group psychotherapy. A psychiatrist agreed to handle two groups for a year for $10 an hour. Again businessmen contributed their money. At the end of the fifteen months we had a good program but much more was needed.

Then, unexpectedly, the mayor called us and said, "The city commissioners are being criticized for not contributing to the program. How much do you need for next year?" We projected $4,400 and the mayor readily agreed to give it. However, we requested only $2,200. We did not want to lose our private financial contributions. Their involvement was important to us. Thus, we started the new fiscal year with a budget of $4,400, half from the city.

By 1965, the program had a budget of $17,000 from the city and about $8,000 from private contributors. The staff included seven retirees who administered the program, twelve part-time professional chief counselors who counseled the probationers and supervised the volunteers, and a part-time staff psychiatrist who coordinated the efforts of thirty-five volunteer psychiatrists and fifteen psychologists and who also made presentence evaluations.[8]

The Royal Oaks program became the subject of considerable interest and research. One study compared the recidivism rates of one hundred Royal Oaks probationers with comparable offenders placed on probation by a court in another state. The Royal Oaks offenders had a recidivism rate less than half that of the other group. Each city was spending $17,000 per year on probation services; Royal Oaks relied extensively on a volunteer staff of over forty persons, but the comparison city was able to employ only one very overworked probation officer for that sum.[9] A second study of the program revealed that Royal Oaks was placing three persons on probation for every two placed by the comparison court. After a five-year follow-up period, 15 percent of the Royal Oaks and 50 percent of the comparison offenders recidivated.[10] According to Judge Leinhouts: "The research simply adds proof to what must be true. Many thousands of hours of intensive rehabilitative services are more effective than one overwhelmed probation officer who can only administer a telephone and letter reporting system."[11]

Judge Leinhouts's efforts to promote volunteerism did not stop with his own court. He was instrumental in developing Volunteers in Probation (VIP), an organization designed to promote volunteer efforts across the United States. In 1972, VIP affiliated with the National Council on Crime and Delinquency (NCCD). VIP no longer represents only volunteers in probation, but also includes volunteers in prevention, prosecution, prison, and parole, as well as designating the "very important person" status of the volunteer.

VIP-NCCD has conducted numerous national forums to promote the volunteer movement and publishes a quarterly newsletter that reports on volunteer efforts throughout the criminal justice system. Today, thousands of volunteer programs operate in every region of the country, assisting offenders and criminal justice personnel at all stages of the criminal justice system.

❑ Service Roles for the Correctional Volunteer

There seems to be no limit to the roles for today's volunteer in community corrections. Schier and Berry have identified ten general roles that volunteers may fill:

1. Support, friendship, someone who cares and will listen
2. Mediator, facilitator of social-physical environment (get jobs, intercede with teacher, open up opportunities, run interference with system)
3. Behavior model, just be a good example
4. Limit setting, social control, conscience
5. Teacher-tutor in academic, vocational, or social skills
6. Observation, information, diagnosis, understanding, extra eyes and ears on the probationer, on the community, or even on the agency on behalf of the community
7. Trainee rather than trainer; intern preparing for a career in the criminal justice system
8. Advisory or even decision-making participation in formulating policy
9. Administrative support, office work, and related facilitation
10. Help recruit, train, advise, supervise other volunteers[12]

Volunteers have been active in recreational, entertainment, educational, religious, clerical, administrative, and support roles in various correctional programs. It appears that the diversity of roles is limited only by the imagination and creativity of correctional personnel and volunteer coordinators.

❑ Advantages of Volunteer Services

One of the principal benefits of volunteer services is their contribution to the personnel resources of correctional agencies. Virtually no correctional program is overstaffed. Most manage to make do by juggling their personnel, and a few seem to be in a perpetual state of crisis because of a wholly unmanageable work load. The use of volunteers can permit the agency to utilize its professional resources as frugally as possible. Volunteers can be used in counseling roles to supplement the agency's limited ability to provide one-to-one assistance to offenders. Volunteers can provide transportation for offenders, clerical assistance to administrators, or other support services to free up professionals for tasks that require special expertise, training, or official rank.

The ability to individualize services is probably one of the most frequently cited benefits of volunteer efforts. For example, probation and parole staff, in Judge Leinhouts's words, often can only "administer a telephone and letter reporting system." Contacts with offenders are generally less frequent than once a month and often last for only a few minutes. Such experiences can hardly be labeled therapeutic or rehabilitative. At best, the contacts provide some semblance of supervision, but they no doubt do little to deter criminal activity. The volunteer assigned to a probationer or parolee can provide the offender with a companion, a role model, or an

Competencies Required for Volunteer Work in Community Corrections

1. Ability to understand and withstand provocative behavior without becoming punitive

2. Development of objectivity in accepting relationships with all clients in a non-judgmental manner, without either punitive or sentimental emotional involvement

3. Ability to accept a person without personal involvement, with neither punitive nor sentimental views, much the same as a physician views a patient—this does not mean complete detachment but rather an empathic relationship

4. Knowledge of on-the-job counseling techniques

5. Ability to say no, with reasons when necessary, and the ability to say yes, with equal reason

6. Sensitivity to pathological behavior as compared with normal random behavior sufficient to permit intelligent referral to professional staff and/or agencies

7. Ability to assess strengths of an individual to determine what there is to build on in the treatment of an offender

8. Ability to make referrals to all staff, community resources, and other specialties with some understanding and sophistication

9. Ability to use tact to avoid creating or aggravating problem situations

10. Ability to use tact to ameliorate developing problem situations

11. Willingness to augment and support the staff of the agency or institution

12. Ability to observe and accurately record (a) individual behavior as pathological or manipulative and which consequently might need referral to professional staff, (b) group behavior signaling the beginning of a potentially dangerous association, and (c) miscellaneous behavior that may be part of illicit activity or regression to earlier behavioral patterns

13. Ability to assess community and family attitudes toward the offender

14. Ability to interpret constructively agency or community attitudes and behavior toward the person on the volunteer's case load

15. Ability to serve as an upward communicator from the offender to the agency or institution with a view toward improving services and policies

16. Ability to maintain discreet silence on some critical issues and "classified" information to maintain (a) staff morale, (b) case load morale, and (c) good public relations

17. Ability to exert external controls by persuasion on individuals who need containment

18. Knowledge of specific procedures that might be modified or elaborated in training programs, consultations, or other ways by which the agency or institutional staff can assist the volunteer in understanding situations and desirable policy

19. Knowledge of the constitutional and civil rights of persons on the case load and ability to incorporate that knowledge into the supervisory process

20. Ability to interpret the system of justice, including laws of arrest, judicial procedure, and a total correctional process, in order to answer correctly questions put by the offender

SOURCE: Vernon Fox, *Community-Based Corrections* (Englewood Cliffs, N.J.: Prentice-Hall, 1977), pp. 252, 253. Reprinted by permission of Prentice-Hall, Inc., Englewood Cliffs, New Jersey.

advisor—whatever he requires to deal with his personal, social, or economic problems. The interaction is not restricted to specific times or places and it need not be limited to the length of the probation or parole period. The assistance is also free from the stigma of authoritarianism that seems virtually unavoidable in corrections. The assistance can be friendly, constant, and lasting.

Volunteers can contribute their special skills and knowledge of the community. Not all volunteers will be skilled in the same manner or degree as the original Royal Oaks citizens, but abilities as diverse as sewing and swimming, motorcycle racing and mountain climbing, and accounting and acrobatics can find a place in correctional efforts. As members of the community, volunteers can contribute their community contacts, facilitating offenders' access to programs and services that might otherwise be unobtainable. One of the problems that persistently plagues correctional programs is lack of information regarding community resources and how to get what from whom. Citizen participation in correctional efforts should broaden the community resources information network agencies use and thus facilitate the resource identification and client referral process.

Finally, citizen volunteers provide possibly the best means available of generating public awareness of correctional programs, issues, and problems. Utilizing their own observations and experiences, they facilitate correctional change by stimulating interest in correctional efforts and a greater sense of community responsibility for the correctional process. Each volunteer can educate members of the general public regarding the problems of crime, criminals, and the criminal justice system. These citizens can generate an informed understanding and interest in issues that too often receive public attention only after crises or scandals make the problems too visible to ignore.

❏ Contemporary Volunteer Programs

A 1979 study of volunteer programs by the National Council on Crime and Delinquency estimated that there were about 350,000 persons working in almost 4,000 volunteer programs across the United States. The survey attempted to identify typical programs but found that the diversity of program operations made such a task impossible.[13]

In 1981, Kratcoski et al. surveyed volunteers in thirty-six programs and reported that most volunteers were white (81 percent) and well educated (84 percent had formal education beyond high school). Although most of the volunteers were female, a significant minority (43 percent) was male. Over half the volunteers were between the ages of 21 and 40; one-third were under 30 years of age. Most of the volunteers were married and worked as professionals, attended school, or were employed in the home. Almost half the volunteers had been working with their program for two or more years. The remaining majority of participants was relatively new to volunteerism.[14]

When asked to evaluate their reasons for entering volunteer work , 81 percent of the respondents reported a desire to help others and other altruistic sentiments. One-fourth of the volunteers, who believed that volunteering would be a rewarding experience, reported personal satisfaction as a motivation. About 10 percent of the participants mentioned the influence of recruiting efforts and career motivations.

The volunteers participated in a wide range of activities (table 12-1). Most of their time seemed to be devoted to the general tasks of providing friendship and personal counsel to offenders. Over two-thirds of the volunteers felt that it was also important for them to engage in such activities as providing employment or educational counseling, educating the public about the causes of crime and delinquency, working as assistants in probation departments or juvenile courts, and working for legislative reform.[15]

The volunteers who participated in the study were evenly divided between programs serving adults and those serving juveniles, and most worked for criminal justice agencies rather than private or independent programs. Four out of five volunteers had received some training before beginning their duties, but only 53 percent regarded their training as adequate. However, virtually all volunteers rated their level of supervision as appropriate.

When asked to assess the problems and satisfactions of volunteering, only one out of five volunteers indicated the existence of any significant problems. These persons reported that there was a lack of communication between volunteers and agency administrators, that clients and professionals sometimes did not take them seriously, and that they received no recognition for their efforts. The greatest source of satisfaction for the volunteers was the feeling that they had helped others and that they had brought about some positive change. In addition, the volunteer experience gave them a sense of being needed.[16]

An earlier study of criminal justice agencies provides us with a different perspective on volunteer efforts. Schier and Berry distributed questionnaires to personnel in 500 correctional institutions and probation and parole departments.[17] Three hundred and fifty of the agencies were known to be operating volunteer programs at the time; the remaining respondents were selected randomly in an attempt to gather data about previously undetected programs.

The survey findings, based on questionnaires returned from 59 percent of the agencies, revealed that approximately two-thirds of the respondents were currently operating volunteer programs. This represented almost a 100 percent growth in volunteer programs over the preceding two- or three-year period. The growth had been particularly pronounced in the area of statewide volunteer coordinating agencies—the survey identified forty.

TABLE 12-1 Volunteer Activities, by Frequency of Participation (N = 545)

Activity	Frequently	On occasion	Never	No information
Shared social events	15%	53%	28%	4%
Referrals for legal assistance	5%	33%	56%	6%
Family counseling	9%	42%	43%	6%
Employment counseling	11%	44%	40%	5%
Assistance in finding a job	12%	47%	36%	5%
Offer opportunity for friendship	66%	26%	4%	4%
Assistance in the formulation of an education program	17%	46%	33%	4%
Actual tutoring in some subjects	9%	23%	63%	5%
Assistance in obtaining psychological attention	6%	37%	52%	5%
Assistance in obtaining medical attention	3%	30%	62%	5%
Assistance in obtaining welfare benefits	3%	25%	68%	4%
Provide transportation	19%	41%	35%	5%
Provide group or individual counseling	54%	31%	11%	4%

SOURCE: From "Contemporary Perspectives on Correctional Volunteerism," by P. Kratcoski, L. D. Kratcoski, and E. Colan, in P. Kratcoski (Ed.), *Correctional Counseling and Treatment*. Copyright 1981 by Wadsworth, Inc. Brooks/Cole Publishing Company, Pacific Grove, California, publisher.

The types of offenders served by the agencies operating volunteer programs were quite varied: 46 percent of the programs served adults, juveniles, and youthful offenders; 60 percent served both males and females; and almost half served both felons and misdemeanants. There were more volunteer programs operating in adult corrections than in the juvenile justice system. There were fewer volunteer programs in the community correctional agencies than in institutional programs.

Most of the programs that used volunteers employed fewer than 25 per month. The typical volunteer met with the agency and/or his client on at least a weekly basis. Only about one-fourth of the clients in correctional agencies that employed volunteer services were actually assigned volunteer assistance.

Most of the volunteer programs relied on relatively passive recruiting measures; less than half the programs had established formal volunteer organizations or recruited through the mass media. They had set neither educational nor experience requirements for volunteers. Virtually all programs screened volunteers through personal interviews. Volunteers selected for the programs were provided with little formal orientation to their jobs; less than one-third received any training whatsoever during their volunteer activities. Supervision of volunteers was also quite limited; although almost half the programs used full-time staff to supervise volunteers, most volunteer coordinators spent fewer than ten hours per week working with volunteers.

Staff in the correctional agencies generally liked and accepted the volunteer programs because they provided more attention to offenders, helped tap available community resources, and improved community relations. A small proportion of staff members was less enthusiastic about the programs, feeling that volunteer programs made it more difficult for staff to control offenders and reduced accountability in agency operations. Sixty percent of the respondents believed that their volunteer programs could be improved. Generally, the agencies expressed a need to develop better control over existing programs (table 12-2).

The need for improvement in volunteer programs was corroborated by another finding of the research. It appeared that volunteer programs typically experienced a 50 percent annual turnover rate. Most volunteers left the programs within six months of entry; 40 percent quit less than three months after beginning.

❑ Volunteer Program Operation

The preceding surveys indicated that volunteer programs can contribute much to corrections. However, inadequate coordination of activities and problems in volunteer-staff relations can impair program effectiveness. These findings prompted the LEAA to sponsor the establishment of a series of guidelines to assist agencies in developing and improving their volunteer programs.[18] These standards address a broad range of issues, including program planning, recruiting, screening, training, job placement, and continuing support for volunteers.

Initial Planning.   The planning of a volunteer program should involve clients, line staff, the agency's director, and the local community. Line staff involvement is especially important because poor staff-volunteer relations are a frequent cause of program failure. Because volunteer programs can cause additional work for staff and because the volunteer's job satisfaction is likely to be influenced by his or her relations with professionals as well as with offenders, positive staff-volunteer relations are essential for program success.

Staff involvement in planning efforts should provide them with an opportunity to ventilate their concerns about the program, such as "Will it be effective?" and "If it's too effective, will staff jobs be endangered?" Staff should have an opportunity to talk with employees in agencies that utilize volunteers and to meet several veteran volunteers. Subsequent planning efforts should seek to maximize staff input and to get real, not just verbal, staff support for the program.

The planning effort should clearly specify program objectives and the roles that volunteers will fulfill. Staff must then be trained to supervise volunteers and to serve as consultants to them to facilitate their work. A director of volunteer services will be required to coordinate volunteer activities. He or she may serve in a full- or part-time capacity, depending on program size.

Recruiting. Recruiting efforts must be aggressive and focused. Citizens cannot be expected to flood the agency with applications for work, at least not in the early stages of program development. The volunteer program must determine the types of persons needed and seek them out. Public speaking engagements and radio, television, and newspaper advertisements can publicize the program. Interested citizens can be invited to visit the agency. Special efforts will probably be needed to encourage minorities and males to volunteer; these groups are traditionally under-represented in volunteer services. After the program has become well established, word of mouth will provide the best method of recruiting; each volunteer can be used as a public relations agent and recruiter.

TABLE 12-2 Improvements Needed in Volunteer Programs

Category	Total response	Percent of programs
1. Better volunteer screening	128	54%
2. More dependable volunteers (high turnover)	107	45
3. More appropriate kinds of people as volunteers	103	43
4. More control of volunteer's relationship with offender	100	42
5. Better reporting of volunteer activities	96	40
6. Better organization of program generally	89	37
7. Other	81	34
8. More money to defray volunteer program expenses	75	32
9. Improve volunteer orientation of training	63	26
10. Allow volunteer more contact with offenders	61	26
11. Improve relations with regular staff	55	23
12. Volunteers take too much staff time	35	15
13. Not enough volunteers	34	14
14. Improve relations with community	33	14
15. Better staff supervision of volunteers	31	13
16. Create more jobs for volunteers	25	11
17. Give volunteers more responsibility and freedom	22	9

SOURCE: Ivan H. Schier et al., *Guidelines and Standards for the Use of Volunteers in Correctional Programs* (Washington, D.C.: Law Enforcement Assistance Administration, 1972), p. 28.

Screening.   The rule of thumb in screening volunteers is *be as selective as if you were paying for volunteer services.* Inappropriate persons and individuals likely to drop out must be identified and weeded out; each candidate must be evaluated and selected with a particular job in mind. Each prospective volunteer should be asked to provide information regarding:

1. The amount of time he or she can donate to the program
2. Familiarity with the community
3. Skills
4. Interests
5. Prior experience
6. Views on crime

No person should be finally selected until after he or she has participated in an orientation program and previewed the job.

Training.   Volunteer training should include the following five components:

1. What the volunteer job is like
2. Overview of the criminal justice system
3. Community resource information
4. What the offender is like
5. Counseling or other job-related skills

Training should also include a ceremonial component—a formal welcome to the agency by its director or a graduation ceremony—to impress upon volunteers the seriousness and importance of their activities.

Figure 12-1 illustrates one agency's approach to volunteer training. The training is divided into three time periods and nine educational components. It is designed to assist the recruit from the initial screening stages to in-service training activities.

Job Placement.   Each volunteer generally must be matched to a job and a supervisor, as well as to an offender. The latter effort should focus on the offender's willingness and ability to work with a volunteer; an attempt must be made to devise a compatible match based on an assessment of the personalities, attitudes, skills, interests, and culture of the two persons. It is also generally desirable to assign offenders to volunteers who live within convenient traveling distance. Most programs attempt to place offenders with volunteers of the same sex and approximate age or older, although both criteria are flexible.

In placing offenders with volunteers, it is important to remember that one-to-one assignments are not the only option available. Volunteers may be assigned in any of the following ways: one-to-many (a single volunteer works with a group of offenders or with an offender and his family), many-to-many (two or more volunteers work as a team with a group of offenders, an offender and his family, or even a more exended group of offenders, persons, and relatives), or many-to-one (a team of volunteers brings their diverse interests and skills to the aid of a single offender).

Continuing Support of Volunteers.   As Schier and Berry note, although the rewards are not financial, *volunteers do get paid.*[19] The payment consists of personal satisfaction and the knowledge of an important job well done. The volunteer program can promote volunteer job satisfaction by special, formal modes of recog-

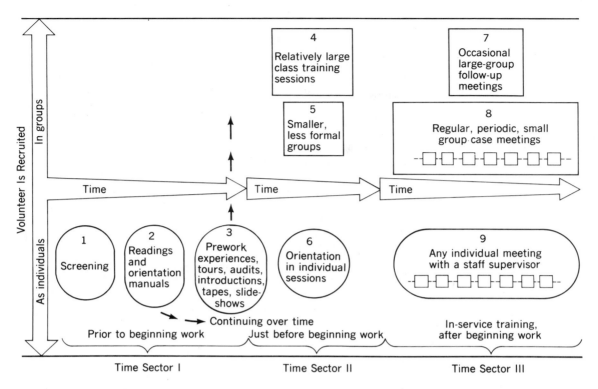

FIGURE 12-1 Court Volunteer Training Opportunities over Time and in Groups or Individually
SOURCE: Ivan Schier et al., *Guidelines and Standards for the Use of Volunteers in Correctional Programs* (Washington, D.C.: Law Enforcement Assistance Administration, 1972), p. 81.

nition (such as banquets for volunteers, volunteer of the month programs, or certificates) and informal, routinely expressed appreciation for volunteer services. No less important is the establishment of a high-quality, challenging volunteer program. In the long run, the opportunity to provide meaningful and valuable service may prove to be the most attractive feature of any volunteer program.

❏ Legal Issues in Volunteer Programs

A number of legal questions surround the administration of volunteer programs.

> Should the volunteer have access to confidential case material, and will his communications be protected by the same degree of privilege as accorded his professional colleague? Should the volunteer be required to sign waivers granting immunity to the agency from his negligent actions?. . . . What happens if the volunteer is an ex-offender? What about situations requiring the arrest of a client?[20]

Problems can also arise concerning the insurance coverage required for volunteers and their use of such government property as automobiles.[21]

To address these potential difficulties, the American Bar Association has recommended the institutionalization of volunteer programs and the establishment of state

A Bill of Rights for Volunteers (Prepared by the American Red Cross)

1. The right to be treated as a co-worker—not just as free help, not as a prima donna
2. The right to a suitable assignment with consideration for personal preference, temperament, life experience, education, and employment background
3. The right to know as much about the organization as possible—its policies, its people, its program
4. The right to training for the job—thoughtfully planned and effectively presented training
5. The right to continuing education on the job as follow-up to initial training, information about new developments, training for greater responsibility
6. The right to sound guidance and direction by someone who is experienced, well informed, patient, and thoughtful and who has the time to invest in giving guidance

7. The right to a place to work, an orderly, designated place, conducive to work and worthy of the job being done
8. The right to promotion and variety of experiences, through advancement to assignments of more responsibility, through transfer from one activity to another, through special assignments
9. The right to be heard, to have a part in planning, to feel free to make suggestions, to have respect shown for an honest opinion
10. The right to recognition in the form of promotion and awards, through day-to-day expressions of appreciation, and by being treated as a bonafide co-worker

SOURCE: Ivan H. Schier et al., *Guidelines and Standards for the Use of Volunteers in Correctional Programs* (Washington, D.C.: Law Enforcement Assistance Administration, 1972), p. 103.

volunteer coordinating offices to provide the legal advice and assistance local programs need.[22] These measures, accompanied by legislation specifying the rights and obligations of volunteers and the agencies for which they work, should permit volunteer programs to function smoothly with no unnecessary complications. Good program planning includes a reassessment of agency insurance needs, efforts to clearly define volunteer roles and their relation to agency staff, and an examination of existing statutes and their potential impact on the volunteer program. These steps are essential if volunteers, agency clients, and staff members are to achieve the full benefits of volunteer efforts.[23]

❑ The Volunteer Probation Officer Program

The Volunteer Probation Officer Program of Lincoln, Nebraska, has been designated an exemplary project by the Law Enforcement Assistance Administration because of its careful screening and training of volunteers and its emphasis on precise matching of volunteers and probationers.[24] Originally, the program attempted to provide youthful (16 to 25 years of age), high-risk misdemeanant offenders with "a structured and intensive learning experience . . . designed to inhibit or 'unlearn' maladaptive behavior patterns."[25] Today the program also serves elderly and mentally retarded offenders as well as female probationers with children who need extra attention.[26] The program lasts for one year; the first two months involve counseling by probation officers and participation in court-conducted educational classes. At this point, offenders are assigned to volunteer counselors.

Counseling assignments attempt to match probationers and volunteers so that the volunteer's skills, resources, and interests match the offender's needs. The

The Lincoln, Nebraska, Volunteer Probation Counselor Program—A Case Study

Person and Offense: W. W. was a 24-year-old male who was charged with two counts of petty larceny. The youth was very upset by the arrests and convictions. He did appear to know the difference between right and wrong but continued to steal despite the first arrest. The current offenses reflected two significant problems: (1) he was exploited by a roommate who manipulated him into stealing; (2) the young man initiated the second theft on his own and appeared to have stolen often in the past.

Family: The youth was rejected by his parents when he was about 6 years old and spent twelve years of his life in the state home for the mentally retarded. Family members refused to allow him to rejoin the family even after he became 18 and had to leave the institution.

Education: Although the young man was mentally retarded, he was able to read and write. He had some minimal abilities with arithmetic.

Employment: The young man had been able to maintain employment as a semiskilled laborer. However, previous to his arrest, a pattern of instability developed. Most recently, the youth decided to quit his relatively well paying job to become a vacuum cleaner salesman. The change in jobs was unfortunate because he lacked the interpersonal skills that a successful salesman should have. He is a dependable worker but does need assistance and direction. He was well liked by his supervisor but had become very sloppy in work habits during the last half year.

Self and Interpersonal Relationships: The youth was sensitive about his mental limitations. He felt insecure about himself yet refused to admit that other people could exploit him. He maintained some social life, participating in planned social acitivities for other mentally retarded persons in the community. However, he had been involved with at least one ex-convict, who appeared to have had a detrimental influence on him. A local clergyman expressed a strong interest in the young man and offered to try to involve him in church-related activities.

Excessive alcohol use may have been another significant problem. The young man was very vague and defensive when discussing his drinking habits.

Relationship Needed: Supervisory. The youth had very limited personal resources. The goal was to maintain the individual functioning in the community.

Volunteer Probation Counselor: A 27-year-old male social work graduate student was assigned to the case. The volunteer counselor was a firm, dedicated, conscientious, persistent, reliable, and concerned person with a great interest in religion. He was married and willing to make his family and home available to the probationer. Although the volunteer counselor had expressed an interest in pursuing counseling as a career, he was perceived by the staff as being somewhat limited in his personal skills. However, because he was a dedicated and responsible person, he seemed well equipped to work with the probationer.

Counseling Relationship: The relationship included dinners with the family, writing budgets and learning how to manage money better, picnics, and assisting the young man in enrolling in night classes when he wanted to attempt to get a GED. Other terms of probation required attendance at alcohol-drug classes as well as writing several essays on topics assigned by the volunteer probationer counselor.

Progress: By the end of the probation period, the youth appeared to have resolved some ambivalent feelings about his father and feelings of rejection by the family, had developed a more favorable self-image, had learned some skills to manage his finances and was able to pay off a number of large debts, and had begun taking additional educational classes. The youth was able to return to his semiskilled job, where he had spent four years working successfully. Problems encountered with other employees and job demands were clarified and resolved. Following completion of the probationary period, a local mental retardation agency was contacted to arrange for a volunteer from their agency to continue to work with him.

During the course of the year, the young man appeared to appreciate the attention and concern shown by both the volunteer counselor and other staff members. All staff members made an effort to talk with the youth whenever he came to the offices.

In describing what he had learned from probation, the youth indicated "not to waste money" and "I am more honest than I was before too." He committed no additional offenses of any kind.

SOURCE: Richard Ku, *The Volunteer Probation Counselor Program, Lincoln, Nebraska* (Washington, D.C.: U.S. Government Printing Office, 1975), pp. 62–64.

program has identified four basic categories of youth in terms of their counseling requirements:

1. *Suitable adult model.* The probationer lacks a suitable adult model with whom he can identify. The youth needs assistance in planning for the future and clarifying his role in the community. By far the greatest number of probationers fall into this category—about 65 percent.

2. *Friend–companion.* Some probationers are unable to relate well to older volunteers. Often the youthful offender is rebelling against the family and/or community. A crucial need is for a dependable friend whom he or she can trust. Approximately 10 percent of the probationers fall into this category.

3. *Supervision.* A small proportion (about 5 percent) of probationers are persons with very limited personal assets. A basic goal is to maintain their functioning in the community outside an institution. They need assistance with very basic skills in living, such as managing finances, obtaining and keeping employment, and finding suitable recreational outlets.

4. *Primary counseling.* The probationer has personal and/or emotional problems that can be aided by talking about them. He is verbal with some insight into himself and the causes of his problems. Furthermore, the youth experiences relief through talking and may be able to make some changes in himself by talking through the problems. Roughly 20 percent of probationers have this need.[27]

Volunteers are matched with probationers on the basis of a number of criteria. Table 12-3 presents the criteria originally employed in the matching effort and the significance of various factors for each type of volunteer-probationer match. For example, the program found that volunteers should be of the same age, sex, and ethnic and occupational background when working with an offender who requires a suitable adult model. These factors are of very little significance when a primary counseling relationship is required; for that relationship, counseling skills are essential.

TABLE 12-3 Importance of Matching Criteria, by Type of Relationship

Criteria	Suitable adult model	Friend/ companion	Supervisory	Primary counsel
Ethnic background	3	3	1	1
Sex	3	3	0	0
Age	3	3	3	0
Education	2	2	0	0
Intelligence	1	1	0	0
Occupation	3	0	0	0
Community contacts	1	1	2	0
Interests	2	3	0	0
Socioeconomic level	2	2	0	2
Counseling skills	1	1	0	3

Note: Code: 3 = Essential for any match (best or second best); 2 = Essential for best match; 1 = Useful; 0 = Not relevant.
Source: Richard Ku, *The Volunteer Probation Counselor Program, Lincoln, Nebraska* (Washington, D.C.: U.S. Government Printing Office, 1975), p. 48.

Today the matching process is somewhat less formal than in years past. The program director, Sammye Henry, reports that the criteria are useful but that many variables cannot be quantified. A case-by-case approach is necessary.[28]

All volunteers are screened through a four-step process. The would-be volunteer fills out a comprehensive application form and is then interviewed by the volunteer coordinator. Each volunteer who passes the interview stage is administered a paper and pencil personality inventory, which is evaluated by psychologists for indications of "gross distortion of personality and . . . other relevant information about personality functioning."[29] The final aspect of screening consists of evaluating the volunteer's performance during the training period. The following are some of the most common reasons for rejecting volunteers:

1. Dishonesty in completing application form
2. Prior criminal offense record, unless the individual is rehabilitated through the probation program
3. Presence of mental and/or emotional problems
4. Poor personal stability, including marginal members of the community who suddenly develop an interest in counseling others even though their own long-term adjustment to the community has been poor, persons experiencing a temporary personal crisis or significant change in life situation, such as going through a divorce
5. Inability to make a commitment for one full year, with the exception of some college students, who may be able to work during the academic school year
6. Joiners (individuals who belong to many different community organizations but rarely bother to contribute much to any one)
7. Inappropriate motivation stemming from personal whim, a desire to reduce boredom, a willingness to be recruited as a personal favor to a friend rather than to any commitment to the program, an axe to grind, or a desire to punish wrongdoers
8. Persons associated with the criminal justice system, including police officers, attorneys, and so forth, are rarely able to function very successfully as counselors. The offender typically perceives these individuals as authority figures and has an extremely difficult time forming a relationship based on trust. However, these individuals may give great assistance with educational classes or in other roles. Also, prominent members of the community are often asked to become volunteer probation counselors. They will often accept the invitation and be genuinely motivated to do a good job as a counselor. Unfortunately, these individuals may be involved with many different kinds of activities so that they simply do not have enough time to be effective as volunteer counselors. Although they probably make a conscientious effort, conflicts in scheduling result in missed appointments or inability to deal with personal crisis when needed.[30]

Volunteer training consists of eight to ten hours of instruction presented over a three-day period. The training provides information about role demands and expectations for the volunteer probation counselor, probation and parole procedures, personal interaction with staff members, the court, the youthful offender, counseling strategies, and crisis intervention techniques.[31] Audiovisual aids are extensively utilized and role-playing exercises comprise a significant element of the training.

Volunteers normally meet with their clients about three times a month. They assist probationers in dealing with employment, educational, and financial problems. Much of their time is spent on recreational activities, which permit the development of a strong, interpersonal relationship in mutually enjoyable surroundings. Both pleasurable experiences and serious problem solving characterize the unique association between volunteers and probationers.

An evaluation of the Lincoln program compared the experiences of high-risk individuals assigned to volunteer probation counselors and high-risk individuals participating in regular probation programming.[32] The high-risk clients were randomly assigned to the volunteer counselor program or regular probation, resulting in forty persons in the experimental group and forty-four in the control (regular probation) group.

During probation, the offenders in the experimental group committed 46 percent fewer offenses than persons in regular probation. Fifty-five percent of the volunteer counselor group committed new offenses during the probationary year, as compared to 70 percent of the control group. Only one in ten of the experimental group committed more than one new offense, but over half the control group committed multiple offenses.

It appears that the preceding achievements were made at relatively little expense. During a one-year period, approximately 350 paid staff hours are devoted to working with volunteer counselors, in addition to the full-time position of the volunteer coordinator and the services of a consulting psychologist.[33] These costs permit over forty volunteers to receive the training and supervision they need to work with their clients and allow the program to carry out the tasks essential to the screening and matching efforts.

❑ Research on Volunteer Programs

A number of studies have attempted to determine the effectiveness of volunteer programs in corrections. An evaluation of the Volunteers in Parole Program established in Illinois is a particularly well designed study of a volunteer program.[34] The Illinois project represented one state's contribution to a larger project developed by the Young Lawyers Section of the American Bar Association. In the program, lawyers volunteered to spend at least six hours a month with a parolee from a state prison. The program was designed to provide limited case load relief to overworked parole officers and to provide one-to-one counseling by a high-status individual in a nonauthoritarian context.

The Illinois volunteers attended a two-day training session that attempted to familiarize them with corrections and parolees. The lawyers were given no further instructions regarding how they were expected to help the parolees.

Parolees who seemed likely to benefit from the program were nominated by their parole officers. Half the persons nominated were then randomly selected to participate in the program; the other parolees served as a control group. Sixteen persons were accepted into each group.

During the nine-month period of research four persons from each group absconded, were arrested, or were revoked from parole. The program also had no effect on the parolees' employment stability; during the course of the program, about three-fourths of the individuals in both groups were working. Parolees who had the assistance of volunteers tended to use community resources more frequently than other parolees, had fewer unrealistic expectations regarding the future, and viewed citizens as more concerned about them than members of the control group. Parolees tended to rely on the lawyers to provide advice on legal and financial issues or parole regulations or simply to be available when they needed someone to talk to.

Although the program was less effective than anticipated, the research provided valuable guidance for future volunteer efforts. In the present program, parolees were not assigned volunteers until six months after release from prison; parolees probably resolved many of their own difficulties during this period and had less to gain from volunteer assistance. Had the volunteers begun their efforts immediately upon the parolee's release, their activities might have proved more meaningful. Additionally, the limited contact between parolees and volunteers may have inhibited program effectiveness—less than one-third of the volunteers met with their clients on a weekly basis; 31 percent of them usually communicated with their clients by telephone rather than in person.[35]

One of the most comprehensive efforts to evaluate the impact of volunteer programs was reported in 1976. It included an assessment of over 250 reports, monographs, memoranda, and so forth pertaining to volunteer program evaluations.[36] Only thirty-five of the studies attempted to assess the impact of volunteer services on agency clients; all but two of the studies focused on community correctional programs.

The assessment concluded that volunteer programs performed as well as or better than formal and traditional correctional programs. The researchers generally criticized the quality of research on volunteer programs and suggested that volunteer programs should state their objectives in a measurable form, specifying who is to be affected by the program, the nature of the anticipated program impact, and how long the effect will last.[37] Such steps would significantly enhance future evaluation efforts.

Paraprofessionals and Ex-offenders in Corrections

Paraprofessionals and ex-offenders working in corrections can also compensate for personnel shortages and offer several advantages over professional staff. Because of their personal experiences and cultural backgrounds, they are often uniquely prepared to assist offenders in rehabilitation and reintegration programs.

❏ Indigenous Paraprofessionals

Indigenous paraprofessionals are drawn from the same community, culture, and socioeconomic status as offenders; some of them may even be ex-offenders. These persons may be expected to share an understanding of the problems offenders face and to possess the ability to communicate with them in a manner difficult to achieve for middle-class professionals or volunteers. The indigenous worker is "a peer of the client and shares a common background, language, ethnic origin, style, and group of interests . . . he 'belongs,' he is a 'significant other,' he is 'one of us.' The style of the nonprofessional is significantly related to his effectiveness, because it matches the clients."[38]

Sharing a background similar to that of the offender enables the paraprofessional to develop rapport with his clients more quickly and spontaneously. The social distance that separates the traditional correctional worker from his or her client is minimized because interracial and intercultural difficulties do not have to be overcome. It has been suggested that paraprofessionals may actually be more effective in working with offenders than professionals.

> The indigenous leader can communicate instantly to the suspicious and distrustful client, avoiding noblesse oblige, in a way that many middle-class professionals cannot do when dealing with disaffected, hostile, anomic youths who see the middle-class agency worker as a part of the system against which he is fighting. . . . Indigenous personnel who "speak the client's language" can form an extremely effective bridge between the milieu of the client and the milieu of the agency; they can make important contributions to the counseling team in contacting the clients to be served, in maintaining them through their agency contacts, and may be particularly effective in follow-up work with the clients in their home, community, and on the job. A client is more likely to report continuing difficulties, after his counseling contacts, to an indigenous worker, than he is to the professional interviewer toward whom the ethic of mutual cooperation and courtesy requires that he affirm the success of the counseling and deny continued problems.[39]

Research indicates that the assistance probationers and parolees perceive as most valuable is provided not by professional probation or parole staff, but by family members, friends, and community resources.[40] Professional staff share this perception; regardless of the intensity of supervision provided, aid received from community members and resources seems more influential than correctional staff services.

Like volunteers, paraprofessionals can supplement professional staff, assuming roles and responsibilities in keeping with their skills, education, and experience. Their presence can enable professional workers to use their time more efficiently, focusing on activities only they are authorized or able to carry out. At the same time, the offender's and correctional agency's needs can be better met because professionals need no longer be torn between what they must do (that is, paperwork) and what they would like to do (work more intensively with their clients). The combined efforts of professional and paraprofessional staff can ensure that no aspect of agency administration or client services suffers because of an unmanageable work load.

❑ Special Role of the Ex-offender

Paraprofessionals who are also ex-offenders have several unique attributes to offer their correctional clients. Not only have they shared the same culture and community as the offender, but they have also confronted some of the same problems, made some of the same choices, and experienced some of the same repercussions. They are thus in a special position to understand and communicate with offenders and to serve as a living illustration of the possibility of reform.

Self-help groups have been found to be particularly valuable in working with individuals who have been unreachable by more traditional therapeutic measures. Alcoholics Anonymous is probably the best known "mutual aid society"; it is one of the few programs to produce consistently positive results with persons suffering from the physical, psychological, and social problems of alcoholism. Several drug treatment programs have adopted the AA model in an effort to assist narcotics addicts in a similar manner.

Although self-help groups may appear to be simply a commonsense approach to rehabilitation, they are based upon sound criminological theory. Over twenty-five years ago, Donald Cressey first identified five principles for changing criminals:

1. If criminals are to be changed, they must be assimilated into groups that emphasize values conducive to law-abiding behavior and, concurrently, alienated from groups emphasizing values conducive to criminality. Because our experience has been that the majority of criminals experience great difficulty in securing intimate contacts in ordinary groups, special groups whose major common goal is the reformation of criminals must be created.

2. The more relevant the common purpose of the group to the reformation of criminals, the greater will be its influence on the criminal members' attitudes.

3. The more cohesive the group, the greater the members' readiness to influence others and the more relevant the problem of conformity to group norms. The criminals who are to be reformed and the persons expected to effect the change must, then, have a strong sense of belonging to one group: Between them, there must be a genuine "we" feeling. The reformers, consequently, should not be identifiable as correctional officers or social workers.

4. Both reformers and those to be reformed must achieve status within the group by exhibition of "proreform" or anticriminal values and behavior patterns. As a novitiate . . . he is a therapeutic parasite and not actually a member until he accepts the group's own system for assigning status.

5. The most effective mechanism for exerting group pressure on members will be found in groups so organized that criminals are induced to join with noncriminals for the purpose of changing other criminals. A group in which criminal A joins with some noncriminals to change criminal B is probably most effective in changing A and not B. In order to change criminal B, criminal A must necessarily share the values of the anticriminal members.[41]

Today these principles have become standard guidelines for offender rehabilitation. If criminals are to be changed, they will be more receptive to influence from persons who are like themselves (but express prosocial values and exhibit conforming behavior) than persons who are very different and represent attitudes and values that are unfamiliar and/or unacceptable. The ex-offender thus acts as the link between the criminal and a new way of life.

Correctional programs that utilize ex-offenders not only better assist their clients, but may benefit ex-offenders as well. Becoming a change agent, a person who facilitates change in other persons, can be an extremely meaningful experience for the ex-offender. For the ex-offender, such work can:

1. Use his knowledge as a resource rather than a liability
2. Involve him actively as a reformer rather than as a perpetual enemy or a persistent dependent
3. Constitute a rite of passage back from a criminal to a noncriminal status

4. Provide him with a career that could be a source of personal and social esteem rather than a source of stigma and degradation[42]

Such experiences may be expected to cement further the ex-offender's ties to the community and law-abiding behavior, as well as to provide him with a meaningful employment opportunity. Today we find ex-offenders most widely accepted and used in the drug and alcohol treatment network. Barriers still exist in many government agencies for the recruitment of ex-offenders as staff.

❏ The New Careers Movement

During the 1960s, a new perspective developed in the field of social services. This approach focused on using persons in counseling and other service roles who had experienced problems similar to those of the people they were helping. It was hoped that such persons would be more effective than professional staff in providing aid to their clients. It was also anticipated that the paraprofessionals would find new careers in the field of social services that would help them improve their socio-economic status, self-esteem, and further their progress up the occupational ladder. This movement was labeled, appropriately enough, "new careers."

The new careers movement began with programs that used self-sufficient persons who had previously received welfare payments to counsel poor or indigent persons presently receiving public assistance.[43] The programs received wide acclaim and the concept spread to the field of corrections. Douglas Grant, president of the New Careers Development Organization, established a program to train inmates for work as program development assistants. The men assumed a variety of positions upon release on parole—"training nonprofessional aides, doing surveys of new careers or job possibilities, and helping set up new career positions within social agencies."[44] Only one trainee was returned to prison for committing a new crime. The New Careers Program identified a large number of roles offenders could perform: in-service training of correctional personnel, research, program planning and development, community relations, rehabilitation services, and advocacy.[45]

In 1968, the Vocational Rehabilitation Act was amended to provide for the funding of New Careers Programs in state vocational rehabilitation agencies. At about the same time, ex-offenders began to be used as probation and parole aides in California. Three years later, the California State Personnel Board developed a career ladder for new careerists so that they could be promoted through the ranks to the position of parole officer.[46]

The federal probation system began experimenting with paraprofessionals as full- and part-time aides in the early 1970s. The demonstration project proved so successful that additional funds were allocated for program expansion. In 1973, the National Advisory Commission on Criminal Justice Standards and Goals took a strong position on the employment of ex-offenders in corrections.

> Correctional agencies should take immediate and affirmative action to recruit and employ capable and qualified ex-offenders in correctional roles.
> 1. Policies and practices restricting the hiring of ex-offenders should be reviewed and, where found unreasonable, eliminated or changed.
> 2. Agencies not only should open their doors to the recruitment of ex-offenders but also should seek qualified applicants.

3. Training programs should be developed to prepare ex-offenders to work in various correctional positions, and career development should be extended to them so they can advance in the system.[47]

❏ Paraprofessionals and Ex-offenders in Corrections

There are no statistics available on the total number of paraprofessionals employed in community correctional programs. We do know, however, that halfway house administrators generally view a mix of professional and paraprofessional staff as the best method of staffing a halfway house program and that paraprofessionals tend to be especially well represented in private community correctional programs.[48]

Although some progress has been made in recent years in hiring ex-offenders in state correctional agencies, there is considerable room for improvement. In 1971, there were 280 ex-offenders working in correctional agencies; eight correctional systems prohibited such employment. Six years later, only four states prohibited employment of ex-offenders and 315 ex-offenders were employed in correctional agencies.[49]

A 1977 survey of correctional administrators' attitudes toward the employment of ex-offenders reported far more advantages than disadvantages. The major strengths of ex-offender employment were their ability to relate to other offenders, their motivation, commitment, and perseverance, their ability to handle stressful situations, and their realistic expectations. The most frequently mentioned disadvantages were the possibility of peer manipulation, poor relations with nonoffender employees, lack of education, the inability to write effectively, and difficulty in communicating.[50] In addition, there is the difficulty of finding suitable candidates.

❏ Probation/Parole Officer Aide Programs

Although probation/parole officer aide programs are few in number, they can be extremely successful. Ohio's Parole Officer Aide (POA) Program, discussed in chapter 8, provides a good example of a well-designed and administered project. The Federal Probation Officer Aide Program, which now employs over forty paraprofessionals in twenty-five judicial districts, is probably the largest single employer of ex-offenders in community-based corrections. The program began with an experimental project in Chicago, which recruited paraprofessionals from the neighborhoods in which probationers lived.[51] They were recommended by probation officers and social service agencies; others made their own inquiries regarding the program after hearing of it from friends or relations.

The aides worked on a part-time basis and were paid according to the number of probationers supervised; no more than three clients were assigned to each aide. The paraprofessionals counseled their clients and provided assistance in securing housing, welfare benefits, medical and mental health services, and employment and training.

The probationers were generally receptive to supervision by aides; black clients were especially responsive to black aides. One chronic offender remarked after meeting "his lavishly dressed and heavily bearded POA for the first time: 'Well, I see the federal probation system is finally hiring some good men!' "[52]

Project staff were also pleased with the performance of the aides, many of whom benefited from their experiences in the program.

> One man, a black nonoffender with a history of alcoholism, was appointed chief counselor and director of a program for alcoholic recovery of employees, sponsored by the U.S. Post Office in Chicago. . . . A white former offender and barber by trade joined the POCA Project and began attending classes at a local junior college. He was later admitted to a major university in the criminal justice program and was hired by the State of Illinois Department of Corrections as an adult parole officer. . . . A black former offender, after serving as a POA, obtained employment with the Illinois Department of Corrections as a youth supervisor.[53]

The project staff concluded that employing indigenous paraprofessionals is a feasible method of supplementing professional staff. Members of the local community were found to be "interested, available, and able to work well under professional supervision."[54] The aides provided considerable assistance to professional probation officers, often being able to intervene in situations where regular staff might have encountered difficulties.

❏ Ex-offenders' Self-help Groups

Although correctional administrators routinely support the employment of ex-offenders in corrections, the practice is not widespread. Not surprisingly, ex-offenders who wish to assist offenders in working through their personal, economic, and social problems have in many cases decided to band together to form their own mutual aid societies. These groups can now be found in most large cities, either as independent, local efforts or as chapters of large, nationally based offender aid organizations.

The largest and best-known offender self-help group is the Fortune Society. Today it has a mailing list of almost 40,000 names and more than 20,000 financial contributors.[55] It was established in 1967 by David Rothenberg, who at the time was producing a play describing the prison experience written by an ex-convict. After viewing the play, *Fortune and Men's Eyes,* audiences were asked to stay and discuss it. Interest in the project grew, especially after judges, ex-convicts, and correctional personnel were invited to participate in the discussions.

As a result of his experiences with the play and its discussion groups, Rothenberg and a few colleagues decided to establish a nonprofit organization to address the needs of ex-offenders. Rothenberg found that his efforts to publicize the program drew the attention of "every ex-con within fifty miles."[56] By 1970, he had abandoned his other activities to focus on prisoner aid and prison reform efforts.

Between 4,000 and 5,000 persons seek the assistance of the Fortune Society each year.[57] About one-third of these persons obtain job placements or other assistance. Fortune Society activities include job development, counseling, housing assistance, vocational training, academic tutoring, photography seminars, and a pen pal project for inmates. The society publishes a newsletter, *The Fortune News,* that chronicles prison problems and identifies potential remedies; for example, the organization strongly endorses community correctional programs. Much of the group's efforts involve speaking engagements and other public relations projects devoted to prison reform.

The Fortune Society

Vinnie DeFrancesco is a good example of a Fortune Society staff member. Now 33, he spent a total of nine years in various New York State prisons, was a drug user for about fifteen years, and has been arrested about twenty times, by his own count. DeFrancesco is a member of Fortune's team of speakers, and when he sits in an office telling his story, his words are persuasive and articulate, though they abandon grammatical perfection in favor of a mixture of street jargon and prison slang.

DeFrancesco has been working at Fortune for three years. Born in Brooklyn, he was the product of a broken marriage. "I had a stepfather who didn't care," he recalls. "I was used as a lever. He was jealous if my mother showed anything toward me—and I was jealous 'cause he took my mother away. I was getting resentful. I was sending out signs like crazy that they should've read."

Some of those signs were constant troublemaking in school and involvement with street gangs, drugs, and alcohol. After several prison terms for drug offenses and robberies, DeFrancesco says, he started to realize that his sentences were getting longer. "It hit me that these months were turning into years." Returning to prison became a familiar routine, and even some of the faces on the inside were becoming familiar. He was greeted by the standard prison jokes, such as "Hey, what took you so long?"

"That's getting institutionalized," DeFrancesco says. "It's 'How many scores did you make?' and 'How much dope did you shoot?' but you get back to your cell and it's reality. I was scared to death. I came out and here I am, four and a half years later."

When DeFrancesco and other counselors talk about their own initial contacts with the Fortune Society, they say that its single most useful and successful function was to serve as a place where excons could become "un-institutionalized." Many former inmates, they say, emerge from prison unable to make the simplest decisions or to perform elementary tasks, like ordering a meal in a restaurant or dialing a phone.

DeFrancesco says he found Fortune a place to talk to people with whom he felt comfortable, a better place to hang around killing time than the street. He says he is always conscious of how easy it would be to slip back into the street scene. After a few months of making time around Fortune's offices, he says, he was told of an opening on the society's own counseling staff. "I couldn't get 'yes' out fast enough," he recalls.

SOURCE: "The Fortune Society—Championing the Ex-Offender," *Corrections Magazine*, 1(5) (1975):18–19. Copyright 1975 by *Corrections Magazine* and Criminal Justice Publications, Inc., 116 West 32 Street, New York, NY 10001.

There are many smaller organizations devoted to the ex-offender's needs. Bill Sands established the Seven Step Program in several cities in the western part of the United States. The seven steps (see box nearby) represent program philosophy, which emphasizes honesty, responsibility, and personal growth.

Some ex-offender programs provide extensive services for ex-convicts. Seven Keys to Freedom is a national organization with over sixty-eight chapters; it emphasizes pre- and postrelease programs, employment assistance, and juvenile programs.[58] Efforts from Ex-Convicts in Washington, D.C., operates a bail bond program, a halfway house, an emergency shelter for newly released offenders who have no place to stay, an employment and training program, and was recently licensed to operate a detective agency employing ex-offenders as security guards.[59] Although their size and services differ, all ex-offender organizations attempt to use the ex-convict's expertise to assist offenders in adjusting to society in a constructive and meaningful way.

The Seven Steps

F   1. *Facing* the truth about ourselves, we decided to change.

R   2. *Realizing* that there is a power from which we can gain strength, we decided to use that power.

E   3. *Evaluating* ourselves by taking an honest self-appraisal, we examine both our strengths and weaknesses.

E   4. *Endeavoring* to help ourselves overcome our weaknesses, we enlisted the aid of that power to help us concentrate on our strengths.

D   5. *Deciding* that our freedom is worth more than our resentments, we are using that power to help us free ourselves from those resentments.

O   6. *Observing* that daily progress is necessary, we set an attainable goal toward which we can work each day.

M   7. *Maintaining* our own freedom, we pledge to help others as we have been helped.

SOURCE: "The Fortune Society—Championing the Ex-Offender," *Corrections Magazine* 1(5) (1975): 19. Copyright 1975 by *Corrections Magazine* and Criminal Justice Publications, Inc., 116 West 32 Street, New York, NY 10001.

Problems and Issues in Employing Paraprofessionals and Ex-offenders in Corrections

❑ Staff Relations

Given the shortage of professionals in the field of corrections, one might assume that agencies would rush to hire paraprofessionals to fill jobs for which the education, experience, or status of a professional is not required. This has not been the case. Several problems that seem to accompany the use of paraprofessionals, regardless of the nature of the field in which they are employed, have inhibited the use of paraprofessionals in corrections.

Some of these difficulties relate to professionals' attitudes toward employing paraprofessionals. To many staff members, paraprofessionals represent a significant threat to personal, social, and occupational status. Correctional workers, particularly probation and parole officers, have labored long and hard to achieve professionalism. Many are extremely sensitive to the idea that some or any of their job functions can be assumed by persons with less education or training than themselves. Using paraprofessionals is interpreted to mean that the work is less complex, specialized, or important than it is; in effect, that the professional is not as essential to the organization as previously thought. At some point, this concern can easily develop into a fear for one's job.

Paraprofessionals generally do not share the same community or personal experiences as professionals in corrections; they are often more like offenders than staff members in terms of ethnic and cultural identity. This may create communication barriers between the two groups. The special rapport that paraprofessionals may be able to develop with their clients can threaten the professional employee.

Concerned and dedicated correctional staff may work hard to overcome cultural or racial differences that the paraprofessional never encounters. Although staff members may admire the ease with which paraprofessionals develop rapport with their clients, they may also resent it.

Paraprofessionals can also have difficulties on the job. Well-defined job descriptions and careful screening efforts are required to ensure that the persons hired possess the skills necessary to fulfill paraprofessional responsibilities and the sensitivity and ability to work with agency staff as well as offenders. Paraprofessionals are, in many ways, in limbo. They are not professionals, with the status and authority of that position, although they perform many tasks identical to those of professional staff. They are not clients, although they have been selected because they have much in common with agency clients. They are expected to act as a bridge or a link between the agency and its clients. They may well be placed under considerable pressure from staff and clients to "act like one of us" or to prove where their real loyalty lies. Maturity, self-confidence, and a sense of personal direction are essential if the paraprofessional is to survive such loyalty tests and emerge from the role conflict as both a valuable employee for the agency and a trusted and helping aide to its clients.

❏ Career Opportunities for Paraprofessionals

If the preceding difficulties can be worked out, an additional problem still remains. Paraprofessional positions are commonly dead-end jobs. The teacher's aide cannot become a certified teacher and the counselor's aide cannot become a professional counselor without meeting educational and other requirements for these positions. Many paraprofessionals, after years of experience, become extremely frustrated when they remain in their same jobs while the agency hires outsiders with less work experience to fill vacant positions.

Two measures are required to overcome these difficulties. First, job requirements for professional positions must be modified to take into account the paraprofessional's experience and expertise. The weight attached to these qualities will necessarily reflect the specific tasks the professional employee performs; it may not always be possible to work one's way to the top without meeting traditional job requirements. One method of dealing with this difficulty is to create new positions superior to that of the paraprofessional but below professional rank. Establishing such career ladders makes job mobility a possibility for most if not all paraprofessionals.

The other essential step in furthering career opportunities for paraprofessionals is promoting educational opportunities for employees. Tuition stipends and educational leave programs will enable the ambitious paraprofessional (as well as regular staff) to take the necessary self-improvement steps to achieve higher employment rank. These programs provide considerable benefits for the agency as well as the employee: The agency obtains a more educated employee with considerable job experience, and good employee morale, an essential requirement of organizational effectiveness, is strongly supported.

❏ The Ex-offender in Corrections

Although some states are adopting more enlightened policies regarding the employment of ex-offenders in correctional agencies and correctional administrators

The Ex-offender as a Youth Counselor

An increasing juvenile crime rate in Baltimore County, Maryland, became dramatically evident in 1974 when 52 percent of all arrests made were of juveniles under the age of 18 years. This figure illustrated the failure of the traditional juvenile justice system within the county and pointed out the fact that the usual methods of arrest, juvenile court proceedings, and attempts at rehabilitation had done little to improve the situation or, ultimately, solve the dilemma. Additional emphasis was placed on the problem when a study conducted by the state's attorney's office determined that 92 percent of all juveniles who were processed by the juvenile court became recidivists.

The Baltimore County Police Department, a recognized innovator in policing procedures, responded to the dilemma in December of 1975 by beginning a program that the news media termed "a bold experiment." A youth counselor, Mr. Peter J. Kambouris, was hired by the police department to counsel and advise juvenile offenders. Ironically, 28-year-old Mr. Kambouris is an ex-

convict and narcotics addict who served four separate terms in state institutions for burglary offenses. By pirating the adage "it takes a thief to catch a thief," Police Chief Joseph Gallen decided to "hire a thief to rehabilitate juvenile offenders."

Despite the fact that, prior to his employment with the police department, the ex-burglar had undergone one of the most extensive background investigations in department history, his acceptance into the confines of the organization was met with great reluctance by many of the officers and outright hostility from others. Perhaps the individual most adamantly opposed to the plan was a former burglary detective who had arrested the prospective counselor on at least three occasions. Even though Mr. Kambouris had been highly recommended by his parole agent and the various youth counseling organizations for which he had done volunteer counseling work, the detective remained steadfast in his conviction that the ex-convict's trustworthiness was subject to question.

generally support these efforts, the practice is still extremely limited. Personal prejudices may be largely at fault, but the explanations may well be more complex. We do not really know how many ex-offenders want to work in corrections; many persons no doubt want to rid themselves of all links to crime and criminal justice after a correctional experience. We also know very little about the actual behavior of ex-offenders as correctional workers; most of the research has focused on the attitudes of the ex-offenders, their clients, and professional staff, rather than on more objective measures of job performance. Finally, most of the programs that utilize ex-offenders use them so sparingly that it is almost impossible to determine whether program results are attributable to the particular persons working in the program or if they can be generalized to other correctional programs.

Clearly, more ex-offenders must be employed in corrections and the advantages, disadvantages, and effectiveness of employing them as correctional employees must be comprehensively evaluated. Without such efforts, correctional administrators' expressed positive attitudes toward ex-offender employment are merely words unsupported either by conscience or commitment.

Future Directions

Perhaps more than any single correctional program, the use of volunteers, paraprofessionals, and ex-offenders offers tremendous potential benefit to the field of corrections. Clients, correctional staff, and correctional organizations can benefit from their

Realizing that even the slightest dissent might jeopardize the future of a project of this nature by impeding public acceptance, the department commissioned the doubtful investigator to conduct an independent background investigation of the proposed youth counselor to determine if, indeed, he had been rehabilitated.

An exhaustive three-month investigation ensued. Continuous surveillance was complemented by a number of in-depth interviews with many of the ex-burglar's former associates, some still in prison. The resulting information convinced the skeptical detective that Mr. Kambouris was truly rehabilitated and guaranteed the program an opportunity to display its usefulness. Peter J. Kambouris, ex-addict, ex-burglar, and ex-convict, subsequently became Baltimore County, Maryland's first civilian youth counselor.

From the more than 1,500 juveniles that the Baltimore County Police Department processes monthly, officers of the youth division select those whom they believe would most benefit from the unique type of counseling program that Mr. Kambouris provides.

Generally, from 30 to 50 cases are referred to the youth counselor each month. The offenses involved cover the entire spectrum of criminal activity, from shoplifting and vandalism to burglary and severe narcotics use. The personal experiences of Mr. Kambouris and the sufferings he endured while in jail enable him to relate to delinquent youth in a previously unheard of fashion. The success of the project to date has been phenomenal, simply because the juveniles and their parents accept the counselor not only for what he is, but because of what he was—a delinquent, narcotics addict, burglar, and convict. Youth acknowledge the fact that, despite his past failures, Mr. Pete Kambouris has become a productive citizen and serves as a model for their future development. To date, of the youths he has counseled, not one has been brought back before the youth division as a repeat offender.

SOURCE: Joseph R. Gallen and Patricia Hanges, "The Effective Use of Formerly Convicted Felons in Police Functions," *The Police Chief* 44(1) (1977): 34, 35. Reprinted by permission.

contact with these persons, whose special perspective on their work can permit them to make unique and immeasurable contributions to many aspects of correctional programming. The resultant opportunity to utilize professional staff more effectively can both improve employee morale and further professionalize the field of corrections.

Even with all the preceding benefits, volunteer, paraprofessional, and ex-offender programs are not failure-proof. Indeed, many problems can and do accompany program operations. All these programs must be sold to correctional staff, their clients, and the community. The programs must be carefully planned, administered, and monitored, with great sensitivity to interpersonal relations as well as task assignment. These programs' future rests with correctional administrators; their willingness or reluctance to initiate, sell, and oversee the programs will determine the growth and success or decline and failure of these potentially dynamic and meaningful correctional strategies.

Summary

Citizen participation in corrections is essential for meaningful correctional programming. Citizens can assist correctional administrators in policymaking, initiate or facilitate reform efforts, or provide direct services to correctional agencies and clients. Most citizens fulfill direct service volunteer roles in corrections, which are easily tailored to any willing participant's skills and interests.

Volunteer efforts are nothing new to corrections, although they did not gain real support and popularity until the late 1960s and early 1970s. Today, thousands of volunteer programs are in operation across the United States, and volunteers serve in many diverse roles. Their contributions permit agencies to make better use of professional staff, individualize services to clients, and increase public awareness of correctional programs, problems, and issues.

Research indicates that veteran volunteers are a dedicated group of individuals who feel they have something special to offer offenders; they view social conditions as the cause of crime and rehabilitation as the goal of corrections. Most volunteer programs are relatively small, perhaps because recruitment efforts are usually low key and volunteer turnover rates are high. Little training is provided to most volunteers, and, although correctional staff generally accept volunteer programs, they feel there is room for improvement.

It appears that improvement is most needed in the areas of volunteer program planning, recruitment, screening, training, job placement, and continued support of volunteers. Some volunteer programs, such as the Lincoln, Nebraska, Volunteer Probation Counselor Program, have been able to overcome these and other difficulties and achieve considerable benefits for offenders. Generally, despite various operational problems, volunteer programs work as well or better than more traditional correctional efforts.

Paraprofessionals and ex-offenders can make special contributions to corrections because of their familiarity and understanding of offender problems and needs. Ex-offenders may be particularly helpful in this regard because they have "walked in the client's shoes" and can serve as role models for reform. Ex-offenders may also benefit from their work in corrections because of the rewarding interpersonal experience, status, and career opportunities provided.

Although there is considerable support for these programs and evidence that paraprofessionals and ex-offenders can achieve positive results, the employment of these nontraditional workers is extremely limited. Negative or ambiguous professional staff attitudes and limited career advancement opportunities are common problems. These difficulties, coupled with a desire to work outside the system, lead many ex-offenders to devote their efforts to self-help, mutual aid societies, designed to help offenders live law-abiding and meaningful lives.

If properly used, volunteers, paraprofessionals, and ex-offenders can significantly improve the quality of correctional programming. Inappropriate or inadequate utilization will limit their function to a "dike-plugging" role, in which their haphazard employment in desperate situations minimizes their potential effectiveness.

KEY WORDS AND CONCEPTS

change agents
direct service roles
Fortune Society
indigenous
  paraprofessionals
job placement

new careers
  movement
personnel resources
planning
prisoner visiting
  programs

rapport
recruiting
screening
self-help groups
training

NOTES

1. National Advisory Commission on Criminal Justice Standards and Goals, *Corrections* (Washington, D.C.: U.S. Government Printing Office, 1973), p. 227.
2. Ibid., pp. 228–230.
3. Ibid., p. 228.
4. Ivan H. Schier, Judith L. Berry et al., *Guidelines and Standards for the Use of Volunteers in Correctional Programs* (Washington, D.C.: Law Enforcement Assistance Administration, 1972),
   pp. iii, 5.
5. Louis P. Carney, *Corrections and the Community* (Englewood Cliffs, N.J.: Prentice-Hall, 1977), p. 283.
6. Ibid.
7. Vernon Fox, *Community-Based Corrections* (Englewood Cliffs, N.J.: Prentice-Hall, 1977), p. 244.
8. Keith J. Leinhouts, "Royal Oaks' Experience with Professionals and Volunteers in Probation," in *Corrections in the Community,* George C. Killinger and Paul F. Cromwell (eds.) (St. Paul, Minn.: West Publishing, 1974), pp. 270–272.
9. Ibid., p. 275.
10. Ibid., p. 276.
11. Ibid.
12. Schier et al., *Guidelines and Standards,* p. 167.
13. National Council on Crime and Delinquency, *Volunteers in Probation. A Report on the National Survey and Questionnaire Conducted by VIP-NCCD on the Volunteer Juvenile and Criminal Justice Movement in the United States* (Royal Oaks, Mich.: National Council on Crime and Delinquency, 1979).
14. Peter C. Kratcoski, Lucille Dunn Kratcoski, and Eileen Colan, "Contemporary Perspectives on Correctional Volunteerism," in *Correctional Counseling and Treatment,* Peter Kratcoski (ed.) (North Scituate, Mass.: Duxbury Press, 1981), pp. 121–133.
15. Ibid., pp. 129, 130.
16. Ibid., p. 130.
17. Schier et al., *Guidelines and Standards,* pp. 1–33.
18. Ibid., pp. 36–120.
19. Ibid., p. 105.
20. Carney, *Corrections and the Community,* p. 296.
21. Ibid.
22. American Bar Association, *The National Volunteer Parole Aide Program, Volunteers in the Criminal Justice System: Rights and Legal Liability* (Washington, D.C.: American Bar Association, 1974), p. 10.
23. Ibid.
24. Richard Ku, *The Volunteer Probation Counselor Program, Lincoln, Nebraska* (Washington, D.C.: U.S. Government Printing Office, 1975).
25. Ibid., p. 2.
26. Personal communication with Sammye Henry, program director, August, 13, 1982.
27. Ku, *The Volunteer Probation Counselor Program,* pp. 14, 15.
28. Personal communication with Sammye Henry.
29. Ku, *The Volunteer Probation Counselor Program,* p. 28.
30. Ibid., p. 30.
31. Ibid., p. 39.
32. Ibid., pp. 69–74.
33. Ibid., pp. 75, 76.
34. John J. Berman, "An Experiment in Parole Supervision," *Evaluation Quarterly* 2(1) (1978): 71–90.
35. Ibid., p. 85.
36. Frank P. Scioli and Thomas J. Cook, "How Effective Are Volunteers?" *Crime and Delinquency* 22(2) (1976): 192–200.
37. Ibid., p. 199.

38. R. Rieff and F. Reissman, *The Indigenous Non-Professional* (New York: National Institute of Labor Education, 1964), pp. 44–48.

39. J. E. Gordon, "Project Cause, the Federal Anti-Poverty Program, and Some Implications of Sub-Professional Training," *American Psychologist,* May 1965, p. 334.

40. J. D. Lohman et al., "An Afterview of Supervision," Research Report No. 10, *The San Francisco Project: A Study of Federal Probation and Parole* (Berkeley: University of California, School of Criminology, 1966).

41. Donald R. Cressey, "Changing Criminals: The Application of the Theory of Differential Association," *American Journal of Sociology* 61 (1955): 118, 119. Reprinted by permission of University of Chicago Press.

42. LaMar T. Empey, "Offender Participation in the Correctional Process: General Theoretical Issues," in *Offenders as a Correctional Manpower Resource* (Washington, D.C.: Joint Commission on Correctional Manpower and Training, 1968), pp. 11, 12.

43. Fox, *Community-Based Corrections,* p. 166.

44. Institute for the Study of Crime and Delinquency, *The New Careers Development Project: Final Report* (Sacramento, Calif.: Institute for the Study of Crime and Delinquency, 1967), p. 1.

45. J. Douglas Grant, "Vital Components of a Model Program Using the Offender in the Administration of Justice," in *Offenders as a Correctional Manpower Resource* (Washington, D.C.: Joint Commission on Correctional Manpower and Training, 1968), pp. 65–70.

46. Carney, *Corrections and the Community,* p. 303.

47. National Advisory Commission on Criminal Justice Standards and Goals, *Corrections,* p. 478.

48. John M. McCartt and Thomas J. Mangogna, *Guidelines and Standards for Halfway Houses and Community Treatment Centers* (Washington, D.C.: U.S. Government Printing Office, 1973), p. 116.

49. Robert R. Smith and Charles M. Petko, "An Updated Survey of Four Policies and Practices in American Adult Corrections," *Journal of Criminal Justice* 8 (1980): 125.

50. Ibid.

51. Donald W. Beless et al., "Use of Indigenous Nonprofessionals in Probation and Parole," *Federal Probation* 36(1) (1972): 13–15.

52. Ibid., p. 15.

53. Ibid.

54. Ibid.

55. "The Fortune Society—Championing the Ex-Offender," *Corrections Magazine* 1(5) (1975): 13–20.

56. Ibid., p. 14.

57. Ibid.

58. Fox, *Community-Based Corrections,* p. 170.

59. Ibid., p. 172.

FOR FURTHER READING

Blew, Carol H., and Kenneth Carlson, *The Ohio Parole Officer Aide Program* (Washington, D.C.: U.S. Government Printing Office, 1976).

Hansen, Stephen, and Ivan H. Schier, *Corrections Volunteer Information Portfolio* (Boulder, Colorado: National Information Center on Volunteerism, 1979).

Ku, Richard, *The Volunteer Probation Counselor Program, Lincoln, Nebraska* (Washington, D.C.: U.S. Government Printing Office, 1975).

Lauffer, Armand, and Sarah Gorodezky, *Volunteers* (Beverly Hills, Calif.: Sage Publications, 1977).

Schier, Ivan H., et al., *Guidelines and Standards for the Use of Volunteers in Correctional Programs* (Washington, D.C.: Law Enforcement Assistance Administration, 1972).

Schwartz, Ira M., Donald R. Jensen, and Michael J. Mahoney, *Volunteers in Juvenile Justice* (Washington, D.C.: National Institute of Law Enforcement and Criminal Justice, 1977).

13: Planning for the Future

IN CRIMINAL JUSTICE, THE 1980s will be known as the decade of the prison-crowding crisis. From 1980 to year's end 1988, the prison population in the United States increased approximately 90 percent, from 329,821 inmates under custody in 1980 to 627,402 inmates by January 1, 1989.[1] It has been estimated that an additional 800 new beds are needed each week just to keep up with the population increases.

Perhaps one of the greatest challenges facing correctional administrators today is the challenge to design, implement, and evaluate community-based correctional programs. United States' correctional systems, long dependent on institutionalization as the most meaningful criminal sanction, are finding it increasingly difficult to maintain the status quo in the face of such problems as severe overcrowding and unconstitutionally inhumane prison conditions. Correctional administrators are finding it necessary to turn to community-based correctional programs to meet some of the demands upon contemporary corrections.

There are many reasons to utilize community-based correctional programs as dispositions for large numbers of criminal offenders. These programs not only offer protection to the community, but they facilitate reintegration, can be less expensive than institutional programs, and can be more humanitarian than incarceration. These advantages become significantly more important when one considers the crisis confronting American jails and prisons.

In 1989, more than forty state prison systems were under court order or consent decree because of overcrowding. Additionally, fifteen states and the District of Columbia were under the supervision of prison monitors or masters appointed by the federal courts.[2] Each of these court orders/legal challenges describes conditions of confinement so inhumane or living environments so overcrowded that they subject inmates to cruel and unusual punishment, in violation of the Eighth Amendment of the U.S. Constitution.

In several states, entire prison systems have been found cruel and unusual in their treatment of inmates; in other states, practices in major institutions have been found similarly unconstitutional. Local jails are also receiving increased judicial scrutiny. In 1988, 12 percent of all jails in the United States were under court order or consent decree because of crowding and conditions of confinement.[3] Throughout the United States, large urban jails as well as small rural jails have been cited by the federal courts for having unconstitutional conditions. If such local intervention signals a trend, we may someday find that most U.S. jails and prisons have at some time been judged unconstitutionally inhumane and been ordered to reform.

How did we reach this desperate situation? Why has it been permitted to achieve such proportions? Although our prisons and jails have never been trouble-free, their problems are often poorly publicized and misunderstood. Because each jurisdiction must manage its difficulties independently, it sometimes appears that the reported problems are isolated and simply represent a new verse in an everlasting song of complaint from persons interested in prison reform. This too common perception is dangerously inaccurate; it has precipitated our current state of affairs. Judicial intervention did not create the prison problem; in fact, current involvement began only after the situation became intolerable and unmanageable. Today, court actions are simply forcing the existing prison crisis into the forefront of community consciousness and requiring action.

Some of the actions taken appear rather drastic. Some states have passed emergency prisoner release legislation to reduce dangerously overcrowded prisons. In other states, such as Georgia, the governor has commuted the sentences of thousands of prisoners. In Texas, when legislators did not act quickly enough to resolve the crowding crisis, the federal court imposed millions of dollars in fines against the state. In Alabama, state officials failed to respond quickly enough to judicial orders to reduce overcrowding. Over the objection of the state attorney general, the court found it necessary to order the early release of almost 300 prison inmates. This action followed orders that restricted the number of inmates that could enter state prisons; at the time the early releases were ordered, several thousand convicted offenders were being held in local jails, awaiting transfer to state institutions.

Alabama's problem is not unique. Across the nation, overcrowded prisons have been placed under court order restricting the entry of new prisoners. The result of such action is that newly convicted prisoners spend many months crowded in local facilities while they wait for empty beds in state prisons. In 1988, seventeen states housed over 14,000 state-sentenced prisoners in local jails. This strategy of robbing Peter to pay Paul, solving the state prison problems at the expense of local institutions, causes serious problems for the local jail, a facility that was never expected to provide long-term housing for felons. What will be the result if the courts now begin requiring humane treatment in local jails across the nation?

One response to this problem is simply to build many more prisons and jails. This strategy has three major disadvantages. First, it is extremely expensive: the per-inmate cost of constructing a new prison ranges from $25,000 to $75,000 per cell, depending on the institution's security classification. Second, it extends and promotes the deleterious effects of imprisonment. Finally, it will inevitably result in a new generation of prisons that will someday also be overcrowded. An alternative response is simply to permit the wholesale release of inmates whenever conditions become unconstitutionally overcrowded. This strategy also has a rather serious drawback: it makes a mockery of the system of justice. At at time when determinant sentences are receiving increased legislative and popular support, it seems somewhat contradictory for the execution of prison sentences to be contingent upon bed space.

Although some prison construction may be desirable and some early releases unavoidable, there is a third and more generally appropriate solution. The planned use of community-based programs, not as a stopgap measure or a strategy to siphon off only low-risk offenders from the prison, but as a serious and permanent alternative to incarceration, can be an effective response to our current prison crisis.

The Importance of Planning

The key is planning. As noted in chapter 1, a poorly planned community-based correctional program can sabotage the goals of reintegration and criminal justice system reform. Poorly planned programs also can lead to an increase in the public's fear of crime and criminals. This fear can easily turn to anger and resistance to future

Community Resistance to Community-Based Corrections: An Extreme Example

First they called Ray Messegee at home and threatened to cut him up with chainsaws. Then the residents of the small town of Elbe, Wash., changed their minds; they decided they would hang him instead.

Messegee, an administrator with the Washington Department of Corrections, has the job of trying to convince the residents of towns like Elbe that they should host work-release centers for convicted criminals. He received the calls soon after he proposed a center eight miles from Elbe.

A few weeks later, after Messegee made his first pitch for the work-release center, a gang of drunken loggers roared into a public meeting at the Elbe firehouse where Messegee was speaking. Outside, they had already threatened to tar and feather him, or perhaps to shoot him. Several loggers broke through a line of police officers inside the firehouse and one grabbed Messegee screaming that he was going to "string him up" for bringing criminals into the town. Outside, rifle shots went off. Police and local officials calmed down the mob and no one was hurt. But Messegee got the idea: The people of Elbe did not want a work-release center in their community. And they did not get one.

SOURCE: Kevin Krajick, " 'Not on My Block': Local Opposition Impedes the Search for Alternatives," *Corrections Magazine* 6(5) (1980): 15. Copyright 1980 by *Corrections Magazine* and Criminal Justice Publications, Inc., 116 West 32 Street, New York, NY 10001.

community-based correctional efforts. This chain of events has been repeated in many communities. Correctional administrators too often have responded by making community-based programming a low priority, saying, in effect, that the public is just not ready. This defeatist position and the chain of events that produces it can be avoided through conscientious planning: the orderly, systematic, and continuous process of applying anticipations of the future to current decision making.[4]

❑ The Planning Process

The National Institute of Law Enforcement and Criminal Justice has developed a planning model for the criminal justice system that describes each component of the planning process (figure 13-1).[5] We use it here as a general guide for planning efforts. The planning task begins with the general question "What are we trying to accomplish?" The task is to determine what should be done and why. The planners' values, philosophies, and judgments play a critical role. This component of the planning effort is known as policy planning. In preparation for the planning effort (step 1), specific roles are assigned to the planning participants and needed information is identified. A description of the current situation is formulated (step 2); it includes an assessment of crime and criminal justice system functions, activities, costs, and an analysis of community characteristics associated with crime. Steps 3 and 4 require planners to project the current situation into the future to determine what is possible, what is probable, and what is desirable. Social, legislative, and political trends must be considered.

Identifying and analyzing problems (step 5) involves efforts to estimate the gap between what is desirable and what is likely to occur. During this critical phase, an effort is made to achieve a full and detailed understanding of potential problems. Specific goals can then be established and priorities set (step 6). These first six tasks are all aspects of policy planning—decisions regarding long-term goals and objectives.

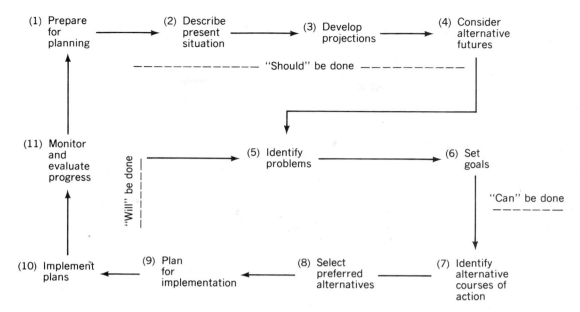

FIGURE 13-1 General Planning Process Model

SOURCE: Robert Cushman and John Wynne, *Criminal Justice Planning for Local Governments* (Washington, D.C.: National Institute of Law Enforcement and Criminal Justice, 1979), p. 32.

The next phase of the planning process can be referred to as program planning. In this phase, decisions that lead to the adoption of specific courses of action are made. The focus here is "What can we do and how?" Steps 7 and 8 involve identifying alternative courses of action by weighing advantages and disadvantages. Contingency plans and guidelines for action are developed at this stage.

Decisions regarding resource allocation are referred to as operational planning. Operational planning seeks answers to the questions "What will we do and when?" In this phase, steps 9, 10, and 11, program implementation is planned and executed and the resulting programs are monitored and evaluated. The evaluation yields feedback regarding program efficiency and effectiveness, which is used to facilitate further planning. The planning process is clearly a continuous effort that focuses on new futures as plans and projections are realized.

❑ Policy Implementation

Implementing policy is not easy, even when conscientious planning precedes program development. The difficulties are especially great when the planning objectives are controversial, poorly understood, or deliberately misrepresented. This is often true in community-based corrections.

Thomas Smith has developed a model of the policy implementation process that explains the types of problems likely to be encountered during the process of turning good intentions into reality. His model focuses on the relationships between four components of the policy implementation process:

1. The idealized policy—that is, the idealized patterns of interaction that those who have defined the policy are attempting to induce
2. The target group, defined as those who are required to adopt new patterns of interaction by the policy (They are the individuals most directly affected by the policy and who must change to meet its demands.)
3. The implementing organization, usually a government agency, responsible for policy implementation
4. The environmental factors, those elements in the environment influenced by the policy implementation (The general public and various special-interest groups are included here.)[6]

These components and their relations are illustrated in figure 13-2, where the policymaking process is seen to produce public policy. During the course of policy implementation, those implementing the policy and those affected by it experience tensions, strains, and conflicts. These tensions lead to policy modifications and result in feedback that will subsequently influence future policymaking.

In community-based corrections, we are generally concerned with policies that mandate the development or increased use of some form of noninstitutional program and/or the elimination or decreased use of some form of incarceration. Target groups may include law enforcement officers, who may be asked to accept ex-offenders back into the community without harassment; prosecutors, who may be asked to drop charges against individuals who have successfully completed diversion programs; judges, who may be asked to change their sentencing practices; and probation, parole, and other correctional workers, who may be asked to re-examine and revise their entire roles. Implementing agencies include departments of correction, individual institutions, probation and parole agencies, and other public and private community-based programs. The general public and special-interest groups (such as neighborhood organizations established to fight the introduction of a halfway house into their community) are clearly affected by the implementation of community corrections policy.

Considering the general process of policy implementation and the particular parties involved here, it seems highly unlikely that community-based corrections plans will be implemented in precisely the spirit in which they are written. Planners and policymakers must be constantly vigilant to ensure that the implementation process does not result in unintended program changes.

❑ Benefits of Planning

Planning is desirable not only when broad changes in correctional policy are being anticipated. Every aspect of correctional administration covering both institutional and community-based programming can be enhanced by planning efforts. These benefits of planning include:

1. Improved analysis of problems. Planning produces the data and analyses elected officials and criminal justice administrators need to improve their decision making.
2. Improved cooperation and coordination. Planning provides a mechanism for increasing cooperation and corrdination among police, courts, cor-

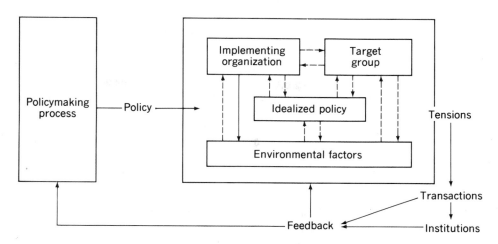

FIGURE 13-2 A Model of the Policy Implementation Process
SOURCE: Thomas B. Smith, "The Policy Implementation Process," *Policy Sciences* 4 (1973): 197–209. Reprinted by permission.

rections, and private service agencies, as well as between different levels of government.

3. Clear goals, objectives, and priorities. Planning permits more precise articulation of purposes and links goals, objectives, tasks, and activities in more meaningful ways.

4. More effective allocation of resources. Planning provides a framework for resource allocation decisions. It simplifies the setting of priorities for the use of resources to achieve criminal justice goals and objectives.

5. Improved programs and services. Planning procedures a clearer understanding of problems and needs. It also makes it easier to formulate goals and objectives and to evaluate and compare alternative programs and procedures.

6. Improved capacity and quality of personnel. Planning focuses organizational effort and provides agency personnel with new knowledge and information. A specialized planning staff can help train criminal justice agency personnel in planning processes and techniques.[7]

Each of these benefits will increase public confidence and support for corrections, a necessary prerequisite for community-based corrections.

Massachusetts provides a good example of a state that appears to have conscientiously planned its policy, programming, and operations with a major emphasis on community corrections. Following passage of the Correctional Reform Act of 1972, the Massachusetts Department of Corrections began implementing a planning effort that established reintegration as the policy and home furloughs, study release, work release, and community-based prerelease centers as the programs. By the department's own assessment, the planning effort appears to have paid off—in 1980, a 10 percent decline in recidivism was reported.[8] This decline in recidivism is directly proportional to inmate participation in community-based correctional programs. It is anticipated that, if inmate participation can be increased, greater reductions in recidivism can be accomplished.

Such results do not come easily. Hostile citizens, legislators, and criminal justice officials can hinder community-based program development. Clearly, planning is even more important when what is being attempted is new and when resistance is firmly entrenched. As Gibbons writes: "Planning moves down a road filled with many switchbacks, detours, and even dead ends, which must be traveled with full anticipation that retracing and retracking will be part of the process."[9]

Reorganizing Community-Based Corrections

One of the most valuable initial strategies for implementing the policy of reintegration is the reorganization and consolidation of existing programs and resources. Reorganization can both improve the delivery of existing services through program coordination and make possible the identification and development of needed services. Too often service fragmentation not only makes it difficult to supervise and assist offenders; it also makes it impossible to determine which services are being appropriately provided, which are duplicated by two or more agencies, and which needed services are altogether absent. Over a decade ago, the following observations of fragmentation in corrections were made:

> Very little is "systematic" about the state-local corrections system. . . . In most situations, administrative responsibility is divided among the state, its counties, and localities; split between agencies at each level that handle adults and those that deal with juveniles; and sliced up within jurisdictions among various functions. Many functions are not even handled by the corrections system but are performed by the courts.[10]

In most communities, little has changed. Too many agencies provide inadequate services because they must serve a diverse clientele. Resources are stretched beyond reasonable proportions; needless duplication of services is the result. What is available is often of little value, and the client who requires something other than the norm is simply out of luck.

Planning efforts should start by making the most of existing personnel, programs, and resources. Reorganization can alter jurisdictional boundaries so that offenders can benefit from an expanded range of services, reduce or eliminate the duplication of services, provide improved services through the reorganization of resources, provide greater consistency in treatment services and philosophy, and result in cost reductions that can make funds available for new programs or other budgeting needs.[11]

The National Institute of Justice has issued a series of guidelines for criminal justice planners considering reorganization that suggests three basic reorganization models. Each is designed to achieve the same basic purpose: knitting together the disparate resources needed for the cost-effective delivery of community-based correctional services.[12]

Under the unified county-administered model, correctional services are locally controlled and financed and administered by a county correctional agency. Comprehensive service delivery is made possible by the consolidation of programs within a single unit of government. The major focus is on goal simplification and clarification and on cost reduction. This model is often employed when states are attempting to encourage local communities to assume greater responsibility for correctional services. The state often provides financial subsidies to encourage local efforts. Adopting this model could result in the unification of all local correctional services; a more likely outcome would be the establishment of a community correctional center or the development of a pretrial service agency.

The regional or multijurisdiction local government model involves the joint funding of a community correctional system by two or more local governments. Reciprocal agreements permit local governments to share institutional facilities (such as jails or juvenile detention homes) and community-based programs when separate funding and services would be unfeasible because of cost or require needless service duplication. This strategy is based on the maxim of the larger the population base, the greater the diversity of services that can be provided. Coalitions most frequently involve two or more counties or a city and county joining to achieve comprehensive service delivery.

Under the state-administered decentralized model, the state funds and coordinates correctional services but leaves day-to-day program operation to local, grassroots authorities. This strategy is especially appropriate in small states where it is possible to maintain an awareness of local problems and needs and to maintain close contact with local authorities. Massachusetts, which contracts virtually all juvenile correctional services, and Connecticut, which contracts all adult parole supervision services from local public and private agencies, are representative of the state-administered decentralized model.

Each of the preceding models is designed to meet a different set of correctional problems; each offers different advantages and disadvantages to the state and local governments involved. Barriers to success can include difficulty in obtaining consensus regarding program objectives and operations among different units of local government or between state and local authorities. The National Institute of Justice suggests that serious consideration be given to seven dimensions of the reorganization effort prior to selecting a specific model:

1. Source of initiative for change. Where does the impetus for unification originate?
2. Values and goals. What values and goals mold its character?
3. Organizational scope. What will be included in the organizational structure?
4. Intergovernmental relationships. What intergovernmental relationships help shape the unification effort?
5. Financing. Where is the money to come from? Who pays for what?
6. Linkages to related services. What linkages are sought between the corrections organization and resource systems in the surrounding community?
7. Service impact. What is the impact of reorganization on service delivery?[13]

Programs/Strategies for the Correctional Planner

❑ Subsidies

Subsidies are payments made by the state to local government to improve community correctional services. Although virtually any type of community-based program may be subsidized by state funds, the term *probation subsidy* is frequently employed because the earliest subsidy programs were specifically designed to improve the quality of local probation services. Probation subsidies are one of the oldest methods of improving community-based corrections and shifting the control and responsibility for correctional programs to local authorities. Today they are still one of the most effective methods of dealing with the problem of prison overcrowding.

There are two basic plans for payment of subsidies. In the first approach, the state pays a flat amount, based upon the local government's reduction in the number of individuals committed to the state correctional system, or a flat percentage of the expenditures involved in operating local programs. The second approach considers the county's ability to pay, as well as the costs of its correctional programming.[14]

The California Experience.

California was the first state to make extensive use of probation subsidies. Established in 1967, the program was designed to reduce prison overcrowding and facilitate the development of intensive supervision case loads for difficult offenders. During the eleven years of its operation, commitments to state prisons dropped considerably, perhaps by as much as 45,000 offenders.[15] This drop saved the state approximately $60 million.[16] The counties that participated in the program received over $200 million to establish local programs.[17]

Under California's program, counties were paid between $2,080 and $4,000 for each offender who, according to the county's past rate of commitment, would have been committed to a state institution. To qualify for the program, its commitments had to fall below a base commitment rate that was equal to its average commitment rate during preceding years. The greater the reduction in commitments, the greater the subsidy per offender maintained in the community. For example:

> If a participating county's base commitment rate were between 40 and 49 persons per 100,000 of total population, it would be entitled to a $2,285 subsidy award per case for a 1 percent decrease in commitments. If its reduction in commitments were 7 percent or more, the county would be entitled to $4,000 per case.[18]

The intensive supervision case loads the counties established were required to serve no more than fifty offenders. Otherwise the counties were on their own to develop whatever local needs dictated. A wide variety of auxiliary services was also developed, including medical and psychiatric care, loan funds, cultural enrichment, and recreation programs.[19] Juvenile programs included specialized foster care, group homes, and day treatment programs.

Despite its success, the program was criticized throughout the years of its operation. There were disgruntled judges who resented their exclusion from community corrections program planning. Sheriffs complained because they received no funds for jail improvement. Even subsidy program proponents were disturbed by the failure of the subsidies to keep pace with inflation; $4,000 purchased significantly fewer services in 1975 than in the 1960s.[20]

In 1978, the program was redesigned to permit the use of up to 10 percent of the subsidies for jail improvement, crime prevention programs, and county training schools, as well as community-based programs. The new legislation also required county supervisors to establish "an advisory group representing all segments of the county criminal justice system to evaluate local needs and recommend to the supervisors how to apply the subsidy funds."[21] In 1980, about two-thirds of the subsidy funds went to probation departments; the remaining funds were distributed to district attorneys' offices, private agencies, sheriffs, police, and the courts.

Although the new legislation was expected to reduce prison commitments, state institutional populations are on the increase. The passage of Proposition 13 and the state's determinant sentencing law are viewed as partly responsible for the growth in the California prison population.

The Minnesota Community Corrections Act.   The Minnesota Community Corrections Act illustrates the second method of calculating subsidy payments. The relative wealth of a community, characteristics of its population, and corrections expenditures are all used in calculating subsidy payments.[22] The Minnesota program differs from California's initial effort in several ways. Counties are penalized $25 per day, to be deducted from subsidy funds, for each day a prisoner sentenced to five years or less spends in state custody.[23] Counties are forbidden to use subsidy funds to replace rather than supplement existing local correctional efforts. These measures are designed to ensure that subsidies will work to decrease prison populations and increase community-based correctional programs.

Minnesota also included two features in its program that exemplify conscientious planning. First, the Minnesota Community Corrections Act provided for development of a statewide master plan for community-based corrections. The plan encompasses virtually all aspects of juvenile and criminal justice and demonstrates a real commitment to local correctional efforts. The state provides technical assistance and program monitoring to the local authorities. Second, Minnesota's legislation provided for establishing community advisory boards that were charged with the responsibility to "actively participate in the formulation of the comprehensive plan for the development, implementation, and operation of the correctional services program and service . . . (and to) . . . make formal recommendations at least annually . . . to the county board."[24]

Although Minnesota's subsidy program is in many ways exemplary, it is not without problems. A study of the Minnesota Community Corrections Act by the Minnesota Department of Corrections and the State Crime Control Planning Board discovered that costs and prison commitments had increased rather than declined between 1975 and 1979.[25] These findings are being hotly debated by corrections officials across the country. On the one hand, critics of community-based corrections interpret the findings as proof that such correctional subsidy programs do not work.[26] On the other hand, supporters of community corrections programs argue that what really happened in Minnesota is that costs and prison commitments increased *less rapidly* than they would have in the absence of the Minnesota Community Corrections Act.

❑ Community Correctional Centers

Community-based correctional centers are multipurpose correctional facilities that combine detention, holding, and prerelease programming with direct service delivery to nonresidential clients. Because of the diversity of programs and services that can be offered by community correctional centers, the National Advisory Commission

Iowa Corrections Official Calls Minnesota Study Biased

To the Editor:

I have read several of the articles in your series on community-based corrections. The most recent by John Blackmore, titled "Evaluating the Minnesota Evaluation," (*Corrections,* August 1981), prompts me to write.

I have been aware of the Minnesota evaluation for some time, and have felt from the beginning that it was an evaluation designed to reinforce traditional (pre-community-based corrections) ideas about correctional supervision, rather than one designed to study objectively the overall results of community-based corrections, as well as its potential.

Iowa and Minnesota developed their community-based corrections systems almost parallel to each other. Iowa, by legislative mandate, chose to make its community system statewide, covering all ninety-nine counties and 100 percent of the population. The system is largely funded by state appropriations based entirely on the workload of the eight judicial district departments of correctional services, which provide all pretrial services, presentence investigation, probation supervision, and a dozen residential facilities in most of the larger cities.

We started in Iowa with the old "Des Moines Project," which is now the Department of Correctional Services of the Fifth Judicial District. It spread from there to cover the entire state by 1977. All the district departments are governed by district boards with majority membership belonging to county boards of supervisors.

From 1970 to the end of 1980, the overall correctional case load, resulting from increasing crime rates, soared more than 300 percent. Prison populations since that time have increased roughly 50 percent. But, and this is where the Minnesota study goes awry, adult community-based corrections populations in Iowa have grown from nothing to almost 14,000, in a state that has a total correctional population of adults amounting to about 17,000.

Institutional programs and parole, operated by the Division of Corrections of the Iowa Department of Social Services, manage about 3,500 persons, with about 2,600 in prison and the remainder on parole. Who could predict such growth? How could it be expected that prison populations would not increase under such a load? Had everything simply remained static from the beginning, prison populations would certainly have declined. In Iowa in 1970, almost 70 percent of all convicted felons were sent to prison.

Today, the figure is down to about 30 percent. I imagine it is much the same in Minnesota. Community-based corrections caseloads are made up of about 30 percent serious misdemeanants, 30 percent aggravated misdemeanants, and 40 percent felons. So, roughly 30 percent of the current Iowa community-based corrections caseload was once managed on the county level, and about 70 percent on the state level. While prison populations have, in fact, risen considerably during the past five years, community-based corrections has still taken almost 90 percent of the overall annual increase.

This year, Iowa's legislature labored with prison overpopulation and resolved to put a cap of 2,650 on the maximum population. When we reach that point, the governor must declare an emergency, which will require the parole board to begin a program of expedited release until the emergency has ended. We do have prison problems in Iowa. But what would they have been

on Criminal Justice Standards and Goals defines community correctional centers in very general terms: "A relatively open institution located in the neighborhood and using community resources to provide most or all of the services required by offenders."[27]

Many community correctional centers are outgrowths of the original local correctional program, the local jail. By endorsing the goals of community-based corrections, opening the facility to the public, encouraging community support and volunteers, introducing community-based services such as alcohol and drug therapy, education, and employment, and providing for diversion, pretrial release, and work release, the local jail can be transformed into a multipurpose community correctional center.

and how much sooner would we have had them had it not been for community-based corrections? By the year 1975, this state would have been engulfed in a crisis of massive proportions, with over 8,000 people under correctional supervision. By the end of 1980, when more than 16,000 persons were under adult supervision, there would have been little hope of ever gaining control. Community-based corrections saved Iowa from those problems and massive institutional building programs costing $150 to 200 million, which still would not have resolved the problem. Community supervision would still have been required on a scale not much smaller than the present.

Iowa's legislature has chosen to continue funding community-based corrections statewide because it has no choice, and because the economics are such that community-based corrections supervision almost pays for itself.

Early this year a study was done in Iowa on the return to the state, as compared to the outlay of cash, for community-based corrections. We found that almost 85 percent of some 13,000 community-based corrections clients were employed at that time, with average salaries estimated at between $7,000 and $8,000 per year. The annual tax return in state employment taxes alone from a $74 million annual payroll was almost $1.5 million. Add to that about 74 percent of federal employment taxes, which are returned to the state, and we add another $4.1 million. That comes to $5.6 million. If we figure that 40 percent of the case load that is employed supports at least one dependent, we add another $6.5 million, which is, in fact, defrayed public assistance costs. If we added sales tax receipts of over $880,000, the total return and defrayed costs would equal more than the $10,600,000 operating cost for community-based corrections in Iowa in fiscal 1981. Those figures were presented to the legislature in their budget deliberations and were acknowledged as reasonable.

Of course, there is additional cost. Iowa's municipalities and counties provide services to community-based corrections clients at an approximate cost of 30 percent of the amount appropriated directly to the department of correctional services for direct operating costs. Mental health services, substance abuse treatment, medical services to the indigent through free or locally subsidized programs, and services that are required for clients through local nonprofit groups and United Way–supported agencies are important in the community-based corrections process, where one objective is to make "maximum use of local resources."

In states like Iowa, and in Minnesota, where large-scale use is made of community-based corrections, it would be chaotic to stop funding.

Pretrial services also have had a direct and profound impact on city and county jails in the state. In my district, those released under pretrial supervision number more than three times the number held in jail, and many more are released without supervision. Without pretrial supervision, jails would be in worse shape than prisons.

The simple economics of community-based corrections alone is enough to more than justify such programs. Costly? Hogwash! Minnesota community-based corrections officials got a bad rap.

James R. (Bud) Kilman
Director, First Judicial District
Department of Correctional Services
Waterloo, Iowa

SOURCE: *Corrections Magazine* 7(6) (December 1981): 7–8. Copyright 1981 by *Corrections Magazine* and Criminal Justice Publications, Inc., 116 West 32 Street, New York, NY 10001.

Benefits of the Community Correctional Center. The advantages of the community correctional center should be obvious. Such programs reduce the fragmentation of services by concentrating them in a single facility or complex of facilities. Service delivery is improved by the introduction of community resources and the assistance of volunteers. When the programs originate at the local jail, the improvement of the jail's physical plant and the professionalization of jail staff are facilitated. Costs of residential services and services to nonresidential clients can generally be reduced because of the enhanced coordination of services. Costs may also be reduced because the establishment of a community correctional center often leads to an increased use of nonresidential correctional dispositions.

Components. As part of its series of program models, the National Institute of Justice has identified ten program components of community correctional centers.

1. Facilities. The community correctional center should have a structured residential component that provides separate housing for pretrial and sentenced offenders. Controlled residency provides both stability to the offender and a starting point for programming his phased reintegration into the community.

2. Programs. The center should have two or more programs; single "treatments" of crime and delinquency have proved unsuccessful.

3. Identification of client needs. Client needs must be identified and resources developed to meet those needs. Needed services may include: supervision in the community, shelter, food, clothing, emergency financial assistance, transportation, medical care, and mental health, vocational, employment, educational, and personal counseling.

4. Delivery of services. Services should be provided by referrals to community resources as well as directly by correctional center staff. The appropriate combination of center and community services should be determined by the availability of resources and assessments of the cost-effectiveness of various service-delivery options.

5. Eligibility. The facility should serve persons in both pre- and post-adjudicatory statuses. Local, state, and federal offenders should be eligible for the center so as to avoid the unnecessary duplication of services.

6. Coordination of efforts. Comprehensive programming requires coordination between criminal justice and community agencies and collaboration between the public and private sector. Interdependence may best be achieved through the development of advisory committees to assist community correctional center planning.

7. Supervision of individuals. Offenders assigned to the facility should be supervised both within and outside the center so that community protection can be ensured.

8. Organizational arrangements. The organizational linkages of the center to the criminal justice and correctional system must be clearly defined.

9. Evaluation and assessment. Organizational goals and objectives should be clearly specified and regularly reviewed. Client and program performance should be assessed utilizing explicit criteria; such assessments should provide the basis for program change.

10. Community orientation. Reintegration to normal community living must be emphasized. The one overriding purpose of the community correctional center is "to ensure that the community becomes the source of social, psychological, and economic support."[28]

Program Models. Following a national study, the National Institute of Justice identified three program models for community correctional centers.[29] The first was the Des Moines (Iowa) community-based corrections model. This model serves the local judicial system as an alternative to jail and/or traditional probation. The Des Moines program provides pretrial and probation supervision, presentence investigations, and residential housing to both male and female offenders. (See chapter 3 for a more detailed program description.) The second, the Montgomery County

(Maryland) prerelease center model, serves offenders who are completing terms in local, county, or state institutions. The program is designed to make possible a graduated release from incarceration. (See chapter 7 for a more detailed program description.) The third, the private community correctional center model, is administered by a private, nonprofit agency. Such programs generally provide a variety of services to a diverse group of offenders.

Talbert House in Cincinnati, Ohio, is representative of the privately administered community correctional center. The goals of the program are

> to provide a proper climate for a fluid transition of the ex-offender from prison to the community; counsel and assist the adult drug abuser (also operate a methadone clinic); deal with the problems of the adolescent drug user; provide an alternative to incarceration; be of assistance to the victims of criminal offenses; provide crisis intervention through a 24-hour telephone switchboard and walk-in center, and counsel/secure employment for the ex-offender.[30]

The program has six residential facilities, including three halfway houses for men, a halfway house for women, an adult therapeutic community, and a residential youth treatment program for juveniles with drug and mental health problems. Other program components include:

1. *COSOAP (Comprehensive One-Stop Offender Aid Program).* Provides a multitude of services under one roof. Includes intake, clinical services and testing, welfare, legal aid, educational and job placement. Funded by LEAA, Greater Cincinnati Foundation, Episcopal Diocese, City of Cincinnati, and CETA. Opened in 1975.

2. *Ex-Offender Employment Program.* Assisting offenders in vocational and job readiness, counseling for vocation training, testing. Works with 5,000 to 8,000 per year. Opened in 1978. Funded by City of Cincinnati CETA funds.

3. *241-WORK.* A temporary day labor program is also a component of this program.

4. *621-CARE.* A 24-hour switchboard and crisis center. Averages 4,500 calls a month. Provides backup services for mental health catchment areas and Community Chest Information and Referral. Funded by 648 Board, City of Cincinnati, Community Chest. Opened in 1971.

5. *Victim Assistance Program.* Opened in July 1976. Provides advocacy services to victims of crime. Counseling by telephone or person-to-person also provided. Over 1,000 victims were served during the first two years.

6. *Methadone Treatment Program.* Program taken over from the City of Cincinnati on July 1, 1977. Provides methadone treatment for 150 drug addicts.[31]

A wide range of adult offenders is eligible for the program; juveniles with drug and mental health problems qualify for the youth treatment program. Referrals are received at the state parole system, the Federal Bureau of Prisons, municipal and county probation departments, and the Treatment Alternatives to Street Crime (TASC) Program. The director of each program, with the assistance of staff and consultants, determines who will be admitted to the residential and nonresidential programs.

The NIJ study revealed that privately operated community correctional centers are more strongly rooted in the community than alternative models. Because they are usually initiated within the community by concerned citizens' groups and are locally financed and controlled, privately administered centers tend to have a greater sense of mission. This attitude was found to encourage competence and promote unified organizational efforts.[32] Private programs were found to be more proficient at self-evaluation and better able to meet accountability demands. The creative funding strategies and sophisticated management control systems that private programs generally develop appear to produce greater cost-effectiveness.

Privately administered programs are not without their disadvantages. Private centers must maintain good relations with local authorities if they are to survive; compromises in program goals are sometimes necessary. Some officials question the ability of private programs to control their clients; it appears that control is a problem whenever no backup jail or prison is available to receive recalcitrant offenders. Another problem results from the policy-oriented conflict between private programs that reserve the right to reject clients or that permit only voluntary admissions and local authorities, who interpret the correctional mandate as sometimes requiring the acceptance of undesirable clients and the coercion of unwilling ones.

Each community will find a different blend of program components and administrative structure. Private centers are most desirable when state and local authorities are indifferent or inconsistent in the administration of corrections.[33] Other models require strong state and/or local support. The private sector can still play a significant role in these publicly operated programs. By contracting for privately administered services, publicly operated programs can greatly enhance the range and flexibility of services available to their clients.

❑ Contracting for Community Correctional Services

As the preceding discussion of privately operated community correctional centers indicated, there are many advantages to using the private sector in community-based corrections. Flexibility, accountability, and cost-effectiveness all seem to be enhanced in private programs. When criminal justice agencies enter into contractual agreements with private programs, they can arrange to provide services tailormade to the needs of their clients. For example, probation departments can contract with different private agencies to provide exactly the number and variety of services probationers require. Although criminal justice agencies can develop similar contracts with public agencies (such as mental health), the advantages are less self-evident. A greater variety of services may be attained, but the burden of service provision is simply transferred from one branch of the public sector to another, with all the standard problems such programs entail.

Theoretically, private programs operate under free market principles: The best survive and the funding of programs of lesser quality is terminated. It has been suggested that the ideal community-based correctional system would be a private system in which offenders are issued service vouchers that they can use as they see fit.[34] The client's or consumer's evaluation of service quality would determine program survival or failure. A variation of this proposal would create an incentive system, in which private agencies receive higher payments for the achievement of greater reductions in recidivism.[35] Both proposals represent attempts to introduce the free market ethos into local programming—rewards are tied to productivity.

At present, the private sector is playing an increasing role in corrections. In most communities, private agencies fill in the gaps between publicly operated programs. In community corrections, the vision of a wide variety of private correctional programs competing for criminal justice agency contracts and referrals has been realized in many states. One problem, however, is that federal regulations specify the nature of programs eligible for funding so narrowly that the pool of eligible service providers is extremely limited. Such competition may also be contrary to the goal of coordinated services. Competition requires program duplication and, too often, a needless waste of resources. The need for comprehensive planning may well restrict the viability of the free market ethos in the provision of social services.

An LEAA-sponsored study of the role of private organizations in providing community-based correctional services revealed a number of problems affecting local programming.[36] Although virtually all criminal justice agencies have the authority to contract with private agencies and many of them are entering into such agreements, few contracts involve private programs specifically designed to meet offenders' needs. More often, the private agencies are receiving most of their funding from other public sources, such as the National Institute of Mental Health, the Department of Labor, the National Institute of Drug Abuse, and the National Institute of Alcoholism and Alcohol Abuse.[37] Generally, criminal justice clients receive the treatment and services designed for nonoffenders with substance abuse, employment, or education problems.

In most communities, the process of referring clients to private agencies is more haphazard than systematic. Little information is available on the characteristics of clients referred, but it appears that there is little difference between referred and nonreferred clients. Factors influencing referrals included the availability of free services (as opposed to these requiring the agency to cover part of the costs), the agency's willingness to accept the referral, and the client's willingness to accept the referral.[38] In most cases, there are no explicit criteria for referrals; each caseworker is responsible for the referral decisions affecting his or her clients.

Generally, there is a need for clearer statements of the services to be provided to clients and greater articulation of the measures of service delivery, program performance, or client response to be used to evaluate programs. These problems represent a growing challenge to criminal justice authorities—the ability to shift from the task of supervising clients to monitoring the performances of agencies to which it has contracted the task of service provision. To address this problem, LEAA recommended the joint development of monitoring and accountability procedures by referral sources and service vendors.[39] Research is needed to learn the characteristics of clients and the ability of programs to supervise them. A logically developed system of referral decision making is necessary to achieve the proper assignment of offenders to programs.

One additional problem may develop when privately administered programs are widely used. Ironically, this difficulty is more likely to occur when small private programs become very successful and expand their operations into neighboring communities, across the state or beyond. Such growth can lead to the creation of a large new bureaucracy, with all the red tape, goal confusion, and resistance to innovation often described as characteristic of public agencies. The privately administered program is often applauded for its grass-roots appeal; it is not clear how much program expansion and replication can be undertaken without the loss of this essential quality.

Florida's extensive use of private probation services began in 1975, when the state legislature turned the responsibility for misdemeanant probation back to the county courts. Faced with the options of developing and funding their own programs, purchasing services from the state, eliminating probation altogether, or utilizing volunteer services, the courts chose the latter option. A volunteer pilot program sponsored by the Salvation Army was so successful that new legislation was subsequently enacted to encourage further private sector involvement in community corrections. The legislation required offenders to pay $10 per month to the approved public or private agency supervising them. This fiscal incentive proved very effective in stimulating the entrance of private agencies into probation supervision.[40]

In 1977, the Salvation Army Act was amended to provide additional financial support to the supervising agencies through purchase of service contracts. Today, SAMP utilizes professional counselors and regular Salvation Army staff to supervise clients, refer them to community resources, and monitor restitution agreements and the payment of fines.

Deinstitutionalization

The unification of community-based corrections, the payment of subsidies, the development of community correctional centers, and the utilization of private resources may be viewed as strategies directed toward the general goal of deinstitutionalization. *Deinstitutionalization,* which was widely supported in the 1960s and 1970s, refers to efforts to reduce a jurisdiction's reliance on incarceration for pretrial detention or as a sentencing disposition. Generally, this objective is accomplished by releasing offenders from institutions, prohibiting new commitments to institutions, or combining these two strategies. We consider three deinstitutionalization efforts. The first two may be considered successes; both resulted in long-term reductions in the use of institutional confinement. The third effort was not so successful. We shall see that the major determinant of a successful deinstitutionalization effort is, once again, planning.

❑ Juvenile Correctional Reform in Massachusetts

The deinstitutionalization of the Massachusetts juvenile corrections system is one of the most widely publicized and researched correctional reform efforts ever undertaken. In the late 1960s, it was becoming increasingly obvious that Massachusetts training schools were neither humanitarian nor rehabilitative. Six major studies of the training schools were undertaken; research revealed a multitude of problems and deficiencies in the ten juvenile institutions.

Civic, professional, and political groups urged reform. As further investigation yielded more evidence of inappropriate treatment and even brutality, support for change continued to grow. In 1969, Jerome Miller was appointed commissioner of the Department of Youth Services and given a broad mandate for reform. Miller's reform efforts were initially focused on turning the institutions into therapeutic communities. Considerable institutional staff resistance brought this move to a halt, and Miller redirected his efforts toward simply eliminating the most repressive and brutal aspects of institutionalization.

Up until that time, the Massachusetts training schools had relied heavily on punishment, deprivation, and personal degradation as the basis of institutional authority.[41] Staff resisted every effort by Miller to change institutional goals and practices, which they viewed as undermining their efforts to control their charges. At the same time, Miller was unable to remove and replace veteran staff members because of civil service regulations. In effect, his hands were tied. What happened next is often mistakenly viewed as miraculous. Miller gave up the hope of ever improving institutional practices; so he closed the institutions and sent the kids home or to community programs—or so the story goes. This view ignores the long and difficult planning process that preceded the closing of the training schools and the development of community-based programs.

Miller's success was made possible because of his use of fortuitous circumstances and his conscientious planning effort. The key components of his general strategy were as follows. First, build upon existing public, professional, and political support for reform. Miller opened the doors of the training schools to visitors and volunteers, knowing that they would not like what they saw and would demand change. Second, obtain fiscal support. Federal support was obtained to supplement state monies. LEAA, Title I of the Federal Education Act, and Title IV of the Office of Manpower Development and Training in the U.S. Department of Labor all provided the fiscal resources Miller required to bring in top staff and create new programs. Third, undertake detailed policy and program planning. Federal funds made possible the establishment of a planning task force that articulated the direction for reform. This task force developed a seven-point plan that called for

1. Regionalization
2. Community-based treatment centers
3. Expansion of the forestry program
4. Relocation of detention
5. Increased placement alternatives
6. Grants-in-aid to cities and towns
7. An intensive-care security unit[42]

This plan became the blueprint for the reform effort.

Miller resigned from the Massachusetts Department of Youth Services in 1973, leaving others to implement his policy and programs. Implementation proved to be difficult. There have been reported problems in monitoring private community programs and a slowly growing number of youths kept in secure detention.[43]

Although there is still some debate regarding the long-term impact of deinstitutionalization in Massachusetts, juvenile recidivism and serious delinquency have not significantly increased.[44] The vast majority of state-committed youth in Massachusetts are able to remain in their communities, often in their own homes. They are able to receive treatment, supervision, and support services without the financial, social, and personal costs of incarceration. (See the discussion of juvenile probation in chapter 10.)

☐ Deinstitutionalization in Vermont

The deinstitutionalization effort in Vermont involved closing the state's only maximum security prison.[45] The Windsor State Prison in Vermont was for many years the oldest operating maximum security prison in the United States. When it closed, it was over 150 years old.

Planning for the closing of the facility began in 1966. By 1975, a concerted effort to expand probation, parole, and alternative programs and the development of four community correctional centers had considerably reduced the prison's population. However, although only 2.4 percent of all persons under correctional supervision were housed in Windsor, operating the facility required one-fourth of the annual corrections department budget. Budget projections indicated that the costs of maximum security incarceration would continue to rise. Because the state was already facing a severe revenue crisis, it was decided that the prison would be closed and would not be replaced. The Federal Bureau of Prisons agreed to accept up to forty of Vermont's maximum security prisoners; the remaining offenders would be served by community-oriented programs. The following objectives were established for the project:

> Eliminate in-state maximum security except for short-term detention; minimize the number of prisoners requiring maximum security; fund the department's anticipated deficit, then projected at approximately 10 percent of the operating budget; increase the staff of the Division of Probation and Parole by 25 percent; double the capacity of the St. Albans Diagnostic and Treatment Facility, a medium security facility; enhance the programs of the four regional community correctional centers; create a classification approach to meet the requirements of the new system, including the development of criteria and process for transferring persons out of state; upgrade volunteer services in the department; increase the capacity of the department's minimum security facility for alcoholics; upgrade other service capabilities around the system—for example, vocational education, psychiatric services, and purchase of services.[46]

Wishing to close the facility as quickly as possible, the Vermont Department of Corrections utilized the critical path method, a technique analyzing networks of activities.[47] This planning aid allowed the department to identify key components of the deinstitutionalization effort and to structure their interconnectedness and timing, to identify potential bottlenecks, and to monitor changes in the component activities. The time necessary to complete the total deinstitutionalization effort was estimated by using a computer program to calculate the time necessary to complete each activity on the critical path. Figure 13-3 illustrates a simplified version of the critical path chart developed by the Vermont Department of Corrections (the actual chart included over ninety activities).

According to Vermont corrections officials, there are many benefits to using the critical path method in planning correctional change.[48] In this project, it permitted administrators to explain the deinstitutionalization effort to correctional staff, budget officials, human service agency managers, the state buildings agency, and the media. By illustrating the time dependencies between necessary events and activities, it facilitated an ongoing review of the activities and created pressure to find the best combination, sequence, and timing of activities. As a computerized planning tool, it facilitated the development of time estimates and made possible the simulation of changes in activity durations and linkages as time estimates changed.

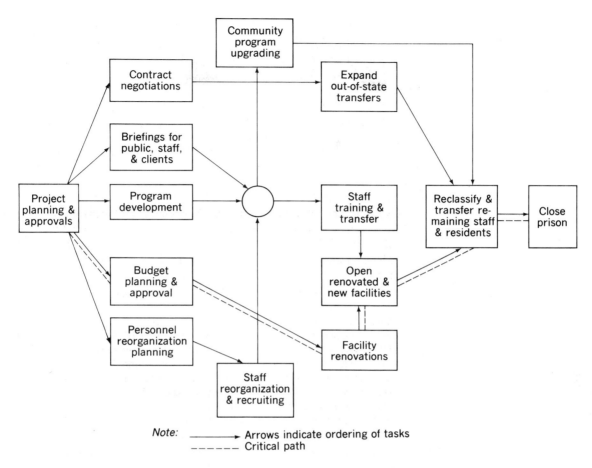

FIGURE 13-3 Prison Closing Project

SOURCE: Cornelius Hogan and William Steinhurst, "Managing Change in Corrections," *Federal Probation* 40(2) (1976): 57. Reprinted with permission from *Federal Probation* (1976).

It is estimated that the critical path method saved two or three months over the course of this project's implementation, a cost savings equal to the prison's personal services and operating budget for that time period.[49] The Vermont case illustrates that deinstitutionalization can be both an effective and an efficient process.

❏ Deinstitutionalization of Status Offenders

The Deinstitutionalization of Status Offenders (DSO) Program consisted of a series of statewide and county programs funded in 1976 by the LEAA. The program's purpose was to reduce the large number of status offenders already in secure institutions and to provide alternatives to the future use of incarceration for status offenders. Eight of the programs have been subjected to intensive study. The following assessment is based on results of these studies, which showed that no program achieved the level of deinstitutionalization mandated by Congress in funding the programs.

Malcolm Klein, who has researched diversion and deinstitutionalization projects for many years, identified six major impediments to successful deinstitutionalization that limited the effectiveness of the national DSO project. These impediments also represent general problems that may confront any deinstitutionalization effort.

1. *Definitional ambiguity.* There was a lack of clarity regarding what types of activities constituted deinstitutionalization and what efforts constituted diversion.

2. *Theoretical rationales.* The theoretical rationales necessary to guide deinstitutionalization programs were not developed. Instead, programs were based on simplistic cliches (for example, keep the good kids away from the bad kids and don't stigmatize kids lest they live up to the stigma).

3. *Client targeting.* The appropriate target group for deinstitutionalization, which was supposed to consist of those status offenders who were incarcerated at the time of program initiation or who would normally be detained or incarcerated, was not consistently defined; methods of identifying such youths from among other status offenders were not uniformly developed.

4. *Service delivery and modalities.* Too few services were offered. Those that were offered were too narrow in character. Counseling and short-term crisis intervention were the predominant modes of treatment; advocacy, skill development, and opportunity enhancement activities were infrequently offered.

5. *Professional resistance.* Law enforcement officers, judges, and correctional personnel, in varying localities and at different times, attempted to shape deinstitutionalization policies and practices in terms of their own professional interests.

6. *Program location.* Too often, DSO project sites were selected because the settings were exceptionally amenable to deinstitutionalization efforts, not because deinstitutionalization efforts were sorely needed. Attempting to guarantee success, the DSO project instead produced little significant change; at best it merely accelerated trends in receptive communities.[50]

All the preceding problems should have been anticipated during the planning of the national DSO project. At each project site, these concerns should have been addressed. What happened? Why was so little achieved by such a massive effort? Apparently, the unexamined good intentions of project administrators, staff, human services workers, and criminal justice system personnel came together in an unguided and confused manner. Good intentions, and there is no real doubt that the persons involved in the projects were motivated by good intentions, were not enough to obtain good results.

❑ A Postscript on Deinstitutionalization

The deinstitutionalization movement, particularly with regard to juvenile and adult confinement facilities, faltered during the 1980s. By the end of that decade, it was evident that the concept of deinstitutionalization had been soundly rejected by criminal justice decision makers and public officials. The confined populations housed in correctional facilities continued to increase. Prisons, jails, and juvenile institutions experienced unprecedented growth, and, as a result, capacity could not keep pace with the inmate population, resulting in overcrowded conditions in all types of correctional institutions.

The concept of deinstitutionalization is not dead, however, merely dormant. While institutional populations continue to expand, criminal justice officials both inside and outside of corrections are beginning to question the policy of incapacitation followed in the 1980s. Strategies such as intensive supervision, electronic monitoring, and home confinement are being experimented with that provide for control and supervision in the community. Both the high cost of jail and prison expansion and the cost of confinement have encouraged criminal justice policy analysts to consider alternative forms of punishments. The Edna Clark McConnell Foundation has spearheaded a movement to encourage the use of alternative sanctions by funding various initiatives in a variety of states dealing with the development of community correctional programs. The National Institute of Corrections has taken a proactive stance in this matter and has published materials and sponsored workshops on developing and implementing community correctional programs as an alternative to crowded correctional facilities.

These materials call for a systemwide strategy for criminal justice reform that brings together a variety of criminal justice decision makers. The American Correctional Association has also recognized the importance of this problem, and sponsors a technical assistance manual for developing and implementing a Community Corrections Act for states to enact. All of these efforts are directed toward reducing the use of institutional corrections and upgrading the correctional services provided in the community.

Summary

The effective use of community-based correctional programs requires planning. Policy, program, and operational planning are necessary if community-based programs are to accomplish the goal of reintegration and overcome the current prison crisis.

There is a variety of strategies available to the correctional planner. The reorganization of local correctional programs can facilitate the most cost-effective use of resources through the coordination of services and elimination of program duplication. State subsidies to local governments encourage local commitment to community-based corrections through the use of financial incentives. Community correctional centers achieve program coordination by centralizing community correctional services in a single, multipurpose facility. Contracting with private organizations encourages innovation, individualization of service delivery, and program flexibility.

Deinstitutionalization is one of the major goals of proponents of community-based corrections. This worthwhile objective can be obtained through conscientious planning. A failure to plan can result in little or no effective change in the correctional system.

KEY WORDS AND
CONCEPTS

accountability	goals	program planning
community	objectives	reorganization models
correctional centers	operational planning	resource allocation
contracting for	planning	service fragmentation
services	policy implementation	subsidies
cost effectiveness	policy planning	
deinstitutionalization	private corrections	

NOTES

1. Bureau of Justice Statistics, *Prisoners in 1988* (Washington, D.C.: United States Department of Justice, 1989), p. 1.
2. The National Prison Project, *Status Report: The Courts and the Prisons* (Washington, D.C.: U.S. Government Printing Office, January 1, 1990), p. 1.
3. Bureau of Justice Statistics, *Census of Local Jails, 1988* (Washington, D.C.: United States Department of Justice, 1990), p. 1.
4. John D. Smykla, *Community-Based Corrections: Principles and Practices* (New York: Macmillan, 1981), p. 280.
5. Robert Cushman and John Wynne, *Criminal Justice Planning for Local Governments* (Washington, D.C.: National Institute of Law Enforcement and Criminal Justice, 1979), pp. 29–33.
6. Thomas B. Smith, "The Policy Implementation Process," *Policy Sciences* 4 (1973): 197–209.
7. Cushman and Wynne, *Criminal Justice Planning,* p. 14.
8. *Criminal Justice Newsletter* 11(5) (March 3, 1980): 1–2.
9. Don C. Gibbons et al., *Criminal Justice Planning* (Englewood Cliffs, N.J.: Prentice-Hall, 1977), p. 119.
10. National Institute of Justice, *Unification of Community Corrections* (Washington, D.C.: U.S. Government Printing Office, 1980), p. 8.
11. Ibid.
12. Ibid., pp. 8, 21.
13. Ibid., p. 20.
14. James McSparron, "Community Corrections and Diversion," *Crime and Delinquency* 26(2) (April 1980): pp. 236–237.
15. John Blackmore, "Behavior Modification for Bureaucracies," *Corrections Magazine* 6(6) (1980): 19.
16. McSparron, "Community Corrections," p. 230.
17. Blackmore, "Behavior Modification," p. 19.
18. McSparron, "Community Corrections," p. 238.
19. Blackmore, "Behavior Modification," p. 20.
20. Ibid., pp. 21–22.
21. Ibid., p. 22.
22. McSparron, "Community Corrections," p. 237.
23. Ibid., p. 239.
24. Ibid., p. 241.
25. John Blackmore, "Evaluation of the Minnesota Evaluation," *Corrections Magazine* 7(4) (August 1981): 24.
26. Ibid.
27. National Advisory Commission on Criminal Justice Standards and Goals, *Corrections* (Washington, D.C.: U.S. Government Printing Office, 1973), p. 233.
28. National Institute of Justice, *Community Correctional Centers* (Washington, D.C.: U.S. Government Printing Office, 1980), p. 79.

29. Ibid.
30. Ibid., p. 78.
31. Ibid., p. 82.
32. Ibid., p. 98.
33. Ibid.
34. C. Ray Jeffrey, "Criminology as an Interdisciplinary Behavioral Science," *Criminology* 16(2) (1978): 166.
35. A. Blumstein, "Free Enterprise Corrections: Using Industry to Make Offenders Economically Viable," *Prison Journal* 48(2) (1968): 26–28.
36. National Institute of Law Enforcement and Criminal Justice, *Contracting for Correctional Services in the Community,* vol. 1 (Washington, D.C.: U.S. Government Printing Office, 1978).
37. Ibid., p. 4.
38. Ibid., pp. 11–13.
39. Ibid., p. 31.
40. Ibid., p. 60.
41. Lloyd Ohlin, Aldin Miller, and Robert Coates, *Juvenile Correctional Reform in Massachusetts* (Washington, D.C.: U.S. Government Printing Office, n.d.), p. 5.
42. Ibid., p. 11.
43. *Criminal Justice Newsletter* 11(15) (July 21, 1980): 5, 6.
44. Robert Coates, Aldin Miller, and Lloyd Ohlin, *Diversity in a Youth Correctional System: Handling Delinquents in Massachusetts* (Cambridge, Mass.: Ballinger, 1978).
45. Cornelius Hogan and William Steinhurst, "Managing Change in Corrections," *Federal Probation* 40(2) (1976): 55–59. Reprinted with permission from *Federal Probation* (1976).
46. Ibid., p. 56.
47. Ibid.
48. Ibid., pp. 58–59.
49. Ibid., p. 59.
50. Malcolm W. Klein, "Deinstitutionalization and Diversion of Juvenile Offenders: A Litany of Impediments," in *Crime and Justice: An Annual Review of Research,* vol. 1, Norval Morris and Michael Tonry (eds.) (Chicago: University of Chicago Press, 1979), pp. 145–201.

FOR FURTHER READING

Coates, Robert, Aldin Miller, and Lloyd Ohlin, *Diversity in a Youth Correctional System: Handling Delinquents in Massachusetts* (Cambridge, Mass.: Ballinger, 1978).
Cushman, Robert, and John Wynne, *Criminal Justice Planning for Local Governments* (Washington, D.C.: National Institute of Law Enforcement and Criminal Justice, 1979).
Gibbons, Don C., et al., *Criminal Justice Planning* (Englewood Cliffs, N.J.: Prentice-Hall, 1977).
McManus, Patrick D., and Barclay Lynn Zeller, *Community Corrections Act, Technical Assistance Manual* (Laurel, Md.: American Correctional Association, n.d.).
National Institute of Justice, *Alleviating Jail Crowding: A System's Perspective. Issues and Practices* (Washington, D.C.: U.S. Government Printing Office, November 1985).

Index

TO THE OWNER OF THIS BOOK:

We hope that you have found *Community-Based Corrections,* Second Edition, useful. So that this book can be improved in a future edition, would you take the time to complete this sheet and return it? Thank you.

Instructor's name: _____

Department: _____

School and address: _____

_____

1. The name of the course in which I used this book is: _____

_____

2. My general reaction to this book is: _____

_____

_____

3. What I like most about this book is: _____

_____

_____

4. What I like least about this book is: _____

_____

_____

5. Were all of the chapters of the book assigned for you to read?   Yes   No

   If not, which ones weren't? _____

6. Do you plan to keep this book after you finish the course?   Yes   No

   Why or why not? _____

_____

7. On a separate sheet of paper, please write specific suggestions for improving this book and anything else you'd care to share about your experience in using the book.

Optional:

Your name: _____ Date: _____

May Brooks/Cole quote you, either in promotion for *Community-Based Corrections,*
Second Edition, or in future publishing ventures?

Yes: _____ No: _____

Sincerely,

Belinda Rodgers McCarthy
Bernard J. McCarthy, Jr.